WITHDRAWN

MEN and
POLITICS

MEN AND POLITICS:

Europe Between the
Two World Wars

LOUIS FISCHER

Harper Colophon Books
Harper & Row, Publishers
New York

CARL A. RUDISILL LIBRARY
LENOIR RHYNE COLLEGE

940.50924
F 52 m
67724
October, 1969

MEN AND POLITICS. Copyright © 1941, 1946 by Louis Fischer. All rights reserved. No part of this book may be used or reproduced in any manner whatsoever without written permission except in the case of brief quotations embodied in critical articles and reviews. For information address Harper & Row, Publishers, Incorporated, 49 East 33rd Street, New York, N.Y. 10016.

This book was originally published by Duell, Sloan and Pearce, Incorporated.

First HARPER COLOPHON edition published 1966 by Harper & Row, Publishers, Incorporated, New York.

This book is sold subject to the condition that it shall not, by way of trade, be lent, re-sold, hired out, or otherwise disposed of without the publisher's consent, in any form of binding or cover other than that in which it is published.

LIBRARY OF CONGRESS CATALOG CARD NUMBER: 66-21165

CARL A. RUDISILL LIBRARY
LENOIR RHYNE COLLEGE

Contents

Conclusion

Introduction

IN the quarter of a century which has passed between the two great wars, few books which have been written upon the subject of international affairs are of such intrinsic importance as Louis Fischer's "Men and Politics." I have welcomed the invitation to write these words of introduction to a new edition.

"Men and Politics" is a work which will never be dated. It is the expression of the convictions of a man who has been afforded an almost unique opportunity for studying at first hand that deplorable world of the 1920's and 1930's. It is the record of the experience of one who has seen much and who has learned much. It is written by a man who possesses to an exceptional degree a capacity for analysis combined with a burning faith in the principles in which he believes.

One of the most curious phenomena of the past decades has been the disinclination of men and women in the United States, and in many of the other democracies as well, to take the trouble to study the lessons to be drawn from history—even very recent history.

A not altogether inappropriate example of that strange inertia is to be found in the fact that there were few even of the responsible leaders in the democracies during the years prior to 1939 who took the time to study, let alone digest, the contents of Hitler's "Mein Kampf." Yet in that verbose and neurotic volume there were presented for all who chose to see not only the clues to the immediate intentions and ambitions of that evil paranoiac but, what was perhaps even more important, the unmistakable proof of the manner in which his diseased mind would react in any given contingency.

In all of the more advanced democracies among the United Nations, the ultimate responsibility for determining whether the peace settlements are to be just and wise, and especially whether they are to be practical, must be borne by the people as a whole. In the United States, for instance, an enlightened public opinion, if it cares deeply enough about the issues involved, as we may well believe it must, can speedily induce its elected representatives to be guided by the views which the majority of the people maintain. But accurate knowledge will be needed before any sound convictions can be formed. And if that knowledge is acquired, the American people will readily reach the conclusion that many of the peace settlements arrived at after the First World War were neither just nor wise nor practical. They will then see clearly that the mistakes made in those peace settlements were just as responsible for the breakdown in world order, for the growth of Fascism and Nazism, for the tragedy of the Second World War, and for the failure of the League of Nations to meet the expectations originally placed in it, as were the sinister ambitions and the ruthless greed of those who wielded power in the Axis Countries, and of the peoples who supported them.

There are a number of books written by some who played a prominent part in shaping the peace settlements of 1919 and of the 1920's, and by others who accurately recorded the events of those days which present in simple form, but in ample detail, the reasons why such decisions were reached. They show beyond the shadow of any misunderstanding the surest way by which the repetition of such errors can now, under not dissimilar conditions, be avoided.

Those pages of history—a history which is vitally important in its bearing upon the momentous problems of the present day—are available to every citizen. The facts set forth are essential to any full understanding by public opinion of the issues involved in the decisions which the people of the United States must now make. But up to the present moment relatively few have realized how much more readily our present course can wisely be set if we avail ourselves of the light afforded by full knowledge of the recent past.

There are also books which have been published in recent years, written by persons with unusual experience or with exceptional qualifications, which to those who will but read them shed a floodlight on what is still to so many of us the murky and confused background of international relations during the past thirty years. In particular, there are only a handful of Americans who have actually lived in the Soviet Union during those first years after the Revolution of 1917 when the Russian people seemed to have retired behind an insurmountable wall of isolation separating them from the Western World. Of these, Louis Fischer possesses the gift of enabling us to obtain not only an understanding but even the actual feeling of those times. And at this moment when cooperation between the

Soviet Union and the United States is imperative, if world peace is to be maintained, comprehension on the part of one nation of the essence of the other is necessary, and an objective appreciation by the people of one country of the weaknesses, as well as of the virtues, of the people of the other country is more than ever desirable. In "Men and Politics" Louis Fischer affords us an opportunity to enlarge our comprehension.

Whatever our own beliefs or conclusions may be with regard to the events and policies which determined the destinies of all peoples during the years between the wars, and with regard to trends and influences which are shaping the course of affairs in the Old World of today, and no matter how sharply the reader may individually disagree with some of the opinions upon these issues which are expressed in "Men and Politics," no one can question that this book has been written by one who possesses full knowledge and authority in the field with which he deals.

"Men and Politics" is a work which deserves the fullest measure of consideration at this time. Its chapters will greatly facilitate a clearer understanding by the American people of the problems with which they are today confronted. Its value in assisting public opinion to grasp more realistically the world issues with which the United States is now undertaking to deal could hardly be overestimated.

SUMNER WELLES

Part One

The Post-War Period
1921 to 1930

1. *The War Is Dead, Long Live the War*

I FIRST visited Europe in 1918. I saw Plymouth and London, Cherbourg and Tours, Milan, Florence, and Brindisi. London had had Zeppelin air raids. The city lights were dimmed at night. Restaurants served little white pills of saccharine instead of sugar. Almost every family mourned a man killed in battle. The women were pessimistic about the war. The Allies had not yet started winning, and laymen said Germany could not be beaten. The countryside abounded with tent camps for khaki-clad Tommy recruits. City hotels were filled with British, French, Rumanian, Italian, and Serbian officers in smartly cut uniforms. Day and night, Piccadilly swarmed with insistent prostitutes.

In the French provinces, women in black stood at railway stations, weeping, as long hospital trains bursting with bandaged soldiers pulled out in one direction and heavy troop trains moved off in the other. It was the fifth summer of the war.

Italy was sunny and beautiful, but sad.

I did not understand much. This was my first look at the Old World, and I was only twenty-two.

Three years later I left America again to see Europe at peace. In the meantime, I had studied history, and on the quiet sands of the Egyptian desert I had read every word of the Versailles Peace Treaty. I had read it with a map.

I arrived in England on the *Aquitania* in December, 1921, and went to London. I did not know then that I would spend eighteen years in Europe. I did not know that I would stay to see the outbreak of a second world war. My eighteen years in Europe were not years of peace; they were an armistice between two wars. Because they are not made in a day, wars are no longer declared. Or they are declared every day for years. Those eighteen years were one long declaration of war. When war came in September, 1939, it was startling news. Most people thought the war had commenced long before.

December, 1921: three years and a month after the end of the first World War. The Kaiser was in exile in Holland. Hitler was an

3

unknown mongrel of Munich. Mussolini stood on a low rung of the ladder that led to heaven in Rome. Only a handful of Bolsheviks knew Stalin. The nations hatched in the incubator of Versailles—Czechoslovakia, Poland, and others—were sprouting wings and strutting in the barnyards of Eastern and Central Europe. Millions hopefully watched the League of Nations set up business in Geneva. England and France were fresh from triumph, and Germany was sunk in defeat. Yet all the elements of the war of 1939 were already discernible.

Part of that month of December, 1921, I spent in London, the London of victory. Able-bodied men in faded civilian suits covered by the khaki overcoats which were all they salvaged from the army, sold pencils on street corners. England, Scotland, Wales, and Northern Ireland—the United Kingdom—counted 1,834,000 unemployed. Most of them were men, and most of the men had served in the war. Mr. David Lloyd George had promised them "homes for heroes." But they lived in disease-ridden slums. They did not even have jobs. Many organized into male choruses and stood on the Strand or in West End squares singing "It's a Long Way to Tipperary" and "Keep the Home Fires Burning." They had sung these songs at Ypres and Arras out of nostalgia. Now they sang for copper pennies. Other ex-soldiers begged without music. Some polished their military medals and wore them when applying for work as bricklayers and bus conductors. They had won the medals after years of blood and mud and lice. They had won the war for their country. But who was the country? Were they part of it? It did not seem so.

Most people I encountered said, "No one wins a war. Who won the San Francisco earthquake?" During the war they had hoped. In peace they despaired. No single idea stirred the country. Workingmen expected big things from the Soviet Revolution. Meanwhile, however, Maxim Gorky, the Russian author, had appealed to the world for food for 25,000,000 starving Soviet citizens. England was tired. London was moved by one consuming passion: to forget.

At the theater, I was tormented by the solid rows of women without men, women who had lost their men in the trenches or who had never had men and now would never have them because the men who might have been theirs were dead in battle. These women had also won the war, for they were of England.

The German fleet lay on the bottom of Scapa Flow where its

own sailors scuttled it, and Britannia ruled the waves. What difference did that make to Briton or German? England and France had acquired some colonies, and Germany had surrendered all of hers. Did this change things for the individual?

The British no longer hated the Germans. They thought Germany should pay reparations because it had started the war and laid France waste; but they were not vindictive. Victory over Germany had shifted the European balance of power in favor of France. The French wanted to perpetuate this advantage by keeping Germany weak. France could do that only with British help. Paris, therefore, advocated a permanent Anglo-French alliance and a League of Nations under Anglo-French control. But that would have made England a tool of French policy, and the British had their own interests. They themselves aspired to be the arbiter of Europe's fate. To curb French hegemony and establish their own the British wished to redress the balance in Europe by restoring Germany's strength.

For generations the international ideal of British statesmen has been a political seesaw with John Bull planted stoutly on the fulcrum, and France and Germany, more or less equal in strength, swinging up and down at either end of the plank and looking to John for balance. Whenever Germany, the naturally more powerful country, succeeded in holding the French end uncomfortably high in the air, Bull left his neutral central position and moved toward France to re-establish the equilibrium. That is the picture behind the war of 1914—and the war of 1939. If Britain and France had worked in harmony after 1919, instead of at cross-purposes between 1919 and 1936, there might have been no war in 1939.

In 1921, Germany was at the mercy of France. That was inevitable after the war. But it was bad for peace. It was bad for business. A bankrupt Germany in the middle of Europe would quiet French fears and ruin Europe. France thought first of her safety, England of her purse. The French said, "If we had a guarantee from England and America we could afford to be lenient to Germany." The British replied, "If you had guarantees you would dare to be harsher to Germany."

Three years of peace had settled nothing and unsettled a great deal. I wanted to see Germany. I had come to Europe to go to Germany. I was going there for no other motive, however, than to join Markoosha, and get journalistic experience. Markoosha was a slim native of Libau, Latvia; she was Russian in her unconventional spirit, German in her education, a pianist by profession, a psychologist by natural endowment. The war had brought her to New York. She had returned to Europe in May, 1921.

It was evening, on December 20, when I first arrived in Berlin. Markoosha was waiting at the Zoo railway station in the West End. But I did not know that Berlin had several stations, and so I continued on to the central terminal at the Friedrichstrasse. When I alighted, Markoosha was not there. No porters were there. I carried my luggage downstairs. No taxis. I tried my schoolroom German on several persons and gathered that the taxis were on strike. The boarding house or pension to which I had been directed was on the other side of town. For a while I waited, not knowing what to do. Then I walked around to the freight section of the terminal. There I saw a big truck marked "Herman Tietz, Department Store." I talked haltingly with the driver but he showed no comprehension. Finally I waved a dollar bill in front of his face and said, "Kaiserallee 15." He cried, "Hop in." He interrupted the loading of the truck and assisted me up to the high driver's seat. From that unusual perch I first saw Berlin. The broad streets were hushed and covered with snow. I had expected more life in such a metropolis. The driver talked incessantly about food, prices, the mark, and the French. That dollar he was earning from me was equal to one-fifth of his monthly salary. "Are all Americans rich?" he asked. "When America entered the War I was at the front and I knew we were beaten," he said. America seemed to him a fairyland.

I found Markoosha at Kaiserallee 15, where she was living. She had reserved a room for me there, too. Though we were constantly together, we remained free until a year later when we were married so that Markoosha could have a baby without too much social inconvenience.

I strolled through the Berlin streets. The building workers were on strike. The post-office employees had met at the Neue Welt hall the evening before and issued a twenty-four-hour ultimatum to the government: if by noon on December 22, the authorities did not raise their salaries they would go on strike after the Christmas holiday. Several industries in Berlin were already shut down by strikes against employers who violated the eight-hour-day law. The *Berliner Tageblatt*, middle-of-the-road democratic paper, complained that numerous factory owners were trying to lengthen the working week.

Blunderingly I found my way to the Kurfuerstendamm and Tauentzienstrasse, shopping streets of the well-to-do. Christmas buying seemed light. Christmas trees were sold out. There had been fewer trees on sale this year, friends told me. In Cologne, according to the papers, one Wilhelm Schoenigen received a sentence of a year's imprisonment and 10,000 marks' fine for selling 600 trees at exorbitant prices. Many similar cases occupied the authorities. Vendors created a scarcity, and then extorted speculative prices.

This was the tragedy of post-War Germany. I soon learned that the spending of money was a fine art—and a complicated science. Foreigners developed a skilled sense. They had to know when to buy money and when to sell money, and also when to shop. Every German hausfrau required financial wizardry to buy potatoes and pay her rent. No person in Germany knew the value of the money he had in the bank or in his pocket. A German workingman brought home his fortnightly salary, say, 400 marks. He went to bed, and while he slept the marks in his jacket pocket were melting away. He woke in the morning, went out, and could buy only half as much food and clothing as he could have bought the night before. Prices had gone up overnight. He therefore said to his employer: You must increase my wages. The employer did so and in turn sold his products at a higher price. Employers accordingly needed more money to meet their wage bills and citizens needed more money to buy goods. So the government printed more money, and the greater the number of marks in circulation the less each mark was worth. That was inflation's vicious circle. Inflation became the German nightmare.

The human being needs security, and he is helped to it by the existence of certain stable points. If he has a job or a friend or a love or a bank account, he plots his course from that fixed position. But no peace of mind was possible when even the money in one's purse refused to stay the same for twenty-four hours. After a while, salaries were paid twice a week and, later, every evening, and people would rush immediately to the stores to make purchases. No one wanted to keep money. The Germans who earned large sums invested in antiques and luxuries, or they traveled and entertained themselves. Night clubs flourished. Germany in those years was governed by the psychology of "eat, drink, and be merry for tomorrow

we die." It left its mark on politics, morals, literature, and art, thinking and popular habits. In years that followed, the German wanted
security above all else, and when a charlatan dictator promised it
many Germans were ready to pay for it with their civil rights. A full
stomach, they said, was better than freedom. Any demagogue could
frighten a German audience by recalling the terrors of inflation.

Pension Wien at Kaiserallee 15 had been a single family's private
apartment, but now each room was occupied by one family or one
person. I had a large room facing the street. For it and three meals
a day and service, I paid 1,000 marks a month. When I arrived in
December, 1921, that sum was equal to approximately six dollars.
After nine months in Berlin, it was equal to seventy cents. Each
month, then each week, accordingly, my rent in marks increased, but
in dollars it kept going down steadily. The rise in prices never caught
up with the appreciation of foreign currency. Germany was a foreigner's paradise. I earned about twenty dollars a week writing for
the *New York Evening Post*, and could hardly spend it.

Next door to me lived an old German couple. The man bore himself with military stiffness. He had owned an estate in Saxony and had
sold it to pay taxes. He always wore the same outfit, striped trousers
and a shiny black coat twice his size. He could insert his big fist into
the empty bulge between his neck and collar; he had simply shrunk
during the food shortage of 1917-1918.

The pension housed citizens of many lands. Several rooms were
occupied by "White" Russians. There were English guests and Polish
visitors, people from Vienna, and a woman student from Italy. Everyone had a tale of war horror, of suffering and privation. Former
enemies now mingled in friendly intercourse.

Meals were served in a dining hall. When you came in you shouted
"Mahlzeit," and when you left the table you shouted "Mahlzeit."
Each time the chorus faithfully answered "Mahlzeit." Every plate
was wiped clean. If half a roll or a segment of cheese or a piece of
meat remained uneaten, it was neatly wrapped up and taken back
to the guest's room to help tide over the long hungry hours between
meals. The German residents budgeted strictly. A ride into the center
of town cost ten pfennigs (one-tenth of a mark) by trolley and
twenty by fast bus. They took the trolley.

We had hot water for bathing only on Saturdays. For a tip of a
few pfennigs, however, any maid would drag numerous pitchers of
water, heated on the gas stove, into the bathroom. On trains or at

the police station the foreigners learned the power of their money. The proverbially incorruptible German civil servant ignored regulations or attended to you out-of-turn if you slipped a mark into his palm. He had to supplement his inadequate salary.

Berlin was short of coal, although Germany normally exports coal. I heard of many pneumonia patients. Children with "war rickets" were natural victims of disease. Germans I met were depressed by these conditions, depressed and humiliated. They blamed the Allies. Gustav Boess, the Mayor of Berlin, warned the world on Christmas day, "If there is not soon a real improvement of living conditions, the health of young and old will suffer. May help come through the comprehension of the powers that be in London, Washington, and Paris! Otherwise it will be too late—for generations."

Peace on earth? Good will to men? It did not take much perspicacity to realize that Europe was drifting rudderless in a choppy sea. It did not require any clairvoyance to foresee that this post-War chaos would exact a terrible vengeance.

Because I wanted to refresh my memories of this first month I spent in post-War Europe twenty years ago, I have recently re-read the *London Times, New York Times,* and *Berliner Tageblatt* for December, 1921. I have made a list of important news items. That simple list reveals all the trends that converged to the terrific clash of 1939. Each event was a portent, each dispatch a warning of the gathering catastrophe. Pieced together, they tell a story that should have made statesmen weep—and act. The handwriting on the wall was clear enough. But statesmen cannot read while they run.

ITALY. *December 1, 1921.* Inkwells, clubs, and chairs fly through the air as Socialists and Fascists clash at a provincial council called to commemorate the death of a workingman killed by Black Shirts. *December 16.* The Socialist party accuses Prime Minister Bonomi of leniency towards the violent followers of Mussolini. The Italian government decrees the dissolution of the Fascist groups of Cremona province. They evade the order. *December 30.* The Banco Italiano Di Sconto, one of Italy's largest financial institutions, closes its doors. Italian businessmen are supremely alarmed.

Italy was marching to Fascism and war.

AUSTRIA. *December 2.* Mobs demonstrating against the high cost of living attack fashionable Viennese hotels, and food stores. The police remain passive. One policeman is quoted as saying, "We are tired of shooting and being shot at. These people are hungry and desperate. So are many of us."

Austria was starving and riotous.

GERMANY. *December 1.* A book entitled *What We Have Lost* has appeared with an introduction by Marshal von Hindenburg. "What has been German must become German again," he exhorts. "This is what you shall bear in mind, O German Youth." (In Paris the book provokes bitter comment. "Germany Contemplates Revenge," warns a French daily.) *December 1.* A pamphlet printed in English and entitled "England's War Guilt" has come from the press. England started the War, it contends, and Germany should therefore not pay reparations. (The *London Times* calls this publication "a pregnant confession of the pure Hun doctrine." Germany can pay if it wants to, asserts the paper. Premier Raymond Poincaré says that if Germany does not pay reparations France ought to take over Germany's customs, taxes, exports, and coal industry.) *December 3.* The Berlin *Deutsche Allgemeine Zeitung* invites the Allies to withdraw their Arms Control Commission because it interferes with industry by inspecting factories to see whether they are making munitions proscribed by the Versailles Treaty. *December 5.* Thieves, many of them women, have been arrested stealing iron crosses, iron eagles, gilded iron crowns, and marble slabs from cemeteries. *December 6.* Chancellor Joseph Wirth asks publicly whether it is "possible, by the terms of a peace treaty, to take a nation like Germany and squeeze it dry as a lemon." *December 9.* At Dresden the Allied Arms Control Commission discovers 353 howitzers made after the War in contravention of the Versailles Treaty. *December 10.* General Max von Hoffmann, commander of the German army in the East, submits that "it is a mistake to disarm Germany as long as the Bolsheviks continue their propaganda offensive." (This is not the last German attempt to gain concessions from the Allies by playing up the Communist menace.) *December 10.* The police in Berlin uncover a secret society aiming to overthrow the democratic republic. *December 13.* The Allied commission in Germany finds a hidden stock of 140,000 machine-gun tubes and 500 cannon. Workingmen, suspecting that these arms caches will be used by German reactionaries against the Republic, are helping the Allied commission find them. *December 22.* Herr von Jagow is sentenced to five years' imprisonment. Jagow was one of the leaders of the Monarchist-right-wing insurrection or

Putsch staged by Dr. Wolfgang Kapp in March, 1920. The rebels expected the army to complete the job they started. But the army remained neutral and the Kapp Putsch failed when labor declared a general strike. This saved the Republic. The Right press in Germany regards Jagow's sentence as too severe, the liberal *Berliner Tageblatt* calls it too mild, and the Socialist *Vorwaertz* demands that General Ludendorff be tried as the real leader of the Kapp Putsch. *December 24.* The Allied Arms Commission finds 342 guns and 247 howitzers behind a plastered wall. *December 28.* In the city of Duesseldorf, French occupation troops arrest thirty members of the secret Ehrhardt society whose purpose is to destroy the democratic Republic. Two of its members, Tillessen and Schulz, had assassinated Matthias Erzberger, German Catholic leader, on August 26, 1921, for defending Germany's signature of the Versailles Treaty. *December 30.* Railroad workers in Berlin and Potsdam go on strike.

Germany was a proud, unhappy, unrepentant pauper.

ENGLAND. *December 1.* Wiring from London to the *New York Times*, Charles H. Grasty says, "It is useless to conceal under the outward forms of the Entente the fundamental differences that now exist between England and France." *December 3.* A British financial expert urges America to use its gold hoard to save Europe's economy. *December 4.* Wickham Steed, editor of the *London Times*, asserts that "the Versailles treaty has left a bad taste in the mouth of the world." *December 24.* In a Christmas editorial the *London Times* writes, "Peace delays its coming. Many still fear that the war which was to end wars has sown the seeds of further wars even more terrible and deadly than the most terrible of all." It discusses the strained relationship between France and England.

The victorious Anglo-French alliance was a thing of the past.

DISARMAMENT. *Washington, December 15.* Japan accepts the 5-5-3 naval ratio proposed at the Washington Arms Limitation Conference. Charles Evans Hughes, Secretary of State of the United States, believes that "this treaty absolutely ends naval competition for all time." *December 24.* The British proposal to abolish the submarine has encountered vigorous resistance from the French delegation at the conference. Albert Sarraut, French representative, affirms that the submarine is pre-eminently a defensive weapon. Sarraut pleads for large U-boats.

Disarmament was a pipe dream.

RUSSIA. *December 8*. Moscow reports two thousand cases of typhus in the city alone. Famine afflicts the Volga and Ukraine regions. *December 19*. Leonid Krassin, a leading Bolshevik, has arrived in London. Plans of a conference to settle the Russian and German problems are being bruited. It may meet at Genoa. The *London Times* writes, "In some well-informed circles the belief exists that Lenin is persuaded of the failure of Bolshevism." (The "well-informed circles" are not very well-informed.)

Soviet Russia was hungry and inscrutable.

All these news items constituted a blueprint of the future. A month's news reports, taken at random, reveal the rotten foundation and the ugly façade of European peace. Europe was winding itself out of one war and getting ready for the next.

Between the summer of 1914 when the first World War commenced, and November 11, 1918, when its Armistice was signed, 5,152,115 soldiers were killed and 12,831,004 were wounded. Germany counted 1,773,000 dead, Russia 1,700,000 dead, France 1,357,800 dead, Germany's ally, Austro-Hungary, 1,200,000 dead, Great Britain 908,371 dead, and Italy 650,000 dead. It takes a lot of charity and wisdom to wipe out so much blood. But there was little charity and less wisdom in post-War Europe.

2. *Proud Poles*

MY first "story" as a foreign journalist took me east from Berlin to Poland. Before leaving America I had called on the managing editor of the *New York Evening Post* and asked him if I could work for the paper. He said they would be glad to read anything I sent and would pay for what they printed. Beyond that he could not commit himself. He was right, of course. I had no reputation and little experience. But I hoped.

Poland was the child of Allied victory in 1918.

Napoleon created a little Poland in 1806 and called it the Grand Duchy of Warsaw. It succumbed to Russia when he limped back from burning Moscow. The Poles boasted a glamorous history. They had fought the Turks; they had died for revolution in Italy and America. They had produced some great men. Statues to them stood, perhaps still stand, in Warsaw: to Chopin, the composer, Copernicus, the astronomer, Mickiewicz, the poet. But the Poland born of the 1919 peace was anticlimax to glory.

Poland included eighteen million Poles and eight million Ukrainians, Germans, Jews, White Russians, and Lithuanians. These eight million non-Poles were that many problems for Poland, for the Poles manifested no aptitude to govern themselves, let alone alien races. But eight million, apparently, were not enough. Marshal Pilsudski, the father of twentieth-century Poland, looked around for more troubles to conquer. He coveted several million additional Ukrainians. He marched into Soviet Ukraine.

It was 1920. Typhus was epidemic in Poland. Herbert Hoover, the American Jewish Joint Distribution Committee, and the Quakers fed millions of Poles with American food. The country had been crossed and criss-crossed by contending armies during the War. Over half a million homes and more than a million barns were destroyed. Poland was chaotic and poverty-stricken.

Pilsudski, in a fantastic bid for power and glory, chose that moment to attack the Bolsheviks. Joseph Pilsudski was regarded as a

13

genius. The Poles said he was mad and afflicted with syphilis, but until he died, they obeyed when he commanded. His war on Russia was a disaster. The Bolsheviks drove Pilsudski back and pursued his fleet troops to the very gates of Warsaw. If it had not been for the "Miracle of Warsaw," the Polish capital might have fallen to the Soviets in 1920. Aided by the French General Weygand and by the Red mistake of advancing too fast, Pilsudski repelled the Russian army. He then faced the tasks of reconstruction after a war that had been a complete waste of time and life.

This Russo-Polish conflict caught the city of Vilna in one of its eddies. Vilna, capital of Lithuania, was in Lithuanian hands when the Poles, following in the tracks of the retreating Russians, approached the city. Fighting broke out between the Poles and Lithuanians. On October 7, 1920, the two hostile camps signed an armistice. Members of the League of Nations Military Control Commission were present to lend authority to the agreement. The agreement gave Vilna to Lithuania. The Poles were to hand over the city on October 10. But on October 9, when the League officials had gone away, Colonel Zeligowski, a Polish army officer commanding Polish soldiers, seized Vilna. Then the comedy commenced. The Polish government called Zeligowski a "rebel" and Pilsudski washed his hands, in public, of Zeligowski's coup, and said the colonel had acted without orders. Did the all-powerful Pilsudski discipline Zeligowski? No. Was Vilna returned to Lithuania? No. Poland declared that Vilna was Polish, and now that the Poles had occupied Vilna it ought to remain Polish. Except to the purblind the farce was wholly transparent.

A little drama was now acted out. Vilna ordered a plebiscite to decide whether it would belong to Poland or Lithuania. I went from Berlin to Vilna to watch the show. It did not take long to see that Vilna was neither Lithuanian nor Polish but Jewish. Jews called it the "Jerusalem of Lithuania." The narrow thoroughfares were filled with Jews, and signs in Yiddish hung above many shops. Polish leaders I interviewed said Jews constituted thirty-six percent of the urban population; the Jews claimed "nearer fifty-five percent."

In Vilna I got my first close-up of government propaganda at work. The Poles were crude. Eleven foreign correspondents had arrived to "cover" the plebiscite. Seven were French, two British, two American. We were fêted every evening by the Polish government press department. Plenty of wine flowed, and when it had done its work, toasts were pronounced to "Poland" and to "the union of the French and Polish nations."

Late Saturday evening, January 7, 1922, the eve of the plebiscite, we were told that the authorities had arranged a special excursion for us the next morning. The journalists would go out in cars to see the peasants vote in the villages. It sounded like a good idea. The automobiles came to the hotel just as balloting started in the city. They were probably the best vehicles available, but their tops were of canvas and the side flaps were open. As we sped along the highway icy blasts blew in; our feet, faces, and hands were frozen. But there was compensation for the acute discomfort. This was the first time I saw northern forests in snow and ice. The woods were carpeted with dazzling white, and every trunk, every branch, every twig and pine and spruce needle sparkled with frost. It was like miles of silvery lace hung high in the air. Farmers passing on their horse-drawn sleighs were trimmed with icicles. We drove for hours, endlessly it seemed. I could not understand why it was necessary to go so far. I had wanted to watch the election in Vilna itself. Finally the cavalcade arrived at its destination, the tiny hamlet of Meshagola. I took two snapshots with my Kodak and I still have them in my scrapbook. They show some of those ice-lace trees, and peasant women wrapped in woolen shawls and woolen headkerchiefs, and men in heavy coats and caps or tub fur hats. All the adult Meshagolans had been corralled to the wooden polling hut, and one photograph shows a Polish official with the official insignia above his vizor and a sheaf of papers in his hands calling out a voter's name. The authorities had found a purely Polish village to prove to us the people's wholehearted participation in the plebiscite.

We returned to Vilna late in the afternoon, and a little while later when I cleaned up and went down into the city streets, the voting was over. We had been taken out of Vilna for almost the entire day so we could not observe what happened in it. All the Lithuanians, White Russians, and Jews had boycotted the elections. They constituted more than half of the citizens. But they knew in advance that Vilna would remain in Polish hands. The Jews felt Vilna should have gone to Lithuania. So did the League of Nations' representatives who lived in our hotel: a Japanese officer, a Swede, and a Frenchman. They made no secret of their views. One of them even told a local newspaper with unbelievable frankness that he was preparing a memorandum for Geneva discrediting the plebiscite. Nevertheless, the League and Europe accepted it.

On the evening of the plebiscite Sunday, a ball took place at the villa of a local grandee, and all the foreign correspondents were invited. The shabby Polish provincial aristocracy was there, aping what some of them remembered of Paris and St. Petersburg, with lornettes—so many nearsighted women!—and trains and little fur muffs and dresses that were certainly pre-War, and the army officers in high leather boots, spurs, and tunics worn so that one sleeve trailed empty behind their backs. The officers clicked heels, kissed hands, flirted, bowed stiffly from narrow waists, and saluted elderly estate owners with great military chic. One thought of Broadway and almost forgot the Vilna soup kitchens. Every now and then a Polish press attaché came over and pointed out the celebrities.

I spent three weeks in Poland on that trip and saw much poverty and squalor. I walked the streets for hours and studied people's faces; I looked into stores to learn the prices and kinds and volume of goods available, into book shops to see what Poles read, and wherever possible I followed the old European custom of looking into the windows of private homes. Sometimes I would leave the hotel and give myself a special assignment: to note the quality of shoes worn, or to count the number of automobiles (they were just emerging in post-War Poland), or to visit churches.

I went to Warsaw, Vilna, Lemberg, the capital of the Ruthenian-Ukrainian province of Galicia, Cracow, and Kattowitz, the great Polish coal-mining center within sight of German territory. Poland was wedged in between two great empires. It had been granted territory which once belonged to both. Its safety and prosperity depended on both. It antagonized both. It attacked Russia in 1920. In 1922, it received a large rich sliver of Germany in Upper Silesia from the Allies. The Versailles peacemakers originally intended giving all of Upper Silesia to Poland. They were persuaded, however, to let the Upper Silesians vote and decide. A large majority of the province's population voted for Germany. But the French would not permit the valuable industries of Upper Silesia to go to Germany. Polish gangs under Korfanty fought with Polish government aid against the German volunteer Freikorps. In defiance of the plebiscite result, France and England—the latter reluctantly—thereupon gave the lion's part of Upper Silesia to Poland. German patriots never forgot that.

On June 16, 1922, when the transfer of territory was made, President Ebert ordered all flags in Germany to be flown at half-mast.

These conflicts with Lithuania, Russia, and Germany were unnecessary and harmful. Partly they arose from Poland's illusions of grandeur. The Poles thought they were a great power. But you cannot be a great power when more than half of your 27,000,000 inhabitants live in straw-thatched huts with walls of mud and floors of dirt. The Poland of 1922 was under-developed economically. Polish railways were poor or non-existent. Poland had no port. Farming machinery was a luxury. Farm methods were ante-Napoleonic. The people were disunited, culturally backward, ill-clad, and impecunious. The political system contrived to keep the ablest citizens, the Germans and Jews, furthest from official posts of responsibility. Throwing Jews out of moving trains and pulling out their beards were approved forms of Polish gymnastics.

This Poland should have looked to its own fences. And if the Poles lacked the sense to mend their ruins and ways, more intelligent leaders of Europe should have told them what to do and made them do it. Nobody did. Poland was another muffed Anglo-French opportunity. The Poles' national vanity was in inverse proportion to their government's ability.

3. *Mourning in Vienna*

WHEN I went to Vienna in 1922, the Danube was black, not blue. The Vienna of waltzes, song, and gala ceremonies had vanished with the first shot of the first World War. By 1916, Vienna knew starvation. Emperor Francis Joseph passed away in that year. He had occupied the throne for sixty-eight years. The old, decrepit empire was as ready for the grave as he; and its actual death after the German-Austro-Bulgarian-Turkish defeat of 1918 was an anticlimax. The peace treaties merely parceled out the property of the deceased.

But the family which could not live together had an even worse time living separately.

Austria and Hungary dissolved their royal partnership. Slices were cut out of each and given to neighbors. The Czechs and Slovaks of the empire, with some Hungarians and 3,500,000 Sudeten Germans, were allowed to create the Republic of Czechoslovakia. Austria claimed those Sudeten Germans at the Paris negotiations, and the map-carvers hesitated. But without the Sudeten mountains, Czechoslovakia could not be defended against German attack. Moreover, economically Sudetenland had much stronger ties with Moravia and Slovakia than with Austria or Germany. So the 3,500,000 Sudeten Germans went to the new Prague state. Another quarter of a million Tirolean Germans became Italian subjects because Italy had guessed right and fought on the side of the victorious Allies. The incorporation of the Tirol into Italy extended Rome's rule north to the Brenner Pass—a good military frontier.

That left little Austria with less than seven million inhabitants. Almost two million of these lived in Vienna. The city that had been sustained in splendor by a vast empire now rested on the flimsiest foundations. One-third of post-War Austrians were peasants who could not raise enough food to feed the nation; one-third were industrial workingmen who manufactured too much for the nation to consume; the last third were officials with no empire to rule, officers with no army to command, and artists, actors, musicians, writers, teachers, doctors, lawyers, and intellectuals whom shrunken Austria could no longer support.

Throughout Europe the Quakers were doing remarkable work for hungry and poverty-stricken people. In Central Europe, in Poland, Spain, and Russia, the Friends saved many lives and spirits by their unselfish, diligent work. Europeans always preferred the Quakers to other relief workers. They trusted them more and did not suspect hidden political motives. In the Quakers' Vienna headquarters on the Singerstrasse, Dr. Hilda Clark was kindness itself. Several times I had lunch there with her eager, idealistic staff. It was through the Friends that I met Professor Hans Ottwald.

Professor Ottwald taught English literature in the university and earned 70,000 kronen, or crowns, a month. "That sounds terrific," he said to me, "but it amounts to exactly seven dollars." A ton of coal cost 50,000 crowns, a decent second-hand suit of clothes cost 60,000 crowns. Professor Ottwald was able to buy a suit from the Quakers for only 10,000 crowns. He rejoiced in his new blue suit. For three years he had worn his old one. After the first two years, it had become shiny and stained, and the edges of its sleeves and cuffs were ragged. For 1,200 crowns a tailor had ripped it apart, cleaned the cloth, reversed it, and sewed it together again. A Viennese in those days no more thought of using only one side of a suit than a newspaper editor would think of printing on one side of his paper.

Professor Ottwald's wife had died during the War. His only son, aged eighteen, lived in Denmark. The Quakers had placed him there with a Danish peasant family in the hope that proper nutrition would help cure his tuberculosis. The professor's two rooms were cold and dark in the evening, and every day at eight P.M. he therefore went to a café. The café was large and roomy and its upholstered seats were soft. Professor Ottwald had his own table, marble-covered like all the rest, and nobody else used it. Friends knew they could find him there from eight to eleven-fifteen. It was his *Stammtisch*. His waiter approached, addressed him cordially by name, chatted for a moment, and went off to bring the cup of coffee and two glasses of water on a metal tray. Another employee in special uniform came over and handed him the *Frankfurter Zeitung*, published in Germany. After a while, the same employee, having observed that the professor had turned to the last page of the *Frankfurter* silently laid the *London Times* on the cool slab. What Viennese individual could afford to buy the clean, beautifully printed *Times?* But the café kept it. Sometimes colleagues paid the professor a visit and they reminisced and laughed or exchanged political gossip. Twice a week, Dr. Ottwald asked for ink and café stationery and wrote a letter to his son. In another corner, two men played chess for hours, a student prepared his physics lesson, a teacher wrote his lectures.

The café in Vienna was home and social club and political arena. Certain cafés were frequented by Socialists and no Monarchist would enter them. The Monarchists had their own café. Other cafés whose high prices kept ordinary mortals out attracted currency speculators. In still other coffee houses long-haired poets and "left-wing prostitutes" abounded. A few of the speculators', or *Schieber*, cafés were closed. Their big plate-glass windows had been smashed in the December food-shortage riots. At that time it looked like revolution. But what political movement would want to take over a bankrupt state and cope with its insoluble problems?

Austria's salvation lay outside its borders. But the map, human stupidity, and sectional interests interfered.

Austria had leather, iron, water power, zinc, copper, salt deposits that had been mined since the dawn of history, a skilled working class, good factories, textile mills, and forests. She could produce abundantly. Given foreign buyers she would solve her problems. But her neighbors wanted to buy less and sell more. Each little country in Southeastern Europe aspired to economic self-sufficiency.

Austria could have prospered if Southeastern and Central Europe had lived a normal life. Instead, Vienna buzzed with spies, gangsters, Macedonian bandits, Turkish dissidents, Hungarian Legitimists, Bulgarian revolutionists, peasant opposition leaders, the rivals of kings—Outs that wished to oust the Ins, and their paid assassins. Vienna was their rialto. Gun-runners and go-betweens darted through hotel lobbies, whispered in cafés, and bribed officials. Customs guards had to be bought or gagged or killed. Foreign governments had their agents here to check on the activities of other government agents. The atmosphere was heavy with possibilities of change. Few accepted the peace settlements as final.

Rumania kept a host of emissaries in Vienna. Rumania's population rose from 7,600,000 in 1914 to 19,319,300 after the War; Bucharest happened to be on the winning side. The Treaty of Trianon between the Allies and Hungary assigned 1,500,000 Hungarians in Transylvania and the Banat to Rumania. Rumania likewise adopted about 700,000 Germans from Hungary. Then in 1918, Rumania seized the

Russian province of Bessarabia. Finally, the Rumanian Crown Prince had marched an army into the Bulgarian Dobruja during the second Balkan war in 1913. Rumania thus had earned the enmity of Bulgaria, Russia, Hungary, and Germany.

Hungary lost territory to other countries than Rumania. One million Hungarians went to Czechoslovakia, and half a million to Yugoslavia. Altogether, Hungary relinquished two-thirds of her territory and two-fifths of her population.

To safeguard themselves against revenge, the three new nations that had ripped strips out of Hungary formed the Little Entente. Hungary listened for their whispers and negotiations at the Balkan crossroads in Vienna.

Bulgaria had also been among the losers. *Vae victis!* By the Treaty of Neuilly (November 27, 1919), Bulgaria surrendered fertile Western Thrace to Greece, England's protégé, thereby forfeiting its outlet to the Aegean Sea; it also lost some strategic frontier segments to Yugoslavia. More reasons for rancor.

The Turks, too, were still a Balkan power and sent their undercover observers to Vienna. Yugoslavia and Bulgaria had admitted several hundred thousand White Russians. Moscow wished to know what they planned to do. Moscow thought, wishfully, of revolutions in Bulgaria, Hungary, and elsewhere. Moscow men made Vienna their headquarters. Vienna was the Balkan conspiratorial incubator. Good stuff for novels but not for peace and business!

The best frontier is three thousand miles of deep ocean, or the Himalayas. But Rumania, for instance, had six contiguous neighbors—Russia, Poland, Czechoslovakia, Hungary, Yugoslavia, and Bulgaria—with Turkey not far off. Even friends were not unalterably friendly; and foes caused each other fear. National economy was distorted, military measures were exaggerated. A stolen province usually meant a frontier hermetically sealed for years. No merchandise could vault over the political barrier. The map fostered poverty.

Maps have always fascinated me. Behind the pink, green, bluish patches I see men, women, horses, officers, soldiers, huts, homes, government buildings. But what intrigues me most about a map is the unrealistic question: How would an altered geography modify history, national psychology, economics, politics? Suppose England, instead of being an island, leaned against France and Holland. Suppose there were no Straits of Gibraltar and Africa were part of Europe. Suppose a sea fifty miles wide separated Germany from

France. Would these two have gone to war so often? Napoleon might have conquered Russia if Spain had been a flat plain. A large island halfway between England and the United States would do what?

Man-made geography likewise shapes the fate of nations.

In modern times, the status of any single citizen is affected by that of all the citizens of a nation. His educational facilities, government services, communications, amusements, and level of life will be worse, even though his home district is wealthy, if the remainder of the country is poor. A California as prosperous as it is today would bolt from the Union if the other forty-seven states were as badly off as Poland. That was one reason for the North's objection to slavery in the South, and it is still a puzzle why the South and not the North seceded.

In a federal union each part strives to improve the other parts; without a federation each individual unit interferes with the progress of all the others. This was especially true of the states in southeastern Europe. Complementary economies were broken up by treaties, conquests, and a suicidal urge toward being nationally self-contained. Each nation was strong enough to resist the natural attraction toward one another. But none could withstand the pull of powerful countries like Germany, Russia, and Italy.

The confusion of races and nationalities in the Balkans is so great that any boundary works injustice. There is no good solution of this problem except decent treatment for ethnic minorities in all countries or a federation of all these countries. Transfer of established populations is cruel.

Vienna mirrored the tragedy of central and southeastern Europe. Vienna mourned. The Friends estimated that half the population of Vienna was tubercular. They took me to a clinic. The low vitality of parents, the malnutrition of mothers, and war-time childhood had raised a harvest of unfortunates. Rickets, heart and nervous disorders of youth and adults, venereal illnesses and rheumatism, filled ward after ward. Many people on the street should obviously have been in hospitals. Mutilated men, wearing "totally blind" or "wounded in Galicia" signs, recalled the terse language of army bulletins: "Successful night reconnaissance." "Enemy trench captured in hand-to-hand fighting." Or even, "All quiet except for occasional artillery fire."

4. *Hitler Is Born*

EUROPE was sick and Germany was its sick heart.

The illness went back to the War. Millions of Germans—perhaps the majority of Germans—never believed that the Allies achieved a military victory. Germany won nearly every battle from 1914 to 1918. As late as the offensive of March-to-May, 1918, General Paul von Hindenburg, the Kaiser's commander-in-chief, bent the Allied lines and penetrated perilously close to the French ports on the English Channel. On May 30, the Germans reached the Marne River again. The Allies started winning only in the second fortnight of July, 1918, but the German war communiqués suppressed the truth until October, and the end came so quickly thereafter that few Germans could adjust their minds to the idea of Germany's defeat on the battlefield. Ludendorff, the greatest German military genius of the War, stated bluntly that the army was beaten. "The war must be ended," he wrote frantically on August 8. By September 29, the German Staff was clamoring for an armistice. "The military situation admits of no delay," Hindenburg declared in a plea for peace. Yet the legend of the unbeaten German army was created at that very moment, and it persisted for years and wrought infinite mischief in the interval between the two great wars. Facts cannot compete with a fiction that is comforting.

The fiction blamed rebellious German civilians for Germany's defeat. To lose the War after having won almost all the battles was so startling and painful to patriots that they invented the "stab in the back" theory. The phantom backstabbers were the Socialists, Communists, Jews, democrats, and pacifists. They allegedly stabbed the nation in the back while the army still held the front. An unintelligent national pride made it seem pleasanter to succumb to the furtive hand of the internal foe than to the foreign mailed fist.

The authors of this myth obscured the simple truth that the last battle is decisive. They forgot that they had been hungry since 1916. Nations do not win wars on a diet of turnips and beets nor in half-paper suits that melt in the rain. Germany's man-power was exhausted. Germany's allies had crumpled. American troops had come into the War to help tip the balance against the Kaiser. But the militarists and reactionaries who had conducted the war wanted to evade the guilt of losing it.

This unhistoric version of Germany's defeat in the first World War had a bearing on the second. It meant that Germany might try again—provided the civilians were under proper control. Moreover, the myth suited the mentality of a public that glories in military efficiency. It suited the army which could hope to dominate the state again if its prestige remained unimpaired. It was a cunning Monarchist weapon against the democrats.

The Allied victory of 1918 brought these democrats into power in Germany. Germany's defeat made Germany democratic. If the Allies and the German democrats had not committed innumerable blunders, Germany might have remained a democracy.

In defeat, the leaders of German militarism scattered. Ludendorff escaped to Sweden. Hindenburg went into silent retirement in Germany. The Kaiser fled to Holland on the advice of his generals. He probably would have been quite safe had he stayed at home. On November 7, when the War was already lost, Kurt Eisner proclaimed a radical republic at Munich, Bavaria. In the first days of November, sailors rioted at Kiel. The military did not try to crush these revolutionary efforts. The army, for the moment, was through. The Monarchist government abdicated. It was through. It peacefully transferred the reins of power to Fritz Ebert, a conservative Socialist. There was no treachery by subversive civilians. There was no German Revolution. The lower strata of society did not rise up and smash the upper crust. Royalty, nobility, and plutocracy, momentarily frightened, took refuge in their lairs and waited. The seats of the mighty simply stood vacant, and those from the depths were thus denied the élan or satisfaction of having fought on the barricades, stormed palaces, and shot traitors. The old was not destroyed. The new had no triumphs. If it was a "revolution," it was a typically German revolution. Nobody stepped on the grass.

The German republic itself was born between spoonfuls of soup. Philipp Scheidemann, bearded Socialist leader, tells the graphic story in his memoirs. "With Ebert, who had come from the Chancery to the Reichstag," and other friends, Scheidemann writes, "I sat hungry in the dining-hall. Thin, watery soup was the only thing to be had."

It was November 9, 1918. The Kaiser and Crown Prince had abdicated the previous day. They had given up the War as lost.

Scheidemann meditated over his tasteless soup. Suddenly "a crowd of workers and sailors rushed into the hall and made straight for our table. Fifty of them yelled out at the same time: 'Scheidemann, come along with us at once. Philipp, you must come out and speak.'

"I refused; how many times had I not already spoken.

" 'You must, you must if trouble is to be avoided. . . . Liebknecht [Karl Liebknecht, the Communist leader] is already speaking from the balcony of the Palace.'

"Well, if I must.

" 'Liebknecht intends to proclaim the Soviet republic.' "

When this information reached Scheidemann he made up his mind. "Now I saw clearly what was afoot," he writes. "I knew his [Liebknecht's] slogan—supreme authority for the Workers' and Soldiers' Councils. Germany to be a Russian province, a branch of the Soviet? No, no. . . ."

Scheidemann then went to a balcony of the Reichstag and spoke to the mass of men below. Carried away by his own eloquence and mindful of the Liebknecht threat, Scheidemann exclaimed, "The old and the rotten—the monarchy—have broken down. Long live the new! Long live the German Republic!"

Scheidemann then went back to his cold soup. When Ebert heard of the incident, he summoned Scheidemann. "Ebert's face," Scheidemann testifies, "turned livid with wrath. . . . He banged his fist on the table and yelled at me: 'Is it true?' . . . 'You have no right to proclaim the Republic.' Ebert to a certain extent was not a free agent." Ebert and Prince Max, the Kaiser's last Chancellor, had reached a secret understanding. They proposed to appoint a regent. Ebert would be "Imperial Administrator" until the people quieted down. Public opinion swept away Ebert's plan. But Ebert remained. He was the Republic's first president. Communist agitation had built a fire under the Socialists and hastened the advent of the Republic. The ferment in the working class convinced Ebert that he could not salvage the monarchy. He stayed to save the capitalist Republic.

The Socialists saved Germany from revolution. They feared the Communists more than the reactionaries. The reactionaries were biding their time while the Communists threatened to act. The Communist goal was a Soviet dictatorship and socialist economics. The moderate Socialists denounced this as "Asiatic Bolshevism." They wished to retain and reform private capitalism, and objected to the violent overthrow of existing institutions.

The Soviet hand had showed itself in Berlin. The Soviet government and the Kaiser's government had signed the Brest-Litovsk peace treaty on March 5, 1918. By its terms Russia abandoned the Allies and ceased fighting Germany. It was a peace at the tip of a mighty German sword. The Kaiser thereupon sent an ambassador to Moscow and Lenin sent an ambassador to Berlin. Lenin's envoy, Adolf A. Joffe, was new as a diplomat but experienced as a revolutionary, one of the founders of the Soviet regime. According to the cold official formula, he was *persona grata* to the German imperial government. Actually he endeavored to overthrow it. He hated it. It was imperialist and he was a Bolshevik. Why should he not work against it? He did. That was the direct honest approach of those days. Years later he told me the story; it was in 1927 when Joffe was forty-four years old. Soviet developments had filled him with anguish and he had decided to commit suicide in demonstrative protest against Stalin's policies. Before he killed himself he asked me to come see him. I had never met him, and had not requested an appointment. But he sent me a message through a mutual friend. He wanted to talk to an outsider for the record. What he revealed was confirmed by his 1919 reports which he took from his files and showed me. His embassy in Berlin, he said, served as staff headquarters for a German revolution. He bought secret information from German officials and passed it on to radical leaders for use in public speeches and in articles against the government. He bought arms for the revolutionaries and paid out 100,000 marks for them. Tons of anti-Kaiser literature were printed and distributed at the Soviet embassy's expense. "We wanted to pull down the monarchist state and end the war," Joffe said to me. "President Woodrow Wilson tried to do the same in his own way." Almost every evening after dark, left-wing Independent Socialist leaders slipped into the embassy building on Unter den Linden to consult Joffe on questions of tactics. He was an experienced conspirator. They wanted his advice, guidance, and money. "In the end, however," Joffe commented ruefully, "they, we, accomplished little or nothing of permanent value. We were too weak to provoke a revolution." He thought for a moment and added, "We probably shortened the war by a month and saved lives. Some generals proposed a fight to the finish rather than accept the Wilson-Foch terms. They wanted to go down in a blaze of glory. Admiral Scheer of the

German navy wished to lead his ships out to challenge the British Grand Fleet in open combat. He knew it was hopeless but he hoped it would be heroic. The sailors at Kiel hoisted the red flag and prevented the vain slaughter. Prince Max of Baden did not send troops, he sent Noske [the conservative Socialist] to quell the Kiel disturbances. That was canny of the bourgeoisie."

The Monarchists withdrew from the scene and let the Socialists subdue the Communists in the streets and face the enemy at Versailles. That placed the odium of the peace treaty on the Socialists who had to sign it because nobody else would—Dr. Bell, a Catholic, also signed—and left the others free to condemn it. Abdication was finally wrenched from the unwilling Kaiser by the argument that German democracy would get better terms from the Allies. He and his friends regarded the Socialists as a protective façade, as temporary seat-warmers. It might have been better to compel the war-makers and war leaders to take their medicine at Versailles. Instead they stepped aside and saved their skins and, many of them, their reputations by a brief vanishing act. The roots of the power of the army, of the estate owners or Junkers, and of the manufacturers and permanent government officials remained untouched. Within two months after the establishment of the German Republic, the Monarchists commenced their attacks on it. In 1920, they attempted to overthrow it by Kapp's insurrection. By 1922, they had enough voting strength, political power, and propaganda-pressure to veto many of the liberal policies of the new democratic regime, and a year later business magnates like Hugo Stinnes enjoyed more influence than a German prime minister.

When I arrived in Germany at the end of 1921, the Monarchy was more in evidence than the Republic. The republican black-red-and-gold flag flew from public buildings, but the yachts and motor boats in the lakes around Berlin as well as many homes consistently displayed the black-white-and-red banner of the Kaiser. The press of the Right described the colors of the republican flag as "black-red-and-mustard," and in private conversation "mustard" became something even more disrespectful.

Strolling through the streets of Berlin or Munich or Hamburg, I would note the firm hold of the imperial Hohenzollern tradition on the minds of the people. Scarcely a stationery store that did not show in its windows, and sell, glossy black-and-white or sepia postcard photographs of "Wilhelm II: German Kaiser"—no one bothered to call him an "ex-"—and portraits of the entire former royal family, especially of "the dearly beloved and much mourned Kaiserin Augusta Victoria." In hotel foyers and hotel rooms, in beer gardens and concert halls, likenesses of the ex-Kaiser hung in pre-War prominence. Berlin street names testified to the timidity of the republic: there was Kaiserallee, Hohenzollerndamm, Koenigin Augusta Strasse, Kronprinzen Ufer, Prinz Regenten Strasse, and so on.

Potsdam, cradle of Prussian militarism, rang with festivities on May 5, 1922. It was the birthday of the former Crown Prince Wilhelm. The town was gay with imperial colors, regimental flags, generals, admirals, and other officers in gala attire, with heel-clicking soldiers and military bands, with male students (embryo men and embryo Nazis) in the bright braided jackets, tight trousers, and bellboy caps of their dueling, militantly aristocratic, anti-Semitic fraternities. General Ludendorff's house in Potsdam—he returned to Germany in spring, 1919, when the anticipated storm was no longer anticipated—served as center of the celebrations, and he himself was the soul of the agitation against Germany's democratically elected government. The Monarchists published numerous daily newspapers, weeklies, monthlies, and books. They had money, position, political security. Their capital was tradition. They strummed the chords of sentiment. They were playing a game for the restoration of what had once been their exclusive world and had now been invaded by workingmen, shopkeepers, men without titles, intellectuals without money, Jews, pacifists, civilians who could not goosestep, women— in a word, by "democrats."

A film was packing several large movie houses in Berlin, breaking all records of attendance—"Fredericus Rex." It depicted the life of King Frederick the Great, father of Prussia's glory. He had been opposed to soldiering. The producer showed his subsequent conversion to militarism. Frederick coined the slogan: "Drill, drill, drill." Each time he uttered the stupid words the spectators clapped vociferously. They were not applauding history, much less art; they were making politics. And then this scene: Frederick in his room waiting to be crowned "Rex." His chief of staff enters, bows low, exclaims dramatically, "Majesty, your people call you." The theater shook with floor-banging and hand-clapping. The noise was obviously a demonstration, a call to another "majesty" not yet dead. Among those who applauded most were youngsters who had just missed the "joys" of fighting at the front, boys who were fifteen or sixteen in 1918 and to whom the war was drums, excitement, and adventure. Many were hooligans who established their manhood by engaging in brawls or by beating up Jews in dark alleys. It was not merely the rambunctiousness of youth, however. They yearned for a Germany that was strong, strong enough to fit them into a groove. They wanted to be cogs in a great machine and grieved because the machine had fallen into a thousand bits.

Daily a Reichswehr guard of sixteen men and an officer marched through busy Berlin streets from its barracks to the President's palace. They were perfect soldiers, polished and clean in olive-green uniforms, tin hats, and leather boots that reached halfway up their calves. They goosestepped in unison like sixteen robots, like one robot. Germans stopped to admire. Women and children marched alongside. Middle-aged men in the somber clothes of merchants or government officials—high wing collar, striped trousers, felt hat— would join the procession and solemnly tap out the left-right rhythm with a cane or tightly wrapped umbrella. They were trying to recapture their youth, perhaps, and see whether they could do what they had practiced twenty years before. But it was more than that. They were demonstrating their identity with the glorious army, merging themselves with it for a moment. Versailles had limited the Reichswehr to one hundred thousand men, but spiritually it numbered millions.

I have seen Britishers watch the changing of the Horse Guards in Whitehall. They looked on it as a brilliant, colorful spectacle, a part, along with fox hunting, of the feudal past, something to gaze upon but not feel about. A similar ceremony in Germany was filled with political significance.

Monarchy also had a popular appeal. It evoked memories of national might, prosperity, and pageantry. The anti-democrats made political capital out of this nostalgia for the irrevocable glory of the past. But for them it was less important to crush the Republic than to control it. If it became their republic, an autocratic, militaristic republic, the Kaiser could saw Dutch wood forever. When Hindenburg was elected President of the Republic on April 26, 1925 (at the age of seventy-eight), the Monarchists ceased sighing for the crown and scepter, the ermine and the purple. Ludendorff, the Monarchist, worked with Hitler who was anti-Monarchist. Differences on the form of the state, on manners and tactics, vanished before a unifying enmity to democracy at home and abroad.

The Junker estate owners, the ex-officers, the Pan-Germans, claimed to be the paragons of patriotism. National unity was ostensibly their highest concern. The Socialists were supposed to be the internationalists. Yet in December, 1921, Otto Braun, the Socialist president of the state of Prussia, appealed to Germans against splitting up Germany. It was an appeal against the machinations of right-wing reactionaries in Bavaria and the Rhineland, who wished to separate from a reparations-paying Germany dominated by Prussian Socialists. Politics and purse were stronger than patriotism. France helped kill these German separatistic tendencies by financing them. In the main, however, it was German socialism which kept Germany intact in the years immediately following the first World War.

In 1919 and until 1924, the moderate Socialists, who called themselves Social Democrats, were the solid core of German political life. No stable government could be formed against them or without their support. The reactionaries on the Right might embarrass the government with propaganda and assassinations but they were too few to rule. The Reichswehr therefore courted the Socialists.

Governments came and governments went in republican Germany, but the hand that guided the German army was never far from, and was often on, the rudder of the ship of state. To safeguard its existence and future, the army adapted its colors to the complexion of the state. It changed during the years from Socialist pink to Nazi brown. It co-operated with the Russian Red Army and the Italian Blackshirts, with Prussian Socialists and Bavarian Monarchists. Political creed mattered less than power. Reichswehr officers, to be sure, had their preferences. Their sympathies were for the Right. But they took what they could get from each government in office so as to build Germany's military might. The Reichswehr wanted law and order and a return to normal conditions. The Socialists gladly leaned on the Reichswehr because they knew the dangers that threatened from people like Kapp, Ludendorff, the Bavarian Monarchists, the Rhineland Separatists, and Ehrhardt's terrorist gangs.

But powerful forces worked for illegal disorder. At the lunch hour on June 24, 1922, I walked out of an office into the street and immediately became aware of an extraordinary quality in the atmosphere. The newspaper vendor at the corner was surrounded by eager buyers as he kept yelling, "*B.Z. am Mittag*, Rathenau Ermordet." The Foreign Minister of Germany had been shot that morning. Europe heard the shot and shuddered.

Walter Rathenau's father, Emil, founded the AEG, or General Electric Company, of Germany. The son was president of the firm. He abandoned business to become foreign minister. He wrangled, sometimes successfully, with the Allied statesmen to reduce reparations. He sought to persuade Germany to live in harmony with the victorious powers. He was diplomat and industrialist, German and Jew, German and European, physicist, chemist, philosopher, and writer. The titles of his books, *The New Society*, *Of Coming Things*, and *Democratic Development* suggest what his dreams were. His long face with its delicate lines reflected the wise businessman and cultivated modern. Even when he addressed the rowdy Reichstag he spoke in a whisper, and the deputies listened. In German life he represented the pole furthest removed from the ruffians who killed him. He was fifty-five when he died on the street.

Every morning Rathenau drove from his house on the Koenigsallee in the Grunewald suburb to the Foreign Office in the Wilhelmstrasse. At 10:50 A.M. on June 24, the car in which he was the sole passenger had reached the intersection of Koenigsallee and Wallotstrasse when an automobile carrying three young men dashed by in the opposite direction. Nine shots were fired at him, and then a hand grenade was thrown into his machine. After the first shot he was seen to rise and attempt to give instructions to his chauffeur. But immediately he slumped back. He was dead before he could be taken home. Three revolver bullets had entered the back of the neck and gone out through the right breast. These alone would have been fatal. . . .

The quest for the murderers started forthwith and extended throughout Germany. A reward of a million marks was offered for information leading to their arrest.

A forest gamekeeper had arrived in Berlin that morning from his province. He was interested in automobiles. He was at the spot of the murder shortly before it occurred, and when he read about it in the paper he reported to the police that he had seen a powerful machine at 10:30 A.M. and, because its radiator was covered so he could not discover the make, and the motor running, he stopped and took special notice of it. He and other passers-by described the chauffeur and the single occupant. Both wore brown leather suits and goggles, and were between twenty and twenty-five years old. A third man walked up and down the street and appeared to be giving signals to the man in the back of the car.

The moment the shots had been fired the car rushed off with the three men in it. The police came to the scene without delay but only bicycles were available for the pursuit. IA, the Police Department of Berlin district, sent word to all frontier posts to watch for the murderers. A detective story, revealing conditions which later made history, began to unfold. It was a preview of Nazism.

Everyone took it for granted that the murder was political. The Socialist press charged that the Nationalists had been planning a St Bartholomew's Day, a massacre of democrats, for July 28. Newspapers said President Ebert, Chancellor Wirth, Rathenau, Scheidemann, and others had been marked as victims.

Several hours after the murder, the Reichstag went into session. General von Schoch, a deputy of the People's Party, a conservative. Monarchist, industrialist group, uttered some jocose remarks about the sudden passing of Rathenau. The Socialists rushed at him yelling "scoundrel." He ran for cover. Then Karl Helfferich entered. He was a leader of the German Nationalist Party, and the day before he had delivered a vicious personal diatribe in the Reichstag against Rathenau. Helfferich opposed conciliation of the Allies and the payment of reparations. As he stepped into the Reichstag now, the Democrats and Socialists greeted him with loud calls, "You are the murderer," "This is the result of your speech yesterday," "Out with the murderers." A score of left-wing Reichstag members approached him, their fists ready. His fellow Nationalists surrounded him to protect him, and finally, white and trembling, he left the chamber.

The same day, Chancellor Wirth, of the Catholic Center Party, visibly moved by the murder of his closest political colleague, rose in the Reichstag and facing right, exclaimed: "Gentlemen of the Right, things cannot continue as they have till now." He read an official proclamation. "There must be a thoroughgoing change. This growing terror, this nihilism which often hides under the cloak of patriotic sentiment, must no longer be treated with consideration. We shall act quickly."

Hundreds of arrests were made as the police scoured the country for the three murderers. Dr. Weiss, chief of police in Berlin, issued a bulletin denying that the hunt was being directed, as in the case of the murdered Catholic statesman Erzberger, by detectives who were Racists (later Nazis). The Erzberger murderers had never been captured. Weiss promised to act with energy this time.

The police were studying scores of threatening letters which Rathenau had received from anonymous writers. Rathenau's secre-

ary turned them over after the murder. The police themselves had
uspected something, and for some time two detectives had trailed
he foreign minister. On the morning of the murder, however, he
was unescorted.

Rathenau had submitted to the detectives' protection, but each evening when he went to dine with his aged mother he slipped away
from them so that she would not be alarmed. During the first three
days after the murder, Frau Rathenau received numerous insulting
letters, and her telephone rang incessantly. She did not reply, of
course, but when the maid lifted the receiver the voice at the other
end would say: "So we got your bastard son." Or, "Serves the Jew
right." Or, "He is only the first."

Three hours after the murder, Werner Flesch, a student, forced
his way into the Reichstag building and delivered a laurel wreath for
Karl Helfferich with the inscription, "To the Savior of German
Honor." Flesch was known as an ardent adherent of Captain Ehrhardt, the chief of a subversive organization known as "O.C." On
June 25, Flesch was arrested. Karl Tillessen, retired lieutenant, and
brother of the murderer of Erzberger who fled to Austria, was also
arrested.

All airdromes received strict instructions from the authorities to
accept no passenger who was not fully identified. In Helsinki, the
Finnish police, at the request of the German legation, arrested three
members of the crew of the German *S. S. Ruegen* in connection with
the Rathenau assassination.

The workingmen in the city of Karlsruhe tore down the "By
Royal Appointment" and "Deliverers to the Kaiser" signs over numerous stores. Crowns on public buildings were smashed. The municipality of Magdeburg ordered the Monarchist names of streets altered to "Rathenau Street," "Erzberger Street," "Einstein Street,"
"Avenue of the Republic," and so on. Similar changes were made in
Berlin and elsewhere.

On June 28, police found the automobile of the murderers. It was
a highpowered Mercedes with modern lines and had been left in a
west-end garage the very afternoon of the deed. The garage manager
was arrested for not reporting this fact. He declared that a chauffeur
had come to him on June 20 and rented space for the car, saying
that he was waiting for his employer to arrive from another city.
The description of the chauffeur given by the manager coincided
with that given by the forester.

In the morning of June 29, Chief of Police Weiss published th
names of the murderers. They were Ernest Werner Techow, chauf
feur, aged 21, born in Berlin, dark blond; Hermann Fischer, also
called Vogel, 25, light blond; Erwin Knauer, alias Koerner and Kern
25, blue eyes, light blond, participant in the Kapp putsch. Weiss
revealed that he had learned the names three days earlier but sup
pressed them because he thought the murderers might still be hiding
in Berlin. Now he had reason to believe they had gone to the prov
inces and he was broadcasting their names and publishing their photo
graphs because he hoped to embarrass their friends to whom they
might come for food, lodging, and money. All three belonged to
Ehrhardt's secret O.C.

Luck brought a specimen of Fischer's handwriting to the police
Fischer had spent the night before the murder in a lodging house in
Berlin. He knew the housemaid there and before coming into town
he wrote her a letter telling her of his impending arrival and asking
her to go dancing with him that evening. He also protested his love
and signed "Hermann." When she saw his photograph in the press
the maid delivered the letter to the authorities who were thus in a
position to include a facsimile of it in the reward placards. Visitor
to inns and hotels had to register, and even if Fischer signed a false
name the way he formed his letters would serve as a basis of comparison.

On June 29, Ernst Werner Techow, the driver, was arrested in
Frankfurt-on-the-Oder and brought to Berlin under heavy guard
His father had been a rich, respected merchant and judge, politically
neutral, who died in 1918. His mother lost the family's money in the
inflation, and from the same cause the pension which the government paid her dwindled almost to nothing. Ernst Werner Techow
the press said, was a member of a "Right Bolshevik association."
(Subsequently, this loose term was translated; "right" became Nationalist, "Bolshevik" became Socialist. Together, National Socialist
or Nazi.) Techow fought in the Monarchist Kapp putsch in 1920
In the same putsch, a younger brother, Hans, then fourteen years
old, organized high-school boys to act as runners and ammunition
carriers. (Hans later became an intimate co-worker of Baldur von
Schirach, leader of the Hitler Youth Movement under the Nazi
government.)

On June 30, Chauffeur Techow confessed. The auto, he declared
belonged to Herr Kuechenmeister, a rich manufacturer in Saxony

who lent it for the crime. On telegraphed instructions from Berlin, Kuechenmeister was arrested. Two mine throwers, six heavy machine guns, four light machine guns, 150 rifles, and thirty cases of ammunition were found in his plant.

Despite this great initial success, the police now lost all trace of the other two murderers. Fischer, born in 1896 in Florence, Italy, where his father was a sculptor, was still at large with his friend, Erwin Kern. Hundreds of detectives searched the countryside. They used motor cars, motorcycles, and bloodhounds who had been given the scent of the murderers' car and of Techow's clothes. But for a week they registered no progress. Suddenly, on July 10, Chief of Police Weiss arrived at Gardelegen, a small town eighty-five miles due west from Berlin, in the big Mercedes employed by Fischer and Kern for the assassination, and set up his headquarters there. Fischer and Kern were seen on that day in the vicinity. A village physician observed them anxiously perusing a map. A schoolteacher reported that the two men stopped him on a road and asked the way to Gifhorn. They were on bicycles. Detectives followed this clue until farmers told them that they had seen two men cycling in the opposite direction. This went on for hours. One person sent the police on one trail and the next person on a totally different one until Weiss and his assistants became convinced that the population was deliberately deceiving them in order to facilitate the murderers' escape. The police thereupon hunted down the informants and arrested them. This was a region of villages and tiny towns whose inhabitants were notoriously Monarchist and Racist. In several small urban centers the reward notices were torn down. The police had drawn a solid ring from Gardelegen to Braunschweig to Brandenburg, but with the aid of local people the two criminals broke through.

To create public sentiment for the Rathenau murderers the reactionary Berlin *Deutsche Tageszeitung* stated that before accepting the offer to become German foreign minister, Dr. Rathenau inquired in Paris whether he should take the post. The Berlin democratic press rejected this canard. The *Berliner Tageblatt* collected public subscriptions amounting to 210,118 marks as an additional reward for those who found the murderers. The government raised its own reward from one million marks to two million. A considerable number of people were arrested on the charge of feeding and housing Fischer and Kern. The people pleaded ignorance, and said they did not read newspapers and had seen no reward placards.

The police were desperate. If the Rathenau murderers eluded the trap set for them just as the Erzberger assassins had, there would be a premium on political terror against republicans, and perhaps a St. Bartholomew's Massacre would indeed take place on July 28. Moreover, the police would be discredited and the hoodlums and swastika patriots encouraged. Weiss increased his force of detectives; nearly a thousand trained men were assigned to the case throughout Germany. Weiss was not dealing with two men, but with two men and untold sympathizers ready to harbor and save them.

On July 12, came news, confirmed by reliable witnesses, that Fischer and Kern had spent the previous night in a flophouse in Schoeningen. They had left at five-thirty in the morning on their bicycles. Weiss sent forty-five policemen to head them off. He suspected they were making for the Harz Mountains. Meanwhile, at headquarters in Gardelegen, hundreds of Germans were being brought in for questioning. Many were later released, a few held. Under persistent cross-examination, a forester in Lenzen admitted having put the murderers up for a night. They had been recommended to him by a rich merchant from Kalies. Thousands of clues kept coming in, some obviously calculated to mislead. Berlin created a new special section of fifty police officials to examine volunteer witnesses.

Detectives investigated every estate and meadow and farm in the vicinity of Schoeningen. Every hut was entered. Several reports suggested that the men were short of money. The police thought the murderers would therefore try to get back to Berlin where it might also be easier to disappear from sight. Accordingly, all roads, main and tributary, from Genthin to Stendal to Brandenburg to Berlin were closed; pedestrians, cyclists, and automobilists had to show identification papers. Every railway station in the area and in Germany was watched. The farming population was warned by proclamation that anyone caught defacing the reward posters would be severely punished. Special "Don't Help the Rathenau Murderers" notices were pasted up.

The police announced that the murderers traveled by night on bicycles and hid during the day. The police could check some of their movements but could not catch up with them. On the night of the eleventh they were in Wismar. They knocked at the door of Herr Otto, a businessman, and retired naval captain. He gave them bread and wine but would not let them stay. From there they went to Neukloster and called on a school comrade named Karl Bauer. He too fed them and sent them on to Herr Wiese, a retired officer. Wiese said they told him they were students on a hike, and gave their names as Funke and Koester. It was impossible to establish whether Wiese believed them or not. In any case, he passed them on to a friend who was chief secretary of the Post Office in Lenzen. The secretary invited them to dinner. He advised them to take a room in the near-by Hotel zur Sonne, which they did. At the hotel it was stated that the two hunted men did sleep there but left early in the morning and crossed the Elbe. They were short of funds and looked weary and bedraggled.

Police established patrols through the Harz Mountains. The innumerable hotels and inns of this great German tourist and vacation area were visited by detectives. Occupants were awakened in the night and searched and questioned on the spot. In one village two young cyclists were arrested. They turned out to be innocent. In another place, reports reached the police that a couple of cyclists were seen studying maps and acting queerly. The police found them, too, but they were not the murderers. The police now felt convinced that the Swastika organizations were sending scores of cycling male couples into the region of search with instructions to behave suspiciously and complicate the task of the authorities.

Berlin announced that Maximilian Harden, famous German liberal gadfly publicist, editor of the weekly *Zukunft* (*Future*), attacked by armed youths on July 3, was sinking from loss of blood. His assailants were also being tracked down.

On July 14, the police arrested a man at Wittenberg, north of Gardelegen. He was a member of the Rossbach, a secret subversive society, and had explosives in his possession. He was not implicated in the Rathenau murder, the police stated, but the government suspected that the Racists were planning to assassinate other prominent republicans so as to divert the attention of the police from Fischer and Kern.

At the city of Hanover the police chased two suspicious men, who escaped to a village in the running fight. One was wounded but both escaped. Were they Fischer and Kern or were they sympathizers trying to mislead the searchers? The police could not answer the question.

The government of the state of Bavaria was putting obstacles in the way of the Prussian police. Count Preger, the Bavarian ambassa-

dor in Berlin, told the Federal Council of Justice that Bavaria wa
tired of being in the Reich federation and insisted on State rights
He denied that Munich could not co-operate in the hunt for Fische
and Kern, but behind these words the police saw a Bavarian intention to create difficulties. The police became feverish. Fischer and
Kern were heading south for Bavaria. If the murderers reached tha
destination the chase would be well-nigh hopeless, for Bavaria wa
also the safe haven of refuge of the Erzberger assassins.

On Sunday, July 16, two young salesmen from Halle, on an out-
ing in the country, came to a hill surmounted by a castle. They inquired from local residents about the castle and were told that it wa
an old structure, dating back centuries. One of its ancient towers wa
a ruin, but the other was inhabited by Count Hans Wilhelm Stein
and his wife who, however, were away on a trip. Saaleck Castle wa
therefore not open for inspection. The salesmen nevertheless climbe
the hill and saw lights in the inhabited tower. They approached the
windows and looked in. Two men were sitting and reading newspapers. They resembled the poster pictures of the murderers. The
salesmen tiptoed away, descended, and informed the police.

On the seventeenth, the hill and castle were surrounded by detectives. This time hopes of success were high. A locksmith wa
fetched from town but the key inside was turned so skillfully tha
he failed to open the door. No sign of life came from the inside
The police retired to the wood surrounding Saaleck Castle and
waited all morning. They waited part of the afternoon. As twiligh
approached two young men stood up on the battlement of the castle
tower, waved handkerchiefs, and cried, "Leave us alone." Then the
retired within. Half an hour later they reappeared and yelled, "Up
Captain Ehrhardt." The police decided to break into the castle. A
they approached, the two men inside shouted, "You cowards, come
on," and fired. The police returned the fire. A moment later, between
blows of a battering ram that was smashing the door, one voice in
the castle was heard exclaiming, "We are dying for our ideals. Gree
Ehrhardt. Long may he live! Hoch!" Then a shot rang out inside
and all was quiet. The police entered. Fischer lay dead on the floor
with a revolver in his right hand. He had put it in his mouth and
pulled the trigger. Upstairs Kern was lying dead in a bed. He had
been felled by a police shot. Fischer had dragged him up to the bedroom and tried vainly to stop the profuse flow of blood. When
Kern died Fischer committed suicide. Both were buried in the Saa-

leck cemetery. (The Hitler regime erected a monument to them.) On their bodies were found three thousand marks. Their bicycles were gone. They had three maps and two bottles of bock beer bought in a store on the outskirts of Gardelegen. Saaleck is one hundred miles south of Gardelegen. Their outer clothing was new. They had discarded the clothing worn in Berlin. Bloodhound recognition, photographs, and every other sign definitely confirmed Fischer and Kern as Rathenau's murderers.

Kern was known to the police as the man who helped Captain Dittmar, a Kapp putsch leader, to escape from prison. Dittmar hid in Saaleck Castle after his flight. At that time, too, Count Stein was away on a trip. Stein was arrested on the eighteenth. He had long been an outstanding member of the Nationalist Party.

The Rathenau murder and this tale of the murderers unfold a map of the ground in which the Hitler regime sprouted and flowered. International developments and German domestic events sometimes fertilized the soil. In other years they killed the plants that grew on it. But the roots never died.

Dr. E. J. Gumbel, higher mathematics professor at Heidelberg University, has tabulated the political murders of Germany. In 1921 and 1922, the Right committed 354 assassinations of leading republicans. No Right leader was killed.

The assassins were often inspired by the older Monarchists, but they themselves were not Monarchist. They were not anything in the early years of the Republic. They had no definite constructive goal, no program. They rebelled against governmental authority but joyously submitted to the rigorous discipline of their own secret societies. They thirsted for adventure, danger, and violence. They detested the soft, liberal, humanistic tones of the Republic. Theirs was a cult of blood, brute strength, and brawn. They despised intellect, business, and the bourgeoisie. No one took these Nazis seriously. But they took themselves seriously, and that is what mattered in the end.

Their Freikorps or volunteer semi-military formations enveloped themselves in a romantic fellowship that had originated in the World War trenches. Upon demobilization from the army they had organized in bands under Captain Ehrhardt and other desperate characters. They had fought in Latvia, Esthonia, and Finland against the Bolsheviks, against the Poles in Upper Silesia, and against workingmen and the Republic in Germany. Ehrhardt was their "Consul." When the government declared them illegal they doffed their uniforms with the Viking ship sewed on the sleeves and reappeared as tourist associations, sports clubs, study circles, chess circles, private detective bureaus, wandering circuses. One group labeled itself O.C., Organization Consul. The Berlin authorities wanted Ehrhardt for high treason. Officially, he had fled to Innsbruck, Austria. It was public knowledge, however, that he came to Munich whenever he wished to instruct his youthful subversive followers. (Count Arco, who murdered Kurt Eisner, was also at large in Munich.) These Freikorps stored arms at convenient hide-outs throughout Germany, but Bavaria was their stronghold because its political climate was most congenial to their anti-government activities. Many of them were later encountered in the Gestapo or secret police, the Brownshirts, and the black-uniformed S.S. guard of the Nazi government.

I visited Bavaria in May, 1922, and went to Oberammergau, in the Bavarian Alps, where the celebrated Passion Play is performed. Up in the mountains above the village, huge crosses cut in rock dominated the vicinity, and one slept on high, downy beds under crucifixes of bone, stone, and wood. The peasants were mild and kindly, soft-spoken, smiling, and eager to please the visitors who even in that disturbed year came from all ends of the earth, especially from Ireland and Italy. The villagers who did not act, made and sold souvenirs. The whole village lived by religion.

Then one descended to Munich, the capital of Catholic Bavaria. Munich was the center for modern art, for a neo-paganism preached in beer-halls, for conspiracies hatched against the state under the open eyes of Bavarian officials. When President Ebert visited Munich he was attended by a heavy bodyguard and he kept out of public sight as much as possible. The republican flag was often torn down and burned.

Immediately after Rathenau's murder, the federal government asked the Reichstag to adopt an emergency Defense of the Republic bill, granting the authorities wider powers to deal with dissident elements and assassins. The act was a pressing necessity, but the Nationalists deliberately delayed its passage until the day after the Rathenau murderers were found dead. The Nationalists wished, above all, to exclude Bavaria from the operations of the new legislation. They failed. But then Bavaria refused to submit to it.

A significant thing happened. Gustav Stresemann's industrialist

People's Party supported the emergency Defense of the Republic Act. The People's Party had been avowedly Monarchist. But no Monarchist party could participate in a republican government. And politicians like to be in office. The People's Party accordingly abandoned its Monarchism when the popular reaction against the Rathenau murder convinced Stresemann that monarchism would always bar the industrialists from controlling the Republic. The loyalty of the Reichswehr to the Republic also influenced Stresemann's decision.

The Socialists put no trust in this sudden conversion. The Center and the Democrats, however, found comfort in the People's Party's modified stand. The Democrats were large and small tradesmen, officials, intellectuals, and enlightened, progressive factory owners—a bourgeois organization. The Center, unlike other German parties, did not represent a horizontal social stratum in the way the Socialists and Communists represented the workers, or the Nationalists the landowners, and the People's Party the big industrialists. It rose vertically through the strata and recruited from all of them on a religious basis. Thus it boasted the support of big, well-organized, and well-led trade unions, largely Catholic in membership, and also of Catholic landlords and Catholic manufacturers, merchants, and Bavarian reactionaries. For this reason the Center party usually had a stable following no matter how swiftly the German political pendulum swung from side to side. It consented to collaboration with Socialists but never relished this role, and it certainly preferred Stresemann to the left-wing Independent Socialists. So when Stresemann protested his republicanism, the Center and some Democrats saw here a possibility of salvation from Socialist preponderance in the government.

The Left tide was running out.

The workers were earning paper money whose purchasing power vanished hourly; tradesmen were being ruined by inflation; the standard of living of officials fell steadily. But anybody who owned property or exported goods abroad sailed on top of the wave. A farmer in 1921 owed a debt or mortgage of one thousand marks. At that time, this equaled the price of two cows. A year later he paid his indebtedness with the proceeds from the sale of twenty quarts of milk. Industrial producers drew even greater advantages from financial chaos. A workingman's average real wage amounted to only thirty-five cents a day. There was little unemployment. Germany's working population was engaged erecting vast industrial empires for Stinnes, Krupp, Otto Wolff, and the rest. These manufacturers produced with cheap labor and exported the product. Foreign countries paid gold, and industrialists kept their gold abroad. They were taking wealth out of Germany, impoverishing their country and its people, but enriching themselves. Mr. Gerard, the pre-War American ambassador to Germany, said in New York in July, 1922, after a two months' trip to Europe, "The only people [in Germany] making money are the manufacturers who are able to sell their products abroad for gold and pay their workers low wages. The Junkers are getting on well."

These circumstances gave the industrialists a stranglehold on the economic, and soon on the political, life of Germany. Certain persons even accused this inner German circle of deliberately keeping the mark down in value so that they could acquire new property inside Germany and gold hoards outside.

Throughout 1922, German housewives staged numerous riots. Haggard and weary, often emaciated and anemic, they stood in their neatly laundered and clean threadbare clothes waiting for hours in long queues. The meager family earnings did not satisfy the family's hunger. Sometimes prices rose while the queue was moving forward and then the housewife had to go home for more money, if she had it, or buy still less. Frequently, their patience exhausted and their nerves frayed, they smashed store windows or beat up storekeepers, damning them as speculators and profiteers. The government was powerless.

How did the Allies behave during the Rathenau murder emergency? Did they help the German Republic bridge the crisis? No. Germany asked for a moratorium. Chancellor Wirth's slogan was, "First bread, then reparations." Germany desired to be excused from reparations payments until December. David Lloyd George, still Prime Minister of Great Britain, would have granted the request. But Premier Raymond Poincaré demurred, and violently. Poincaré was a small man and a lawyer. It was said of him that he knew everything and understood nothing. Native of Lorraine, a province recovered from Germany in 1918, he feared and hated Germany. His view was narrowly national, "We ask only what is due us." German reparations payments had been included in the French government's budget as an income item, and if Germany failed to pay, the French government could not meet its obligations. But suppose Germany defaulted? Then sanctions. Poincaré carried around a plan for the invasion of the Ruhr.

The bulk of reparations, when paid, went to France and Belgium for they had suffered most property damage from the War. Reparations and inflation were strangling British foreign commerce. Some London economists realized that reparations were economic madness. On July 10, 1922, the *London Times*, the rhythm of whose editorials often beats in unison with the heart of the London City, or financial district, published an editorial entitled "The German Crisis" which said, "It is high time for Great Britain and France to take sober and earnest counsel together against the gathering menace to the fruits of our common victory." In the peculiar *Times* elliptical style this was going far, but a week later it actually resorted to the rude word "controversy." A controversy was raging between London and Paris. The British government favored a moratorium for Germany. It invited Premier Poincaré to come to London and talk it over. He postponed the reply; then he accepted "in principle" but delayed fixing the date of the trip. Finally he arrived on the seventh of August. There was the usual fanfare when a great statesman boards trains and alights from trains. Poincaré and Lloyd George attended numerous "momentous" ceremonies. History was supposedly being made in secret conclave. But after seven long days of behind-the-scenes bickering, during which Germany held its breath and stock-market tickers oscillated nervously, the Anglo-French conversations broke up in officially announced disagreement. Poincaré wanted control of German mines and forests, and would not hear of deferring Germany's reparations installments. Europe was left to drift. The dollar bought 840 marks on August 4. It bought 1,440 marks early on August 24. During business hours on August 24, the mark fell so much that in the evening a dollar bought 1,975 marks.

The German people suffered. Private homes equipped with electricity and gas used kerosene lamps because they were cheaper. Cities groaned from overcrowding, and foreigners rented the best apartments. Coal was rationed. Markets and second-hand stores overflowed with musical instruments, carpets, paintings, and fine books sold by impoverished members of the middle class. Thousands of amateur music teachers, masseuses, typists, waitresses, salesgirls, recruited from formerly comfortable families, depressed the standards of pay in these and similar professions. Night cafés, cabarets with naked dancers, gambling dens, and vulgar vaudeville shows attracted large clienteles of splurging, ostentatious profiteers, get-rich-quick inflation millionaires, and the social flotsam and criminal scum that move in their wake. Fortunes made in a day were dissipated overnight. Prostitutes complained of heavy amateur competition. Frequent robberies occurred in the apartments of foreigners. Public-school pupils lacked the means for the purchase of pencils, books, and paper. Sometimes teachers contributed these from their own slender salaries. Physicians with diplomas organized against quacks and miracle healers. Suicides multiplied. Most suicides employed gas because it cost little. Many newspapers and weeklies suspended publication on account of increased expenditures and reduced circulation. Paper cost fifty times the pre-War price. Innumerable Germans gave up buying flowers, and Germans love flowers. A medical examination of school children in Berlin showed 15.7 percent normally fed, 17.1 percent well-fed, 67.2 percent underfed. Children frequently fainted in class.

Germany's light was going out.

The German people suffered, and yearned for messiahs and panaceas. Astrologers did brisk business. They advertised extensively in newspapers. Louis Haeusser, like Ribbentrop, was a champagne salesman. He lost his money and became a wandering preacher. He called himself "The New Christ." He taught celibacy and the pure life. "Suppress your sex," he yelled at meetings. Thousands listened wherever he went.

In its illustrated section, the *Berliner Tageblatt* printed a photograph of a tall man with high forehead, dark unkempt hair that fell to his shoulders, and long beard down to his chest. He wore sandals over his stockingless feet, a skirt with ragged hem, and a cape. He was distributing leaflets to pedestrians. The newspaper called him another specimen of the "messiah plague" which was afflicting Germany.

In Munich, a man of thirty-three with less hair—he had only a small mustache and tiny beard—but possessing a hypnotic voice and queer manner and who did not have much sex to suppress was making speeches to small audiences. His name was Adolf Hitler. His father's surname was Schicklgruber. He hated workingmen and Jews and had not as yet distinguished himself by any love of truth. He, too, promised redemption.

Hitlers and Haeussers, "Christs" and pagans, itinerant mystic consolers, political assassins, and conspirators reflected the spiritual travail and material troubles of a nation in adversity. On the somewhat higher plane of philosophy, Oswald Spengler, the German thinker, simultaneously glorified physical strength, force, race, the state, and war, and derided culture and individual personality in his *The Decline of the West*. Privations and national humiliation bred immorality, vulgarity, and despair.

The friends of the Rathenau murderers were waiting for a leader.

5. *Lenin's Russia*

THE Allies were afraid that Germany would succumb to Bolshevism. "Ordinary common prudence," Prime Minister Lloyd George said in 1922, demanded that England and France treat Germany decently in order to save her from Communism. Russia, one heard, was prostrate after eight years of war and famine. Yet at the mention of Soviet Russia some men quaked and some cheered. The truth about Russia was apparently elusive.

Russia had always fascinated me. In my youth I had read the great novels of Count Leo Tolstoy and Dostoevsky and many of the stories of Turgenev, Gogol, and Maxim Gorky in English translation. Russia emerged a land of mysticism and misery. At the age of twenty I avidly devoured Prince Peter Kropotkin's *Memoirs of a Revolutionist*. There seemed to be a wealth of ideas and art in poor, downtrodden Russia. Russia was large, empty, distant, eastern, and apparently so civilized yet uncivilized.

From Berlin, in 1922, I saw Russia at closer range. A revolutionary regime had supplanted the world's symbol of reaction. Iconoclasts had taken over the country of the ikon. The strong brute groped for modern weapons. East was being dragged westward and the West feared it. Russia, ever visionary and missionary, talked about reshaping Europe. If Europe had needed no reshaping it would not have been so worried.

Bolshevism was a protest against the Europe that had made the first World War and the peace that followed. It was a protest too against the future war implicit in that peace. My vague sympathy for Soviet Russia was first of all a reaction against the chaos, disunity, dishonesty, and despair of the rest of Europe. I never thought of Soviet Russia as a Utopia. I knew, when I first went there in September, 1922, that I was going to a land of starvation. If I had mistakenly expected a paradise I would have been disillusioned after the first glance. In Lenin's Russia of 1922, I looked not for a better present but for a brighter future. I also expected clean politics and a foreign policy that rejected conquest, colonies, imperialism, and the lying that is often synonymous with diplomacy. I anticipated an equality between people and politicians. I had read the statements of Lenin, Trotzky, Chicherin, Litvinov, and other Soviet officials. They were frank and strong. The notes of Foreign Commissar Chicherin to foreign governments shot holes in the screen of hypocrisy behind which bourgeois statesmen tried to hide their activities. They threw a searchlight of humor, logic, and truth into the blackness of world affairs. I suspected that Moscow would be fun.

Soviet Russia, moreover, was conceived by its creators as the kingdom of the underdog. Evolution is the survival of the fittest; civilization is the survival of the unfittest. The Bolsheviks undertook to serve civilization by aiding those handicapped by poor parents, inadequate education, bad health, and slave psychology.

I was born in the Philadelphia slums to poor parents. My father worked as a laborer in a factory and then graduated to selling fish and fruit from a pushcart. I can still hear his cry, "Peaches, fresh peaches." Sometimes I hauled the empty pushcart to the stable. My mother took in washing. The family moved whenever it could not pay rent—which was often. Until I reached the age of sixteen, I never lived in a house with electricity, running water, or an inside lavatory, or any heat except from a coal stove in the kitchen-living room. We frequently starved, and for many years the only good meal my sister and I ate each week was the one given us by a rich aunt on Friday evenings. A long, intimate acquaintance with poverty killed my dread of it. In later years, I could always reduce my needs to my means and I never craved security. But life as I had seen it could certainly stand improvement. Especially did I feel that society has an obligation to help us overcome the accident of birth. It does so often, but not often enough.

Yet for some reason that I cannot explain to myself now, the two Russian Revolutions occurred without making the slightest impression on me. I do not remember the abdication of the last Czar in March, 1917. I was in the United States and must have been reading newspaper accounts of this historic change, but my memory did not register it. When the Bolshevik Revolution occurred on November 7, 1917, I was in Canada, a volunteer in the British army. During the "Ten Days that Shook the World," I was learning to form fours and fire a rifle. Lenin and Trotzky stirred no ripple in my calm existence.

But in Europe, in 1921 and 1922, Russia could not be ignored.

Russia exercised all minds. Foreign Commissar Georgi Chicherin, accompanied by Maxim Litvinov, Christian G. Rakovsky, Adolf A. Joffe, Karl Radek, and others had passed through Berlin—where Chicherin hired Markoosha, expert typist and translator, to do part of his secretarial work—and gone on to the Genoa Conference. It was Bolshevism's first formal appearance on the European stage. What manner of men were these? Did they wear black beards and hold knives between their teeth? In Genoa, they argued long among themselves before deciding to don tails, top hats, and white ties or tuxedos as the occasion required. Chicherin bowed low to a king and clinked glasses with a Catholic archbishop aboard an Italian man-of-war.

"What is your opinion of the Versailles Peace Treaty?" a journalist asked Rakovsky at a press conference in Genoa. "Treaty of Versailles?" "Treaty of Versailles?" said Rakovsky, as though trying to recall some faint memory. "Treaty of Versailles?" this highly cultivated European and intellectual repeated. "I know nothing about it." The Soviets dissociated themselves from the European peace. That was a point in their favor. The words of Rakovsky won Germany's collective heart, and he stirred warm emotions for his country in many others, myself included.

At Genoa, the Allies refused to talk sense with either the Germans or the Russians. The Germans and Russians accordingly concluded the Rapallo Pact of friendship between themselves. Russia began to play an important role in world affairs. I decided to go and see.

I first went to Russia, via peaceful, prosperous Stockholm and sleepy Tallinn, without a word of the language, and with two letters of recommendation from Markoosha—one to Asya Finger, a Russian friend, another to Eliena Krylenko, secretary of Litvinov, sister of the Soviet attorney general and later the wife of Max Eastman. On the train I met Sidney Hillman of the Amalgamated Clothing Workers of America with two advisers, W. O. Thompson and Dean Howard, who proposed to recondition several clothing factories and show the Russians how to run them. Hillman spoke Russian and when we reached the Moscow railroad station he got me a horse cab and told the driver to take me to the Savoy Hotel.

The Savoy was full, but I knocked at the door of Jim Howe, Associated Press correspondent, who let me sleep in one of his two beds until a vacant room became available. American correspondents abroad are a fraternity. The fraternity has no name, no officers, no meetings, no dues, and no fixed membership. But whenever an American newspaperman arrives in a foreign capital he has friends whom he has never seen. He need only telephone one of the resident American journalists and say, "This is Charles X of the Chicago so-and-so," and the reply will be, "Where are you? Come on over. Will you know how to get here?" and he will be handed around to other colleagues, and introduced to officials and given meals, teas, and information. There is fierce competition among them, but also cordial collaboration, and the visiting writing "fireman" who just drops in for a fortnight or weekend is never lost in the strangest environment.

They were killing giant rats in the corridors of the Savoy at the time, but it was the only accommodation open to bourgeois foreigners who had no private apartments.

What a strange city! I walked the streets of Moscow for hours each day. Red Moscow was in the grip of an orgy of capitalist business.

From 1918 to 1921, Soviet city people and the army lived on rations given to them by the government. The peasants had to sell their crops to the government. The government paid with paper rubles. Paper currency is good if you can buy something with it. But all the stores were closed. So the peasant did not want to sell his produce, and the Bolsheviks, faced with the possibility of starvation in the army and cities, sent troops into the villages to requisition food. This stifled the peasant's natural desire to plant. Coupled with a drought, the result was a famine in the Volga region and the Ukraine where millions died. The peasant planted less, hid his harvest, and sold it only to private individuals who slipped out of cities with sacks full of old clothing, shoes, tobacco, or interior decorations. Bigger objects too found their way into the countryside in exchange for food, and traveling through Russian farm regions in later years, I saw pianos, gramophones, books, paintings and rugs, which lowly muzhiks had received from hungry law-breaking city folk during that difficult period. But this bootleg business was a thin unsatisfactory trickle. It could not meet the needs of millions of urbanites nor offer a regular market to a hundred million peasants. In 1920 and 1921, peasants in many districts openly displayed their displeasure at the restrictions on the sale of their crops. Revolts broke out in several provinces and among Kronstadt sailors who were peasants'

sons for the most part. Lenin quickly grasped the significance of
this. In March, 1921, he readmitted capitalism into Soviet Russia; he
introduced the New Economic Policy—NEP.

Lenin called the NEP a retreat. It superseded a system which
was in part "military communism"—a war necessity—and in part
militant communism: the state ran the munitions plants, railroads,
banks, mines. In lesser degree, the same system had been tried in
the United States during the first World War—with this difference:
in capitalist countries the capitalists were temporarily denied complete supervision over their properties. In Soviet Russia they were
permanently dispossessed and exiled or imprisoned or shot, thus
leaving a clear field for socialism. Under "military communism,"
moreover, the peasants tilled nationalized soil, which they held in
usufruct. And private business was proscribed. The NEP altered
one situation; private business was legalized.

I saw private trade take its first faltering steps in Communist Russia.
Here a red-faced woman in white headkerchief stood on the pavement holding five pairs of cotton gloves in one hand and half
a dozen neck scarfs in another. She was launching a business career.
A wrinkled veteran had managed to scrape together ten packets of
cigarettes and a few boxes of matches. A board suspended by strings
from his shoulders was his showcase—and there he stood, a capitalist.
Perambulating bookstores, pushcarts filled with luscious fruit from
southern regions, and cobblers repairing shoes and nailing on rubber
heels in the autumn cold completed the picture of open-air capitalism.

Every day also saw the reopening of shops shuttered and barred
since 1918; many were being renovated. Moscow's carpenters, plas-
terers, and glaziers could scarcely cope with the job of lifting the
big city's face. Very often a store would emerge only gradually
from its four years of hibernation. First one window was plated
and behind it the owner might display powders and perfumes imported from Paris in 1914. The next week his cap and hat section
exposed itself to public view. Diamonds, fur coats, silks, valuable
carpets, marble statuary, and ordinary wearing apparel were then
put on sale. These were old stocks. The merchants had carefully
guarded them during all the long years of revolution, civil war, and
undernourishment. In one window I saw an unused typewriter
marked "Ithaca, 1913," a microscope, opera glasses, and medical instruments.

To children pressing their stub noses against plate-glass windows all this was strange indeed. They had never known what trade meant. There were more curious observers outside the stores than buyers inside, and cash registers played slow, intermittent music. Most Muscovites could afford little more than food and bare necessities—if that. The new capitalists or Nepmen, however, bought from one another, and their tribe increased. Soon Moscow scenes reflected the change. Through streets filled with ragged thousands, ladies decked in satins and sables rode safely in horse-drawn droshkies. Under the old system they would not have dared. Men began coming to the theater in evening dress, and from the performance they drove in smart, racing droshkies to cabarets where waiters in black served endless, costly meals and champagne while fat gypsies sang and danced. The most sumptuous cabarets were The Empire, Hermitage, Weep Not, and Cheer Up. The obeisances and the old-fashioned subservience of the waiters revolted me. When my income permitted, I also went to the gambling casinos. Nepmen crowded around the roulette and baccarat tables from which the state raked in a percentage of each pot. But occasionally one could also see a sallow, nervous player, obviously a government employee, who either was trying to win some money for himself by using official funds, or had already lost part of these state rubles and wanted to recoup. Agents of the secret police, sometimes in the guise of Nepmen, watched eagerly for such easy prey.

Three-fourths of the Nepmen engaged in retail trade; the others manufactured food, clothing, sanitary articles, hardware, and kitchen utensils. The Nepman looked for quick turnover and profits. He did not wish to invest in basic industries. He wanted to "travel light," so as to be able to jump off the train in case the government changed its mind again and prohibited private enterprise.

Big factories remained in the hands of the state. These sold their output to two kinds of wholesalers: Nepmen and state trusts. Both sold to Nepmen retailers. But the state trusts themselves also opened retail stores. All competed with one another, and the cheating and confusion were great.

The government owned all property. Small industrial undertakings such as printing presses, bakeries, restaurants were leased to private capitalists. The workingmen complained that these Nepmen violated the labor code, paid low wages, and even defied the trade unions. A Communist writing to the Moscow daily *Pravda* protested against such injustices, but his story indicated the extent of the Bolshevik dilemma. When the authorities insisted that the Nepman pay better salaries he simply closed the factory. The workers asked for six weeks' pay as compensation. The Nepman pleaded no funds. They took him to court. The court found that he was really penniless. "What can be done with such adventurers?" the *Pravda* correspondent asks. Put them in prison? "That's a good thing, but what will the proletariat get out of it? . . . In this case the government should help the dismissed laborers."

Minors employed in petty handicraft shops worked ten to twelve hours a day at miserable pay. Conditions "are simply intolerable," said an official investigator. Piatakov, a leading Soviet industrialist, declared publicly that "the Nep vermin" created a chaotic market and irrational economics, and drove many Communists into "black melancholy."

The Nepmen demoralized state officials by setting a tempting example of high living or by direct bribes or by their mere presence. The Nepmen had their spies in state trusts. Apartment houses owned by the Moscow Soviet (the municipality) often preferred Nepmen to workingmen. The houses were managed by tenant committees who had to pay for maintenance and repairs. When their funds were inadequate they sold the right to rooms or suites to merchants who gladly agreed to higher rents as well. "Help!" cried the headline of a *Pravda* article, "the Nepmen are driving workers out of the best houses." Women angered over apartment disputes tore out one another's hair or threw hot pots at one another in communal kitchens. Russians committed murder for rooms. Yet in the midst of it all, a Nepman would walk in with his billions and lease three rooms, for any corner of which poorer citizens would have given their eyeteeth.

The government had been advancing the running expenses of factories. But "the government can no longer allocate funds to subsidize industry," wrote *Pravda* in September, 1922, the month I arrived in Moscow. It would concentrate on improving transportation and on assisting the peasantry with loans. Immediately plants began closing down. Unemployment rose.

Peter Bogdanov, chairman of the Supreme Economic Council, told a Soviet congress in December, 1922, that Soviet Russia was producing only four percent as much iron as Czarist Russia. The next day Gregory Sokolnikov, Commissar of Finance, informed the saddened delegates that the government's revenue amounted to only one-hundredth of its expenditures. The other ninety-nine percent poured from the overworked printing presses which turned out rubles by the trillions. The Bolsheviks were living on, and quickly exhausting, the capital they had inherited from Czarism.

It was a vicious circle. Lenin's bold experiment of putting socialism and capitalism in one crippled cage did not yield a mongrel, for they refused to mix. It retarded the growth of each, for they stole food from one another.

Meanwhile, the peasants, to quiet whose grumblings the NEP had been introduced, continued to grumble. I visited villages. The peasants said, "Before the war, we sold one pood [36 pounds] of grain and could buy 8 arshin [yards] of cotton goods with the proceeds. Now we receive only two arshin for a pood." The Bolshevik press published the same figures I heard from the illiterate plowman. In one village I asked the wife of a former justice of the peace what difference the Revolution had made. She replied, "People talk more."

The NEP encouraged anti-Bolsheviks to dream of the complete restoration of capitalism. Some workingmen became apathetic. Communists resigned from the Communist party. Communists committed suicide in despair. Peasants ambushed Soviet village journalists and killed them. Meanwhile, Lenin lay in bed after his first stroke. His illness lasted six months. Millions of hearts trembled lest he never return to work and leadership. He recovered in October, 1922.

I first saw Lenin that same month at a session of Central Executive Committee, a kind of senate consisting of delegates from municipal and village soviets. The meeting took place in the throne room of the Czar's great marble palace situated inside the red-brick walls of the Kremlin fortress. The walls of the Kremlin also encircle several Greek Catholic churches, an arms museum, barracks for the guards, and houses once inhabited by the royal servants and priests, which are now the homes of top-rank Bolshevik leaders.

The Czar's palace itself had remained unaltered. The thick doors plated with green malachite were intact. In the throne room the ten massive chandeliers suspended from the ceiling with their thousands of tiny pointed electric bulbs, the huge rectangular marble columns decorated with heavy gilt wood designs, the imperial crowns, crosses, and double eagles were just as the Czar knew them. Only the throne was gone and in its place was a long table covered with a red cloth at which the presidents of the assembly sat. While

Nicholas Krylenko, Federal Attorney General, was delivering an address from the podium, Lenin walked into the hall unescorted and sat down unnoticed on one of the yellow folding chairs near me. I had a few minutes to observe him. His head was round, almost bald, and luminous, with a high domed forehead, high cheek bones, a reddish mustache, little red beard, and slanting, Mongolian, twinkling eyes. His lips played with a smile. Soon the delegates noticed him and whispered, and then the whisper "Lenin" became a loud cry drowned in applause, and Lenin, almost running, moved up to the platform. Immediately, Krylenko interrupted his long report, and the chairman, Mikhail Kalinin, President of the Soviet Republic, said simply, "Comrade Lenin has the floor." The applause lasted exactly forty-five seconds; Lenin raised his hand, the clapping stopped and the delegates resumed their seats. He held a watch in his palm and said that the physicians had given him permission to speak fifteen minutes. He spoke fifteen minutes, all the while squinting nearsightedly at his watch. His tone was conversational, rapid and informal. He gesticulated freely but there was no striving for effect. The audience laughed or grew emotional or settled into seriousness just as he apparently wished it. I understood only a few words.

When Lenin finished, the meeting adjourned and more than a hundred delegates crowded into an anteroom adjoining the ex-Czarina's bedroom for a photograph. The photographer had as much trouble getting them seated and quiet as if they were a high-school class and not the Bolshevik rulers of Russia. In the center row sat Leo Kamenev, Lenin, Zinoviev, General S. Kamenev, Kalinin, myself, Savel Zimand, an American free-lance writer, F. A. Mackenzie of the *Chicago Daily News* and George Seldes of the *Chicago Tribune*. We foreigners had simply pushed a bit and got where we wanted to be. All around, the other men—there is not a single woman in the picture—stood, sat, and sprawled on the floor. Among them were Leo Karakhan, assistant Commissar of Foreign Affairs, Tomsky, leader of the trade union movement, Bogdanov of the Supreme Economic Council, Yenukidze, a Georgian Bolshevik and Secretary of the Central Executive Committee, and Demyan Bedni, the poet laureate. Many of the delegates were still in old military uniforms and leather army jackets. A considerable number wore white collars, but more had on Russian blouses.

Lenin spoke again in the same place several weeks later—November 13, 1922—and this time I understood, for his speech was in German. It was an address to the congress of the Third International—the Comintern. Representatives of Communist parties throughout the world had arrived in Moscow for the event. Their faces were all shades of white, yellow, and brown. Born Christians, Jews, Moslems, Buddhists, Brahmans, pagans, this was Mecca for all of them. And Mohammed delivered them a lecture. On this occasion the physicians allowed him to speak an hour.

While Lenin talked, impish Karl Radek sat at his feet, and whenever Lenin lacked a word in German he lowered his head and gave the Russian expression to Radek, and Radek turned his ugly face upward and offered the German equivalent. Several times Lenin did not like Radek's translation and threw the Russian word into the audience and waited till the delegates shouted a suitable German synonym. The address was full of humor. Lenin quoted something he had written in 1918 and added, "Of course that was said when we were more stupid than now." The Bolsheviks would continue to make "a colossal number of mistakes." "Nobody can see that better than I," implying that many were his own. Why? Because Russia was backward and had been denied help from the outside. The Bolsheviks, moreover, had been forced to take over old government officials who detested the new regime. In February, 1921, "disaster threatened"; the "great mass of the peasants were against us" and many workingmen as well. The Soviets had gone too far towards socialism without sufficient preparation. Therefore the NEP. "We must always be ready to retreat." The last eighteen months showed some progress. To be sure, more than "a quadrillion rubles" were in circulation. This figure, though astronomical, was unimportant. "You can always cross out the zeros." It was more important to stabilize the ruble and they had stabilized it for three whole months. They had to reconstruct heavy industry, for "without it we die as an independent country." It would take several years. To finance reconstruction of plants and railroads "we are economizing on everything, even on schools."

Enemies would rejoice in his admission of errors, Lenin predicted. But when the Soviets miscalculated it was in saying two times two are five; when the capitalists went wrong they said "two times two are a tallow candle." The capitalists supported Admiral Kolchak, the anti-Bolshevik White whom the Red Army had completely

smashed. They dictated the Versailles peace. Those were political
blunders of world dimensions.

Leon Trotzky, Commissar of War, followed Lenin. He spoke two
and a half hours in exquisite German. Immediately thereafter he
delivered the same address again in fluent, rich French. And then
he gave it a third time in Russian. It was a seven-and-a-half-hour performance with only two brief intermissions.

Trotzky was fiery, flamboyant, penetrating. The congress cheered
him wildly. This was the last Comintern congress which admitted
non-Communist correspondents. In the press box sat an American
artist drawing a sketch of Trotzky. At first he made Trotzky look
like a Mephistopheles. Then he tore it up. There was more of the
tenor in Trotzky—the peacock, performer, charmer.

The historic struggle between Stalin and Trotzky had not yet
commenced, and Trotzky was recognized as the organizer of the
Red Army. But though still the head of the army, Trotzky had
too much dynamic energy to make it a full-time job in peace. He
had taken over the ruined railroads of the country and was trying
to bring order out of their chaos. He wrote long, half-page reviews
in the daily press on European and Russian books (he was one of
Russia's outstanding literary critics), delivered numerous speeches,
and, in addition, preached puritan morals. Urging "a new life,"
Trotzky attacked swearing and those three-ply Russian "mother"
oaths which, incidentally, Lenin used on rare occasions and Stalin
often, but Trotzky never. "Cursing," Trotzky thundered, "is a
heritage of slavery."

A strong puritanical streak runs through Communism. It denies to
the individual for the sake of the whole and the future. Loose living
is discouraged not as sin but because it softens the soldier fighting
the social war. Besides, the NEP was corroding morals as well as
socialist economy, and puritan self-restraint seemed a necessary corrective. I attended a dance recital directed by Goleizovsky, former
ballet impresario. It was crude pornography. The police would
have been summoned if anybody had done horizontally what the
performers executed under the guise of dance. A Soviet critic declared this "thickly erotic style" incongruous "in our harsh revolutionary epoch." But these things were an attempt to escape from
harshness. Trotzky and Bukharin prescribed the antidote of puritanical discipline. Bukharin, stormy petrel, thirty-five-year-old editor of *Pravda*, beloved by the youth and by Lenin—though Lenin

publicly castigated him for false theorizing—issued a warning to the younger generation to forget the despair born of the NEP and to crusade against drinking, smoking, and "certain sexual laxnesses." "Nihilism," Bukharin insisted, "has no place among us." He suggested the creation of a "Communist Pinkerton." Yes, detective stories; Karl Marx used to read them and liked them. They had need too of revolutionary romanticism and civil-war tales, Bukharin continued, for their political discussions were dry and left the soul cold.

Entertainment frequently conforms to the pattern of work. People bombarded with numerous strong sensations during the day crave more during their evening leisure. Nepmen who gambled for fortunes in their markets gambled away fortunes in the casino, and private capitalists perilously poised on the rim of the Soviet volcano were in no mood for contemplative music or fine literature or delicate political satire. Peaceful coexistence with this resurrected internal capitalist enemy subjected Bolshevik morale to stress.

In 1922 and 1923, nevertheless, the fires of Bolshevik idealism from which the 1917 revolution rose were still burning high. The Kremlin's task was to keep them so. The call to a better world came from leaders who shrank from personal adulation. The fifth birthday of the Soviet government was certainly cause for congratulation; the Bolsheviks had expected to be crushed long before that. Yet the press refrained from personal tributes. Victory was the achievement of all. I have read carefully the anniversary issue of the *Pravda* of November 7, 1922. On the first page is a facsimile quotation from Lenin but no other mention of Lenin or of any other Bolshevik. Half of the second page is devoted to a survey of the civil war by General S. Kamenev. Not a single personal name occurs in it. A calendar of five years of the regime contains two casual references to Lenin, one to Trotzky, and one to Krylenko. Then there is an article by S. Zorin in memory of the Mensheviks who died in making the Revolution. The Mensheviks were now sworn enemies of the Bolsheviks. They opposed dictatorship and Soviet principles. But the official *Pravda* gave them the credit they deserved. For "they too" says Zorin, "participated in the memorable days of the Revolution." Such an honest tribute became inconceivable in later years.

The rest of the *Pravda* issue carries an article by Zinoviev which quotes Lenin's statement that "every housewife must learn to run the government," but has no other reference to Lenin or anybody else; an article by Bukharin with two mentions of Lenin but no praise of him, and no mention of any other individual; a poem by Demyan Bedni, also purely impersonal; and a feuilleton by Sosnovsky, in which he reminisces intimately about the early period of the Revolution. In this article Lenin is mentioned seven times, Trotzky two times, Antonov-Avseyenko twice, Rakovsky twice, and Zinoviev, Sverdlow, Voroshilov, Manuilsky (a Comintern official), Bukharin, Joffe, and Chicherin once each. Further contributions to the paper likewise abstain from personalities. Eulogies are conspicuous by their total absence. Stalin's name does not appear at all in this holiday publication. The *Pravda* issue of February 23, 1923, commemorating the fifth anniversary of the formation of the Red Army, was equally devoid of personal references, of tributes to Lenin or Trotzky, and of any mention of Stalin.

For comparison I have selected at random a latter-day *Pravda* anniversary issue, that of November 7, 1937. Stalin's name occurs eighty-eight times, Lenin's fifty-four times. The adjective Stalinist is used fifteen times. Lenin's name is almost always coupled with Stalin's. President Kalinin writes, "The Bolshevik party, educated by Lenin and Stalin . . .," "the banner of the party was held by the strong hands of Lenin and Stalin. . . ." Another hymn to Stalin reveals that, in 1917, "the working class of Leningrad, led by Lenin and Stalin, conquered for the Soviets." A contributor waxes ecstatic, "Today I shall see Stalin. I know his face . . . that exalted figure of a human being." Stalin is "the great Stalin." War Commissar Voroshilov is mentioned twice, Kalinin twice, General Budenny once, Dimitrov, head of the Comintern, once. No other leaders are mentioned. But Kalinin twice assails Kamenev, Zinoviev, and Rykov as "traitors." Trotzky and Bukharin invariably are linked together in spluttering epithets: "The Trotzky-Bukharin bandits, spies, wreckers, plotters, and murderers"; "The Trotzky-Bukharin agents of Japanese-German fascism."

There was in Lenin's Russia an unwritten but strict Bolshevik code against exaltation of the individual, no matter how great his services. Biographical facts on Soviet personalities were rarely published, and it was bad taste to refer in public to the wife or children or family or habits or travels of any outstanding Bolshevik. That was his private affair. His wife's rating in society depended on her merit as a citizen and worker; the marriage certificate itself brought no honor or social position, much less publicity. For foreign journalists whose editors wanted "human interest stuff," the Bolshevik press was a desert without oases.

My life as a correspondent was divided between Moscow and the provinces. Once Henry G. Alsberg, brilliant occasional contributor to the New York *Nation* and official of the American Jewish Joint Distribution Committee, went for an inspection tour of the Ukraine. Because the ordinary passenger cars were infested with typhus-bearing lice, he used a private railway car which had belonged to one of the Czar's brothers, a grand duke. George Seldes of the *Chicago Tribune*, Sam Spewack of the late *New York World*, who has become a successful playwright, and I gladly accepted Alsberg's offer to go along. Both Seldes and Spewack were very anti-Soviet. Each of us had a comfortable compartment to sleep in, and we ate in a large salon. We had corn flakes, canned milk, G. Washington coffee, and other luxuries of home which had been bought in the special Moscow canteen of Herbert Hoover's American Relief Administration—or Ara, as the Russians called it.

Our special car stopped at Kharkov, the capital of the Ukraine, at Kiev, Vinnitsa, and Kamenetz-Podolsk. In Kharkov, I visited a crowded hospital where a big hole in the roof made the top floor uninhabitable and allowed cold and rain to fill the whole building. A woman in one ward seemed too plump to be very ill but the doctor explained that she was swollen from hunger. In near-by Crimea, two hundred thousand had died of starvation. Authorities assured me that the cholera epidemic "had been mastered" and typhus "reduced to normal dimensions."

The Ukraine with its thirty-odd million inhabitants was a world of tragedy. A million homeless waifs orphaned by war and famine roamed the steppes, starved, rode the rails, spread disease, and committed crimes. Every section of the country had tasted war. Some towns like Berdicheff changed hands eighteen times. Few places saw fewer than six or seven changes. Each change meant an attack by the assailants, shelling and shooting. Then the retiring forces would take away as much as they could carry and the incoming victors would loot the rest. The victors would set up their own government and introduce its money. The peasants and townspeople were compelled to accept this money in return for goods. A month later that government would be driven out of the town, and the money would become worthless. The succeeding government then brought its money, and again the population surrendered crops and materials for another paper currency which again became so much colored printing matter when a third conqueror came along. In villages, peasant women carefully untied large bright handkerchiefs and asked me hopefully whether their accumulation of bills, representing years of labor in fields and barn, would ever have any value. They showed me Czarist rubles, Kerensky rubles, Petlura bills, Denikin bills, Polish money, Makhno money, Grigoriev money. Every bandit chief, every rebellious general, impoverished the inhabitants of his area with this financial literature.

With rare exceptions, all anti-Bolsheviks pogromed the Jews. About two million Jews lived in the Ukraine. Thousands were murdered, and hundreds of thousands robbed of all their goods and driven away from their homes. The eyes of those who remained revealed it all. In Fastov, a small town near Kiev, a boy of twelve who led me around pointed to a beautiful young Jewish woman who passed us and said, "She was raped by eighteen Cossacks." Her eyes showed it, too.

On a subsequent trip to Minsk, Homel, Vitebsk, and other centers in White Russia, near Poland, I saw similar pictures of crushed souls, torn families, ruined railroads and bridges, idle factories, desolate farms, and ignorant bewildered officials. What a job the Soviet regime had undertaken!

Most foreign correspondents in Moscow met this difficult Russian situation with little sympathy. I had made the acquaintance of one Russian family of government officials and one Jewish NEP family. Occasionally, a visitor like Max Eastman dropped down from the Communist planet. A translator read me the newspapers in the forenoon. For the rest, I spent my time with my professional colleagues. We correspondents were one big, almost permanent poker party. Seldes would say, "Here, hold my hand, I have to get off a story," and an hour later, his dispatch censored and filed for the enlightenment of waiting Chicagoans, he returned to resume the real business of life. During this first stay in Soviet Russia I learned much less than I should have. In general, the unfriendly anti-Soviet attitude of almost all the correspondents, which seemed based less on knowledge than on prejudice, had the paradoxical effect of creating a generally friendly attitude in me.

One fine day, Mr. Ketchum, a roving correspondent of the *Lon-*

don Daily Express, arrived in Moscow. He asked his colleagues for the "lowdown." I tried, with the woefully inadequate data at my disposal, to give him a picture of conditions. He listened for a few minutes, and then said with a smile, "Before I left London, my chief, Lord Beaverbrook, called me into his office and said, 'Now Ketchum, you are off to Russia. We don't care what Lenin is thinking or what Trotzky is doing. What we want to know is whether the girls in Moscow wear drawers.'" Ketchum had a generous expense account.

I myself had no expense account and no salary. I lived from check to check. I had an assignment, for irregular pay, from the Jewish Telegraphic Agency, but I soon discovered that the fate of Russian Jewry was a by-product of larger Soviet developments. I devoted myself to a study of the broad scene. I wrote on it at odd intervals for the *New York Evening Post.* I wrote to the *Post* from Berlin, Warsaw, Vilna, Stockholm, Riga, Tallinn, and Moscow. After mailing each article I waited until the newspaper with the printed contribution reached me in Europe. Then I sent another article. For several years I could not get myself to write a correspondence before I was sure that the preceding correspondence had been accepted. I needed the encouragement of publication. This meant that I wrote less and earned less and had more time for investigation. I think my strongest instinct is curiosity. When aroused, I suffer if I do not know what I want to know, and Moscow aroused me powerfully. Under the bombardment of its kaleidoscopically changing events there could be no intellectual laziness or complacency. I read a lot, traveled, and talked with those foreign journalists who felt Moscow's excitement. They were, particularly, Paul Scheffer, of the *Berliner Tageblatt,* a cultured German, Walter Duranty of the *New York Times,* and William Henry Chamberlin.

William Henry Chamberlin of Philadelphia, educated at Quaker Haverford, wrote for the *Christian Science Monitor,* one of America's best dailies. His hobby was baiting America, and nothing amused him more than quoting at length from H. L. Mencken's "Americana" which he did to the accompaniment of laughter and with a rhythmic wiggle of one finger. Though classmates probably never thought of him as rugged and though he is the scholastic type, he played poker eagerly with a glacial Japanese expression, and usually won. In Moscow, where food was limited, he faced special difficulties; he had to have two meals of meat per day, and he ate his weight in chocolate each year. If he did not have chocolate his energy lagged. Fortunately, the Soviet government gave him special permission to import it in adequate quantities. Sonya, his wife from Vinnitsa who had taught French in a New York high school, kept the chocolate and rationed him in accordance with his literary output, which was prodigious anyway. Chamberlin had worked with Heywood Broun on the *New York Tribune* and contributed to a Soviet publication in America. He was very pro-Soviet. Not so Sonya. She was an eager hostess and whenever she met anybody she was quick to invite him for tea. Chamberlin was one of the few serious students of social conditions among the Moscow correspondents. For most of them Moscow was a hated, uncomfortable assignment which, they hoped, would serve as a stepping stone for promotion to Berlin, then London or New York.

Popular journalistic topics were opium and alcohol. On a redbrick wall near the Red Square in Moscow, the Bolsheviks had cut a slogan in stone, "Religion is the opium of the people." Authorities attributed it to Marx.

The Bolsheviks are anti-religious and anti-church. The Russian religious leaders knew that Bolshevism boded no good for them. The church did what it could to defeat the Soviets during the civil war. The Soviets accordingly treated the church as a political foe. But political opposition apart, the Bolsheviks regard all religion as an unscientific anachronism. Their goal was depicted in a large colored poster: a sturdy workingman, hammer in hand, having smashed churches, synagogues, and mosques on earth, was seen mounting a ladder to heaven where Jesus, the Greek Catholic god, Jehovah, Allah, and a fire-breathing black demon stood frightened at his approach.

On Soviet earth, in fact, many religious institutions had been closed but many remained open; religious worship was officially free but actually under very strong social pressure. Bukharin and Preobrazhensky affirmed in their *ABC of Communism* that "the campaign against the backwardness of the masses in the matter of religion must be conducted with patience and consideration. . . . The credulous are extremely sensitive. . . . To mock . . . would hinder the campaign against religion." Nevertheless, mockery prevailed over patience. Every religious holiday called forth an antireligious carnival. On Christmas Day, 1922, I watched as young Communist paraders sang parodies of church hymns in the streets of

Moscow. Floats drawn by horses portrayed priests, rabbis, and mullahs performing rites while sticking one hand behind them to receive their pay from capitalists. A devil chased a priest who hid under the broad skirts of a peasant woman—reminder of the profligacy and licentiousness of the Greek Catholic church which Count Leo Tolstoy and others had exposed. One float represented a typical Russian village: large, stone church with gilded bulbous steeples and gold cross in the midst of crooked, unsanitary mud huts. A young Communist on a cart yelled, "There is no god, and if there is let him strike me dead right now." Women made the sign of the cross as he passed; he seemed to be the one part of the parade that impressed them. In the evening, effigies of the gods of all religions were burnt in a square near the railway station while couples danced.

A writer in the Soviet press protested that such lampooning antagonized the devout without even convincing the actors. Don't make the church a martyr, he cautioned. He proposed lecture courses under the slogan, "Down with god. Long live science." Within two years anti-religious processions and public spectacles ceased. Persecution of churchmen continued. The Greek Catholic, Roman Catholic, and Jewish churches bore the brunt of the direct Bolshevik attack. But in the peripheral territories of the culturally more retarded Christian and Moslem racial minorities, greater caution was exercised. The followers of Allah received special treatment because the authorities feared a violent reaction to repression. In Ufa, Siberia, for instance, an all-Russian Moslem Church congress (there must be about ten million Moslems in Soviet Russia) was permitted to convene in June, 1923, and it actually sent a resolution of greetings to Lenin which appeared in the Bolshevik press. It stated that all the faithful would pray to Allah for his health.

The Bolsheviks did not confine their efforts to persecution and atheistic propaganda. They endeavored to split the Greek Catholic church. In opposition to the central conservative church presided over by Patriarch Tikhon, two schisms took place; one result was, the "Living Church," led by Archbishop Yevdokim of Nizhni Novgorod, Bishop Krasnitsky of Moscow, and Vedensky, an eloquent cultured priest whom on several occasions I heard preach to packed congregations and whom I once heard debate publicly with Anatole Lunacharsky, federal Soviet Commissar of Education; the other was the Church of the Resurrection guided by Metropolitan Antonin of Moscow. Both groups wished to be reconciled to the

Soviet regime and hoped in return for better treatment. No doubt, spontaneous movements towards the reform of the corrupt Greek Catholic church were natural under the impetus of the Revolution. But I suspect the GPU had a hand in these schisms. I cannot prove it. Yet knowledge gained in later years about Soviet secret police methods makes me wonder whether these trends towards the purification of Greek Catholicism did not find some of their inspiration, or at least some of their financing, in the spacious Lubianka headquarters of the GPU.

Next to religion the favorite theme of many correspondents was Russian drinking habits. The United States was "dry" as a result of the Eighteenth Amendment and by the same token it was swamped with bootleg liquor. Soviet Russia, too, lived under prohibition and drank samogon, or home-brew. Under the Czarist regime, vodka, a beverage with forty percent alcohol content, more or less, but never much less, was manufactured and sold as a government monopoly. Lenin and other Communists regarded this as one of Czarism's most heinous crimes. In 1914, the Czar enacted prohibition because he knew that otherwise the Russian propensity for drunkenness would paralyze every military effort. The Soviet regime continued this wise measure. But the Russians yearned for vodka, and particularly in the villages the muzhik brewed his own from wheat. The government established a special commission headed by Smidovitch, an old party idealist, to combat samogon. Its production was punishable with death. Bootlegging was counter-revolution. A *Pravda* article mercilessly flayed a certain Professor Ozerov who, in the Moscow *Economist*, advocated restoration of the government vodka monopoly. Under the Czar, the party organ thundered, "drunkenness was a social calamity. It poisoned the national organism." After the famine and suffering and consequent undermining of Russian physique, vodka now would "in several years convert the country into a cemetery." Ozerov promised the state an income of two hundred and fifty million rubles in gold from the vodka monopoly. The *Pravda* spurned this polluted lucre and intimated that it regarded the professor as a sly counter-revolutionist. In 1923, the Soviet government, however, introduced the making and distribution of vodka as a government monopoly. It bowed to the reality of bootlegging—"the peasants are wasting their grain on it"—it wanted the gold income, and it had to give the population something on which to spend its earnings. No shoes or apartments or pants? Then at least alcohol.

Lenin was of course big news for every foreign journalist. On March 12, 1923, the *Pravda* took the unusual step of publishing an extra edition announcing that Lenin had had another attack. His blood circulation was again irregular and that interfered with the movement of the right leg and right arm. Speech was slightly impaired. Complete rest was ordered. He would not even see newspapers because they made him want to participate in politics.

Who would succeed Lenin if he died? Everybody guessed a different person. Going through my files, I find that, writing from Moscow to the *New York Evening Post* of April 12, 1923, I reported, "Stalin is the least known abroad, yet the most likely to wear Lenin's shoes if anybody will." I do not remember how I reached this conclusion, for Stalin was also little known in Russia. He had played a role in the early days of the Revolution and in the civil war. Subsequently, he quietly ran the Commissariat of Nationalities, an important but not a pivotal job. Why should I have expected him to be preferred over Trotzky, Rykov, Kamenev, Djerzhinsky, Zinoviev? The reasons became clear later.

The correspondents faced a problem. If Lenin died the censorship would certainly stop journalists from sending the news abroad until it had been published inside, and that might be delayed pending measures of security. Isaac Don Levine, of the Hearst press, went to London at this time and agreed with his office there that when Lenin died he would send a telegram asking for one hundred and fifty pounds. (When Lenin died the censorship did retard dispatches, Levine cabled for the one hundred and fifty pounds, but his office cabled back that he was overdrawn and not entitled to another advance. It had forgotten the code and it lost a world scoop.)

Once F. A. Mackenzie gave a luncheon in honor of Robert Hodgson, the chief of the British Mission in Moscow. We all drank to the health of King George V. We drank to the health of Warren Gamaliel Harding. Whereupon, Isaac Don Levine, who was something of an *enfant terrible*, suggested that since we were in Russia we might also drink to the health of the chief of the Russian government who was ill and perhaps needed it. Consternation. Could His British Majesty's agent drink to the Bolshevik dictator, and would a lot of anti-Bolshevik newspapermen also drink to him? Clouds on numerous faces and smiles hidden behind others. Was the polite party breaking up? Arthur Ransome saved the day. Ransome was the regular correspondent on the *Manchester Guardian*, a typical Britisher with long mustache, pipe, lanky legs, and broad accent. He understood politics and had reported the Revolution from its inception; he was the friend of Lenin, Trotzky, Chicherin, and Radek. But he was also the author of wonderful children's tales. And so now he started telling a children's story about a snake and a frog, and on and on it went, humorous and piquant, with no point, just beautiful words and a laugh now and then and shrewd observations on animals which might be applicable to human beings. When he concluded the narrative, the tranquil atmosphere of polite society had been restored, and the guests dispersed.

Lenin, severely handicapped, with bullets from a woman assassin's revolver still lodged in his body and weighed down by paralysis, saw further than any other Bolshevik. Two problems occupied his mind: administration and culture. He realized that theory and philosophies availed nothing without efficient government service. He feared the rise of a bureaucracy. All his articles in the last year of his life concentrated on the twin problem of bureaucracy and culture. Unless Soviet Departments functioned with obvious benefit to all, Lenin insisted, the peasant would abandon his alliance with the workers and collaborate with the Nepmen, and that would spell catastrophe for the Soviets. "Better Less, but Better" was the title he gave to one essay on these questions. In social, political, and economic matters "we are terribly revolutionary," he sneered, but when it comes to office management the Bolsheviks were worse than conservative. Russia was less educated than other countries. The Bolshevik goal must be. "First study, second study, and third study; study and check what you have studied."

The movement towards world revolution, he said, was being thwarted by the enslavement of Germany. Russia herself "lacked sufficient civilization to pass directly to socialism." The Bolsheviks therefore had to build a state which could withstand a long siege and that was only possible with efficient administration. And again, in another article: "To build socialism it is necessary to be civilized."

Lenin put great trust in co-operatives. "The simple growth of co-operatives . . . is identical with the growth of socialism." Co-operative stores could defeat the private Nepman who was the great danger. The peasants and workers must participate in these co-operatives. Without mass participation in economic enterprises there is no socialism. Lenin advised a radical alteration of outlook. "Formerly we put the primary emphasis on the political struggle, on the seizure of power. Now the center of gravity has shifted for us to peacetime cultural work." Furthermore: "Complete co-operation is only possible after a full-fledged cultural revolution." From more culture to more co-operatives and then to socialism. Finally, and these are the last published words of Lenin, he quoted Napoleon's saying and used the original French, "On s'engage et puis on voie." This is a typical Leninist dialectical proposition. Lenin translated it freely, "First you enter a serious struggle and then you see what happens." The Bolsheviks staged the 1917 Revolution without knowing what would come of it. Now they knew and they had won a victory. But the future of the Russian Revolution, Lenin continued, could not be found in a textbook on revolution.

Lenin was profoundly Russian. He sensed Russia and had made exact studies of its conditions, literature, and history. But Western Europe was his spiritual home. He had lived in it during many years of exile and he respected its attainments. Hitting hard and straight as usual, he wrote on January 4, 1923, in *Pravda*, "While we are talking nonsense about proletarian culture and comparing it with bourgeois culture, statistics show how bad things are [in Russia] in the field of plain reading and writing. We have made little progress in this respect since the Czar fell. This shows how much real hard work we must do before we rise to the level of the ordinary civilized country in Western Europe." So they were capitalist yet civilized!

Lenin mingled a high appraisal of western culture with the expectation that socialism would improve it. The Bolshevik goal of world revolution springs from a conviction that socialism is better. This consciousness of a mission to spread the Red gospel throughout the "heathen" bourgeois world antedates 1917. It had nothing to do with the fact that Russia went Bolshevik. But when Bolshevism did conquer Russia a second reason for world revolution became operative: to save Soviet Russia. In the beginning, nobody thought that a Communist Russia could exist as an island in a capitalist sea. Either one or more of the important countries would adopt socialism and break the solid capitalist front against Russia or the Revolution in Russia would succumb. That is why a faction among the

Bolsheviks rejected the 1918 Brest-Litovsk peace with Germany. They thought that if the Kaiser invaded proletarian Russia the workers of Germany would revolt in protest and rescue Bolshevik Russia. Signs of ferment were visible in Germany at the time, and a war on the Soviets might accelerate the process, they contended. But Lenin refused to gamble. "Germany," he said, "is only pregnant with revolution whereas here in Russia a perfectly healthy baby —the socialist republic—has already been born, and we may kill it if we start a war." This "bird in the hand" principle implied no renunciation of world revolution; it was simply a keen assessment of probabilities. As the Soviet regime grew stronger and older the readiness to sacrifice it or its interests to foreign uprisings diminished. But while Lenin lived, the official attitude was that "the fate of the Soviet government is directly related to the fate of the world revolution."

Accordingly, every ray of revolutionary sun in Europe or Asia was focused by a huge Bolshevik magnifying glass to warm Russian hopes. In mid-January, 1923, Poincaré sent a French army into Germany's greatest industrial region—the Ruhr. He expected French bayonets to collect reparations and dig coal for France. Chicherin called it "a crime." Excitement reached white heat in Moscow. I saw several hundred thousand truly enthusiastic workingmen parade through the capital. Similar processions defiled in provincial cities. A fortnight later, "events in Central Europe," had convinced the *Pravda*, "that without a revolution, society is condemned to perish. Decay costs more than revolution. Many countries cannot be saved without new regimes." And within a few days: "Only the proletariat can save Germany. The bourgeoisie has sung its song." The wish is always father to the thought with sanguine people. As long ago as 1848, Marx and Engels, the father and mother of socialist science— Marxism—imagined that "a specter is haunting Europe—the specter of Communism." Their disciples have frequently, and just as mistakenly, taken each portent for the event itself. Karl Radek, German in education and habits of mind, was sure in 1923 the Russian and German proletariats would soon unite to begin a new phase of history. But Russia was weak. The Soviets could do only two things: they sent half a million poods of bread to the Ruhr workers—that was approximately twenty-one pounds per man, very nice, nobody else did as much, but still only a gesture; and they warned Poland not to take advantage of the French invasion by marching into Germany. Moscow hinted action if this happened. The Poles had mobilized their army. Roman Knoll, the Polish Chargé d'Affaires in Moscow told Radek, who passed it on to Chicherin, that if Germany went Communist, Poland would not object—provided she could annex German East Prussia. Thereupon Chicherin summoned Knoll and advised Poland to keep hands off. Czechoslovakia also found a way of informing Chicherin that she would not intervene against a Communist Germany as long as Czechoslovakia's territory remained secure. Poland and Czechoslovakia were allies of France. They would not have taken such diplomatic steps without France. It was obvious that France calmly contemplated the prospect of a Communist Germany in the belief that revolution would disrupt Germany and undermine the traditional foe. Poincaré and the Comintern dreamt the same dream—in vain. Nothing happened.

In the summer of 1923 I returned to Germany. The mark had outrun the ruble; inflation made Germans nervous and physically sick; everybody speculated in currency; kids talked about the rate of the dollar and pound. Food riots in numerous towns kept the police busy. But it was summer and I was tired after nine months in Russia and I went to the seashore. Living costs had fallen so low for "dollar princes" that I could maintain a wife, a first son, his nurse, and myself in a good hotel on the Baltic Riviera.

Between swimming and tennis I wrote five articles on Soviet Russia and with these in my suitcase I set out to "conquer" America. From the Manhattan pier I went straight to the *Nation* office at 20 Vesey Street. *The Nation* had been my ideal goal when I dreamed in youth of becoming a writer. At the office I asked for Lewis Gannett, one of the editors. He was attending a staff conference, the telephone girl said. I asked for Freda Kirchwey. She was out of town. So instead of leaving my five valued manuscripts, I took them home and sat on them for months. I did not know that literary agents existed, and I had no connections. Finally, on the repeated suggestions of friends, I bravely telephoned Freda Kirchwey. She was very gracious but informed me that a special Russian issue was about to go to press. In the near future, there would not be much room for Russian material, but she would like to see mine anyway. I sent them in. In a few days I received a summons to appear at 20 Vesey Street, and Ernest Gruening, managing editor, later Governor of Alaska, told me they would take three of the five. I was surprised and delighted.

Charles Evans Hughes was then Secretary of State, and he opposed diplomatic recognition of the Soviet government because it fomented world revolution. I wrote a four-hundred-word note on the subject and brought it in to *The Nation*. Lewis Gannett and Freda Kirchwey read it as I sat there. Lewis said, "I don't think it's convincing." Freda said, "I think it is convincing." Lewis made several wise and constructive suggestions which I accepted, and the article appeared in the next issue under the editor-given title, "What Mr. Hughes Needs to Know." In it I reported what Karl Radek had said to me in Moscow, "Revolutions are not carried in suitcases." A country must be ready for revolution before revolutionists can do anything about it. And I had heard Trotzky assert at a public meeting that no revolution threatened the United States. I simply made the point that there existed among the Bolsheviks two points of view—the national and international—and "a constant struggle in the Communist party" went on between them. In the Internationalist wing I included Radek, Zinoviev, and Bukharin, who would stake the safety of the Russian regime in order to effect a revolution in some European country. The so-called "nationalists"—I did not mention names and did not give Stalin's view—felt that unless they were a success in Russia no nation would be willing to follow their example. It now seems clear that, for 1923, that was a sound analysis of the coming struggle for Bolshevik power.

My problem was to finance the trip back to Europe. Henry G. Alsberg advised me to offer my services to *The Nation* as Russian correspondent and ask for an advance. This appeared to be too wild an ambition, and I did not attempt it. The weeks dragged on, however, without anything happening, and in despair one day I made an appointment with Freda Kirchwey. She promised to consult Oswald Garrison Villard. When I returned the verdict was that I could be staff correspondent, without an advance, although they would undertake to accept a certain number of contributions. This was good news; I felt it a great achievement to establish such a contact with the magazine. A week later I sold an article on religion in Russia to *Current History* and another to the *Menorah Journal*, and the income was just enough for the transatlantic passage with a few dollars to spare.

I was walking down Chestnut Street, Philadelphia, on January

21, 1924, when the afternoon papers blazoned the news of Lenin's death. In one hundred and forty years Europe had produced two figures to whom history will devote more than a paragraph when the nineteenth century and the first quarter of the twentieth are as ancient as the Greek era is to us. They were Napoleon and Lenin. Napoleon was a brilliant failure. He failed in Egypt, he dreamed in vain of India, he lost in Russia and met defeat in Europe. Final judgment of Lenin must be suspended. The best biographies are of dead men. When the effect of a man's work lives long after him the definitive biography waits. Lenin's niche in history will be defined by the next three-fifths of the twentieth century.

What really made Lenin great is what he wanted. When the goal is limited, success is apt to make one a big little man. Lenin wished to forge a new world, and the stupendousness of Lenin's conception enhances his concrete achievement. Lenin spurned personal triumphs and functioned through an impersonal weapon—the Communist party. His power lay in his selflessness, unusual will, singleness of purpose which sometimes amounted to mania, and in an uncanny faculty of seeing and doing the right thing at the right time. He set the date of the Bolshevik Revolution. If it had been attempted several weeks earlier or two months later it might have failed. History revealed itself to him and he made himself its servant.

Did Lenin make history or did history make Lenin? A hundred Lenins could not have produced a Revolution in November, 1917, if Russia had not been ripe for it. Lesser men like Zinoviev and Kamenev would have missed the opportunity; Lenin correctly diagnosed the symptoms and applied his cure at the right juncture.

Lenin brought to politics passion, faith, and instinct. But these were effective because he harnessed them to a scientific mind. Lenin respected facts. Again and again he told his followers that theories deduced from books or brewed by intellectual alchemy were worthless. Political theory not based on a deep knowledge of life was barren, he believed. Lenin could understand the daily thinking of a peasant, a soldier, a workingman as well as of a French politician. He combined a comprehension of broad issues with a knack for detail. And he could grasp the inner meaning of ordinary things like bread, fatigue, peace, hope, personal dignity.

In politics Lenin never lied and he told as much of the truth as possible. No statesman tells the whole truth. Lenin won popular support by demonstrations of wisdom. If he thought he was right, mountains could not budge him. In Lenin's brain, now preserved in Moscow and being studied under the microscope, agility fathered opportunism. His opportunism represented a compromise with conditions, rarely with principles. Lenin was characterized by a complete disregard of first public reactions to acts that apparently compromised him. He accepted the gift of the sealed railway car from General von Ludendorff in order to get back to Russia from Switzerland and lead the Revolution. He wanted help from the Allies, too. Lenin was plastic if necessary, and adamant if necessary. "Ulianov is a bull-dog; he has a death grip," a Bolshevik once said of Lenin. Very true. But he knew at what moment to let go. That is what made the New Economic Policy a stroke of genius.

Now Soviet Russia faced an enigmatic future without Lenin. A battle for the succession was inevitable.

6. Six Lost Years

*E*UROPE *seemed on the verge of collapse at the end of 1923. The collapse did not come. Improvement came instead. The Cassandras, Communist and otherwise, were wrong. Stabilization lasted six years until the end of 1929.*

Between 1924 and 1929, Russia, Germany, and most other nations registered progress. Living standards rose. Peace reigned. Encouraged by these phenomena, statesmen, economists, and businessmen attacked fundamental problems, too. Here they failed—and it was the world's last chance. In those six quiet years between 1924 and 1929 no solid base was built for European and international life. The second World War of 1939 started where the first left off, in 1919, but it did not loom as a definite menace until 1930 when the period of stabilization closed.

During the six fat years from 1924 to, and including, 1929 the Soviet Union lived under the sign of the Trotzky-Stalin feud. Germany struggled with reparations, England and France struggled with one another and, on the question of war debts, with the United States. Disarmament was in the air, but it never came down to earth. Economic panaceas were debated in Geneva, London, Paris, and other centers. Nothing came of them. Italy jogged on under Fascism. China boiled. India was in turmoil. The United States counted its stock and bond profits.

The era of unprecedented prosperity in America was terminated by the stock-market crash of October, 1929, and the subsequent business depession. Three lean years followed, preparing the United States for President Franklin D. Roosevelt and the New Deal. Roosevelt first took office on March 4, 1933.

Soon the same economic slump reached Germany. The Reich slid steadily downward from 1930 to 1933. At the bottom of the toboggan was Adolf Hitler. He assumed office on January 30, 1933. Different countries, different solutions, different leaders.

In Soviet Russia that uneasy symbiosis of capitalism and socialism called NEP or New Economic Policy, which began in 1921-23, reached a dead end in 1929. That year marked its grave and the launching of the high-pressure industrialization effort known as the Five Year Plan. It also marked the emergence of Joseph Stalin as the undisputed master of Soviet destinies.

The era of 1933 and after was dominated by Stalin, Hitler, and Roosevelt.

PART ONE: STALIN VERSUS TROTZKY

The feud between Stalin and Trotzky was a battle of giants that rocked the Soviet Union for many years and profoundly affected world events. It was a relentless combat in which neither man relaxed his grip. Only death could separate them. With his last breath, Trotzky flayed the dictator who prevented him from succeeding Lenin. There was venom, force, and the rage of inhibited genius in Trotzky's verbal thrusts against the master of the Kremlin.

But Stalin? Stalin won. He was master of the Soviet Union. Yet he never suspended hostilities; unremittingly he pursued Trotzky. Not content with exiling him to Alma Ata, thousands of miles from Moscow in Central Asia, Stalin deported him to Turkey. Under Stalin pressure, the Turkish government then expelled him. Thereafter the Kremlin frowned whenever any European government with which it maintained diplomatic relations seemed inclined to grant Trotzky asylum. Finally Norway braved Stalin's wrath and took in the famous exile. On Moscow's insistence, the Norwegian government also asked Trotzky to go. He went to Mexico. Accordingly, the Soviet government refused to establish diplomatic relations with Mexico.

The Moscow trials were first of all trials of Trotzky in absentia. Trotzky in Norway, Trotzky in Mexico was the chief defendant in the legal proceedings under the klieg lights in Moscow's Hall of Columns. The purges were directed against Trotzky's friends, against friends of those friends, against Communists who might be or might become Trotzkyists. The blood feud between the two revolutionists went on.

Tens of thousands of men and women have been shot and imprisoned or sent to rot in frozen wastes because of this war between Trotzky and Stalin. Soviet domestic and foreign policies were perverted by it. History has been rewritten and changed because of it. And the whole labor movement of the world was rent and weakened by the Trotzky-Stalin enmity. In 1939, I discussed the Soviet purges and Moscow trials with John Strachey, the British popularizer of Marxism. He said, "They helped to bring on Munich." Hitler's victory over Czechoslovakia, perhaps even the second World War, reflects this fantastic bout between the Ukrainian Jew and the son of an illiterate Georgian cobbler.

Was this historic duel personal or was it a clash of ideas? Trozky admitted that he had a violent dislike for Stalin. "He always repelled me," writes Trotzky in his autobiography, adding that Stalin's characteristics were "a narrowness of interests, empiricism, psychological crudeness, and the peculiar cynicism of a provincial." The long controversy between the Stalinites and Trotzkyists concerned itself with the world revolution, the Chinese revolution, and the Kremlin's economic policies in Russia. It descended to ugly diatribe and invective but always against a background of impersonal ideology and theory. Yet years before any of these problems had arisen or could have arisen, Stalin was intriguing against Trotzky, and Trotzky was appealing to Lenin against Stalin. Stalin appears to have been jealous of Trotzky from the very beginning. In the autumn of 1918, General Yudenitch, a White Russian leader, advanced from Esthonia on Petrograd. Trotzky personally led the defense. For his successful efforts, he was decorated with the Order of the Red Banner. Trotzky himself describes the session of the Politbureau, the highest Communist authority in Russia, at which this distinction was decided on. Leo Kamenev, assistant premier under Lenin, proposed that Stalin be granted the same decoration. "What for?" exclaimed Mikhail Kalinin, later President of the Soviet Union.

"Don't you understand?" Bukharin elucidated. "Lenin thought this out. Stalin can't live if he hasn't got what the other fellow has. He can't forgive it."

As early as October 4, 1918, Trotzky, then at the front commanding the Red Army, telegraphed to Lenin, "I insist categorically on the removal of Stalin." Stalin was at Tsaritsin (later christened Stalingrad) on the Volga acting as the political support of Voroshilov who was in charge of the Bolshevik troops there. Trotzky accused Stalin and Voroshilov of creating a little military kingdom for themselves and of refusing to obey orders from headquarters. Stalin was removed and transferred to the southern front in the Ukraine. There Voroshilov soon joined him. Again Trotzky and Stalin collided. January 10, 1919, Trotzky was telegraphing to Moscow that "the Tsaritsin methods which had led to the complete disintegration of the Tsaritsin army cannot be permitted in the Ukraine. . . . The tactics of Stalin, Voroshilov, and Company will mean the collapse of our whole undertaking." Lenin advised Trotzky to compromise with Stalin. But no compromise could be effected between these two. In June, 1919, the course of the war in the Ukraine was running against the Bolsheviks. Stalin urged the Communist Central Committee in Moscow to dismiss Trotzky from the Red Army command. Trotzky thereupon offered his resignation. It was not accepted.

Trotzky was direct and merciless in his criticisms. Either he ignored individual psychology or else he did not understand it. He stepped on people's toes. And, says Trotzky, Stalin systematically collected those on whose toes Trotzky had trod. Trotzky could not subordinate himself to anybody. He even found difficulty in submitting to Lenin and declined to be Lenin's right-hand man. He preferred a field of activity for himself where he would be first.

Trotzky was an erratic, capricious individualist. Trotzky's speeches and articles warmed and thrilled multitudes, but in his personal relations he was cold. People were cold to him. Even Lenin, of a friendly, sunny disposition, could not get close to Trotzky and wrote to him as "Esteemed Comrade," instead of "Dear Comrade." Chicherin used to say to me, "Trotzky was a prima donna." There was something of the pedant in Trotzky. He was a master administrator and organizer and insisted on the execution of instructions and on the strictest attention to details. In his personal dress and habits he was neat. His desk was a model of order. He tried to teach Russians punctuality. These elements in his character made him a successful army leader but a poor politician. He never obtained a hold on the party machine, and there is no evidence that he ever tried. In his consciousness of superiority, he placed himself above the battle and therefore lost it.

When Lenin suffered his first stroke in May, 1921, Trotzky was convalescing in a village just outside Moscow. Lenin might have died. Trotzky was the next ranking leader in Russia. Yet for three days Trotzky was not informed about Lenin's illness. Trotzky believed that Stalin, Zinoviev, and Kamenev, already intriguing against him, deliberately kept him in ignorance. But where were Trotzky's secretaries? Did he have no party henchmen who could have rushed out by car to tell him and bring him into town? Trotzky held his head so high above the clouds that his feet never stood on the solid ground of party organization. He was a Gibraltar without a hinterland, a lone lion, a dreadnaught sailing the seas without escort. He was therefore easily vulnerable to attack. The enemy could creep up on him in stealth. Stalin is not nearly as good a speaker or writer as Trotzky, and has much less education, culture, and Marxist training. But the party secretaries were his lieutenants. That counted for more than a million striking phrases.

When Lenin died in January, 1924, Trotzky had gone for a cure to the Caucasus, then a four-day trip from Moscow. He did not return to the capital for the funeral. But this was of only minor importance. Stalin, Zinoviev, and Kamenev had already prepared the ground for their attack on Trotzky's political future. They controlled the pivotal Central Committee and had so out-maneuvered Trotzky that he was the Opposition. But his was a strong Opposition. The government offices were honeycombed with Trotzkyites. The university students, who always played an important role in Russian political life, staunchly supported Trotzky. A resolution of the Red Army's Communists, dated January 18, placed them behind Trotzky. Factory meetings and provincial organizations telegraphed approval of his views. Yet when the regular National Conference of the Communist party met in Moscow the fourth week of May, 1924, Trotzky did not have a single delegate. He himself failed of election as a delegate.

In addition to Trotzky, the Opposition had other able leaders. This is what the Stalin-Zinoviev-Kamenev triumvirate did with them before the National Conference convened:

V. V. Osinsky, scintillating Bolshevik economist, scion of the princely house of Obolensky, was kept in Stockholm as Soviet trade representative.

Sapronov, a young workingman who had forged his way to the front rank of the party, was ordered to Vladivostok, a ten-day rail trip from Moscow.

Antonov-Avseyenko, untamable revolutionary with untamable hair, who had stormed the Petrograd Winter Palace on November 7, 1917, was dispatched on a mission to China.

Preobrazhensky, co-author with Bukharin of the *ABC of Communism* but now seeing Communism differently from Bukharin, and from Stalin, received instructions to participate in the Anglo-Russian negotiations in London.

Simultaneously, commissariats, offices, and universities were rigorously combed of pro-Trotzky elements. In Trotzky's absence and without his knowledge, Skliansky, his first assistant in the War Department, was discharged, and Frunze appointed in his stead. Frunze straightway attacked his new chief in the press. General Muralov, loyal friend of Trotzky, commander of the Moscow garrison, found himself in a distant military post. Stalin was taking no chances.

These and similar shifts destroyed, neutralized, or terrorized the Trotzkyists. The national party conference of May, 1924, therefore gave the triumvirate leadership a unanimous vote of confidence. But Trotzky was not yet finished by any means. Stalin, Zinoviev, and Kamenev might hold the party machine, but Trotzky still had a powerful appeal to the youth, the army, and the rank-and-file Communist and workingman. The "Lenin and Trotzky" legend shielded him. At the conference, Nadezhda Krupskaya, Lenin's widow, an old party leader and educator, rose to Trotzky's defense. Likewise Boris Souvarine, representative of the French Communist party, asked for the special privilege of the floor and, speaking French, said, "To the working class of the world Trotzky's name is synonymous with the revolution." Stalin knew this was true. It was too early to take Trotzky's scalp.

Stalin continued diligently to dig the ground from under Trotzky's political feet. Trotzky moved away and did not even snipe back. Suddenly Trotzky fired a broadside at his enemies; he published a book. It appeared at the end of 1924 and the dust storm it raised did not subside for years. The two-volume work was entitled *1917*; it reviewed the exciting events preceding the Bolshevik revolution. The dynamite was in an introduction called "Lessons of October." (The Bolshevik Revolution occurred on October 25, according to the old Gregorian calendar, November 7, Julian style.) Trotzky recalled that Zinoviev and Kamenev opposed Lenin and sought to dissuade the Communists from seizing power. He cited Lenin's denunciations of these "deserters." If they, and Rykov, Nogin, Miliutin, and other fainthearted Bolsheviks had had their way, Trotzky emphasized, there would have been no Soviet regime.

Trotzky was not born yesterday. The major part of his forty-five years had been spent in active politics. And he must have known that those whom he assailed would strike back. He attacked with the best weapon he had, his pen. He was the artist in politics. But their arsenal did not lack ammunition, either; it contained wire-pulling devices, intrigue, unscrupulousness, demagogy. Hitherto Stalin, Zinoviev, and Kamenev had condemned Trotzky for trying to convert the party to Trotzkyism. But they did not define Trotzkyism. They said he wished to organize his own fraction within the party, and that is treason against the Communist code: the party must be a "monolith," solid. But these charges were vague. Now Trotzky gave his enemies a wonderful opportunity. For he was pulling down the prestige of two party leaders, and the motive could be none other than political, a step to the fulfillment of his own ambition. Thousands of like-worded resolutions poured in from Communist and non-Communist groups condemning Trotzky's "aggression." He had raked up old sins. They would, too. Had he not quarreled with Lenin in those hair-splitting, tempest-in-a-teapot theoretical discussions of the pre-Revolution emigration? Once he called Lenin "unscrupulous." Lenin had branded Trotzky an "empty phrasemonger." These squabbles were forgotten in 1917 and during the subsequent years of intimate collaboration. Now the Stalinists refurbished them. Trotzky had been a Menshevik—cardinal sin. He had entered the Bolshevik party for the first time in 1917. Cautiously, moreover, Stalin, Zinoviev, and Kamenev commenced to minimize Trotzky's part in the Revolution and civil war. Stalin once had declared publicly, "All the practical work of organizing the insurrection was conducted by Trotzky." That did not make it impossible to assert the opposite a few years later.

The anti-Trotzky barrage worked so successfully that in January, 1925, the triumvirs put Frunze in Trotzky's place as war minister.

Luck now played a cruel trick on Trotzky. His temperature rose and stayed abnormally high for months. He took to his bed and could do no work. The Stalin leadership exploited this interval. Still Stalin did not dare to destroy Trotzky completely. Trotzky's name fired the imagination of millions. In 1925, Trotzky asked Bukharin, who was doing much of Stalin's thinking at this time, why the party had become a lifeless mechanism. Bukharin replied, "We are afraid of you. That is why there is no democracy in the party."

Spring, 1925. Trotzky, unemployed, knocked at the Kremlin gate for a job. He got three: chairman of the Chief Concessions Committee, chairman of the Electro-Technical Authority, and chairman of the Industrial Commission for Scientific Research—all subordinate tasks requiring meticulous attention to a million minor matters. Stalin wished to bury Trotzky under a mountain of detail. If Trotzky slipped on one detail it would be magnified into a mountain and be made the subject of an attack on him. Trotzky nevertheless welcomed his new role. He hoped to wait till the ill wind blew over. He regarded this early phase of the New Economic Policy (NEP) as the revolutionary ebb. His turn would come with the inevitable resurgence of revolutionary élan, he thought. He conceived of himself as cast for the role of generalissimo in smashing offensives. A mediocre major could manage things in a muddy trench. . . . This was one of Trotzky's many political blunders; history kept Bolshevism in the trench for many long years.

Trotzky wanted opportunities offered to youth to enter government and party service. He feared that sclerosis would harden the arteries of the Soviets and conduce to conservatism. He wanted the lid lifted on criticism within the party ranks. He was afraid of the NEP. He had advocated it long before it was enacted. He voted for it. Now it alarmed him. The hundred million peasants were that many private capitalists. The new privileges brought them by the NEP made them stronger economically. They would encroach on the socialist city and crush the Bolshevik revolution. All Bolsheviks, Stalinists as well as Trotzkyists, were disturbed by this menace, and Stalin introduced the first Five Year Plan in 1928, to destroy it. But the time factor and personal temperament were elements in this controversy. Trotzky's culture and nerves made him a westerner. He was impatient. While the party leadership boasted of its economic achievements, Trotzky complained of the slow pace of progress.

The dilemma was that progress created problems. One of Russia's blights was recurrent famine. The Bolsheviks proposed to stamp it out and they began by trying to restore the peasant's initiative. But if he raised more he would have more money for the purchase of manufactured goods and the government was not yet producing sufficient industrial goods. Of course, the government could import the commodities which the peasant wanted to buy. But if everything the peasantry earned went abroad to buy foreign articles then the Bolsheviks could not finance their own domestic industrialization program, and Russia would remain an agrarian country. It was the historic function of Bolshevism, however, to industrialize Russia, increase the number of factory workers—the proletariat—thereby making Russia more independent economically and less vulnerable to outside attack.

To the Trotzkyists the peasant, being a private capitalist, was an enemy of socialism. In a poor, technically backward country like Russia, they argued, with seventy-five percent of the population residing in villages, you could therefore never have socialism. At best, the city could become industrialized at the expense of the peasants, and meanwhile the Bolsheviks could hope for and foment revolutions abroad. The sovietization of western industrialized Europe would save Soviet Russia from being engulfed by its capitalistic peasant masses. This was Trotzky's theory of "Permanent Revolution." But the attempt at a revolution in Germany in 1923 failed. No other major and successful revolution seemed to impend. This meant that the Russian peasant would have to be antagonized and milked indefinitely. The Kremlin could not face such a problem with equanimity. Neither could it solve the problem.

It tried hard. By the end of 1926 most of the old factories had been reopened and reconditioned. New factories were being built. Workers' wages had mounted to ninety-one percent of pre-War wages. The ruble was stable, and the billions and trillions were gone. A gigantic Soviet effort from 1921 to 1927 had brought Russia back to 1913 economic levels. But with the slack taken up the rate of advance diminished. The government accordingly curtailed its industrialization program because it refused to squeeze the peasant inordinately. This infuriated the Opposition.

Preobrazhensky, a Trotzkyist economist, showed that in 1925 and 1926 the workingman was spending six percent of his annual income on vodka because he had nothing else to spend it on. The six percent represented half of his wage increase. The Trotzkyists insisted that to cut the Gordian knot they had to industrialize with fierce rapidity, introduce western technique, and thus ultimately produce an adequate supply of manufactured goods at lower prices. If this entailed inflation they were reconciled to it.

The city workers wanted more industrialization because it promised more jobs and more goods. The peasants wanted less industrialization. But some peasants were migrating to the cities because of the empty shelves in village stores and the chances of work in town. In 1924, 1,672,000 peasants moved to urban centers, in 1925, 2,780,-000, and in 1926, 3,200,000. The government had to employ them or invite an economic crisis with political implications. To employ them it had to industrialize. To industrialize it had to make the village pay by giving it less goods at higher prices. That would induce further migration from the villages and, thus, further industrialization. This was the inevitable vicious circle produced by the NEP. The Stalin leadership was endeavoring to break through the circle.

At the end of 1925, a startling development occurred. Zinoviev and Kamenev deserted Stalin and joined Trotzky. Trotzky boasted that they had been converted to his political program. But he himself once remarked sarcastically that Kamenev and Zinoviev "lacked that little detail called character." They turned their coats several times, and Zinoviev was especially disliked despite his talents. It is, of course, quite conceivable that the intimate knowledge of Soviet affairs gained as members of the ruling triumvirate convinced them that the government's policy was leading the country into a morass. But it is also likely that they suspected Stalin of plotting to get rid of them, and hastily formed self-protective alliances with Trotzky whom they had previously maligned and persecuted. Trotzky was not above grasping the proffered aid.

Stalinist spokesmen admitted that capitalism was growing in city and village, but they argued that socialism's growth exceeded that of capitalism. This provoked an indecisive battle of statistics. Even the naked eye, however, saw a new class of rich peasants or kulaks. In 1925, Bukharin, the right-winger, said to the peasants, "Enrich yourself." In the same year a federal decree permitted the renting of land. This was a reactionary innovation. Land had been nationalized on the first day of the Revolution. Nobody owned land. Nobody could buy or sell land. Now it could be rented. The authorities submitted that they merely legalized an existing situation; poor peasants who lacked equipment or hands to till their fields had been leasing it to wealthier peasants under myriad guises—fictitious marriages, fake partnerships, false co-operatives.

The enrichment of the peasantry really signified the enrichment of one or two small upper classes of peasants and the impoverishment of the others. Class differentiation had overtaken the countryside— the Soviet countryside! "Is this what we fought for?" Communists asked. The Soviet record from 1921 to 1926 showed a series of concessions which the farming population had wrung from the unwilling Bolsheviks by passive weight rather than by political action. This was ominous.

What to do? In the city the government started taxing the private capitalistic Nepmen out of existence. The assessor would enter a store and demand 3,000 rubles in taxes. The Nepman claimed that his whole enterprise was worth less than that. "I'm sorry," was his only comfort. I knew personally of several cases in which the storekeeper simply walked out of his premises and never returned. Co-operative and state stores took their place. The Nepman went "underground" and speculated.

To crush capitalist competition in the village, kulaks were arrested, heavily taxed, and dispossessed. By so doing, the Soviet regime often killed the goose that laid the golden eggs. The moment a peasant produced a large surplus for city consumption he became too prosperous for the safety of socialism, and so he was economically decapitated.

A good deal of this went on under the pressure of the Opposition's propaganda. But such negative, destructive methods of "building socialism" could not be applied for a long time without deleterious results to the national economy and without spreading disaffection among the peasantry. The peasant who was not a kulak hoped to become one. Who could blame a man for wanting to earn more? But when he saw the fate that overtook the kulaks he lost his ambition, and the state consequently lost crops. In 1928, all cities were short of bread.

Economic difficulties in 1926 and 1927 encouraged the Trotzkyists to intensify their efforts. At party meetings Opposition spokesmen interjected remarks and attacked the Stalin leadership. At a meeting in the Moscow Avtopribor factory which produced automobile accessories, Radek, Piatakov, Sapronov, and Zinoviev spoke—certainly important leaders—and at one in the morning Trotzky arrived and took the floor. The work of the Opposition seemed so methodical as to create the impression of an organized fraction inside the party. Communist psychology is hostile to fractions.

On one occasion the Communist Central Committee discussed a motion to exclude Comrade Osovsky from the party for proposing the legalization of a second political party in Soviet Russia. Trotzky and some of his friends opposed Osovsky's exclusion; it was voted by a large majority nevertheless. Logically, the Opposition's tactics, if long tolerated, would have implied acceptance into Soviet life of a second Communist party—as the Republican party is a second capitalist party in the United States. But that was inconceivable under a dictatorship. The Opposition's obstructions at meetings caused considerable resentment among workingmen and Communists, and Trotzky himself saw the necessity of beating a retreat. On October 16, 1926, the Opposition published a declaration promising to refrain from fractional work.

The truce was short-lived. Soon the Opposition returned to the fray. This time the battlefield was not within party meetings. The Opposition commenced calling its own secret meetings. Gatherings took place in workingmen's homes or in factory cellars and were attended by a few score or a few hundred people. Trotzky says he sometimes addressed four such meetings a day. The great orator who had spoken to whole divisions of troops at the front before sending them into the firing line and whom I had heard addressing thousands in big Moscow halls, now appeared in small apartments in the proletarian districts. With the bed pushed into one corner and baby's crib piled on the bed, chairs and tables removed, sweating humanity packed tightly into dingy quarters to listen to Russia's Demosthenes. It must have reminded him of his youthful activities under the Czarist regime. Sometimes, too, the Opposition dared to call large open meetings which attracted thousands.

The Opposition proposed a ten-billion-ruble forced loan from the kulaks, Nepmen, and non-Communist government officials. They advocated, in addition, the seizure of two and a half million tons of grain from prosperous peasants. They advocated super-industrialization. But they could offer no constructive suggestion as to how to do it without driving the peasantry, which paid, into an anti-Bolshevik fury. Trotzky correctly diagnosed. He was a brilliant analyst; that made him a great orator and journalist. But he could not prescribe. His own followers felt this. The country felt it, too.

Events abroad now exacerbated the Stalin-Trotzky feud and hastened Trotzky's doom. In May, 1926, the British coal industry was paralyzed by a strike. The General Council of the British Trade Union Congress called a general strike to help the miners. Moscow's heart skipped a beat. Was England marching to revolution? The Soviet Trade Unions telegraphed large sums of gold for the relief of the striking miners. The general strike, however, aroused violent public hostility in Britain. Inspired by Winston Churchill, volunteer groups and the authorities took stringent action. Soon Ramsay Mac-Donald, J. H. Thomas, and other conservative figures in the Trade Union movement called off the general strike, and before long the miners had to go back to work.

The Trotzkyists tried to pin the failure of the British strike on Stalin. In 1925, at the suggestion of Tomsky, leader of the Soviet trade unions and a right-wing Bolshevik, the Russian and British trade unions had formed an Anglo-Russian Committee. This collaboration, it was hoped, would check hostile moves by the British government against Soviet Russia and strengthen the working-class movement in Europe. Trotzky first approved, but then decided that such co-operation with an organization led by conservative labor leaders hampered the growth of Communism in foreign countries. He wanted the Communist party in England to go out into the open and fight the MacDonalds and Snowdens. He had no faith in united fronts. The collapse of the British strike apparently proved him right. Actually, however, the setback in England was a setback for the Trotzky Opposition in Russia; it showed that the prospect of revolution in an advanced European country was not bright, and yet one of the pillars of the entire Trotzky platform at home was the belief in revolution abroad.

In 1927, the Chinese Revolution crumpled. The Soviet peoples have always had a keen sympathy for China. One school of Bolshevik thought assumed that "the infantry of the East," the teeming hundreds of millions in Asia, would make the first assault on the capitalist rear after which "the cavalry of the West," Europe's organized workers, would finish the job by a frontal drive. Hopes therefore rose high when the Chinese Nationalists under Dr. Sun Yat-sen established a government in the southern Chinese city of Canton. Dr. Sun openly advocated intimate collaboration with Moscow. The Soviet government sent a large sum of money to finance a military training school headed by General Chiang Kai-shek at Whampoa, Canton. The Soviet government delegated Michael M. Borodin, formerly of Chicago, as its representative in southern China. Before long he was the real leader of the Chinese Revolution. General Galen, a Russian officer who became better known later as Marshal Bluecher, went to China with a military staff to assist Borodin. The Chinese Nationalists won signal successes.

During this period, the Chinese Communists, on instructions from Moscow, were members of the Kuomintang, the Chinese Nationalist party which included rich merchants, provincial war lords, peasants, bankers, workingmen, and coolies. Stalin told the Communist International on November 30, 1926, that "the exit of Chinese Communists from the Kuomintang would be the gravest error." He likewise questioned the wisdom of organizing soviets in China in opposition to the Kuomintang government. The Trotzkyists advocated both these measures.

Foreign Commissar Chicherin later told me of a debate on China in the Politbureau which he attended. Radek predicted that Chiang Kai-shek would betray the Revolution. Stalin vehemently disagreed. The next day news came from China that Chiang was executing the Communists and left Kuomintangists. "That is why," Chicherin said to me, "Stalin then took the Trotzkyist line in China." Chicherin asked me not to publish this until he died.

The Stalin leadership thereupon adopted the policy of fostering peasant soviets in China. The Trotzkyists crowed in triumph. Stalin countered that when the Opposition wanted soviets it was too early. Radek, the Opposition's China expert, said: But you wanted them too late, when reaction was in flood throughout China. When the Trotzkyists proposed forming Chinese soviets, the Communists and left-wingers still had influence and arms. Now they had lost them.

The Bolshevik majority probably miscalculated the tempo of Chinese events and stuck too long to Chiang Kai-shek. But I doubt whether the Chinese Revolution could have been saved by Trotzky. The counter-revolutionary forces in China, foreign and domestic, were stronger than the Revolution. The Trotzkyists could try to convince Russia that they had been right and Stalin wrong. But politics is not a matter of having the correct answer. The crushing of the Chinese Revolution was a fact, and it diminished Trotzky's prospects in the Soviet Union for, one after the other, the hopes of world revolution were fading. In Russia there was economic stability if not prosperity, and progress despite poverty. Moreover, unity is a Communist fetish and Trotzky threatened to split the party. Many followers of Trotzky left the Opposition because they disapproved of its methods even when they accepted its ideas. They objected to its secret printing press, its clandestinely distributed pamphlets and street demonstrations.

Nevertheless, Trotzky resisted political death. The stars of the Bolshevik firmament—Trotzky, Kamenev, Rakovsky, Zinoviev, Radek, Osinsky, Alexandra Kollontai, Muralov, Smilga, Preobrazhensky— were still in the Opposition. Krupskaya, Lenin's widow, did not stand with either side. But she knew Lenin's last testament. It was a political document. (He had had no property to give away.) He put it in her safekeeping in December, 1922. In it he wrote, "Comrade Stalin, having become general secretary of the party, has concentrated tremendous power in his hands, and I am not sure he always knows how to use that power with sufficient caution." On January 4, 1923, Lenin asked Krupskaya for the testament and added this striking postscript, "Stalin is too rude. . . . I propose to the comrades to find a way of removing Stalin. . . . This circumstance may seem an insignificant trifle. But I think that from the point of view of preventing a split in the party, and from the point of view of the relations between Stalin and Trotzky . . . it is not a trifle, or it is a trifle that may acquire decisive significance." Lenin foresaw the great contest. His testament is to this day unpublished in the Soviet Union. Krupskaya read it twice to meetings of the Central Committee. Once Stalin himself had to read it aloud at a secret session. It has been carried by word of mouth—but not very far, strangely enough. Few Russians of my acquaintance ever heard of Lenin's will.

The Trotzkyists were a large group of generals leading a small army. Yet they were difficult to vanquish. Stalin required another weapon before he could administer the final blow. He found it in the foreign situation. The relations between the Soviet and non-Soviet worlds were marked by mutual suspicion and hatred. But Russia was weak and needed outside aid and a respite from hostility and therefore sought to get along with the other governments. As early as 1925 I had been able to report that the Communists were "ready to scrap political principles for practical prizes." The great powers, on the other hand, failed to realize that Europe could never settle down until it settled with Moscow. Direct anti-Soviet military intervention was now out of the question. Mussolini, striving to be first, recognized the Soviet government in 1923; Ramsay MacDonald followed suit in February, 1924; France exchanged ambassadors with Red Moscow in October, 1924; the Soviets scrapped an oil concession they had granted Harry F. Sinclair in Northern Sakhalin and gave it to Japan, thus paying for Tokio's recognition in January, 1925. Nevertheless, the Soviet regime continued to be the object of financial embargoes, trade boycotts, social hostility, and diplomatic frigidity on the part of bourgeois nations.

The great powers explained their uncompromising attitude toward Soviet Russia by the Kremlin's refusal to pay debts. But they themselves did not shine by example in this matter. Moreover, when they subsequently needed Russian support they forgot the debts. They explained it, further, by Communist propaganda and the existence of a Bolshevik menace to the capitalist countries. Why should they build up a real or potential enemy? Communist propaganda has undoubtedly been a serious irritant, and the British were especially annoyed by Moscow's role in China and in the coal and general strikes. Governments must of course take steps to counteract influences they think harmful. But statesmen who wished to pacify a continent, prevent another war, and salvage world economy should have seen the larger aspects of Soviet Russia's role in world affairs. Neither Communism nor the Soviet government has ever been a serious threat to the British Empire or Great Britain, or to British capitalism. Czarism was a much greater threat to India, yet England and the Czar became war allies. If anything, the Communists made British labor more anti-Communist. The same applies to other bourgeois nations. Viewed in the perspective of history, and forgetting Moscow's stupid day-to-day sniping at other world powers, the non-Soviet nations have committed innumerable blunders in their relations with Soviet Russia. They were blunders because while they hurt Russia they hurt the blunderers no less.

On May 24, 1927, the British government severed diplomatic relations with Russia. The ground was propaganda. The move got the British nowhere. They subsequently were forced to resume these relations. Lord Balfour said that a break with Russia "carries with it obvious dangers. Does it carry with it obvious advantages? . . . I fail to see them." Prime Minister Baldwin and Foreign Minister Sir Austen Chamberlain (half-brother of Neville Chamberlain), in a solemn matter that concerned not only England and Russia but the peace of hemispheres and the lives of millions, frivolously vented their emotional animosity towards Bolshevism and overlooked the practical considerations. The British initiative soon spoiled Franco-Soviet relations, too.

I arrived in Moscow from a trip abroad in June, 1927. On all sides Soviet acquaintances plied me with questions: "When will the war break out?" "Will they attack us through Poland or where?" I said, "You're crazy," to intimate friends and argued with but did not convince high Soviet officials. Moscow was panicky. The peasants bought salt. From time immemorial they have done this when they fear war. Villages held back their grain. The cities felt the shortage. Yet all this commotion was artificially created by the Stalinists to crush Trotzky. When I spent eight days with Foreign Commissar Chicherin in Wiesbaden, Germany, in 1929, he said to me, "I returned to Moscow from western Europe in June, 1927. Everybody was talking war. I tried to dissuade them. 'Nobody is planning to attack us,' I insisted. But then a colleague enlightened me. He said, 'Sh! We know. But we need this against Trotzky.'"

Later too Maxim Litvinov told me he did not think the British government was attempting to organize a war against Russia in 1927. "That was merely idle gossip here of some people and the press." He continued, "It is wrong to suppose, as many of us do, that Russia is the center of all international affairs. England broke with us because she hoped that others would follow her example and that as a result the Soviet government would become more amenable to British pressure." But Stalinist propaganda created the impression that war was coming tomorrow. Having done so, the party leadership demanded of the Trotzky Opposition what it would do in case of war. Would it continue its assaults on the party while the capitalists fought the fatherland?

How did Trotzky answer? I will not relent; I will be like Clemenceau, Trotzky said. When the Germans were marching on Paris in 1917, he explained, Clemenceau assailed the French cabinet for its ineptitude, and ultimately brought about its fall. He then led France to victory. Trotzky promised to do the same. He would defend the Soviet Union under the present Stalin leadership if the enemy attacked. But he would at the same time attack Stalin. The party leadership used this admission to sow further prejudice against Trotzky.

In the midst of all this, with a number of other Americans, I spent six and a quarter hours with Joseph Stalin. Professor Jerome Davis of the Divinity School of Yale University conducted a group of Americans to and through the Soviet Union in the summer of 1927. The Russians called it "the American Labor Delegation," but most of its members, I believe, represented nobody but themselves, and only John Brophy of the Miners' Federation and James Maurer of Pennsylvania were labor leaders. The group included Stuart Chase, Paul H. Douglas, economist, Rexford G. Tugwell, Robert Dunn, radical labor research student, and I. Israels, New York lawyer. When they went for their interview with Stalin on September 9, 1927, they invited Anne O'Hare McCormick and me to go along. We saw Stalin not in the Kremlin but just outside it in the headquarters of the Central Committee within Moscow's old Chinese wall.

We entered Stalin's large reception room at one o'clock in the afternoon. We sat with Stalin until seven-fifteen in the evening. During all this time Stalin never once left the room. He never once sent out a message or received a message. There was no telephone in the room. Here was the man at the helm of Soviet Russia. All threads ended in his hand. Yet he had deliberately cut himself off from everything and everybody for almost an entire working day. He had so organized his work that he could devote himself exclusively to his visitors. This concentration is characteristic of Stalin.

Twice during our prolonged stay, on instructions previously issued, a typical Russian working woman brought in cheese, sausage, and caviar sandwiches and a large steaming samovar—the word means "self-cooker"—with tumblers for tea with lemon. This woman was the only person to enter the room.

When we arrived Stalin gave each of us a sharp, energetic handshake and invited us to occupy chairs around a long table covered with green felt cloth. He wore high black leather boots, and a civilian khaki suit the trousers of which were stuffed into his boots below the knee. His body is solid but not fat and he moves quickly and softly. If I had seen him without knowing who he was, he would never have impressed me. He looked like any one of a million Soviet workingmen.

Stalin sat at the head of the table. I sat first on his left making bad pencil sketches of his head and keeping notes which I now have before me. My notes read, "Deep pock marks over his face," "crafty eyes," "low forehead," "thick bushy black hair," "ugly, short, black and gold teeth when smiles." He smiled little. He was busy. But at conferences and public meetings, during periods of relaxation, I had seen him laugh uproariously.

Trotzky waves the magic wand of a magnetic personality and captures his interlocutor. Stalin does not. But as he talked to us hour after hour my respect for his strength, will, and faith grew. He built up this impression as he built up his political position—slowly, methodically, brick by brick. Nothing Stalin said throughout the interview was brilliant. He was pedestrian, solid and simple. His statements interested professors of economy and would have been intelligible to factory hands. The questions had been submitted to him in advance, and he probably prepared the answers in advance. Sometimes he did not grasp the meaning of the question, and rambled before he reached its pith, but finally he did get to the point. His replies were always long and thorough. His mentality lacked the witty epigram or the remark with insight which can light up a whole field of thought. He plowed long and deep. His complete composure, the complete absence of nerves, and his calm voice reflected inner power. One could see that he might be a man of iron.

The questions posed to Stalin dealt with theoretical Marxism, Leninism, and imperialism. He would not allow himself to be drawn into a discussion of his differences with Trotzky. That was not a subject for a Communist leader to discuss with non-Communists. He did say this: Lenin "proved that it was possible to construct a complete socialist society in a land of the dictatorship of the proletariat encircled by imperialist states." I do not know where or how Lenin proved that socialism could be established in one country. It was the bone of contention between Trotzky and Stalin. Trotzky's view was diametrically opposed to Stalin's. Both Trotzky and Stalin cited Lenin in support of their conjectures, but I do not think that a case is won if it can lean on a quotation from Lenin or an interpretation of a quotation from Lenin. To date, socialism has not been established in the Soviet Union. That may or may not mean that it cannot be.

More questions to Stalin. Is there personal incentive in Russia? Does the American Communist party get its orders and money from Moscow? He said it might under certain circumstances. Must a Communist be an atheist? While he was answering this question the chiming of bells in a church across the street drowned out his voice. He smiled and we laughed. (In later years, church bells were silenced by decree.) Yes, a Communist must be an atheist.

These questions and more questions were put to Stalin. After three hours one could see delegates sitting on the edges of their chairs, and Jerome Davis was getting ready to say something like, "Thank you, Mr. Stalin, for your kindness in granting us so much of your time," but Stalin never gave him a chance. Finally, at the end of four hours, Davis did deliver his speech. But Stalin said, "No, no. I have answered your questions. Now you must answer mine." And for two and a quarter hours he asked questions and the Americans answered. He inquired why so few American workers belonged to trade unions, whether unemployment insurance existed in America as in Russia, why there was no labor party in the United States, and why the American government had not yet recognized Soviet Russia. That was all. He gave each one a second bone-crushing handshake and we left. I felt that Stalin was typical of many Bolsheviks—unsentimental, steel-willed, unscrupulous, and irresistible.

A few weeks after this interview Stalin started Trotzky on the trek which ended near Mexico City. Trotzky knew that his defiance of party discipline could not continue much longer with impunity. He had to win or succumb. On November 7, 1927, ten years from the day he, with Lenin, and others had made the Revolution, he made another bid for power, this time not against a bourgeois regime but against the Stalin regime. There were rumors on the eve of the anniversary that the army, massed in the Red Square in front of the Lenin mausoleum for the annual parade, would demonstrate against Stalin. Some courageous soldier or officer would cry out "Down with Stalin," and others would echo the slogan. Nothing happened. But the mood that day was tense. The Chinese students of Moscow's Sun Yat-sen University, participating in the march, formed a long, sinuous dragon. In the middle of the square they threw Trotzkyist proclamations in the air. The GPU arrested some of the Chinese. In the afternoon, pictures of Trotzky were torn down from buildings. At one place near the center of town, early in the afternoon, Trotzky himself came out on a balcony and commenced to address the civilian parade of workingmen as it moved towards the Red Square. Russians climbed up and stopped him. Later I saw Trotzky and Kamenev slowly driving down the Tverskaya Street toward Strasnaya Square in a big black limousine. What were they thinking? They had failed to rouse the population; the match had not met any fuel. Their doom was near.

Several days later the Communist party expelled Trotzky from its ranks. For a Communist, membership in the party is everything. It is his ticket to work, political activity, and happiness. Outside it he exists only as a shadow. A cardinal ex-communicated by the church, a king forced into abdication and exile—these mildly suggest the tragedy of a Trotzky deprived of his red membership card in the Communist party.

That very day I received a telephone summons to visit Adolf A. Joffe, the Soviet diplomat, former Ambassador to Germany and China, negotiator of the Soviet peace with Poland and of numerous treaties, among them the Rapallo Pact, long an intimate friend and warm admirer of Trotzky. Joffe was in bed, very ill. He had been suffering for many months. He looked like a Jewish rabbi, with very high brow, thin black hair and beard, delicate thick fingers, pale face, and sad, sad eyes. He almost frightened me. I could not imagine why he had asked me to come. I had never met him before.

Apparently he had read my *Oil Imperialism* which dealt with his work as chairman of the Chief Concessions Committee, and we had an intimate mutual friend who must have talked to him about me. He asked me about conditions in Europe and America. Did I think a revolution possible in Germany?

I said, "No." Germany had regained her social equilibrium.

China? I was pessimistic there, too.

But England had had the General Strike, he argued. The workers were displeased with their reactionary leaders. I replied that I had sensed little revolutionary sentiment in England. He rested often during this conversation and appeared to be in constant pain. He would stop and swallow hard, or prop himself up on one elbow and pour himself medicine from one of a dozen bottles which stood on his little night table. He inquired about American conditions. I spoke of stenographers wearing silk stockings and playing the stock market.

It was then that Joffe showed me papers relating to his personal activities while Ambassador to Germany in 1918, which I have already described. He had fostered and financed revolution there, the papers proved. "Would not the possibilities of revolution be enhanced," he suggested, "if certain forces did more to encourage the European proletariat?" This was the nearest he came to a direct criticism of Stalin. I said I could not of course guess what might happen in different circumstances but I had not observed any mounting tide of revolution anywhere. We talked on this subject for a while. Pain obviously tortured him. I went home.

Five days later Joffe committed suicide. He left a letter addressed to Trotzky. Joffe killed himself because he was very sick. But he was also sick at heart. Too sick to help the Revolution with his life, he wished to aid it with his death. He wished to arouse anger against the Stalin leadership. If he had seen any prospect of revolution abroad he might have been reconciled to a prolongation of his physical agony. But he knew just as well as I did that the chances of world revolution were slim.

Joffe's body was laid out in the conference chamber of the Commissariat of Foreign Affairs. Chicherin, Litvinov, and Karakhan, as chiefs of the commissariat, stood near the door to greet mourners. Trotzky, Kamenev, and Radek, walking abreast, passed Chicherin, Litvinov, and Karakhan and completely ignored them. Such was the bitterness.

The funeral took place at a cemetery near Moscow. Thousands of Trotzky sympathizers attended without interference from the police. Very soon any such demonstration would become unthinkable. Trotzky, Zinoviev, Kamenev, and others spoke. All the while a dear friend of mine, George Andreichin, Macedonian peasant turned Bolshevik, lay on a limb of a tree just above the open grave yelling at intervals: "Long Live Trotzky," "Long Live the World Revolution," "Down with the party bureaucrats," "Up the youth. . . ."

The ceremonies finished, everybody crowded towards Trotzky to give him an ovation. Appeals were made to the people to go home. They stayed, and Trotzky for a long time could not get out of the cemetery. Finally young men linked elbows and formed two human chains facing one another with a narrow corridor in between through which Trotzky could pass to the exit. While this operation was proceeding Trotzky waited alone in a kind of wide brick shed opening on the cemetery. But he never stood still. He walked like a pacing tiger, zigzagging all the time. I was near by and had the definite impression that he feared assassination. When the chains were finally formed the crowd surged in the direction of the corridor. Trotzky thereupon rushed in the opposite direction through an almost empty part of the cemetery and jumped into a waiting auto. That was the last time I saw Trotzky.

On January 16, 1928, the foreign correspondents went to the railway station. Trotzky was leaving for his Central Asia exile. A tremendous mob filled the station for a sympathetic send-off. Rakovsky was there. Trotzkyists climbed on to the train and led the cheering. But why doesn't the train leave? It is long past its scheduled departure. The assembled multitude calls for Trotzky to appear. No Trotzky. Finally the train leaves. We went home disappointed. Days later we discovered that the GPU, seeing the demonstration, the last of its kind in Soviet Russia, canceled Trotzky's departure. He left the next day in secret. Trotzky refused to walk. GPU men carried him down the stairs from his apartment into the car, and from the auto into the sleeper.

A political gulf separated Stalin and Trotzky. But the personal rivalry between them cannot be overlooked. Even when two persons are ready to give their lives for the same cause or spend their energies for the same organization they may hamper one another's work or destroy one another out of petty considerations. Lenin's authority might have kept Stalin and Trotzky at peace.

Emphasis has often been placed and misplaced on the theoretical chasm between Stalin's position and Trotzky's. In many cases, however, the cleavage was a question of speed and timing. Both Trotzky and Stalin wanted soviets in China, Trotzky earlier, Stalin later. A few months, to be sure, may make all the difference between success and failure. But if Trotzky and Stalin had not been political enemies moving at cross-purposes they might have arrived at a compromise on the China issue.

Trotzky advocated suppression of the rich peasant kulak in 1926. Stalin suppressed the kulak after he had suppressed Trotzky in 1928. Stalin's Five Year Plan in 1929 provoked little adverse criticism from Trotzky. The honest Trotzkyist, Christian G. Rakovsky, went into exile for his anti-Stalin opinions in 1928 and sincerely repented and backed Stalin's program in 1934. Trotzky's violent words and Stalin's violent acts made reconciliation between their followers difficult.

At one period, Stalin's Moscow headquarters branded all foreign Socialists as "social fascists." A little while later these same "social fascists" were eagerly sought by the Communists as allies. Another year elapsed and those allies in the Popular Front were spattered with Moscow's blackest mud. Trotzky, too, objected to compacts with non-Bolsheviks. Once he had favored them. Once Lenin had favored them. Lenin supported Kerensky against the armed revolt of General Kornilov, choosing the smaller of two evils. On the eve of the Revolution, Lenin urged a compromise with anti-Soviet Russians. What then is the "correct" Communist line on the question of Popular Fronts? There were similar shifts in the Bolshevik attitude toward many other questions, shifts due to time or greater intelligence or more experience or changes in the world situation.

It is possible, therefore, to exaggerate the importance of theory and policy in the struggle between Stalin and Trotzky. Lenin refused to recommend Stalin for the Bolshevik leadership not because he disapproved of Stalin's ideas on economics and social philosophy but because of Stalin's rudeness and power-hunger. Stalin and Trotzky were much closer politically than Stalin and Bukharin or Stalin and Rykov. Yet Stalin could work with Bukharin and Rykov.

The Trotzky-Stalin controversy crippled the Bolshevik Revolution. Trotzky often stirred the Communists to a realization of threatening dangers. That was his service to the Soviet Union. But under his assaults the Stalinists developed an unfortunate defense; since Trotzky charged that Stalin was always wrong the Stalinists insisted that Stalin was always right. Trotzky said Stalin was inferior and mediocre. The Stalinists replied that Stalin was a superior genius. Out of this arose the doctrine of Stalin's infallibility. Stalin at the summit seemed to become another person; instead of shrinking from the limelight as he had in the early phase of his career, he was forever seeking it. These new psychological manifestations in Stalin have affected history, and Russia is a sadder place as a result.

As soon as Trotzky was banished from Moscow a new alignment of Soviet political forces began to crystallize. Stalin had occupied a central position between Trotzky and the more conservative leaders like Rykov, Bukharin, Sokolnikov, and Tomsky. While Stalin fought Trotzky, the Right applauded Stalin. He helped to thwart radical anti-NEP and anti-kulak tendencies. Stalin appreciated their assistance against Trotzky. But with the elimination of Trotzky, Stalin was furthest Left. Now he proceeded to tax and arrest kulaks and private Nepmen. A strong right-wing opposition to Stalin emerged. Yet this right-wing tried to form a coalition with Zinoviev and Kamenev, who had first been centrist friends of Stalin and then leftist friends of Trotzky.

At 9 A.M. on July 11, 1928, Gregory Sokolnikov rang the bell of Kamenev's Moscow apartment without previous appointment and asked to see him. He remained an hour and while he was still closeted with Kamenev, Bukharin arrived, likewise unheralded. When both departed, Kamenev wrote out a detailed memorandum on these conversations. Several of his friends were later allowed to make copies of this report, and within very few days one copy reached me. I took full notes which I still have.

This meeting draws aside the curtain to reveal an intimate view of the higher realms of Soviet internal politics. Sokolnikov called early in the morning in the hope of evading the watchfulness of the GPU. Bukharin had not telephoned because he did not want to be detected by wiretappers of the secret police. The understanding between Sokolnikov and Bukharin was that if Sokolnikov did not return to Bukharin within an hour Bukharin would join them at Kamenev's.

Sokolnikov, in his preliminary tête-à-tête with Kamenev, stated that Bukharin had definitely broken with Stalin. Bukharin preferred Kamenev and Zinoviev to Stalin. Sokolnikov said this twice to make it more impressive. Bukharin was offering Kamenev and Zinoviev an alliance against Stalin. Sokolnikov declared that Bukharin was in a tragic position and feared another Kamenev-Zinoviev-Stalin bloc. Tomsky and Rykov, the Right oppositionists, were more and more hostile to Stalin's leftist trend. They condemned Stalin as inconsistent. He wanted to retain the NEP and destroy the Nepmen, kulaks, and foreign concessionaires.

At this point, Bukharin arrived. Bukharin was extremely nervous and spoke for three-quarters of an hour without stopping. He stated that Stalin's policy was undermining the Soviet regime. His differences with Stalin were now deeper than ever. Bukharin had not talked to Stalin for several weeks. Politbureau meetings recently had been very stormy with members calling one another "liar" and "scoundrel." Stalin, he said, was completely unprincipled, and his main purpose was to subject everybody to his power. Bukharin affirmed that he, Rykov, and Tomsky aimed to bring Kamenev and Zinoviev back into the Politbureau and to oust Stalin. The Stalinites, Bukharin predicted, would soon apply to Kamenev for help. "You can't put a single document into Stalin's hands without his using it against you." Bukharin suspected that Stalin would soon try to remove him from the editorship of the *Pravda*. Stalin now would propose a stricter policy of exploiting the peasantry. Since the peasants would resist and since civil war might result, they needed strong united leadership. Bukharin told Kamenev that he was not talking to him in the interests of a personal conspiracy or to make a palace coup; the fate of the Revolution was at stake. In matters of Comintern policy, Stalin was very Right and conservative. He had expelled the Comintern from the Kremlin.

"Stalin will destroy all of us," Bukharin exclaimed.

"What are your forces?" Kamenev probed.

Bukharin declared that Tomsky, Rykov, Uglanov, and Andreyev were with him and against Stalin. The Leningrad party organization opposed Stalin but was afraid to have him removed lest the regime be weakened. Stalin had won the favor of the Ukrainian Communists by removing Lazar Kaganovitch, Moscow's chief representative in the Ukraine, whom they disliked for his Jewish origin.

Yagoda and Trilesser, high officials in the GPU, would also side with the anti-Stalin forces, according to Bukharin. Kalinin and Voroshilov had deserted them. Stalin held them by "special tongs."

"Molotov," Bukharin said, "is a fool. He tries to teach me Marxism."

Bukharin added that Stalin wanted very much to be recognized as a theoretician. "Stalin," he said, "is an opponent of the Genghis Khan variety and has no scruples." There was no point in starting a discussion in the Central Committee of the party because if they accused Stalin of driving the country to hunger and crisis he would charge them with supporting the kulaks. The trouble was that the state and party were united in one bureaucracy and that the police would be used to suppress any ideological party opposition. Stalin is revengeful and adept in the art of "knifing in the back." Recently when Stalin divined that Bukharin was about to attack him at the Politbureau session he had addressed Bukharin endearingly as "Bukashka" and said, "Bukashka dear, you and I are the Himalayas. The others are pigmies." When the Politbureau assembled, Stalin launched into a violent personal attack on Bukharin. Thereupon, Bukharin revealed Stalin's statement about their being Himalayas. Stalin countered that Bukharin had invented the whole conversation in order to turn the Politbureau against him. Stalin, Bukharin said, had converted the Politbureau into an advisory body for his own acts. He would lead the country to civil war and then suppress the insurrection which he himself had provoked.

Bukharin asked Kamenev to keep in touch with him but not to use the telephone. He explained that only Rykov and Tomsky knew that he had gone to see Kamenev.

One by one Prime Minister Rykov, Bukharin, Zinoviev, Kamenev, Sokolnikov, and other right-wingers were deprived of every vestige of authority or political power. They lost their jobs. By 1929, Stalin was supreme dictator. One by one, in subsequent years, they were tried in Moscow and sentenced to be executed. They were purged because in a dictatorship they dared to deviate from the opinions of the dictator. In democratic countries such deviations lead to factions or intrigues within parties or to the formation of not very dissimilar parties. In Soviet Russia they led to the execution cellar.

Stalin now entered upon the "great offensive," the great adven-

ture, the great experiment in smashing capitalism in one country
and setting up a socialist economic system. That was the Five Year
Plan.

PART TWO: SEMI-SANE INTERLUDE

Watch a man playing tennis or arguing with a waiter and you
may be able to judge how he conducts his business. Human psychology is not departmentalized. Hitler's first important political act
revealed the man.

It was the evening of November 8, 1923. Commissioner von Kahr,
Governor of Bavaria, and General von Lossow, commander of the
Reichswehr in Bavaria, defying the federal government, were setting up their own regional dictatorship. Kahr and Lossow called a
meeting in the Buergerbraeukeller (Citizen's Beer Cellar), a large Munich assembly hall, to explain their action.

Germany threatened to fall to pieces. Chaos ruled in Bavaria. The
situation had revolutionary possibilities. Adolf Hitler resolved to ex-
ploit them. He had talked passionately to groups of Ehrhardt Freikorps members, to Racists and extreme Nationalists. He had oratori-
cal talents. He was one leader of a small party. But "voices" told
him he would be master of Germany.

Three thousand listeners packed the Munich beer hall. Governor
von Kahr and the giant von Lossow were on the stage. Kahr was
speaking. "Hitler . . . noiselessly entered the hall," writes Konrad
Heiden in his biography of Hitler. "Pistol in hand, he rushed toward
the platform where Kahr was standing. . . . He gave the impression
of a raving lunatic. His men posted a machine gun at the entrance
of the hall. Hitler himself, now hardly in command of his senses,
leapt on to a chair, fired a pistol-shot toward the ceiling, leapt down
again, and dashed on through the hall to the platform." He climbed
up on the stage. His lips covered with white foam, he announced
that the "national revolution has begun"; his Storm Troopers were
in occupation of the barracks of the Reichswehr and police. This
was a lie. "Then, in peremptory tones," writes Heiden, "he summoned Kahr, as well as Lossow . . . to follow him." They followed.
After all, there was no sense in being shot by a maniac. Hitler locked
Kahr and Lossow in a room and delivered a long speech to them.
He aimed his revolver at them. He declared that he was removing
them from office and appointing himself Chancellor of Germany
and Ludendorff chief of the army. Then he put his pistol to his own

temple and cried out, "Unless I am victorious tomorrow, I shall be a dead man."

Hitler had only three hundred men at the Munich beer hall. He had, however, his own hysterical courage and a revolver. With his sense of the dramatic and his boundless egotism and self-faith he had assumed that if he subdued for a moment what was in front of him the whole battle would be won. By surprise he paralyzed his opponents. But soon they recovered. Hitler had to release Kahr and Lossow. The Reichswehr refused to join the insurrection against the Reich. Its monocled commander-in-chief, General von Seeckt, telegraphed from Berlin that "he would have the Putsch suppressed." The next day, a Hitler-Ludendorff march on Munich ended in blood-shed and Hitler's flight. He was arrested three days later. Three days after he had declared himself Chancellor of Germany he sat in a prison cell.

Hitler's personal Blitzkrieg in the Munich beer hall bears all the marks of Nazi war strategy in 1939 and 1940 and, too, of his conduct in home politics—the blood purge of June 30, 1934, for instance. Hitler tore down the aisle in the beer hall just as his motorized columns cut ribbons through Poland and just as his army raced to the English Channel ports without regard to what was at its flanks or rear. Hitler always believed in the paralyzing effect of lightning action. To startle is to win half the battle. To give the impression of strength is to win strength. It worked often. In 1923, it landed Hitler in jail.

The Nation of June 3, 1925, published an article of mine from Berlin saying, "Legal justice in Germany, as in Soviet Russia, is class justice. In Moscow a member of the bourgeoisie and a member of the proletariat commit the same crime. The worker receives the lesser punishment. In Germany Hitler arranges a Putsch and the Communists plan an insurrection. Hitler spends six months in a palace-prison and is then released to continue his activities; the Reds get ten or fifteen years' hard labor."

This article was shown to Hitler and translated to him, for he reads only German. On looking through my old clippings recently I was astounded to find in *The Nation* of September 2, 1925, a letter from Adolf Hitler complaining against my statement about him. I had, of course, seen the letter at the time, but I had forgotten about it and so had the editors of *The Nation;* Hitler was one of many

insignificant German gang-politicians. *The Nation* printed his letter
and threw the original into the wastebasket.

Hitler's letter read as follows:

Uffing, June 28

To the Editor of *The Nation:*

Sir: In your issue of June 3 Mr. Louis Fischer says that 'Hitler spent
six months in a palace prison and was then released.'

I was in prison at Sanberg a.S thirteen months in all. A special decree
on April 1, 1924, deprived me of all previous privileges. All privileges
theretofore granted the prisoner were either abridged or wiped out.
Count Arco was still benefited by these alleviations.

—ADOLF HITLER.

Two things are of interest: Hitler's insistence on being credited
with a longer prison term, and his jealousy of Count Arco, who
murdered Kurt Eisner. Hitler was delivered to the prison on November 11, 1923. He was sentenced to five years' incarceration on
April 1, 1924. He was released on December 20, 1924. Hitler, therefore, spent thirteen months in prison. This time Hitler told the truth.
But he served only nine months of a five-year sentence. I had mistakenly put it at six months. R. T. Clark says in *The Fall of the
German Republic* that Hitler "was treated more as a guest than as a
prisoner." The real point is that Hitler was released after a short
sojourn in jail and allowed "to continue his activities." What if he
had remained under lock and key for the full term—until April 1,
1929? Would that have altered the world's fate?

The failure of the Ludendorff-Hitler revolt induced the reactionaries to submit to the Republic. Submission was now easier because
the Socialists no longer dominated the Reich. On August 13, 1923,
Gustav Stresemann, leader of the moderate right People's Party, had
taken office in Berlin. That placated the extreme Right.

This recession of the threat to the Republic from the Right coincided with the collapse of violent Left opposition. In the autumn of
1923, the German Communists planned a revolution. Preparations
progressed far and a number of Russians arrived to help. But Moscow
vacillated. It decided on the revolt and then revoked the instructions. Later it again gave the signal to proceed, only to cancel it a
second time. This last order was delayed in reaching Hamburg, and
some workingmen of that port erected barricades, seized streets and
warehouses, and fought the police until a messenger arrived from
Berlin countermanding the struggle.

CARL A. RUDISILL LIBRARY
LENOIR RHYNE COLLEGE

The defeat of leftist and rightist violence against the democratic Reich coincided with the defeat of the Reich's own violence in the Ruhr. Young Nazis and Communists had committed acts of sabotage against the French occupation of the Ruhr. Factory owners had obstructed French efforts to normalize industrial production. The German federal treasury had covered their losses and was bankrupting itself in the process. Stresemann knew this strategy of passive resistance was doomed, and he peremptorily stopped it.

Germany entered a period of relative tranquillity. In 1923 it had looked like the end of the Republic. Suddenly, in 1924, there was peace. The Ruhr episode exposed the folly of an openly anti-Allied policy. The endeavors of Rathenau and Wirth to co-operate with England and France had been regarded by many Germans as a national crime. Now the majority began to see Allied-German collaboration as a national necessity.

Germany had to heal the wounds of war and inflation and pay tribute to the Allies. Poincaré had invaded the Ruhr on the excuse of German non-payment of reparations; that convinced the Germans they must pay.

The Allies had saddled Germany with reparations until May 1, 1956. Statesmen and nations took that seriously. The motive behind such a prolonged indemnity, obviously, was not to repair war damages. Its first purpose was to punish Germany for having started the War. But the Germans angrily denied that the war guilt rested solely upon them, and cited secret diplomatic documents to demonstrate that the roots of the first World War lay in the conflicting ambitions of empires. Its second purpose was to keep Germany too weak to start another war. But a weak Germany could not pay reparations. By 1924, it was generally agreed that Germany was unable to pay reparations unless she received foreign loans. Apparently, then, it was necessary to strengthen Germany with credits in order to weaken her by reparations.

America furnished most of the credits. With the credits, Germany would pay reparations to the Allies. With the reparations the Allies would pay their debts to America.

This attempted business solution of the reparations muddle was called the Dawes Plan after Charles G. Dawes, Chicago banker, former United States Vice President and Ambassador to London. It was administered in Berlin by S. Parker Gilbert, an American, who

CARL A. RUDISILL LIBRARY
LENOIR RHYNE COLLEGE

graduated from that job to a partnership in J. P. Morgan and Company. He ran the show because his country was paying the bills.

The Dawes plan went into effect on September 1, 1924. In 1924-25, Mr. Gilbert collected one billion marks from Germany. (The mark had been stabilized at 4.2 to the dollar; this sum therefore equaled approximately two hundred and thirty-eight million dollars.) The next year he got one billion two hundred and twenty million marks; and one and a half billion in 1926-27. For 1927-28 the prescribed total rose to two billion marks, and in 1928-29 the peak was reached with two and a half billion. This was the "standard year": and the two and a half billion would be paid annually until 1956. It was the plan of an optimist.

Where did Germany obtain these colossal sums? She pawned her railways to the Reparations Commission and levied a railway tax which increased fares and freight rates twenty-seven percent and correspondingly reduced traffic; she taxed the coffee, tea, cocoa, tobacco, and whiskey which her citizens consumed; she cut her budget; she taxed her industries. All the proceeds went to S. Parker Gilbert. Germany also gave France coal and labor for nothing.

Mr. Gilbert deposited the marks in a Berlin bank. The Allies, however, wanted the money in their own countries. That was not Germany's concern. The transfer abroad was Gilbert's affair. But he knew that if he bought pounds, dollars, and francs with his marks and shipped them out, the heavy loss of capital would cripple Germany's economy unless she could get in foreign countries at least as much money as he sent to foreign countries. One way of getting money abroad is by exporting goods. But world commerce languished and countries were limiting their purchases of German goods. Germany accordingly had recourse to another way of getting money abroad; she borrowed it. She borrowed it from America, and to a lesser extent from England, Holland, and Switzerland so that she could pay reparations to the Allies. During the first four years of the Dawes Plan, Mr. Gilbert reported, Germany paid five and a half billion marks in reparations and borrowed, on long terms, six billion marks. Germany paid out less than she took in. The Dawes Plan was thus a moratorium based on the assumption that after a period of economic recuperation, and as a result of building up her own trade and financial surpluses, Germany could pay reparations without foreign loans. That day never arrived.

Both sides complained.

The Germans complained. Reparations depressed the German standard of living. Germany counted 1,900,000 fully jobless and 600,000 part-time workers in 1926 despite the foreign money pouring into the country. The money remained partially uninvested in industry—already overexpanded during inflation—and floated around on the stock market where it stimulated speculation and easy profits. The mere interest on foreign loans was mounting so rapidly that it constituted a brake on economic recovery.

The British complained. During 1925-26, Great Britain received sixty-three million dollars from Germany in reparations: in 1926-27, twice that much. Yet here is a typical British reaction: the British Electrical and Allied Manufacturers' Association published a pamphlet on German economic conditions which said, "It is essential for manufacturers in this country to press for a drastic revision or even abolition of the Dawes Plan in their own interests." "In their own interests" Britons wanted less for Britain. Why? Because a contracting domestic market and the need of increasing exports to repay loans and pay services on loans were compelling Germany to push her exports and compete against British producers throughout the world and even in England proper. Traditional free traders in England were beginning to favor protective tariffs at home and in their empire to keep out foreign commodities.

The British also hoped that along with reparations all international indebtedness would be stricken from the cumbersome ledgers.

Others also favored debt cancellation. Newton D. Baker, U. S. Secretary of War during the World War, advised cancellation. Irving Fisher, Yale economics professor, and Thomas N. Perkins, a New England banker, urged cancellation. The *New York World* and the *New York Times* urged it. But the bulk of Americans could scarcely understand why money which they had loaned to foreigners should not be repaid.

The inter-Allied debt agreements were to continue in force until 1986. They have long ceased being worth the scraps of thick white paper on which they are printed. Yet for many months, busy financiers, government officials, and economists worked on every comma, digit, and syllable of these documents. The relations between nations were embittered or ameliorated, international trade was facilitated or thwarted, and the value of moneys and savings fluctuated in accordance with whether or not these debt negotiations were proceeding smoothly.

Suppose a wise statesman had foreseen the ephemeral nature of the debt agreements and their threat to peace and world business, but his country had given him no mandate to cancel them. He could have tried to mold public opinion. Suppose, as is likely, he had failed. What could he have done? History shows that he would have been right to cancel. Yet in a democracy he could have done nothing.

In this respect, the American political system is no different from European democracies. A British cabinet pursuing an unpopular policy could the same day be ousted by Parliament. An American president could not be. But he would need congressional approval and might not find it. Moreover, presidents and legislators have their ears close to the ground, not only in an election year, and they rarely make a move against the ascertained opinion of the majority of the electorate. Often, indeed, a minority has deterred the executive and the legislature from taking a novel though desirable course, desirable in the light of subsequent events and in the subsequent view of the public itself. Democracies are handicapped by the time-lag of public opinion.

Is dictatorship the cure for this democratic dilemma? The dictator might very well adopt a wrong policy. Unchecked, he might lead to disaster. I do not know the solution to this problem. But with regard to reparations and war debts it never arose. No statesman had sufficient vision. America insisted on debt payments and France insisted on reparations payments.

As long as the United States imposed a high tariff on European imports, the European debtors could not meet their obligations. "I say without hesitation," asserted Senator Reed Smoot of Utah, "that the loans we made to foreign countries and that the banks are now making to foreign countries cannot be paid." Smoot knew because he was the co-author of the tariff law. Professor Ernest M. Patterson of the University of Pennsylvania proposed that "instead of raising American tariffs we should carefully but definitely lower them." Nobody listened; Americans wanted to have their tariffs and eat debt payments too.

Debt payments just lapsed, while reparations were annulled by common consent in 1932. But at least from 1924 until their disappearance, reparations stayed the rough hands of French generals and politicians. The Dawes Plan failed to solve all of Germany's economic problems or to satisfy creditor and debtor nations. But it kept the German mark stable and improved German business conditions. If the impression of national prosperity was somewhat illusory, the Dawes era seemed like heaven to Germans who had experienced war and inflation. The ruins of the past were repaired and there was much new construction. The nation's nerves enjoyed a vacation.

Politics reflected the change. 1924 was a sane interlude in the history of Europe. The narrow-mindedness of hobnailed, saber-rattling reactionaries gave way to British, French, and German governments whose thinking was tinged with internationalism; the post-War years had proved that nationalistic introspection made bad matters worse. In England, Ramsay MacDonald, the head of the Labor Party, and in France, Edouard Herriot, leader of the Radical Socialists (who were neither radical nor socialist), came into office. In the new atmosphere, an idea was born which took shape in the treaties signed at Locarno, Switzerland, on October 16, 1925, by Chancellor Luther and Foreign Minister Stresemann for Germany, Vandervelde for Belgium, Briand for France, Austen Chamberlain for England, and Mussolini for Italy. Formal signature took place in London on December 1, 1925. By the terms of the Locarno Pact, Germany renounced forever all claims to the provinces of Alsace and Lorraine which she had taken from France in 1870 and held until November, 1918. A strip of German territory fifty kilometers wide east of the Rhine River would be perpetually demilitarized.

Versailles was a dictated peace. But at Locarno, Germany voluntarily accepted much of what she had acquiesced to under duress at the Paris Peace Conference. She did so in order to wean the French from their intransigent hostility towards the Reich. As a reward for Locarno, Germany was admitted into the League of Nations with a permanent seat in the League Council. For the first time since 1914, Germany and the Western Powers met as equals, not as vanquished and conquerors.

Editors and politicians throughout the world hailed the Locarno Pact as the dawn of a glorious era of peace. "The spirit of Locarno" was invested with miraculous healing qualities. "Locarno" became a symbol of good will. But "the spirit of Locarno" was in part a product of imaginative wishful-thinking. European rivalries persisted. The French army still occupied the German Rhineland.

Locarno was something, but not enough. The War increased the number of countries in Europe from twenty-six to thirty-five and lengthened Europe's frontier's by seven thousand miles. That meant more armies and fortresses to guard them. It meant more walls over which merchandise had to jump—after paying heavy duties for the privilege of jumping. Each new nation in Europe wanted to build its own factories and protect them by barring foreign goods. This hurt the old exporting nations like England, Germany, Austria, and France, and it ruined the new industrializing little states which could scarcely afford expensive plants producing inferior commodities at high cost. Economic nationalism was the curse of post-War Europe.

Some minds grasped this truth between 1924 and 1929. But first it was necessary to modify economic geography. The peace agreements were drafted under the sign of national self-determination. Wilsonism, as incorporated in the peace treaties, was a license to European racial jealousies to run amuck. When self-determination could be implemented at the expense of the former enemy, the Allies were the most enthusiastic Wilsonites. But self-determination never stopped the Allies from giving the South Tirol Austrians to Italy, the Upper Silesian Germans to Poland, and Hungarians to Rumania. The peace of 1919 was political. To set up a counterweight to Germany, and, secondarily, to Hungary, the peace conference carved out new countries whose safety required them to enter the French military orbit. Czechoslovakia, Poland, Rumania, and Yugoslavia owed their lives to this conception. Wilsonism helped to establish a new French solar system of armed security. As far as possible, except for the Germans and Hungarians, attempts were made to concentrate races under a single flag so that one part of a nationality did not remain on one side of a frontier and another part on the other. But it mattered little to the map-designers if iron were separated from the coal needed to smelt it or if industries were cut off from their markets. Soon, the farsighted understood. Rectification of frontiers, however, was impossible in Versailles Europe without force or the threat of force. The only feasible revision, and the revision needed most urgently, was the opening of frontiers to the free passage of goods.

Before the first World War, Germany enjoyed a practical world monopoly of potash. The peace treaty transferred large German deposits to France. That fostered wild competition between the two countries. Finally, a meeting in Lugano, Switzerland, on April 10, 1926, launched the International Potash Syndicate. German potash producers would not sell in France nor French potash producers in Germany. Of the rest of the world market, Germany got seventy percent, France thirty percent. Prices and profits rose. Buyers did not like it. American interests protested and refused to participate in a gigantic loan floated by the Potash Syndicate. But London took up the issue and oversubscribed it many times within a quarter of an hour.

On the same principle, and likewise in the 1926 "Spirit of Locarno," the electric-bulb manufacturers of Germany, the United States, Holland, France, Denmark, Sweden, Norway, England, Italy, and Japan, the bottle-makers of England, Germany, Czechoslovakia, and Scandinavia, and the iron-pipe producers of Poland, France, Germany, Belgium, and Czechoslovakia formed international pools.

These were preliminaries. The test was the European iron and steel industry. Always it had been Englishmen, like John Maynard Keynes, and Liberal and Labor leaders, who criticized the Versailles Treaty. Lloyd George, one of its authors, now regarded it skeptically. Ex-Premier Nitti of Italy pleaded for its emendation. The French and Belgians, on the other hand, swore by every letter of it. Suddenly, everything changed.

On September 30, 1926, the heavy industrialists of the German Ruhr, the French Comité des Forges, and the Belgian and Luxembourg iron and steel magnates formed an international cartel, or trust, to co-ordinate production and exports. This "Steel Locarno" followed the Locarno Pact even as Stresemann had suggested Locarno twenty-three days after the Dawes Plan went into operation.

Germany joined the League of Nations on September 6, 1926. During this League session, Gustav Stresemann and Aristide Briand slipped away from Geneva and crossed the French border to a charming restaurant at Thoiry. Amidst good food and fine wine and enveloped in the smoke of Stresemann's fat cigars and Briand's ceaseless cigarettes, they talked five hours. An American journalist lunching downstairs was unaware of the informal proceedings on the second floor, but soon the polyglot correspondents' corps at Geneva learned that somewhere, but exactly where they did not know, a world-shaking event was taking place. A man-hunt started. The French and German foreign ministers, still "ex-enemies," in 1926, were actually enjoying a friendly meal together. The fact itself was invested with far-reaching significance, but it soon appeared that their conversation, too, encouraged optimists in hoping for a Franco-German entente, or, at least, an end of hostilities. With their cigars and cigarettes, Stresemann and Briand were smoking the pipe of peace.

At the same League session, Sir Austen Chamberlain represented Great Britain. From Geneva he did not go straight home; he went instead to Livorno, Italy, and met Benito Mussolini. The British papers nonchalantly called it a "pleasure trip." The Italian press, more honest sometimes because controlled, intimated that Livorno aimed to offset Thoiry.

What happened on the Duce's yacht at Livorno? The *Giornale d'Italia* affirmed that France and Germany could not alter the Versailles Treaty without Italian and British consent. England, said this authoritative Fascist organ, was first among the nations to recognize the "progressive character of Italian Fascism"; England at Versailles had obstructed Italian claims less than other powers; both nations had similar interests in the Mediterranean. The daily *Lavoro* cautioned Germany and France against the steel pact which infringed on Italian as well as British interests.

The Diplomatic Correspondent of the *London Daily Telegraph*, often the voice of his Foreign Office, reminded Italy that "the recent development of her metal industries, and her lack of native coal resources, would render any Franco-German coal and steel combine a matter of serious economic concern for the peninsula." A few days later he warned Italy against supporting any revamping of Versailles or any "cash settlement" for the evacuation of the Rhineland. His hint to the Italians to remain aloof from the Franco-German iron and steel cartel mirrored a strong British opposition to it. England imports iron and exports coal, and she feared that a dovetailing of Rhineland and Alsace-Lorraine industries would give the continental trusts an advantage over her. Judge Gary of the U. S. Steel Corporation said the cartel was a blow against the British steel industry. British influence therefore persuaded Polish coal and steel manufacturers to shun the cartel. Poland was normally anti-German and pro-French. But when France moved closer to Germany, Poland moved closer to England, especially since the London City could become either the source of loans for the money-starved Polish industries or the intermediary between Wall Street and Warsaw.

Herein lay the tragedy of Europe. Every action provoked an equal and opposite reaction. Find a friend and you made an enemy. No sooner did Briand and Stresemann contemplate a step towards pacification than Chamberlain and Mussolini, suspecting it might be aimed against them, as indeed it might have been, rushed to sabotage it. No sooner did France and Germany plan to lower an economic frontier than England, Italy, and Poland complained.

International obstacles to a European settlement were reinforced by discordant intra-national tendencies. Stresemann's rightist enemies at home resented his cordial approaches to France. And the moment Briand succeeded in establishing a relaxed atmosphere by breaking bread with Stresemann at Thoiry, his superior, Premier Poincaré, delivered a sizzling anti-German speech at Bar-le-Duc, stressing the point which always offended Germans most, Germany's war guilt. The German press thereupon attacked Poincaré for stabbing peace in the back, and Stresemann at Cologne demanded the evacuation of the Rhineland. To aggravate matters, a French lieutenant in the German town of Gemersheim shot a German civilian, and at Neustadt in the occupied zone a French soldier was killed by a German. Chauvinist elements in both countries made political-party capital out of these and similar incidents. Germans said they were reasons for evacuation; Frenchmen said they were reasons for continued occupation.

The yearning toward economic internationalism and political sanity tried to overcome these obstructions. In 1926 and 1927, the prestige of the League of Nations was at its peak. Peace hopes mounted high. They fed on talk. A floundering continent groped for a solution that would save it. The International Chamber of Commerce issued a manifesto declaring that "trade barriers are working havoc throughout Europe. . . . They should be abolished wherever possible, or at least greatly modified." These were the constructive ideas: customs unions, reduced tariffs, and international cartels. Briand paraded as the prophet of USE—the United States of Europe. Others called it Pan-Europa. In France, progressives broached a scheme for a European federal reserve bank to control all currencies. At The Hague conference on reparations in 1929, Gustav Stresemann lifted his voice—the German dailies devoted special attention to the idealistic tone of his voice—and attacked the "barriers which barred the emergence of a world economy and, particularly, of a European economy." But editors in western capitals asked whether Stresemann's goal was a Utopia or, perhaps, more foreign trade for German businessmen. Even in England, mother of free trade (and, therefore, of parliaments?) an intelligent industrialist like Lord Melchett seconded Lord Beaverbook's campaign for free trade within the empire—which meant keeping foreign competitors out of it—

and protectionism against the rest of the world. Britain took this course. In spite of idealistic outpourings, the trend was away from a European customs union and towards more protection.

Economic internationalism is no cure-all. But without it there could be no solution in Europe. Economic nationalism is wasteful. Raised to the ultimate degree it is Fascism, striving for autarchy or self-containment. The vague outline of two possible choices open to the capitalist world began to come into focus in 1929: either the world would pool its resources and distribute its goods through unhampered channels of international trade, or some countries, no matter what they preached at the time, would try to produce and own everything they required and to seize what they required but did not own. The first signs of the threatening struggle between Fascism and non-Fascism were discernible a decade before the two came to bloody grips.

Intellectuals, hardboiled bankers, radicals, and statesmen aired plenty of plans for economic salvation and war prevention. But the very fact that these blueprints remained on paper deepened pessimism and social discontent. The longer the proposals for European peace were discussed in public the more obvious it became that governments had not yet converted them into reality. This applied equally to disarmament.

The Preparatory Commission for Disarmament met intermittently at Geneva from May 16, 1926 to April 26, 1927, and again and again up to 1929, and after. Experts attempted to determine which end of a cannon was defensive and which offensive, whether commercial airplanes could serve military purposes and whether fortresses were for attack or defense. Diplomats jousted in marble-halled lists with brilliant phrases as lances and memoranda as armor. All lost. By the spring of 1929, the League of Nations had published fourteen thousand pages of reports on disarmament debates, but not a single soldier or gun or ship or plane had been eliminated from the world's military establishments. On the contrary, all nations had accelerated the pace of reamament. It seemed to me then that all Europe was arming and that the Allies' ambitious international effort to reduce Germany to a military nonentity had failed. If Europe had wished to disarm, it might have seized the opportunity in 1919 and 1920 when Germany was practically a military zero. Nothing had been done then, and now it was too late.

The Kellogg Pact was signed in Paris on August 27, 1928. All the great powers, including Russia, Japan, and Germany, and scores of smaller states joined the United States in renouncing war as an instrument of national policy. But when U. S. Senator Capper proposed legislation for an embargo on arms shipments to any aggressor who had violated this solemn and almost universal pact he found little support. People preferred a peace without teeth. And they never really put any faith in the pact, for the year of the Kellogg accord marked a sharp rise in armaments.

Hopes inflated by talk were deflated by acts. The war psychosis born of the first World War had barely yielded to the peace psychosis in 1925 when the nations started preparing for new wars. Idealism turned sour and disillusionment spread. The disappointment was not so much with 1914-18 as with 1919-29. The war was a gruesome calamity. But it was the dismal aftermath that made it a complete waste. If out of the war a better Europe, and even a better life, had risen, the bloodshed might have been condoned or forgiven. But the utter bankruptcy of governments and statesmanship in the post-War era impelled people to re-examine the War and mark it down in value. Many of the anti-war novels and plays really reflected the failure of the peace. Consciously, or by an instinctive reaction, authors, intellectuals, and others found the horrors of the war more ghastly as they realized that in liquidating the first War the ground had been prepared for a second.

All Germans believed the peace wronged them; some took the view that they must oppose the efforts to carry it out. Most post-War German governments, however, acted on the assumption that fulfillment of obligations would help Germany, and, incidentally, Europe. But every economic difficulty in Germany, every refusal of the powers to unite the continent, and every step toward European rearmament undermined the position of those Germans who favored collaborating with the Western Powers. The German Social Democrats, for instance, voted against the appropriation for a pocket cruiser. The Nationalists had only to publish official Anglo-French news about naval and army expansion to weaken the appeal of the Socialists.

Niccolo Machiavelli gives advice in *The Prince* on how to treat defeated adversaries; they "must either be caressed or annihilated." The Allies did neither. They could not or did not want to annihilate Germany, and their rough caresses irritated more than they placated. Reparations, the French occupation of the Rhineland, and the Versailles Treaty were symbols to Germans of their inferiority, and weapons, therefore, which the reactionaries could use against the democratic Republic.

Gustav Stresemann, the author and administrator of German foreign policy from 1923 to his death on October 3, 1930, once outlined his diplomacy to me when I cornered him at a tea in the Foreign Office. He said, "The three objects of German policy are to achieve the evacuation of the Rhineland, to reduce and ultimately abolish reparations, and to alter the anomalous status of East Prussia separated from the Fatherland by the so-called Polish Corridor. The occupation of the Rhineland," he continued, "does not harm us economically, but no minister can remain in office who does not strive to clear the province and thus comply with the wishes of all Germans. With respect to East Prussia, there can never be perfect relations with Poland. Here Russia renders us invaluable assistance.

"In view of our immediate aims: Reparations, Rhineland, East Prussia," Stresemann added, "we cannot forego our policy of an understanding with France." The omission of England was glaring and I called attention to it. Franco-German collaboration was his pet child and his words revealed resentment against London for interfering with it. He intimated that England feared the economic rise of Germany and the probable renewal of spirited Anglo-German commercial rivalry.

To millions of Germans, however, reconciliation with France was an inglorious and constant reminder of Germany's defeat. To justify it and to win sufficient votes for his policy Stresemann had to produce results all the time. When the Allies made no concessions to him, his political opponents on the Right asked what sense there was in his kowtowing to Paris. But the more the Allies gave, the more encouraged the Germans felt about asking. As long as the Allies held hostages in Germany in the shape of reparations and the Rhineland occupation, the German government had to be a democratic one based on co-operation with the Allies. This restrained the Nationalists. They enjoyed the luxury of demagogy but could not run Germany. When, however, the Allies had nothing more to give, this restraint was lifted. Having got all the cake, further reason for good behavior disappeared. At The Hague reparations conference in 1929, the Dawes Plan was superseded by the Owen D. Young Plan, and the reparations annuities, theretofore unlimited in number and amounting to approximately $600,000,000, were now fixed at $492,000,000 for the next thirty-seven years, and $408,000,000 for twenty-two years after that. Thus was Germany's fate to be settled until 1988! In pursuance of the Young Plan agreement, the Allies immediately commenced to evacuate the Rhineland; their last soldier departed in June, 1930. This represented all the Allies could surrender as far as their physical presence in Germany was concerned, and for the moment at least, the limits of concessions on reparations had also been reached. The Stresemann policy of reconciliation accordingly appeared less useful because it could yield no tangible fruit, and from 1930 the descent to Hitler grew very marked. Hitler supposedly rose to office on a high wave of resentment against German enslavement. As a matter of fact, he only became possible with the disappearance of the Rhineland occupation and, in 1932, of reparations. It is a paradoxical truth, therefore, that Versailles kept Germany democratic whereas Allied leniency freed those German forces which ultimately opened the road to Fascism. As somebody has put it, Germany was freed from her enemies so that she might become her own enemy.

That a basis for Fascism existed in Germany is clear from the assistance and adulation given to the Rathenau murderers. The humiliation of the defeat and the peace stored up animosity for the Republic which treated in friendly fashion with the traditional enemy. The insult of the Rhineland occupation added to the economic injury of reparations. Desperate, disgruntled persons, especially young persons, moved to an extreme in which security became ugly philistinism and employment an irksome bar to participation in the adventure of Nazism. Because they suffered from the absence of work and security they grew to abhor both, and an unsettled life of strife became an object in itself.

But these were the minority of the population. The vast bulk of Germans lived in relative prosperity during 1924 to 1929. They saw improvement and hoped for more. Art, the cinema, the theater, the sciences flourished. The liberal elements of the nation spread their beliefs. It is a fallacy to suppose that Fascism was Germany's inexorable destiny. To regard anything in politics as inevitable is a fatalism which ignores the dynamic laws of society. Man is not entirely free, but within broad limits he can affect and alter his fate. As in all countries in modern times a tug-of-war went on in Germany between Right and Left, between employers and labor, between conservatives and progressives. The outcome of this conflict was not preordained, and the elements of peace, democracy, and decency might have won.

Part of the responsibility for their defeat and the consequent advent of Hitler rests on the shoulders of the rest of Europe. The German Republic succumbed because the War-winners did not do enough to save it. They operated against one another, against European unity and against Germany. With England, France, Russia, and Italy, as well as the minor nations, working at cross-purposes, Germany was the first big casualty.

1930 opened the decade of aggression, Fascism, and appeasement which ended in the second World War. Several of the dikes which might have stemmed the dark tide were pierced or removed in 1929.

One dike stood on the other side of the muddy Tiber in the city of Rome. The second was on Wall Streeet, New York.

The Lateran Treaty between Pope Pius XI and Benito Mussolini was concluded in February, 1929, and went into effect on June 7, 1929. It restored to the Pope his temporal power over the one-sixth of a square mile included within the gray walls of the Vatican which thus became a unique little state. Since 1870, the Vatican had had no terrestrial authority. In that period its spiritual authority had increased enormously. In 1929, it regained its terrestrial authority.

"The whole force of the Italian Catholic Church is now to be placed behind the Mussolini dictatorship," commented *The Nation*. Mussolini had encountered serious obstacles in consolidating Fascism in Italy. The Socialists and Communists interfered, and so did the Catholics. Fascism's ambitions are total; it does not merely wish to rule certain acres. It aspires to conquer the heart and mind, particularly of youth, and on these the strength of Roman Catholicism was founded. A fierce struggle accordingly ensued between Catholicism and Fascism. On the part of the Church, it was fought subtly. Mussolini used repression and propaganda.

The Lateran Treaty was a peace treaty between the Roman Church and Fascism. It strengthened Mussolini who needed the popular support which amicable relations with the Vatican brings to a government of Catholic Italy. He paid the Vatican a large sum of money and conceded its right to sovereignty.

The repercussions of this pact reached to Germany, Poland, Spain, and Portugal where Fascist movements were striving for influence over Catholic populations. Hostility to Fascism ceased to be the unalterable tenet of Catholics after the Pope became reconciled to the Duce. Innumerable German Catholics, to be sure, persisted in their abhorrence of Fascism, and Cardinal Faulhaber of Munich pursued the struggle against Nazism with rare courage. Nevertheless, prominent Catholic politicians now began to lean further towards Hitler; and it was von Papen, a leader of the German Catholic Center Party and owner of its daily newspaper *Germania*, who actually opened the door for Hitler's entry into office.

American capitalism had served as another bulwark against Fascism. But in 1929, American capitalism ran into a little trouble. It had been warned by men like Paul M. Warburg who, criticizing the Federal Reserve system in March, 1929, declared that "if orgies of unrestrained speculation are permitted to spread too far, the ultimate collapse is certain not only to affect the speculators themselves, but also to bring about a general depression involving the entire country." Some people pulled out and lived happily ever afterwards, but the American stock-market public as a whole was too money-mad to pay attention to dull economists. Installment plans, eighteen million bathtubs, and millions of automobiles, symbols of the Coolidge Age, were as destructive of sobriety as bootleg liquor, and the crash came on October 24.

The American stock-market collapse and the subsequent economic slump had more to do with the advent of Hitler than the Treaty of Versailles. The boom Germany experienced between 1924 and 1929 was stimulated by borrowing abroad, chiefly in the United States. Germany borrowed abroad, approximately, in 1925, 1,250,-000,000 gold marks; in 1926, 1,750,000,000 gold marks; in 1927, 1,650,000,000 gold marks; and in 1928, 1,500,000,000 gold marks; but in 1929, only 400,000,000 gold marks, and after that it tapered off even more sharply. With what results? German stock-market values rose from 100 in 1924-26, to 148.8 in 1928, but dropped to 133.9 in 1929 and 49.6 in 1932. German production was 100 in 1928, 101.4 in 1929, 83.6 in 1930, 69.1 in 1931, and 55.3 in 1932. Then came Hitler. Unemployment stood at 1,913,842 in 1929, and 5,737,000 in 1932. That helped Hitler. Unintentionally, and in consequence of what appeared to be purely American events, the United States contributed to the coming of Fascism in Germany.

7. Personal

GOING to Russia from Germany or France was like going to another planet. Probably nothing would please an astronomer more than to fly to Mars or some other star, and there set up his telescopes and measuring paraphernalia to observe our planet's movements. From Moscow, one got a better view of the chaos on non-Soviet planets.

Soviet Russia was not-Europe and not-America. Each time I left Russia I understood it better. Each time I got disgusted with Russia I had only to return to central and western Europe. The disgust dwindled.

The Russian Revolution was a vast churning process. What had been on top was ground to the bottom, and what had been on the bottom ruled. The mass of peasants and workingmen, long separated from light and sun by a thin crust of royalty, aristocracy, and plutocracy, pushed lava-like to the surface and flowed far and wide, covering the former upper stratum as it moved.

I had never been in Czarist Russia. But when I first visited Soviet Russia in 1922, much of Czarist Russia still stood intact. Czarism in its ugly elegance was too brittle to change, too dumb to improve, too selfish to share. Czarism made the Bolshevik Revolution and handed it to Lenin. Revolution is always the old cook's last meal; he prepares the ingredients, the new cook puts them on the fire. The contrast between palace and slum hovel, and between manor house and tumbled-down peasant hut supplied the fuel of Russia's rebellion. By 1922, the Revolution had not yet removed the hovels and huts. It therefore took all the more pains to preserve the palaces. The peasant in homespun shirt and with shoes made of wood-shavings, who timorously toured the gorgeous homes of the Romanov kings felt better when he returned to sleep under his thatch roof while the cow mooed in the next room. He felt superior because he had ousted his superiors. The concrete proof was that he and his wife had just visited the Czarina's bedroom. The worker was fed on dreams, theories, and hatred of the past. The Bolsheviks told him that everything belonged to him; it was his factory, his city, his summer resort, his government, his future. It gave him an illusion of wealth. He believed it because no other owner existed; the former capitalists, landlords, and nobles had been exiled or killed.

In a village near Kharkov the peasants asked me whether I knew the Rudenskys. The family had owned the land of the entire village. During the civil war, the peasants had murdered Rudensky and his wife. Two sons, officers in the White Russian army of Denikin, died fighting. But one son escaped abroad. He worked as a waiter in Paris. Did I know him? Ivan Rudensky, the only heir to their land. The Soviets had nationalized the land. It had ceased to be private property. The peasants saw the strength of the Soviet regime. But they would have felt more comfortable if Ivan were dead instead of washing dishes in Montmartre. The business of the Bolsheviks was to prove that the past was irrevocable.

One of my most memorable early experiences in Russia was the trial of Boris Savinkov. It contained more drama than many of the later trials staged when Moscow had learned the tricks of publicity. A strange, startling individual stood in the dock answering charges punishable by death. But actually the trial was a funeral; an anti-Bolshevik chapter of Russia's past was about to admit bankruptcy, commit suicide in the witness box, and be publicly interred.

Boris Savinkov was a terrorist, a revolutionist, and a good novelist. He had tried to assassinate Lenin and had made plans to blow up Trotzky's train. He staged a three-day anti-Bolshevik uprising of the Right Social Revolutionaries in the town of Yaroslav in 1918. He admitted all this at his trial on the evening of August 21, 1924.

Savinkov testified that he had stolen into Russia a week before from Poland and the GPU had caught him in a house in Minsk. The courtroom held about 150 people. Among them were Djerzhinsky, first chief of the secret police, Leo Kamenev, assistant prime minister, Chicherin, Radek, Karakhan, and other Soviet celebrities. Proceedings were taking place before Russia's Supreme Court. At the press table, I remember Walter Duranty of the *New York Times* and Albert Rhys Williams, who understood what was Tolstoyan in the soul of the Russian peasant.

Savinkov sat in the witness box between two soldiers with fixed bayonets. He was about fifty. The right side of his face looked as though a hand had pushed it upward, and in the left cheek there was a deep gash from cheek bone to jowl. His eyes gave the impression of looking at something they had looked at before—death. By the time I arrived he had been testifying for three hours. He told of his pre-revolutionary activity; he had participated in the assassination of the Czarist Minister Plehve and of the Grand Duke Sergei. "I also took part in many other terrorist attempts. I am a man who worked all his life for the people and in their name. . . . I loved Russia and felt deeply devoted to its working people."

Then why had he fought the Bolsheviks? Because they had suppressed the democratic Constituent Assembly and because "I thought the masses would not follow the Communist party." In that he admitted his error. "The majority of Russia's workers and peasants are for the Communists." This statement was worth the trial, for Savinkov had a name in Russia and here he was in court making his obeisance to the Soviet regime.

"I am a revolutionary. I am not a criminal," Savinkov exclaimed, and those present listened with a respect that echoed agreement. "I am a prisoner of war. I fought and lost. Judge me as you wish. Right or wrong, misguided or not, the Russian people is my people and I submit to its will."

He resumed his seat. Chief Justice Ulrich, young, pudgy, jovial (I interview him a few days later), and his two associates retired to pass sentence.

We waited. Savinkov waited in front of us. An hour passed and then two. We waited from nine to midnight. Savinkov was waiting to know whether a bullet from the rifle of that soldier who guarded him would smash out his brain. Almost every ten minutes the two soldiers escorted him to the lavatory. He was nervous. Once I was in the washroom with him. He glanced around bewildered like a baited animal—a strong man, not frightened but afraid.

One o'clock. Bolshevik leaders in the audience suggested that the verdict would not be delivered until tomorrow. Tomorrow! How would Savinkov sleep tonight? Uncertainty would be worse than an immediate firing squad.

Shortly after one o'clock, a tall sailor came in and shouted, "The court is coming." We rose. Ulrich began to read. "Whereas" and he read a list of Savinkov's admissions, "whereas" and he listed Savinkov's sins against the revolution, "whereas" and he enumerated the proletarian lives that Savinkov's activities had cost, "whereas" and "whereas" and "whereas." The air throbbed. My heart knocked hard against my ribs. It was difficult to listen. I stood about four feet from Savinkov. How was he able to stand upright? ". . . is sentenced to death," I heard Ulrich say. Before anyone had time to react, Ulrich went on, "Nevertheless, in view of . . ." It was like a sudden discharge of pent-up electricity. A cold hand had ceased clutching at the heart. In view of Savinkov's confession of guilt, in view of his readiness to serve the Revolution, the death sentence was commuted to ten years' imprisonment.

I watched at the exit door to see Savinkov leave. In his black overcoat pocket was a large whiskey bottle, half-full. His guards had allowed him to gulp from it during the long wait.

I wondered why Savinkov should have wanted to enter Russia in 1924 and risk a death sentence or a life in prison. He must have known that there was no chance of crushing Bolshevism. I have a conjectural interpretation of Savinkov's act which is probably very near the truth, and it is based on the adventure of another anti-Bolshevik. In 1924, Vitali Shulgin, a Russian Monarchist politician and writer, entered Russia. We know this story because it has been told authentically. Shulgin had left Russia in 1920. In the same year, his son who fought in the White armies was reported missing. After that, Shulgin lived in European exile. In 1923, a Russian came to him with a letter of introduction and informed him that his son was living in Soviet Russia under an assumed name. Did he want to see him? Yes, but how could he? Well, he could go to Russia illegally. There were many Monarchists in Russia who would be glad to see him. In fact, there might be an opportunity of restoring the Czars. Shulgin was eager to accept. But his informant told him that the road was difficult and expensive. Shulgin borrowed the money. His new friend escorted him to the Polish city of Rovno, near the Soviet frontier. Here several fellow-Monarchists housed them. They told Shulgin he must grow a beard to avoid detection and practice running in the woods in case the GPU border guards should fire at them as they crept into Soviet territory. Shulgin grew the beard and became a skillful dodger. Finally, they made their way into Russia, avoiding the GPU. His friend brought him to Kiev where a number of Monarchists came to see him. Shulgin also traveled to Moscow, and after looking up old political associates he left Soviet Russia by stealth.

But Shulgin learned later that it was the GPU that had arranged every detail of his "illegal" trip. The Russian who originally suggested the idea was a GPU agent. He had advised on the beard and the running exercise to make the whole thing seem more plausible. The "Monarchists" who talked with him in Kiev were officials of the GPU. The GPU also facilitated his easy exit without visa. The GPU did this to find out whether Shulgin had any of his own contacts in Russia, and the people he interviewed in Moscow were caught in the GPU's net.

It seems certain that the GPU also brought Savinkov into Russia. He did not suspect it. GPU men led him into Russia and straight into the arms of the GPU in the house in Minsk where he had expected to find anti-Soviet conspirators. The purpose was to get his confession of past sins and his tribute to Soviet power.

The *Encyclopaedia Britannica* reports that Savinkov died in prison in 1925, the year after his trial. The Soviet government made no announcement of the fact. We in Moscow knew that he had thrown himself out of a window in the top story of the GPU prison on Lubianka Square. Savinkov, restless, dynamic, adventurous, could not dwell in a cell for ten years. He had hoped, Bolsheviks told me, to be reprieved and to give the Red Army the benefit of his experience as a military leader. When he saw this was an illusion, life lost its meaning and he committed suicide.

Not often did sensational events like this Savinkov trial enable one to get a close-up of the Soviet riddle. To know more about it I tried to become acquainted with Soviet statesmen and with ordinary people. The Bolsheviks were pleased to see a serious approach to the life of their country. Moreover, politicians talk freely when they are certain they will not be quoted—some politicians, I should say—and I gave proof in Moscow that I could be discreet. What I was told in secret I kept secret. I went on the good journalistic principle that a statesman's information is his own until he releases it for publication. (Death also releases.) Besides, I am good listener, and most men will talk about themselves or their work to a sympathetic listener.

But the ordinary person's reaction may be a much safer guide to national sentiment than the views of an official. The "man-in-the-street," however, rarely walks the streets of a capital city. Moscow is not the Soviet Union, Berlin is not Germany, Paris is certainly not France, and Rome never was Italy. So I traveled a great deal, and in Russia I traveled year in and year out to the same towns and villages to meet the same workingmen, minor officials, and peasants. That enabled me to gain their confidence, to understand them better, and to make comparisons. One often goes to a place the first time in order to go there the second time. I liked especially to visit the warm Caucasus. I never go north if I can go south, and I worship the sun. My interest in oil politics took me frequently to Baku, the hot city on the salty Caspian, "the finger," as Chicherin once said, "that points to Asia."

In 1926, *Oil Imperialism*, my first book, was published. Ernestine Evans called it "a political detective story." It traces the intrigues and schemes of governments and international oil trusts to obtain control of the oil fields of Russia, Persia, and Turkey. (Russia's petroleum resources are as great as those of the United States.)

Oil moves navies, merchant marines, automobiles, factories, and airplanes. Lord Curzon, British Foreign Minister, said in November, 1918, that "the Allies floated to victory on a wave of oil."

I became interested in oil politics during the Genoa Conference in 1922. The protocols of the conference show as little reference to petroleum as to helium gas. Officially, none of the world's diplomats who attended the sessions ever mentioned oil. Nevertheless, oil was the key to its deliberations. Samuel Spewack first called attention to this fact in sensational dispatches from Genoa to the *New York World*. Sir Henri Deterding, of the Royal Dutch Shell, and Walter C. Teagle, with whom I subsequently discussed oil problems, never came within earshot of the conference, and lesser oil agents avoided the limelight while they pulled wires unseen. But when one followed the wires, and fitted together the pieces of the puzzle it became obvious that Moscow's refusal to surrender its oil wealth was the bar to a reconciliation between Russia and the rest of Europe. The oil companies stood in the way of a diplomatic settlement. Genoa was part of an intriguing network. Petrol magnates hampered statesmen and inspired statesmen.

I worked on the book for eight months, starting in Moscow, continuing in Berlin and London, and finishing in New York. I ransacked libraries in two continents.

I met many oil men. They talked little and knew a lot. Mr. Boris Said, for instance, represented the Standard Oil in London. Quite casually, one day, he suggested that there was in the Soviet Embassy in London a letter from the British Foreign office showing how Lord Curzon had attempted to obtain a concession from the Soviet government for the Royal Dutch Shell, Standard's rival. I persuaded

Counsellor Bogomolov to give me the letter and printed it. Mr. Ivy Lee, the Rockefellers' clever counsel on public relations, also helped me with information and documents. Publication served his purposes and mine, too.

Oil Imperialism was published in New York and London and translated into French, German, and Russian. The income from the book was small yet by my standards substantial. As an author, I got more lecture dates in the United States. More people had heard my name even if they had not read the book, and my journalistic work was thereby facilitated.

Unfortunately but naturally, the fact that an official has seen your name in print may mean all the difference between an interview and no interview, or between talkativeness and reticence. A card of introduction from a chance acquaintance may open a diplomat's door which all your knowledge of his subject could not unlock. Indeed, even the print on the card may make a difference. Once I was talking in the German Foreign Office on the Wilhelmstrasse with M. Schlesinger, in charge of commercial negotiations with the Soviet government. A liveried attendant brought in a card and handed it to Schlesinger. "But who is he?" Schlesinger said, with some irritation. "I don't know him." The lackey shrugged his shoulders. Then Schlesinger moved his finger back and forth over the name on the card. The letters were embossed. "All right," he instructed the lackey, "ask him to wait."

This reminds me of an interview I had with Joseph P. Kennedy, U. S. Ambassador in London, in October, 1939. I thought it might be interesting to listen in wartime to an American ambassador of the Roosevelt administration who had out-Chamberlained Neville Chamberlain during pre-War appeasement. I telephoned for an appointment and received it. As I was about to enter the ambassador's office, Bill Hillman, formerly of the Hearst news service, now European representative for *Collier's Magazine* and NBC, walked out, and we quickly arranged to meet that same evening at the Café Royal. Inside, Mr. Kennedy's bespectacled, strawberry-colored face wore a bored look, as if to say, "What does this fellow want? Why does he come to bother me?" I was sure he had never heard of me and was merely seeing me as a courtesy to an American journalist. I tried to make him talk. I asked questions about the situation in England and he said, "You can know as much about that as I do." I asked him about certain official acts of the British government and he said, "If I knew, I wouldn't tell you." I attempted to tell him something and he showed lack of interest. After about fifteen minutes of this, I felt I was wasting my time and his, when suddenly his whole manner changed. He spoke freely and fluently, expressed his views on Germany's power and on the differences in the British cabinet, answered queries, asked me about Russia, Germany, and Turkey, complimented me on my analysis of European affairs, and said he would get my books and would like to hear me lecture. I stayed for forty-five minutes after the first horrid quarter of an hour and we parted cordially.

In the evening at the café, Hillman said, "Did you notice the note I sent in to Kennedy?" I did remember that at one moment in the interview the ambassador's kindly old secretary brought in an odd-shaped slip of white paper on which I could see a large pencil scrawl. "Yes," said Hillman, "I wrote, 'Fischer is an interesting fellow. Talk to him.'" Hillman was a veteran London newspaperman who saw Kennedy almost every day. He could permit himself such liberties with the ambassador and the ambassador could trust him. It was only after he read Hillman's message that Kennedy became communicative.

Before writing *Oil Imperialism*, I visited Baku, the largest oil city in the world. I traveled with Paul Scheffer, of the *Berliner Tageblatt*. Scheffer, working for this liberal, democratic, Jewish-owned, and Jewish-edited German daily, was a pro-Soviet German Nationalist. He was pro-Soviet because of his German nationalism. Germany's defeat in 1918 convinced him, as it had convinced his ambassador in Moscow, Count Brockdorff-Rantzau, that Germany's salvation lay in Russia, red or white. Rantzau descended from an old Prussian noble line. His very tall, straight figure, his long, thin pale face, his sparse hair parted in the middle, his high, stiff wing collar, his abhorrence of physical movement, his love of classic allusion and philosophical digressions during political conversation, and the cloistered womanless life he led with his twin brother—all these stamped him the aloof aristocrat. He recoiled from fleshy, smelly, earthy Moscow and the heavy tongues, heavy boots, and heavy manners of average Bolsheviks. I saw him often through the years in his Moscow embassy or his home near the Tiergarten, Berlin, and he always gave the impression of being above the storms and stresses of life. Yet his whole post-War political career was based on German-Soviet collaboration. Under his seemingly casual glance, German army officers supervised the manufacture of airplanes, tanks, hand grenades, and other munitions in Soviet factories because Anglo-French stipulations prevented them from being produced in Germany. He tried to foster Russo-German trade and understanding. Scheffer tried to help.

Scheffer was the ruddy, rotund, round-headed Rhinelander—a connoisseur of wine and food. Rantzau preferred whiskey. Both alike endeavored to put love of country above the sharp distinctions which separated the German Republic from the Soviet regime. Scheffer inveighed against the Bolshevik dictatorship and argued that the backwardness and innate cruelty of the Russian made possible a rigorous repression which the culture of Germans ruled out. Yet he favored an eastern orientation of German diplomacy and sought to convert Berlin statesmanship to his and Rantzau's policy.

Scheffer and I traveled together in the same railway compartment for two and a half days from Moscow to Tiflis. We flew together to Baku, rode horses together along mountain trails, slept in the same room in the Oriente Hotel in Tiflis, and did most of our journalistic work in common during that six-week Caucasus tour. In subsequent years, we met frequently, indeed regularly, in Moscow to eat and argue and exchange information and opinions.

(On January 1, 1936, Ambassador William E. Dodd gave a New Year's party in the United States Embassy in Berlin. I was talking to Mrs. Dodd when Scheffer came up, greeted her, and kissed her hand. He did not know me; he had become the editor of the Nazified, Hitlerized, *Berliner Tageblatt*.)

Scheffer and I took our Caucasus trip to see Baku but also to investigate conditions in Georgia where a Menshevik uprising had just taken place against the Bolshevik regime. Reports reaching foreign papers said it had been suppressed after much bloodshed.

The Caucasus, cradle of the white race, is a museum of nationalities. Here live Georgians who claim kinship with the Basques of Spain (Lloyd George once told me that the Basques and Welsh were related); Moslem Turks in Azerbaijhan; Armenians made hot by the winds of the Persian desert and cool by the breezes from two-humped Ararat; Kurds near Batum; Circassians of Greek blood near the Black Sea; mountain Jews who speak ancient Hebrew; Ossetians; Dagestanians; Abhazi; Adjari; and literally hundreds more. Many of these races still practice the blood feud. The Swannetians saw airplanes fly over their mountain fastnesses before they had reached the wheel stage of culture. To all these peoples Bolshevism brought schools, cleanliness, centralized government, and peace. Czarism sometimes fanned tribal hates so that it might rule the divided. Under Bolshevism, in contrast, Armenians intermarry with Tatars—which is like saying that the southern colonel's daughter married a Negro—and other ancient enemies are mingling their bloods and talents. The Bolsheviks gave this welter of nations perfect cultural freedom but no political or economic independence. There are native officials, and the local resources are developed to the fullest. But Moscow rules the furthest crag and corner.

Women in Baku still wore the veil in 1924, and mullahs taught boys the Koran in the sing-song I had heard in Cairo, Jerusalem, and Damascus. "May God give me fleshiness," those women prayed, "rosiness I can buy for myself." They lived for men, and tastes differ with climes. But the chains were falling with the veils, and the new woman paced the street in boy's cap and short skirt with a volume of Marx under her arm and a worker on it, while her covered sister slipped quickly from harem to shop and back.

In the mountains of Georgia, Scheffer and I saw Hevsurs who wear coats of mail and claim to be descendants of the Crusaders. At a church in Allahverdi, eastern Georgia, we heard troubadours extemporize ballads to tunes from their two-string instruments inlaid with mother-of-pearl. Stately couples, dressed in velvets and embroidery handed down through generations, performed wild tribal dances in a provincial marriage mart that assembled around the church now closed by decree. Into this strange world, the Bolsheviks injected Bolshevism. Their caution notwithstanding, explosions had to take place. In Georgia, one out of every seven inhabitants was a prince like the Mdivanis, which meant that he was a peasant who owned a three-room house on stilts and a horse and two goats. This little capitalist objected to socialist encroachment. Workingmen, raised in the traditionally strong Menshevism of Georgia, abhorred Bolshevism. Moreover, the Georgian had a passionate dislike for the Russian. Stalin and Orjonekidze might rule in Moscow, but Moscow remained Russian and the nationalities on the periphery had not yet made their peace with federalism. Scheffer and I were being toasted in a wine cellar at Tsinandali on an estate confiscated from the Grand Duke Nicholas. The head of the GPU lifted a ram's horn filled with claret and said, "To our three guests."

"But," demurred Tchaikovsky, commander of the Red Army cavalry brigade of the district, "I am not a guest."

"Russians are always guests here," the toastmaster replied.

This was the background of the insurrection we were investigating, and it was the background, too, for a study of the vast task undertaken by the new regime. Journalistic work in such a country taught one history, psychology, government, economics, ethnography, geography; a university education free. New situations regularly challenged the mind.

I devoted much time to internal Soviet problems, read Marx and Lenin, read more than I wrote. But my pet subject remained foreign policy. I decided to write a history of Soviet foreign affairs. I expected to do it in eight months. It took three years and grew into two big volumes.

My task in preparing the book involved picking the brains and memories of Bolsheviks who had formulated and administered Soviet foreign policy. These included Chicherin, Foreign Commissar, Litvinov and Karakhan, assistant commissars, Soviet ambassadors like Krestinsky, Sokolnikov, and Rakovsky.

Maxim Litvinov is the coldest Bolshevik realist. Slogans never misled him. He has cast off all illusions. "The prospect of world revolution disappeared on November 11, 1918," he said to me. The corollary was that the prospect might reappear when a second war commenced. Bukharin and others held this thesis, but Stalin frowned on it.

Litvinov would always accept a compromise if the alternative meant hurting the nation for a principle. Yet he is a fighter and several times refused to yield to Stalin. He won his point against Stalin; indeed, Soviet foreign policy between 1929 and May, 1939, followed the pattern of Litvinov's mind more than of his chief's. In the last two years during which Litvinov was Foreign Minister— 1937 to 1939—this was due to inertia and the absence of an opportunity to launch a different policy.

Litvinov's foreign policy was to avoid trouble. Truest revolutionist, he wished to keep Soviet Russia at peace so it could develop internally. He did not want to spend money on a Red fleet, he told me. He sought to develop Soviet foreign trade. He endeavored to enhance Moscow's prestige by Soviet participation in conferences, pacts, and agreements. Disarmament at Geneva was his "baby." Chicherin never liked it. Assistant Commissar Litvinov fought for Soviet adherence to the Kellogg Pact. Chicherin, the Commissar, fought against this. The Soviets adhered. It did no good, and Litvinov did not expect war to be outlawed. But he wanted Moscow to appear on the world stage.

It used to be a subject of mirth with my friends among the younger Soviet officials that if Chicherin said "Yes" Litvinov would say "No" and *vice versa*. Yet the two of them worked in the same office toward the same goal. Chicherin carried over into Soviet diplomacy some of the traditional Russian suspicion of the British Raj in Central Asia. Persia and Afghanistan were important to him, and to Stalin, and to Lenin. Indeed, Stalin, the Georgian, was more Great Russian than many Russians, just as Hitler, the Austrian, was the real Greater German. Maxim Litvinov, on the other hand, was a westerner and he simply did not see the wisdom of spoiling Russia's relations with European powers for the sake of Soviet influence in small Asiatic countries. He said to me in March, 1929, "I think an agreement with England about Afghanistan and the East generally is possible, but the government takes a different view."

On August 9, 1929, at the end of a long interview with Litvinov in the Berlin Soviet Embassy, I told him I was going down to Wiesbaden, Germany, to see Chicherin. Litvinov said, "Is that so?" And after a moment's hesitation he added, "His memory isn't as good as it used to be." In fact, Chicherin's memory remained startlingly photographic. Rivalry and jealousy heightened differences of temperament and culture into clashes of policy. It was so in the conflict between Stalin and Trotzky, too. It is difficult to determine where the personal leaves off, and the political begins.

Statesmen, and kings and queens and presidents, are human and may be petty. Chicherin was queer and a genius. He usually remained above the battle in a world partly of his own private construction. But Litvinov is full-blooded, virile, and tempestuous. He never likes big men around him, and when he became Commissar, succeeding Chicherin, in 1930, he managed to get rid of Gregory Sokolnikov and Leo Karakhan, both assistant commissars and both extremely well-connected in the highest Soviet spheres. Sokolnikov was sometimes summoned to Politbureau meetings to give advice on financial and international questions. Litvinov did not like that. Karakhan hobnobbed with the Caucasians on the upper level, Anastasias Mikoyan, Ordjonekidze, and Stalin. That gave him the possibility of going over Litvinov's head. So Karakhan was sent away as Ambassador to Ankara.

Nor did Litvinov have any affection for journalists. He unbent a little in Geneva and other foreign cities, but in Moscow it was almost as hard to get to him as to Stalin. Journalists know too much, he used to explain, and interfere too much. It took me a long time to win his confidence.

Litvinov saw me in his office but more frequently in his home in the "Sugar King's Palace." This was a big villa on the bank of the Moskva River just opposite the Czar's palace in the Kremlin. Here the Soviet government had housed prominent foreigners like Enver Pasha; Claire Sheridan, the British sculptress and friend, at one time, of Leo Kamenev; Sidney Hillman of the Amalgamated Clothing Workers' Union; and others. Later it became the British Embassy. Built by a pre-revolutionary Russian millionaire it bore the marks of Czarist culture; it was ornate, huge, gaudy, dark downstairs and bright upstairs, and appointed with expensive French period furniture, clocks, china, and innumerable paintings by European artists. A cellar and two detached wings had furnished quarters for the sugar king's servants. For a while, I lived in part of one wing with my family. Our neighbor was Rita Klymen, correspondent of the *London Daily Express*, whom the Bolsheviks expelled for using offensive language against the Red Army. This palace and scores of other Moscow villas had been expropriated by the Soviets; they were administered by the Bureaubin which rented them to embassies and individual foreigners.

Litvinov occupied three rooms in the second story of the main house with his wife Ivy, British-born, a lively, witty, and acute woman. They had two children, Misha, aged thirteen in 1929, a wild boy, and Tania, aged eleven in 1929, a beautiful, shy girl. Often when Litvinov came home in the evening he would have to listen to tales of Misha's fights and escapades. Ivy could not manage Misha and left the trying job to the burly, irate commissar father. But Litvinov loved his children. Occasionally, Tania would sit in his lap and Misha by his side while he told me of his meetings with Briand, Chamberlain, and Lloyd George. Litvinov likes the movies and goes to them often in Moscow and abroad. He would take Misha and Tania and explain the captions and plots to them. Misha grew up to be a tall, lanky youth studying engineering, and Tania is an artist.

Litvinov knows English well but speaks it with a horrible accent.

At League of Nations meetings in Geneva all the delegates and correspondents would troop into the hall when Litvinov rose to deliver an address, for he invariably said something curt and profound which gave endless pleasure to the bulk of the journalists' corps by expressing their cynical disrespect of the fatuous, self-defeating, pusillanimous anti-war efforts of the League. But how the audience strained to understand Litvinov! He talks quickly on the platform and swallows at least one syllable in each word. He wrote every one of these speeches—rare feat for a statesman—wrote them in Russian and had them translated into English by Ivy or Andrew Rothstein. Owner of a great mind, Litvinov is cruelly critical of blunders and intellectual folly, and his subordinates often feared to go before him to report. But they admired him and he was loyal to them, and many remained in the commissariat for long years until the purge took them from him.

Litvinov had told me the story of Soviet foreign relations as far as the important Anglo-Russian conference in Lodon in 1924. But when he finished discussing these negotiations he added, "I have told you everything I remember. The man who really knows what happened is Rakovsky."

"But Rakovsky," I protested, "is in exile."

"Go see him," he snapped in his characteristic bark.

I was startled by this suggestion from a commissar to visit a banished Trotzkyist. "How can I find him?" I asked.

"He is somewhere in Saratov. His daughter can give you the exact address," Litvinov advised.

Rakovsky's daughter was married to the Soviet poet Utkin. She bubbled with joy when I called and told her of my proposed journey. She gave me her parents' address and begged me to take a letter and a suitcase of books to them.

Suddenly it occurred to me that although Rakovsky knew me he might not reveal important unpublished matter to me unless he was sure that Chicherin, Litvinov, and others were doing likewise. I regarded Rakovsky as a loyal Bolshevik despite his official sins and did not expect him to disclose diplomatic secrets without permission. I went to Litvinov with these doubts.

"But what do you expect of me?" he replied. "I cannot write a letter of recommendation for you to a banished Trotzkyist."

"Then there isn't much point in going," I said sadly.

"Well," Litvinov said, "let me think about it."

Two days later a courier brought me a letter. I still have it. It was signed by Litvinov and addressed, not to Rakovsky, but to Feodor Rothstein, Litvinov's assistant and chief of the press department of the foreign office. Litvinov asked Rothstein to give every possible assistance to me in the preparation of my book on Soviet foreign policy. Rakovsky would know that this letter was intended for him first because a letter from Litvinov to Rothstein would otherwise not be in my hands, and, secondly, if Litvinov wanted to give such instructions to Rothstein he would give them orally, for they met a dozen times each day. Their offices were just one floor apart.

I arrived in Saratov, ancient Volga town. I was so busy that I never saw the Volga during the eight days I spent there. On the black bulletin board of Saratov's best hotel, on which guests' names were written in chalk, I read "Christian G. Rakovsky" and again "Christian G. Rakovsky." He had two rooms.

I knocked at Rakovsky's door. Rakovsky had studied and practiced medicine in France before the Revolution. He possessed great erudition. He had been Soviet Ambassador in London and Paris. I had seen him last in the London Embassy. The Soviet government maintains its foreign diplomats in the grand style befitting their station and their exposed position in the bourgeois world. They live in fine villas, drive in big limousines, serve sumptuous meals, and arrange great receptions. In London, Rakovsky donned silk breeches and attended royal parties in Buckingham Palace. When I knocked at his door in Saratov he came out in a vest and stocking feet. He had been sleeping. I explained the purpose of my visit and pulled out Litvinov's letter. He glanced at it hurriedly and pushing his lips upward into a scornful expression handed it back, saying, "I don't need that."

Then began eight exciting days. I would come to Rakovsky's room at noon. He would talk to me for two hours while I took down the voluminous notes that now lie on my desk. Then he would go to lunch. Sometimes I walked with him to the lunchroom; men would bow as he passed and raise their hats. For this political criminal in exile was the most prominent and, I suspect, the most revered resident of Saratov. I would come back to his room at six in the evening, when he resumed the thrilling narrative. At about seven, a young man would come in, nod, sit down, and listen. A few minutes later, another man entered, and another. By seven-thirty, six or seven people were in the room. These were Rakovsky's fellow exiles gathering daily to exchange views with their leader. He would then suggest that I excuse him and return at midnight. Midnight! I like to keep regular hours. Fresh as a young man, Rakovsky, aged fifty-six, would start at midnight and go on until two in the morning. Then the electricity in the great provincial city of Saratov would be turned off, and Rakovsky would light some candles. At three he would extinguish them, for it was morning and the sun was rising. At four he would say, "Well, I suppose you want to go to bed." I did.

In Rakovsky's room stood a tremendous trunk full of documents and letters. I was astounded to find that he had been able to take to Saratov the secret protocols of the Anglo-Soviet conference in London in 1924. He allowed me to copy what I wanted out of them and this material was first published in *The Soviets in World Affairs*. He also had with him seven letters he had received from Chicherin. They were all written in pencil between March and May, 1919, when Rakovsky was Prime Minister of Soviet Ukraine, and Rakovsky was sure Chicherin had never made carbons. Two of the letters dealt with William Christian Bullitt's mission to Moscow in 1919, and the others with secret Polish overtures to Moscow. Bullitt had been sent by President Wilson to Lenin to patch up a peace with Russia. Young Bullitt acquitted himself nobly. Accompanied by Walter Pettit of the U. S. Military Intelligence Service and Lincoln Steffens, he saw Lenin, Chicherin, and Litvinov. Chicherin wrote to Rakovsky urging him to support an understanding with the Allies. "The decision is very important," he declared. "If we don't try to get an agreement the policy of blockade will be pressed with vigor. They will send tanks . . . to Denikin, Kolchak, Petlura, Paderewski. . . . We want [the Allied troops of intervention] evacuated before the signing of the peace. . . . They want us to reduce our army before that." Four days later Chicherin informed Rakovsky that Bullitt "does not believe that big concessions can be won for us in Paris. But he hopes to carry this proposal through. . . . France knows nothing about it. This must be kept absolutely secret." The Soviets were eager for an agreement with the Allies, and Bullitt left with decided pro-Bolshevik sympathies. But when he returned to Paris he found that Woodrow Wilson "had a headache" and refused to receive his own emissary. Nothing came of the entire mission. Wilson, according to Colonel House, was too preoccupied with the German peace to think of Russia. That was unfortunate because peace was indivisible, even before Litvinov coined the phrase years later.

Rakovsky had a marvelous memory, and what he could not recollect he was often able to reconstruct on the basis of documents. He would dig for them in his suitcases and trunks, and if he failed to find what he wanted he would go into the adjoining room, wake his wife, and ask her about such-and-such a file, and she, rather than leave it to him, would put on a dressing gown, come in sleepy-eyed but smiling, with some disparaging remark about the helplessness of the male sex, and take up the search herself.

In accordance with the accepted code, I avoided references to Soviet party politics. A Bolshevik normally skirts around this subject in conversation with foreigners who are not Communists. (Radek made an exception with me and so, occasionally, did Chicherin.) One afternoon, however, Rakovsky himself broke the rule. There had been a knock at the door, and the hotel manager, obviously pleased to have a reason for seeing the great man, delivered a telegram. Rakovsky opened it and blanched. After a moment, he said in a voice filled with contempt, "This is a message from Radek, Smilga, and Beloborodov [leading Trotzkyists in Siberian exile]. They are going to make their peace with Stalin, confess their errors, return to Moscow. They want me to join them. Never. I shall not desert Trotzky. I love him personally and I admire his policies. Stalin has betrayed the Revolution."

In those mild and distant days, it was enough for an Oppositionist to recant and beat his breast publicly to be taken back into the party. But Rakovsky was adamant, and he remained in exile many more years.

The telegram broke the ice, and thereafter Rakovsky spoke several times of internal party strife. He said Stalin had deported Trotzky as an indication to foreign governments that the Kremlin intended to pursue a conservative foreign policy divorced from the revolutionary aims of the Third International.

Rakovsky was part-Rumanian, part-Bulgarian, and the Bessarabian question interested him enormously. In his talks with me in Saratov he revealed facts whose significance then evaded me but which have acquired new meaning in recent years. In January, 1918, when the Bolsheviks were weak and otherwise occupied, Rumania marched into the Russian province of Bessarabia and annexed it. Late in 1920, after the Bolsheviks had defeated the last of the White generals, Frunze, war commissar of Soviet Ukraine, wanted to reconquer Bessarabia. Frunze was a Moldavian. He argued that it would be hard to demobilize the Red Army quickly, that many of the units were ethnically Moldavian and Bessarabian, and that they would participate enthusiastically in a war on Rumania. Voroshilov supported Frunze. Lenin consulted Rakovsky, who had studied the Bessarabian problem before the Revolution and written a pamphlet on it. Rakovsky opposed violence. A Russian offensive against Rumania would arouse all the major powers against Moscow. Moreover, Rakovsky submitted, if Rumania collapsed Russia would have an open Balkan problem on her hands and that would involve the Bolsheviks in more than they were then ready to handle with their limited resources.

But this did not end the matter. In the summer of 1921, Trotzky proposed recognizing Bessarabia as part of Rumania and closing the open wound. Rakovsky demurred. He argued that by keeping the Bessarabian problem unsolved Moscow could keep Rumania permanently on tenterhooks and thus influence the whole Balkan situation. Bulgaria was anti-Rumania and so, to an extent, was Yugoslavia; by quietly opposing Rumania, the Russians would win sympathies in Bulgaria and Yugoslavia. Rakovsky contended that even Czarism had been regarded as a liberator in the Balkans; Bolshevism could play the same role.

At about the same time—mid-1921—Stalin telephoned Rakovsky in Kharkov and asked him to come to Moscow for crucial deliberations. Djerzhinsky sent a special train to fetch Rakovsky. Lenin received Rakovsky with smiles and eager inquiries. A White general named Sloschov, who had escaped with thousands of soldiers from Russia in 1920 was now in Istanbul (Constantinople) and had offered to come over to the Bolsheviks and march his army of armed veterans from Constantinople through Bulgaria, Rumania, and Bessarabia, conquering as he went in the name of Russia. On reaching the Ukraine, Sloschov would be granted amnesty by the Bolsheviks and receive a commission in the Red Army. Rakovsky jumped at the idea, and Lenin approved it. Lenin chuckled especially at the thought of taking Constantinople from the British, who were then its real masters, and restoring it to the Turks.

But, Rakovsky continued, the British authorities learned of the

Sloschov plan and obstructed it. Sloschov later come to Soviet Russia and joined the Red Army.

When the Turks were hard pressed by the Greeks in the Anatolian war in 1922, Leon Trotzky, Soviet war lord, favored rendering them unstinted aid. Stalin, Ordjonekidze, and other Georgian and Caucasian comrades, Rakovsky told me, were afraid, however, that Turkey would grow too strong. The Caucasus borders on Turkey, and the Caucasians were therefore pro-Turk with moderation. They recalled that in March, 1921, Turkish troops actually occupied Batum, a seaport in Georgia. It is interesting and curious that such regional considerations contributed to the formulation of Stalin's ideas on foreign policy.

In 1924, and on several subsequent occasions, too, Litvinov wished to recognize Rumanian sovereignty over Bessarabia. Litvinov was always the businessman in diplomacy and he did not like to have an unfinished account. Latent hostility with Rumania made it difficult for eastern Europe to settle down and Litvinov wanted to heal the sore. Rakovsky and Litvinov quarreled on this matter. When Rakovsky went as Ambassador to London he would write regularly to the Politbureau in Moscow recalling the necessity of Russian watchfulness in the Balkans and of perpetuating Bessarabia as a "Soviet Irredenta." When Rakovsky stopped writing on the subject because negotiations with Great Britain absorbed all his time, Chicherin inquired by letter why Rakovsky had left him to fight the battle alone. Thanks to Chicherin's and Rakovsky's insistent propaganda, the Soviet press on January 26, 1928, the tenth anniversary of Rumania's seizure of Bessarabia, called Bessarabia "the Alsace on the Dnieper." Trotzky and Litvinov were reconciled to its loss. Rakovsky, Chicherin, and Stalin were not.

With the hindsight allowed by the passage of years and in the perspective of events just before and during the second World War, I find many of Rakovsky's disclosures startlingly revealing. One sees here the first signs of Soviet expansionism, the beginnings of the conflict between Chicherin and Litvinov and also the origins of the break between Stalin and Litvinov in May, 1939. Litvinov had no interest in territorial acquisitions. Stalin had. Indeed, Stalin's tendency to extend Soviet power manifested itself in 1921. Then it was ignored as a momentary aberration. But it evidently ran deep.

In February, 1921, Persia and Soviet Russia signed a treaty of friendship which required Moscow to evacuate the province of Ghilan in northern Persia. Red troops had entered this province in 1920 while pursuing counter-revolutionary units. Lenin favored the liberation of Ghilan, especially since British withdrawal from south Persia was contingent on Russian withdrawal from the north, and it was in Moscow's interest to have a free, independent Persia. Nevertheless, Stalin and Ordjonekidze, both Georgians—Georgia is contiguous with Persia—sabotaged the agreement and sent arms and Soviet personnel to local chieftains in Ghilan with exhortations to organize Soviets.

Feodor Rothstein, then Soviet Ambassador in Teheran, wrote to Lenin protesting against these Georgian efforts. He submitted that Persia was poor, archaic, and retarded, and had no working class to speak of. For the Bolsheviks to export a revolution to such a country would cause endless complications with the Shah and England without, however, producing a Soviet Persia. "It seems to me you are right," Lenin asserted in reply to Rothstein.

Rothstein thereupon urged Riza Khan, the virtual ruler of Persia—later Shah—to march into Ghilan and suppress the tribal leaders and notably a certain Kuchik Khan, who had obtained support from Georgia. Kuchik Khan was defeated and froze to death hiding in the mountains. Riza cut off his head and displayed it in Teheran. "Among the prisoners Riza took," Chicherin told me, "were Russian peasants from the province of Tula. Those were the soldiers of Stalin's Ghilan Soviet Republic," Chicherin sneered.

In Moscow, Stalin stormed. His protégé had been killed. He blamed Rothstein. The question was brought up at a session of the Politbureau. A person present at this meeting described the scene to me. Stalin pressed his complaint.

"Good," said Lenin with a gleam in his eye, and he dictated to the stenographer. "Strict reprimand to Comrade Rothstein for killing Kuchik Khan."

"No," someone said, "it was Riza who killed Kuchik Khan."

"Good," Lenin exclaimed. "Strict reprimand to Riza Khan for killing Kuchik Khan."

"But we cannot reprimand Riza. He is not a Soviet citizen," Stalin objected. At this, Lenin burst out laughing and so did the others. The matter was dropped. In his tactful wisdom, Lenin had reprimanded Stalin. In 1939, no one could reprimand Stalin.

Karakhan was in charge of Soviet relations with Asiatic states. Litvinov watched over Europe. Chicherin supervised. Karakhan was himself an Asiatic, a handsome, attractive Armenian, a lawyer by training and son of a rich family. He had a fine head of hair, a pitch-black, well-trimmed beard, perfectly manicured nails, large white teeth, a ready smile. He was the best-dressed Bolshevik. He was free, informal, and friendly, and he could laugh at himself. He once told me this story:

At the beginning of his diplomatic career, Karakhan served as secretary to the Soviet delegation which negotiated the enforced peace with the Kaiser's government at Brest-Litovsk in 1918. Trotzky had refused to accept Imperial Germany's terms. "No peace and no war." The Bolsheviks would not fight because they could not, but they would not sign a humiliating treaty. In reply, Ludendorff simply ordered a German army into Russia. Thereupon, Lenin resumed the negotiations. Trotzky refused to go to Brest-Litovsk. Joffe, Sokolnikov, Chicherin, and Karakhan did go. Meanwhile, however, the Germans and their allies, the Turks, had increased their demands. The Turks were now asking the cession of Kars, Erzerum, and Ardagan. Karakhan wired this information to Lenin and signed his name. When the telegram arrived it read that the Turks wanted Kars, Erzerum, and Karakhan. Lenin laughed aloud and said, "Well, that's all right. I'll give them Karakhan any day."

Karakhan did a good job as Ambassador in China. The Chinese and most others liked his cordiality and relative absence of restraint. He was much younger than Chicherin and Litvinov. (He was forty-eight when Stalin had him executed in the big purge of 1937.)

Once while telling me about his work in China, Karakhan said, "I have something for you," and went into his inner office and brought out a file of original letters which he and Chicherin had exchanged with Dr. Sun Yat-sen, the father of the Chinese Nationalist movement. I asked what I could do with them, and he replied, "Take them home and copy them." I was afraid that they might be lost or stolen or burnt and so I sat down in his anteroom and made the copies. I did not publish them in *The Soviets in World Affairs* because I thought Karakhan might get into trouble. One letter in English, signed "L. Karakhan" and dated Moscow, September 23, 1923, read, in part, "Dear Dr. Sun: The absence in Canton of a permanent and responsible representative of our government has long been keenly felt at Moscow. With the appointment of M. M. Borodin an important step has been taken in this direction. . . . Please regard Comrade Borodin not only as a representative of the Government but likewise my personal representative with whom you may talk as frankly as you would with me."

The point is that Borodin, who led the Chinese Revolution until 1927, was not supposed to be an official of the Soviet government. The Soviet government always disavowed him and claimed that he represented the Third International (Comintern).

A little while later Karakhan addressed Dr. Sun as "Dear Comrade," which is the natural salutation for a Bolshevik to use in correspondence with one who is a friend and not bourgeois. Sun Yat-sen, in reply, wrote "Dear Comrade" to Karakhan.

Dr. Sun's letter of September 17, 1923, to Karakhan in Moscow included this paragraph, "What follows is *rigidly confidential*. Some weeks ago, I sent identic letters to Comrades Lenin, Tchitcherin, and Trotzky introducing General Chiang Kai-shek, who is my chief of staff and confidential agent. I have dispatched him to Moscow to discuss ways and means whereby our friends there can assist me in my work in this country." Chiang got what he came for. Moscow gave him money, arms, and military advisers. The marriage of convenience between him and the Bolsheviks lasted until 1927, when Chiang broke with the Russians, the Chinese Communists, and the Left Kuomintang, including Mrs. Sun Yat-sen, widow of the man who had dispatched him to Moscow. Borodin himself had to flee across the Mongolian desert to Moscow.

Soviet Russia's part in the Chinese Revolution is a sensational chapter of Kremlin foreign policy. Michael Borodin knew the whole story. Others knew pieces of it but they refused to talk. So I had to tackle the big man himself. I made my first attempts in 1927 and did not succeed until 1929. A naturally secretive person, Borodin had been made even more cautious and elusive by his work in Chicago and China. My first interview with him took place on February 26, 1929. I saw him again on March 13, March 25, April 15, May 23, May 24, May 27—he was growing interested in the telling and our talks, each of which lasted three or four hours, became more frequent—May 29, June 4, and June 26. Never once did he give me a definite appointment. He would say, "Telephone me Friday evening." I would do so. His wife Fannie, or his son who worked for the GPU, would answer, consult him, and return to say, "Comrade

Borodin would like you to phone him tomorrow morning at nine."
I would do so. He would come to the telephone and say, "Call me
again in twenty minutes. I may be summoned to a meeting." Often
he canceled appointments already made. But when I finally got to
him, the reward was rich. He liked to talk and act the oracle. Our
interviews usually took place in the morning. He would slip out of
his pajamas and dress in my presence, consume a breakfast of tea,
and then stride up and down the huge room in the Supreme Economic Council house in Sheremaytivsky Street while I scribbled notes
with muscle-cramping speed. The maid came in to clear the floor of
mattresses on which people had spent the night. Sometimes a little
gray mouse gaily disported itself about the room.

Borodin is tall and broad-shouldered with a shaggy head and a
thick walrus mustache. He speaks a good English intermixed with
American slang and frequently throws in a phrase like "You know
what I mean, eh?" or "Get me?" He impressed all who met him in
China as a person of exceptionally high caliber. He impressed dis-
cerning Americans like Lewis Gannett and the agents of Standard
Oil, as well as the Chinese. He dangled Chinese war lords and twisted
them around his fingers. Years after Borodin left China his name still
awed Chinese statesmen and workingmen. He was the real dictator
of Nationalist China. He departed in haste because Chiang turned
the Revolution towards the Right and threatened to decapitate his
Soviet aides.

"We will be back in China," Borodin predicted in 1929, and he
quoted approvingly a statement by George Sokolsky that "Chiang
Kai-shek can do nothing without the Russians." Both prophecies
came true. But, Borodin added, "This is not a personal matter." He
knew his bolt had been shot, and when Chiang did again plead for
Soviet assistance Borodin stayed in Moscow.

Borodin contained an honest mixture of Trotzkyism and Stalinism.
He said with Trotzky that every "middle" peasant wanted to become
a kulak or rich peasant just as "every little pig wants to become a
big pig." The Russian peasant therefore had to be "de-peasantized,"
industrialized. Borodin declared, "There can be no question of making the Russian peasants happy or of a union between workers and
peasants. The Soviet government must put the workers on short
rations, industrialize agriculture, and meantime wait for world
changes that are sure to come in five or ten years." That was the
Trotzkyist position. But he affirmed that Radek, the Trotzkyist ex-

pert on China, "was caught in a maze of contradictions." (Favorite Communist lingo.) "How," Borodin exclaimed, "can Radek expect us to establish a socialist state in far-off Kwantung in southern China when he thinks a socialist state cannot succeed in one country, not even in Russia?" A Soviet China was a dream, and when Chiang refused to co-operate in creating a liberal, populist China in which the peasants had land and from which the foreign imperialists had been expelled, the Communist game was up. The workers and peasants alone were too weak. Without Chiang, that is, without the bourgeoisie, nothing could be achieved. Chiang could do nothing without the Russians; it was equally true that the Russians could do nothing without Chiang.

When I mentioned difficult economic conditions in Soviet Russia, Borodin concurred and said, "There is probably no solution until revolution comes in another country." He meditated for a moment. "But not in the East. An eastern revolution, in China, for instance, would be an added responsibility for Moscow. It would not be a bad thing, but what we really need is a revolution in England or in Germany."

Borodin was studying India during the period I saw him. He said the British Empire was old. "The British Commonwealth of Nations," he said wishfully, "is just another name for a family in which the children, the dominions, are growing up and will soon go their own separate ways." When I once said to Chicherin, "Bolsheviks think too logically," he corrected me and said, "You mean, too primitively."

Essentially the book I was writing was the story of Chicherin's life-work, for after Trotzky resigned as Foreign Commissar in 1918, Chicherin took over and he had held the post up to this time. Chicherin understood my aims and did all he could for me within the limits set by public policy.

He had an astounding memory. For months he received me every Sunday afternoon. In the intervening six days he had, of course, seen an endless stream of diplomats, assistants, and Soviet officials. But when I came into his spacious office he invariably said, "Last time I was saying," and resumed practically from the sentence where he had left off the preceding week.

Chicherin was born in 1872 of noble stock. His mother was the daughter of Baron George Meyerdorff, an explorer in Central Asia.

His father, an estate owner in the province of Tambov and brother of the Russian philosopher, Boris Chicherin, served as counselor in the Russian Embassy in Paris. Further back, the Chicherins are pinned to the family tree of the Narishkins, who were related to the Czars. Georgi lifted himself out of this background to become a Bolshevik commissar. He studied history with distinction at St. Petersburg University, worked as an archivist in the Russian Foreign Office, wrote on the Crimean War, and then for reasons of health went abroad where he fell in with Marxists, and joined them. When the Bolshevik Revolution occurred, Chicherin was serving a sentence in Brixton Jail, London, for anti-war propaganda. Trotzky demanded his release. The British refused. Trotzky thereupon announced that no Briton would leave Russia. The British government released Chicherin and he became Trotzky's first assistant. It was the cabinet of Lloyd George that had incarcerated Chicherin. A few years later Chicherin negotiated with Lloyd George in Genoa.

Chicherin lived the life of a recluse. His apartment adjoined his office and he rarely left the building except to go to the Kremlin for cabinet or Politbureau meetings. One Sunday afternoon, after he had talked to me for over an hour, he asked me whether I would take a ride with him. We drove out the Tverskaya towards the airport. There he ordered his car to stop, stepped out on the left side, walked around the hood, re-entered the auto on the right side, and ordered the chauffeur to return home. He had taken his day's, perhaps week's, exercise and air.

Chicherin suffered from diabetes, bad eyesight, and muscular trouble in his right leg. In addition, he was a hypochondriac. He never wanted to be far from his physicians. In 1929, he went to Berlin for a cure. I followed him. He stayed incognito in a Grunewald sanatorium. I asked Soviet Ambassador Krestinsky to arrange an appointment for me with Chicherin. He did so and Chicherin revealed history to me in the midst of thermometers, medicine bottles, and insulin needles. A week later I requested Krestinsky to get me another date. Krestinsky said, "I'll do it, but if you want to see Chicherin you must not tell him he looks well. He made a scandal last time." Last time I had remarked, "You are looking better."

In August, 1929, Chicherin let me come to Wiesbaden during his cure. He would spend two or three hours a day reading the almost completed manuscript of The Soviets in World Affairs, and then for two or three hours he would comment to me on what he had read, pointing out errors, filling in gaps in my information or just reminiscing. It was a great intellectual experience for me. To him it entailed physical strain, and at the end of each interview his outer suit was wet with perspiration.

Because of his illness Chicherin had to eat enormous quantities of food. I sat with him once through dinner, and wrote to my wife about it as follows, "This is what he ate. One big cup of soup, a whole boiled trout that hung over both sides of the plate, a whole spring chicken with fried potatoes, a small plate of string beans, cheese with black bread, and a large orange. He drank a half bottle of red wine and a bottle of Fachingen mineral water. He was in a very fine mood and told me interesting things for my book. After this tremendous meal he ordered the waiter to bring him tea and a liqueur in the bar."

The bar was a long room. We occupied a table near one end. Opposite the table was a window with iron bars. Chicherin had been telling me about the Third International and the way it interfered with his work. "It was never so stupid as at present," he declared. "The whole disarmament business at Geneva is merely designed as slogan for Comintern propaganda and internal politics. It enables us to say we are being threatened." Just then a dog stood up outside the window with his front paws against the bars and barked. "There, there," Chicherin exclaimed jeeringly, "that is an attack on the Soviet Union. The dog provides the Comintern with a slogan."

Chicherin told me in Wiesbaden he would soon resign on account of illness. The illness was partly physical and partly political. When Litvinov succeeded him as commissar, Chicherin had to leave the apartment and office he had occupied for eight years. I was back in Moscow then, and Chicherin sent me the following letter by messenger under date of August 16, 1930:

DEAR COMRADE,

I am preparing to leave the house very soon and to go to a private lodging. Please do not forget to send your book when it comes out. I thought it would be ready in March. I send you my farewell greetings and hope to be in touch with you in future. My greatest joy remains to me: playing Mozart. He is for me the world in extract and the incarnation of the beauty of life. I am mostly in a very bad state, with some life coming back for a short time usually late in the evening.

Yours truly,

G. CHICHERIN.

This letter is one of twenty-five Chicherin wrote me in 1929 and 1930, and which I have withheld from publication until now. All were in English by hand in ink. Some ran into many pages.

Chicherin played the piano beautifully. Once, during the Lausanne conference, he rendered selections for the Soviet delegation. But usually he played alone. For a Bolshevik to say that only music remained to give him joy is a sad note indeed. Chicherin, a scholar, wrote only one book, a short volume on Mozart. A few people in Moscow read the manuscript, Education Commissar Lunarcharsky, Constantine Oumansky, and others. But Chicherin would not allow it to be published.

Chicherin poured all his talent into music and work. He had the broad vision of a truly great man and the petty meticulousness of an old maid. Markoosha describes how he would regularly come into the secretariat at the Genoa Conference and examine the addresses on envelopes and, in some cases, even write the addresses. He put the same intense concern for detail into his reading of the corrections I entered into my manuscript after seeing him at Wiesbaden. Five to ten times he wrote to Philadelphia telling me that I had misspelled names. Thus, September 30, 1929: "The Catholic bishop was *d'Her-bigny*. The Polish negotiator was Wieckowski. . . ." October 20: "The names are d'Herbigny, Wieckowski (delegate, not head of delegation), Giulietti, Moncheur. . . ." He also carefully checked dates for me and verbal formulas. Thus: "Pechenga (Petsamo in Finnish) was granted to Soviet Finland by the treaty of March, 1918," and then the Bolsheviks, he explained, could not refuse to give it to Bourgeois Finland. And: "The Chinese government discouraged trade, handicrafts, and agriculture of *Mongolians*, but Chinese did all these things in Mongolia, sucking the blood of the people." The aristocrat who had only rare contacts with the masses had a profound sympathy for them.

When he read the corrections I mailed to him, new facts came to his mind and he included them in letters which followed me across the Atlantic. "Do not write me any more here. Your letters will not find me here. What will happen with your letters I cannot foresee. I sent you many letters, one very long on many sheets. The steel was not to be transported abroad, but to the interior [a reference to Allied intervention in North Russia in 1918]. Many other things." His interest in my book was touching and almost painful. Once a passage in a German book he was reading struck him as important for me and he copied out a whole page of it and sent it to me.

In February, 1930, I returned to Moscow. Chicherin was in Moscow, too, still Foreign Commissar. I asked him for an interview. A messenger immediately brought his reply, "Dear Comrade, Have you come for a long time? I am at present invisible. Please write. When will the book appear? . . ." And he added some historic material about the Locarno negotiations which I included in the book.

Again I asked to see him, and I asked him to write an introduction to my book. The same day he sent me a very long letter. He wrote, "For what purpose do you wish an interview? Perhaps later on, not now. In my present condition I cannot write anything. But there is another consideration. . . . Nobody of us can write prefaces to this book. It is independent. And it is impossible to write a preface for a book where there is the false affirmation about the Sowjetgranaten [an allusion to my story about shipments of Soviet munitions to Germany]. In many places, you referred, in answer to some objection of mine, to other sources, also non-Russian sources. Ergo, the book is independent." There followed more new material, and then this postscript, "Have you utilized Trotzky's *Mein Leben* [Trotzky's autobiography]?"

I replied that I knew my facts about the Soviet munitions were correct, but if he wanted to deny them officially I would print the denial. I said I thought he could write an introduction to an independent interpretation of Soviet foreign policy. He refused. February 9, 1930: "We cannot indorse in the form of a preface standpoints of yours differing from ours. Or else the book should have been another one." And again corrections and more information. He intimated, too, that he would be interested in seeing the proofs of the book. I had already read and returned the bulk of them, but I promised to show him the remainder.

Apparently seeing the thing in actual print stirred Chicherin more than my typescript. Or was it his situation in Moscow? In any case, he began to hit harder. With reference to my interpretation of Soviet Russia's collaboration with King Amanullah of Afghanistan, Chicherin, always the romantic in Eastern affairs, wrote me, "Page 793, lines 27-31, is *politically* on the wrong track. Our aid was *politically* impossible. Our adversaries spread the rumor that a red army detachment was on the way to Kabul. Teheran was immediately on its feet in utmost wrath. Soviet soldiers in Kabul!!! Immediately we assured

Persia it was untrue. Russian soldiers or artillery in Kabul would have meant war with England: so near India!! If in 1885 peace hung on a thread because Russian soldiers appeared to be going south of Kushk on the road to Herat [Afghanistan], what would have taken place in England after Russian soldiers had appeared near the Khyber Pass!! England operated against Amanullah with mullahs and feudals; we had no such elements at our disposal. There is no Thaelmann in Afghanistan." Thaelmann was the German Communist leader.

In another letter, he said, "I spell Tchitcherin, the Britishers spell Chicherin."

A letter from Chicherin, dated February 14, 1930, contained a little bombshell and revealed his political position and the reason for his dismissal. In my concluding chapter I had said: "Moscow's policy in 1930 was more radical than at any time since 1924, and while fluctuations and zigzags are not excluded, the regime promises to retain its present anti-capitalist, anti-imperialist, and proletarian character." Then I sketched the Five Year Plan and the Kremlin's hope to improve conditions. Chicherin commented, "You speak like a Stalinist: your book, your responsibility." That did not mean that he was a Trotzkyist. He simply anticipated sharper departures from the policy of 1930 than I had thought conceivable.

To this letter Chicherin appended a postscript about Soviet government relations with the Third International. "It is quite wrong," it read, "to leave unexplained the difference between the Komintern and the Soviet government. Our Politbureau is not the dictator of the Komintern. The fact that our party is stronger and richer than the others is also the reason for much *opposition* among the fraternal parties against ours. . . . The Soviet government joined the Kellogg pact, and the Komintern opposed the Kellogg pact: complete difference." In later years this difference, whether complete or not, was completely wiped out.

In August, 1930, I sent Chicherin the printed volumes of *The Soviets in World Affairs* with a sincere but, I felt, inadequate inscription of gratitude. This evoked a terrible letter from him. "I am in the greatest possible despair," he wrote. "I am near to suicide owing to your blow." And he asked me "to repair the immense harm you have unjustly done to me." I was thunderstruck and mortified, for he was ill and had certainly deserved well of me. This explosion of Chicherin's anger was touched off by my treatment of Allied intervention in North Russia in 1918. I had written, "The Bolsheviks, harried as they were, could scarcely prevent an Entente landing in the North. Chicherin therefore made it clear to the ambassadors that while the Bolsheviks objected to intervention, they would resist foreign landings only in case they were directed against the Communist government," but not if "they moved inland in the direction of Finland against the German forces there." Chicherin had told me this himself. But he now cried, "Your exposal is absolutely false, it puts me down as a traitor." Further: "You represent me as having favored the entente landings, provided they would have declared their aim at the Germans. I would have been the greatest traitor and the greatest idiot if I had done so."

But I had not said he "favored" them. I said the Bolsheviks could not stop them and so he tried to divert them away from Communist territory and against the Germans. Even in the cool objectivity of the present day, I do not think I did Chicherin an injustice or pictured him as supporting foreign governments' attacks on his own country. Nevertheless, I apologized and sought to mollify him. He would not be comforted, and wrote me long, sad letters. He feared that "the thing can make a noise already now abroad and in our ruling circles, so that an explanation can very soon become inevitable. This misfortune outweighs for me everything else." At this point he opened his heart, and out of it welled forth all his physical suffering, his mystic passion for music, and his concern for posterity's verdict. "In general," he wrote me in a long letter, "my condition is much worse than a collapse. In the morning at 8½ or 9 A.M. I am a little fresher, I read the papers and speak to the secretaries, Korotkin or Nikolayev, then after 1½-2 hours (at 10½ or 11) begins the great Qualzustand [torment]. I am lying down immovably, boundless feebleness, not so much sleeping but principally half-dozing, partially hallucinating, subdelirante Zustaende [sub-delirious condition]; pain in everything; with the greatest difficulty I rise for dinner and supper and eat almost nothing. About 9 or 10 or 11 P.M. the period of pause comes, some little renewed vitality for several hours, when I read papers, write letters, attend to the small practical matters of existence. During this period of interlude I looked into your book (very insufficiently) and am now writing this letter. During this period I also play Mozart, the best thing I have had and have in life, my ideal of beauty, the incarnation of cosmic universe-feeling and of fiery real life, of human psychology and of immensity without shores, true nectar and ambrosia filling with complete satisfaction. In these few hours

I play and read and write and eat. But it is for a short time always. So it is not only delicate health, it is immensely worse—when and how the conclusion comes—is unknown. But I will not go down to posterity as having encouraged entente landings, which is completely untrue. Unfortunately the one paragraph in cause gives this wrong impression."

He continued to write to me on this and other subjects. In one letter he declared, "I am and always have been an absolutely undiluted, unmixed, unwavering, unswerving enemy of our joining the League of Nations."

September 30, 1930, he broke off a many-page letter with the remark, "I am obliged to stop, because my pain becomes again stronger."

He had expected a "scandal" from what I had written about the Entente landings in northern Russia. Russians are terrified by a "scandal." But no critic or reviewer, or anti-Bolshevik or Bolshevik leader, noticed anything unusual or wrong or derogatory in what I had said about Chicherin's attitude, and so Chicherin took a quieter view, and his last letters to me were again friendly, personal, and warm.

I never visited Chicherin again. He received only his doctors and Karakhan and Korotkin. Karakhan told me that Chicherin frequently praised my book. Occasionally, I would see Chicherin walking on Arbat Street, Moscow, and I would stop and gaze at him from a discreet distance full of somber thoughts. He wore dark glasses, carried a cane, seemed shorter and much much older, and usually held under his arm a bundle of old books bought from an antiquarian. He always read a great deal and even in these final years he spent all the foreign currency the government allowed him on the latest books of English, French, and German literature. His misery dragged on. He died on July 7, 1936, long after he had expected the end, and the torture of those years was written on every feature of his head and hands as he lay in his coffin. Men who had worked with him cried, but no important Soviet leader came to the funeral, the press gave little notice to his death, and Assistant Commissar of Foreign Affairs Krestinsky who spoke at the services paid a halting tribute and mixed it with criticism. It was the saddest kind of end.

In 1928 in Berlin, Alex Gumberg, a remarkable American who died in 1939, said to me, "I had lunch today with a dictator, a foreign minister, and an ambassador." The only foreign minister in Berlin that day was Chicherin. I guessed he would be accompanied by Ambassador Krestinsky; but I could not guess the name of the dictator. "Parker Gilbert," Alex said. One of Alex's functions in the world was to bring different worlds together whether it was on Unter den Linden or Fifth Avenue, and in this case he helped establish a contact between official Moscow and the American who held the threads of German economic life in his right hand. I interviewed Parker Gilbert several times. This tall, modest man possessed incisiveness and penetration and an amazingly detailed knowledge of affairs. He usually kept to the subject of reparations when we talked, but sometimes the conversations ranged to Russia and America. He believed the Bolsheviks were making a mistake in industrializing so quickly. They ought, he felt, to export more grain and import more consumers' goods.

Parker Gilbert favored American recognition of Soviet Russia. He expected that if Hoover were elected and if he appointed Dwight Morrow Secretary of State a settlement on debts and other matters could soon be reached between Moscow and Washington. "Morrow or Owen D. Young," he stated, "could soon solve the problems. But a lot of people in the State Department have little minds and lack vision." Amen.

"Hoover," Gilbert said, "is Mr. Fix-It!" He had discussed Russia at length with Hoover. Hoover had great faith in the Slavs and felt Russia and America had a big common future. "But he is Mr. Fix-It," Gilbert repeated, "and he likes to settle matters according to his own formula and get the credit and praise for it. Morrow, on the other hand, would efface himself even when every bit of the solution was his own. That's the way he acted down in Mexico." As to Calvin Coolidge: "He is a small man but his brain is not so small."

In Berlin I also paid visits to high officials of the German Foreign Office like Mr. Gaus, the chief treaty writer, Mr. von Dirksen, later ambassador to Moscow, Mr. Schlesinger, and Mr. von Buelow. I sat at the feet of Chancellor Luther and Foreign Minister Stresemann at the regular Foreign Office press teas. Once Count Brockdorff-Rantzau came in to such a tea. He was red and nervous and he sat down beside me and hastily gulped a cognac. A little while later Stresemann arrived. Rantzau said, "I just had a stormy session with him." Rantzau had offered to resign from the Moscow Embassy and Rantzau was a man of great influence, especially with President Hindenburg. Rantzau objected to the Locarno pacts and to Germany's impending entrance into the League of Nations. So did Chicherin, and Rantzau and Chicherin saw eye to eye on these matters. They believed in Soviet-German collaboration. Rantzau feared that Germany would turn away from Russia and barter Russian friendship for chimerical Allied favors. Stresemann reassured him and Chicherin later admitted to me that his own apprehensions were unfounded. Germany's policy did not become pro-Ally or anti-Russia. The man who foresaw this was Stalin. Where Chicherin stormed against Germany's entrance into the League in 1926, Stalin saw its advantages for Russia. Moscow, Stalin said, would now have a friend in the councils of the great powers, and it is a fact that in 1927 when Sir Austen Chamberlain urged a European bloc against Russia, Stresemann torpedoed the scheme. Chicherin told me about Stalin's prevision in Wiesbaden and I inserted it in my manuscript. This alarmed Chicherin. He had told it to me in secret. He wrote a letter to me to Philadelphia saying, "It is quite impossible to name the person who favored Germany's entrance into the League, it would be a scandal." Always the fear of "scandal"! That was September 30, 1929. On October 9, 1929, he again asked me by letter not to mention Stalin's name. On October 20, again. On October 31, a fourth time. I had to delete Stalin's name. Now I can mention it.

In Berlin, too, I talked at length with De Witt Clinton Poole of the United States Embassy about the early revolutionary days when he was consul in Moscow. He suggested that I see Bruce Lockhart, who was British envoy in Moscow at the same time; he gave me a letter of introduction.

R. H. Bruce Lockhart, author of *British Agent*, tells his own story in that book. When I met him in London he did not seem the figure of romance that rose from his pages. He rather appeared the typical Englishman. But flair for romance often invites romance, and the maiden of the South Sea Isles and Mura of Moscow were undoubtedly not ladies of his dreams only. I have met Mura in Berlin and Paris. She is the Countess Budberg, and how she got to Moscow and Lockhart the archives may some day reveal. Subsequently she lived with Maxim Gorky at Capri, and still later with H. G. Wells. She is a highly intelligent woman.

Lockhart took me to his London flat and read to me from his old Moscow diary. He quoted Colonel Raymond Robins of the American Red Cross in Russia, as saying that "Trotzky was the greatest

Jew since Jesus." On March 26, 1918, Lockhart had an audience with
Lenin. The Germans threatened to conquer Soviet Russia and Lenin
asked the Briton for British military assistance. But the British, Lenin
predicted, would not give it. "Your ways are not our ways and our
ways are not yours." Lockhart was getting depressing wires from his
London superiors. They had no sympathy for the Bolsheviks. Lockhart himself would have helped the Russians in order to hamper Germany on the western front. The London geniuses, however, were
moved by their social prejudices, and they refused to assist Communists even if that meant assisting themselves.

When United States Ambassador Francis came to Moscow, Lockhart wrote in his diary, "Francis doesn't know a Left Social Revolutionary from a potato." Francis was a provincial who got his ambas-
sadorial appointment on the strength of a large campaign contribution to his political party. He played poker well.

As the writing of *The Soviets in World Affairs* drew to a close I
began to think of photographs. I first went to Chicherin who had a
mania for photographs. He liked to be photographed, preferably in
costume, and usually kept numerous copies of his own and other
people's pictures. Korotkin, Chicherin's faithful personal secretary,
allowed me to search Chicherin's file of photographs. I did it in
Korotkin's presence, and he had stories to tell about many of the
snapshots. With his permission, I took one showing Chicherin in an
ornate Mongolian costume. The paunchy commissar was enveloped
in a rich silk Mongol kaftan. On his head stood a high-crowned
turban which ended in a commanding peak, and around his waist he
had buckled a jeweled sword. He looked like one of his ancient Tatar
forbears. Korotkin recounted that several years before, an official
delegation from the Outer Mongolian republic which rested under
Moscow's protecting wing arrived in Moscow to negotiate with the
Soviet government. Its first act was to be a formal visit to Chicherin.
But five days passed and they made no request for an audience. When
the interview finally took place, Chicherin had decked himself out in
the colorful Mongol regalia shown in the photograph, but the Mon-
gols appeared in the coarse three-piece European street suits which
a Moscow tailor had hurriedly made to their order. Moscow to them
was the West.

In Chicherin's archives I also found a photograph of Karakhan
playing tennis doubles in the Crimea. Karakhan's doubles partner was

King Amanullah of Afghanistan. "No," said Korotkin, "I can't give you that. A Bolshevik leader playing with a king! How would that look? Besides, Amanullah has been overthrown and is now in European exile and our government maintains cordial relations with the monarch who ousted him. I am afraid it will get Karakhan into all sorts of political trouble."

But it was a marvelous photograph for just those reasons, and I wanted it. So I walked into Chicherin's office and repeated Korotkin's arguments and requested him to overrule them. Chicherin replied, "This is a matter for Karakhan to decide. He knows the political implications best." I went upstairs to see Karakhan. I reminded him of the photograph with Amanullah and explained that Korotkin objected to publication on several grounds of policy.

"You bring me the photograph," Karakhan replied. "If I am holding the racquet correctly you can use it." His grip was right, and the highly unusual photograph appeared in the book.

Maxim Litvinov gave me the original credential signed by "V. Oulianoff (Lenin)" appointing him Ambassador to the United States in June, 1918. On receipt of this document in London, Litvinov applied for an American visa and was refused. He nevertheless prided himself on the Lenin autograph and made me promise faithfully to return the paper immediately I had a facsimile.

Markoosha gave me a group photograph of the Soviet delegation to the Genoa Conference. She herself was on it, as Chicherin's secretary, and also Eliena Krylenko, Litvinov's private secretary, Bronya Shmoish, later Krestinsky's private secretary, as well as a galaxy of Soviet diplomats, including Chicherin, looking like a young priest, Litvinov, Krassin, Boris Stein, later Soviet Ambassador to Italy, Jan Rudzutak, fated to be a member of the Politbureau and executed in the purge, Vorovsky, shot in Switzerland by a reactionary Russian, Sapronov, an Opposition leader, also purged, Preobrazhensky, also purged, and many others.

For the frontispiece of the first volume I used a photograph of Trotzky at the front. He is seen before his famous railroad car giving instructions to an aide-de-camp dressed in leather from heel to neck who does not stand to attention. Trotzky—with his boots, greatcoat, woolen helmet decorated with a five-pointed Soviet star, revolver, pince-nez, and black mustache—looks the intellectual Mars.

For the frontispiece of Volume Two I used a pen drawing of Stalin. It makes him look crafty, sly, and oriental. Soviet friends first thought it a caricature, but I had the perfect reply; it was the cover of a book I bought in Soviet Baku.

I was very proud of the job I had done on *The Soviets in World Affairs*, and when Litvinov once said to me, "I keep your book on my desk for reference," I felt I had been rewarded for a lot of hard work. The book was translated into French and published in Paris. A German firm translated it and paid me advance royalties, but Hitler came to power before the printing commenced. The Soviet publishing house Litizdat also contracted for its publication, and gave me a sizable advance payment in rubles. Markoosha translated it into Russian. Radek agreed with enthusiasm to write an introduction. He actually wrote it and I have a copy. But printing was delayed many months. Radek twice mislaid the manuscript. Finally, he told me he could not sponsor such a book on his own responsibility. He did not wish to court danger. He would have to ask Stalin whether the translation could be published. Later he told me he had asked Stalin and Stalin said no. The reason is not far to seek; John Reed's *Ten Days That Shook the World* is prohibited in Soviet Russia, although it had sold hundreds of thousands of copies and although Lenin wrote an introduction to it saying, "Unreservedly do I recommend it to the workers of the world." It is suppressed because Reed told the truth about Trotzky's historic activities in those ten days and ignored Stalin's minor role. My book also cleaved to the record and did not accept the legend beginning to be current in the late twenties that, besides Lenin, there was only Stalin, while Trotzky moved somewhere far in the rear fishing in turbulent counter-revolutionary waters.

8. *Life with Foreign Correspondents*

LIFE would have been pretty dreadful if it had consisted exclusively of work and talks with diplomats. I believe in regular surrenders to laziness, and it is a favorite theory of mine that man spends too much time in a perpendicular position. In Moscow, Berlin, Paris, London, and New York I loafed, played tennis, met journalists, family, relatives, and friends and played poker with passion. Once in Berlin I participated in a correspondents' all-night poker game in which I won one hundred and twenty-five dollars. It seemed like a million in those days. The next morning I bought my wife a fall coat and twenty-four hours later I was flying to Moscow. Usually, however, I lost at poker.

Journalists always talk shop because their shop is the whole world. The stars of the writing firmament crossed and recrossed Europe in those years. The *Chicago Daily News* sent to Moscow men who would become famous. Negley Farson succeeded Junius Wood, one of the most fantastic figures in American journalism. Junius, gray-haired, ruddy-faced, smiling, and looking as though he had just arrived from Nebraska's farms or Kentucky's hills, was a peripatetic encyclopedia and a doubting Thomas. He smoked Mahorka, a cheap, pungent variety of Russian tobacco, in corncob pipes, of which he had about thirty, fixed his own vodka with lemon peel, and conducted a long polemic with the Soviet Postmaster General about the size of the Soviet Union. The postmaster claimed his country covered one-sixth of the dry surface of the globe and Junius contended that it was only one-seventh. Nobody won, but Junius kept us all amused with details of the controversy. Once Chicherin's secretary phoned the correspondents and asked them to come for an interview with the commissar that evening. When the correspondents arrived the elevator man handed each one a mimeographed copy of a statement by Chicherin. Junius wired his story somewhat in this fashion, "The elevator boy of the Soviet Foreign Office today gave me an interview on Bolshevik foreign policy. . . ."

Negley Farson has told of his Moscow stay in his bestselling autobiography; he was considered a "transgressor" even by his not too puritanical colleagues.

John Gunther came next in line for the Chicago paper. Big and made bigger by baggy suits, jovial, friendly, he was good company. He was writing a novel in those days, and he did not yet realize the public would prefer books psychoanalyzing continents to novels psychoanalyzing individuals in love.

The dean of the Moscow journalists' corps, Walter Duranty, one evening in 1927, invited Rayna Prohme, Dorothy Thompson, James Vincent Sheean, and me to dinner. Rayna, a girl from Chicago, had edited the Hankow *People's Tribune* before the Nationalist collapse in China, and Sheean wrote intelligently on China for *Asia*. Duranty and Dorothy did most of the talking. Jimmy Sheean busied himself looking for alleged mistakes in my *Oil Imperialism* and underscoring them for Rayna's benefit. At one point Jimmy left the room and when he came back he said, "Charming cook you have, Duranty."

"You leave that cook alone," Duranty snapped, smiling to soften the asperity of the reply. Katya was charming indeed, and she later became the mother of Michael Duranty, a lovely Anglo-Russian entente with noble features.

Duranty likes to talk, especially about wars (he was at the front in the first World War), blood, and women, and he does it extremely well. Dorothy was not yet the famed Dorothy Thompson, and she listened. I first met Dorothy in Berlin in 1924 through the Grossmans, mutual Jewish friends. Later we used to see one another at the Friday teas in the German Foreign Office and, rarely, in cafés by appointment. She was good-looking and well dressed. She was unhappy in those years, and unhappiness can make a person more attractive because less arrogant. But Dorothy, if hard and cold, is courageous and intelligent.

About a week after our dinner, Duranty invited the American colony to his apartment to meet Sinclair Lewis. The early part of the evening Lewis discoursed in endless periods. I believe he recited a piece that went into *The Man Who Knew Coolidge*. After a while, however, he lay down on the broad couch in Duranty's living room and fell asleep. Dorothy covered him with a rug. The guests trooped in and Lewis slept. Nobody dared wake him. Hours passed and still he slept. The guests started going home. When I left at midnight Lewis was still snoring. Everybody was impressed. A lesser person would not have been so brave.

Duranty was dean of correspondents by reason of his long experience but also because of his brilliant pen and social grace. Duranty is a bundle of paradoxes. He is a cynic yet a romantic. He sees the drama in politics but detests the theater and rarely attends a performance of the opera or ballet. This Englishman who for years was America's outstanding foreign correspondent does not really care what happens to the world. His interest in politics stems from his love of spectacles—and what bigger spectacle is there? "King of reporters," as Bernard Shaw called Duranty, his ambition, nevertheless, is to write fiction. Whereas the French journalist hoped to graduate into politics the American journalist's goal was usually Hollywood, Broadway, or a literary career. With H. R. Knickerbocker of the International News Service, Duranty wrote several short stories, and one of his own earned one of the annual O. Henry prizes. He never knew Russia thoroughly, and the theory and economics of the Stalin-Trotzky affair bored him. He understood Soviet politics, however, through an uncanny faculty of distilling a situation out of the political atmosphere, and at times he sensed the trend of events without possessing any concrete data. He broke many a lance for Stalin yet he is the mild Cambridge don with a love for good literature and for curdling detective stories.

Duranty played much bridge, and poker if the stakes were high enough. He also entertained much. To him came foreigners of all nationalities and even a few Russians. Among the foreigners, during this period, were the Chens.

The four Chen children stirred Moscow's curiosity. They were born in Trinidad, British West Indies, where their rich Chinese grandfather owned cocoanut plantations. They received their education, such as it was, in private schools in England, and visited China for the first time in 1926, to bask in the brief sun of their father, Foreign Minister Eugene Chen. Their language was English with an English accent, and the moment they learned a few words of mispronounced Russian their Russian vocabulary was larger than their Chinese. Percy, the eldest son, joined a Russian Red Army officers' training academy, then took up journalism, later sold automobiles; he did not inspire confidence. Jack is serious and has gifts as a cartoonist. Yolanda studied cinematography under Eisenstein, and married a Soviet film producer. Sylvia made the greatest hit. The blood of French Napoleonic generals and West Indian Negroes coursed in her mother's veins, and Sylvia's dancing combines the delicate brush lines of the body-shy Chinese with the wild rhythm of the jungle. Her skin is darker than Chinese yellow and lighter than Negro brown, and the slit of her eyes is just sufficiently Chinese to be intriguing. She moves with exquisite grace and merely to see her walk is pleasurable. In Moscow she at first danced the Charleston and jazz to Moscow's delight, and the big Opera House went wild when she did her Spanish fan dance. Before long, however, the Communist bug bit her. That might have been all right had it stayed in her head, but it went to her legs, and she took to dancing Marxism. The Moscow public frowned. For an interpretation of the theory of surplus values one does not go to Terpsichore.

Shortly after I met Rayna Prohme I left for a trip to the Crimea and the Ukraine. She asked me to let her use my room while I was away, and I did. Rayna occupied it for three days, and then the landlady, whose Nepman husband was in prison, put her out; she didn't like women. A week after I returned to the capital Rayna fell sick. She fainted while visiting some friends in the Europa Hotel. Officially they said she had the grippe, but Dr. Link, the physician of the German Embassy, tested her vision by holding matches before her eyes and knew otherwise. The curtains of her room in the Hotel Metropole were closely drawn all day and in the evening electric bulbs were shaded. But she discussed China problems with a startling insight and planned to write a book with Borodin. I dropped in every afternoon for a chat. There was a strange fascination in her. She owned a tremendous head of tousled red hair and intelligent eyes; one felt that she was the kind of woman who belonged to no one, not even to herself, but to social movements. She asked me numerous questions about Russian conditions and Bolshevik theory, and she was obviously thinking of joining the Communist Party.

Jimmy Sheean was very perturbed by Rayna's health. One evening, after a week of her illness, the Veps, a Russian couple who had known her in Hankow and who were now sleeping on the floor of her room and nursing her, telephoned and asked Jimmy to come over immediately. I was with him and we went over together. They told us that Rayna had asked for Jimmy but was again unconscious and had lost control of her bodily functions. For some reason the meaning of unconsciousness did not register in me and I sat down on her bed, took her head in my hands, and tried to wake her. She was pale and cold, and did not wake.

The next day I went to the Metropole Hotel early and the elevator boy said to me, "She's dead."

The job now was to take care of Jimmy; William C. White, who had turned journalist after studying law in Moscow, and I undertook it. The procedure consisted in filling Jimmy with vodka so he could sleep; but Jimmy has an endless capacity for alcohol. Neither White nor I drank, and so we would talk for hours while Jimmy emptied one carafe after another. After imbibing what would have put any normal human being under the table, Jimmy was still wide-awake and uncomforted.

Jimmy was tortured by the idea that she never knew he loved her. I tried to convince him that a woman always knows. "Besides," I said, "you remember when you and Rayna strode arm-in-arm across the Red Square on November 7? I had not seen her since my return from the south and I yelled to her, 'Are you happy,' and she yelled back, 'Yes.' Why was she happy?" I asked Jimmy.

On the afternoon of the funeral, Rayna's friends met at the second Moscow University. Madame Sun Yat-sen, Eugene Chen and the Chen quartet, other Chinese, Russians, but not Borodin, and at least one hundred Americans, including Dorothy Thompson, were there. The coffin, covered with red cloth, was placed on a cart drawn by a horse. In front was a military band that played quiet revolutionary tunes and Chopin's and Beethoven's funeral marches, then the catafalque, then the mourners. Men removed their caps as the cart passed. One Russian workingman asked Bruce Hopper (now teaching at Harvard) whether "the deceased was ours"—meaning whether he or she had been for the workers—and when Bruce answered "yes" the Russian joined our ranks.

I had not cried since I was a boy of fifteen, but now I broke down and wept. When the procession arrived at the crematorium, darkness had set in. The Moscow crematorium has an all-white interior with high vaulted ceiling and looks like a streamlined cathedral. The coffin had been opened to reveal Rayna's face surrounded by flowers. It rested on a slightly raised platform.

We took seats and listened to speeches. Jimmy sat slouched down in his chair, his overcoat collar up, and his head pulled down into his coat so that only his hair was visible. He cried all the time, and so did many others. Anna Louise Strong, the American journalist, this time rose to a great emotional height—as she did in some of her stories like "Head High in the Wind"—and moved herself and us with a few sincere sentences. She called Rayna "China's John Reed," "a second American contribution to world emancipation," "a soldier for freedom."

All now assembled around the open bier, and slowly, almost imperceptibly, it began sinking into the cremating furnace. This was an awful moment. It seemed much more irrevocable than interment in an earthen grave, and I think I saw Jimmy sway forward as though to hold Rayna back.

Jimmy could not remain in Moscow after that, and he moved heaven and earth—in this case, the Soviet Foreign Office, the Moscow Soviet, and the various foreign consulates—to get out and go abroad early the next morning. He has never gone back to Russia since. He wrote Rayna's story in *Personal History*, a book which has become the cultural Baedeker of a generation of Americans.

The episode of Rayna's death has attached me, forever apparently, to Vincent Sheean. I rarely see him, and we are very different persons, but I remain deeply fond of him always.

Several weeks after Rayna's death, Bill Prohme arrived in Moscow. Anna Louise Strong had telegraphed him in Manila and promised him that all Rayna's papers and effects would be taken care of. She likewise advised him against risking the long trip from the warm Philippines across the murderously cold Siberia of winter to below-zero Moscow. Bill Prohme was a consumptive. But although he knew he would arrive long after the funeral, he came nevertheless. And then he did this: he saw every play and cinema and opera that Rayna had seen, he talked to all the people she had talked to, and he visited every place she had visited. He even wanted to go to the room I had loaned Rayna for three days and where I no longer lived.

It seems to me that two kinds of women move men to great love: women who give very much and women who give nothing as women. I imagine Rayna was the second kind. But that was not all; she was an extraordinary human being with a spark that is rare, and people close to her felt its magnetism.

Maurice Hindus came frequently to Moscow and wrote some excellent books. He could never bear Moscow for more than a week or so, and soon he would sling his shoes over his shoulder like the Russian peasant—the peasant did it to save his shoes but Maurice to save his feet—and tour the countryside. He is simple and loves simple people. He is a farmer and loves the soil. Hindus has a tremendous capac-

ity for warmth and affection. He participates in the suffering and
joys of others; and he frequently empties his purse to friends. He was
born in a Russian village and appreciated what the Bolsheviks were
doing to lift the villages out of the Czarist mire. Doubts frequently
tormented him, as they did all of us, but when they tormented him
he was disconsolate and grim and yearned either for frivolity or, more
frequently, for a soul-interview with a kindred spirit. In Markoosha
he occasionally found that kinship. They would take down their souls
and have a wonderful time. He understands emotions and ignores economics. He despised Communist terminology and Marxist logic and
admired the Soviets only for what they did to uproot and give new
life to humanity. Hindus is humble, and honestly avows his limitations,
accepting assistance when he needs it. He is an American lecture audience's ideal: dramatic, passionate, personal, romantic-looking, and
not too high-brow.

Eugene Lyons, Moscow correspondent of the United Press, lived
on a social island to which a certain type of Soviet citizen rowed over
from the Soviet mainland in search of the warmth and light that come
with good food, dancing, and pleasant hosts. On the mainland, real
life evaded those citizens and Lyons. He rarely if ever visited Soviet
factories which were social, political, and cultural centers as well as
production units, and when he visited a village it usually was to buy
antique furniture. He had a real grievance; he had expected the Bolsheviks to open their arms and homes to him, for he had been a radical in New York. But when they treated him as they did all other
non-Soviet foreigners he was quite disappointed, and that colored his
thinking and ultimately changed his views. Nobody who depends on
society life can be very happy in Moscow. Lyons writes well and has
an irritability which can be mistaken for moral indignation. But he
makes no pretense to profundity, and when he enjoyed the rare privilege of an exclusive interview with Stalin he talked about his little
daughter Jeanie and he let Stalin talk about his little daughter Svet-
lana, and he never put a single serious question to Stalin. Lyons admitted this later and kicked himself for it.

In Berlin, I often met Guido Enderis of the *New York Times*, a
German from Milwaukee who wore suits of big vivid checks and
liked to bet hundreds of marks on two deuces; Edgar A. Mowrer,
brother of Paul and uncle of Richard, who wandered amid mystic
ideas until Hitler made him a fiery, effective anti-Fascist; H. R.
Knickerbocker, whose books were bestsellers in Europe but scarcely

stirred a royalty ripple in the U. S. A.; and the United Press man, Frederick R. Kuh, my closest friend, whose contacts were better than those of any other correspondent. I often marveled at the way Kuh would telephone a member of the German cabinet or ambassador and inquire about the newest sensation.

Discussing German politics with Berlin colleagues I often said, "Whenever President Hindenburg puts on a top hat and striped pants and goes around the corner to dedicate a building or open a door, that's news for you. But a few million unemployed, the intrigues of East Prussian landlords, and the gangsterism of the Nazis doesn't even deserve a 'short.' " One of them countered wisely that readers and editors wanted dispatches on subjects already known. Just as an audience applauds most the arias and symphonies it has often heard, so the public asks news about people and situations with which it is acquainted. The popular British press meets this attitude by making their correspondents news. Thus the *Daily Express* announces that Sefton Delmer, its veteran news ace, has arrived in Prague, and thereafter it is Delmer's doings that are of interest and only incidentally his coverage of the Czechoslovak crisis. By writing news the journalist becomes news. It is not so stupid, either. I often go to a paper to read Edgar Mowrer's or Helen Kirkpatrick's or Stoneman's or Leland Stowe's reactions to events because I know them and can sometimes judge the events by their reactions.

While writing *The Soviets in World Affairs*, I continued to contribute to newspapers and magazines for I had no other source of income. With the exception of teaching school in Philadelphia for half a year in 1917 and work in a New York news agency in 1920, I have never held a job and I have always tried hard not to get one. Once when I weakened for a brief moment and thought of applying to the *New York World*, Markoosha warned me off. She always supported herself and the children while I free-lanced, and it was not till 1929 when by doing just what I wanted I earned more than I needed for myself that I accepted partial financial responsibility for the family. Markoosha made some money by translations. I never owned any property—beyond a typewriter and now a steel filing cabinet—or any stocks or bonds. I have never held any insurance of any kind. I have never been a member of any political party or of a trade union or, after my youth, of any club. I am essentially a libertarian and resent shackles, even personal ones. I can impose discipline upon myself but I would fight its imposition on me by others. This applies especially to intellectual discipline. For me the question of joining the Communist party never arose because I would not allow another person to tell me what to write or what to think.

I nevertheless sympathized strongly with the Soviet regime out of a conviction that, despite all the repression, it had brought a new freedom to workingmen, peasants, women, youth, and national minorities, and that, in time, the dictatorship would yield to a democracy which would be real and better. That was my big mistake. I will discuss this later.

To supplement literary earnings I lectured in the United States each year. I spoke on Russia, on American relations with Russia, and also on general European conditions. In 1927, my subject was "The Eclipse of Europe." It is interesting to look back at records. I find that Philip A. Adler of the *Detroit News* interviewed me that year and wrote, "Another European war and then the complete eclipse of Europe as the leader in the world's civilization was predicted by Louis Fischer. . . ." And: "He took exception to the optimistic reports of Europe's economic and political status brought by prominent Americans. Fischer could point no way out of the difficulty. 'One thing is certain,' he declared. 'While the nations of the world are talking disarmament they are all engaged in a mad race of armaments. All are preparing for the next war.'" In a New York lecture that same year, I asserted, according to a notice in the *Times*, that "Europe is falling into a flabby state of decrepitude. It is like an old man who has been in a fight and cannot regain his breath, and the younger people seize his wealth, influence and power. Europe has no goal." That was in the days when America was being blamed for all of Europe's ills— "Uncle Sam Shylock," the European papers said; and Oswald Garrison Villard editorialized in *The Nation* about an Anglo-American war. So when F. P. A. saw the *Times* account he wrote in his "Conning Tower" the next day, "Back from a trip abroad, Louis Fischer says that Europe has no goal. It probably will be charged against America that we stole the goalposts."

Europe was descending fast into the abyss of crisis and war, and on account of our own troubles and prejudices we did not try to do enough to save it.

Part Two

World Crisis and World War
1930 to 1940

9. *The Peaceful Death of a Democracy*

HOW did Hitler come to power in Germany? Hitler's policy, at home and abroad, has always been to reveal his plans. Hyper-suspicion of propaganda, however, led many people to doubt what he said. The Nazis boasted that they would rule Germany, and Hitler painted a picture of his future game. "Heads will roll," he said. He would destroy democracy. Yet democracy tolerated him and helped him take office in order to destroy democracy. This peaceful death of German democracy is one of the strangest chapters in history, and it is of special interest because the suicidal propensities of democracy are not uniquely German. German democracy marched to its grave with eyes wide open, and singing, "Beware of Adolf Hitler."

Soviet Russia pays a high price for its one-party system. Republican Germany paid a heavy price for its many-party system. The abuses of proportional representation allowed small groups of voters, representing small regional or economic interests, to send parliamentarians to the Reichstag. And since the existence of German cabinets was sometimes a matter of a few parliamentary votes, these parties could individually or in combination overthrow a ministry or blackmail it by threatening overthrow. When minorities frustrate the majority, faith in majority rule is shattered and the road is clear for dictatorship.

This was one difficulty. But greater difficulties harassed German democracy. Democracy is temperate. Its foe is extremism. In Germany, extremism was the thermometer of a sick social system and an ailing economy. The two extremes in Germany were the communists and the Hitlerian National Socialists—the Nazis. Both fought democracy and urged dictatorships.

The voting strength of the Communists and Nazis rose and fell with bad business and unrest. In the elections of May, 1924, the Nazis won thirty-two seats in the Reichstag. But in December, 1924, the domestic calm following the adoption of the Dawes reparations plan reduced the Nazis to fourteen. In May, 1928, they had only twelve.

The Communists had sixty-three Reichstag deputies in May, 1924, but only forty-six in December, 1924, and fifty-four in May, 1928. Came the 1929 economic crisis. On September 14, 1930, the Nazis went up to one hundred and seven seats, the Communists to seventy-six. These polls were the temperature of the patient, Democracy.

What shook and finally upset the German Republic was the struggle for stability. The German craved stability because he liked it and lacked it. More than most people the German enjoys discipline. He prefers the calculable. I was in a Berlin barber shop one day and heard the barber ask a square-headed Prussian customer how he wanted his hair cut. "Make it two millimeters in the back and four in the front," the Prussian replied. Meticulousness is congenial to the German. President Hindenburg was shaved every day for forty years by the same barber who came each morning at the same minute, stayed the same lenth of time each day and departed at the same tick of the clock. Germany is a country of straight lines. I have flown over it many times. The scene from the plane is usually one of geometric forms. Nature is occasionally permitted to add soft curves. Every patch is carefully tilled, every hedge neatly trimmed. (So different from the rambling English countryside.) German forests and woods look like painfully tended parks. No fence may be nonchalant. Everything wild is tamed by man—except man himself.

I do not believe that one race is inherently good and another inherently bad. But climate, occupations, and economic wealth do help fashion national characteristics. The Egyptian fellah must be different from the Ukrainian muzhik, fisherfolk in Cornwall are unlike California orange growers, and the Prussian farmer acquires a set of psychological reactions that are not those of the tanned, wine-drinking Provence peasant. Political events may even modify physical characteristics; the hardships of the last twenty-five years in Russia have shortened stature, and the tall, straight, oval-faced Russian woman with the alabaster skin and hair demurely parted down the middle is no longer as typical as a shorter, hardier, peasant-like working woman with powerful pelvis, stocky legs, and much bosom. The daily bath, freedom, good food, sports, care, leisure, and better gynecologists have made American women the best-looking in the world.

Life on a given territory does mold national character, and Germans in the between-wars era were nervous, uncertain, and tired, and they yearned more than ever for a strong hand to guide them. In the relatively tranquil years—1925 to 1930—President Hindenburg, dull and stolid, with flat-topped head and very broad shoulders, towering above all men around him, was a symbol of solidity, slow change, and loyalty to the past and the law, and he sufficed as a reassuring, stabilizing force. In the midst of the whirl of cabinets he stood still, the source of authority, the peg that held the whole structure. Behind him were the Reichswehr and the Junker landowners; the industrialists marched in step.

But in 1930 came confusion. The timbers creaked. Little pilots lost their direction and looked for some beacon to help them ride out the storm. Hindenburg was no longer enough, for he backed the Owen D. Young reparations plan and summoned the nation to unity behind the democratic Republic—for which "sins" Hermann Goering, Nazi, viciously attacked him. In time of turmoil, people turn to the parties of despair which aver that they have the only solution and that it lies in new men, new methods, new institutions. This seems logical to those who are suffering from the failure of the old. Mounting difficulties thus proved to be wind in the sails of the Communist and Nazi extremists.

The Nazis had this advantage: the Communists summoned citizens to rise and fight on the barricades against ruling cliques and mighty groups of business magnates. They anticipated bloody civil war, sacrifices, death, and initial chaos and poverty. Hitler, on the other hand, announced blandly that he would perform the task for them. If they believed in him they would be saved. He promised salvation without participation, and cure by faith. He was wise enough to insist that he would attain power by "legal" means. Actually, the Nazis established their regime not by revolution or big pitched battles as in Russia. They were peacefully inducted into office by the last blind abdicating politicians of democracy, and before and after this startling event there was just enough murder and loot to please the sadists and frighten the non-Nazis. Without excessively offending the German love of order, Hitler satisfied the passion which some Germans, along with many others, have for shedding blood, inflicting cruelty, avenging past inferiority, and lording it over the unfortunate ones who do not possess rifles, rubber truncheons and party membership cards.

Hitler's appeal, moreover, was wider than that of the Communists. The Communists looked for adherents chiefly among workingmen. But although they won over some Social Democrats, the solid core of the German proletariat remained Socialist, and not Communist, during the pre-Nazi years. The Communists likewise found friends among the advanced intellectuals. A few pauperized peasants and impoverished small middle-class businessmen also joined.

Hitler, however, appealed to every German. He promised each one something different. He did not care if one promise conflicted with the other. The bigger the lie, he said, the more acceptance it would find. He promised the militarists a large army and conquests. He promised the Nationalists an expanded Germany and a resurrected nation. He promised the spinsters husbands. He promised the capitalists protection against trade unions, and he promised the workingmen whatever he thought workingmen wanted.

To the peasantry Hitler said, "The peasantry is the foundation of the people. The German people can live without towns; they cannot live without peasants." To the workers, Goebbels said, "You are the aristocracy." To the little man who had lost his savings Hitler ranted against the bankers. To bankers, Hitler promised measures against their Jewish competitors. He offered the small storekeeper support against the chain stores and monopolists, but addressing the monopolists he declared that "our big industrialists have worked their way to the top by reason of their efficiency. In virtue of this selection, which merely proves their higher race, they have a right to lead." Hitler, himself a Catholic, cultivated the Catholics, but a Nazi agent in Switzerland, quoted in Heiden's biography of Hitler, told Protestants that Hitler was fighting Catholic domination of Germany. All of them he would rescue from Communism and the wicked peace treaty. From all of them, therefore, and from Jews, Hitler could collect money for his party treasury.

In the contest between the two extremes, the Nazis were bound to win against the Communists. The Commuists had a head start, and in the beginning the triumph of the Soviet Revolution brought them many recruits. But the Nazis quickly took first place after the 1929 slump. The Communists proposed the dictatorship of the proletariat, Hitler the dictatorship of the German. The Communists marched under the banner of Marx; Hitler under the banner of Hitler. The Communists were atheists. Hitler associated God with his political mission. The Communists preached internationalism, which is a higher concept; the Nazis preached nationalism. The Nazis were anti-foreigner, anti-Jew, anti-Versailles; the Communists anti-capitalist. But the majority of Germans were either big or little capitalists or expected to become big or little capitalists. Or they were officials and professional people who identified themselves with the middle class, rather than with the workers.

Germany was not Russia. The German Social Democrats who stood athwart the Communists' path to power were stronger than Russia's moderate socialists. The German owning classes were stronger than the Russian owning classes. The Bolsheviks destroyed big business, but the German "revolution" never tried, and it is possible that it never tried because big business was so much bigger in highly developed Germany than in backward Russia. Moreover, the peasants played a primary role in the Bolshevik Revolution—they hoped to get land—whereas the German farmer would oppose a revolution for fear of losing his land. The broader the distribution of wealth the less likelihood there is of a Communist upheaval.

In an advanced industrialized country with millions of farm-owning families a revolution is impossible until the apparatus of government, the police, and the army have been annihilated in war or through famine or some vast natural catastrophe, and until millions of property owners have lost their property and the hope of regaining it. The German bourgeoisie knew this after 1929. It knew too that without allies the Communists could not have a preponderance of power, and with allies they could not make a revolution, for the allies would be either anti-revolutionary proletarians or non-proletarians.

The Nazis were never needed as a bulwark against a Communist regime; the Communists could not establish their regime. The weakness of the German Communist movement is demonstrated by the fact that it did not lift a finger to prevent the Nazis from taking office in January, 1933, or from consolidating their power in the months that followed.

The Communists did not have arms and were unfriendly to the army and police who had them. The only conceivable Communist weapon was the general strike which, however, depends for success on its being general. But with millions of unemployed, and millions of Social Democrat workingmen sticking to their work because they opposed such a strike and its revolutionary implications, and with the Fascist Nothilfe organization of trained scabs, a Communist strike could not paralyze national life. It could not therefore be the prelude to revolution.

The German Communist party suffered from other impediments. I knew few if any German Communists in the early years. My sympathy for Soviet Russia did not result in any special interest in foreign revolutions. This was probably due to my skepticism about the chances of such revolutions. I always regarded the Bolsheviks as dynamic and creative and the foreign Communists as their pale marionette reflections. I judged the German Communists by their press and deeds and these were execrable. The Berlin *Rote Fahne* was a doctrinaire, sensational newspaper, and Communist dailies in other countries were little better. More serious Communist periodicals had quality, and I always enjoyed R. Palme Dutt's incisive editorials in the London Communist *Labour Monthly*. But nowhere did the Communist movement develop a serious original thinker or leader. No Lenin or Trotzky or Stalin or Bukharin emerged. I believe this is largely attributable to dependence on Moscow, not so much for orders and money but for ideological cues. If Moscow purged its right-wingers the foreign Communist parties launched crusades against their right-wingers, and turned logical somersaults to explain the procedure; if the Soviet Left had aroused Stalin's ire the Communist Left was persecuted in Chile and China. When the Kremlin attacked formalism in Russian literature and art, the French and Greek Communists did likewise in widely different situations. Parrots cannot become leaders.

The German Communist party was purged several times on instructions from Third International headquarters in Moscow. Once when the German Communists obviously wished to get rid of its leader, Ernst Thaelmann, Moscow reinstated him. Subservience took precedence over ability. The close ties and intimate collaboration with Moscow had their uses—the foreign Communists could lean on a functioning revolution for strength and influence. They could say, "Communism is already working in one country." But it hampered the exercise of free will and independent judgment, and the Communists outside Russia never knew what tactic they would follow until those inside told them. In case of disagreement, Moscow's view prevailed, and the foreign Communists either submitted or quit. Many of the best young German intellectuals were at one time members of the Communist party. They joined and left in unending stream. They joined in hope, they left in bitterness.

During some of the most crucial periods in the history of the German Republic, when the fate of Germany absorbed all Germans, the Communists would devote a considerable portion of their energy to "Hands Off Soviet Russia" and "Hands Off China" campaigns while neglecting German problems. On a day when a burning domestic issue riveted German attention, the *Rote Fahne* might appear with a tremendous first-page story about the visit to Constanta of a British cruiser which allegedly but not actually menaced Russia. Working-men became disgusted. Russia had their sympathy, but Germany was their life.

Further dissatisfaction with Communist policy sprang from the numerous instances in which Communists and Nazis took the same stand in the Reichstag or state legislatures and even in popular elections. Too often the Communist goal was to defeat the government, or embarrass the government and foster chaos. The ultimate consequence—that the Nazis would benefit from the government's inability to act—did not seem to concern the Communists. Many German Communists were convinced that Fascism would open the road to Communism. Instead it opened the road to the concentration camp. Too often the Communists' first desire was to square themselves with their followers, to show that they were in the opposition and would never never support a Catholic Bruening or a Social Democrat Hermann Mueller. In the end they got a Hitler who did not need their support. Many Communists abandoned the party when they understood this implication of Communist policy.

Big business and others did not subsidize Hitler to prevent a Communist revolt. That was the pretext; it made a popular slogan. Rather they wanted to undermine the power of the mighty German trade-union movement, reduce wages, increase hours, rid themselves of the irksome necessity of bargaining collectively with their workingmen, cut social security expenditures for labor—and multiply armaments. The Nazis could serve all these ends. The capitalists saw the Nazis as a big and growing mass movement of protest. They hoped to tame it, perhaps break it, but in any case bend it to their purposes.

Under the German Republic, the political parties canceled one another out, and all governments were more or less impotent. Real power therefore resided with the army commanders (the Republic was too pacifist for them), the industrialists (the Republic was too socialistic for them), the big landlords (the Republic was too liberal for them), and the permanent officials (the Republic was too democratic for them). But these four estates did not have the votes. And they could be blocked by those who had. Now here came Hitler amassing millions of votes. He might, if properly treated, bolster their power with ballots.

After the birth of the German democratic Republic, nothing was done to crush the power of the giant trusts, the big landlords, the army and the bureaucracy. The trusts in fact became richer and bigger, the latifundia were not parceled out, the army wielded tremendous influence, and the permanent officials enjoyed enlarged prerogatives because of the inexperience and ignorance of quickly changing ministers. They were four states-within-the-state. United, they constituted a super-state. The battle of 1930-33, was not between Hitler and the Republic. Superficially, it did assume that aspect. But the deeper questions were: Which of the four states-within-the-state would harness Hitler to its chariot? Which would defy him? Which would endeavor to escape defeat by bowing to him? For Hitler the issue was simply this: Which could help him to victory? These questions shaped the record of the pre-Hitler years.

1930

On March 6 bloody riots of unemployed took place in Berlin. The next day Reichswehr Minister Groener issued a decree prohibiting Nazi cells in the army. On March 19, the Reichstag passed a law providing for fines on persons who insulted the Republic, the Republican flag, or the Republican government. On March 27, the cabinet of Chancellor Hermann Mueller resigned, chiefly because it lacked Parliamentary support to enact the federal budget. Three days later Heinrich Bruening was appointed Chancellor in Mueller's place.

Bruening was forty-five when he became head of the German government. He was a conservative Catholic. He concentrated on financial problems that brooked no delay, and was apparently too busy to see or to cope with the tremendous changes taking place in German life. He was stern, matter-of-fact, and honest. Those are important virtues, but they did not constitute adequate equipment to ride the German storm.

Chancellor Bruening faced a new budget deficit on July 1. His attempts to cover it by additional taxation found no Reichstag majority. He thereupon warned Parliament that under Article 48 of the Weimar Constitution, the President of the Republic could decree emergency legislation without a Reichstag majority.

Now the fun—and disaster—begin!

On July 16 Hindenburg issued a presidential edict providing fresh sources of revenue. Within forty-eight hours the Social Democratic Party, resenting this attack on parliamentary government, moved a resolution in the Reichstag to annul the President's decree. The motion passed by 236 to 221 votes. Who voted for it? The Nazis, Communists, and Nationalists—all enemies of parliamentary democracy. They were glad to intensify the political confusion. Bruening then persuaded Hindenburg to disband the Reichstag and order new elections. This is just what the Nazis wanted.

In July the government of the state of Prussia issued an order prohibiting its officials from joining Nazi or Communist organizations. This was a wire stretched across a torrent. During the months of July, August, and September, Germany seethed with an ugly election campaign filled with recrimination, violence, threats of dictatorship, and avowals of patriotism.

Fifteen parties participated in the national elections of September 14, 1930. Ten of them won fewer than thirty seats in the Reichstag. The remaining five fared as follows: the Social Democrats dropped from 153 to 143; the Nationalists dropped from 73 to 41; the Catholic Center rose from 62 to 68; the Communists jumped from 54 to 76, and the Nazis polevaulted from 12 to 107.

The Berlin stock market collapsed. The world press was shocked. The Social Democrats promised to support Bruening as the sole hope of democracy. Bruening again became Chancellor.

At this point, I stopped in a bookstore on the Kurfuerstendamm and bought an armful of Nazi literature, including *Mein Kampf*. I found this Hitler opus wild, disjointed, written in bad German, and completely unimportant as a political book. It was important only because a man who now controlled 107 Reichstag deputies had written it—in prison.

The economic situation deteriorated with increasing rapidity. Factories in the Ruhr shut down. Capital fled abroad in fear of internal disorders. The government endeavored in vain to reduce prices. Employers reduced wages.

The new Reichstag opened on October 13. The 107 Nazi deputies entered Parliament in brown semi-military uniforms, marching in goosestep. Stormy scenes accompanied the election for speaker. Nazi Deputy Heines, known to have murdered political opponents, repeatedly played on a fife. A Communist deputy countered with loud whistling. Communists and Nazi legislators rushed at one another at frequent intervals. Newspapers referred to the session as "a carnival parade," and "a barbarian performance." Social Democrat Loebe was elected speaker.

On November 12 Gutehoffnungshuette, German's giant steel cor-

poration, declared a ten percent dividend. In 1929 it had a seven percent dividend. Rheinmetall, another steel company, likewise announced bigger dividends.

December 15: 3,977,000 unemployed.

Throughout December a film based on Erich Remarque's *All Quiet
on the Western Front* was being shown in many theaters in Berlin
and other cities. Incensed by its pacifist implications, Nazis attacked
spectators as they entered the theaters, smashed electric signs outside
the movie houses, and threw stink bombs inside. Nazis paraded in uniform to places where the picture was being shown. There was so
much Hitler pressure that the government finally banned the film.
The *Berliner Tageblatt* wrote, "This was done not on the basis of the
law but at the command of the street. This affair too proves that the
only danger which threatens Germany is not the growth and mouth-
heroism of Nazism but the flabbiness, the spirit of retreat, and the
vacillation of the so-called 'bourgeoisie.' " The *Berliner Tageblatt* itself was bourgeois.

The disease was correctly diagnosed. The spread of the disease worried the doctors. But the plague marched on.

1931

At the end of 1931, the number of unemployed reached a Hima-
layan high: 5,773,000. Big national banks crashed and the government
had to take them over or save them by tremendous grants. The specter of inflation rose ominously and Germans thought with trembling
of the horrors of 1921, 1922, and 1923. The stock exchange was
closed for many months. Industrial output for the year fell to the low
level of 1922 and 1923.

Storekeepers, farmers, families who lived on small fixed incomes,
and professional people saw their incomes and property going or
threatened. Many joined the Nazi and Communist parties. Sometimes
they joined the Nazis first and then went over to the Communists.
Sometimes they moved in the reverse direction. Inter-party shuttles
were heavily-laden with people whose misery made them search and
whose honesty made them shift.

The Nazis registered great gains in the states of the German Reich.
In Thuringia, Braunschweig, Saxony, Hesse, and Oldenburg the Hit-
lerians became the major party. Hitler promised to prevent inflation.
Prince August Wilhelm, grandson of the Kaiser, said in a speech at

Braunschweig, "Hitler was sent to us by God." His imperial grand-father thought exactly that about himself.

Nazi violence stirred the country. Nazi rowdies intimidated villages and towns. The police was either afraid to suppress them or closed an eye out of sympathy.

Nazi violence was deliberate. The Nazis applied it on principle, for its effect, not out of necessity. They believe that violence impresses the timid and suppresses the brave. In any nation the timid outnumber the brave. *Mein Kamp* had one notable contribution: a prescription on how to delude the masses. Small doses of simple ideas; repeat endlessly. Repetition breeds credulity. It exasperates only the intellectually élite and they are few.

The French army had evacuated the Rhineland. This made Hitler's rise possible. Now Bruening was trying to abolish German reparations payments. He had to try; German economy demanded it. But if he succeeded he would open the way to Hitler's success. The effort to abolish reparations made Franco-German collaboration necessary. The end of reparations would end the collaboration. Germans would not trust Hitler to maintain friendly relations with Paris. But they would trust Hitler when those relations became unnecessary.

Everybody was working for Hitler. On March 31, 1931, the German Foreign Minister Curtius announced an impending German-Austrian customs union. Bombshell. Neither France, Czechoslovakia, Rumania, nor Yugoslavia had been consulted. Briand said, "I will not permit it." That killed it. This gave point to Nazi propaganda against Versailles. France, like Italy, resisted the Anschluss between Austria and Germany because it would have made Germany bigger and stronger. But a stronger Germany would be a stronger republican Germany, while defeat of the union meant aid to Hitler. Hitler benefitted coming and going: Concessions to Germany on reparations made it easier for him to rule Germany; a rebuff to Germany on Austria brought him new followers.

A congress of West German industrialists on June 3 demanded wage reductions and the curtailment of trade-union rights. The Nazi newspaper, *Essener Nationalzeitung*, hailed this congress as an approach to Hitler's program. *Der Deutsche*, a publication of the Catholic trade unions, spoke of industry's plots to supplant the government with a directorate of business.

Guenther Stein declared in a *Berliner Tageblatt* editorial of July 7 that a prominent German industrialist had said to him, "We must revert to 1904 in matters of social services. Wages have to be cut twenty percent. Bruening is right-wing but not conservative enough." At a congress of the German Nationalist Party, Hugenberg, its leader, attacked Bruening for obstructing Germany's movement to the Right. At this same meeting, Fritz Thyssen assured Hugenberg of the support of the western German industrialists. The Congress sent a greeting to the Kaiser at Doorn. The extreme Nationalists did not yet know whether they preferred Hitler or Kaiser.

Riled by Nationalist hostility, Chancellor Bruening resigned on October 7. Since there was no alternative as yet to Bruening, he formed a new cabinet on October 9. But Bruening was now Chancellor by the grace of Hindenburg. He governed by the President's emergency writ. He was what the Germans called "a presidential chancellor," which meant that Hindenburg was dictator. Bruening, the democrat, served the dictator. He did so because Hitler was the alternative dictator. A struggle was brewing between Hindenburg and Hitler.

1932

This was the fateful year. All the antagonisms reached boiling points.

Hindenburg's term was to expire in April, and his friends were eager to avoid at national poll. They feared internal disturbances and their effect on the delicate negotiations with foreign powers for the cancellation of reparations. Also, they were not sure of the election results. But Hitler, too, felt uncertain and when Reichswehr Minister Groener, Hindenburg's friend, summoned Hitler, he duly presented himself. On January 7, secret talks took place between Hitler, Bruening, and Groener. Would Hitler consent to a postponement of the presidential elections for a year or two? Hitler wavered.

Violent clashes shook the Nazi party. Goebbels and Goering insisted that Hitler run against Hindenburg. Hitler's negotiations with Groener and Bruening to cancel the election broke down. On February 15, Hindenburg announced his candidacy. "I feel it my duty to do so," he declared. The Communists immediately nominated Ernst Thaelmann, and on February 22, Goebbels simply told a Nazi meeting at the Sportspalast that Hitler was their candidate.

The German Nationalist party of Hugenberg then put up Theodore Duesterberg, a leader of the Stahlhelm, or Steel-Helmets, World

War veterans of conservative view. The Socialists named no candidate. They had no affection for Hindenburg, but much less for Thaelmann and Hitler, and if they did not support Hindenburg, Hitler might win.

The results on March 13 were:

Hindenburg: 18,654,000

Hitler: 11,341,000

Thaelmann: 4,982,000

Duesterberg: 2,558,000

Hindenburg lacked 0.4 percent of an absolute majority, and a second poll therefore had to take place according to the German Constitution. On April 10, the results were:

Hindenburg: 19,361,000

Hitler: 13,419,000

Thaelmann: 3,706,000

Hindenburg was re-elected. Over a million Communist voters, more intelligent than their leaders, had sensibly stayed at home. The Nationalists had split, more going to Hitler than to their own national leader, Hindenburg.

It was possible to say: Hindenburg has won decisively; we anti-Hitlerites now have power and the mandate to stop Hitler and take drastic measures for a radical cure of Germany's ills. But it was also possible to say: One cannot destroy a party that musters over 13,000,-000 votes and keeps growing all the time; we must come to an understanding with Hitler.

The heads of the cabinet determined on the first course. Three days after Hindenburg's election, Groener banned the S.A. The S.A. was Hitler's army. Republican Germany never had national boy-scout and girl-scout movements. Each political party had its own youth organization. The juveniles from the ages of six to eighteen were trained in party hatreds and inter-party warfare. I often watched them in the country marching to and from railway stations or camps with their packs on their backs and, the boys at least, steel-pointed canes in their hands. If a rival group passed each would try to drown the singing of the other, and yell abusive epithets. Sometimes they came to blows and then the canes were useful. When this younger generation reached maturity it was equipped with all the bitterness and narrow-mindedness required for the last fight for and against the German Republic.

Young adults were organized along similar party lines. The Communists had the Rotfront militants, good strapping workingmen and excellent street fighters. The Social Democrats had one of the largest organizations called the Reichsbanner. Two other groups of a semi-military character were usually regarded as potential dangers to the state because they had arms or could get them in an emergency; they were the Nationalist Stahlhelm, war veterans who had developed paunches and poor breathing since 1918 but nevertheless maintained a nation-wide union led by energetic men, and the S.A., the Nazi Brownshirts who had mastered, from much practice, the technique of breaking up meetings, staging little pogroms, throwing stones into windows and running away, waylaying old Jews on dark corners. Now Groener outlawed the S.A.

The S.A. received regular pay and regular military training. It lived in barracks, wore uniforms, and saluted. It was a second army, 600,-000 strong, whereas the Reichswehr was restricted to 100,000. Groener acted, he believed, for the Reichswehr when he ordered the S.A. disbanded. Armies are notoriously jealous of their power and rights. The Red Army resented the rivalry of the GPU which had its special armed forces. The Japanese army eyes the Japanese navy with a jealous eye. There is even a semi-friendly, semi-serious jealousy between the army and the navy of the United States. Many generals and officers of the Reichswehr objected to the Nazi S.A., and Groener was their mouthpiece. They were contemptuous of the Austrian corporal who had defamed their noble Prussian marshal. It looked as if the Reichswehr, one of the four states-within-the-state, had taken sides against Hitler.

Chancellor Bruening also considered the moment well-chosen to introduce reforms designed to save the republic. He tackled the land problem. Large, densely populated farm regions were in distress, whereas many East Prussian estates owned by Junkers raised little and did little work. Hindenburg was one of the Junkers. He was Junker Number One. Many permanent officials in Berlin, Koenigsberg, and other cities hailed from these ancient noble families with the "von" between their Christian names and surnames. The Junkers wanted money—who does not?—and their friends were near the exchequer. "In 1932," says Konrad Heiden, "12,000 peasant farms received 69,000,000 marks [in subsidies from the German government] while 722 big landowners received 60,000,000!" Baron von Oldenburg-Januschau, Hindenburg's close friend and neighbor, himself took 621,000 marks from the federal exchequer because his three vast estates were ostensibly insolvent. With this money he immediately bought a fourth.

The estates had to be broken up, and the scandal of the Osthilfe—the subsidies to East Prussian land magnates—investigated. Chancellor Bruening planned a frontal attack. He had worked himself into ill health campaigning for the re-election of Hindenburg because Hindenburg was a pillar of the Republic. Hindenburg had indeed remained loyal to his oath to serve the Republic. But he was a reactionary in economic questions, and Junker cronies had his ear. These estate owners hated Bruening because he accepted assistance from the moderate socialists. They even thought of Bruening as a "socialist," for he had worked intimately with Adam Stegerwald, leader of the Catholic trade unions, and they believed a trade union was always a trade union, and always bad.

Chancellor Bruening went to Neudeck in the middle of May, 1932, to lay his land reform before President Hindenburg. Neudeck was the old Hindenburg family's last Prussian estate.

Hitler set no store by the breaking up of the estates. He deleted from the Nazi Party program the plank favoring confiscation of estates without compensation. He wrote in *Mein Kampf* that Germany needed the Ukraine for agrarian colonization. The East Prussian spaces, he said, would not do for that purpose. To the landlords he thus gave the bird in the hand; to the peasants he promised two in the Ukrainian bush.

When Bruening brought Hindenburg the plan to accelerate agrarian resettlement in East Prussia, the Junker coterie in and around Neudeck made a choice: they were for Hitler and against Bruening.

President Hindenburg, then 85, was still sturdy but he kept audiences short because he had to leave the room often. Weighty matters of state were accordingly dispatched in a few minutes. Bruening stood before Hindenburg at Neudeck and outlined his proposed new presidential emergency decree:

HINDENBURG: "I am told that the decree also includes a Bolshevik resettlement plan. How about that?"

BRUENING did not reply. He read on.

HINDENBURG: "You deal with finance questions, too? I thought you were confining yourself to Bolshevism."

BRUENING read on.

HINDENBURG: "But my dear Mr. Chancellor, this will never do. We cannot introduce Bolshevik wage laws and Bolshevik settlement schemes. The two trade unionists must leave the government."

BRUENING wondered who the two trade unionist ministers were.

HINDENBURG: "Yes, I mean you and Mr. Stegerwald. Of course you can remain as Foreign Minister."

BRUENING: "Thank you, Mr. General Field Marshal. I cannot remain with a broken neck."

Bruening resigned on May 30. On June 2, Baron Franz von Papen, owner of the daily *Germania*, organ of the Catholic Center Party, and leading figure in the conservative political Herrenklub (Nobles Club), formed a new cabinet on Hindenburg's instructions. His cabinet was called the Cabinet of Nobles. Minister of Interior, Baron von Gayl; Foreign Minister, Baron von Neurath; Finance Minister, Count Schwerin von Krosigk; Agriculture, Baron von Eltz-Ruebenach; Minister of Food, Baron von Braun; and Reichswehr Minister, General von Schleicher. The East Prussian aristocrats had defeated the Bruening republicans; Schleicher had defeated Groener.

I spent an afternoon with General Groener in his Berlin apartment on December 20, 1932. He did not wish to talk about current German events but read to me instead from his War diary, and discussed his work in the Ukraine in 1918 when he commanded the German army of occupation. The next day, on his recommendation, I had a long interview in a Grunewald villa with Hetman Skoropadsky, German puppet ruler of the Ukraine. Groener thought Germany need not have lost the World War in 1918. He urged Ludendorff to remain passive on the western front, where they did not have sufficient troops to break through; it was wrong to launch the spring, 1918, offensive. He would have captured Moscow instead and overthrown the Bolshevik government. He advocated, if necessary, a slow retreat towards a reinforced Hindenburg line in the West. This would have required the American army to take the offensive, and since the Americans were inexperienced, inadequately trained, and enthusiastic they would have been smashed and would disappear as a factor within a few months. The German general staff, however, insisted on an offensive in the West, and thought it could win in the summer of 1918. That caused Germany's downfall, Groener said.

While Groener spoke to me, I heard "Nurmi" crying in a near-by room. Groener had recently married, and a baby had arrived so few months thereafter that his enemies said it broke all records for speed; they christened it Nurmi. The story of Nurmi went the rounds in all political circles, and somebody made sure to plant in Hindenburg's slow-witted cranium the idea that the army resented such frivolous immorality on the part of its chief. Nurmi was a factor in the downfall of Groener.

The fall of Bruening and Groener had been engineered by General Kurt von Schleicher. He negotiated secretly with Hitler, Roehm, the head of the S.A., and Goebbels. He was Groener's assistant minister in the Reichswehr. When Groener banned the S.A., Schleicher had walked up to his chief at the Reichstag session and told him the army would never stand for this. Schleicher and General Hammerstein then forced Groener to resign. Groener reflected one Reichswehr tendency: loyalty to the Republic coupled with a desire to make it conservative and law-abiding. But a big unit may have several tendencies. The Reichswehr included young blood, new officers imbued with the Hitler spirit of military expansion, conquest, dictatorship, anti-Bolshevism. Moreover, on Bruening's public insistence, oddly and ironically enough, the powers would soon recognize Germany's right to equality of armaments. A new opportunity was dawning for the Reichswehr. The German army now saw the long-awaited day coming. Schleicher spoke for them, and he was stronger than Groener. Schleicher intrigued with the Nazis, with the Junkers, and with the big industrialists to bring in Papen. Papen opened the way to the Hitler regime.

Thus the landed aristocrats, whom the Republic had treated with gentlemanly moderation in 1918, and the militarists whom the Republic had restored to posts of power, bided their time for fourteen eventful years to slay the Republic at the first opportunity. It was easy because they had made sure to man the pivotal jobs from president to general to judge to police commissar. (*A Berliner Tageblatt* cartoon showed a typical Prussian magistrate examining a prisoner. "Are you a Republican?" he asks. "If so, I can dispense with your defense.") It was easy because the working class was divided between Socialists and Communists and because a part of the bourgeoisie put economic privileges above democratic rights.

Hitler played on the bourgeoisie's fears by luridly and hysterically painting the great red specter of Communism. More than anything else it was the appeal to anti-Communism that ruined German democracy. The forces which German Communism could not destroy in

1918 and certainly could not destroy in 1932, nevertheless used the bogey of Communism to destroy the Republic in 1933. They talked against Communism; they meant trade unions and liberalism. The antagonism of German big business, landlords, and militarists to the liberalism and pacifism of German democracy wrecked German democracy. When Hitler laid siege to the German Republic he found a multitude of his friends within the gates. Papen merely warmed the chancellor's seat for Hitler.

Papen performed numerous concrete services for Hitler: On June 16, the S.A. ban was lifted. On June 17, at the Lausanne reparations conference, Papen demanded the scrapping of reparations and offered to pay three billion marks in final settlement thereof. The offer was accepted. On June 18, the S.A. asked the government for arms. On July 20, using Reichswehr troops, Papen suppressed the socialist government of Prussia. On July 30, Reichstag elections took place. They had been ordered by Papen who hoped that every election would be a step towards a Hitler cabinet.

Election results: Nazis, 230 Reichstag deputies; Socialists, 133; Communists, 89; Catholic Center, 75; Nationalists, 37. The moderate parties of the middle and right practically disappeared. Seven parties obtained one to seven deputies.

So there was a new Reichstag after a national election which cost several dozen lives. It met on August 30, and elected Hermann Goering speaker. Only twelve days later, it voted non-confidence in Papen by 512 against 42 ballots. What did Papen do? What did Hindenburg do? They disbanded the Reichstag and called new elections. Again meetings, election brawls, political murders, and uncertainty.

But—these elections brought a slight surprise. The Nazis dropped to 196; the Socialists won 121 seats; the Communists, 100; the Center, 70. Von Papen remained Chancellor, meanwhile negotiating with Hitler and pulling wires with Hindenburg and his coterie in order to have Hitler succeed him. On December 2, however, Schleicher succeeded Papen. This was unexpected. What had happened?

It takes money to finance an election and to pay a huge army like the S.A. The Hitler party was bankrupt. The industrialists were tightening their purse strings.

There had been a small but marked economic improvement in Germany during the latter half of 1932. More significantly, Schleicher was playing his own game. No man at the pinnacle or near it selflessly yields to another. Power is very sweet. Schleicher had a plan;

he wanted to split the Nazi organization and form a government based on the trade unions and the anti-Hitler Nazis. Gregor Strasser did not altogether approve of Hitler's compacts with the industrialists. The Nazis were National Socialists. But Hitler was a Nationalist and anti-Socialist while Strasser toyed with socialism and therefore took an anti-Hitler line. Strasser and Schleicher conspired together against Hitler and Papen. The industrialists took fright. They had thought they could manipulate the Nazis by financing Hitler. But now it seemed that Hitler did not control the Nazis. (Gregor Strasser paid for all this. He was shot in the blood purge in 1934. So was Schleicher.)

On December 3, the Nazis lost half their votes in the state of Thuringia. Throughout December Schleicher released numerous pacifists and democrats from jail and rescinded some restrictions on freedom of the press. December 22: Entry in Goebbels' diary: "In the party there is a great deal of discord and unpleasantness to be got rid of. The financial calamity continues."

Was Hitler's sun setting before it reached zenith?

1933

I arrived in Berlin in January. My friends in the American Embassy, my friends in the Soviet Embassy, American journalists, German journalists, everybody said, "Hitler is through." But on January 30, Hitler was Chancellor.

Things had happened behind the scenes. On January 4, Hitler held a secret rendezvous with Papen in the Rhineland. Papen then took him to a meeting of industrialists in Duesseldorf. From one of the participants I have an eye-witness account. Hitler was not in brown shirt but in full evening dress and white tie. Hitler told the industrialists that Schleicher was dangerous; "But I am a friend of German economy." He ranted and beat his stiff white shirt. Seeing this hysterical mediocrity, the shrewd businessmen—and bad politicians—thought he would be easy to manage. As Fritz Thyssen, President of the Vereinigte Stahlwerke corporation, admits in a letter in the *New York Times*, June 9, 1940, Hitler "held out to us the promise of complete freedom in handling the problems for which he was not competent." Hitler called Schleicher the "Red General." Strasser, he said, had no following. Schleicher was an adventurer who wanted to seize the estates à la Bruening. Time pressed. It had to be soon or never. He needed power to save them and Germany. He also needed a little money. The big businessmen applauded and drank toasts to Hitler and gave him money. Thyssen had supported the Nazis from 1923 onward.

It now remained to convince Hindenburg that Chancellor Schleicher was willful and ambitious whereas Hitler was "legal," patriotic, and ready to talk terms. A rumor was circulated (or was it true?) that Schleicher held the Reichswehr garrison at Potsdam in readiness to stage a coup d'état against the government. Papen maneuvered indefatigably for Hitler. He lived under the same roof with Hindenburg, and each chance he got he dinned into the old marshal's ear, "Only Hitler can guarantee law and order"; "Hitler has lost votes and we can now handle him." On January 30, Hindenburg summoned the Austrian corporal and made him head of the government. That is how German democracy died.

Who is this Hitler?

Marxists whose analyses are often correct, and as often incorrect, say Hitler is "the agent of monopoly capitalism," the false-face of big business. I find this too crude a simplification to fit the complicated facts.

There is a tendency among intellectuals, Marxist and otherwise, to substitute glib generalizations for careful study, and aphorisms for facts. I recall a speech by Felix Frankfurter at a Zionist convention at Cleveland in 1924. The audience was hostile to him and he kept saying, "You must have facts, facts, facts." Every time they heckled Frankfurter, he shouted, "Have you the facts, the facts, the facts?" I thought then that he was overdoing this insistence. But now, when I have forgotten the details of the controversy, I remember his sage advice. To simplify is not always to clarify. It is wrong to say that Hitler is the slave of German big business because it helped him achieve power. The facts do not support this generalization.

Hitler was the raucous voice of German discontent. His millions of supporters were neither workingmen nor rich men, but middle-class people afraid of social and economic demotion. Until the first World War, people looked to the capitalist class for prosperity and economic well-being. More recently, however, capitalists have had to look to the state for assistance. (Capitalists sometimes resent this even when they originally asked for it or made it necessary.)

When the capitalist, once economic king and autocrat, fails to create satisfying conditions, the mass turns to the government and cries, "What can you do for us?" The state acquires more meaning for the people. It ceases to be a mere policeman, tax collector, and soldier. It becomes the source of jobs, bread, and checks. Who then dominates the state is a matter of tremendous significance. Politics is no longer "a game." It is life.

The German middle class wanted a strong state that would save it. German big business wanted a strong state that could help it. The Republic was too chaotic and disunited to be of much use to either. The capitalists could dominate the German state but they could not make it strong. They hoped Hitler would. Having failed to rally popular support to their conservative parties they had recourse to the demagogue. Thirteen million Nazi votes looked like a guarantee of stability and strength. The permanent civil servants asked for a master worthy of their respect. The army wished to serve a great power. Germany was a nation yearning for potency. That is why Hitler attacked Versailles and ascribed Germany's weakness to it. That is why he impressed listeners when he promised to eliminate political parties because they weakened the state.

Who would hold sway in the coming big-fist state? Big business entertained hopes. It had ties with Hitler. But the middle class was not enamored of big business. The little man rarely is. This dislike was the extent of the German middle class's anti-capitalism or "socialism." The German middle class had lost faith in the upper bourgeoisie's ability to provide security and profits for the entire nation. The little men themselves aspired to power. Hitler was their little man. Astutely sensing their psychological and economic needs, he made his party their mouthpiece and agent. To attain his goal, big business co-operated with him. Each remained on guard. "Who would fool whom?" Fritz Thyssen now avows that he was fooled. In 1939 he fled into foreign exile in the footsteps of so many unhappy Jews, Communists, Socialists, pacifists, Catholics, and other Germans whose brutal persecution he had paid for. His property was confiscated like the lesser fortunes of a Kohn or a Levi. Other members of his class, however, still collect uncertain benefits in the fatherland.

How did Hitler's class—the middle class—fare? The pleasures of strict rationing have been conferred on it, and its sons and daughters were honored with compulsory labor camps, party jobs, *Kraft durch*

Freude picnics, military regimentation, and glorious death for "Gott und Hitler" on land, sea, and in the air. The gains, if any, are wiped out by the Gestapo and swallowed into the maw of Mars.

The sacrifices which every German, rich or poor, magnate, landlord, soldier, priest, worker, or peasant, makes to the insatiable Moloch of the authoritarian state are the answer to the question of who won in Germany. No class won. Moloch won. Hitler won. There are no more Communists and no more trade unions, but also no freedom and no solid peace, no relaxation, no safety; only strain and pain and tribute.

Governments today wield many weapons of unprecedented effectiveness. The arsenal of the dictatorships—secret police, propaganda monopoly, jobs, huge funds—is so endlessly awe-inspiring that no individual or group dares to challenge authority. Governments are taking over functions formerly performed by economic classes. The more numerous a government's duties, expenditures, and employees the more powerful it is. Our era is characterized above all else by the emergence of governments which are mightier than the classes that created them and which can therefore defy or ignore or betray the classes that created them. No class rules Nazi Germany. Hitler oppresses all classes.

10. *Revolution Comes into Its Own*

A REVOLUTION, whether Nazi or Bolshevik, does not like to stop. It gets sick when it stops. It has an irresistible urge to move on toward the goal for which it was born.

The Bolshevik Revolution aimed to wipe out all private capitalists and erect a socialist economy. Between 1918 and 1920, civil war interfered. Between 1920 and 1928, internal weakness interfered. In 1929, came the revolution for which the Revolution of 1917 was made. Sufficient experience and reserves of wealth had been accumulated under the NEP to initiate a new phase of socialist activity. Immediately there was a terrific outburst of long pent-up destructive and creative energy. Lustily, happily, the Communists went to work smashing what they did not like and setting up what they conceived to be the new society. The dynamic of revolution had been let loose, and it was like a hurricane, like a giant on a rampage. Obstacles did not exist. Costs did not matter. The only thing that mattered was the attainment of the original objective.

"*Za shto borolis*" was a popular Communist saying. "Is this what we fought for?" When they saw rich capitalist Nepmen dining in government-managed cabarets, when they saw workingmen employed by private factory owners, when they saw peasants living in rickety barns and plowing with the same wooden stick, they asked, "Is this what we fought for?" And now the Kremlin gave the answer: "No, not for this," but for new cities, new mammoth factories, new socialist villages, new universities, new schools, new roads, a new life, for the Five Year Plan and for agrarian collectivization. Whatever stands in the way must perish.

"There are no fortresses which Bolsheviks cannot take," Stalin proclaimed. The fear of cruel punishment if you failed and the hope of reward for yourself and the nation if you succeeded further accelerated the tempo of Soviet reconstruction. The great adventure had started. 1929. "We will overtake and outstrip America." The first five-year plan, a grandiose scheme for doubling production and introducing millions of new hands into industry, was not enough.

"The Five Year Plan in Four," became the new goal. But this was not enough. There would be a second plan, and then a third, each more ambitious, each requiring more effort and more zeal.

The keynote of the period was "more." Comrade Margolin, the student-like manager of a government grain farm in the steppes of northern Caucasus, took me in a new Buick to one end of his land, then drove fifty-four miles in a straight line to the opposite end. An hour's dash by express train across one farm! But near by was Gigant, another, bigger, "grain factory"; there the manager used an airplane to get from one part of his farm to the other. A Stalingrad plant started in 1930 turned out tractors at the rate of 21,000 a year. In 1931, a sister plant in Kharkov commenced operating at a greater speed, and a third tractor plant was already then in construction at Cheliabinsk, Siberia. Before the Kharkov unit was finished they began enlarging it. At Magnitogorsk in the Urals the government built what it claimed to be the biggest steel mill in the world. Simultaneously, it laid the foundations of others of equally imposing dimensions. At Dnieperstroi, the workingmen boasted that their dam and hydro-electric power station had no peer for size even in America. But it was small compared to Angarastroi that would start going up next year on the shores of Lake Baikal. And they would dam the Volga too. Russia, the giant, had stirred from his slumber. He would break records—and other things, too. Every mounting curve of production had to be pressed upward still further. Excelsior.

A motto of the period was "Leftward, Ho." Socialism in the village meant not only no private renting of land, no private ownership of horses, plows, but also socialized chickens and pigs. Socialists could not eat like Czarist muzhiks. No individual pots and pans! Only communal kitchens! The peasants, whether in earnest or jest, spread a story that the government was manufacturing mile-long beds and blankets under which all families would sleep together. New houses in some cities had no facilities for cooking. The socialist state would make meals for them. If the old life was to be scrapped it had better be done completely, quickly, now. Pouring new wine into old bottles is conservatism. The revolutionist smashes the old bottles before he has new ones, then he makes new bottles—and then he looks for new wine. Rotten vestiges of the past would contaminate the new. "Nothing succeeds like excess," the vibrant Bolsheviks said. Flabby democrats and milk-and-water social democrats sought a mean that was not gold, but dross. Wages, which had never been equal in Soviet Russia, must be equalized! Private practice of medicine was frowned upon. "Socialism overnight by fiat!" The roof and façade must be communistic even though the structure and base rested in poverty, inefficiency, illiteracy, cultural backwardness. There was a lot of childish desire to show off in all this, but also a feeling that it was beneath a Bolshevik to respect obstacles or considerations of expediency or the wishes and comfort of the population. The population would appreciate it all later on.

The Communists did not spare themselves any more than they spared others. They neglected their health and families. They behaved as they would at the front. This was a war, too, a war against an old society. Of course there would be pain and blood and dirt. Birth—the most glorious process in nature—is accompanied by blood and dirt. What does an individual matter, the Bolsheviks asked, when a whole world is being remade? Human beings did not count when a better world was being built for human beings.

The entire Soviet Union felt inspired in the presence of this spectacle of creation and self-sacrifice. I too was swept away by it. I saw old ugly walls totter and new walls rise. A whole nation marched behind a vision. Tourists to Mexico waxed enthusiastic over the bright colors and primitive life of the native who suffered from disease and poverty. But in Russia the factory was conquering. If the profit would be bathtubs, better clothing, sufficient food, more doctors, more disinfectant, more books—fine. I had lived in Ukrainian villages. I had stood at train windows during night hours of horrid wakefulness crossing the flat face of Russia. No light. Hundreds of miles of darkness. People lived in that all their lives. I had done high-school lessons by kerosene lamp. It doesn't kill you, but bright light is better. To this day I hate to turn off a light. Lenin wrote, "Socialism equals Soviets plus electricity." Now the electric bulb was invading the bleak black village; steel and iron were vanquishing Russia's wood civilization. I translated Five Year Plan statistics into human values. Europe was stuck in the mud. Russia was trying to lift itself out of an ancient mire. This juxtaposition and contrast bred the radicalism of the Left during the early thirties.

Outside Russia, the years beginning in 1929 found governments confounded by deep crisis, with able workingmen in bread lines, farmers seeing their precious crops plowed under or destroyed by dust, and intellectuals in a quandary. An endless stream of thirsty minds flowed into Russia from the capitalist West. How did Russia do it? Was it because of planned economy? Can capitalism plan? Can the governments of the United States, of England, of France, do some of these things without a revolution? Why must American and German engineers help build up the Soviet Union when there ought to be plenty of opportunity for the application of their talents at home? There had never been so little faith in orthodox capitalism. John Strachey, British pro-Communist Marxist, swept the American petty bourgeoisie off its feet into the fellow-traveler class. In Washington, Boris Skvirsky, unofficial Soviet representative, was one of the most popular foreign figures. Future New Deal braintrusters sat eagerly at the feet of Peter A. Bogdanov, Russia's trade commissioner in New York. What was the secret of Bolshevik success and capitalist failure? Books on the Five Year Plan headed the bestseller list. Parlor Bolshevism and pink cocktail parties were the vogue. If all this now seems difficult to believe it remains, nevertheless, an authentic picture of those days, and I recapture it easily when I think back of the visitors who then crowded into crowded Moscow.

They included intellectual slummers and dissatisfied women—for to have been to Moscow had become as necessary in some circles as to have sat on the terrace of the Café de la Paix; but most of them were serious inquiring professors, teachers, writers, social workers, and politicians.

Among the authors of books on Russia was Will Rogers, America's comic sage, with whom I tramped the streets of Moscow. He imported a plentiful supply of chewing gum. Between chiclets and chuckles he explained that he had always worked for a living, was a proletarian, and never made a cent on his investments.

Theodore Dreiser was a great American tragedy. He lost his passport. Sensationalists inflated the loss into a Soviet plot. He cabled to Berlin for a new passport. And then he recalled that he had handed it to the hall porter for registration. He resented defective plumbing and wrote anti-Soviet articles. Later he forgot about the discomforts and became friendly with the American Communists, who were willing to forget his earlier sins.

William Allen White, observant and wise, visited Moscow with his wife. They saw much and said little. I think they learned much and liked it a little. Mr. White edits his *Emporia Gazette* at Emporia, Kansas, and Emporia is not New York, Washington, or Chicago. But a vital artery of the nation passes through Emporia and the Whites have a finger on the national pulse.

In July, 1930, I received a telegram in Moscow from Berlin signed "Kuh." I had received many like it before and so had other foreigners. It told me that *"Margaret Bourke White Young American Industrial Photographer"* had been waiting five weeks in Berlin for a Soviet visa and wouldn't I please *"stir up."* I had never heard of anybody named Margaret Bourke. Why should he be wiring me that she was white, young and industrial? I wired back and asked her name. Margaret Bourke-White, one of America's greatest photographers. Markoosha and I became her fast friends. She was high-strung and hard-working. The Russians respected her devotion to work. She took pictures all day and bathed them in her bathtub all night, and if that prevented her from bathing, it didn't matter. The picture's the thing. When she photographs, her eyes are transformed. Nothing else exists. The eyes reflect a passion and mania. The eyes see more and so do the pictures. Peggy (now Mrs. Erskine Caldwell) started her career by photographing industry—steel, glass, machines, and pipe organs. She could not take faces. (She certainly failed to take mine, wasting eighty plates!) As her personality unfolded and mellowed, so did her art, and her photographs of human beings in the American South, in Czechoslovakia, in Russia, are the work of genius. Russia, to which she returned, made her think socially and unsealed a deep well of sympathy for the plain suffering citizen of the world. She has a strong character harnessed to terrific energy, yet she tends to merge her identity with others and to submerge her personality in work. The mellowness of maturity and the relaxation of happiness intensified the first tendency and moderated the second.

Russia always had a partiality for Negroes. Russians are color-blind; distinctions of race mean nothing to them. When Roland Hayes sang in Moscow, the big Conservatory scarcely held his audience. He rendered Debussy and Chopin faultlessly while it yearned for more spirituals. "Sweet Chariot" and other religious hymns were freely translated on the Russian program as cries of proletarian revolt. Waylin Rudd, another American Negro, danced superbly, and acted in the Meyerhold Theatre and in Soviet films. He became a Soviet citizen. But of course Moscow lost its heart, as most cities and individuals do, to Paul Robeson.

I first met Paul Robeson in his London apartment. He had just played the leading role in *Saunders of the River*, a propaganda film for British colonial imperialism, and though somewhat ashamed of his contribution to that cause he was still immersed in Black Zionism, and the rooms were filled with African masks, weapons, trophies, and jungle knickknacks. At the same time, Paul had already learned Russian and sang it beautifully. Discussions with him were pleasant for many reasons but also because he would frequently break into song to illustrate an argument. I predicted that Moscow would cure him of his African nationalism and suggested that he go there. But Essie, his beautiful wife, said, "Baby, you can't do that." At which point, the six-foot-six baby, All-American football star, exploded into a loud rolling laugh. Later he did go to Russia, and so did Essie, and then Essie put little Paulie to school in Russia and sent her mother to take care of him there, and Paul Robeson abandoned his solution for one race and continent and moved into the radical movement in England and sang many free concerts for Left causes. But he remained an African nationalist and because Moscow was pro-Negro Paul felt that it could do no wrong, even when it joined hands with Hitler who was anti-Negro. Paul has a big body, a big mind, and a big heart. He would be a great artist in any skin. Jacob Epstein did a bust of him. But it was almost unnecessary. He is a perfect bit of sculpture himself.

Alexander Woollcott overshadowed all of Moscow's best conversationalists. (On one trip across the Atlantic, he talked at great length to me, for some unknown reason, about Charles Dickens.) But the real distinction for which he has gone down into the history of foreigners in Moscow—apart from not writing a book on Russia—was his appearance on the Red Square for the November 7 anniversary parade without an overcoat. That day the army turned eyes right on Woollcott instead of Stalin. The long hours in the grandstand on November 7 were always murderously cold and it was all I and most others could do to stand it until the most interesting part of the demonstration had passed. But Aleck stuck his paunch out and his hands in his pants' pockets and watched immovably. At the opposite extreme was Linton Wells of the International News Service, who one year brought not only a heavy woolen shawl and a heavy overcoat but a big bottle of Scotch in the overcoat to keep the temperature up. In the beginning I disliked Wells, and once we quarreled. It was at an interview in Moscow with Colonel Lindbergh who, with Anne, had swept gracefully down on the Moskva River in his plane and then refused to talk. The correspondents, especially Linton Wells, insisted that he reveal his plans and Lindbergh said he wouldn't. I suggested that special circumstances had created in Lindbergh an attitude of mind towards publicity which we ought to respect, whereat Lint said, "Nuts." But later we were reconciled. I began going to his parties. He lived just one flight above us and if I didn't go I was kept awake anyway by the dancing and prancing upstairs. He was also increasingly appreciative of Soviet efforts at reconstruction and serious about his work, and he often came down to talk about news stories. Sad experience taught him to bring his own drinks, and if he rang the bell and arrived with a glass in his hand I understood he had come for a short while, but if he brought a bottle I settled down to longer confab. (I met Lindbergh again several years later at the estate of Thomas Lamont, Morgan partner, where he argued in favor of a strong American navy capable of taking the offensive against Japan if the need arose.)

Elizabeth Hawes, pink Schiaparelli, hoped to teach the Russians to dress well. The Russians found her styles too radical and continued to wear their conservative clothes. The Bolsheviks tend toward quiet conformism in everyday personal life. For that matter, modern revolutionists are obedient conformists in politics, too.

Sholom Asch, Jewish author of *The Nazarene*, was interested almost exclusively in the Jewish villages of the Ukraine and Crimea and in those villages he was almost exclusively interested in what the Jews thought of Sholom Asch. He would ride in an auto across the hot steppes and if he saw a Jewish farmer off in the broiling fields he would have him summoned. "Do you know Sholom Asch?" was his first question in inimitable Yiddish. If the reply was negative he drove on, if affirmative he asked which books he had read, and what he had liked in them, and then how the new agricultural life affected city Jews.

Josephine Herbst, sensitive novelist, and Mary Heaton Vorse, veteran of many strikes, were deeply interested in what was going on in Soviet Russia. So was Ella Winter, then Mrs. Lincoln Steffens, subsequently Mrs. Donald Ogden Stewart.

I gave Ella the idea for a book, and sketched it with her chapter by chapter in New York. It was to be a *Humanity Uprooted* brought up to date, humanity striking Soviet roots. Being a serious industrious person, Ella went to Moscow and did it.

Margaret and Corliss Lamont also wrote an enthusiastic book

which they meekly entitled *Russia Day by Day*. I have always liked these two people. Margaret, scrupulously honest, is a Socialist, her husband, son of the Morgan partner, stands close to the Communists. They do not merely give money to radical causes; they give time, work, and heart. Ideological blunders and naïveté do not weigh as heavily in the balance as stubborn devotion to one's ideas. Both are Christian reformers, the type that modestly fights for principles and has a religious sense of social duty.

Will Durant, popularizer of the lives of philosophers, produced a book too. He crossed Siberia in a train, then spent several days in Moscow; he called his book *The Tragedy of Russia*. 1933. William Henry Chamberlin, reviewing it in *The Nation*, lambasted Durant's "efforts to rear a formidable structure of sweeping generalizations . . . on a narrow base of factual observation." He might have added that Durant had a lot of company.

Professors came in great numbers to the Soviet Union. Among them were John Dewey and his daughter, Ben Cherrington, executive secretary of the University of Denver and later chief of a section of the State Department, Professor Heber Harper, Professor Samuel Harper of Chicago—an annual visitor and careful student, and Professor George S. Counts of Teachers College, Columbia, whose *Soviet Challenge to America* was the best book I had seen on the first Five Year Plan. These professors saw the havoc which the depression was working in western capitalist countries. They reflected the disgruntled view of university youths who were graduating into joblessness or into jobs at filling stations. That is why Counts' sympathetic book on Russia was a message to depressed America. (Walter Lippmann asks Professor Counts to explain that attitude. But Lippmann, the historian, has forgotten his history. Counts does not have to justify his critical attitude to a society which produced two wars in twenty-five years, not to mention the distress and unemployment between wars. It is not Counts' fault that his students are disillusioned. Those students merely observe the world in which they live.)

I have looked back at the magazines and newspapers of that period and at the books which were being published. It was a time of search and doubt. Liberals were dropping *The Nation* and *The New Republic* and reading *New Masses*. Miles Shereover sold vast quantities of Soviet gold bonds to Americans who had faith in Russia's ability to pay and diffused their investments as a guarantee against collapse at home. Intellectuals played with technocracy, government by an oligarchy of engineers. Others toyed with planning.

In a New York trolley a poster said, "Don't worry. The pendulum always swings back." This was the transit company's contribution to the solution of America's economic problem. An American tobacco firm advertised as follows, "The economic situation is bad. BUT KEEP SMILING. SMOKE HAVANA CIGARS." Many American intellectuals turned from such advice to a study of Soviet ideas and economic devices. The torrent of books on Russia reflected and fed this interest.

Moscow's long list of foreign callers included Waldo Frank, mystic rebel and fine but sometimes opaque stylist who lavished admiration equally on Soviet idealism and Soviet women; Emil Ludwig, who wrote good biographies of Germans but who wrote inadequately on Russia; Roy W. Howard, who had an historic interview with Stalin; Lion Feuchtwanger, whose Russian stuff was very poor; Julian Bryan, photographer, who annually filmed Soviet progress; Dr. Harry M. Sigerist of Johns Hopkins, soft-spoken intellectual, fierce fighter, and stiff-necked friend of the Soviets; Mary van Kleeck, Colonial Dame, Russell Sage economist and pro-Communist; Professors Kingsbury and Fairchild of Bryn Mawr, academic twins who captured the minds of Soviet planners; W. W. Lancaster, liberal legal adviser of the National City Bank, who took time off from hopeless negotiations to look at hopeful social experiments; Romain Rolland—his *Jean Christophe* had thrilled me in my youth and now I was excited to see him, at Gorky's home, in the flesh— adamantly pro-Stalin; Julio Alvarez del Vayo, Spanish Socialist diplomat, journalist, and his Swiss wife Luisy, who, on being introduced to King Alfonso in a private house in Madrid, said, "How do you do, Monsieur"; André Malraux, whose arguments in my Moscow apartment displayed a morbid interest in death—we met often later in Madrid near death, in New York, and in Paris during the second World War; Sherwood Eddy of the American Y.M.C.A., a friendly critic of and commuter to the Soviet Union; Cass Canfield of Harper's, and his wife; Efrem Zimbalist, violin virtuoso, and Alma Gluck, opera singer, who enrolled their daughter in the Moscow Conservatory of Music and their son in a Soviet high school; Professor Harry F. Ward of the Union Theological Seminary, whose Christianity led him towards the Communism he hoped to see in Russia; Rabbi Israel Goldstein, friend of my youth in Philadelphia, who found that Moscow lay on the road from Jerusalem to Brussels; Elmer Rice, social playwright who came with his whole family, and then came back again; and a host of others. For thousands of intellectuals and intelligent people a trip to Russia had become a compulsory summer course with credit.

Even the British were not immune. One London group consisted of the three young Laborite M.P.'s, John Strachey, Aneurin Bevan, and George Russell Strauss, plus Celia Simpson and Magda Gellan. Another included David Low, the Labor cartoonist; Yeats-Brown (*Bengal Lancer*), Yogi in India, Nazi in England, and Kingsley Martin, editor of the *New Statesman and Nation*. Low—three letters that are a hallmark of political wisdom and draftsmanship—illustrated a book on Russia which Martin wrote. Low, with no Soviet background, saw more at a glance than many people after years of study. Intuitively, he goes to the heart of a problem and finds its essence wrapped in comic paradox.

In the summer of 1931, George Bernard Shaw visited Moscow for nine days. He was accompanied by Lady Astor, striving hard to be the *enfant terrible;* Lord Astor, quietly embarrassed by his wife; David Astor, whom his parents scarcely saved from Communism; and Lord Lothian, whom we had known as Philip Kerr, a weighty journalist and Lloyd George's right-hand finger. But certain Britons have a strange way of vanishing suddenly and reappearing in a totally different incarnation, and one day Kerr disappeared forever and became the Marquess of Lothian. The Astors arrived with Mr. Tennant, their private Christian Science healer, who took sick, and with Maurice Hindus, and through Hindus I joined them and ran around with them a good deal to factories and parties. As their autocade passed through city streets men stopped and tipped their hats to Shaw. The press too featured Shaw. The Astors and Lothian were "also present." In Moscow, at least, the aristocrats of the blood trailed far behind the aristocrat of art.

I was standing outside the Metropole Hotel one afternoon with Hindus when Lady Astor, returning from an excursion, stopped to talk to us. Then she said, "Well, I must be going. I promised Mrs. Shaw to wash G.B.S.'s hair with Lux twice a week." She had brought several boxes of Lux with her from London.

Shaw publicly admitted that he was in fine fettle. Towering above a group of devotees that surrounded him one morning in the lobby of the Metropole, he roared, "This Russian black bread is wonderful. I never evacuated so well in all my life." He celebrated his seventy-fifth birthday in Moscow but behaved like forty, always eager to go places, ever wide-awake and ready to sell his grandmother or son—had he had either—for a pun.

With Litvinov, Jacob Suritz, Soviet Ambassador to Turkey, and others, we visited the Bolshevo Commune, several miles from Moscow, where the government gave young criminals, mostly thieves and mostly boys, complete freedom and an unique opportunity to remold their lives. We sat in a garden surrounded by hundreds of them and now Litvinov, now I, translated the colloquy. Shaw told them he had once been a thief and gave them the details. It is all right, he advised, until you're found out. He might have wrecked the commune.

For many years, I spent one day each year at the commune. The girl ex-thieves had their own dormitory which was much cleaner than the boys'. One girl had a tattoo on her forearm which read, "There is no happiness in life." It was made in prison. Another girl hid her right hand behind her back when I asked her to let me see the tattoo on it. Finally, blushingly, she yielded. It read, "This hand will avenge Kolya Svertkov's deed." She refused to tell me what the deed was, but announced triumphantly that Kolya Svertkov had been shot.

During the Shaw visit to Bolshevo, the visitors organized a team to play the Russians' favorite game of volley ball. Shaw did not play but Lothian did, and this was the only time during the nine days that I saw him come out of his reserve and calm. Lady Astor played on the thieves' team.

Shaw and his titled friends had an interview with Stalin. When the American correspondents later asked G.B.S. for comments, he said, "I shall get $1 a word from one of your foolish newspapers to write about this interview. Why should I tell you?" But as usual some things trickled out. Lady Astor asked Stalin when they would stop killing people; he replied, "When it's no longer necessary." Stalin said Winston Churchill would lead England in a crisis, perhaps as a Fascist. Whereupon Lady Nancy—in the days of Cliveden appeasement some of her enemies called her "Lady Nazi"—exclaimed, "No, we don't like too clever people." Lord Astor kept his counsel but asked penetrating questions.

Before leaving Moscow, Lady Astor was quoted as saying that

Russia was "the best-run country on earth," while Shaw said, "I was a Communist before Lenin." But since then the Communists, as usual, had come to him, and they were no longer Communists, but Fabian Socialists.

Lothian, when still Philip Kerr, had given his opinion long before, in the *London Observer* of September 22, 1929. He wrote, "Russia has dethroned usury from the altar on which it now stands in Western civilization, has rendered it almost impossible for anyone to live, or at least to live comfortably, except by the fruits of his own work, and has made the great engine of economic production and distribution function for the general good and not for private profit."

Lord Lothian told the London School of Economics when he got back from Russia that he was "inclined to think that behind the Russian revolution lies a body of fundamental economic idealism which is going to have a prodigious influence on the history of mankind." Thus, what he saw in Russia in 1931, confirmed what he had thought of Russia in 1929. This was true of so many visitors: they came to see what they wanted to see, good and bad; they came to find corroboration of views previously held and opinions previously expressed.

Bernard Shaw, of course, is the young-old playwright playboy, incalculable and impressionistic, loving above all to shock. But Beatrice and Sidney Webb were old and trained social scientists whose work had influenced a whole generation of British thinking. They were founders of Fabian Socialism, socialism by evolution, and their doctrine was "the inevitability of gradualness." They too came to the Soviet Union. Beatrice Webb was born in 1858 and her husband in 1859. At such advanced ages, the system usually rejects change and conduces to conservatism. But they came and saw and were conquered.

This ancient British couple, who had written scores of classic works together—they were always "the Webbs," though I suspect Beatrice is the bigger Webb—looked strange in Moscow. They traveled extensively in the country gathering material but making less noise than an ex-governor of Kansas and certainly less than the Shaw-Astor-Lothian troupe. At dinner in our apartment, they told of one incident in Tiflis. Every Bolshevik of course knew "Sidnay and Biatriche Vebb" because Lenin had translated their book on *Trade Unionism*. But that was back in 1900, and when they were introduced in Tiflis, someone said with spontaneous surprise, "Why, I thought you were dead." They were so much alive, however, that they commenced to write a major opus on *Soviet Communism: A New Civilization?* which ran to 1,174 pages. In 1934, aged 76 and 75, they came again to Soviet Russia for more data.

In 1935 Mrs. Webb—she never allowed anyone to call her Lady, and he very reluctantly submitted to "His Lordship" only while he was minister in the British Labor government—invited me to lunch in their country home at Passfield Corner, Hants. They plied me with questions for a whole morning. We sat in their library, one extensive wall of which was covered with shelves containing their own publications. At lunch, I had to ask repeatedly for more food because I was being served the meager vegetarian ration which they, and Shaw when he dropped in from his near-by farm, munched slowly. After lunch Mrs. Webb put on a lace night cap and said she would retire for a nap, while Sidney took me for a walk in the woods. Roley-poley body on short legs, he led me a merry race until suddenly he cried, "Here I cast myself upon the ground." And he did. He stretched out on the barren December earth and relaxed and inhaled deeply, and two moments later resumed his walk at breakneck speed.

Harold J. Laski visited Moscow with his wife in 1934. He was then a friendly critic of Communism and a left-wing laborite, Left enough to be permitted to lecture at the Moscow University but not Left enough to escape the jibes of planted hecklers of high academic standing. Laski is brilliant and witty. Labor audiences and classes at the London School of Economics hear him to be entertained and go away enlightened. He knows everybody and has the pardonable frailty of revealing it on every occasion. "And I said, 'Now Stanley . . .' And Baldwin said to me, 'Harold . . .'" Or: "I said, 'F.D., what you think of . . . ?' and the President laughed and asked me to tell him about . . ." The point is, it's true. He has spoken to everybody of importance in England, knows the best minds in America, and has met the statesmen of the continent. In Moscow he had a talk with Lazar Kaganovitch, second most important man in the Soviet Union who is rarely seen by foreigners. A remarkably retentive memory and a unique choice of phrase enable him to character-sketch prominent personalities by stringing their statements on a silver thread of his own. The British Labor Party, of whose inner executive committee he is a member, avails itself of his services in formulating political programs and manifestoes. He is a younger

Webb, streamlined by the twentieth century and America. Laski, apart from all else, is a great journalist whose sentences are not only epic in phrasing but epic in meaning.

Throughout the crowded years in Russia, I met many kings of the spirit who visited it from every land. I met Dr. Fridjhof Nansen, whose tales of Arctic explorations won my boyhood fancy and who after the War became a great relief administrator; Sir Rabindranath Tagore, the Indian poet and sage who liked Moscow despite his pacifism and its violence; Jawaharlal Nehru, the Hindu leader; Karin Michaelis, the Danish author; Henri Barbusse, who talked to me chiefly about Jesus Christ; Agnes Smedley, who channeled a passionate temperament into politics, a brilliant writer and journalist, bravest of all American foreign correspondents for she braved China's diseases and wars and the Chinese gunmen who wanted to earn the Japanese reward for bringing her in "dead or alive"; Mrs. Sun Yat-sen, true and noble revolutionist who hid Miss Smedley when the gunmen came too close—and many many others with lesser names but fine hearts and a devotion to mankind which sent them searching in Russia for an indefinable something.

Many thousands of Americans, Britons, Germans, wished to settle in Russia during those years. Many hundreds did, and many more would have but for restrictions imposed by the Soviet government. Frequently men and women entered on tourist visas and tried to stay, but the police would not let them. The authorities wanted only regulated immigration and were prepared for only a small trickle of that. Sometimes I felt like an employment agency. "I am anxious to live in Russia for a year," read a typical letter, this one from an executive director of an educational association in New Jersey and an old friend of mine. "What are the possibilities of my finding employment?" I advised him to learn to drive a tractor. But he rejected this wise counsel, came to give English lessons, became a correspondent of British and American papers, became a Communist, and named his son Karl—after Marx or/and Radek.

Critics of the waste and high social cost of capitalism, these tourists-to-an-ideology wanted to see a society groping toward its goal without benefit of private bankers, holding companies, business magnates, and stock markets. Many of them were fascinated by the phenomena of growth and popular enthusiasm in Russia. Where there had been nothing, a factory or a whole city or a giant farm had come into being for everybody. The hum of creation stirred them. Other nations had built just as quickly and much better than Soviet Russia. While they built, individualism ran amuck and victory was to the strong, sometimes to the corrupt. The Bolsheviks, however, aimed to guide individual ambitions into the national energy fund for the common weal.

In 1932, the managing directors of Soviet "giants"—the new mammoth industrial plants—were summoned to Moscow for a technical conference. Inevitably, one session was a banquet to which foreign correspondents received invitations. In Russia, there are no introductions by a third person; each person gives his own name. When the directors introduced themselves to me, they did not say "Dibetz" or "Svistun." One shook me by the hand and said "Dnieperstroi" which was the name of the big hydro-electric station and dam on the Dnieper. Another said, "Autostroi," which was the name of the automobile factory on the Volga; another "Magnitogorsk," the huge magnetic steel city in the Urals.

"*L'état c'est moi*," a girl college student from Leningrad said to me. "You see, I am the state. Its problems, troubles, and victories are mine. Our minds are turned outward," she explained when she heard that the depression turned many American minds toward psychoanalysis and glands. "I would be bored to death if I had only myself to think of and take care of."

Walking barefooted down a dirt road, a Russian boy said to Maurice Hindus, "We have put the word 'riches' into the museum." A Soviet arithmetic teacher gave the class this example, "If a man buys six dozen apples at eighteen kopeks an apple and sells them at thirty-six kopeks an apple what does he get?" A boy waved his hand wildly and exclaimed, "A jail sentence." This illustrated a basic principle of Soviet economics but also a basic change in Soviet psychology.

In the summer of 1932, I spent a week at the Putilov factory in Leningrad. It is one of the oldest and largest steel and machine-making plants in Russia, covering an area of seven square miles. I lived on the premises in a workingman's dwelling, went swimming with the workers, visited their homes, attended their meetings, ate with the personnel, talked to an endless array of employees, interviewed the director several times, and inspected many of the workshops where they made locomotives, turbines, freight cars, dredgers. I went back the next summer and again the next summer and then a fourth time so that I could gauge progress and change. The Putilov people knew me and I knew many of them. They took pride in their factory. They pointed out to me the new trees and flowerbeds planted since my last stay, the new foundries erected, the new million-ruble clubhouse built near the plant for the 28,000 workers, and the volumes acquired by the tremendous library. As I walked around the place, men would call out to me, "Look at this. This wasn't here last year."

Many expensive imported lathes functioned in the turbine shop. Each one had an inscription painted on it like this: "Comrade, your lathe costs 17,500 gold rubles. Take care of it." I asked whether this really meant something to the mechanics. One of them answered, "If I spoil my machine the government will have to export more of our butter and eggs to buy another." In a sense it was a factory with 28,000 bosses.

The director's chauffeur told me that he previously worked in the foundry but had to be transferred on account of his bad lungs. I said, "This is much better, isn't it?"

"No," he replied, "there I was producing. Here I am merely serving somebody."

Soviet citizens knew that they were making history and paying the cost. I used to visit the Dnieperstroi construction every year. In 1930, I clambered over the red granite boulders which form the bed of the broad Dnieper. The river had been checked and diverted. Five years later I drove by car over a road on top of a wall 110 feet high. The wall rested on those boulders. The wall was the Dnieper dam creating 810,000 horsepower of electricity. At the official inauguration of the dam and the industrial city that rose round it, I stood on the periphery of the crowd which consisted of the workingmen who had built it and the peasants from near-by villages. I heard one typical Russian laborer say as he watched the water rush in a Niagara cascade over the lofty concrete dam, "Now I know where my butter and boots went." He had made an investment in the economic upbuilding of his country. The whole nation had invested heavily, invested lives, health, nerves, and faith. A regime which accepts such an investment from depositors accepts a tremendous responsibility. The inspiration of the Five Year Plans was better food, clothes and shelter—a better life tomorrow. But not a too distant tomorrow. For Russia had lived in misery since 1915. From 1915 to

1935—for many people that represented a whole lifetime, a whole lifetime spent in hardship.

The Nazis said bluntly: Your butter is making guns. Guns lead to war. The German people cannot have been surprised or disappointed on September 1, 1939. But the Bolsheviks said: Your butter will make electricity, steel, and coal. The electricity, steel, and coal will make shirts, shoes, houses, transportation facilities, books, defense weapons, peace, and freedom. That was the hope which inspired the effort of the years from 1929 to 1935. The added investment exhausted most Soviet citizens. But toward the end of 1934, and especially in 1935, they saw material improvement and relaxation of the terror. The country was better protected against attack. Russians felt they would have peace. In 1917, Lenin promised peace and bread. The promise was now beginning to be fulfilled.

11. *At Home*

EACH year I came home from Europe to lecture and refresh myself with friendship.

Lecturing in America helped me to write. It was difficult to write five thousand miles from my editors and seven thousand miles from some readers. Lecturing is more intimate, especially since I have the disconcerting faculty of seeing hundreds of faces while I stand in front of them and talk. And I occasionally remember those faces when I meet them again and wonder where I have seen them before. I find that most American audiences start out with a sympathy for the speaker which he forfeits only by his own grievous fault. The size of an audience, its interest in what is being said, affect the quality of a lecture. Question time is the best because one comes to grips with the listeners' minds. In radical groups there are always a few who make speeches instead of putting questions, but usually questioners seek enlightenment or helpfully try to keep the ball rolling.

Lecturing in America has also helped me to see America. It has taught me geography, regional history, psychology, and a few more things. I was in Detroit in 1933 when all the banks closed. I had no money and no one I knew had money. Checks were no good and nobody knew when they would be good. So the hotel manager simply told me to leave without paying my bill. In cities and on trains the emergency created a camaraderie, unity, and universal loquaciousness that were comforting and heartening.

The first time I visited San Francisco, kind hosts showed me the city and its environs. They asked me how I liked it. I said it was one of the finest places I had ever seen. They asked whether it wasn't more beautiful than Los Angeles. I said I had never been to Los Angeles. No, but surely, they insisted, Los Angeles couldn't be as beautiful as this. I repeated I couldn't tell. They were deeply disappointed and I realized that a deadly feud existed between the two great cities.

I am fascinated by the ties that exist between Iowa and Nebraska and Southern California, between New England and Cleveland, between Florida and Spain, and between New England and England. The portraits on the walls of a dining room in a Hartford mansion took me right back to the eighteenth century.

Lecturing is usually tranquil. But sometimes there were storms. For instance: March 20, 1932. The ballroom of the Bellevue-Stratford Hotel in Philadelphia. Foreign Policy Association luncheon. Chairman: Francis A. Biddle, noted Philadelphia lawyer, later United States Solicitor General. Speakers: Calvin B. Hoover, Professor at Drake University, Eve Garret Grady, wife of an American engineer formerly employed by the Soviet Government, and myself. Subject: Russia.

The luncheon became front-page news.

Mrs. Grady had just published a book about the Soviet Union entitled *Seeing Red*. She contributed articles to the *Saturday Evening Post* and other magazines and spoke over the radio—always against the Soviets. What she said was so glaringly unfair to her readers, to listeners, and to Russia that I decided to take this opportunity to expose her. Mrs. Grady spoke first and indulged in her usual denunciations of the Soviets. Then I spoke.

"Truth," I said, "is the highest of moral values. Honesty is greater than politeness. In view of conflicting presentations of Russian conditions, and since America is so far from Russia that few Americans have their own basis for judgment, the veracity and character of the reporter play an important role." While she lived with her husband in the Soviet Union, I continued, Mrs. Grady wrote favorable articles for the *Moscow Daily News*, a Bolshevik publication. At one period she published an article giving luscious details of the abundance of food in the mining district where she lived. But after leaving Russia she published an article in an American magazine and referring to the same place and the same period she declared that there had been a serious lack of food. I read excerpts from both articles. Moreover, Mrs. Grady had written that she was expelled from Russia for circulating a joke about Stalin. "That is untrue," I declared. She left Russia because her husband was dismissed by the Soviet government. I then read the copy of a telegram sent by Mr. Grady to a high Soviet official declaring that in case the Soviet government did not renew his contract he would conduct propaganda against it in the United States and stating that he had numerous influential friends in America, among whom he named Senator Borah. The Soviet government, however, did not renew his contract and when he and his wife left, Mrs. Grady commenced fulfilling the threat which was contained in her husband's telegram. At this point I dropped the subject of Mrs. Grady and proceeded with my address on Moscow's foreign policy. When I sat down the Chairman gave Mrs. Grady a chance to reply. She rose and said, "It has frequently been said that to be true to one's self one has to be a cad. I think that Mr. Fischer is being true to himself."

"Francis A. Biddle, the Chairman," according to the newspapers, "leaped to his feet, hammered with his gavel and interrupting Mrs. Grady, rebuked her." "I will not sit here," he declared, "and listen to that kind of veiled insults in this hall." "Whereat," said the *Philadelphia Inquirer*, "there was loud applause." Mrs. Grady sat down. Mr. Biddle offered her another opportunity to deny my charges or dispute my facts, but she refused.

Hoover leaned over to me and whispered, "While you were talking Mrs. Grady said to me, 'What would you do in such a situation?'" And Hoover replied, "I wouldn't get into such a situation."

Mrs. Grady sat at her place for a few moments weeping. Some people said she fainted and was escorted out of the room. Actually she walked out at least an hour before the luncheon was over and never returned. But more important: after this luncheon Mrs. Grady ceased writing, ceased speaking on the radio, ceased appearing publicly. Since then I have never heard one word about her nor has any one of the many people of whom I have made inquiries.

During a Pacific Coast tour in 1933, I spoke in Spokane at the convention of the Inland Empire Education Association. Lincoln Steffens and I were the guest speakers and each of us delivered three addresses.

"Make 'em laugh," Steffens advised. "Then you can say anything. You can tell Americans to go to hell provided you do it with a joke or anecdote. I always preach revolution," he confessed. "But I make it funny and they don't mind." They didn't, and he went much further than I did, while I got into trouble. For, as one paper said, I was advocating American recognition of Soviet Russia: "FISCHER WANTS HAND EXTENDED TO RED RUSSIA." The S.A.R. (Sons of the American Revolution) adopted a protest and published it in the press. The D.A.R. passed a vote of horror (though some of them came backstage and said they agreed with me). Most indignant of all, it seems, was Turnbull—"School Speaker Roils Turnbull with Russ Talk"; Turnbull was Alex Turnbull, president of the Board of Education, and he got so angry after my morning speech that he wanted to stop my speech in the afternoon.

A reporter rushed into the breach, and the following brilliant interchange took place. I quote:

"Dr. Fischer"—a lecturer usually becomes Doctor, it's more impressive—"we are informed the Daughters of the American Revolution are keeping a close check on your movements. It is said they believe you are in the employ of the Russian soviet. You undoubtedly know about these things. What have you to say?" . . .

"Junk," Dr. Fischer replied; "just junk! Similar charges were made against Senator Borah and others who have visited Russia and have told the facts about Russia. Such charges are the work of closed-minded reactionaries."

"Are you advocating a Communist form of government for the United States?" the interviewer asked.

"I am not mentioning America in these lectures. I don't know anything about America."

"Are you not an American?"

"Yes, I'm an American, but I don't know anything about America."

"Do you mean to say you know more about Russia than you know about the United States?"

"I do. I have been in Russia ten years making a study of Russia. I have never made a study of the United States."

The parting blow was the worst of all. "Your statements," the reporter asserted, "differ with those made by Will Durant who lectured here recently." I pleaded guilty.

What I really thought about revolution in America was correctly quoted, with approval incidentally, in the Scripps-Howard *San Francisco News*. I said:

"No Communist revolution is possible in any country until the whole middle class is impoverished. We still have a huge middle class, and we have as yet no proletariat, which means a class of workers who own no property and have no hope of owning any.

"Steps toward revolution are the development of a proletariat, the rise of a large class of tenant farmers, and the impoverishment of the middle class. We have the beginnings of all three, but we still have the utmost confidence in our ability to check them by a resort to state capitalism and even to state socialism.

"The greatest element of stability in any social order is hope, and we have tremendous reserves of hope. Not until hope is lost is a people ready for the desperate expedient of revolution."

During the many years in which I wrote and lectured about the Soviet Union I was of course accused of being a Soviet agent, the recipient of Soviet gold, and a Communist. Such gossip never bothered me. I asked for the proof. There could be no proof because it was and is untrue. If I had been a Communist I should not have been ashamed or afraid to affirm it. I was never an official or an unofficial representative of the Soviet government or of the Comintern or of any branch or department of either. I never carried out any mission for Moscow or anyone in it. In 1925, I worked for four months in the Soviet Telegraphic Agency (TASS) office in London in the capacity of journalistic expert on international politics, much as Colonel Hugh Cooper and other American specialists worked for the Soviet government. That was the closest and the last connection I had with the Soviets. I was pro-Soviet when I thought the Soviet government was doing good, and I am anti-Soviet now because I think the Soviet government is doing more harm than good.

But it is interesting to scrutinize those who made these charges. They had not a shred of evidence and had only their anger to guide them. Because I was pro-Soviet I was accused of being in the pay of Moscow. What does that mean? That one could not be pro-Soviet except for pay. That seems to me to reflect sadly on the character of the persons making the charges. Is it not possible to take a stand out of conviction and deep belief? Apparently with some people only money counts and they cannot understand anything except in terms of price. Or, not being able to answer an observer's statements, they try to smother him in mud.

I have all my life been devoted to one cause or another. I cannot imagine life without something higher than myself in which I can have faith. Naturally that colors my writing. But who is objective? Only a jellyfish has no prejudices. I endeavor to reduce mine to a minimum. Truth with me is a passion, and I do not hold that a cause is worth much if it must live on lies. I write as I please and what I believe to be true. I was a passionate partisan of Loyalist Spain. But my first article on Spain at war was so unfavorable that the Madrid censor refused to pass it. I nevertheless had it smuggled out and published.

I advocated American recognition of Soviet Russia because I believed it would help Russia and, at least, do no harm to America. I regarded Soviet Russia as important to the future of the world. The French Revolution was opposed and maligned, but it made a tremendous contribution to civilized life. I expected good to come of the Bolshevik Revolution. Recognition would assist Russia, and therefore the world, to greater peace and prosperity. It would establish normal relations and normal channels of information between two peoples. I cannot see that it has, to this day, done the slightest damage to the United States. On February 25, 1933, I debated with Congressman Hamilton Fish, Jr., at the National Republican Club in New York on recognition, and he said: "Recognition of the Soviet would be an antagonistic move against Japan. It would bring about a situation where the United States would find itself policing Manchuria and fighting China's battles all alone." The only answer to that would have been: "Mr. Hamilton Fish, Jr., you're a fool." But he was a congressman and I a mere journalist, and we were in a polite gathering. Yet how silly that sounds today. "Policing Manchuria." The fact is that Russia fought China's battles against Japan while the United States did not. Mr. Fish also stressed the menace of Communism. The best answer was Roy W. Howard's in a letter to Reeve Schley of the Chase National Bank. "Personally," Howard wrote, "I think the menace of Bolshevism in the United States is as great as the menace of sunstroke in Greenland or chilblains in the Sahara."

Even men like Chief Justice Hughes have enjoyed visiting Alexander Troyanovsky, the first Soviet Ambassador, and lesser men have been pleased to talk there with his lesser successor, Constantine Oumansky. Until 1939, the Soviet Embassy received a high rating in Washington society, and congressman crashed the gate at its receptions. Matrons and debutantes pulled wires to receive invitations. It was considered piquant and slightly naughty to have partaken of Stalin's food.

"Concerning the Russian reception, the lucky 800 who received invitations (it is said that 4,000 requests were unfilled) have talked of little since but the aplomb of the Troyanovskys, the excellence and abundance of the food and wine, and the good taste of the furnishings. To hear the talk, one would suppose that they expected to find the Ambassador in a smock and leather boots. The fact is. of course, that the Soviet government has maintained diplomatic establishments in foreign capitals for many years, and so far as I know, their social conduct has always been unexceptionable. At any rate, the Ambassador's evening clothes were impeccable, and debutantes who arrived in red gowns especially ordered for the occasion were somewhat chagrined to find Mrs. Troyanovsky in a modish creation of peach. Heywood Broun seemed uncomfortably conscious of his dinner jacket until ex-Senator Brookhart showed up in shiny blue serge. (None of his friends' evening clothes fit him.) To me the rarest sight of the evening was that of a Republican congressman from Massachusetts leaning against a bust of Lenin, with a glass of Soviet champagne in one hand and a hunk of Soviet caviar in the other, gravely discoursing on the red peril in America as disclosed by the Wirt charges. Judging from appearances he was feeling no pain, and what he lacked in a sense of humor was made up in appetite. Grizzled dowagers who had not been out since General Grant's inaugural ball smirked and waved their reticules frivolously at one another, and all was merrier than the wedding bell. There is doubtless some salutary, if not shocking, moral to be drawn from all this, but thus far I have been unable to discover it. I had a swell time— partly, perhaps, because I didn't run into Ham Fish."

That was Paul Y. Anderson in the *Nation* of May 2, 1934.

Soviet diplomats can be very irritating in negotiations, and Soviet-American relations never filled in the blank check that Roosevelt, Bullitt, and Litvinov wrote for them. But I can discover no detriment caused to America. Only a few opportunities missed on both sides. Relations between states are not based on mutual approval of their acts at home or abroad. If the United States maintained diplomatic contacts only with governments whose policies all Americans admired we would have a much smaller foreign service, and on the same principle there might be fewer foreign diplomats on the Potomac. Diplomacy is not love; it is business. It is impossible to know when America will need Russia's co-operation somewhere. With an eye to that day, contacts, however cool, must be maintained.

One Saturday in January, 1931, I attended a lunch at the National Republican Club where the late Senator Bronson M. Cutting and Anna Louise Strong spoke for American recognition of Soviet Russia while Matthew Woll, trade-union leader, and Paul Scheffer spoke against it. Both sides argued so poorly that I thought there was room for a book on the subject. On Monday, I went to see Harrison Smith, my enterprising publisher, and sketched the outline of the book. On Tuesday, we signed the contract, and a month later the book was ready for the press with the title, *Why Recognize Russia?*

The person who first interested me in United States recognition of Soviet Russia was Senator Burton K. Wheeler, of Montana. I interviewed him in April, 1923, in the Sugar King's Palace in Moscow, where he and Mrs. Wheeler were staying as guests of the Soviet government which, in view of the scarcity of decent accommodations, was a sensible thing to do. The kind senator, seeing my inexperience, practically dictated the interview to me, and its first sentence, as printed in the *New York Evening Post* of May 28, 1923, read, "There is absolutely no reason in the world why the United States should not recognize Russia." After I thought about it a little I felt the same way.

Colonel Raymond Robins, a rib of the real America, ex-Governor Goodrich of Indiana, Senator Borah, and innumerable wise citizens made recognition their fight. It was, to say the least, bad politics and bad common sense not to be in touch with a power which was half of Europe and which occupied a most important strategic position in relation to Japan and China.

I met Colonel Robins at dinner at Alex Gumberg's, which was a second home to me in the United States. Alex was a Russian-Jewish immigrant married to Frances Adams of the New England Adamses. In Alex, Russia and America merged in a remarkable synthesis. He had a profound loyalty to the Bolshevik Revolution—perhaps because he witnessed its birth in Petrograd. In the early romantic months, Alex, working with Colonel Robins of the American Red Cross, often interviewed Lenin, Trotzky, and other high Communist officials, and until his premature death in May, 1939, he treasured letters from them. The Soviet government arrested and exiled his younger brother, S. Zorin, writer and Trotzkyist. It later arrested an older brother and sent him into prolonged exile. When the *Pravda* attacked his older brother, it also slandered Alex. (Alex had the satisfaction of seeing the *Pravda* print his letter of refutation, something the infallible Olympian *Pravda* did about once a decade.) Intimate friends of Alex's, among them Serebjakov, were tried and executed. Others, like Valeri Mezhlauk, Vice-Prime Minister of the Soviet Union and Chairman of the State Planning Commission, who used to come to the Gumberg apartment in East Seventeenth Street, New York, disappeared in the big purge. Alex was puzzled along with the rest of us, but he remained pro-Soviet even when he noticed, and commented on, my cooler attitude. I think he could not forget the glorious auspices under which the Revolution started and could not believe that the seeds then sown had all grown into tares.

After the Revolution, Alex presided over the office of the Soviet Textile Syndicate in New York. He bought cotton for Russia. American businessmen recognized his talents. Later he became a highly paid and highly appreciated member of the Atlas Corporation. His life thus spanned the variegated stream of American society. A Morgan called him in for consultation. Dwight Morrow, U. S. Ambassador in Mexico, asked him down to talk over the situation there. Communists came in to hear his anti-Communist views in a parlor within a stone's throw of Union Square, for though he liked the Soviets he disliked the tactics of the American Communist Party. Senators Borah and Robert La Follette were his close friends. Philip La Follette and his fiery wife often visited the Gumberg apartment. There, staid university professors met Communist authors, ship captains told their tall tales to society ladies, financial writers from Wall Street mingled with poets, and Socialists and Communists and Trotzkyists debated at the fireside while bankers and editors and teachers listened. John Dewey, at an age of over seventy, used to love to come—and dance. Businessmen got acquainted with artists, corporation lawyers with Bohemians. For many Americans, Alex was the bridge to Soviet Russia. But subsequently he helped Russia understand America. Floyd Dell, Stuart Chase, Joseph Wood Krutch and his wife Marcelle (in fact the whole *Nation* family), the Van Dorens, Louis and Stella Adamic, Reeve Schley, Lewis Gannett, Kenneth Durant, Rebecca and Oscar Bernstein, Samuel Zemurray of the United Fruit Company, Josephine Herbst, George Britt, Joseph Freeman, Paul and Julia Blanshard, Amy and Walter Charak, Edith Christensen, and May Cameron were steady visitors. Frankie, Alex's wife, contributed an unostentatiously efficient and cordial hospitality. Alex was a good conversationalist who unfailingly went the longest way around a circle to get to the point of his story. His great art, however, consisted in provoking others to talk, and in ragging everybody, so that there were no dull moments unless you created them in a corner by yourself. He possessed warmth and a deep understanding of human beings. He had the mellow wisdom of age and the mischief of a boy. He helped many people with advice, sympathy, and hospitality. Death at fifty closed a full life but also left many pages unturned.

Thanks to Alex and his friends, my circle of personal and journalistic acquaintance in America grew wide. Alex brought me to Senator Borah and S. Parker Gilbert. And it was through one of Alex's banker friends that I got an appointment with Secretary of State Henry L. Stimson.

I saw Mr. Stimson on several occasions. When he received me in his office on February 3, 1933, he seemed deeply disappointed, as if he were being torn from something he did not want to leave, and my impression received confirmation later that day from an assistant secretary. What Stimson said indicated clearly his anti-appeasement attitude toward Japan and his support of Russian recognition. He asked me about conditions in the Soviet Union. I talked of industrialization in European Russia, and in Siberia particularly. He said, "I think Russia's military position is not as strong as it looks." This point had apparently entered into somebody's apology for America's policy toward Japan. If Russia was weak, America could not take grave risks in the Far East.

From Stimson's office I went to Senator Borah's. He told me of a conversation he had had with Stimson that summer under the trees of the Borah mansion. Borah believed Stimson was leaving office with a heavy heart because of things undone, one of those being recognition. Stimson, Borah declared, would have recognized Russia but for President Hoover. In Borah's opinion, Hoover was hostile to Russia because the Bolsheviks had confiscated his properties (the Urquarht holdings), and because "Hoover is such a colossal individualist and conservative."

Borah thought Roosevelt would recognize Soviet Russia soon after the Inauguration despite the fact that Bernard Baruch opposed it. Owen D. Young was for it, and so was Cordell Hull, who, Borah predicted, would be the new Secretary of State.

During those days the high officials of the Department of State were busy handing over to their successors; one of them, who was going back to his university, said to me, "This is a queer system where a man has to quit just when he has learned his job." He told me Stimson was suffering under the strain of the transfer.

I returned to the Department of State after the first Roosevelt administration had taken over. It was the most chaotic institution I have ever seen. Raymond Moley, Hull's assistant, told me he favored recognition of Russia. I talked to him about the Chinese Eastern Railway and its importance to America's position in the Far East. He asked me to send him a memorandum on the subject (which I did) for submission to Mr. Roosevelt. He made it quite clear to me that there was just the President and himself and nobody else. An English diplomat, watching Moley function, said: "Moley, Moley, Moley, Lord God Almighty." But in subsequent years white, translucent, single-track Cordell Hull succeeded in eating up all the young upstarts who thought he was only an old congressman from Tennessee. Nothing so reveals the immaturity, or so undermines the position, of young men on the periphery of others' greatness as the temptation to boast.

On one of my trips to Washington I took a path across the White House enclosure to cut from one street to the other. Hundreds do it every day. If I had not lived so long in Russia, it would not have seemed remarkable to me. I once sat in the square opposite the White House with a Soviet journalist. He commented on the same thing, and said, "Democracy, by God."

For many years I contributed regularly to that dignified, excellent paper, the *Baltimore Sun*. Opposite its fine editorial page it printed double-column mail feature articles from a galaxy of celebrated correspondents like H. N. Brailsford and "Pertinax," and I was proud to be in the distinguished company. I appreciated the paper and the treatment accorded my correspondences—never a word altered or cut.

During a lecture visit to Baltimore, Paul Patterson, owner of the *Sun* papers, invited me to an editorial conference. Men with honored names in American journalism were present: John W. Owens, editor of the Sun papers, Hamilton Owens, editor of the *Morning Sun*, John H. Adams, Frank R. Kent, veteran columnist, H. L. Mencken, and others.

The conference devoted most of its attention to a bill pending in the Maryland legislature on the licensing of Christian Science healers. The *Morning Sun* wished to oppose the licensing of healers. But Mencken of the *Evening Sun* expressed the belief that if "boobs" wanted to be healed by healers that was their business. Probably no one has lampooned and burlesqued Christian Scientists, Mary Baker Eddy, and healers as much as Mencken. But his loyalty to freedom exceeded his aversion to "quackery." The meeting soon developed into a debate on liberty. Mencken did most of the talking and no one objected. His wit, dirty jokes, and scientific animadversions kept all entertained. When Mencken tired or dried up, others present, including myself, were asked for opinions. Absolute freedom, I thought, meant anarchy and danger to the community. Suppose somebody started a magazine to advocate murder and rape? In the end, the conference ruled that each *Sun* paper could do as its editors decided, and, in principle, each editor could write as he pleased. Since murder or rape was not involved this certainly followed the great journalistic tradition.

I appreciate the value of freedom more than most Americans because I have lived so long in countries that have no freedom. There were years when I pooh-poohed liberty and said, "Liberty for whom?" But in Russia where the Bolsheviks began by denying liberty to their enemies, they ended by denying it to everybody. In many ways, absences from Russia made me fonder of it. But in many other ways, the West made me doubt Russia. More and more, the great question for me was: Can the Soviet dictatorship gradually evolve into a political democracy?

12. *Stalin and the GPU*

SOVIET RUSSIA continued for many years to attract intellectuals and workingmen from western countries. Indeed the rise of Hitler in 1933 multiplied the number of foreign friends of the Soviet Union. They saw in Russia a counterpoise to German might and Nazi ideas.

To be sure, some people whom one would have expected to see in Moscow never put in an appearance. Senator William E. Borah, for instance, told me in 1933 that he would have liked to visit Russia and Germany but didn't go because as chairman of the Senate Foreign Relations committee he would have had to pay his respects to England and France and he hated them. I believe Borah did not go abroad once during his entire official career.

Despite my repeated urging, Freda Kirchwey, editor of *The Nation*, also failed to visit Moscow. Once, with her husband Evans Clark, former editorial writer on the *New York Times*, now director of the Twentieth Century Fund, she got as far as Vienna, and from there they sent me a classic telegram, reading, "NO TIME FOR RUSSIA."

But often it seemed as though everybody I ever saw or heard of in America turned up in Moscow at some time or another during those hectic years of Soviet reconstruction. One summer day a bus drew up in the narrow little side street where we lived, and out of it issued Maxwell Stewart's tourist group of teachers and social workers bent on asking me questions. Occasionally, correspondents would hand visitors from one to the other. And what a jumble of Duranty-Ralph W. Barnes-Fischer-Lyons-Spencer Williams-Habicht they must have carried away with them to mull over on the Atlantic before telling waiting reporters, relatives, and pupils the "real truth about Russia"! Some tourists returned to Moscow on their way out and then I would cross-examine them, for they often saw things with their fresh eyes that had become invisible to me. The final question from me or Markoosha was, "Is there any clothing you could leave for our friends?" and we would go over to their hotels and pick up slips, silk stockings, shirtwaists, suits, shoes, and what-not for Soviet

216

acquaintances to whom these cast-offs meant more than the latest Alix or Schiaparelli creation could mean to tomorrow's debutante. We had Soviet women friends who would come to the apartment just to feast their eyes on the old clothes that tourists wore for roughing it in Russia. One would say, "Do you think she could leave that scarf?" These Russians were ready to pay any amount of money for such hand-me-downs, and occasionally the foreigners took rubles because they needed them for their travels.

I saw so many tourists that I finally decided I might as well have some of my own, and in 1934, I accepted an offer from John Rothschild to lead an Open Road tourist group through the Soviet Union at so many dollars per head. I did this for three summers running, and the last time, just before going off to the Spanish War, I earned $2,000 for five weeks' travel with stimulating people.

Maurice Wertheim was my star pupil in 1934. He had been commended to my attention by Freda Kirchwey. (He later bought *The Nation* from Villard and, soon, sold it to Freda.) Wertheim is a wealthy man, with large holdings of many kinds. He lives in a penthouse in New York and has an estate at Cos Cob where he maintains a handsome establishment. He takes pride in his collection of Picasso "Blues" and other French moderns including Despiau sculpture. Good capitalist, he bought a river in Canada so he could catch his own salmon. Yet this man said he came to Russia "to find a social philosophy." Bolsheviks had a hard time understanding the friendly reaction of this millionaire investment banker, this "Wall Street" man, to Soviet conditions. On long hot train rides across the Russian steppes, when he was not winning at chess or anagrams, he studied Marx and then provoked arguments with me and our little redheaded Soviet interpreter, Vera Bakhanova, who was a young Communist and an eager Soviet gospel-spreader. Or he read Soviet statistical reports and State Bank statements.

To understand what this trip meant to Maurice Wertheim I had to wait until the winter of that year when I lived as a guest in his big penthouse and estate. What contrast!

In Russia, Wertheim had slept in a stuffy upper berth with three others in the compartment, had taken afternoon naps on trains in his clothes, jogged over rough Russian roads in buses with bad springs, and jumped up a minute after meals when I summoned my flock for the next factory or village excursion. "Ah, let's sit still for a minute," he would beg sometimes, but there was no time, and he obeyed like a sport. He had never felt better in all his life. I called the cure extroversion. The big thing was that Soviet Russia had taken him out of himself and made him forget America, business, and all the rest of it.

At the opposite pole from Maurice Wertheim was Jim Ferry. Wertheim was Harvard, a horseman, yacht-owner, director of the Theatre Guild, friend of President Conant, of Sam Behrman, of Joseph Krutch. . . . Ferry, red-faced Irishman, graduate of a primary school, spoke a workingman's idiom. He had been a workingman most of his life, but was now a contractor of underwater construction in Atlantic City. He looked the embodiment of toil and common man. He helped the group a lot. He smelled the concrete in new Soviet buildings, he touched brick and iron for us, he told us whether a job was well-done or not. I do not know whether he had ever read a book. Certainly Marx was Martian abracadabra to him. But he loved the Russians immediately because he saw workingmen on top, and his round Farley-face broke out into a smile when laborers at a Soviet resort boasted of facilities for vacations which he knew were denied similar people at home. With Ferry and an Armenian engineer I waded thigh-deep, in appropriate clothing, through the Moscow subway then under construction. He told me what they were doing more expensively, what better, what worse, than in America. But he said their concrete "is mixed with love." "They build for themselves," he repeated, "whereas at home we build for a boss under contract." (Years later Ferry turned up in New York with the huge typewritten manuscript of a novel he had written on Russia.)

Wertheim, Ferry, Miss Blanche Hull, Dr. Dorothea Moore of Cambridge, Massachusetts, and the other members of the party raced after me through Leningrad, Moscow, Kharkov, Tiflis, Baku and numerous villages and by the time they had seen a long chain of factories, farms, new parks, children's homes, hospitals, office buildings, apartment houses, on tours which were not conducted because they could choose the places they wanted to see and by the time they had talked to scores of executives, workingmen, peasant women, students, and soldiers, they were so enthusiastic about Russia that I had to suggest the existence of certain aspects of Soviet life not so visible to the naked eye. At one of our regular meetings at which I lectured or answered questions or led discussions, Wertheim asked that we give some time to these aspects. It was in Odessa at the end of the tour. We had just returned from a swim in the Black Sea which had been followed by a brief interview with William C. Bullitt, then on vacation in Odessa. Our group spent four unbroken hours analyzing the seamy sides of Soviet affairs. My own contribution to this séance was devoted to the GPU and Stalin.

GPU are the initials of Russian words meaning State Political Administration which is a euphemism for Russia's special political police. The "O" sometimes found in front of these letters stands for federal, but it is not used in Russian conversation. Russians always say "Gay Pay Oo." So as not to say "Gay Pay Oo" too frequently, some foreigners refer to the special police as "the three letters" or "the YMCA."

My first personal contact with the GPU was in 1923. It was then the custom for foreign correspondents who wished to take their clippings, carbon copies, and letters out of Russia to bring them to the Narkomindel (Soviet foreign office) and have them examined there by a GPU official. By appointment I brought my files and met the man who had been summoned from the big GPU headquarters just across the street from the Narkomindel. He was young, tall, and blond, and spoke perfect German. His mother was Austrian and he had received part of his education in Vienna.

His perusal of my papers was perfunctory and we talked as he paged through them.

"Have you ever killed anyone?" I inquired.

"Yes," said the GPU official quietly.

"Killed or executed?" I asked.

"Killed and executed," he said quietly.

"I understand," I ventured, "how a man might kill in battle. But for a government official to approach a defenseless prisoner from behind and fire a bullet through the back of his neck—how could you do it?"

"Listen," he exclaimed. There was excitement in his voice, and he had dropped my papers. "In 1919, I was in the Red Army fighting Kolchak in Siberia. Fifteen hundred of us were captured. The Whites divided us into three groups of five hundred each. The first group received shovels and were ordered to dig a trench. When it was finished they stood in front of it, and machine guns pumped lead into them and they fell into the long common grave. The second group was forced to pick up the shovels and cover their dead comrades with sod. Then they dug a second trench. A second time the machine guns opened up and mowed down the second five hundred. I was in the third group," the GPU man continued, and by this time the telling had become hard for him. "We had to cover the dead and dig our own grave. We had not been allowed to exchange a word. But we knew what we were going to do. We rushed the machine gunners and hacked them dead with our spades. We were mad. One hundred and forty-two of us were killed. The rest escaped into the woods. Then I volunteered to work in the GPU. Do you think I would hesitate to shoot a White?"

Sadists and perverts undoubtedly find their way into the secret police units of dictator states. But this GPU official and many of his colleagues were inspired by revolutionary fervor. Work in such an organization is dangerous. The enemy may strike you down or a false step or a false word can subject you to the severest punishment by your own government. The GPU operates under a code of strictest individual secrecy, discipline, responsibility, and self-sacrifice.

The secret police saved the Bolshevik regime from defeat in the Civil War. It suppressed conspiracies and ferreted out hidden enemies. It also had to deal with foreign spies, who were always plentiful in Soviet Russia. Some of these subsequently showed in their memoirs how they tried to interfere with the Bolshevik defense program.

Even in peacetime, the Soviet government needed to be on guard against internal and external enemies. But after a while, and particularly in peacetime, a secret police tends to become a vested interest. The GPU had power to act quickly and summarily. It was inevitable that this power should be abused. The corrective would have been public criticism or public discussion. But this was not permitted; the GPU was an untouchable. The *Pravda* of November 15, 1922, contained a letter by N. Podvoiskaya accusing a GPU official named Volkov of killing V. G. Marts, a schoolteacher, in order to get the latter's room. Three days later the paper printed a communiqué from the GPU charging N. Podvoiskaya with giving false information and declaring that Marts was killed not by Volkov but by I. N. Naoumov. Below this official statement, however, the *Pravda* published an article by N. Mehonoshin, a prominent army officer, in which he contradicts the GPU's facts. He reveals the circumstances: Marts, the murdered man, occupied an apartment of three small rooms with a large family. Regulations entitled him to that floor space. But Volkov who lived in the same house coveted one of Marts' rooms.

He terrorized Marts and coerced the house committee into giving him the room. The court issued an injunction. When the litigants left the courthouse, Volkov and Naoumov, a friend of Volkov, set upon Marts, and Naoumov drew a revolver and shot him. Such a public airing of an illegal act by a GPU official and, more to the point, such public contradiction of a GPU communiqué were precluded in later years. The GPU had become inviolable.

I once had a brush with a GPU official. Taxis were always difficult to obtain in Moscow. Sometimes, taxi drivers just refused to take you where you wanted to go. A Moscow paper printed a caricature one day showing a pedestrian loaded down with a pack, a fat briefcase, a stove pipe, and a bundle dangling from a finger. He approaches a taxi, tips his hat obsequiously to the chauffeur and says, "Pardon me for troubling you, honored comrade. But perhaps by accident you will soon be going in the direction of Pluschiha Street?" The driver returns an indignant stare and doesn't budge. When one found a taxi one held on to it. One day I got into a taxi standing at its rack in Theatre Square. I gave my address to the driver. Just then a man opened the door and said to me, "Citizen, this taxi is for me." I said I had been here first. He insisted. I sat still. He said he was on official business and said it with a tone which meant, "You can imagine who I am." Lest I fail to see his point, however, he added, "If you don't vacate soon you'll find yourself in those cellars," and he stretched out his arm in the direction of the near-by GPU prison on the Lubianka. I sat still. He pulled out a whistle and summoned the traffic officer. A crowd had gathered. He showed a badge behind his lapel and asked the traffic officer to order me to leave the taxi. The officer said he had no right to do that. He repeated that he was on official business. I said, "If you're on official business you should have an official car. You take your turn for a taxi like everybody else. Right here you have no more rights than I have." From my accent as well as from my unaccustomed tone he realized that I was a foreigner and went away.

I was not being brave. I knew nothing would happen to me. Chicherin assented when I once said to him that foreigners, especially Americans, tacitly enjoyed extra-territorial privileges in Soviet Russia. But no Soviet citizen would have dared to behave as I did. No one defies the GPU. The GPU has hundreds of thousands of employees in all parts of the country. It is represented in every factory, office, and house. Its arm is long, its vengeance swift, its memory excellent, and there is usually little recourse from its decisions. It seizes persons without a court warrant, and can send them into exile without a trial, and at times it executes without trial and without judicial judgment. No one wants to monkey with even an insignificant cog in such an omnipotent machine. Little men and big fear it. It thus becomes a law unto itself. The fear deters some enemies. But it also paralyzes the initiative and creative spirit of many loyal citizens. Visitors to Moscow used to ask whether socialism (by eliminating the profit motive) kills personal initiative. No. But the GPU does.

During the early years of the New Economic Policy (NEP) from 1921 to 1926, Nepmen were arrested and banished to Siberia, but the average pro-Soviet person remained unmolested. The terror eased. Then came the Stalin-Trotzky conflict. In 1927 Stalin began to employ the GPU against the Trotzkyites. I regard this as a fatal crossroads in the history of the Soviet dictatorship. For it demonstrated that the GPU swept out not only anti-Bolsheviks but also Bolsheviks who were contending for Stalin's scepter or merely questioning his omniscience and infallibility. The popular mind grew cynical about the GPU's function. To combat this cynicism the regime branded Trotzky and all anti-Stalinists as counter-revolutionists and Fascists. That greased the toboggan to the big trials and purges of later years.

The power of a secret police depends on the volume of its work and on the nature of its work. If it arrests few people and shoots fewer it cannot be politically strong. If its work is open to criticism and inspection, if its activities move on the plane of legality and are confined by respect for civil rights, it cannot become a state within a state.

The new revolutionary phase of Bolshevism, which commenced in 1929, gave the GPU new business. The Soviet government had entered upon an epochal task of industrial construction. The regime was in a hurry. In the most efficient country in the world—which Russia was not—mistakes would have been counted by the thousands. Soviet mistakes were myriad. Some of these were committed by anti-Soviet engineers who did not want the Five Year Plan to succeed. The bulk of Russia's technicians, however, was loyal, and yet things went wrong; here the plan remained unfulfilled, here there were fatal accidents, here a factory turned out inferior goods. The population which suffered privations because of shortages looked for an explanation.

But as dictator, Stalin could do no wrong. The dictatorship was beyond reproach. The principles of socialism had to remain above criticism, and the national economic plan itself naturally was perfection incorporated. Someone had to be punished for falling production and defective machinery; someone, preferably the guilty one—but not necessarily. It was like a political campaign in a democracy where one side is lily white and all the difficulties, from unemployment to crop failures to earthquakes, are blamed on the other side, except that in Russia, the "campaign" was conducted in the night by the GPU and the accused in the Black Marias could not answer back. The GPU sought the scapegoats on the slopes below the summit. At times it reached perilously close to the dictatorship's peak but it never touched the fountain of authority whence the revelation was brought down the mount, and no GPU step could suggest that Stalin or those whom he shielded at the moment were at fault. The arrests were designed to prove that others were at fault.

Many tens of thousands of engineers, managers, technicians, and officials in industry were arrested and exiled. The GPU expanded into a vast spying organization of dimensions unprecedented even in Russia.

Simultaneously, agrarian collectivization converted the GPU into a huge economic establishment. The GPU arrested and exiled vast hordes, possibly millions, of peasants from their homes to distant regions of the Soviet continent. I saw them at work in Kazakhstan and elsewhere. Many of these were kulaks or richer farmers who forcibly or indirectly obstructed socialism on the land because it meant their death as private capitalists.

The banishment of the kulaks made those who remained less recalcitrant; it thus facilitated collectivization. The GPU thereby became an important instrument of government economic policy. Moreover, the wholesale, compulsory migration of kulaks supplied the authorities with labor for large construction projects in far-off, sparsely settled realms. The kulak arrests were, in part, a deliberate form of colonization. In view of the sullen attitude of the exiles, they were put under the care of the GPU which actually conducted the work of construction. The GPU became a railway builder, canal digger, desert irrigator, timber cutter. It employed vast armies of skilled and unskilled workers, and engineers, all of them exiles, as well as free citizens. These tasks still further enhanced the GPU's influence and power. It was the most potent single institution in the country, too potent for Stalin's liking.

It would have been natural for Stalin to want to curtail the authority of the GPU, but the only way of doing it would be to curtail its work, and having introduced construction by exiles and espionage by GPU agents in industry this could not be done with ease.

Moreover, some of the GPU's jobs had been of questionable legality and had been motivated by the dictator's desire for personal power. The secret police in a dictatorship knows too much. In a dictatorship, it is often dangerous to have certain types of information acquired in the course of legitimate official duty. If this information embarrassed superiors or could be used for purposes of blackmail, its owner might find that his luck had changed for the worse. One of the reasons why some people were purged was they had purged others and knew how it was done. Thus purges beget more purges.

A secret police is of the very essence of a dictatorship. It evokes the fear which is the motor fuel of dictatorship. The relationship of the Soviet population to the GPU was therefore of endless social significance, and I always watched this carefully. The GPU employs hundreds of thousands of uniformed and non-uniformed men and women. But over and above these, it regards all persons as unpaid collaborators. According to the basic tenet of the GPU, it is the duty of every Soviet citizen to report to the GPU whatever he believes might be of value to it. If it is ascertained that any person knew something of importance and did not report, that person is liable to punishment for complicity. The question has frequently arisen whether such and such a Soviet ambassador or trade representative is an employee of the GPU. Foolish question! They all are, some directly, but all indirectly in the sense that they must—if they can—give the GPU information it might want to have. The GPU also has collaborators in non-Soviet embassies and even in the families of bourgeois diplomats.

The average Russian is a mild, easy-going individual, trusting and talkative. He does not take well to GPU methods of spying. Especially after 1929, few persons privately condemned anyone carried off by the GPU. The GPU became identified in the public mind with political expediency rather than with justice. No one took for granted that the victim had sinned against the Revolution. People did not say, "The scoundrel." They said, "What a pity!" This was one of the Kremlin's most serious blunders; it blunted its sharpest weapon. The GPU was originally conceived as a bulwark of the Revolution. But the GPU was more interested in the feeling of insecurity and terror which its acts engendered. The Soviet citizen did not merely say, "What a pity!" when a friend disappeared in the night. He said, "If he has been taken away maybe my turn will come soon too."

Fear also killed something which the government wanted. Numerous engineers were so frightened of making an error that they tried to do as little work as possible. Engineers told me on the oilfields at Baku that they grew nervous as they approached the end of well-boring. For the well might be dry and then their failure would be charged to ill will even though some borings must bring in nothing just as some bring in gushers. An engineer whom I knew in Moscow quit his factory job to drive a taxi; that involved no risks.

The multiplicity of arrests among technical personnel so decimated the ranks that Sergo Ordjonekidze, a Georgian friend of Stalin's and Chairman of the Supreme Economic Council, went to Stalin and told him that it would be impossible to conduct normal industrial operations unless the GPU ceased molesting engineers. He also complained that whenever the GPU required an engineer for a Siberian or Turkestan project it simply arrested him because it knew that, what with the scarcity of trained industrial leaders, this was the only way of getting him.

Stalin saw the point, and he himself had accounts to settle with the GPU. On June 23, 1931, therefore, Stalin called a halt to the pogrom of intellectuals and professional people in a speech hailed as the "Magna Charta" of the intelligentsia. "These comrades should not be discouraged," he ordered. Within a fortnight Stalin reshuffled the leadership of the GPU.

Stalin, first of all, demoted Yagoda. If we knew more about the backstage struggle between Stalin and Yagoda, it would, I believe, be almost as absorbing as the conflict between Stalin and Trotzky. The battle represents the attempt of a dictator to rid himself of the mechanism which made him dictator. Stalin wanted to be free. Yagoda, the Bolshevik Fouché, threatened to become indispensable.

The titular head of the GPU was Menzhinsky, who was physically and mentally unfitted for the post. Genrich Yagoda did the real work; he was a thin man with furtive look and a Hitleresque mustache who rarely appeared in public. He started and ended his career in the GPU.

Yagoda had been first assistant to Menzhinsky. Stalin now reduced him to second assistant and placed Akulov over him as first assistant.

Akulov was a friend of Lenin's, a supporter of the party's Central Committee rather than a typical official of the secret police. He was mild instead of ruthless and he believed in "revolutionary legality" instead of wholesale arrests. He immediately stopped the mass arrests of engineers and intellectuals which had provoked resentment in that class and also among workers who saw the havoc it wrought in industry. He dismissed overzealous and unscrupulous officials of the GPU, replacing them in some cases by workingmen with a simple but healthy revolutionary psychology.

Meanwhile Yagoda sulked. He remained in his villa outside Moscow and rarely came to work. Within four months, however, Akulov was pushed out of the GPU and received the comparatively unimportant post of Communist party secretary in the Donetz coal basin. Yagoda resumed his job as boss of the GPU. As the Russians say, "the apparatus ate" Akulov. The GPU machine refused to co-operate with him. And apparently Yagoda, though inactive inside the GPU, was working hard elsewhere, pulling wires. He had purged the Trotzkyites. He had purged the Rykov-Tomsky right wing. He knew the secrets of those sealed volumes. In 1931, Stalin had many enemies. The right wing was not completely annihilated. Yagoda might have joined them. The country was in an unsettled state due to industrialization and collectivization. It would not do to alienate Yagoda. Stalin could shoot him or reinstate him, but the shooting of important leaders had not yet commenced. Stalin was not yet almighty.

So Yagoda went back into the GPU. But Stalin does not easily admit defeat. Vengeful Georgian, he never forgets anyone who has defied or crossed him. Almost two years elapsed. On June 20, 1933, Stalin brought Akulov to Moscow again, and placed him not within the GPU this time, but over it. The special post of Federal Procurator, or Attorney General, was created for Akulov, and the decree which did so, signed by the President of the Republic Kalinin and Prime Minister Molotov, stated that he would exercise "supervision . . . over the legality and propriety of the acts of the GPU." Akulov thus became the supreme judicial officer of the Soviet Union. His first function consisted in curbing the GPU, and primarily Yagoda.

Akulov could stay any sentence passed by the GPU. He could ask for pertinent files on any case. He could re-investigate any case.

His headquarters were beleaguered day and night by relatives of imprisoned citizens. People began coming back from exile. He commuted several death sentences, to my personal knowledge. One concerned the elder brother of Alex Gumberg. Ambassador Troyanovsky asked Yagoda what Gumberg's fate would be. Yagoda said he would be shot. Troyanovsky asked Akulov. Akulov said he would not be shot, and he wasn't.

Orders were given to the GPU not to arrest any engineer without a special warrant or without consultation with the Central Committee of the party. The same restrictions were placed on the GPU with respect to officers and men in the Red Army.

The latter half of 1933, but particularly 1934, witnessed a general easing of the atmosphere. Of course, the GPU still kept busy. But repression tapered off perceptibly. People talked more freely. Literature reacted to the change.

Other factors operated to undermine the GPU's position. Litvinov's star was rising. Soviet diplomacy played an increasingly glorious role in world affairs. And Litvinov did not brook the interference of the GPU in foreign policy. It had in the past arrested foreigners without warning the Soviet Foreign Office and had thus caused complications. Its agents abroad meddled in business that was not theirs and brought official representatives into disrepute. Litvinov resisted the GPU's penchant for ubiquity.

The Red Army resented the GPU's desire for omnipotence. The GPU was itself an army, an élite corps, and its officers regarded themselves as higher than army officers. But Russia was arming heavily; army prestige grew commensurately and the GPU dropped in the scale.

A spy story struck the GPU between the eyes just at this moment when its stocks were lowest. In 1920, the Poles attacked Russia; Russia drove back the Poles and advanced on Warsaw. In the ranks of the advancing army was an Ukrainian Communist named Konar. The Poles captured him and shot him and gave his papers to a Polish spy named Poleschuk. Poleschuk took the name of Konar and went into the Soviet Ukraine to do intelligence work for Poland. The confusion resulting from war, famine, and economic collapse made his task easy and he found a job with the Soviets. He rose quickly in the Soviet hierarchy. He rose to front rank in the Ukraine and then, being very capable, was transferred to Moscow where he ultimately became Assistant Commissar of Agriculture in the federal government. As such he attended meetings of the highest political bodies and submitted memoranda to Stalin and other high Bolsheviks. He also reported to the Polish government. He kept touch with numerous Polish spies throughout Russia.

In 1931, Konar married a Soviet film star. She was tall and beautiful. He was happy and had almost reached the pinnacle in the Soviet Union. The Polish ties were now a nuisance and danger to him. He decided to break them. But the Poles would not let him. Such a man could be of endless service to them just because he ranked so high. They had him in their power because one word from them and he would be arrested by the GPU and shot. Konar therefore continued to work for them.

One day at a big committee meeting in Moscow, Konar was introduced to an Ukrainian official. The official did not understand. He had known Konar well. This was not Konar. He watched throughout the meeting, and then carried his suspicions to the GPU.

The GPU spied on Konar. A GPU agent with a concealed camera took a photograph of him in a commission shop in Moscow where he went to deliver papers to the Polish military attaché, Kovalevsky. Konar was shot; Kovalevsky was recalled.

I can imagine the conversation between Stalin and Yagoda at this point. "What good are you," Stalin would have yelled, "if you can't keep foreign spies out of my own office? You have your people everywhere but you couldn't spot a spy who was with us for thirteen years!"

Economic conditions improved. The country was quiet. The GPU was doing a bad job and its opponents pressed the case against it. In January, 1934, accordingly, the Soviet government transferred some of the judicial functions of the GPU to civil courts; henceforth the shorn GPU would carry the name of Commissariat of Internal Affairs.

Normally, when a commissariat is established, the commissar is appointed simultaneously. But the new commissariat remained without a commissar for six months while a brisk struggle proceeded behind the scenes. Rumor had it that Stalin favored Jan Rudzutak, a Lettish Communist, for the job. Rudzutak was numbered among the upper ten Bolsheviks. (Later he was executed.) But Yagoda fought for his own retention. Maxim Gorky supported him. Gorky and Yagoda were friends, and a complicated personal relationship existed between them. Gorky exercised great influence over Stalin who respected his culture and was pleased to have Russia's greatest artist among his supporters. In July, 1934, accordingly, Yagoda received the appointment of Commissar of Internal Affairs. He had won again.

But Commissar Yagoda's power was smaller. He was small physically, too; all the recent GPU heads have been small men. I saw him looking smallest one freezing morning in December, 1934, on the Red Square, several days after an assassin named Nikolaiev killed Sergei Kirov—Bolshevik No. 4—in Leningrad. Nikolaiev had been demoted at his government office and he blamed it on Kirov and shot him in the back of the neck.

The Soviet government immediately ordered the execution of one hundred and three persons who were in prison when the crime occurred. They could not have had anything to do with Kirov's death. But suicides are notoriously contagious, and the Bolsheviks felt that assassinations were, too. The Soviet press has always been cautious about the way it reports attempts on the lives of foreign statesmen. It does not want to suggest anything to individuals in Russia who may be harboring the same idea. The shooting of the one hundred and three, most of them foreign spies but some young dissident Communists, was a coldblooded act of intimidation. *The Nation* commented on this event in an editorial paragraph. I criticized it in a letter to Miss Kirchwey from Moscow (*The Nation* may have thrown away Hitler's letter, but it kept all of mine, and I now have them for reference.): "Your editorial paragraph in the issue of December 19 is mild, and I would have made it stronger. . . . I cannot excuse the executions, and what is more I haven't seen a good explanation. . . . I think it is all very artificial, this new search for heretics who are so scarce these days. Moreover, you cannot shoot 103 Whites thus giving the impression of a 'White Guard' plot and then exile Zinoviev . . . as the inspirer of the deed."

When the news of Kirov's murder reached Moscow, Stalin and Yagoda took the next train for Leningrad. Stalin then did a strange but logical thing; he talked to the assassin alone for several hours. It must have been important for Stalin to understand the mind of a Soviet citizen and Communist who would shoot one of Russia's most popular leaders.

Nikolaiev had been a follower of Zinoviev, and an ex-Oppositionist. "Stalin," I wrote in an article, "came to the conclusion: 'Once an Oppositionist, always an Oppositionist,' and although his power is supreme and unquestioned, Stalin decided to proceed immediately with the complete annihilation of the small remnant of unhappy Trotzkyists and Zinovievists who, through recantation, had crept back into minor posts in the party and in the government." I believe this helps to explain the subsequent Moscow trials. Almost all the defendants in them were ex-Oppositionists. Stalin was afraid that they would turn against him in a crisis. His naturally suspicious mind told him that men who had been loyal to Trotzky or Zinoviev or Kamenev would not really be loyal to him despite all their protestations.

Kirov lay in state in Moscow. Stalin kissed the dead man on the lips and later he, and Kalinin, Voroshilov, Kaganovitch, and others carried the urn with the ashes through the streets and the Red Square to the wall where it was immured. I stood very close to this group as it passed and my farsighted eyes had an excellent view. Stalin was really sad, for Kirov was his bosom friend. But I watched Yagoda more. Yagoda marched near the urn, and his eyes were now on Stalin now on the guards who guarded Stalin. He looked like a hunted animal himself. Stalin must have given him a good drubbing. Stalin's first act in Leningrad had been to dismiss the highest GPU officials in the city for neglect.

At events on the Red Square, a number of leaders precede Stalin to the reviewing stand on Lenin's beautiful marble mausoleum. He arrives a bit late—whether by design or not I do not know. This day Stalin walked up the steps first, and alone, and stood alone on the stand for a minute, turning his head slowly from one side to the other as if to say, "Here I am. I am not afraid." Then the others ascended. The Red Army had placed special guards on the Red Square for the Kirov funeral to supplement the GPU which always had a monopoly on that duty. The guards wore fresh uniforms with no insignia.

Stalin can wait. He possesses consummate patience. It is one of his crowning virtues; he owes much of his success to it. He built up his own position slowly. He tears down his enemies and rivals in installments. If he can negotiate a distance in two jumps he prefers them to one, and three are still better. He destroyed Trotzky in six stages, Zinoviev and Kamenev in four, Rykov and Tomsky in three; he took the Baltic states in two lunges. He is like an animal of prey which first paws its victim to feel out its strength, then strikes to cripple and steps back to watch the effect, and finally kills. In his mind there must be a ledger page marked "Unfinished Business" in which are entered the names of those men who have not been finished. Here he put down Yagoda several times and here also in 1934-35 he inscribed all ex-Oppositionists.

By 1935, the GPU had been deprived of its special prerogatives and cowed. This was part of a healthy process of democratization which Stalin did not try to arrest. Anti-Bolshevik classes and groups had disappeared. The kulaks were no more an important social factor. Indeed many of them, emaciated and contrite, now commenced returning to their villages. The intellectuals, as a body, were pro-Soviet. Non-Communist engineers were elevated to high positions in industry. Party membership ceased to be a special privilege, and non-Communists were not necessarily suspected of less loyalty than Communists. Distinctions between groups grew thinner. The Nepmen were no more. A recession from official lawlessness manifested itself everywhere. Draconian measures did not cease altogether, but the trend was definitely in the direction of moderation. The Kremlin apparently realized that arbitrary acts and violence could not permanently replace wise civil administration. More and more, the regime now appealed through persuasion to self-interest.

Despite the Kirov assassination, 1935 marks the high-water mark of personal freedom in the Soviet Union. It almost coincided with the point of greatest prosperity. Both coincided with the maximum restrictions on GPU ruthlessness.

The curbs on the GPU were attributed by Bolsheviks to the wisdom of Stalin. They are attributable to that and to his intolerance of competition. Stalin's policy has always been the greatest possible concentration of authority in himself and the greatest possible diffusion of administration among others, so that nobody becomes too strong. Soviet embassies abroad have on occasions telegraphed Moscow for permission to hold afternoon teas. No individual or institution in Russia is allowed to acquire too much popularity or authority. Stalin tries to monopolize the popularity and authority and to lend them to subordinates whenever the needs of administration require it, but always in such a way as to be quickly retractable and rigidly controlled. Prime Minister Molotov and Lazar Kaganovitch and others carry out important functions and bear heavy burdens. Stalin cannot do all the work himself. But they are his tools and he can unmake them at will.

Stalin is a genius at organization. He has assembled a tribe of lieutenants who depend on his favor and who are too small or too grateful or too slow or too frightened to make a move against him. Any display of excess individualism or excess ambition, or excess popularity, will get them into trouble. They know it. This shows in big things and in little things. A foreign photographer once came to Moscow to take pictures of the Bolshevik chiefs. When War Commissar Voroshilov was approached he asked whether Stalin's picture had been taken. He waited until it had been and then he posed. Frederick Kuh of the United Press, returning from a trip to Manchuria, once had an interview with Voroshilov at which I was present. Voroshilov took Kuh's dispatch to Stalin for censorship. He did not venture to do it himself. Kuh wrote, by way of describing the scene, that a revolver lay on Voroshilov's desk. Voroshilov thought it would not be wise to let that appear in print abroad. Stalin said, "Why? A military man, a revolver." I have these facts from the third person present.

Stalin supervises the little things so as to train his subordinates not to do big things without him, and they end up by not doing little things without him. Stalin receives literally thousands of letters daily from all parts of the country. He reads many of them himself, and each letter receives a reply either from him or from the department concerned. He encourages this letter-writing. It makes him popular. It advertises his role as dispensor of favors and arbiter of fates.

When Boris Pilniak wanted to go to the United States on the invitation of the late Ray Long of *Cosmopolitan* he applied for a passport in usual fashion to the GPU. He received a rejection. He applied a second time and was refused. Then he wrote a personal note to Stalin and the next day a messenger brought him a letter from Stalin promising that he would "intercede" on his behalf with the authorities. The many friends who entertained the gay, carousing Pilniak in America know that Stalin's little "intercession" worked.

The Baseches episode reveals another Stalin technique.

Baseches was a little ugly man always picking the sores on his forehead. He said, proudly, that he was an illegitimate son of the Austrian Emperor Francis Joseph. When he forgot he said, equally proudly, that he descended from Hungarian nobility which in that case must have been Jewish. Apparently he was—but you could never be sure—a lieutenant in the Austro-Hungarian army of occupation in the Ukraine in 1918. He spoke Russian well, having been graduated from a Moscow high school. He came back to Russia in 1922 as correspondent of the Vienna *Neue Freie Presse* and wrote an excellent book on Soviet economy. When cafés opened in Moscow a new life commenced for him. He spent every evening, literally, in the Metropole Café, and when you came in with a woman he came over and kissed her hand whether she liked it or not, and sat down whether you asked him or not. Out of habit he would ask for a loan, and some gave it to him. He knew many people and dug up odd bits of information from the flotsam of the Russian bourgeoisie. These he put into articles once too often, and Moscow decided to deport him. Soviet dealings with foreign correspondents were the reserved province of the highest Politbureau. No lesser authority could take any important decision about them. And it was the Politbureau which voted—they always voted and signed their names to the resolutions they adopted—to expel Baseches from the Soviet Union. An excerpt from the Politbureau minutes was sent to Chief of the GPU Yagoda and that was tantamount to an order to escort the Viennese correspondent to the frontier.

Podolsky heard about it. Podolsky was assistant head of the press department of the Foreign Office. He had studied philosophy in Switzerland and France, spoke German, French, and English perfectly, was moderate, quiet, sometimes brilliant, always tired; he had three little children and a sick wife and he loved his children as no man ever has and would disappear frequently from his desk, rush down the Foreign Office stairs, with milk can and shopping net in hand, to join a queue in the hope of buying the family some food. One summer he got a month's vacation in the Caucasus. But he stayed no more than a week. He missed his two little daughters and his son. So this baldheaded Jacob Podolsky learned that Baseches was to be deported. He went to see his chief, Litvinov. He explained that he wanted to hold no brief for Baseches. He disliked him and abhorred his anti-Soviet views. But if the Soviet government expelled Baseches, Podolsky argued, the outside world would say that Moscow tolerated only those correspondents who were pro-Soviet and banished all others. Podolsky therefore thought the Politbureau decision a mistake. Litvinov said in effect: Mind your own business; who are you to question the fiat of the supreme Bolshevik authority? Podolsky was just a minor official even in the Foreign Office. Anyway, Litvinov added, the matter is now in Yagoda's hands, and Baseches will be on his way tomorrow.

Undaunted, Podolsky telephoned Yagoda. That required a lot of courage. The average Soviet citizen and official stands in mortal dread of the master of the GPU. Podolsky told Yagoda his doubts about the wisdom of deporting Baseches. Yagoda probably could not believe his ears, but he instructed Podolsky, in direct, rude language, to keep off the premises. The GPU had received its instructions, and that was all.

By this time it was midnight. Baseches would be leaving the next morning. Podolsky telephoned Stalin's apartment in the Kremlin. A woman's voice answered the telephone. Podolsky told her who he was and asked her to remind Comrade Stalin that he had been to Stalin's office as an interpreter for foreign interviewers. She came back with the request to call again in twenty minutes. Podolsky waited, nervous but determined. He dialed again; the same woman's voice; she said, "Just a minute," and in a minute Stalin said, "Yes?" Podolsky, overwhelmed, spoke what he had hastily rehearsed many times: Baseches was a "Svoloch" (scoundrel), but by expelling him the government would undermine the authority of those journalists who remained. Stalin listened, with an occasional "Da" (yes) which became friendlier as Podolsky developed the argument. Finally Stalin said, "I cannot change Politbureau decisions. But we can reconsider the matter at our next session. Meanwhile Baseches can stay on." The Politbureau reconsidered, and Baseches was not expelled. (Podolsky disappeared in the big purge of 1938. I saw Baseches in Paris after the war started in 1939.)

The Baseches episode shows some of Stalin's virtues. He is accessible to persons and to common sense when he wishes to be, and he is not rigid in his thinking. In fact, he is given to zigzagging in major policy. He experiments, and if he fails he pursues another course. But through it all he knows best how to maintain his own throne on the apex of the Soviet pyramid.

In Moscow they tell this story which certainly is untrue: Stalin is sitting in his office in the Kremlin. He summons Lazar Kaganovitch, Bolshevik No. 2. After initial greetings, Stalin says:

"Have you been seeing Molotov of late?"

"Yes," Kaganovitch replies.

"How do you get on with him?" Stalin inquires.

"Very well," Kaganovitch replies.

"I have been noticing something very queer," Stalin says. "Molotov tells everybody you are a Jew."

"Well, I am a Jew," Kaganovitch declares.

"Yes," Stalin agrees, "but why should he say it? He must be up to

something. Why should he keep emphasizing the fact that you are
a Jew when everybody knows it?"

"That's right," says Kaganovitch wrinkling his brow. "I wonder
what Molotov is planning to do!" He goes out.

Stalin summons Molotov. After initial greetings, Stalin says:
"Have you been seeing Kaganovitch of late?"

"Yes," Molotov replies.

"How do you get on with him?" Stalin inquires.

"Very well," Molotov replies.

"I have been noticing something very queer," Stalin says. "Kaganovitch tells everybody that you stutter."

"Well, I—I—do st-stutter," Molotov stutters.

"Yes," Stalin agrees, "but why should he say it? He must be planning something. Why should he keep emphasizing that you stutter
when we all know it and don't mind it?"

"That's right," says Molotov wrinkling his brow. "I wonder what
Kaganovitch is up to!" He goes out. Stalin rubs his hands gleefully
and exclaims, "Now I can work."

However fantastic the story, it describes a method which Stalin
has employed more than once. All dictators fear rivals. But Stalin
removes them with uncommon thoroughness and ease, and he is undoubtedly more powerful in the Soviet Union than Hitler is in Germany or Mussolini in Italy.

The wish of a dictator to enjoy unchallenged support is normal in
a dictatorship. But there is a side of Stalin's personality which is
decidedly abnormal. Stalin's entire life as a statesman has been directed
towards destroying one duality—Lenin and Trotzky—which history
accepted, and substituting another—Lenin and Stalin. He pursues
this goal with a relentlessness and pettiness which are epic, and pathological.

Stalin is a big man, else he would not be where he is. But big men
are not immune to the emotions and weaknesses of lesser men.
Jealousy, wounded pride, the desire for publicity, the ambition to
disprove inferiority, revenge, and the urge to open closed doors actu-
ate great politicians as well as lawyers, merchants, and college grad-
uates. Indeed, the passion, temperament, and drive which raise a
politician to the heights also intensify and magnify these personal
frailties until, as in Stalin's case, they mold history.

Trotzky was many things which Stalin would have liked to be.
Trotzky was a magnetic figure, a brilliant writer, a great speaker, a

master theoretician, and a noted historian. He had glamor and fire. He was unusual and not pedestrian. Moreover, he had treated Stalin with the contempt and disdain of a superior. Lenin had assumed that Trotzky would succeed him. Lenin's last testament contained some barbed criticism of Trotzky's shortcomings, but it denounced Stalin and asked that he be removed from the post of party secretary which he then occupied.

To prove to himself, Russia, and the world that he was entitled to wear the mantle of Lenin, to prove that he was not the inferior of Trotzky—these became Stalin's personal goals. They spurred him to great effort, to success, to achievement, and to cruelty, dishonesty, and ruthlessness.

First of all, every mention and memory of Trotzky had to be stamped out. In Russia today none of Trotzky's books can be obtained even in the libraries for reference. All Soviet citizens have burned or otherwise destroyed all books by Trotzky, all magazines, articles, and pamphlets that contained statements by or in favor of Trotzky, and all photographs of Trotzky. To own a picture of Trotzky in Russia would be tantamount to writing one's jail sentence. All Soviet histories and encyclopedias have been revised and republished so that Trotzky's role in Soviet life has either been entirely eliminated, or blackened and distorted. Authors have contrived to write histories of the Red Army without using Trotzky's name once although he was its organizer and the first Bolshevik War Commissar. Without special permission it is even forbidden to quote Trotzky in order to attack him, for it could easily be alleged that the quotation, although used ostensibly to condemn, was really intended as Trotzkyist propaganda. (Boris Mironov, a Soviet friend of mine, a Jew, and a fervent Bolshevik and anti-Nazi, wrote a book of sketches of Nazi leaders and necessarily cited the words of Hitler, Goebbels, and others. The book was published in Moscow with official approval, but later the Soviet press accused Mironov of writing it for the purpose of making Nazi propaganda in Russia.) John Reed's *Ten Days That Shook the World* has been suppressed and cannot be found in any Soviet bookstore or library despite the fact that Lenin read it twice and wrote an enthusiastic introduction for it. For years it was considered the finest Communist propaganda and was used abroad as such. But no more—because it pays tribute to Trotzky's part in the birth of the Revolution and ignores Stalin. The new legend, however, omits Trotzky as a character in the Bolshevik Revolution. He was just not there, according to all recent Soviet publications. And no longer could anyone read the classic stories of the Revolution, like John Reed's book, which told of the intimate collaboration between Trotzky and Lenin. Trotzky can only be spoken of in Russia as a Fascist, an assassin, a counter-revolutionist, a person who tried when he was in Russia and after he left to wreck the Revolution.

Stalin, on the other hand, was the organizer of the Red Army; he it was who always stood by the side of Lenin. Recent films show Lenin turning to Stalin and asking for his advice in difficult moments. Children's books contain the same perverted view. To exterminate every trace of Trotzky, Stalin has felt it necessary not only to remove every Trotzkyist from circulation, and also to remove any person who ever dared to attribute mistakes or weaknesses to Stalin.

Today, Stalin must be hailed in Russia as the source of all good, the originator of all ideas, the father of every successful enterprise. Few writers finish an article or book without quoting profusely from Stalin. I have opened at random a volume of the Great Soviet Encyclopedia. In the article on "Mythology," eighteen lines out of one hundred and sixty are devoted to Stalin. The article on "Metaphysics" says, "In the country led by the genius of Stalin, leader of all peoples, the struggle against metaphysics rests on a materialistic base." The article on "Mehring" quotes Lenin twice and Stalin twice.

The tasteless fawning adulation of Stalin which I criticized in print as early as 1930 seems mild compared to the heights, or depths, of sycophancy attained in subsequent years. In 1934, the Soviet icebreaker *Cheliuskin* came through a truly heroic adventure in the Arctic. The whole world applauded. Of course, Stalin did it. The workingmen of Leningrad sent a letter to Stalin saying, "Thanks to your wise leadership this epic ended with victory. . . . You are the great collaborator of Lenin and now continue his work. . . . Beloved Comrade Stalin . . . gifted leader of the world proletariat . . ." Thousands of resolutions in the same style were published throughout Russia's press stories of the *Cheliuskin*.

But Stalin is not merely an Arctic explorer. He is also the father of Soviet sport and gymnastics. An article on the "Purity of Newspaper Language" quotes Stalin's language as a shining example. President Kalinin said, "Ask me who best understands the Russian language and I reply—Stalin." He is also the greatest general. An editorial on the Red Army dated November 19, 1934, explains that during the Civil War, "the inexhaustible strength of Stalin reigned at the front. The party entrusted him with the most dangerous tasks in the first line. . . ." Peasants greet Stalin, "Our first word of love, of greeting, we send you, our own Stalin, our beloved friend, our teacher. . . ." The women of the country announce that "Stalin's name arouses a wave of delight, love and devotion in us. . . . We thank Comrade Stalin for a free, joyful life. . . . We thank Comrade Stalin for the wonderful path and aims which his strong hand points out to us." The national slogan of Russia's children is, "Thanks, Comrade Stalin, for a happy childhood."

Nine cities and towns in the Soviet Union have been named after Stalin, and the post office must have a lot of trouble with Stalingrad, Stalinogorsk, Stalinabad, Stalin, Stalino, Stalinir, Stalinissi, and Stalinaoul. Thousands of clubhouses, streets, factories, farms, mountain peaks, ships, coal mines, oilfields, railway spurs, and sport organizations—but, significantly, no children—have been given Stalin's name.

This well-conducted symphony of personal glorification served as the musical accompaniment to the establishment of the leaning tower of Stalin's personal dictatorship. With the hindsight and perspective I now have, I can understand what happened in the years between 1931 and 1936 in Soviet Russia. There were two lines of development; they moved in opposite directions. One line was towards the devolution of the terror, the undermining of the GPU, the guarantee of civil rights. This line reached its point of culmination in the Constitution of 1936 which I shall discuss in a separate chapter. The trend towards democracy was fostered by general economic improvement and the decimation and conversion of anti-Bolshevik elements in the population. Those who remained could be accorded better treatment. The second line led to Stalin's personal dictatorship. In the beginning, this tendency required the harnessing and constricting of the GPU. But having attained his goal, Stalin needed a mighty secret police to keep him there, and he therefore resurrected the GPU, annulled the Constitution in fact, resurrected the terror with unprecedented ferocity, and instituted the big purges and the Moscow trials. Thus the progression towards Soviet democracy was killed by Stalin's own ambition.

I always felt a lusty antipathy for the GPU. I knew too intimately many of the decent people it had destroyed or paralyzed by fear, to approve its excesses. I greeted with joy and recorded in my articles each successive measure by which Stalin clipped its wings. My repugnance to the dithyrambic chorus of Stalin praise never remained a secret. I aired it on numerous occasions in conversations with Mironov, with Radek, with Mikhalsky, the *Izvestia* editor who visited America, and with many others. They attributed it to my "Trotzkyism." I was never a Trotzkyist. My spirit simply reacted against falsely picturing one man as the acme of all virtues and hammering all others on the head so that only pigmies remained all about him.

In Stalin's favor I chalked up: One, the erection of new factories and cities and the rise of an industrialized country based on village collectivization designed to banish recurrent famine. Two, the relaxation of repressive measures which tapered off perceptibly after 1933. Against Stalin I held the concentration of power and the oriental, fawning exaltation of one infallible, indispensable, inevitable, omnipotent all-high. But I did not foresee that his yearning for supreme power would cancel out his own encouragement of the movement towards freedom. I did not realize that it would destroy the moral character of the nation, demoralize every citizen, crush the capacity to think, and pave the way to a regime which, beginning in 1937, was less democratic than Russia had ever been under Bolshevism or Czarism.

Yet I still feel that even Stalin has not been able to kill all the good that came out of the Revolution. Whatever is left has no real expression in Soviet politics. It cannot influence present-day policy. In fact, a prolongation of Stalin's rule, by him or his successor, may completely destroy it. But if a different and better world ever emerges out of the welter and chaos and blood that mar our lives today it will find in Russia allies who are now silent and unhappy.

13. *Palestine Revisited*

MOSCOW is bitter cold in the winter. It gets dark at three in the afternoon. I hate cold and darkness. The Moscow winter begins in October; and one year it snowed on May 1. In January, 1934, this was too much for me, and I decided to go in quest of the sun. I chose Palestine. I left Moscow in mid-January during a fierce blizzard and eleven days later I was swimming in the Dead Sea.

I went from Moscow to Odessa by train and there boarded the Soviet steamer, *Novorossisk*. She was forty years old and full of big rats. At night I had to burn a light overhead to keep the beasts from my face. Occasionally I felt them on the blanket but there was just nothing to do about it. At Constantinople I got off, rested, and walked the city streets for two days; then I boarded an Italian luxury liner for Athens, where I discovered to my horror that the *Novorossisk* had caught up with me and was the only boat scheduled to leave Greece for Palestine in the near future. Off Crete we almost foundered in a storm, but the rats apparently never got seasick. The democracy of the Soviet crew offered some compensation for physical discomforts—the best quarters were occupied by the sailor's club and the stokers ate with the captain; nevertheless, I was glad when we landed at Tel Aviv.

In Palestine again!

I had spent fifteen months in Palestine in 1919-20. In 1917, I volunteered to serve in the Jewish legion which the British government was then recruiting in the United States to help reconquer the Holy Land. After experiences in Canada, England, France, Italy, and Egypt, we finally got to Palestine when the War had ended, and our unit saw no fighting. But my friends said I did plenty of fighting with the British officers. I complained about the worms in the dog biscuits that were given to us in lieu of bread; I protested against being "paraded" to synagogue every Saturday. What riled me most was the spirit of this army that had just won the War for democracy. At Alexandria I saw a British officer, embarking for demobilization in England, make a special trip down the ship's gang plank, kick an Egyptian of the labor corps, and say in my hearing, "This was my last chance."

I was a corporal, and regulations required private soldiers who wished to speak to an officer to be "paraded" before him by a non-com like myself. Once I escorted two privates to an officer, clicked heels, saluted according to the manual, and said, "These gentlemen would like to talk to you."

"In the British army," he declared stiffly, "the only gentlemen are the officers." Well, I didn't like that and my conduct showed it. Everything went more or less smoothly, however, until I was elected a member of the battalion committee. Then my captain decided to take revenge. I used to go on leave without permission rather regularly. The Jewish legion excelled in that form of indiscipline. Usually they never bothered to catch us. Now my officer reported me absent and Captain Harvey sentenced me to a fortnight in prison at Kantara, on the Suez Canal. They took the trouble to transport me from Palestine to Egypt across the country which the Israelites had passed in the opposite direction, and confided me unlovingly into the hands of a brutal-faced sergeant. The food was miserable, the hours long, the treatment colonial. Some prisoners were beaten. The camp was situated out in the desert. In the morning we did all sorts of "fatigues," and then, when the Egyptian sun was high, we put on full packs—thick leather straps, haversack by the side, shovel and packed bag on the back—and did knee bending, jumping in position, arm and leg calisthenics. Afternoons, we filled straw baskets with loam dug from the desert, carried them about one hundred yards and made a mound. When it was large enough the sergeant ordered us to take the loam back and fill in the holes. I slept in a tent with tough Scotsmen of the Black Watch regiment, and only their wit and tales of personal adventure in the late war prevented me from becoming permanently embittered against the British people. When I returned to my battalion in Palestine I tried to be demobilized so I could live in the country as a civilian. But army law did not allow that, and I remained a British soldier until 1920.

In soldier's uniform and hobnailed boots I went literally from Dan to Beersheba. Near Dan, the Jordan began, and I heard its youthful rumble in the distant hills while standing night guard at blockhouses in the Jewish colonies of Tel Hai and Cfar Gileadi, which were being besieged by Bedouins. A young settler named Shor was killed at my feet while Arab bullets whistled all around.

Taking advantage of a three-day leave from the army, I had made my way to Upper Galilee to participate in the defense of those isolated Jewish points. On my return to the battalion after seventeen days' absence, the sergeant marched me into Captain Jaffe's tent for "trial." "I missed my train in Tiberias," I pleaded, and while the sergeant and I tried to keep a straight face, the Captain shouted, "Dismissed." Later he called me to inquire how things were going up there.

I met most of Palestine's Jewish labor leaders in those years: Beril Katzenellenson, Ben Zwi, Yavniali, Ben Gurion, Dov Hoz, Gollomb, and others. I visited many of the collectivist farms where young emigrants from Russia, Poland, Rumania, and other lands led a rustic Rousseauan life based on egalitarian principles. The streets of Palestine's Jewish cities were paved with ideals and the soil of Jewish farms were fertilized with Jewish blood. Never had a downtrodden people attempted to build a haven for itself at such cost and sacrifice. Yet that long stay in Palestine dimmed my Zionism, and Soviet Russia later extinguished it.

Zionism is Jewish nationalism nailed to a territorial objective, and I know now that I have never felt deeply Jewish. The fate of Jews in Nazi Germany does not touch me any more, nor any less, than the hardships of German pacifists, or socialists, or Catholics. I have asked myself whether this is really so; I have tried to study my emotions about it, and I am sure I am telling the truth. The plight of one wartime refugee is just as distressing to me as that of another—whether he be Jewish or French or Spanish. Palestine and Jews never stirred me as much as the Spanish Republicans in their struggle against Fascism.

Some of my best friends are Jews, and some are not. I was born and raised in the Jewish Ghetto of Philadelphia. From an orthodox Jewish family background one step took me into the Zionist movement. It was not conviction but just glide. Most American Jews remain in the Ghetto even when they move to the fashionable suburbs and join country clubs. Their personal, social, and even business contacts with non-Jews are astoundingly few. It is not always, perhaps it is seldom, their fault. This, therefore, is no plea for assimilation. It takes two to make a bargain. And even after the bargain has been sealed and delivered a Hitler or a Mussolini or a Coughlin may remind Jews of ties they had hoped to forget.

Jewish segregation was greatest in Poland and Czarist Russia which excelled in discrimination. But it is far from negligible in free countries like England and the United States. It tends to create a special Jewish emphasis on Jewish problems. I do not doubt their importance or the necessity of coping with them. But other problems are larger; they encompass the world and are therefore more alluring. Indeed, as I studied the Jewish question in Soviet Russia, Poland, and Germany, I felt more and more that Jewish problems never stand by themselves, but are the by-products of vaster problems. Jews are the symptom of a malady. The malady's the thing. As I moved out into the world and seized opportunities to investigate the major world trends in politics, economics, and sociology, I became less interested in specifically Jewish matters. Jews often told me that this was a "crime" and a "sin."

I explained to my friends in Palestine in 1934 that I had not come to gather material for articles, but merely to luxuriate in the warm air, and I picked Palestine because they were there. Mrs. Irma Lindheim, a rich New Yorker, telephoned me from a Communist farm in the North and asked me to come study their new life. I told her what I told all others, "I'm loafing." They either did not believe me or they politely suggested that I was a "traitor to my people" or they attributed a sinister purpose to my trip. Some assured me that I had strayed from the fold but would return like so many others.

I stayed with Gershon Agronsky and his wife Ethel, Philadelphia friends of my youth. With three delightful children they inhabited a fine old Arab house in the Arab quarter where few Jews dared to live. But Gershon, editor and publisher of the daily, English-language *Palestine Post*, is a mildly romantic, mild Don Quixote, and stayed on in the district even though women who ventured to come unescorted in the evening arrived with palpitating hearts from much running and with tales of lurking Arabs. Later, I am told, Gershon relented and moved to the Jewish suburb on top of a Jerusalem hill. He had been trying—perhaps subconsciously—to prove a point: that a Jew could live wherever he wished in the Jewish homeland, and that Arab and Jew could mix.

In Tel Aviv, I renewed a pleasant acquaintance with Maurice Samuel, a Zionist who thinks, a wit with ideas, and in Jerusalem I saw

Dr. Schmarya Levin, his daughter Enya, and a friend Eiga Shapiro whom I had known well in New York. To Gershon's house came young Moshe Chertok, official of the Jewish Agency, and others bearing Zionist politics. I enjoyed most several visits to Dr. Judah Magnes, Chancellor of the beautiful Hebrew University on Mt. Scopus, and several times trudged up to visit him. Every time I went to see Magnes, Gershon figuratively gritted his teeth and actually exploded into invective. For Magnes had propounded an Arab-Jewish peace pact, and Gershon and his Zionist colleagues wanted peace with the Arabs only on Jewish terms and only when the Jews had become a majority in Palestine. Magnes, a former New York rabbi, wrote a book on the Soviet-German Brest-Litovsk peace negotiations. He is one of those persons who is religious enough to take his religion seriously. "Love thy neighbor as thyself" led him to sympathize with working people, at one time with Communists, and at all times with the Arabs.

Everything I heard and saw in Palestine in 1934 confirmed the opposition to Zionism born during my earlier stay. There are enough national hatreds and inequalities in the world. A movement conceived in high idealism as Zionism undoubtedly is should not create more.

Louis Lipsky, Abe Goldberg, and other Zionist leaders in America had always insisted that there was no Arab problem in Palestine; just a few effendi landlords, they said, who conducted anti-Zionist propaganda from comfortable hotels and cafés in Cairo or Paris while making lots of money selling Jews their Palestine estates. But they were deluding themselves to give themselves false comfort.

Imperialism usually benefits the colonials it oppresses. Yet it nurtures nationalism in the oppressed. Zionism intensified this effect of British imperialism.

In 1919 and 1920, the young Jews I knew—the two Grazovsky boys, Hoz, and others, many of them first generation Palestinians or arrivals from Eastern Europe—spoke Arabic. Tel Aviv ate vegetables from Arab truck gardens and Jewish merchants operated in the adjacent city of Jaffa. In Jerusalem even more Jews knew Arabic, in fact Arabic was the native tongue of some Jews. Jewish agricultural settlements employed many Arabs.

But in 1934, the young generation knew no Arabic. Gershon's son Danny had picked up a few words in the street; he did not learn it in school. Yet Arabs are the majority in the country. I saw Arabs in Tel Aviv very rarely and then they seemed to be on a voyage of discovery, while for Jews to go to Jaffa was an adventure. In this little land, two races, both Semitic, both laying historic claim to it, lived in separate circles; their chief contacts were through stones, clubs, and rifle shots. At the exquisite Hotel David in Jerusalem, we went to dance Saturday evenings on a floor of stone slabs as smooth as silk. The Jews sat in one part of the room, the Arabs in another, the British officers in a third. The officers danced with Arab women and occasionally even with Jewish women—but Arab with Jew? I am sure it was never, but I will say almost never.

There are always effendis, and paid agents of various foreign countries stirring up trouble, but Arab nationalism had become real. Arab "Boy Scouts" in shorts were men training as an anti-Jewish army, while Jews engaged in running guns from Belgium because they had to be prepared.

As Gershon Agronsky was the unofficial press spokesman for the Zionist movement, so another "G.A.," George Antonius, correspondent of the Crane Foundation, expressed official Arab views. "Lives in the mufti's house," Gershon sneered when I went to lunch with Antonius and his beautiful Egyptian wife, sister of Mrs. Smart of the British Residenecy in Cairo whom I met later in Moscow. Antonius talked about an emerging and unifying nationalism in the entire Arab world—Syria, Transjordania, Iraq, Egypt, North Africa— with support from the Moslems of India. The Jews were building a rich new home in the crater of a volcano. Heroic? Yes. But was it wise?

In Tel Aviv I saw shops that seemed to have been transported straight from the Kurfuerstendamm in Berlin after the advent of Hitler, shops filled with expensive house furnishings, modernistic glass ornaments, Rosenthal chinaware—it all appeared so incongruous in a poor pioneering country. Meanwhile, the British High Commissioner, according to newspaper reports, was going among the Arab villages remitting taxes; there had been a crop failure. Of course, some Arabs were also fabulously wealthy.

The Jewish economy of Palestine was abnormal and unsound and depended on regular financial injections from outside. Because of land speculation, which contrasted sharply with the advanced policy of the Jewish National Fund, orange groves were planted that promised to yield three times as much fruit as available markets would absorb, and I was asked when Soviet Russia would buy Jaffa oranges. Strange source of support for Zionism! Gershon said,

"We don't worry. Anti-Semitism will always save us. Now the German Jews are bringing their capital into Palestine. Later it will be Austrian Jewish capital. And South Africa. And maybe French." There would always be new bricks to buttress the artificial structure which, nevertheless, would remain artificial.

Palestine is part of a huge, feudal, Arab continent. Zionism is an attempt—daring but difficult—to unhook it and float it over to Europe.

I went to a Jerusalem concert where the Casadesus quartet played on antiquated musical instruments. When it was finished I stood up and found that I was the only one on my feet. For everyone had remained in their seats because the British High Commissioner had not risen. This was unimportant but symbolic. England and Ireland were then negotiating and quarreling about annuity payments and trade. Gershon's *Palestine Post* took the British side. Astonished, I asked why and he replied, "We must support the British empire." By force of circumstances and inevitably, Zionism is tied to the apron strings of British imperialism. This is a source of both strength and weakness. Bayonets are not good to lean on for a long time, and the bayonets may be withdrawn, or they may be knocked down by a stronger arm. Zionism's alliance with England doubled Arab hatred for Zionism and England. It was a liability to the British and a danger to the Jews.

Given the stubborn insistence on Palestine and no other place as the Jewish homeland—an insistence that can be criticized but not condemned, for only the stubborn win—Zionist security lay in an understanding and close collaboration between Jews and Arabs. That is easier said than done, but many Zionists agreed when I argued that they never tried very hard. Even Jewish labor leaders, very enlightened, advanced, and sentimentally internationalist (they were collecting huge sums while I was there for the Viennese Socialists whose tenements had been shelled by the Austrian government) made only a brief perfunctory attempt at organizing bi-racial trade unions. Chertok, the efficient laborite, unconsciously gave me the reason when he said his nationalism came far ahead of his socialism. Low Arab living standards and wage levels, to be sure, are a serious bar to mixed organizations. But when the fate of a movement and of hundreds of thousands of people depends on success in bridging this gap, the stubborn ones should have been stubborn, here too. The gulf between Jew and Arab is wider than ever, the efforts to

close it fewer than ever, and conciliators like Dr. Magnes invite abuse
and contumely.

The Zionist dilemma was clear in 1934, but a major Jewish occupation in Palestine was that of pooh-poohing dangers and Cassandra-
like prophecies. It improved the mood. And I am bound to say that
a surprisingly large proportion of the Jews I encountered there were
happy. This is endlessly important on a planet so immersed in misery. It is perhaps the best answer to some of my jeremiads. Some.

Even if Zionism were a paradise for the few Jews in Palestine,
the Jewish problem, involving as it does millions of Jews, cannot
be solved in so small a territory. Small geographically, Palestine is
merely a pinhead politically. The Jewish future in Palestine and
elsewhere will be determined by the outcome of a much vaster struggle of free people against totalitarian slavery. Until the Norwegians,
Dutch, Danes, and French—aye, until the Germans, Italians, and
Spaniards are free, a Jewish Palestine is a chimera and Jews in all
countries will suffer mounting disabilities and cruelties. We are all
citizens of one big but closely knit world. Liberty and decency are,
like peace, indivisible. Racial prejudice is the most contagious of
man's diseases.

They asked me in Palestine about Russian Jewry and about the
Jews of Poland. I told them that in the Soviet Union Jews were
equal. A rabbi was persecuted in the same manner as minister, priest,
or mullah. Jewish merchants suffered the same restrictions as Tatar
or Russian or Ukrainian or Turkoman merchants. Jewish workingmen, peasants, or officials had the same rights, advantages, and duties
as the Ukrainian, Armenian, Kabardian, Georgian, or Chuvash
proletariat. Any Jew could join the proletariat and thereby become
equal. Many former Jewish tradesmen, industrialists, and landowners
had done so by finding employment in factories or by settling in one
of the Ukrainian and Crimean colonies fostered by the American
Joint Distribution Committee and directed in Russia by that saint
among men, Dr. Joseph A. Rosen.

Innumerable Jewish merchants just dropped their former pursuits
and lived with their children who might be Communists or Soviet
officials or workingmen. Others persisted in long-ingrained habits,
and I told friends in Jerusalem of the case I knew of a Jew in Kursk
who collects old tin cans and stamps crosses out of them and sells
them, secretly, to peasants or, wholesale, to priests for anywhere
from five to fifty rubles. He markets about two thousand crosses a

month and had been in business for a year. Sometimes he visits Moscow looking for tin cans. When he is caught, as he inevitably will be, he will be punished not as a Jew but as an illicit businessman.

Anti-Semitism in Soviet Russia, I told them, was counter-revolutionary. Anti-Semitism is a hardy plant, and Czarism had fed it well. But the Bolsheviks cut it down and tore out its roots one by one. The vestiges that remained were being attacked with a view to total eradication. Why? Because Bolshevism is essentially a doctrine of internationalism. Nationalism and nationalistic hates are foreign to its conception. But also for a more practical reason. Soviet internal peace required that the two hundred or more racial units live harmoniously together. If the Bolsheviks tolerated Jewish inferiority, the Tatars could argue that the Armenians were inferior and the Georgians might want to dominate the Ossetians, and then the Russians, largest national agglomeration, might claim hegemony over them all. Anti-Semitism would undermine the Soviet state and transform its character. Inevitable under the Great Russian supremacy of Czarism, anti-Semitism is unthinkable as long as the Leninist principle of equality of nationalities prevails. Just as the dogma of Deutschland Ueber Alles brings anti-Semitism and must inspire Nazi attempts at foreign conquest, so the Soviet policies of no Russian nationalism, no discrimination between nationalities, no foreign conquests and no anti-Semitism are all tied together, all part of the same cloth. This was the lesson I preached in Jerusalem in 1934.

Moshe Chertok suggested that the Nazis simply wanted the jobs of ousted Jews. It went much deeper. The Soviet Union stood on the foundation of class war. What distinguished a man in Russia was not the color of his skin or the temperature of his blood or the length of his nose but whether he worked for his living or exploited others. Hitler, however, wished to blot out class differences. Employer and employee must be part of one racial fellowship. To erase class distinctions he emphasized differences of blood.

At Gershon's table, in Magnes's apartment, at Dr. Levin's chessboard in the Vienna Café, it was not sufficient, however, to prove that the three million Jews of Soviet Russia were physically safe and economically and politically as well-off or as badly off as the next non-Jewish fellow. What about Jewish culture and the Jewish religion? Why were Zionists persecuted and imprisoned?

I gave them the answer I gave Judge Julian W. Mack at a *Menorah Journal* dinner in New York in 1932. Maurice Hindus and I spoke

on the Jewish situation in Russia, and in the question-period Judge
Mack sent Chairman Henry Hurwitz this note (I stuck it into my
pocket and kept it), "Unlike most Zionists I had thought I understood and while deploring could explain the reasons for anti-Zionist
activity by the Bolsheviks. But if, as Mr. Fischer says, no one asks
him about Palestine, if as he says, Zionism is dead among Russia's
Jewish youth, why this continued harshness against what must, on
this assumption, be but an insignificant number of Jews—those who
do advocate Zionism?"

I replied that the Bolsheviks were consistent. They objected to
Zionist activity because it was a bourgeois, pro-imperialist movement,
and because in Russia bourgeois social and political activities were
proscribed. Only the proletariat is entitled to organize itself. It doesn't
matter how many Zionists there are and what influence they exercise.
Their work is illegal and when they engage in it they do so knowing
the attendant risks. I myself had in 1922 and 1923 attended meetings
in Moscow of Socialist Zionists. Zionists who were not bourgeois
could function, but it soon developed that these Zionists began to
stress their Communism more than their Zionism, and then they
ceased being Zionists and became professional Jewish Communists.
The Jewish Communists were the spearhead of anti-Zionist persecution.

"Then what of Jewish culture and religion?" they persisted in
Jerusalem.

"Dead or dying," I said. Remnants persisted, but the young generation was lost to the synagogue as to the church and mosque. The
Bolsheviks encouraged the teaching of Yiddish as the popular Jewish
tongue. Several Yiddish daily papers and many big editions of the
works of Sholom Aleichem and Sholom Asch were published. The
government maintained schools where Yiddish was the language of
instruction. "But," I added, "Jewish parents do not want their children to attend such schools." They prefer schools in which Russian
is used. That opened larger possibilities for future professional activity. Moreover, intermarriage was very prevalent and Jewish men
were at a premium; they stayed sober and made good fathers.

"That means assimilation and submergence," they concluded.

I said, "Some day, maybe."

"And will Armenians or Georgians be assimilated?"

"Probably not so soon if at all."

I agreed that the dispersal of Jews accounted for the difference.

The Armenians sat on their own territory. This proved the Zionist contention that Jews must have a homeland, they argued.

"Which would you rather have," I asked unfairly, "the threat of assimilation in Russia or of annihilation in Poland?" I had studied the Jewish situation in Poland in 1922 and devoted a month of research to it in 1926 in preparation for a special series of articles in the *Menorah Journal.* Since then I have from time to time visited Poland, interviewed its statesmen, journalists, diplomats, businessmen, and farmers. The Jewish situation deteriorated steadily after the birth of the modern independent Poland. It was worse in 1926 than in 1922 and worse in 1934 than in 1926. And always it was hopeless.

The Jews of the world are caught in the toils of waxing nationalism. In a weak national state like Poland they were the scapegoats, in a strong national state like Nazi Germany they are the victims. The more nationalistic the majority the greater the cruelty inflicted on a national minority. For nationalism is parochial, intolerant, and egoistic. The true Jewish solution is not in setting up another nationalism but in breaking down all nationalism. The Zionists answer, "And what happens to Jews in the meantime?" We know what happened: destruction of bodies through murder and suicide and the endless, aimless wanderings of refugees, mangling of spirit, and smashing of cultural centers.

Poland before the second World War was a one-story hut with no facilities. The Poles did not say we must build us a better house. They said there are too many Jews in our mud-thatched cabin and they must get out and go as far away as possible. The Poles said there were too many Jews in the cities but refused to grant them farms. The Polish peasants said there were too many Jewish traders and boycotted them, and then patronized new Polish merchants who stepped into the Jewish stores.

So, as we sat discussing in sun-lit Palestine, the outlook of the three million Polish Jews seemed dark, and to Zionists the outlook of Russian Jews was dark, and to me the outlook for Palestine was dark. I had a good month's vacation nevertheless. Hot sun in February! The short automobile run from cool Jerusalem to torrid Kallia on the Dead Sea was like sliding down a chute into a cauldron, and many people get sick at their stomachs. A Scotsman who lives there led a woman to the beach and said, "Now you are the lowest woman in the world." We were furthest below sea level, and on the horizon, in brown haze, were Amman and Moab. One relived the Bible and one's religious-school youth. I rowed over to the spot where the Jordan flows into the briny lake, and again at Jericho we watched Arabs on donkeys cross the narrow Jordan bridge to Transjordania. A single open aqueduct built by the Romans still makes Jericho a big green patch in a bleak, yellow alkali desert. Dates and diminutive bananas and vegetables grow profusely. Here the Arabs are darker and interspersed with black Bedouins and Nubians. Outside the tiny city, these sons of Esau did the spadework for archaeologists who were exposing to view the ancient walls of Jericho. The small bricks of pressed mud obviously had had to crumble at the puff from Joshua's trumpets.

Sir Herbert Samuel, the first British High Commissioner, had owned a winter home in Jericho, and when he went back to England he presented it to a group of the Jewish intellectual élite who took turns at weekends in it. The Agronskys invited me. The servants were old Russian peasant women from the province of Tver. They had come in 1913 to kneel at the Holy Sepulcher, and the War had left them stranded.

Reluctantly, for I was enjoying myself, I boarded at Jaffa a fast French liner for Marseilles. We lay over for a day in Alexandria where I had lived as a soldier. I had an errand to do. In Moscow a Jewish dentist had given me a family portrait to deliver to his sister. When the civil war and the pogroms drowned the Ukraine in blood in 1919, he fled with his father to Moscow, and she with her mother to Egypt. She was a dentist, too. They were separated for life. To go to Russia from Egypt meant to brand yourself a Bolshevik, and the Soviet government did not allow its citizens to go abroad. The earth had become a world of walls made of stouter material than mud or even granite, and the walls were guarded by stupid humans with machine guns.

14. *Mediterranean Russia*

IN 1933, Markoosha's purse was stolen on a Moscow trolley. Some such accident happened to her about once a year. This time the purse had contained her passport, a lot of foreign money, some Soviet money, and my United States passport. When I got home she was nervous, and I had to comfort her.

Since the United States had not yet recognized Russia, I wrote to the nearest American consulate, the one at Riga, Latvia, reported the theft of my document, and asked for another. The answer was that if I presented myself in person they would issue a new passport. But how could I travel to Riga without a passport? Well, some friendly diplomat in Moscow might give me a certificate of identification. While this correspondence proceeded my passport turned up. This was not unusual. Moscow had a lot of skilled pickpockets for whom Markoosha was no match. They knew that the GPU would persist in the search for the purloiners of an American journalist's passport but might not be so zealous hunting down some dollars and pounds. They accordingly mailed the passport to the GPU who forwarded it to me. It was stained and moldy but not seriously damaged and I traveled on it to Palestine, Egypt, and Marseilles.

From Marseilles I planned to go to Spain. Even in those peaceful days the Spanish consul required the approval of an American consul before allowing an American citizen to enter Spain. This amounted to a perfunctory stamp always granted without any questions. But when I submitted my passport for the stamp in the U. S. Consulate in Marseilles, I waited endlessly in the outer office. I complained to the clerk but she was no help. When I began to lose patience the consul himself came out and invited me into his cubbyhole. How was I and how were things in Palestine? What school had I attended in Philadelphia? When had I been in New York last? How long had I lived in Moscow? Did I know so-and-so there and how were conditions there? Expertly suppressing a vast accumulation of anger I finally asked what all this had to do with giving me a free, routine, unimportant, rubber-stamp for Spain. Then the consul explained.

They had been informed when I lost my passport several months ago and they wanted to make sure that I was the authentic owner of the document. My hat was off to the American consular service. For this meant that through the Riga consulate every U. S. consul in the world had received a notification about my lost passport and a caution to be on guard against an imposter.

I expected money in Marseilles from *L'Europe Nouvelle*, a Paris weekly to which I contributed regularly. But it did not arrive. I phoned Paris and was told that there had been a regretted delay and I could have the remittance on Monday. This was Saturday. I had lived rather well on the trip and was now very low in funds, and the problem was whether to wait in Marseilles or try to reach Madrid on the few dollars I had left. I decided to go on. I lived that day on two orders of hot chocolate and buttered rolls, and carried my heavy luggage to the train for Barcelona. I arrived in Barcelona in the morning and would leave that evening for Madrid. But there was a bullfight in Barcelona that afternoon, and I had never seen one. I saw it at the expense of my food.

The bullfight was physically exciting. My teeth chattered. When I thought about it, I did not like it. But my emotion soon stopped the thinking.

I learned something about Spaniards at the bullfight and I saw it confirmed later in other bullfights, in politics, in Spanish journalism, and in the conduct of the Spanish War of 1936-39. It matters a great deal to a Spaniard how a thing is done. Style and form are terrifically important. If the matador touches the bull's flank while escaping his horns he elicits loud approbation. If he shows nonchalance and rolls his cape in graceful waves when the bull dives to gore him the spectators like it. The final kill must be clean, executed with one straight plunge of the sword. A Spaniard would rather die than show fear. A Spaniard wants to die beautifully and to live with dignity even though in poverty. "Better to die on your feet than to live on your knees," Pasionaria's dictum during the Spanish War, was typically Spanish. Manner ranks high in Spain's list of virtues. Sometimes the manner is superficial and finds expression in a flourish; sometimes it is deep and ethical.

In Madrid I called on Luis Araquistain, former Spanish Ambassador to Germany, to whose monthly *Leviathan* I had contributed. He took me to Largo Caballero, "the Spanish Lenin," leader of the trade unions and the Spanish Socialists. He also introduced me to his brother-in-law and neighbor, Julio Alvarez del Vayo, son of a general, former Spanish Ambassador to Mexico. Araquistain was the right-hand man of Caballero and del Vayo was the left-hand man, or vice versa. Araquistain had married a Swiss girl named Trudi Graa. Del Vayo had married her sister Luisy. A third Graa sister married a Spanish finance minister. Through their husbands, Trudi and Luisy played considerable roles in Spanish affairs. They were handsome, blonde, and energetic, and at least as intelligent as their spouses; their policies were the condensed, sharpened, and indelible copies of their husbands' policies. During the war, a bitter enmity, based on complicated personal-political motives, broke out between Araquistain, Loyalist Ambassador in Paris, and del Vayo, his superior as Loyalist Foreign Minister. Then the two sisters, who loved one another dearly, broke off relations, too.

I had one letter of introduction from Frederick Kuh to Lester Ziffern, the Madrid United Press correspondent. Through Ziffern I met the other correspondents, and through them I met many Spaniards and foreigners. Outstanding as a United States diplomat was Claude G. Bowers, United States Ambassador. He first ate half of his cigar and then lit and smoked what remained of it. His shoes were old and misshapen. He banged out his own dispatches to the State Department with two fingers. He was a democrat in the finest American tradition, democratic in thought and treatment of his fellows and in his approach to international problems. Naturally, therefore, he sympathized with the Republican liberals and Socialists but loathed the aristocratic Monarchists with whom he associated. He initiated me into the intricacies of Spanish domestic politics and blessed me as I left for a tour of Spanish villages.

My trip to the villages and cities of Spain made me love Spain. Indeed, Spain for me was love at first sight. It also opened my eyes to the penury of the Spanish people. I knew instinctively that this country would experience turmoil and bloodshed because conditions were intolerable.

"I am not hungry today. I ate my cat." I thought he was joking. But the villagers who stood about nodded in confirmation. A woman of twenty-seven, who had five living children and looked forty-five, said, "Recently a horse fell dead on the road and we ran out and cut strips of meat from it." One peasant said, "The last time I ate meat was at the funeral of a city friend."

"And butter?" I asked.

"We don't know what it is," the women replied. "Even the children never get milk."

I went into at least a dozen huts and looked for food supplies.

No family had sugar. In one earthen house I found two small bunches of scallions, four potatoes, a small, half-filled bottle of vegetable oil, and nothing else: no bread. The authorities had distributed free bread on the three previous days but none on this day, and so there was none.

Clothes were ragged. Shoes of canvas with rope soles. The inhabitants looked more bedraggled than in a poor Ukrainian village.

I made a note of all the articles in one mud hut: three wooden chairs, a wooden table, a few pots, spoons and plates, a pan for washing clothes, a wooden bed with straw pallets, and that was all. In other huts it was the same.

This was the village of Pueblo del Rio, thirty minutes by direct electric trolley from the much advertised tourist city of Seville in Andalusia, rich in land and water. At first I had not wanted to go to a village so near a city. In Russia I knew that a village too near a city was not typical. And, in fact, the peasants of Pueblo del Rio told me that the situation in other villages was much worse.

The villagers I met owned neither horse nor cow nor pigs nor poultry nor sheep. They did not even possess enough land for truck growing. This was the condition of the great mass of Spanish peasants. All the soil of Pueblo del Rio belonged to three owners. The farmers worked about four months each year. One man told me that he had earned nothing for the last six months.

This was not a bad year. It was a normal year. These people and hundreds of thousands of other Spaniards lived in a permanent state of semi-starvation. Tens of thousands of Spanish peasants inhabited caves. I could see those caves as I traveled through the countryside and I could see the children and the adults near their mouths. Those people subsisted on spinach and other grasses. Whole districts were known for their underfed cretins. This had been going on for decades. The most distressing feature was not so much that conditions were horrible as that nothing was being done to remedy them. I saw poverty a-plenty in the Soviet Union. But that poverty, even the 1933 Ukrainian famine, was the concomitant, in part the result—sad paradox—of prodigious effort to give the country a new and permanently healthy agrarian base. In Spain, however, the poverty had stimulated no effort to destroy it.

"What are you waiting for?" I asked at Pueblo del Rio.

"We are waiting for death," a middle-aged peasant woman replied.

"What has the Republic done for you?" I asked.

"Damn the Republic," one of them said. They all wanted land and the Republic had not given it to them.

I asked why they did not seize the land. They all had one answer in two words, "Guardia Civil." The guardias, middle-aged militias, too pot-bellied to run but reactionary enough to shoot straight at peasants, deterred tempestuous spirits. Graves covered those who had defied the law.

Later, in Madrid, Ogier Preteceille, a Spanish-Frenchman who worked as correspondent for a British daily, took me to see Manuel Azaña, a moderate Republican and Prime Minister of the Republic from October, 1931, to September, 1933. We went to his home for he was no longer in office, and he received us in a darkened room. "Spain's strong man," they called him. But I gathered the impression of a man with a big head and a soft well-cushioned body. On the eve of the civil war, he was again Prime Minister and during the war he was President of the Spanish Republic. He was the kind of politician in whom excess intellectuality paralyzes will power. Educated in a famous Catholic monastery, he became a prominent jurist and literary figure. He wrote several plays, three novels, and an autobiography of his youth entitled *The Garden of the Monks*, which is still one of the gems of the Castilian language. He also translated Borrow's *The Bible in Spain* into Spanish. Subsequently many Spaniards regretted that he had not limited himself to fiction and eschewed political reality.

I asked him why he had not introduced a new land law to change conditions in the villages. He told me he had worked on the land-reform law for eighteen months while in office. And just when he had finished it he was overthrown.

I laughed. "A year and a half to write a law?" I exclaimed.

"Yes," he sighed. "Social problems had to wait. We were busy fighting religious and political enemies." So Spain's greatest problem, land, waited. The Socialists, too, had curbed their eagerness for economic change in order not to embarrass the Republic, and now the reactionaries were in office again and had wiped out all the wage increases, all the progressive laws, and many of the educational advances of the long Azaña regime.

One very sunny Sunday morning, Dr. Juan Negrin and Jay Allen, the American correspondent, took me by taxi to the little town of Colmenar Viejo, twenty miles from Madrid. The taxi waited to take us back. Negrin was a member of the Cortes but he had never opened his mouth in it—partly out of shyness and lack of confidence, partly from a sense of the futility of it. Who was he to speak in the presence of Indalecio Prieto, Calvo Sotelo, and Manuel Azaña? Negrin and I spoke German together. He had been graduated from the University of Leipzig where he wrote a treatise on the sympathetic nerve system. Now he taught medicine in the University of Madrid and conducted a special metabolism laboratory. He is a native of the Canary Islands, soft and fleshy; he loves to live and eat well, and he frequented the best Madrid restaurants.

We stopped at the piazza in Colmenar Viejo. We had come to see the life of workingmen in a small provincial city. Colmenar has stone quarries. In the piazza workingmen, no women, stood around in groups. Under broad sombreros their faces were pinched by hard work and malnutrition, and dried by the sun. Their corduroy suits had been brushed for the Sabbath. Trouser legs showed patches from thigh to shin. Elbows were similarly adorned. They stood close together and talked little and the predominant color was black.

Jay introduced himself, then Negrin, then me. They complained of low wages, but chiefly of unemployment. Conditions were becoming intolerable. In reply to a question practically all of them said they were Socialists. We asked who their leader was. They said, "Largo Caballero." Did they know any other Socialist leaders? No, never heard of any, and this was twenty miles from the Cortes where they all made speeches. Would they follow Caballero into a revolution? Yes, they would follow him anywhere, and the sooner the better.

One man volunteered to show us his house. We tramped down a road covered by inches of dust and entered a cool, stone hut, poorly furnished, almost empty. The worker's wife was stirring something in a pot on a low open fire. "Black lentils," she said. "This is our steady diet. Black lentils and black coffee. No milk, no sugar, little bread. Can you expect a mother to nurse a child on such a diet?" Two of her children had died last year of pneumonia, she said. In an aside to me, Negrin suggested it was probably due to undernourishment. A baby of seven months lay in a crib near the stove. She said it was sick with hernia. Negrin opened the covers and looked at it and I saw from his mobile face that he gave it no chance. The woman said she just did not know what to do. They were burdened with mountains of debt. The grocery store gave her a little food on credit. Neighbors helped but they themselves had next to nothing. Her husband had worked twenty-five days in the last six months. The employers were deliberately refusing to operate the quarries. I asked what they thought should be done. The workingman declared the government should force the capitalists to give them work. "Anything else?" No, that was what they all wanted.

The husband had not gone to church for years. "The priests take and never give," he said. His wife stopped attending mass after both children died. But she berated her husband when he launched into a tirade against the church. Both spoke as from hollow chests and weak bodies. Their protests echoed undermined physiques. "Nothing happens for years," they said.

When we left, Negrin stuck a silver duro or five-peseta piece into the woman's hand. Seventy cents. As we walked down the road we heard the woman screaming and running towards us. The duro was counterfeit like so many others circulating in Spain. Negrin exchanged the coin.

We dropped Jay at his home and then Negrin drove me to my hotel. In the taxi he said, "Do you think we could get arms from the Russians?" I said I didn't know but he might try. I felt, "This man is serious."

The earth and the pavements throbbed with discontent. The air was heavy with foreboding and rumor. As I walked through the streets with Ziffern he would say, "There are machine guns on that roof." Everybody expected trouble. Caballero told me he had read Lenin in French and Trotzky's great *History of the Russian Revolution* in Spanish. "This," I wrote, "is indispensable preparation, but arms are as important, and I think the Spanish revolutionists have too few of them and too little money." It turned out that they had no arms at all. The Monarchists, however, had sent a delegation to Mussolini, and the reactionaries who failed in the Sanjurjo revolt in 1932, were resolved not to lose next time.

I had the impression that I was in a civilized country. In that village of Pueblo del Rio the peasants had something which the peasants in a Russian village lacked. I wondered what it was. The Spaniards begged; some of them were illiterate; they were dirty and unkempt. Yet the most miserable among them bore himself with a personal dignity and self-assertion which the Russian and Ukrainian peasant did not show. The Spaniards seemed to stem from an old culture. The workingmen in blue denim shirts, small, puny men, wore a proud look. Their eyes said, "I am a man," even though life was treating them like dogs.

On the other hand, the Spaniards had mutilated the famous mosque at Cordoba by building a Catholic cathedral over it and into it. Where did such vandalism come from? Spanish princes violated the exquisite, but somewhat garish Alcazar of Seville by decorating its walls with vile untalented paintings and introducing vulgar, ugly furniture into its rooms. The incomparable Moorish Alhambra at Granada had been defiled by the heavy reforming hands of Isabella and Ferdinand of Castille. Yet cities like Cordoba and especially the blue patios of its well-proportioned homes were filled with calm dignity. Was it Arab culture and Arab blood that accounted for the grace and the pride? In Granada I entered a café with a woman. She was the only woman there, and all the men eyed her. Spanish women enjoyed civil rights, but custom decreed that they stay at home. When a Spaniard courts a girl he "eats iron," because he stands on the street with his face in the bars of a window and his beloved is on the other side in her house. This too suggested Arab segregation and feudalism.

The cafés of Madrid and Barcelona were packed with slim young men in tight suits, their hair slicked down with much oil and their faces insipid, waiting to shout remarks at young women who would pass.

I felt an intuitive dislike for them. They were not all bad and some of their kind I later saw at the front in the Loyalist army. But most of them were born in the other camp. Then women came along to sell lottery tickets; they represented another Spain. Their black hair was drawn back tightly to a knot on the backs of their heads and they wore black woolen shawls with fringes. My mother had always worn such a shawl, only hers was gray. It cost less than a coat. When the wind blew cold they wore it as she had—over the head and shoulders and around the chest. These Spanish women's faces were deeply lined and prematurely old from privation. They were the Spain of the fields, mountains, and factories.

Spain often reminded me of Russia. Like the Russia of the Czars it was a country of extreme distinctions of wealth and power. Those who had power were effete and those enjoying moral health stood close to the soil and soul of the nation but their stomachs were empty.

The Spaniard has a Slav indifference to time. With all his solar temperament, the Spanish peasant is as docile and patient as the muzhik. When the maid in the Victoria Hotel in Madrid started telling me her life story instead of making my room, I harked back to Moscow's Savoy. The common people of both Russia and Spain are trusting, simple, warm, and communicative. They like to stand and move in groups. In Soviet Russia such groups melt into a mass. In Spain each individual remains distinct.

But above all in its social development Spain was the Russia of the Mediterranean. In 1917 Russia was a backward, feudal autocracy with an established, corrupt church. Eighty percent of Spain's 23,-000,000 inhabitants lived in villages in 1934. The Russian percentage was seventy-five. Both countries had radical proletariats, weak middle classes, influential aristocracies, rotten monarchies, weak armies, little industry, and heart-breaking poverty. Russia and Spain had defeated Napoleon and successfully defied the French Revolution. In 1917, Lenin first staged a French Revolution—he destroyed feudalism by dividing the estates and banishing the aristocrats. Then he proceeded to make the Bolshevik Revolution. In 1934, Spain yearned for a French Revolution. For one hundred and fifty years it had waited and its progress was that much retarded.

The Spanish Republic arrived in April, 1931. Its function was to bring the French Revolution to Spain. But when Azaña tried the reactionaries stopped him. An outworn class had placed itself athwart Spain's current of life. Either the class would be smashed or there would be a flood.

15. *Free Lance at Large*

MY income from work is my means of doing more work. In 1935, I wanted to make a round trip through Europe, for things were evidently brewing fast. I wrote *The Nation* suggesting a series of ten articles at one hundred dollars apiece. My expenses, I assured them, would amount to no less than $1,000, for I intended going from Moscow to Poland, Germany, France, England, Italy, Switzerland, Austria, Czechoslovakia, ending up again in Moscow. *The Nation* agreed. It never has much money but always manages somehow to scrape together as much as it needs.

I stopped first in Berlin but found that I could not start the series with an article on Germany because Germany was not quite the key to European events. I went on to Geneva. It was not the graveyard I expected. The League of Nations had adopted sanctions against Italy on a signal from Great Britain, and Geneva veterans were somewhat more optimistic. Frederick Kuh gave me a reception in the apartment of Wallace Carroll to which "all Geneva" came, the permanent correspondents and many League officials. Of the former there were Robert Dell, *Manchester Guardian*, Andrew Rothstein, *Tass*, and Clarence K. Streit, *New York Times*, author of *Union Now;* of the latter, Dr. Ludwik Rajchman, chief of the League's Hygiene section, a Pole who had been adviser of the Chinese Nationalist government, Mr. Tirana, an Albanian in the League's economics department, and Konni Zilliachus, son of an American mother and a Finnish father.

Zilliachus was born in Japan, went to elementary school in Sweden, secondary school in England, and was graduated from Yale University. In the World War, still a Russian subject, he volunteered for service with the British Army in Siberia which helped Kolchak. He thereby became a British citizen. In Siberia he married the daughter of a Polish revolutionary exile. In Siberia, too, he learned to respect the Bolsheviks. He spoke the languages of all the countries his life had touched—except Finnish—and in addition, French, German, Spanish, Danish, and some Turkish. For many years he worked in the

261

League's Information Department. While maintaining the proper
neutral decorum of a League official he wrote explosively critical
pamphlets about the League and the British Conservative government's international policy. Later he resigned from the League's press
bureau to become a left-wing Parliamentary Labor candidate, an
editor of Sir Stafford Cripps's radical *Tribune*, and, during the second
World War, a British censor. Even he was slightly less cynical about
the League in 1935 than at most times.

Other Genevans hoped that the League had discovered a prescription for keeping alive by doing something. Of course, it acted as a
façade for British imperial interests, but if the product was good
they were willing to forget its origins. The real question was how
long Italy could hold out under economic sanctions. Tirana and his
friends exhibited columns of figures on Italy's gold, imports, exports,
and production. But even the best statistician who can use a logarithm
to determine probabilities may be a bad prophet, and some of them
knew better than to project themselves perilously into the future.

Marcel Rosenberg was in Geneva. He had come to the League as
assistant secretary. A hunchback with deep flaming eyes, he had made
a big impression in Paris as Counselor of the Soviet Embassy, and
Paris salons angled for his visits. Several times he took me along. It
was Rosenberg on the Soviet side and Edouard Herriot on the French
side who prepared the ground in France for the Franco-Soviet military pact. He thought I knew Russia. In 1930 and 1931, I argued
with him regularly against certain Soviet domestic policies. He, good
Bolshevik, automatically defended them. When they were discarded
as recognized blunders, he took me more into his confidence on
Soviet foreign policy.

Also, he knew I knew how he came to be appointed to Geneva.
Stalin's candidate as Soviet assistant secretary in the League of Nations (each major power in the League Council could designate a
member of the secretariat) was Gregory Sokolnikov, ex-Commissar
of Finance, and a man of big caliber. But he was too big for Litvinov,
too big to be Litvinov's obedient instrument. Litvinov, however,
could not reject Stalin's candidate outright. He could present his own
candidate, Constantine Oumansky, chief of the Foreign Office press
department, shrewd and subservient. Stalin said that to send Oumansky would offend the League. He was too young, and had never
held a high post. But by suggesting Oumansky Litvinov had indicated that it was unnecessary to send a person of Sokolnikov's stature.

Moreover, having turned down Litvinov's candidate, Stalin could not insist on his own. That was another reason why Litvinov had offered the name of Oumansky. They then agreed on Rosenberg, who had been Litvinov's choice from the beginning.

As a Soviet diplomat, Rosenberg had received a salary of approximately $2,500 a year. But the League paid Rosenberg $25,000, a large part of which he contributed to the treasury of the Communist party. He had a large villa, two limousines, a battery of secretaries, and a nice new wife, daughter of Emilian Yaroslavsky, Soviet Atheist No. 1 and an elder Bolshevik statesman. I sat with Rosenberg for many hours in the evening. He too saw a flicker of hope for the League because it was obstructing an aggressor. Yet it was all because London had so willed it, and I decided to stop in Paris only a few days and start my "Arms over Europe" series with a survey of the British situation.

Britain was divided. The British government's actions were contradictory. It put one foot forward and then recoiled. It apparently wanted to stop Mussolini from grabbing Ethiopia. Sanctions were applied. But the policy was half-hearted. The British government also helped Mussolini grab Ethiopia.

This dichotomy was deepened by two elections, one of which was not an election. It was the Peace Ballot. The British League of Nations Association, led by Lord Robert Cecil, had conducted a voluntary nation-wide poll in which 11,559,165 adults enjoying official franchise participated. This was more than half the number of votes cast in national elections for Parliament. According to the result as announced on June 27, 1935, 10,027,608 favored economic and other non-military League of Nations sanctions against aggressors. On military sanctions, 6,784,368 voted in favor, 2,351,981 against. Almost everybody—over ten and a half million peace balloters —wanted all-round reduction of armaments.

The Peace Ballot shook Prime Minister Stanley Baldwin's conservative cabinet into a pro-League pose. Ten million votes for sanctions could not be ignored. So the League of Nations adopted sanctions against Italy. Having done this, Baldwin shrewdly ordered national elections.

I spent part of the campaign period in London. I went with Harold J. Laski to hear him deliver speeches for Labor candidates. (Laski himself has consistently refused to run, or, as the British say, "stand" for Parliament.) I also accompanied D. N. Pritt, left-wing Laborite and famous lawyer, and his wife—wives almost invariably stump with their husbands in England—George Russell Strauss and his wife, and Dorothy Woodman on their election campaigns. Pritt and Strauss were elected; Miss Woodman was defeated.

The candidates could say that the British government was not sincere about sanctions. But they could not prove insincerity, for Baldwin had actually forced sanctions on Europe.

The Baldwin government won the general election on November 14, 1935. Four hundred and twenty-one government supporters were elected to Parliament against 179 of the Opposition. The popular vote, however, was 11,570,179 for the government, and 9,930,460 for the Opposition. It was a close vote and Baldwin's advocacy of sanctions made the difference which spelled victory.

Having won a substantial majority in Parliament on a pro-League platform, Stanley Baldwin immediately proceeded to carry out an anti-League policy. I hesitate to make a charge of double-dealing or playing false with the electorate, but the Conservative party had been helped into office in 1924 by the forged "Zinoviev letter." In his unfinished book on the League of Nations which Robert Dell confided to me before his death, he charges that Sir Samuel Hoare, the British Foreign Minister, was only waiting for the elections to sabotage sanctions and that Laval said privately he expected British policy to change after the elections. Negley Farson, in *The Nation* of November 13, 1935, undertook to defend British policy against American liberal critics, yet he predicted "that the British government will almost certainly make no peace dicker with Mussolini until after the general elections in November." The peace dicker was tried in December.

The Peace Ballot showed Baldwin he would lose the general election unless he paid lip service to the League of Nations during the election campaign. Sanctions against Italy were another "Zinoviev letter" for the British Tories. Sanctions enabled the Tories to win the elections. Stanley Baldwin, speaking to the House of Commons "with the utmost frankness" on November 12, 1936, practically admitted that he had lied to the electorate in 1935.

The British government persuaded the League to apply sanctions to Italy in October, 1935. But when it was found that these sanctions were insufficient it did not apply oil sanctions which would have been decisive. Nor did it close the Suez Canal. The expedient of closing the canal would have saved Abyssinia and collective security and vindicated the League. The British held Suez. If they were in earnest about Abyssinia how could they allow Mussolini to crush Abyssinia with men and materials that went through the canal?

But they failed to close it, allegedly, because the canal was operated by an international stock company whose statutes stipulated that it must remain open at all times, in peace and war. Rubbish! When Italy went to war in 1940, England immediately closed the canal.

The British contended that if they pressed Mussolini too hard he would make war on Britain and sink the Mediterranean fleet. This meant that Baldwin and Hoare were not very serious about sanctions. They would court some minor inconveniences for the sake of Ethiopia, but they would not take risks. By not taking small risks they got themselves into bigger troubles later. The course of the second World War has shown that it is not so easy to sink the British fleet in the Mediterranean. The chance of Mussolini starting a war on the British Empire when he had no allies was very slight. Germany was anti-Italian on account of Austria and was not yet sufficiently armed.

The British government's failure in the Ethiopian crisis was due to a fear of destroying Mussolini's regime and to a lack of indignation over the rape of Abyssinia.

Pro-League sentiment in England stemmed chiefly from Labor and Liberals, and was accentuated by the rise of Hitler and Italy's aggression against Abyssinia. Labor and the Liberals were inherently anti-Fascist. The League of Nations for them had become an instrument to check the spread and successes of Fascism. But the British government had no such attitude towards the League because it had no such attitude towards Fascism. Many supporters of the Conservative government were pro-Hitler and pro-Mussolini.

On February 6, 1934, for instance, Sir John Simon, British Foreign Secretary, told the House of Commons that "Germany's claim to equality of rights . . . ought not to be resisted. There is little likelihood of peace in the world if you try to put one country or race under an inferior jurisdiction." For the sake of peace, then, Germany had to be allowed to rearm. He made the argument sound plausible, but actually it was stupid. Sir John was saying: let Hitler arm and he will keep the peace. Subsequently, bombs over London wrecked Simon's "logic" but not his high position in British public life.

And there was the Marquess of Lothian, who had reacted favorably to Soviet Russia. He went to study Nazi Germany and visited Hitler. When he returned he wrote two articles in the *London Times* of January 31, and February 1, 1935. He too found a sympathetic explanation for German rearmament. "National Socialism," he declared, ". . . is a movement of individual and national self-respect." That statement was not calculated to strengthen anti-Fascism among the typical *Times* readers, or in the British nobility. "The central fact in Europe today," asserted Lord Lothian, "is that Germany does not want war and is prepared to renounce it absolutely as a method of settling disputes with her neighbors, provided she is given real equality." ("Real equality" had already been given to Germany during Bruening's chancellorship.) But Hitler told Lothian personally that "Germany does not want war" and Lothian believed, and repeated it to the British public. Hitler told Lothian many things. Lothian repeated them too. Hitler told him "finally and most vital, that he will pledge Germany not to interfere in his beloved Austria by force."

Lothian came away fully convinced by Hitler. "I have not the slightest doubt," he wrote in the *Times*, "that his [Hitler's] attitude is perfectly sincere. Hitler's Germany does not want war. Hitler does not want it not because he is a pacifist, but because he knows what war means, because he can only carry out his plans for training and disciplining and uniting the young generation in peace."

Lord Lothian therefore urged "treating [Germany] as a friend." For Germany "is not imperialist in the old sense of the word. . . . Its very devotion to race precludes it from trying to annex other nationalities."

Bloody events have supplied the commentary on Lothian's journalism.

British rearmament was an issue in the November, 1935, British elections. But how could they arm when they were being disarmed by assurances of Hitler's pacific intentions? A nation puts its money and heart into rearming only when it knows the name of the potential enemy. But Hitler was being pictured as a friend. He had no hostile intentions against his neighbors, much less England. Perhaps he was thinking of a trial of strength with Russia. That would be all to the good. "It is an open secret that Hitler, while unconcerned about the Russia of today, is deeply concerned about the Russia of tomorrow. . . . What will Russia be when it is organized, strong, and equipped and Stalin is no longer there?" Thus Lothian after his talk with Hitler. Hitler was facing east; England need not worry.

Granted, Hitler is a convincing talker. But Lothian was no gullible youngster. Many democrats, pacifists, socialists, Communists, and liberals were instantaneously anti-Nazi. They instinctively reacted against the Hitler dictatorship. Not so Lothian. He did not admire Nazi methods, of course. But he believed Hitler; he wanted to be-friend Hitler. The first reason why the governments of England and France did not resist Fascist aggression, and why they were not pre-pared for the big war was that they were not anti-Fascist. They did not understand the nature of Fascism. They underestimated Fascism. They were soothed by Hitler's lullaby that he was a "bulwark against Bolshevism."

The British, and the French, accordingly, continued to play the old balance-of-power game. England, in November, 1935, rocked merrily in numerous cross-currents. The military, apparently, favored an alliance with France, and rumors told of secret Anglo-French staff talks about Germany. On the other hand, the British government took the world by surprise in negotiating the Anglo-German naval agreement of June, 1935, which gave Hitler a green light on naval construction up to a limit. (When he reached the limit he scrapped the agreement.) The French howled. They had not even been in-formed that this treaty was under consideration, and they said quite openly—"Pertinax," for instance—that it was aimed against France.

This move to appease Hitler was considered by some a necessary preliminary to throwing down the gauge of battle to Mussolini. The Anglo-German naval pact had no sooner been signed than Anthony Eden rushed to Rome and told Mussolini—before the invasion of Abyssinia—that he could have only a part of Abyssinia. Herewith the British government entered on its course of giving away what did not belong to it. Nevertheless, Eden's policy required resistance to Rome's maximum demands.

The opposite school of thought was represented in the British Foreign Office by Sir Robert Vansittart, hard-looking yet handsome, a poet, a scenario writer, and England's best professional expert on international politics. He saw Hitler as the greater menace, and hoped to keep Italy in the British camp. If Mussolini was forced to fight for the Abyssinian desert three thousand miles away, he would not be able to protect the green garden in his backyard—Austria—against

Hitler. It was Italy's military moves that had kept Hitler out of Vienna in 1934. Vansittart would have been happier if Mussolini had never ventured into the desert. But was the desert worth the loss of Italy's friendship? Sir John Simon, great statesman, went further, and declared that if Italian Fascism were thwarted it might be overthrown and then Italy would go Communist. Beginning with Karl Marx in 1848 many people have seen the non-existent "specter of Communism."

So some said, appease Germany in order to stop Italy; and others said, appease Italy in order to check Germany. Until June 10, 1940, when Mussolini went to war against Britain and France, high British officials, including Lord Halifax, Foreign Secretary, still dreamed of appeasing Italy.

Small wonder that England's efforts on behalf of Abyssinia and the League were half-hearted. Geneva had harbored sanguine hopes, but in London, my friends suspected that the British government would betray the League, Ethiopia, and England's interests. Not all Conservatives were lukewarm about opposing Italy's conquest of Abyssinia; not all Laborites believed in the wisdom of sanctions. Every line demarcating divisions of public opinion is a zigzag. But, generally speaking, the cleavage was perpendicular and separated Right from Left. The Left stretched from Conservative but dissident Lord Robert Cecil to Harry Pollitt, the secretary of the Communist party. The Right consisted of reactionaries called Liberals like Sir John Simon and Liberals writing for Conservatives like Lord Lothian. The Left militantly demanded peace measures which their opponents branded "warlike"; the Right championed "peaceful compromise," which in several years drove Great Britain to war.

London muddled along, but it always gave me the feeling of being the center of the earth. Not only was it the hub of an empire and the focal point of innumerable news channels that displayed their names on Fleet Street, the world's greatest newspaper artery; it had strength. England was part of Europe yet not of Europe. It had stakes everywhere but stood alone and proud. They tell the story of a headline in the *London Times* which read, STORMS OVER ENGLAND; CONTINENT ISOLATED. London boasted more Rolls Royces and slum homes per square mile than any town in Christendom. After the theater the Strand filled with men and women in evening clothes. Around the corner were areas of debasing filth and poverty. Yet London thought and changed money and shipped goods for half

the world, did it with a quiet dignity and self-assurance. Respect for
tradition here was compounded of stodginess, a consciousness of
inner power, and obeisance to a successful past. Moscow is very old
and very new. Berlin is new. But in London everything that is new
seems old and everything that is old is very old. The soot on its
buildings, the top hats on its messenger boys, the winding alleys, the
names of streets and inns one knew from Dickens and Thackeray,
the Victorian and Georgian red-brick houses where an earl or an
admiral or a poet was born, blur and bridge the centuries. New York
is. Chicago will be. In London you can never forget what England
was.

The symbol of London might be a Bobby or a John Bull or
Colonel Blimp. A Prussian grenadier could stand for Berlin. Moscow
is a worker with dark cap on his head and hammer in two hands.
Even Vienna in its good days was a man with a feather in his green
hat, a cape over his shoulders, and a gold chain across his bulging
vest. All these cities are men. But Paris is a woman, a woman who
knows how to choose her clothes.

It is not merely that each building in Paris has beauty. Whole
areas of the city have design and architecture. There is nothing on
the planet like the cluster of the Arc de Triomphe at the Etoile, the
Champs Elysées, the Place de la Concorde, and the Tuileries at evening. Parts of the city are not just tacked on to one another. They
grow into and out of one another. France loved to live. The artists
of all nations converged on Paris, but Paris had learned, and sometimes taught, the greatest art of all, the art of living. That is not why
it died—for a short while, one hopes. France was not less soft, wine-
guzzling, and smiling in 1914.

When I went from England to France at the end of 1935, I wrote
an article on "The Tragedy of France." The German shadow was
dark on the face of France. Winston Churchill said in October,
1935, "Germany is already well on her way to becoming incom-
parably the most heavily armed nation in the world and the nation
most completely ready for war. This is the dominant factor which
dwarfs all others, and is affecting the movement of politics and diplomacy in every country in Europe."

As I moved from one country to another, war was railroad talk,
parlor talk, newspaper talk, breakfast, lunch and dinner talk. A strong
country, well-organized and technically advanced, with a big, virile,

and able population was concentrating most of its attention on military preparations. There were years when a different spirit in Europe, a different policy in London and Paris, and happier circumstances within Germany might have prevented German rearmament. But now it had commenced, and the French had to decide what to do about it. France's three choices were: to crush Germany immediately; to make terms with the presumptive aggressor before it was too late; or to organize a defensive combination of powers against him for the future. France had no stomach for an invasion of Germany. The desire in France for a rapprochement with Germany was widespread. The Fascists, the reactionaries, the middle-of-the-road politicians like Edouard Daladier, and even many socialists advocated an understanding with Nazi Berlin.

If Hitler had been willing there could have been Franco-German friendship in 1935. But the secret emissaries like Count de Brinon whom Pierre Laval sent to the Wilhelmstrasse did not always receive a cordial reception. France had too little to give Germany. A French promise not to attack was worthless. Hitler knew France did not intend to attack. Frence guarantees of Germany's frontiers were equally superfluous; no one planned to take territory from Germany. If Hitler hoped to get a loan he would apply to London, not Paris. The redistribution of colonies likewise depended on London. Hitler's *Mein Kampf* mapped the destruction of France after a German pact with Britain. Hitler wanted England's friendship, not France's. At times, he gave the impression of courting France when it served his diplomatic purpose. But it was never an important reality.

Without abandoning hope of worming himself into Hitler's good graces, Laval therefore explored the third choice: a union of powers against Germany. What were the possibilities here? England, Russia, and Italy. The United States was not to be had for such combinations, and Japan was too far away.

On May 2, 1935, Laval signed a treaty of mutual assistance with the Soviet government. On May 16, 1935, Czechoslovakia, France's ally, signed a similar agreement with the Soviet government and the two documents were linked by a clause which said that Russia would help an invaded Czechoslovakia only after France marched to her assistance. Hitler screamed with anger. He was being encircled. On numerous occasions he insisted that the Franco-Soviet pact be canceled. He declared that the existence of that pact made amicable relations between him and France unthinkable. This suited many

Frenchmen who disliked the pact because, they said, it helped French Communists and the French Left generally. Nazi Propaganda Minister Goebbels warned the French, "Whoever treats with Bolshevism will end by being devoured by it." In Paris this was regarded as a good bit of friendly advice. It was always Hitler's strategy to obstruct friendly relations between the Western Powers and Russia.

The French government, however, did not drop the pact. It merely failed to invest it with real content. The treaty presupposed military consultation and collaboration between Russia and France. The Russians were willing. The French never were. The treaty remained a scrap of paper. This irritated the Russians, but it did not win the Germans.

Similarly, France irritated England without winning Italy. On February 3, 1935, British and French statesmen met in London with an eagle eye cocked on Germany and agreed to work intimately together for the pacification of Europe. In April, 1935, England and France met with the Italians at Stresa and all three decided to deal in concert as far as Germany was concerned. Italy feared German encroachment in Austria. Mussolini was the patron of Austria. If Hitler got Austria he would look down on Italy from the Brenner Pass, and Il Duce did not want to be haunted by those eyes and that mustache. Stresa seemed like the achievement of a triple entente.

All this love-making followed a little friendly visit by Laval to Rome in January, 1935. Laval then made it clear to Mussolini that France would not object to Italian occupation of Abyssinia. Laval gave Italy 2,500 shares in the French railway which runs from Djibuti to Addis Ababa together with two strips of French territory, one adjoining East Eritrea, the other adjoining Libya. Laval likewise renounced, in writing, the French rights under the Anglo-French-Italian spheres-of-influence convention of December 13, 1906.

The Italian invasion of Abyssinia was thus Laval's baby. He knew it was coming. He encouraged Mussolini by concessions. The best one can say about Laval's intentions is that they were designed to keep Italy's friendship and to keep Italy in the front against Germany. This was mistaken strategy. Retreat in the face of Fascist aggression encouraged further Fascist aggression. This is not hindsight; it was for this reason that anti-Fascists favored collective security and sanctions against Italy. The Left foresaw what actually happened: a succession of surrenders to totalitarian dictators ending in a major catastrophe. For the aggression of the dictators was inspired by their disrespect for democracy. There was never a "March on Rome." Mussolini rode to Rome in a Pullman sleeper and received power peacefully from the King and pusillanimous Prime Minister Facta. Italian democracy abdicated and invited its own destruction. Hitler did not fight for power either. He was inducted into office by the officials of a democracy, inducted when his popularity was declining, inducted lest it decline too far. Taught by these experiences at home to hold democracy in contempt, they soon found that foreign democracies too had no guts. Every evidence of democratic weakness in relation to Mussolini merely convinced Hitler that he also could defy the democracies with impunity. Laval's effort to stop Hitler by mollifying Mussolini merely spurred Hitler on to emulate Mussolini. If Laval wished to keep Mussolini's friendship he should have prevented Italy from seizing Abyssinia.

Two basic ideas were in conflict in the Europe of 1935, balance of power and collective efforts for peace. Balance-of-power jugglery inspired the inept steps of the British to court Hitler and of the French to court Mussolini. The alternative was firm resistance to Fascism wherever it tried to extend its black might. But to be unalterably opposed to Fascism one had to be anti-Fascist, and Laval was not, nor was Sir Samuel Hoare, nor Stanley Baldwin.

Laval, like many Frenchmen, acted on the assumption that England would have to be pro-French in a crisis because it could not allow Germany to conquer France without endangering its own existence. France thought she could not lose England, but might lose Italy. This was more balance-of-power psychology. Events proved that British sentiment against France on account of French disloyalty in the Abyssinian affair helped to create an atmosphere in London which facilitated Germany's subsequent remilitarization of the Rhineland.

Laval was right in supposing that if war came England would have to fight by the side of France. But until then both France and England could be seriously weakened by successive Fascist encroachments.

It might be argued that Laval could not have foreseen that Abyssinia would be followed by further totalitarian attacks on the empires of democracy. This defense could have been made in 1935. But the Lavals, Flandins, and the other French, and British, reactionaries continued to appease the Fascists when these further totalitarian attacks eventuated in 1936, 1937, 1938, and 1939.

On that trip to Rome in January, 1935, Laval began digging the grave of France.

The train from Paris moved quickly through Switzerland and over the cold, snow-covered Alps into spring-like Lombardy. Vegetation was green and the lakes blue despite the winter. I got off at Milan to see Italy before I saw Rome. I slept in the Hotel Cavour.

I went to the Milan Cathedral first thing in the morning. Beautiful outside with, the guidebooks say, a thousand marble statues on the small spires and in the niches of its walls, it is monumental and moving within. Every time I have come to Milan since then I have visited the cathedral. Sunday mass is particularly impressive. The archbishop in an elevated loge, the priests and choir chanting and circling on a raised dais looked to me like figures on a cloud; it was a scene of crimson and silver lit up by broad rays of thin soft light that contrasted sharply with the enveloping darkness of the dimmed church. It is easy to see how such a service fills many people with awe. A hard-working peasant in Italy or Spain, leaving his plow and lowly hut to enter his village church, a giant edifice of granite, gold, and color that towers above his own life and whose cool dampness and calm unworldliness are mysteriously unlike his daily drudgery, cannot but be fascinated or frightened by the authority he does not understand. Poor countries always have dominant churches, and an authoritarian church may prepare the mind for authoritarian politics. Submission to dogma, dictatorship, and the doctrine of infallibility easily filter from the clerical realm into the temporal. In this sense, Greek Catholicism was the precursor of Bolshevism and Roman Catholicism removed the psychological barriers to Fascism.

Milan was plastered with anti-sanctions posters and Mussolini pictures. Mussolini scowling, frowning, pouting, smiling; Mussolini fencing, shooting, swimming, strutting, flying, speaking, fiddling; Mussolini on a cannon, on a tank, on a horse, on a balcony; Mussolini bald, Mussolini in Roman helmet, in steel helmet, in flier's cap; Mussolini, Mussolini. That evening I went to a cinema. In Rome, several days later, I went to a cinema. No applause for Mussolini. A movie is dark and you can do as you please. War scenes from East Africa. No applause. Once one man clapped his hands. The silence thereafter was impressive.

I asked a Milanese workingman who had been in America why he was not fighting in Abyssinia. He said, "Let others fight." I put the same question to an employee in the hotel. He said, "Let those fight who have no jobs." He regarded the war as a sort of unemployment relief measure.

I could discover no enthusiasm for the war against Ethiopia, and that despite the propaganda and despite the real resentment against the British for imposing sanctions. War posters were torn from walls or defaced. I observed this closely, checked it in various sections of the city, and made sure it was not the work of children. An Italian nobleman in Milan, whom I visited in the dark of night at the suggestion of a British viscountess, told me that his friends detested Mussolini because he had humiliated the King of Italy.

One of Italy's outstanding aristocrats, Prince Filippo Doria, was arrested for his anti-Fascist remarks and his disapproval of Italy's costly Abyssinian adventure. He was not alone in disapproving and not alone in the concentration camp.

In the super-rapid electrified train to Rome, Blackshirt militiamen patrolled the corridors, and when one of them approached, the eyes of the Italian passengers signaled a kind of silent warning, and conversation stopped while faces froze into immobility. The landscape was beautiful, the villages poor, the women invariably in black, in mourning, presumably, for their own past and their sons' future.

All Rome is divided into three parts: the servants of the Pope and God in black cassocks or brown robes and sandals, the civil servants of the dictatorship in mufti, and the armed servants of the King and Il Duce in gaudy pale blue, black, and green uniforms with an infinite variety of headgear from tasseled aviator caps to broad hats topped by rooster plumes.

Every footstep in Rome echoes history. I was torn between ancient Rome that had made so much history and modern Rome that was making so much trouble. The Colisseum, for some reason or other, had fixed itself in my imagination as a boy, and I paid it my first visit. It was even bigger than I had expected it to be. Rome brought back the distant days when I had studied Latin. In the arena of the Colisseum I heard American-college English, and saw American college boys. But instead of slacks and decorated slickers they wore long black robes reaching down to high laced shoes. On their heads were flat-crowned, broad-rimmed black felt priest hats. They asked me about America. I asked them about the war. They wrinkled their noses to indicate its unpopularity.

Through a Communist friend, I frequently met in Paris with a German Jesuit preacher, well-known as an anti-Nazi, who had taken up permanent residence in France. This Jesuit gave me an address in Rome and told me to go there without previous appointment. He gave me a name. It was the name of a German Jesuit professor who spent several evenings a week at the home of Cardinal Pacelli, later Supreme Pontiff. They had met when Pacelli was Papal Nuncio in Berlin. The Catholic professor told me of widespread grumbling against the war, and in this he confirmed the testimony of Soviet Ambassador Boris Stein. On my first visit the Jesuit professor did not talk much. I understood his inhibitions and asked few questions. At a subsequent meeting he seemed very sad. Catholic bishops of Italy were presenting their gold crosses and rings to Mussolini for the prosecution of the war. The German Father felt that the church should remain aloof.

The Vatican did not condemn the Ethiopian war. In fact, the Pope indicated that there might be just and unjust wars. The church had a stake in Abyssinia. The Ethiopians are Christian, but Monophysitic like the Copts of Egypt and the Armenians of Russia. The Vatican hoped to convert them to Roman Catholicism.

An American correspondent introduced me to Macartney of the *London Times*. He took me to Sir William MacClure, the press attaché at the British Embassy. He handed me on to Sir Eric Drummond, the British Ambassador. I also saw Count René de Chambrun, the French Ambassador, proud of being an American citizen by virtue of his direct descent from the Marquis de Lafayette, and Mr. Breckenridge Long, the United States Ambassador. I interviewed all of them again when I returned in April, 1936.

When I asked my friends who among the Fascist leaders would be interesting to talk to, several said, "Rossoni." The Foreign Office press department arranged it for me. Edmondo Rossoni was Minister of Agriculture and Forests, and a member of the Grand Fascist Council. People estimated that he was No. 4 or No. 5 man in Italy. He had worked as a laborer in the United States and France, and spoke English and French, English as the Italians spoke it in the Washington Avenue neighborhood in South Philadelphia where my family had lived for several years. He was short and compact, with a round strong head, sunburnt face, black hair—the type one sees stripped to the waist and leaning on picks and shovels when the train

passes over a stretch of track that is being repaired. I felt rather excited to be interviewing a big Fascist chief.

He started to tell about his achievements as Minister of Agriculture while I kept trying to get him to talk about America. "I know
all about American prosperity," he said. "I was an I.W.W. I know
all about it. I knew Bill Haywood. He was not a man. He was a
big boy of fifty. He was a guy with an immense love of man, not
a politician. He was an Italian—same temperament. We got many
types here like Big Bill." Then we moved to Abyssinia. I took copious
notes on his official stationery. At the end of the interview he asked
me to submit the text for his approval. I did so and he sent it back
with corrections and with his card initialed with an underlined
"R." Looking now at the notes and the text and his deletions I think
perhaps that some of the words he crossed out, and which I therefore did not publish at the time, were among the most interesting.

"We have increased wheat production for the whole country," he
had begun, "and also increased the land under cultivation." He
handed me the appropriate statistics.

I said, "You have a dictatorship. Why don't you nationalize land?"

"A dictatorship," Rossoni replied, "is a political matter, not an
economic or social matter. We cannot take the land away from
the landlords." The government could only buy the estates of those
who wished to sell and then the peasants could buy these lands with
federal loans. In this way, Rossoni estimated, they could find work
in the next five years for 400,000 families.

But this process was slow. Many landlords had grown fabulously
rich by selling their huge latifundia at fancy prices. Besides, the
peasants hesitated to assume the responsibility of heavy debt payments for twenty years. That is why "crowded" Italy had a great
deal of untilled land: the landlords did not cultivate it; the peasants
could not buy; the government would not take it. On December
7, 1935, the *Osservatore Romano*, newspaper organ of the Vatican,
reported a Rome congress of peasants who urged that the estates
be divided. I therefore persisted and said to Rossoni: "Instead of
conquering Ethiopia which you hope will accommodate surplus
Italians, why don't you attempt to take care of them at home by
introducing a land reform?"

Slightly irritated, Rossoni replied, "The Abyssinian war perhaps
has economic reasons. But chiefly the reasons are moral and political.
France did not acquire colonies because she was overpopulated. Nor

did England." He was saying just what I should have wanted him to say if I could have planned it. There was never any truth in the claim that economic necessity or the need of new lands for settlement, or even the need of raw materials, compelled the so-called "Have Not" countries to expand. Rossoni also had admitted that Italy behaved like any other capitalist country in relation to its rich landlords. The interview was going fine.

"Italy can make a new contribution to civilization," Rossoni continued. "Italy must carry civilization to the entire world." He blackpenciled that last sentence, perhaps as being too immodest.

This did not satisfy me, and I said, "You have a dictatorship. You can send people to war, maybe to their death. Why can't you take vacant land from the estate owners and give it to the peasants?"

Signor Rossoni, to my delight, was now thoroughly aroused and replied with equal candor, "That is demagogy. Peasants must be directed. 'Give land to the peasants.' That is a phrase. There must be organization. We are Fascists, not socialists."

Then what was the Fascist economic program? He replied, "Corporations." Italy was a corporative state. I did not know what that meant. "The Italian corporations," he explained, "unite capitalists, technicians, and workers. The technicians must organize and direct industry. The technicians must not be the slaves of the capitalists. [He later changed "slaves" to "instruments."] They must guide the workers. The technician is the bridge between worker and employer. [I recalled the American technocrats.] The worker himself has no executive ability. If he is talented he soon lifts himself up to the capitalist level. I know socialist leaders who, when they recognized their own abilities, passed over to the capitalist side. [I wondered whether this was a dig at Mussolini, ex-socialist.] Workers must be well-organized and not free to be crazy. A strike is an act of folly. I am not bourgeois. I am a worker. [He crossed that out although he had said it.] Mussolini was a worker. [He crossed that out.] We are anti-bourgeois."

I asked him whether Italy would not take Abyssinia and then ask for more territory. He replied, "It would be foolish to hypothecate the future."

Then Rossoni dictated a speech to me. "Some people think the world stands still. The dynamics of history is a big thing. I believe in imperialism. But the imperialism of the future will be different. It will be moral, and represent the domination of able peoples over the world. It will not be materialistic as British imperialism is to-day." He added, "We do not want war. The war we want is work. Mussolini said that.

"I think democracy is working for war," Rossoni affirmed emphatically. "Not Japan, not Germany, not Italy. Democracy."

We talked about democracy and the social system. "Ah, the ballot is not interesting," he said. "Cannon is interesting. We are not anti-capitalist. We are anti-capitalism. We change the name of capitalist to factory-Fuehrer just as the Nazis have done. Money is merely opinion. Gold is not indispensable."

He asked me many questions about Soviet Russia, and then expressed his own view. "The Bolsheviks are no longer revolutionaries because they are in accord with the western democracies. They are lost."

At the end of more than an hour, I rose to go. He shook my hand warmly and said, "Don't you find us quiet despite the war?"

I said, "Quiet but worried."

He said, "No, united and eager to work." And he pointed to large oil paintings of farm scenes that covered the walls of his spacious office. He asked me to come back, and I did that same week for another hour, and I talked with him again at length in April, 1936.

It would never have occurred to me to ask Mussolini for an interview. There was no use inviting a refusal. But several journalistic colleagues said to me, "Have you seen Mussolini?", and when I said no they urged me to apply. Several friends in the American, British, Soviet, and French embassies put the same question to me and gave the same advice. They said he was very much interested in Soviet Russia and had copied from the Bolsheviks. Towards the end of my stay, therefore, on December 10, 1935, I wrote this letter:

To His Excellency,
Signor Benito Mussolini,
Chief of the Italian State.

DEAR SIR,

I would like to talk to you about the international situation, and you will decide whether it will be an interview, or a conversation which is not for publication.

I am an American journalist and have spent the last fourteen years in Europe, mostly in Russia, Germany and England. I have written a number of books, one of them a two-volume history of Soviet foreign policy which has been translated into French.

Now I am writing a series of articles on the situation in Europe. I have come here after a fortnight in England and a fortnight in France. Those two stays have supplied the material for my first two articles which I have shown to Signor Macia.

I am, and have been for thirteen years, the correspondent of the New York *Nation* which is liberal and anti-Fascist. I too am anti-Fascist. But I am completely cynical about England's attitude and about the position taken by the League of Nations. I will state the Italian case fairly.

Since the plan of my series requires me to leave Rome by Sunday, I take the liberty of urging you to give me your reply very soon. I hope very much that the reply will be in the affirmative.

Very respectfully and sincerely,
Louis Fischer.

A reply came the same day. It came from a secretary who spoke for Mussolini and wrote, "Much to His regret, the Chief of the Government, will be unable, between now and Sunday, to grant you an interview. I am sorry not to have been able to arrange this and hope it may be possible on some other occasion."

That day Mussolini had received the Hoare-Laval proposal, and I was not surprised that he should not have wanted to see me in the next four days. But the rejection almost contained a promise. (When I returned in April, I tried to collect the interview but the same secretary said he had read the articles on Italy which I had published in the meantime.)

Sir Samuel Hoare and Premier Laval proposed to give Mussolini part of Abyssinia. The proposal had been drafted secretly and sent secretly to Mussolini. Then England was not serious? It was ready to compromise. But the proposal leaked out because it had enemies inside the British government. A revolt of British public opinion, unprecedented demonstration of virile democracy, rose to such heights that Prime Minister Baldwin had to scuttle either himself or Hoare. He chose Hoare. Then England was serious? Mussolini could not quite tell. Meanwhile the British prayed for early rains in Abyssinia, but when the Abyssinians asked Britain for arms they got none. Italy poured its wealth and men into the mountainous wildernesses of East Africa in return for which the Fascist papers promised gold, platinum, coffee, cotton, jobs, copper—in fact, Abyssinia was a marvelous treasure house. (A stay in Italy in November, 1939, convinced

me that Abyssinia had given Italy a few bananas and a lot of head-
aches but nothing else.)

From Italy I moved, via Venice and thrilling Austrian mountain
scenery, to Vienna. The Rome-Berlin axis had not yet been forged,
but the forge was being built. The fire that beat plowshares into
swords also shaped the axis.

A free Austria was the peg of European peace. Austria dammed
the Nazi flood. If Austria fell, Nazism would pour over southeastern
Europe. But Austria itself was Fascist. Its trade unions, parliament,
free press, and free elections had disappeared. Mussolini safeguarded
it against Hitler. Yet Mussolini had destroyed its inner democratic
defenses against Hitler.

I made a beeline from the railway station to the home of M. W.
Fodor, *Chicago Daily News* correspondent. He knew everything
and everybody. When he was not at home one could be sure to find
him at the same table every morning at eleven in the Imperial Café.
I likewise spent profitable and pleasant hours with George Messersmith, American Minister, whom I had first met when he was
Consul General in Berlin. Messersmith never disguised his revulsion
against Fascism and wrote long letters to his chiefs in Washington
warning of dangers which so many Europeans in high democratic
places watched with treacherous equanimity. G. E. R. Gedye, brilliant pent-up Englishman with the Hungarian name who worked
for the *New York Times,* also led me through the maze of Austrian
politics as did little Scheu of the *London Daily Herald,* and others.

Most observers agreed that the Schuschnigg government enjoyed
the support of as much as three percent of the population. One-
third of all Austrians were socialist or Communist, chiefly the former, one-third were Christian socialists, chiefly Catholic, and thirty
percent were Nazi. The infinitesimal remainder constituted the popular backing of the regime which was authoritarian but had no authority. The government, however, did not bother about votes. It
had no intention of calling elections and it sat on the bayonets of
Prince Starhemberg's Heimwehr while Mussolini scowled protec-
tively.

Mussolini protected Austria and ruined it. In February, 1934, the
Austrian government turned cannon on the beautiful modern apart-
ment-house settlements of the Socialist party in Vienna. Morreale,
Mussolini's agent in Vienna, inspired that attack. The Socialists were

crushed and driven underground. In July, the Nazis made a bid for power. They assumed that the crushing of the Socialists paved the way for them. Mussolini was alarmed. The Nazis almost succeeded. Diminutive Chancellor Dollfuss was killed. (Hitler later honored the murderers.) Mussolini expected the Reichswehr to follow in the footsteps of Hitler's Austrian puppets. He mobilized the Italian army. That stayed the Nazis' hand. Mussolini spoke Hitler's language, the only language Hitler understands, the language of force. But Hitler merely bided his time. When his time came, on March 13, 1938, Chancellor Schuschnigg hastily distributed arms among the workers of Vienna. Schuschnigg realized that the workers were his natural friends, the natural bulwarks against Fascism. But it was too late. He had killed their spirit and their organizations, and banished their leaders. He could not repair in a morning the damage of four foolish years.

The Czech government understood. They knew their turn would follow Austria's and they tried to buttress Austria's domestic defenses by keeping in touch with the Austrian socialist movement. I learned that in this way: I wished to see Otto Bauer, the gifted theoretician and leader of the Austrian Socialists who had been forced to emigrate. I asked correspondents where he might be found but they did not know. I asked everybody I met, and had no success until I asked Schrom, the secretary of the Czech Legation whom I had known in Moscow where he worked as a journalist. He took out a little date-book from his vest pocket and gave me Bauer's address and telephone number in Bruenn, and his wink told me—as did his words subsequently—that Prague was not neglecting the best prop Austrian independence could have had. But the Czechs alone could not save Austria from the Austrian government, Mussolini, and Hitler. Only a democratic Austria had a chance of survival. But the Fascist Mussolini did not want a democratic Austria. So he killed Austrian democracy, and thus killed Austria and thus killed his own independence and became Hitler's tool.

The Austrians are supposed to be a gentle, "gemuetlich" people and many of them are. But no generalization about a nation is correct. The shelling of the Viennese tenements was an extremely brutal act, without parallel in history. Muenichreiter, a Viennese Socialist, was wounded seriously in the arm and head during the fighting. Nevertheless, he was sentenced to death. They carried him, unconscious, to the gallows on a stretcher, and they put the noose around his neck while he still lay on the stretcher. An eyewitness described the scene in the *Prager Mittag* of February 17, 1934. It was one of many gruesome executions in the Vienna of waltzes.

Czechoslovakia was among the few civilized countries of Europe, and if Neville Chamberlain did not know where it was that was his loss. Lying between the Teutonic and Slav areas of the continent, it was a nation whose people had the efficiency of the German without his hardness, harshness, and submissiveness, and the peasant warmth, dreaminess, and spiritual health of the Russian without his uncouthness, cruelty, and backwardness. Prague was paved with culture. It was the one European city where I went on a rubberneck tour; the sights revealed the living past of the nation.

In the Hradjhin, the medieval castle which seemed to be constructed of superimposed layers of the country's history, I interviewed Eduard Beneš, President of Czechoslovakia, successor and intimate co-worker of Thomas Masaryk, the Republic's founder. He was of Europe's first minds, a skilled diplomat, writer, internationalist. His country's fate, to be sure, depended on internationalism and on the fruition of the idea on which the League of Nations should have been founded. But that was also true of France and England. Beneš was an internationalist because he was a good Czech. Laval and Baldwin too would have served their nations best by serving Europe first. Beneš made the mistake of assuming that Europe was ruled by Benešes. Too expert to be naive, he nevertheless trusted the good intentions of men who looked like gentlemen. He trusted in the articles of international treaties. And he expected the speeches he heard and the speeches he made to produce a situation which would justify his incorrigible optimism. Very late in the short sunny day of his country's freedom he went to Moscow where I first met him. He nursed a real cultural and political entente between Moscow and Prague. It was hampered by domestic reactionaries who feared the ascendancy of the left. It was hampered by Hitler who declared that the Bolsheviks were upon him. Beneš told me in Christmas week, 1935, that he would gladly negotiate with Hitler but Hitler had rebuffed every initiative. Later, in Berlin, Mastny, the Czech Minister, and Camille Hoffman, his press aide, gave me concrete details on Germany's disinclination to settle potential disputes amicably.

Beneš dreamed of a modified Danubian federation, and curbed his liberal hatred of Mussolini in the hope that Italy would again save

Austria, which also meant saving Czechoslovakia, from Germany. Czechoslovakia's future thus hung on Rome's attitude to Germany. If the two Fascist states took the same road, Czechoslovakia was doomed. But Rome's attitude to Germany would reflect its relations with England and France, and those depended on the outcome of the Abyssinian conflict. Prague's eye was glued on distant Addis Ababa. Though his whole world rested on the frail reef of Geneva, Beneš therefore had his doubts about sanctions, and would have been pleased to see the success of some patchwork of peace like the Hoare-Laval vivisection of Abyssinia. He needed Italy. Yet if the League failed in Abyssinia it would be weaker in Europe, and the European status quo would be endangered, and Czechoslovakia was part of it. That was the dilemma of the Slav statesman of Prague. The answer would have been an aggressive peace policy by England and France, but even Beneš could not hope for that. He knew that France had sabotaged sanctions. He had no guarantee that after balking Mussolini in East Africa, England would be ready to check Hitler in Central Europe. Indeed, what he heard from Jan Masaryk, his Minister in London, must have made him uncomfortably suspicious of England's pro-German orientation.

The beginning of aggression was the end of Czechoslovakia. The attack on Haile Selassie sent Beneš into exile and Europe into war. A shot fired at Sarajevo brings Wisconsin farmers to Archangel and the Marne. Frontiers and oceans disappear for war. Internationalism bursts into full flower when the cannons roar. In peacetime it vanishes. When it vanishes in peacetime there is sure to be a wartime in which it can reassert itself.

A non-stop express train took me from Prague to Berlin—280 miles —in eight hours. As I entered the lobby of the Hotel Adlon, the porter yelled, "Ach, Herr Fischer, Moscow is calling you," and I talked with Markoosha over the telephone. In view of Hitler's well-known views on Moscow at the time, this was not a very auspicious beginning for a stay in Nazi Germany. But I never kept my opinions or connections a secret in Berlin, and called and visited the Soviet Embassy as often as I wished. It is better not to seek to avoid detection in a dictatorship, and I had nothing to hide anyway. If sleuths shadowed and spied upon me, I was not aware of it. I always left my suitcase open to ease the task of any inquisitive Gestapo agent, and if I had personal mail which I did not want copied for the dossier, I kept it in my jacket pocket.

I requested an interview with Ribbentrop and he sent a titled lieutenant to look me over and report on my Aryanism or lack of it, I presume. His relative Dieckhoff, later Nazi Ambassador in Washington, was apparently not so allergic and consented to talk to me in the Wilhelmstrasse. He said Germany wanted a plebiscite in Austria on the question of "Anschluss." Hitler was ready to sign peace treaties and non-aggression pacts with everybody except Lithuania and Russia. When I asked Dieckhoff whether that might not lead to war with Russia, he said, "Jawohl." Nazis were always ready to reinforce the impression of their "anti-Communism."

I arrived in Berlin fourteen years almost to a day after I had first seen it, in December, 1921, from a department-store truck. I had been in Germany every year since 1921, sometimes for several months at a time, sometimes less. I had never known it so pessimistic, not even in the worst years of inflation when the suffering was greater. Germans of all classes fought for their pessimism and insisted that any optimism achieved by an effort of will would vanish at the first touch with today's reality. They were sad and they were resigned. They had been called on to make sacrifices which were only beginning. They were shouldering the heavy burden of peacetime rearmament in order that they might carry the heavier burden of war.

When will the war come, every German asked. "Germany," I wrote in *The Nation* of March 11, 1936, "must wait until the new millions are molded into soldiers fit for long and trying battles. When will that be? Some specialists say 1937, most say 1938, some say 1939. The Reichswehr today probably numbers 800,000 commanders and men. In 1939, it will count one million men under arms and two and a half million freshly drilled reserves. This is about the right amount of cannon fodder for a beginning."

One would have thought, in view of Germany's obvious preparations to go to war in 1939 or before, that the democracies also would make preparations. Instead, they talked peace and friendship with Hitler, and jogged along at an amiable, old-man peace pace.

Germany had begun to resemble an armed camp. I noticed an increase in the number of Reichswehr cars and uniforms since my last visit. The army trucks were painted with camouflage. That was part of the practical business of getting ready for war. But it was also part of "the psychological preparation which goes on with unrelenting intensity every hour of the day in the press, radio and schools." There was no secret about it. If I knew it, foreign governments knew it or should have known it. Conscription had been introduced on March 16, 1935.

But foreign observers who wished to be deluded overlooked Germany's military measures and quoted Hitler's pacifist speeches. He delivered one such on May 17, 1933. "No new European war," he declared truly, "could create conditions better than the unsatisfactory conditions of today. . . . Germany is always ready to assume further security obligations of an international character. . . . Germany would be prepared to abolish its entire military establishments."

Why did Hitler utter these palpable lies? Because in April, 1933, Pilsudski, frightened by the rise of Hitler, occupied the Westerplatte, a small peninsula in the Danzig harbor, and wanted to invade Germany. Pilsudski asked France and England to co-operate. On May 16, 1933, President Hindenburg wrote to his State Secretary Meissner, "These days you can of course get into touch with me at any time of the day or night." (Normally, the old man could not be disturbed from his sleep.) The day after this note was written, Hitler made his pacifist speech. He wanted to call off Poland. Yet it was quoted as an earnest of good Nazi intentions. The Western Powers were impressed by Hitler's speech, and vetoed Pilsudski's preventive war.

Hitler made another much-quoted pacifist speech on May 21, 1935. It had two motifs: friendship for England and hatred of the Soviets. Three weeks later England signed the Anglo-German Naval Agreement. Hitler was bidding for it in his speech. A day after this speech, which contained fierce, unbridled attacks on Bolshevism, Hjalmar Schacht went to the Soviet Embassy and offered the Soviet government an official German credit of one billion marks. That is the way the Nazis conducted their foreign policy.

Meanwhile, Hitler told the powers how to behave when he went to war or when he took something without going to war. He disliked any "international network of intersecting obligations"—in other words, collective security. Instead, if two nations fight, "the other nations withdraw at once from both sides at the outbreak of the conflict rather than allow themselves to be involved in this conflict from the outset by treaty obligations." For example: Germany attacks Czechoslovakia. All nations stand aside. No nation helps Germany, no nation helps Czechoslovakia. Hitler threatens Austria. "All other nations withdraw at once from both sides." Neutrality. It is fantastic that Hitler should have the effrontery and gall to suggest a procedure which so obviously would make German conquest so easy. But it is much more fantastic that the Western Powers later adopted just that procedure. "To face an adversary in detail," writes General Douglas MacArthur, U. S. Army Chief of Staff from 1930 to 1935, "has been the prayer of every conqueror in history." Hitler advertised that this was his dream, too. He wanted to divide his victims and smite them individually. He said he would do it. They let him do it.

Through Miss Martha Dodd, daughter of U. S. Ambassador Dodd, I met Armand Berar, a secretary at the French Embassy in Berlin, and he took me for an interview with his Ambassador, M. François-Poncet. He had had an audience recently with Hitler. The Fuehrer devoted most of his time to attacks on the Soviet Union. On December 13, 1935, Sir Eric Phipps, the British Ambassador, had had a three-hour session with Hitler. Hitler devoted most of that long period to a raving diatribe against Bolshevism. They wrote home to Paris and London, and Paris and London were reassured. "Hitler means no harm in the West," they whispered. They did not want to see that East and West should unite. Hitler's purpose was to separate them. He succeeded.

Conversations in embassies were conducted as far as possible from a telephone, and even then a pillow was usually pressed over the telephone. The assumption was that the Gestapo had so wired the telephones that its dictaphones functioned even when the receiver was on the hook.

I had always been very much attached to Berlin and to Germany. I loved the language and I respected the nation's scientific and cultural achievements. I hated to hate Germany. I walked down a street with Boris Smolar, correspondent of the Jewish Telegraphic Agency. Two tall S.S. men passed in black uniform, marching in step. I asked Smolar whether he hated them. He said yes. I didn't. Smolar had felt the cruelty of the Gestapo. He had been persecuted and arrested, even though he was an American citizen legitimately reporting for American publications. Only the persistence and courage of United States Consul Raymond H. Geist saved him from long detention and a horrible fate. Yet I too knew enough of the tortures in Gestapo cellars, the brutality of its concentration camps, and the cynicism of its murders. Even after years of Nazism, however, I still liked Germans too much to place the blame on individual Germans. Populations cannot be held responsible for the crimes of their governments although they have to vote for and serve those governments.

I stopped and talked to a man selling toy balloons on a street corner. He greeted prospective customers with a resounding "Heil Hitler" and wore a Swastika in his buttonhole. But he was bitterly opposed to the Nazi regime and complained to me about its deprivations and war preparations.

Many Communists and Socialists had entered the S.A. Brownshirts for protective coloration. A Communist told me he had joined the S.S. in order to enter the university. An S.A. man I met in a private German home told me he had recently started studying Marx. I have known many Communists who became anti-Communists and I doubt that Hitler's following must always remain loyal. A few fundamental loyalties are unalterable, but political attitudes are not.

Berlin friends told a story of a visit to a factory by Hermann Goering. He gathered the workingmen around him and said he wanted to speak with them heart-to-heart. They could be candid. Nothing would happen to them. He turned to a gray-haired mechanic and said, "Tell me, how do you stand politically?"

"I," replied the old fellow, "I have been a Communist for years."

"Are you still a Communist?"

"Yes."

"How many Communists work in this plant?" Goering inquired.

"Oh," several men volunteered, "only about thirty percent of the force."

"What are the rest?" Goering asked, hopefully.

"About fifty percent of the total are Social Democrats," he was told.

"And the remaining twenty percent?" Goering pressed.

"They are Catholic trade unionists."

"But then where are the Nazis?" Goering insisted.

"Ach," came the reply, "we are all Nazis." Protective coloration warded off "protective custody."

Hitler has millions of supporters in Germany but also millions of enemies who vote "Ja" at every election out of fear. I saw and heard enough anti-Nazis in Germany to feel certain that great masses of Protestants, Jews, Catholics, pacifists, democrats, socialists, and Communists continue to abhor the Nazis. When Hitler gains Norwegian territory or French territory he wins some Germans at home. Success helps every government. But when the drums stop beating, the people take stock and wonder who is paying for all this and what vengeance the future has in store for them. Above all, I found many Germans who were ashamed of their country, ashamed because Germans were torturing Jews, ashamed because Germany was reviled abroad, ashamed because German science was cut off from the main world-currents of invention and research. Goebbels' propaganda dissipates some of this sentiment, but Germans are ashamed of Goebbels too.

I asked for an all-wool sweater at Gruenfeld's department store. The salesgirl asked, "Don't you know there is nothing all-wool in this country?" I asked a salesman in a bookshop on Unter den Linden for some good political literature. He said, "Good?" I complained to a waiter at Kempinski's on Kurfuerstendamm that a bad egg seemed to have gone into the ice cream. He said, "No, sir, that is impossible. It couldn't have been a bad egg. We use only egg powder." All of them and so many others took special delight in making statements that were correct but derogatory to the government. A taxi driver complained that business was bad because night life had disappeared. "The Nazis who go out at night have their private cars," he sneered. I asked a waiter at the Bristol Hotel how they had made out New Year's night. He said, "Not so bad." I said the guests must have been mostly foreigners. He replied, "No, foreigners can scarcely afford our prices. They were mostly Nazi officials."

There was plenty of opposition to the Nazis. I believe it has not died. But it was and is impotent. Its effectiveness has always been exaggerated. Revolutionary and subversive movements are powerless in a dictatorship which does not hesitate to arrest and shoot suspects. People are not convinced—they merely conform—when their friends are carried off to jail in the night. By the end of 1935, Germany had had three years of Hitler and not a single economic problem solved. The problems are still unsolved. "Guns instead of butter." They gave their health for the guns, then they would give their lives with the guns. The Nazis had succeeded in turning Germany into a prison camp which they were succeeding in preparing for war. That was the sum of Nazi progress. Nazism did not transform all Germans, nor most Germans, into Nazis. The nation sullenly watched as the dynamic gangsters tried to run the show. The enjoyment of democratic privileges sometimes breeds Fascists. The joys of dictatorship could easily breed democrats. When French democracy collapsed, many French Fascists dropped their democratic masks. There are many Fascist masks in Germany.

In Warsaw in January, 1936, I had several long conversations with U. S. Ambassador John Cudahy. In 1924, in Warsaw, I called on the American Minister, John W. Stetson (of the Philadelphia hat firm). In 1931, I talked in Warsaw with U. S. Ambassador John N. Willys (of the automobile interests). He was followed by Cudahy of the meat-packing family, and he in turn by Anthony J. Drexel Biddle (of the Philadelphia banking house) whose home and furnishings were smashed by Nazi bombs. I have never met Biddle, but of the rest only Cudahy understood what it was all about.

Cudahy was a member of the United States expeditionary force to North Russia in 1918, and there he had observed the behavior of American soldiers fighting the Bolsheviks. He wrote an anonymous book criticizing the American expedition and I believe his memory took him back to those years when he compared American army men with the Nazi troopers in Belgium in 1940.

Cudahy likes to hunt. He told me of an adventure while hunting in Soviet Russia. Through the American Embassy in Moscow, he had arranged to go to the forests of Central Russia to hunt bear. The GPU prepared him a bear for the slaughter, but the GPU's dogs were overzealous and drove the bear away, and Cudahy returned empty-handed.

In Poland, Cudahy hunted with Polish aristocrats on the huge estates of East Poland, and he knew their psychology. Through his excellent connections he was well-informed, and information digested by a high intelligence made him one of the best American diplomats in Europe. He disliked Polish Foreign Minister Beck and entertained doubts on the wisdom of Polish foreign policy. He told me of the intimate relations between Poland and Nazi Germany as he observed them in the manors of Polish nobles where Prussian Junkers came to hunt and Nazi officials to intrigue.

Cudahy also saw the base poverty of the Polish peasants who could not but contrast their dismal existences with the opulence of the fortunately born. While Cudahy hunted with titled snobs he did not forget the miserable millions. He told me that many peasants looked across with envy into Soviet Russia where collectivization had improved farming conditions.

Poland's economic plight was appalling. Its rotten condition showed in these figures: 540,000 employed workingmen, 330,000 unemployed workingmen, 330,000 government officials, 271,510 soldiers.

Finance Minister Kwiatkovsky on December 5, 1935, announced in the Sejm—Poland's parliament—that Polish peasants with twenty-five acres of land spent on the average of eight dollars a year. (In 1929, they had spent $22.40 a year.) But they were millionaires compared to the peasants who held only ten to twelve acres and who constituted thirty-one percent of the population, and another thirty-four percent who owned even smaller "dwarf households." He said, "Ten million persons stand completely outside the realm of economic life." They neither bought nor sold. Jews, Poles, and Ukrainians who received three dollars a month from American relatives could become businessmen on that money.

The peasants were reacting violently against their poverty. In May, 1935, a serious insurrection in the province of Volhynia had to be suppressed by the army. Likewise, a revolt in Central Poland in December, 1935. Peasant disturbances were a chronic disease. Anti-Semitism spread. Bombs were thrown into synagogues, Jewish houses burned, Jews beaten and killed. The government did not suppress such atrocities, perhaps because it did not try too hard.

Pilsudski was dead and the Poles felt his absence. Marshal Ridz-Smigly now wore Pilsudski's mantle but it was too big for him. Poland's second great man was Foreign Minister Joseph Beck. He received me in the ministry, and before he had talked five minutes I thought of an eel. It was impossible to pin him down, and when I believed he was pinned down to one point he had evaded my question and delivered a disquisition on an abstraction. I knew I would never know what he had said when he got through, and I therefore stood up and reached for a sheet of paper in a little stationery container on his desk. He stood up too, reached the paper before I did, took out a folded sheet, tore it in two at the fold, and gave me the half that did not have the imprint of the ministry on it. When I had covered that paper I rose again, he rose again, and repeated the performance. Beck had been a Polish intelligence officer in Paris and the French decided to deport him because he had allegedly stolen military documents. He looked on others, apparently, as others had looked on him.

(In 1938, I entered Cordell Hull's office to keep an appointment with the Secretary of State. Mr. Hull's secretary came out into the waiting room and told me I would have to wait a few moments. Since I had just seen George Messersmith in the Department and wanted to make notes on our conversation I asked the secretary for some paper and he said, "Here, take this," and he gave me a pad which I had seen before on the table. It was Mr. Hull's stationery with the imprint: *Department of State*—THE SECRETARY.)

Having squeezed much water and circumlocution out of my Beck interview notes, I find this, "Pilsudski said, 'Always have a fluid policy.' . . . Don't build a roof when you haven't got the walls. . . . The world is tired. No nation has temperament. Fortunately, no nation has temperament . . . I believe in realities. We have no desire to attack Russia. No attack on Russia can be made without us. . . . People formerly exaggerated the German-Polish problem. It is impossible to concentrate all of Europe's difficulties into the realm of German-Polish relations. [This was a hostile reference to France's attempt to keep Poland out of the German orbit.] . . . Europe is accustomed to minimize the power of Poland. This will now change. . . . I am sure that when the present atmosphere clears Franco-Polish relations will improve. . . . War is always possible but the world is tired and too preoccupied with domestic problems. The world is too optimistic. It thought its problems could be solved at Geneva. But the League was never all-inclusive. . . . I don't believe in a crisis in Europe. There is too much nervousness—Poland will not join the Soviet-French bloc."

In plain English: Beck proposed to cultivate Germany, ignore the League of Nations and collective security, and pay lip service to good relations with Paris and Moscow. Having spoken with him, with Finance Minister Kwiatkovsky, with General Burhart-Bukachki, Inspector General of the Polish army, with Colonel Matushevski, editor of *Gazetta Polska*, a government organ, and member of the "Colonels Group" that Pilsudski had reared, with American businessmen, Soviet Ambassador Davtyan, Jewish merchants, Polish journalists, German Jews writing for Nazi dailies in Germany, Foreign Office officials, and many others, I checked my impressions with Cudahy and Colonel Albert Gilmor, the American military attaché.

(Whether it was Lieutenant-Colonel Philip R. Faymonville in Moscow, or Lieutenant-Colonel John Magruder who explained the Abyssinian war to me at Geneva, or Colonel E. R. Warner McCabe who did the same at Rome, or Major Truman Smith in Hitler Germany, or Colonel Stephen O. Fuqua who followed the Spanish War with the zeal of a young man, I have always found that United States military attachés are keen, able observers who do a better job than many of our ambassadors—perhaps because they know maps and weigh realities while eschewing the diplomatic racket.) Then I wrote in *The Nation* of March 18, 1936: the Poles believe that "if Germany goes to war, enough nations will remain aloof to enable Germany to win. Poland's benevolent neutrality might then be handsomely rewarded. . . . For selfish considerations Poland would hardly welcome a German attack on the Soviet Union. . . . Poland would undoubtedly prefer German expansion in the direction of Austria and Czechoslovakia. The Poles would presumably receive Teschen and the Hungarians Slovakia; thus a common Polish-Hungarian frontier would be created."

With some changes—Germany did not go to war but broke up Czechoslovakia without one, and Hungary got the Carpatho-Russ instead of Slovakia—this was a description of the Munich episode in September, 1938, and its aftermath. Poland won its common frontier with Hungary, although why anybody should have wanted it is beyond me. It is obvious from what I wrote then that the Poles anticipated the demise of Austria and Czechoslovakia, anticipated it and did nothing to prevent it, and prepared the way, by conduct that was pleasing to the Nazis, to benefit from it. Poland's foreign policy reflected Beck character, pure opportunism. It also reflected Poland's history. "Poland," I said, "must decide whether it stands with the violent revisionists or with those who want collective security." If war came, Poland "might easily be the battlefield . . . and be ruined.

"Poland, in my opinion, is playing a doubtful diplomatic game based on the idea that since war is inevitable it might as well get something out of it." Ultimately, it got a fourth partition, and death, destruction, and cruel suffering for the good farmers and working-folk who never had seen Beck or Ridz-Smigly or the hunting lodges of Volhynia. The Jews, street-car conductors, and little storekeepers of Warsaw were better Poles and better men than Ridz-Smigly.

I bought a hand of bananas in Warsaw for my boys in Moscow. They were not sold in Russia and do not grow there. At the Soviet border, the customs guard who had never seen such objects, said to me, "Are these made or do they grow?"

I bought postage stamps in every country and in the post office on the roof of the Vatican for my son George, aged eleven. Having returned home, I had to tell both boys what I had seen in Europe. There was no use saying, "It's too complicated for you to understand." Markoosha had once said that to Victor, George's junior by exactly 365 days, when he asked her the meaning of a political cartoon in *Izvestia*, and he replied, "With simple enough language you can explain anything you really understand." (He is that kind. I once scolded him in Russian for a misdeed. He listened intently and when I was finished he pointed out a grammatical mistake I had made.)

We went to the big wall map on which the boys had followed my trip, and I outlined the relations between various states. They were born in Berlin and had gone to school in Czechoslovakia, and that facilitated my task. They put peculiar questions.

"Isn't England stronger than Italy?" George asked. When I assented he wanted to know why England could not stop Italy.

I told him about divisions within a democratic country which were not possible under a dictatorship. "Then isn't dictatorship better?" he pursued.

"But the dictatorships in Japan and Italy have made wars because they don't have to consult their people, and Hitler will go to war too," I elucidated.

"Why can't the peace people in all countries get together?" Vitya asked. I tried to cope with that.

"I think the Fascists will attack the Soviet Union," George announced and returned to his stamp collection. He had been taught that in his Moscow school.

I went to see Karl Radek, the best Soviet publicist. I noticed he spoke of Stalin as "starik." Theretofore he and everybody else on the inside or close to the inside had referred to him as "Khozayin," the boss. Now with instructed spontaneity he had become "the old man," which was softer and more affectionate.

Radek told me that he was seeing Stalin regularly. I asked whether Stalin read Hitler's speeches in full, as well as the speeches of other statesmen. He said, "Of course, we supply him with translations of everything." Radek's words about Stalin were most rapturous, too rapturous for good taste in private conversation.

Radek believed Russia would be attacked. I expressed doubt. He said, "You have always doubted it."

"So far I've been right."

"It's the one time you'll be wrong that counts."

"I've read Lenin and remember him despite Bolshevik propaganda today. Lenin always emphasized the contradictions among the capitalist powers. The capitalists are more likely to cut one another's throats than yours."

He disagreed.

I made the rounds of Soviet and foreign diplomats in Moscow. I have never tried to be diplomatic with diplomats. They are too adept. A non-conventional approach is more likely to break down their reserve. With my friend Frederick Kuh I went to see the Turkish Ambassador in London in October, 1939. An important Anglo-Turkish treaty of military co-operation was about to be signed, but Tewfik Rushdi Aras told us he knew nothing about it. "The negotiations are being conducted in Ankara," he said. I interrupted this well-worn twaddle by saying, "Surely, Mr. Ambassador, your government would not insult you by keeping you ignorant of such crucial talks with the government to which you are accredited." Kuh nudged me delicately with his elbow, but Rushdi, somewhat taken aback by this unceremonious sally, could not admit that his chiefs kept him in the dark, and he revealed some of the salient facts of the treaty. If one is devious, indirect, and shrewd the diplomat will outmaneuver you and send you home with sweet nothings. I either refrain from mentioning certain subjects necessarily surrounded by secrecy or I differ and argue with a diplomat as I would with a friend.

On September 9, 1932, I spent three hours at the Japanese Embassy in Moscow, half the time with Ambassador Koki Hirota (Prime Minister of Japan from March, 1936 to February, 1937) and the other half with Eiji Amau, his counselor, later Foreign Office spokesman in Tokio and Japanese Minister in Switzerland where I saw him at League of Nations meetings. During the second World War, I crossed the English Channel with him through a cordon of British protective destroyers; Amau was on his way to assume the Japanese ambassadorship in Rome.

In Moscow, Amau's special duty was to report home on the Soviet internal situation. He began by asking me about domestic conditions. I said they were rather difficult. He said: "Who, in your opinion, is next in power to Stalin?" and while I guessed he gave me his own answer, in true indirect Japanese fashion, by telling me that a German professor had recently examined Kaganovitch and found him rather nervous. When we left Soviet politics and discussed foreign affairs he did not contradict when I identified Manchukuo with Japan.

But Hirota denied it and said Manchukuo was an independent state. I laughed. He said, "Like Egypt." I said, "Like India." He said, "Perhaps like Nicaragua."

Hirota commented angrily on Secretary of State Stimson's disinclination to recognize Manchukuo. "But Mr. Stimson," Hirota screeched in a high voice, "is only one person. The real ruler of the United States is President Hoover. Does Mr. Castle [then Assistant Secretary of State] say that America will not recognize Manchukuo?"

I ventured to explain that although American officials might differ on foreign policy it was not usual for high members of the United States government to enunciate divergent foreign policies. But he measured American affairs with his Japanese yardstick, for he asserted unreservedly that he, for instance, represented the army "which is," he added, "the real power in my country." "General Araki," he said, "is only a figurehead. The real men are the young officers, the colonels, who, unfortunately, still have no leader. . . . But they will not make war on Russia," he insisted. "While I am here, there will be no war." He pounded the desk.

I suggested that sometimes ambassadors were recalled.

"No," he declared, "I am here for the army, and the army will not fight Russia."

The Ambassador affirmed that Japan did not fear Communist propaganda. Japanese economy has suffered and the government would cope with that, but the Japanese Communist movement was weak, and the weaker the Communist movement, the smoother the relations with Moscow. He gave Turkey and Italy as other illustrations thus proposing the paradox that a Fascist country which suppressed its Communists might be on better terms with the Soviet government than a democracy that was irritated by them.

Sir Esmond Ovey, the British Ambassador, formerly Minister in Mexico, usually took a friendly stand towards the Soviet government. I used to see him often. Once I was at lunch with him and Lady Ovey in the Sugar King's Palace, when an attendant announced that "Mr. Greenway has just returned." Mr. Greenway was the Secretary of the Embassy. Ovey asked him in for coffee. Greenway told the story of an extended trip he had just completed through the Soviet provinces. His impressions convinced him that the Soviet government would soon fall. He knew definitely that all Bolshevik leaders, with the exception of Stalin, had deposited large sums abroad so as to live in comfortable exile. Seeing my skeptical smile he assured us that his information came to him "from unimpeachable authority." It always does. Ovey, however, kept his head, although once his attitude was such that Litvinov felt compelled to tell him, with characteristic gruffness, that "this is not Mexico, you know." Greenway had served in Brazil before his transfer to Moscow.

My best Moscow contact in the diplomatic corps—until Hitler spoiled it—was with the German Embassy. And even after Hitler arrived, several high German officials in Moscow told me to come to the Embassy even though they would have to stop inviting me to their homes. About once a month I went to lunch at Ambassador von Dirksen's place. When the waiters came in to serve he kept quiet or strung out empty words. Sometimes there were only the two of us. But often Mrs. Dirksen was present. She was a treat—tall, unconventional-looking and unconventional-acting.

After lunch, the Ambassador would tell the waiter to serve coffee in the parlor. That was a signal for Mrs. Dirksen to disappear, because the Ambassador wished the real political talk to commence. But she generally refused to be shelved and his grim face, with the typical German saber cut and the monocle, grew graver still. For, much to my delight, she did not remain quiet. Once, he kicked her under the coffee table—gentle reminder to be discreet—and she kicked back, and both of them noticed that I had seen this affectionate exchange. Dirksen was pedestrian but efficient and not without flashes of wit. He continued in the Brockdorff-Rantzau tradition of friendship for Russia until Hitler made it impossible and removed him to Japan. The ambassadors of dictatorships have no enviable lot.

Generally speaking there have been no great ambassadors in Moscow or elsewhere in the between-wars period. The day of the diplomat in foreign capitals who makes his own policy is gone. It vanished when the radio, airplane, and transatlantic telephone came upon the scene. When a prime minister can get into a plane and fly to see a dictator, when a president can pick up his telephone and talk to a foreign minister in Europe, an ambassador becomes a secretary and reporter. But since newspapermen are often better reporters, this diplomatic function too is circumscribed. Since 1919, foreign ministers have been crossing frontiers and holding international conferences with a frequency that is unprecedented in all history. Whenever anything of importance occurs the ambassador's boss comes on the scene to clinch the deal, to sign the document, to straighten out difficulties. Much of the fun has gone out of diplomats' work and they therefore devote more of their time to fun, entertainment, polishing the social graces, showing national movies, and carrying messages. An ambassador is a glorified errand boy and, if capable, a propagandist too. He can also pervert his government's policy.

The Bolsheviks in 1935 and 1936 were still obsessed with the fear that Germany and Japan would attack them simultaneously. They therefore wanted better relations with England, France, and America. But England had offered only weak resistance to Italy in Abyssinia and how could one expect her to be resolute against Germany? Yet Moscow was most anxious to improve relations with London. France cold-shouldered Russia. America held aloof. The Russians therefore continued to arm frantically and to advocate the Popular Front whose aims were: anti-Fascist governments in democratic countries, maintenance of the geographic status quo against Fascist assaults, and to this end, the strengthening of the League of Nations. On their part, the Bolsheviks were prepared to collaborate with bourgeois governments, and to soft-pedal the world revolution.

But I submitted to Moscow friends that the Soviet government had to do more. "I believe," I wrote in a *Nation* article on foreign affairs, "that the democratization of the Soviet Union would weaken the enemies of peace." Raya Oumansky had just served us a plentiful lunch in her apartment on the Spiridonovka, and the men—Oumansky, Boris Mironov, his assistant in the press department, and I—retired to another room where I read them this sentence from my article in order to provoke a discussion. Mironov agreed with me. But Oumansky, always the official, said it was irrelevant. (Oumansky is now Soviet Ambassador in Washington, and Mironov, my best Soviet friend, was shot.)

It was very relevant. A democratic Russia would have assisted anti-Fascist elements in France and England in getting rid of their Chamberlains and Bonnets. Instead, the purges and the Moscow trials helped produce the second World War.

16. The Extended Hand

WHEN the news of American recognition of Soviet Russia reached Moscow in November, 1933, Stalin said, "*Ne Razkhlebatsa,*" which in his unique Russian meant, "Keep your shirt on. Don't display our excessive glee." And "*Ne Razkhlebatsa*" was the slogan which went out to the whole country as instructions to editorial writers and speakers. Be dignified. The Soviet Union is a great power. Keep your shirt on.

Ambassador William Christian Bullitt got a warm welcome from the Kremlin. He had been a consistent friend of Soviet Russia since his very creditable performance in Moscow in 1919—the best thing he ever did—and, partly as a reward, partly to ascertain what was the potential of Soviet-American relations, Bullitt received an invitation into the holy of holies where few foreign ambassadors have trod, and had a long conversation with Stalin about which he always maintained a difficult silence.

William Bullitt came from Rittenhouse Square, the rich aristocratic center of old Philadelphia. I was born not very far away—somewhat nearer the Liberty Bell—above a delicatessen store in the fish and chicken market at Fourth and Monroe Streets. Kenneth Durant, a mutual acquaintance of Bullitt's and mine, also hailed from Rittenhouse Square.

Bessie Beattie, one of the first Americans to write eyewitness accounts of the Bolshevik Revolution, and author of *The Red Heart of Russia*—tells this story. She returned from Russia in 1918. Before going home to San Francisco she went down to Washington to collect literature on the war in George Creel's make-the-world-safe-for-democracy government propaganda bureau. A pleasant young man helped her and engaged her in conversation. Where had she come from?

She said, "Russia."

He asked what she thought of it, and she said it was fine.

Suddenly he ran out and called another young man. "Listen," he exclaimed, "this lady agrees with us about Soviet Russia and she's

299

been there." One of the young men was Kenneth Durant, who for many years has been New York correspondent of the Soviet telegraphic agency TASS and adviser of the Soviet Embassy in Washington and of other Soviet agencies. The other young man was William C. Bullitt.

The day Bullitt arrived in Moscow I phoned him from the lobby of the Hotel National and asked whether I could come up. He greeted me very cordially with his red-and-gold smile. He seemed intelligent and very pro-Soviet with an air of "Well, we succeeded in the end in getting recognition." He used one phrase that stuck in my mind. He said, "After all, the President, Jack Reed, and I are of the same American strain."

Later that day somebody called Bullitt from the lobby and informed him that Harpo Marx was downstairs. Bullitt descended in a jiffy, pumped Harpo's hand, and appeared pleased that Mr. Marx had done him the honor. Harpo talked in Moscow, talked very much, and regaled all parties with jokes and antics.

In due course, the Russians arranged a public performance in which Harpo Marx would show his art. We went to the Myusik Hol, as the metropolitan vaudeville theater was called. First, Harpo had to be shown Moscow's variety, and so the regular performance dragged on for many hours with about one laugh per hour. Finally, it did end. Now for Harpo. Yes, but . . . Harpo Marx had to be introduced to the Soviet audience. Accordingly, Pudovkin, successful Soviet cinema producer, rose in front of the curtain and delivered a speech punctuated with appropriate quotations from Lenin, Stalin, and Engels on the role of humor in society, on the social significance of Hollywood, and finally on the real meaning of Marx, Harpo.

At last the curtain went up—it was nearly midnight—and Harpo in his famous straw wig appeared in a two-actor sketch. It was one unending laugh. Several times the performance was interrupted because the heroine just couldn't stop laughing. The Russians, whose laughing muscles had grown flabby from insufficient exercise, held their sides and asked for more. Harpo, among other things, did his renowned cutlery trick. Dozens of knives, spoons, and forks dropped from his sleeves. Then he took a huge quantity of silver from inside the actress's dress.

After the show many foreigners and Soviet friends went backstage. Among them was Maxim Litvinov, with his wife and son and daughter. And here it developed that Litvinov's pockets were filled with knives, spoons, and forks which Harpo discovered. Maxim grinned broadly and little Tania clapped with joy.

Comedy does not grow profusely in the orchard of dictatorship. Back in 1922, Bim and Bom, the Russian Amos and Andy, produced a sketch in which Bim came on the stage with photographs of Lenin and Trotzky.

"What are you going to do with those?" Bom asks.

"Hang one and stand the other against the wall," Bim replied. But that sort of thing was soon prohibited.

Sergei Eisenstein is the great genius of the Soviet cinema. His silent movie *Potemkin* is still unsurpassed. I have known him well for many years and we frequently exchanged visits. He is a natural comedian. His culture and reading, his knowledge of languages, art, and politics are above the average of even the most advanced circles. His big head, surrounded by a thinning corona of long blond hair, is crammed full of weighty facts. But his natural bent is comedy. Every gesture, every grimace and movement of the hands is mirth-provoking, and his jokes and puns are myriad.

He once planned to do a comedy about the Soviet bureaucrat. Here was a subject born for comedy—the blundering, helpless official worshiping papers, files, and numbers. . . . A Soviet journalist once received an assignment to write up an insane asylum. He came to the entrance of a building and heard one man say to another, "This is an insane asylum," so he went inside. He asked to be taken upstairs in the elevator. The elevator man sat immovable on his little stool and said, "That's not an elevator. That's a cage and only lunatics go into it to be stuck between the floors." The journalist decided that this was certainly the right place, and walked to the second floor. In the corridor, he saw women with papers rushing in one direction and a moment later he saw them come running back in the opposite direction, their fingers in their hair, shouting, "Oi, oi." He peered into an office. A disheveled man in shirt sleeves was banging on the telephone and yelling, "I am the director of a trust, do you understand? The director of a trust." The journalist made a note, "A case of false identification." He stopped a person who looked important and might be the doctor and said to him, "I have come here to write up the insane asylum. What shall I do?" "You stay right here," the man replied. "You'll get all the material you want." And in this manner the journalist went through the entire building, then returned home and wrote up the story, and added a postscript, "Later I learned that it was the Commissariat of Trade."

Eisenstein would have packed such a situation with rollicking fun, but the Soviet government refused him the permission. It was all right to print an occasional article ridiculing bureaucracy. Mikhail Koltzov and other feuilletonists did that. But a movie reached millions in towns and villages and made too big and permanent an impression.

During the first five-year plan an anecdote went from mouth to mouth in Soviet Russia: Two workingmen in their own airplanes met in the air. "Where are you going?" says the first. "I'm on my way to Odessa to buy a dozen eggs. And where are you going?" "Ah," he replies, "I hear there are men's socks to be bought in Leningrad." As Markoosha once said, "The best subway in the world and no needles in Moscow." But you cannot burlesque Soviet economy on the stage or silver screen. The mature can laugh at and criticize themselves. But when the Bolsheviks introduced *Samokritika*, or self-criticism, it was confined to rasping criticism of others. This does not mean that Soviet citizens never smiled or laughed or that Soviet art confined itself to barren tragedy and tough political fare. *The Little Golden Calf* by Ilf and Petrov would take a prize in any international competition for mirthful satire. *Squaring the Circle*, written by Katayev, Petrov's brother, entertained audiences in Berlin and New York as well as Russia. But such specimens were rare. Koltzov, the editor of the Moscow satirical weekly *Krokodil*, once asked me about Will Rogers. Among other things I told him that Rogers sent a daily syndicated telegram of some ten lines to the newspapers and they regularly contained two or three laughs each. "Hm," Koltzov commented, "I'd be happy if we had two laughs in a whole issue of *Krokodil*."

There are two things in a dictatorship: the dictatorship and its enemies. It is sacrilege to make fun of the dictatorship. Nor can you make light of its enemies. You can't shoot a man after you've dismissed him with ridicule.

When Harpo Marx said good-by, leaving Soviet cinema directors dejected and jealous, the American colony settled back to work, and the American Embassy got down to business. John C. Wiley, the Counselor of the Embassy, took care of the difficult routine without neglecting diplomacy and society, while Bullitt established contacts and felt his way towards a policy. Bullitt is an erratic personality and has an erratic intelligence. He is brilliant at times and quite lacking in normal good judgment at other times.

In Moscow, Bullitt built up a strong friendship with the Polish Ambassador Lukashevitch, and I noticed in 1935 that Bullitt manifested an increasing sympathy for Polish foreign policy which kept step with Hitler's.

Bullitt often told me that President Roosevelt was, like himself, pro-French, but that the State Department tended to be more pro-British. Bullitt's affability and superficiality are very French. He is too temperamental and expansive to like the stolid, heavy-jawed British.

At first, the United States Embassy was the sun of Moscow's diplomatic heaven, and Bullitt was social king. But soon a cloud dimmed and chilled the scene. The Russians said Bullitt was "not serious," and to a Russian that is a serious charge. Part of the trouble lay in a cordial, mutual dislike between Bullitt and Foreign Commissar Litvinov. Litvinov several times told me of his regret that Washington had not sent a career diplomat instead of an "ambitious and impatient" one who hoped to rise to fame on success or failure in Russia. There were no laurels to be reaped by Bullitt in Moscow. He had legitimately hoped there would be, and he was disappointed through no fault of his own. The two great fields in which Soviet-American relations could develop were trade and the Far East. But trade did not reach high levels for business reasons, while the United States was not then ready to collaborate with Russia to save China from Japan's love.

The petty irritation between the American Embassy and the Soviet Foreign Office reached an explosive climax in August, 1935. That month a Congress of the Third International (Comintern) convened in Moscow—the first since 1928. The Comintern had been moribund because there were no revolutions or potential revolutions, and that being the case, the Soviet government did not wish to spoil its foreign relations by releasing the raucous voice of the Third International. But a new phenomenon tormented Stalin in 1935: Hitler.

When Hitler took power in 1933, Moscow kept very quiet about Nazi barbarism. When Moscow keeps quiet it is afraid—that is a pretty safe rule to go by. Throughout 1933 and during part of 1934, I used to plead with Radek, with Rayevsky, the foreign editor of *Izvestia*, with Boris Mironov, assistant censor in the Foreign Office, and numerous other Russians. "The whole world is protesting against the Nazis," I said. "Mass meetings, demonstrations and parades protest against the burning of the books, the persecutions of Jews and other minorities, the atrocities in concentration camps. . . ."

I told them of a procession I had seen in New York where marchers carried banners such as "Down with Nazi paganism," "Down with Hitler," while the Jewish undertakers passed with a big placard which read, "We want Hitler." But the voice of Moscow was not heard in this universal chorus of anti-Nazi indignation. My friends' usual reply was, "Wait." Moscow feared a Nazi-Japanese attack.

My impatience was rewarded toward the end of 1934. Soviet domestic conditions had been normalized and the Nazis were looming as a grave menace. Germany was arming. Moscow looked around for friends. On May 2, 1935, the Soviet and French governments signed a mutual assistance treaty which most men regarded as a military alliance. Both felt threatened by Nazi Germany. A few days later Pierre Laval, Premier of France, arrived in Moscow. The Foreign Office gave him a grand evening reception at which "all Moscow" was present. Bullitt stood and talked with Marshal Tukhachevsky, assistant War Commissar, and then whispered long with Laval's companions. Laval spent most of his time talking to War Commissar Voroshilov through an interpreter. I watched Laval's face for a long time. He has the face of a French provincial butcher. It is the face of a man who trusts no one and would be surprised if anyone trusted him.

Stalin never came to such affairs. Nor Molotov. The host was Litvinov and he danced with the youngest and prettiest. The Bolsheviks wore full dress or military uniforms with their decorations, but leaders like President Kalinin or Trade Commissar Mikoyan came in street attire.

Laval had an audience with Stalin, Molotov, and Litvinov where they were photographed in smiles, and then a famous communiqué was issued. "Comrade Stalin," it read, "understands and fully approves the national defense policy of France in keeping her armed forces at the level required for security." Why should Stalin approve the French government's policy of national defense? Was that not the business of Frenchmen? Yes, and some Frenchmen, the French Communists, had theretofore disapproved of French defense measures and refused to vote in favor of appropriations for the construction of the Maginot Line. But what was the use of Communist Russia entering into a military alliance with France if French Communists did their best to keep France militarily weak? There was obviously no logic in that, and through this communiqué Stalin gave instructions to the French Communists to change their strategy—which they immediately did. Frenchmen in Laval's retinue made no secret of the fact that France could not fight a war successfully unless the French Communists supported it, and now Stalin had guaranteed that the French Communists would not be anti-war if war came; they would co-operate with the French government.

Laval's visit to Moscow was thus the prelude to the Popular Front. That French reactionary's chat on the Red Olympus ushered in world-wide collaboration between liberals, democrats, socialists and Communists—a collaboration which, ironically enough, eliminated Laval from office until Hitler conquered France.

In many countries, something like the Popular Front was ripe. In the spring of 1935, Margaret Marshall and Muriel Gray, of the *Nation* staff, gave me a party at their Greenwich Village apartment. Benjamin Stolberg was among those present, and he drew me aside and said, "Wouldn't it be a good idea if you arranged a little lunch for me and Earl Browder?"

I did not then know Browder; I met him later. I said, however, that Browder might object because of the accusations Stolberg had leveled against the American Communist party in the New York press. But the fact that Benjamin Stolberg thought Earl Browder would consent to talk to him is interesting as evidence that an anti-Communist believed there had been a real change of heart among Communists towards their opponents. Stolberg's suggestion was merely one small reflection of a new attitude on the part of very many non-Communists and anti-Communists. Sentiment was crystallizing towards a union of the foes of Fascism. The rise of Hitler called for a mobilization of forces against him. Democratic disunity within Germany had led to Hitler's victory at home. A widespread conviction prevailed that disunity outside Germany would lead to Nazi victories abroad.

Moscow observed this yearning toward unity. Moscow's own interests turned it in the same direction. The Bolsheviks needed allies among foreign governments and foreign popular movements.

The formal adoption by Communists of the Popular Front took

place at the Seventh Comintern congress held in Moscow during August, 1935. Moscow extended its hand to the world's non-Communists. Bullitt chose that moment to break with Moscow.

Bullitt regarded the Comintern congress as a personal insult. He had been closeted in the White House with President Roosevelt and Commissar Litvinov in November, 1933, when United States recognition of the Soviet government was arranged. Litvinov gave certain promises. Mr. Roosevelt gave certain promises. Litvinov later told me that Roosevelt had broken his promises, and Bullitt later told me that the President was angry because Litvinov had broken his promises. At any rate, when the White House conferences were concluded, an exchange of official letters between Roosevelt and Litvinov appeared in the press. Every detail of these letters had been gone into during the conferences. Litvinov's letters pledged the Soviet government "not to permit the formation or residence on its territory of any organization or group—and to prevent the activity on its territory of any organization or group of representatives or officials of any organization or group—which" . . . and there follows a description of the American Communist party. This was a water-tight undertaking, and its literal interpretation would have required the Soviets to disband the Comintern and to bar all American Communist delegates from the Soviet Union. But when American correspondents asked Litvinov at a big press conference whether this pledge applied to the Comintern, he replied, "The Comintern is not mentioned in the documents. You should not read more into the documents than was intended." Litvinov contended in 1935, moreover, that he had informed President Roosevelt that the Soviet government accepts no responsibility for the Comintern. Nevertheless, the text of Litvinov's letter to Roosevelt stands as a solemn Soviet commitment. And so, when American Communists came to Moscow and reported at the Comintern congress on labor conditions and strikes in the United States, the State Department was warranted in protesting. Indeed, the American government would have been entitled to discontinue relations with Moscow.

The protest called attention to a broken Soviet pledge. But when the United States failed to disrupt relations it meant that the United States did not take the pledge seriously—unless Bullitt believed that after his warning Stalin would shut down the Comintern and the American Communist party. But this would have been too naive. The Russians have a proverb, "If you say 'A,' you must be ready to

say 'B.' " Washington said "A" but had no intention of saying "B,"
and so America accused, Moscow denied the accusation, and nothing
happened except that the atmosphere between the two nations was
clouded with bitterness.

A statesman would have paid more attention to the new moderate
policy of the Comintern than to the cold, two-year-old text of
Litvinov's letter. The Comintern's resolutions on the Popular Front
made it plain that the world Communists were wheeling to a new
strategy. The Comintern instructed Communists in all countries to
"form a united front with Social Democratic and reformist organizations as well as with mass movements of national liberation and religious, democratic and pacifist groups."

Was this sincere or was it a maneuver? There is nothing permanent
in any government's policy and expediency enters into all official
decisions. But the policy of the Popular Front was a natural growth.
People everywhere yearned for it, Communists and non-Communists.
All politics is a choice between two evils. Those who can stand no
evil are not in politics. The menace of Fascism made it ridiculous
for anti-Fascists to be squabbling among themselves while the enemy
moved up on them. Non-Communists were prepared for the Popular
Front by Hitler, by economic difficulties in capitalist countries, by
Russia's successes, and by a desire to see the Soviet experiment proceed without molestation from the outside. The Popular Front also
pleased most Communists. I talked to hundreds of Communists during the Popular Front period from 1935 to 1939, some rank and
file, some the highest, and I found that the alliance with non-Communists was congenial to them all. To be sure, it felt strange. "Social
Democrat" had been a term of abuse automatically interchangeable
with "Social Fascist." To call anyone a "reformist" had been to
insult him. Religious and pacifist organizations had always been
fought as enemies of the working class. The Comintern's sharp
reversal drove some Communists into the Trotzkyist camp. But the
bulk of them liked it even though the hostility towards non-Communist allies never disappeared altogether. The Popular Front gave the
Communists a wide field of activity in national life. They became
important. Lenin always taught that Communists must keep contact
with the masses. The Popular Front presented a golden opportunity
for such contact. Moreover, much had changed since the 1928 Comintern congress predicted "a new cycle of revolutions and wars." Wars,

yes. But no revolutions. The Comintern realistically recognized in 1935 that the impending wars could only be prevented if Communists forsook active advocacy of revolution and extended their hand to all parties and persons who wanted to stop Fascist aggression. This was the sense of the Comintern congress of August, 1935; yet it was on an issue raised by this congress that Bullitt broke with the Soviet Union and departed from his pro-Soviet traditions. While the Russians were intransigent foes of everything capitalistic he sympathized with Moscow. When the Russians, for selfish reasons, became conciliatory and proposed collaboration to check Hitler and Japan he turned away from them. If the Popular Front had been a prolonged success the second World War could have been prevented. It might have been a success. But if it had been only a possibility it was much more important than registering impractical protest against speeches delivered by three insignificant Americans in the Kremlin.

Ambassador Bullitt did not merely deliver his note of protest to the Soviet Foreign Office. Energetic individual, he launched a fierce propaganda campaign in Moscow against Moscow. He met the American correspondents every day and urged them by their dispatches to fan the flames of anti-Sovietism in America. He ignored precedents and summoned non-American foreign correspondents to do the same thing in their own countries. He also worked on foreign diplomats to have their governments protest against the Comintern congress. Some did so without Bullitt's vehemence and with no conviction that it would help.

After that, Bullitt's presence in Russia became impossible and he withdrew to Paris in a cyclone of dust. It was the mistake of his life. He might have served the cause of peace. Instead his anti-Communism propelled him into the arms of the appeasers in England and France. More on that in a later chapter.

Mr. Bullitt was succeeded by Joseph E. Davies, a very wealthy man, who took a pro-Soviet line in Moscow and Washington. Usually he sailed his big yacht in the Baltic and Black Seas, leaving the hard work in the Moscow Embassy to Loy Henderson. But he supervised. Once, in 1937, while passing through Paris, he invited me to his flower-laden apartment in the Ritz and asked me to give him my view of purges, trials, and GPU. He thought my opinion too unsympathetic to Russia and we argued long until Mrs. Davies called him to dinner.

When I arrived in Marseilles from Palestine in March, 1934, I bought all the British and French newspapers I could find in order to catch up with the news. One item in the *London Times* from Moscow startled me. Later the Soviet press confirmed it. Christian G. Rakovsky had recanted and returned to Moscow as a Stalin supporter.

With the perversion of a journalist who must rush his opinions into print, I suspended my study of Spain long enough to write an article on Rakovsky's change of heart. *The Nation*, responsible for most of my titles, called it "The Tragedy of Trotzky." From my contacts with Rakovsky before and during his exile it was not difficult for me to comment on the causes that had brought Rakovsky back from Siberia into a Popular Front with Stalin.

In Saratov, Rakovsky was well treated. But his adamant refusal to confess his sins and accept Stalin's leadership led to his exile to a hole in the cold barren ground called Barnaul. Some American prospectors came there once and since Rakovsky was the only person speaking foreign languages he was hauled out as their interpreter. When they left they gave him a dollar tip. But Siberian conditions and humiliation could not break Rakovsky. He was made of the stern stuff of those who languished for thirty years in Czarist exile and died there rather than deviate from their principles.

In 1928, he had told me he would always remain loyal to Trotzky. He insisted that Stalin had betrayed the Soviet Revolution. Now he had returned to work with Stalin. I visited him twice in his apartment in Moscow in 1935, and Madame Rakovsky served me tea as she had at Saratov. I also saw him three or four times in his office in the Commissariat of Health where he had taken over the direction of all the commissariat's scientific research institutes. (He was a physician by profession.) What I heard from him in Moscow confirmed what I had written in Madrid. Exile had not broken him. But he looked out upon Europe from Barnaul and found no revolution. "It is an indisputable fact . . . that the world revolution is as far away as when Lenin and Trotzky directed the Third International. Fascism . . . creeps from country to country. The intensity of human distress is equalled only by the ferocity of political reaction. Europe never looked so dark and beyond hope as the present time. Yet Communism makes no headway. The Comintern is a dismal failure." This is what I wrote from Madrid. Coldly reassessing the situation, I would say the same thing about it today.

Rakovsky wrote from Barnaul, "The differences which separate me from the party lose their significance in view of the growth of international reaction." Hitler brought him back to Stalin.

When *The Nation* with my article on Rakovsky arrived in Moscow, a Bolshevik friend phoned and asked whether I knew Bela Kun, the ex-dictator of Communist Hungary and now chief of the Comintern. I said I didn't. He said it would be interesting for me to meet him. I said I had no objection—but did nothing about it. The next day a German acquaintance phoned and asked whether I would like to see Bela Kun. I said, "Yes." Then a bourgeois foreign journalist who knew Kun came to my apartment and asked me whether I knew Bela Kun, and when I told him no, he dialed my telephone and made an appointment for me with the Comintern leader.

Kun had the *Nation* article spread out in front of him. He was very cordial and excessively polite and I hated it and told him so. He said, "You wrote 'the Comintern is a dismal failure.'"

"Isn't it?" I demanded. That set a new tone for our conversation. The upshot was he wanted me to explain why I thought the Comintern was a failure. I offered a string of reasons. The Communists were preaching world revolution which was not practical politics. They preached it in a language that was translated from the Russian and superimposed on Marx's involved German so that not even intellectuals, let alone workingmen, understood it. The Communists were sectarian and dogmatic, a sect with its own Esperanto. The Communists ignored national issues in their own countries and talked too much about Soviet achievements. This was a matter of bad emphasis, not a fundamental error. The Communists had antagonized the labor unions by organizing their unsuccessful trade-union international. Dual unionism weakened the workers in their struggle with employers and the workers resented this and blamed it on Moscow. The Communists had two kinds of paint: red for themselves, black for everybody else. Socialists were Fascists, liberals were "rotten," pacifists were "a menace," and so on. "This," I said, "is pure bunk." "*Quatsch*" was the word I used in German. At any rate, that was not the way to win friends and make converts.

Bela Kun agreed only about the Esperanto. Yet about the whole he said, "You will see. We have already decided to pursue a new strategy. Things will change." Thereafter, I saw Bela Kun many times. (He disappeared in the big purge.)

Bela Kun was one of the engineers of the Popular Front. I am sure he believed in it. In all of the years of the Comintern's uncompromising revolutionary attitude what depressed the Communists most was their isolation from the working-class masses abroad. The Soviet government, too, had never really been able to cement any friendship with bourgeois governments. Now Moscow turned a new leaf and wrote Popular Front.

As part of this new mental attitude, the Soviet government joined the League of Nations which it had formerly reviled. It offered military collaboration to France and Czechoslovakia and sought to cultivate England and the United States. The League of Nations was wedded to the territorial status quo of Europe. Russia now accepted that status quo and was ready to defend it.

The Popular Front, similarly, was an acceptance of the social status quo in capitalist states. It meant not revolution but, instead, collaboration with non-revolutionary and reformist parties which wanted social change by democratic means.

Moscow's Popular Front strategy was designed to stop Fascism. Unless the anti-Fascist forces in England, France, and elsewhere were strongly organized, the appeasers in bourgeois countries would make concessions to Hitler. The alternative, therefore, was Popular Front or appeasement. The choice was: Oppose or appease. Oppose meant oppose through the Popular Front and in conjunction with Soviet Russia. This is what Bullitt did not understand.

17. *Appease or Oppose*

EUROPE now interested me more and Russia less. Europe was on the eve, although no one knew when night would set in. Soviet developments tormented me. Economic conditions continued to improve in the first part of 1936, but a conflict was in progress between a trend towards political liberalism and another trend towards cruel repression. Things were happening which made me sick and kept my fingers out of the typewriter. I preferred to wait before I condemned, at least until I got completely fed up. So after only two months at home I sallied forth once more in March, 1936, and went to Berlin as the first stop in a journey which I expected would take me to Spain and Italy again.

Once when I arrived in Nazi Berlin from Moscow, and got into a taxi to find the streets looking strangely empty, an idea suddenly occurred to me and I said to the driver, "Is today Sunday?" He must have thought I was crazy, and answered, "Of course." Russia had abolished Sundays and introduced a six-day week, and we therefore never knew the days of the week in Moscow. At first it used to be difficult to get accustomed to them abroad. In the Soviet Union the days were distinguished by their numbers in the month, not by their names in the week. Now it was Sunday and everybody in Berlin would be away. I had a letter of introduction from Ambassador Bullitt to Ambassador Dodd, and I was so determined to present it immediately that I could not stop myself from trying. I went straight to the telephone and called the United States Embassy. To the voice which was apparently handling the switchboard that Sabbath morning I said, "Will you please tell me how I can reach the Ambassador?" and the voice replied, "This is Mr. Dodd." I drove without delay to the Embassy.

A southern Jeffersonian democrat, William E. Dodd was naturally anti-Nazi. While teaching in the University of Chicago, he was called to the telephone one day by President Roosevelt, who asked him to be Ambassador to Berlin. Mr. Dodd could not have been more surprised than any one of several hundred distinguished history professors in American colleges who had never been in politics and never came near diplomacy. Dodd was the antithesis of a diplomat because he said what he thought. He told Adolf Hitler in person what he thought and it amounted to a scorching denunciation of the Fascist dictatorship. He was equally opposed to all forms of dictatorship and discoursed passionately on Thomas Jefferson.

In Nazi eyes, the Ambassador's disinclination to entertain them and shake their hands made him "peculiar." But he knew his business; indeed the President had told him what his business was by appointing him. To send Professor Dodd to Berlin was a slap at Hitler. The Ambassador found it all the more difficult to understand how American oil companies were permitted to build aviation oil refineries for the German government at Hamburg when he knew they would be used by Goering's aggressive bombers. Nor could he approve when the United States sold Germany tremendous quantities of magnesium which the Nazis were converting into airplanes and aerial bombs. Douglas Miller, the United States commercial attaché in Berlin, America's best expert on German economic conditions, and no less anti-Nazi than Mr. Dodd, supplied the Embassy with the data on American participation in Germany's rearmament, and Mr. Dodd would pound these reports with his bony finger and declaim against the unwisdom of nurturing Germany to military greatness.

The Ambassador was kept well-informed by highly placed German officials who were none too pro-Nazi, and also by non-Germans. On March 6, 1936, I saw him in his residence and he told me that Hitler would speak to the Reichstag the next day and announce some great event, probably a Reichswehr advance into the Rhineland. The next day Hitler convoked the Reichstag.

Berlin hung out all its flags, and soldiers and secret police patrolled the center of the city. The short distance between the Chancellor's palace and the Reichstag meeting place was black with people, mostly uniformed guards, but also some spectators. I posted myself in front of the Adlon Hotel on Unter den Linden to see Hitler go by. Down the entire length of the street stood S.S. men in black suits. They stood arm to arm and shoulder to shoulder forming a solid human wall facing the street. Back to back with these men stood another human wall facing the houses. The same arrangement was repeated on the other side of the cordon through which Hitler's car would pass. Suddenly they all sprang to attention. From the shouting I knew Hitler approached. Now I had my own little problem. There were of course secret service men among the foreigners who watched at the entrance of the Adlon. There might also be an assassin. To be above suspicion I felt that I had to keep my hands out of my pockets. But a person who fired at Hitler might drop his revolver into my jacket pocket or, to get me into trouble by provocation, the police might put a weapon into my pocket. I knew from experience that the police in a dictatorship are always very nervous when the dictator exposes himself to the public. Harry Jaffe, an American radical, was once pounced upon by a GPU agent because he pushed in order to get a closer view of Stalin. They found nothing on him and he was released a few hours later, but Jaffe really never lived it down. Nor did I know that the Gestapo would be as gentle with me or that it would not wish to seize me on this propitious occasion. In any case, once arrested for an invalid reason they might invent another reason to keep me. I pondered the alternatives. I folded my arms on my chest, but that left my pockets open. Hands behind my back did not clearly demonstrate innocence or inactivity. (Later an American friend told me he went through the same calculations himself.) Finally I had the solution. I clasped my body tightly at the waist with my elbows—that took care of my jacket pockets. My forearms covered my trouser pockets and I locked my fingers on my abdomen. It felt uncomfortable but it lasted only a moment, for Hitler's automobile, with armed sleuths on the running boards, dashed by in two seconds as he gave the arm-erect salute sitting in the back of the car. I went immediately down the block and heard Hitler's speech on the radio in the Soviet Ambassador's private apartment. Ambassador Suritz was very gloomy.

That day opened a new era in European history. On that day, the German army took over the Rhineland. By the Treaty of Versailles this area was demilitarized. But it had been a forced peace agreement. By the treaties of Locarno, Germany voluntarily accepted the demilitarization of the Rhineland, and then Hitler specifically subscribed to it. Now Germany broke her word and sent troops into the Rhineland.

March 7, 1936, was Hitler's first lunge towards world conquest. How did the powers deal with this new phenomenon of Germany defiant? Plenty of people in England and France, especially the latter, demanded that France mobilize and march into the Rhineland. They realized that a fortified Rhineland would put all France's eastern friends at the mercy of Berlin. For if Germany had a western wall, France could not come to the direct assistance of Poland, Czechoslovakia, and Austria. The whole system of French continental hegemony depended on France's ability to attack Germany effectively in the West in the event of German offensive action in the East. In 1919, Marshal Foch even wanted France to take the left German bank of the Rhine. He said, "Whoever is not on the Rhine has lost everything." But the civilians of the British and French governments disagreed.

And now, Germany had re-established the Watch on the Rhine.

It has been stated on the best authority, and accepted as true by statesmen, diplomats, and publicists, that the German officers who led the Reichswehr into the Rhineland had orders to retire if they met an advancing French force. It has even been stated, with less authenticity, that the German soldiers carried no ammunition. But this information is really unnecessary. The French army could easily have repelled the German army in March, 1936. The Reichswehr numbered only 100,000 plus the first year's conscripted recruits, and Hitler's air force and armored divisions were in embryo.

The French cabinet decided, lukewarmly, to take military action. But first they consulted the British. Perhaps they consulted the British knowing that the result would be negative.

Pierre-Etienne Flandin, French Foreign Minister at the time of the Rhineland occupation, revealed history in an article in the *London Sunday Times*, March 26, 1939. "The French government," he declared, "had informed Great Britain that it proposed to resist by force; it raised no question of British intervention in an action which it intended to take for its own account."

This is pretty definite. France decided to act. French public opinion was divided, but the government was resolved to stop the remilitarization of the German border province. England was not asked to participate, but simply to approve.

"But," wrote Flandin, "the British government, faithfully reflecting its own public opinion, and profoundly imbued with the principle of the equality of rights of all the peoples, and imagining that all peoples were equally inclined to observe the principle of right and justice, asked the French government to renounce this policy."

England asked France not to march into the Rhineland. "It will be possible to find later, in the records of the Quai d'Orsay, the proof that France warned England at that moment of all that might happen in Europe. Much of the French prediction has unfortunately come true."

Flandin could never have written this in a British newspaper if there were any doubt about the truth of his statements. The Germans have now read those records in the Quai d'Orsay although they knew in advance what was in them. The French prediction dealt with the difficulty of defending Austria, Czechoslovakia, and Poland after Germany had fortified the Rhineland. This being the case, the British should not have held France back.

Having remilitarized the Rhineland, Hitler started building the Siegfried Line. That predetermined the fate of the French continental system of little allies. Czechoslovakia's life-line ran from Prague across Germany and the Rhineland to Strasbourg and thence to Paris. On March 7, 1936, Hitler moved into a position where he could cut it. The chapter that ended with Adolf Hitler touring the sights of Paris opened four years earlier in the Rhineland. The Rhineland episode is the watershed in the history of Europe between the two wars. After that, Germany gained one advantage after the other.

Then why did the French do nothing? Where was the French instinct of self-preservation? Observers would ask that question from the spring of 1936 to the spring of 1940. If war had come in March, 1936, France would have won easily. Germany would have been attacked by France, Czechoslovakia, Poland, and probably Russia. That might have been the end of Fascist aggression—not only in Europe.

Later in 1936, 1937, and 1938, when Spain, Austria, and Czechoslovakia were at stake, the appeasers said, "We are not prepared. We are too weak. We cannot fight now." That this was only a part-truth and, really, a lame excuse, becomes clear from the Rhineland affair. For in the spring of 1936, France alone was much stronger than Germany. Appeasement was never a matter of a weak arm but of a weak brain.

Why did Paris look on supinely?

One of the answers is England. (There is rarely one answer to a political question.) "Versailles had left a bad taste" in the British mouth. Hitler, the British said, was eliminating one of the treaty's least defensible provisions.

France, to be sure, could have stopped Hitler without British aid. But the French had occupied the Rhineland once before. They had punitively marched into the Ruhr in 1923. They had insisted on the pound of reparations flesh from Germany. The result was nil. The Poincaré method had to be abandoned because in the long run it was objectionable. In 1936, the French government was not prepared to revert to the crude anti-Germanism of the Stresemann and Rathenau periods. It had turned over a new leaf. The treatment France should have meted out to republican Germany, it accorded Nazi Germany. France now was in a defensive, unaggressive mood. Germany could not be destroyed forever. Pacifism was sweeping France. Even the defensive spirit limped. The first World War had been a disappointment. It had brought some territorial acquisitions and some indemnities, but even this costliest of all wars, in which France had bled herself white, had not rid France of the eternal German menace. Maybe it could not be done by warlike means. In any case, Germany under Hitler had launched out on a new career of militarism. If France had seized the Rhineland and then marched out again it would have been worse than nothing for it would only have irritated the Germans. Was France then to march in and plow up the whole country and occupy Berlin before the Nazis reached their militaristic goal? Not a single French leader advocated such action. France had no stomach for life-and-death combats. Could not a peaceful settlement be reached? Any delay of the ultimate struggle was desirable. Another day lived is a day gained. Most Frenchmen probably took the fatalistic view that some day they would have to meet Germany again on the battlefield. Then the later the better; in the meanwhile, reinforce the Maginot Line. For that final test of strength, Anglo-French collaboration was necessary. Britain must not be unalterably alienated. France decided not to over-ride the British veto and act alone. Having angered England by taking Italy's side in Abyssinia, France's chief purpose was now to worm itself back into the good graces of the British public.

But that was only part of the story. Just as Hitler had won friends in high British circles, so he found defenders in important French groups. Hitler's chief aim in life, they contented, was to crush Bolshevism. He had repeatedly assured French journalists and politicians that he had no ambitions in the West. *Mein Kampf?* Yes, but that was merely a propaganda book written by a young man in prison. Had not Hitler forever renounced all claim to Alsace and Lorraine? Of course, his remilitarization of the Rhineland opened rather unpleasant possibilities. But perhaps it was not really as bad as it looked. If Hitler marched on Russia, as they hoped he would, he had to cover himself in the Rhineland against an attack from the West. Instead of enraging Hitler by signing military treaties with the Bolsheviks, France should encourage him to concentrate on the East; then France would be relieved of pressure and danger. If Hitler attacked and defeated Soviet Russia it would be the end of Communism in France. French anti-Communists should therefore encourage Hitler in his anti-Bolshevism. If France, on the contrary, whipped up anti-Fascist sentiment as a preliminary to resistance to Hitler, and to Mussolini, that would be wind in the sails of the French left. A victory over Hitler would weaken Fascist tendencies and reactionary forces in France.

There can be no divorce between foreign policy and domestic conditions. The domestic situations in the democracies always helped Hitler and the other aggressors. By precipitate action in the Rhineland, Hitler had deepened the disunity with France. It would not be the last time.

Laval and the reactionaries had defied England and acted against England in the Ethiopian affair. Now these same reactionaries made teamwork with Great Britain the keystone of their politics. If England opposes our marching into the Rhineland, they contended, we must not do it. This looked like a pro-British attitude. It was actually a pro-German attitude.

So instead of doing something about the Rhineland, and because they did not intend to do anything, they called the League of Nations together to deliberate on what to do. The League Council would meet in London on March 13. By assembling in London rather than in Geneva, the French politicians furnished themselves with an alibi. They had been coerced by the British, they would say. You could not be impolite to your host. The French put themselves in the British hand, and King Edward VIII, reputed to be pro-German, lent one of his own palaces for the purpose. I went to London along with that swarm of international correspondents that swoops down wherever the statesmen foregather.

Royal palaces were not built to accommodate hundreds of working journalists and only a few of us could stand at the entrance of the chamber where the delegates—Eden for England, Flandin for France, Litvinov for Russia, Beck for Poland, Ribbentrop for Germany—sat at a horseshoe table. A few others could see and the remainder had to listen to the amplifiers in the rear rooms. When Ribbentrop spoke I was among the five or six at the door, and at that vantage point I was about twenty feet removed from the delegates. Ribbentrop was nervous and pale. Litvinov wore a studied look of contempt and read a newspaper while Ribbentrop spoke. When Ribbentrop sat down it was obvious that the League would do nothing.

After the session, the delegates came out into the corridors, and then statesmen, journalists, and distinguished visitors milled around in one thick mass. It was in these intervals that newspapermen posed questions to the delegates and exchanged views among themselves. The evening before, walking down Whitehall, I had met Dorothy Woodman, an Englishwoman, Parliamentary Labor candidate, vegetarian, pacifist, and dynamic revolutionist. She was accompanied by Senator Georg Branting, Swedish Socialist, for whose daily paper, *Sozialdemokraten* I wrote irregularly. In the interval that followed Ribbentrop's speech I walked up to a man, extended my hand which he took, and said, "Hello, Branting."

The man said, "I am Ribbentrop."

I quickly dropped the Nazi's hand and turned on my heel almost straight into Beck's arms. He must have thought I had been talking to Ribbentrop for he seemed anxious to stop and chat with me. I declared that it was an outrage to take this thing lying down and he replied, "We can do nothing alone," which in diplomatic language meant that Poland had been prepared to take steps if France did. I think that was the case. Nobody could do anything alone and therefore they did nothing collectively. Nobody could do anything alone except Germany. After Beck went off I was introduced to Madame Genevieve Tabouis, French journalist, whom I met often in later years, and listened to sharp quips from an Englishwoman acquaintance who wrote biting political verse in the *New Statesman and Nation* under the pseudonym of Sagittarius. Most of the journalists were very cynical about "the mighty French" and "the bloody British" and the "great League of Nations."

I saw Litvinov in the Soviet Embassy where he was living. He said, "The British have paid the French back for not supporting them on Ethiopia." After Abyssinia, the Rhineland. "A few more blows like this," he said, "and where is the League of Nations?"

Several times I left the sessions with Marcel Rosenberg, Russian assistant secretary of the League of Nations, Gershelman, Litvinov's private secretary, and Rosenblum, Litvinov's aide on commercial treaties. "Your good life is ending," they twitted Rosenberg. They felt the League was doomed after its failure on the Rhineland. I walked around with Rosenberg for a time after the other two left us and then we went into seven stores—we counted—until, on the Strand, Rosenberg found exactly the pair of yellow suede gloves that suited him.

Among most of my Liberal and Labor friends in London the sentiment was that it would be unjust to prevent Germany from exercising full sovereignty in the Rhineland. In abstract reason, of course. But practical politics must consider consequences and not only ethics. Germany's remilitarization of the Rhineland was ethical, the results were most unethical—the results were the seizure of Austria, the crushing of Czechoslovakia, the war on Poland, the war on France. But no one saw that far although many of us were beginning to say, more and more, "Fascism is War." Leland Stowe wrote a book with that title.

The more immediate effects of Hitler's march into the Rhineland were a change in the foreign policy of Poland, which now commenced to feel still more at home within the German orbit, and a change in Belgium's foreign policy. On October 14, 1936, young Leopold, King of the Belgians, startled Europe by announcing a future attitude of neutrality as between Germany and France. This looked like non-partisanship. But actually it implied that Belgium would be equally friendly towards Germany which might attack her and to France which could only defend her. France having disclosed her weakness, the League having proved its bankruptcy, Belgium had decided that it could not antagonize Germany by being too pro-French. Consternation ruled in Paris. The French and Belgium general staffs could now no longer consult as they had in the past under the Franco-Belgian military treaty. These consultations were not resumed until December, 1939, when Belgium feared imminent invasion, when the Battle of Flanders was not far off. But generals cannot repair in six months what was lost in three years. In 1936, France commenced losing the battles of 1939 and 1940. In 1936, France should have commenced extending the Maginot Line to the sea. It did not.

March 7, 1936, also made the Italo-German axis a black reality. Hitler delivered his blow in the Rhineland while the British were engrossed in the Abyssinian affair. The British did not want to quarrel with Germany and Italy at the same time. Nor did the French want to quarrel with Mussolini when they saw Hitler approaching. This demonstrated to the two dictators the virtues of synchronization and co-operation. Anglo-French irresolution in Abyssinia reinforced Hitler's resolve to take the Rhineland. The mild reception accorded in London and Paris to this epochal event told the axis powers that they could go further. The conviction that Germany "could get away with it" encouraged those Nazis who believed in circuses when there is too little bread.

Hitler in the Rhineland was a blow to the French Right which was in office at the time but did nothing to check him. The anti-Fascist Left made political capital out of this. France wanted a new deal at home and abroad. The new-born moderation of the Communists had produced a real Popular Front, and the Left entered the parliamentary elections with bright hopes. Balloting took place on two successive rainy Sundays, April 26 and May 3, 1936.

I was impressed by the way the French cast their ballots. They came, husbands often with their wives, as though to perform a solemn religious rite. This civic duty obviously meant something very important to them, and as I went in pouring rain from a rich district in the center of Paris to one of the proletarian faubourgs and then to a middle-class arrondissement my feeling grew that love of democracy lived in France. I could not help thinking back to my youth in Philadelphia. My family resided at one time on south Sixth Street in the heart of one of Bill Vare's solidest wards. He had contracts to collect ashes and keep the city clean, but if he did keep the city clean, which was doubtful, it was in the streets and not in its politics. On normal election days my father received two dollars for his vote, but in years when there was a sharp contest the price went up to five dollars. Such an amount bulked in the family budget and we all knew about it. Election day to me brought not only big bonfires for which we boys collected old mattresses, planks, boxes, from the entire neighborhood, but also a little extra food and perhaps a nickel in my pocket. Democratic politics are never immune from unscrupulous politicians, and there were notorious cases in which votes were purchased in France too. But not as a regular procedure, and then on a limited scale. In England and in republican Germany it would have been altogether inconceivable.

The elections gave the Popular Front a decisive majority in the Chamber of Deputies, and on June 5, 1936, Léon Blum became Premier. By elevating him to its highest administrative office French democracy was defying Hitler, for Blum was both Jew and Socialist.

He enjoyed the parliamentary support of the Radical Socialists to the Right of him and the Communists on his Left.

Blum had an anti-Nazi mandate. The French electorate was tired of French kowtowing to Fascist aggressors. It was tired of Fascist Leagues at home too. The attempt on Blum's life in February had roused Paris to a white heat of anger. Now a Left government had taken office to end such things. The Popular Front had triumphed. It had triumphed in Spain too at about the same time. These two regimes were destined to be tragically interlinked.

The job of Blum and the French Popular Front was to arm against Fascist aggressors. But Blum introduced radical social reforms and improved the status of labor. That antagonized the French capitalist class. It was determined to overthrow him. It resisted everything he tried to do. It resisted his rearmament efforts.

After the Rhineland, France should have armed feverishly. It failed to do so.

After the Rhineland, France should have cultivated Russia. For since the French army, even had it wished, would have experienced difficulty in getting through the German fortifications in the Rhineland to help Austria, Czechoslovakia, and Poland, these little countries needed a big friend on the other side of Europe, and the only friend available was Soviet Russia. It was the national duty of France to cement the bonds with Moscow and include Russia in the French defense system. Russia had announced her readiness to co-operate. But the French bourgeoisie opposed this. And soon Spain became an additional stumbling block toward good relations between France and Russia.

18. *Before the Battle*

IN London I made an arrangement with Sydney R. Elliott, of *Reynolds News* to send weekly messages by cable or telephone from any place I visited. *Reynolds* is a large-circulation Sunday newspaper published by the British co-operative movement. It would pay me thirteen pounds per story. With my other sources of income this promised to make me rich, and I opened a checking account with a London bank. For I had been developing a personal syndicate which took the form of mailing eight or nine carbon copies of my *Nation* articles to publications in various European countries. The London *New Statesman and Nation* printed many of them, so did the Paris *L'Europe Nouvelle*, a Prague daily, a paper in Oslo, one in Stockholm, and the Prague German refugee weekly, *Weltbuehne*. Sometimes I placed contributions in Holland and Belgium too. At times the total income from one article amounted to $250. Now I had *Reynolds* in addition.

On my arrival in Madrid I wanted to make good with *Reynolds* and sought an interview with Prime Minister Manuel Azaña. I asked Alvarez del Vayo, the Socialist deputy, to speak to Azaña. Azaña had read my write-up of our talk in 1934. At that time I had laughed when he told me it required eighteen months to write a land law, and I said in my article that I had laughed. When del Vayo spoke to him, Azaña said, "Ah, Fischer, the man who laughed at me! But not more than I laugh at myself. Let him come." He fixed the date of April 4, 1936.

Constancia de la Mora, who later wrote *In Place of Splendor*, consented to act as my interpreter. I had met her at the del Vayos' and at the Araquistains'. She was a handsome dark Spanish woman, in revolt against her aristocratic, Catholic upbringing, who ran an antique and folk-art shop opposite the Cortes. Her grandfather was a Maura and a Prime Minister of Spain; her husband, Ignacio Hidalgo de Cisneros, served in the Spanish air force and, she told me, slept at the airfield several times a week lest the Fascist pilots seize it as part of a reactionary insurrection. Constancia was an excellent translator because she spoke English perfectly and understood the political subject matter as well.

Everything Azaña said he allowed me to publish—except the most interesting and piquant part of the interview.

The following is what I suppressed, at his bidding. I said: "Why don't you purge the army?"

"Why?" he asked, feigning innocence.

I said: "Some of the generals are opposed to your government."

"No," Azaña assured me, "they are all my friends."

"A few nights ago there were tanks on the streets and you were in the Ministry of Interior on the Puerta del Sol until two in the morning. You must have feared a revolt."

He denied it and attributed his presence there to another reason.

I told him I had heard stories of impending trouble by army generals.

"That is café gossip," he laughed.

I said I had heard it in the Cortes.

"Ah," Azaña declared, "that's a big café."

"Besides," he added as an afterthought and with a smile, "if it were true I wouldn't admit it to you."

He knew I knew and I knew he knew that the chiefs of the army were up to something. Azaña, in fact, took the ineffective precaution of shifting some of the most powerful and least dependable generals. Franco was moved from Madrid to the Canary Islands, Goded to the Balearic Islands and Mola to the Navarre province in Northern Spain. From these new posts they plotted the rebellion far from the eyes of the central authorities in the capital. If Azaña had arrested thirty disloyal generals, a million Spaniards might not have died in the war of 1936-39, and the country would not have been ruined, and Fascism would not have been encouraged to make new sallies against free countries. But Azaña was a liberal democrat and Spain was a liberal democracy, and Spaniards said they do not kill in cold blood.

Azaña, however, went so far as to admit that the moment was serious. He said, "The reactionaries of the Right have lost the capacity to rule Spain. They are half-republican, half-monarchist and they agree among themselves only upon the necessity of squeezing labor and perpetuating outmoded forms of land ownership and industrial management. They provoked the Asturias uprising in autumn, 1934, in order to justify draconic measures against the Left. They brushed aside the Constitution. As a result, we republicans were convinced that we would all be condemned to destruction unless the terror of the Right ended soon. The fruit of the conviction was the Popular Front which brought this cabinet into office."

On February 16, 1936, the Popular Front had won the national elections. It was not the first time and probably will not be the last time in a Latin country, however, that the losing side disputed the election figures. The Right, defeated by ballots, decided on bullets. Planning commenced immediately.

On election day, Portela Valladares was Prime Minister of Spain. At the beginning of the war, he sided with Franco. When the Italo-German invasion of his native land became too much for him, this tall, thin man with curly gray hair returned to his people and sided with the Loyalists. I heard him tell the October 1, 1937, session of the Cortes in Valencia that when the deputies before whom he stood were "legally elected" on February 16, 1936, leaders of the Right came to him and sought to dissuade him from surrendering his office to Azaña. The Right wanted Portela to ignore the democratic verdict. He refused. They thereupon prepared to use other means.

I asked Azaña how he proposed to rob the reactionaries of their power to keep the hands of the clock from moving. He outlined a mild land reform. He would strive to maintain the Popular Front fusion ticket intact and, for the rest, he would see. "The only Spaniard whose views are always right is Azaña," he suggested with an unliberal immodesty. "If all Spaniards were Azañistas everything would be all right."

I said, "That's what all dictators think. But if I judge you aright, you have no ambition to be a dictator."

Constancia argued with me on the wisdom of translating this literally, but I told her to go ahead.

"No," he replied, "I am no dictator. Yet what I said is true. I am no dictator but I would like everybody to agree with me out of his own free will."

I suppressed a laugh. Only dictatorships achieve "unanimity."

I rose to go. He sent greetings to Cisneros, Constancia's husband, and gave me an autographed photograph of himself.

I told him I hoped to be back in Madrid a year from now. "Will you still be here?" I asked.

"Yes," he replied, "if I don't get bored with politics."

Azaña was not a strong man. But he was in a strong position. The

Left hoped that his moderation would deter the Right from violent action against the Republic. Without Azaña's middle-of-the-road republicans the Left would have had no majority. To keep Azaña, the Left therefore stuck to middle-of-the-roadism. Azaña was thus a bulwark against radicalism, and some members of the Right appreciated his contribution to stability. Through Azaña Spain tried to avoid revolution. Spain needed a thorough reorganization of her national economy. Spain needed a French Revolution to drag it from the eighteenth century into the twentieth. Azaña expected to make this revolution by democratic evolution. Skeptical, the Socialists and Communists supported him because the alternative was terror from the Right.

But Spain's hope of internal peace was fast vanishing. The day before I saw Azaña I interviewed Francisco Largo Caballero who for forty years had been the leader of the Socialist and trade-union movements. "The reactionaries," he said, "can come back into office only through a coup d'état."

That was the key to the entire Spanish situation. The Right did not have a majority in Spain. It had economic power but not enough votes to get political power. It feared that without political power there would be encroachments on its economic power. When the republicans were divided, parliamentary manipulations had allowed the Right to oust the republicans. But now the republicans had formed the Popular Front bloc, and democracy offered no way of bringing the Right back into office. The Right's alternative was violence.

Spain had to do something about her poverty. "Hunger and unemployment," wrote Mr. E. G. de Caux, the pro-monarchist Madrid correspondent of the *London Times*, "are driving the inhabitants [of rural districts] to despair."

I wanted to see the countryside, for the peasant problem molded Spain's life. I discussed the matter with Minister of Agriculture Ruiz-Funes, and he arranged it. He gave me a car and a guide—Demetrio Delgado de Torres, a 1927 graduate of Cornell University. Jay Allen joined us. We traveled twelve hundred miles through the heart of peasant Spain.

Lester Ziffern, United Press Madrid representative, supplied me with figures on big landholdings in Spain: The Duke of Medinaceli owned 195,680 acres, the Duke of Peñaranda 104,345, the Duke of

Alba 89,625, the Duke of Comillas 42,795, and the Duke of Lerma 25,560. But millions of peasants did not even own a potato patch.

The trip reinforced my affection for Spain and my feeling that a storm was gathering around her head. As we drove along the highway and through villages, some people gave us the outstretched-arm Fascist salute. We were in a swell limousine. Our chauffeur said, "No, Señor, I am not that kind," and answered with the clenched fist; he was a Socialist. Elsewhere adults and children greeted us with the clenched fist. I had seen the same thing in Germany between 1930 and 1933.

The peasants were bitter. At Barcarrota, one Sunday afternoon, we chanced upon a Socialist meeting. Margarita Nelken, a member of the Cortes, had promised to speak but failed to appear. A crowd of 300 men and women were gathered in the Casa del Pueblo (people's house) with nothing to do and nobody to listen to.

"Jay," I said, "let's take over the meeting."

"How can we do that?"

"We'll ask them questions. I've done it in Russia often."

The local chairman was happy to have anything happen, so we marched up to the rickety wooden platform. Jay made a little introductory statement, explained who we were and that we had no political affiliations and only sought correct information, and then I put the questions.

"Why are you Socialists?"

"Because we want liberty," one woman replied.

"Because we don't want to starve," another added.

"Don't you eat enough?" I asked. The reply was a burst of laughter. I suggested that those who ate meat twice a week, raise their hands. No hand went up.

"Who eats meat once a week?" Not a hand went up. A woman rose and explained that the regular diet of most of them consisted of vegetable soup, black coffee, bread—when they had it—and sometimes sardines.

"Don't the children have milk?" I inquired. Several mothers with babies on their arms, pointed to their breasts.

"Yes," one said, "while they get it from us, but not later."

I now came to the subject which interested me most.

"Have you received land from the new government?"

Yes. All of them had received land. They hoped now they would live better. But they had to eat until the new crop came in and they had no money. Moreover, they would need money for tools, animals, and seed.

"We have land now, but it is too little for a decent living," one man volunteered. Applause greeted this statement.

"How is it," I probed, "that Azaña, who is a bourgeois, has given you land?"

"The Socialists forced him!"

"We made him do it!"

"He had to!"

These exclamations expressed the sense of the meeting.

"And won't you all now become little capitalists?"

This provoked much mirth.

"Maybe we will some day live like human beings instead of animals."

"What about the landlords?" I asked. Derisive laughter.

"Let them weep a bit as we have been weeping all our lives," a mother proposed.

"Suppose the Rights came back and took the land away," I asked.

"They will have to kill us first!"

"They will never be allowed to come back to office."

"They cannot force us to starve any longer!"

The peasants wanted something and quick. They did not know how long the Popular Front regime would last. To forestall trouble, the official Institute of Land Reform published a circular in the province of Caceres asking landlords to rent some of their land to landless peasants. Rent it! A month later, when I spoke to Señor de la Fuente of the Institute he told me that not a single proprietor had replied. One fine morning, therefore, the peasants who owned a yoke of mules—the "yunteros"—but no land, marched to the estates in a body with their animals and plows, and each marked off a modest parcel as his field. He tilled it and paid rent for it. This was illegal. But it showed the mood of the country, and the Institute thereupon did its best to legalize the peasants' acts. The Civil Guard, now subject to the orders of a progressive government, did nothing to obstruct the farmers.

In the neighborhood province of Badajoz, hard by the Portuguese frontier, which we visited, agricultural conditions were even worse than in Caceres. Eighty-five percent of the population lived by the land. There were 175,000 families in the villages. But 2,946 individuals owned forty percent of the soil. Here too the yunteros took land in the spring of 1936 and then signed leases for it.

In Caceres, 41,499 yunteros were settled on estates in this fashion during March and April, 1936, and in Badajoz, 24,702. That was the extent of the land reform. In other provinces it had scarcely started.

We talked to peasants everywhere, in fields behind the plow, in mountain villages, in churches. We interviewed landlords and estate managers.

I sat on a stone post in the central square of the white town of Badajoz waiting for Torres, Jay Allen, and a Spanish official who had gone into the café for a drink. I made these notes in my black diary: "The peasants are no longer in a desperate or violent mood. Azaña's modest reform could inaugurate a period of peace and adjustment in the countryside. The peasants will not allow themselves to be driven off the land. They will support the Popular Front and resist the politicians of the Right.

"But—the feudal barons of Spain are wedded to the ancient Roman concept of property. They will not brook the slightest interference. Devoid of social outlook, they see in the forced renting of part of their estates the doom of the divine right of landowners. Caceres and Badajoz are a portent to them. For the moment, they cannot resist the government. They will hate it the more."

If the landlords had employed the peasants and tilled all their land they might have insisted on their property privileges with at least a show of justice. But when a country is being ruined by a small group of private owners there is a higher morality and patriotism which warrants change. Spain or the landlords? That was the question. The landlords answered: To hell with Spain. We are the only Spain.

That was the cause of the war in Spain.

I returned from the provinces to Madrid and then proceeded to Barcelona whence I planned to go to Italy. On April 16, 1936, writing to *The New Republic,* I reported that the Right reactionaries were depressed and disorganized, that their chief hope was a violent coup d'état with the aid of the army and the Civil Guard.

That hope was fulfilled. With the aid of German and Italian consuls and other agents in Spain—the pertinent documents were seized in the German consulate in Barcelona when the War started and have been published in book form—the reactionaries marshaled their forces, and started their propaganda barrage abroad.

Meanwhile, the Republic slept.

19. *England Helps Mussolini*

THE Columbus was the most expensive hotel in the city.

But in Genoa one had to live in the Columbus, especially since it was not far from the harbor waters which the Navigator had sailed.

If Mussolini had used the money he spent on the conquest of Ethiopia to pull down the slums of Genoa and build homes for the poor, more Italians would have found work and happiness than can ever go to Abyssinia.

In the window of the *Corriera della Serra* in Rome, the gold cross of a Catholic bishop was displayed. He had given it to finance the war in Africa. The Queen contributed her wedding ring. The peasant woman in black contributed her wedding ring.

Two shots of propaganda in the arm seem to be worth one more hole in the belt. The war in Ethiopia caused some unrest in Italian industrial towns—baby riots in Spezia, Milan, Turin, and Genoa—but Mussolini knew how to arouse the patriotism of the masses. Abyssinia left them cold. Positive propaganda failed. But "Hate England" propaganda worked.

Sanctions would have worked, too. Factories were closing down for lack of imported raw materials. Food was scarcer. An officially inspired cookbook taught housewives how to prepare "sanction recipes."

On the streets of Rome, I saw many posters showing a turkey and a rabbit eating lettuce leaves. The leaves were shaped to form the word sanctions. Turkeys and rabbits, that is, would destroy the effect of sanctions. (I know nothing about turkeys. But I know that rabbits are anti-Bolshevik. During the first Five Year Plan the Bolsheviks distributed a poster depicting the rapid breeding possibilities of rabbits. Two rabbits soon become eight, eight sixty-four, and before long rabbits would replenish the Soviet earth and compensate for the slaughter of cattle following collectivization. But the rabbits, inspired by Trotzky or someone else, refused to breed. I had a suspicion in Rome in April, 1936, that rabbits might also be anti-Fascist.)

330

The sanctions applied by the League of Nations late in 1935 could ultimately have paralyzed Italy's economy which is naturally weak. But Italy was winning the war in Ethiopia with greater speed than Anthony Eden had anticipated, and the rains did not come. For quicker effect, an additional sanction was needed: oil. Without oil there is no modern war. Mussolini had reserves, but if the big sellers of petroleum stopped selling it the Italian expeditionary force in Ethiopia would be checked.

Breckinridge Long, the United States Ambassador in Rome, told me that he opposed the application of oil sanctions. He worked against their application. He submitted his views to Washington. And since the United States is one of the largest oil exporters, America's attitude would be decisive, for if one country continued to supply Italy, all would. On the day that the idea of oil sanctions was definitely shelved Mr. Long told me he was very happy because he had helped avert a European war. I wonder. Sanctions had not induced Mussolini to go to war against England and the other nations which applied them. But oil sanctions were more serious and might really cripple Italy in Africa. Therefore, the argument ran, Mussolini would go to war. Because oil sanctions would cripple Italy and force Mussolini to stop the war in Ethiopia he would attack Europe. That was not very logical or realistic but it helped the Fascist dictatorship to its first sizable conquest.

When I interviewed Sir Eric Drummond in the British Embassy he seemed to be in a daze. He had become the ambassador of a defeated country. England defeated by Italy. England defeated by England. Ramsay MacDonald and Sir John Simon could give the British public all kinds of excuses. But in Rome everyone knew what had happened. Drummond knew. Mussolini knew. Drummond, a few months ago the mouthpiece of Britain defiant, now was very small and uncomfortable. Italians laughed and said to me, "When the British lion roars you can see his false teeth."

Mussolini worked hard against the British. When the question of oil sanctions was acute, he summoned the Soviet Ambassador, Boris Stein, and argued against the wisdom of Soviet collaboration with England. Mussolini showed Stein a telegram from Ambassador Grandi in London on Great Britani's pro-German orientation. "Here," Mussolini said, handing him the wire, "those are your British friends."

Count René de Chambrun, French Ambassador, who each time we met reminded me that he was an American, too, sat in the glorious villa built by Michelangelo and was amused. The whole situation made him think of a play that was running in New York called *Idiot's Delight*. "I'm one of the idiots," he exclaimed.

Mussolini had his soul's desire, Abyssinia. The British comforted themselves with the thought that he would have to come to them for the money to develop it. Another British fallacy.

The Italian people gained glory and a reduced standard of living. Edmondo Rossoni, the fascist Minister of Agriculture, admitted it. But it was really not so serious, he added. "We Italians don't need as much as you Americans. I agree with the Catholics that you cannot have happiness on earth." I gathered up my notes and said good-by.

He said, "Now we will have peace."

I said, "I hope so but I doubt it."

20. *The Statue of Liberty*

THERE is a statue of liberty in Moscow. It stands opposite the building of the Moscow Soviet, and on its base is inscribed the text of the Soviet Constitution.

Even the rigidly dictatorial Bolsheviks have painted freedom and democracy as their goals. Freedom has always been man's great ideal.

The experience of the Soviet Union and of all dictatorships has demonstrated that without freedom there can be no full stomachs. Nor can there be any economic security without civil rights. What is a job when you can be lifted out of it by the secret police on no charge or on an unknown charge and imprisoned or shot without open trial and without friends or relatives knowing anything about you? Sometimes a Soviet official disappears in the night. His wife immediately begins leaving food parcels for him at the GPU prison. She has asked no questions because she will get no answers. Then one day, the guard at the gate rejects her parcel. That is how she learns that her husband has been shot. She never sees the body.

Citizens of dictatorships want most of all to be free. In 1935, when Moscow announced a forthcoming constitution which would introduce new liberties, real happiness pervaded the land.

It is possible to explain or excuse a dictatorship or condone its sins. But nobody except those who dictate ever like a dictatorship. I was pro-Soviet despite the dictatorship. I knew its crimes better than most because I mingled with Russians more than most foreigners. But I always looked forward to the growth of democracy at the expense of the dictatorship.

I realized the difficulties. Democracy was not born overnight in England or France.

Russia's cultural backwardness militates against democracy. In 1930, I went to Kazakhstan to witness the opening of the Turkestan-Siberian railway. It traverses country through which the legions of Genghis Khan and Tamerlane marched to India. It is on the borders of China. The railway was built, for the most part through desert, by kulaks from Russia and by moon-faced Kazaks. Those Kazaks had

333

never seen a railroad. Bill Shatoff, Chicago I.W.W. who supervised the job, said that the men had lady fingers from riding horses all their lives. Women do the hard work among Kazaks. The women are great beauties. On that trip, I visited Samarkand, Bokhara, and Tashkent. I stood by the tomb of Tamerlane.

I had gone down in a special train with foreign correspondents—Duranty, Lyons, Jim Mills, Mollie Cogswell, William Henry Chamberlin, Deuss, Smolar, Baseches, and several Germans who were afraid to ride across one of the new railway bridges and walked over while Americans, including Mrs. Eugene Lyons, rode jubilantly on the locomotive fender—and with a group of Soviet authors, among them Pilniak, Leonov, and Vsevolod Ivanov. The train had a de luxe diner with large mirrors in its walls. At station stops, the Kazak women came on board, and when they discovered the mirrors they were mad with delight. They had never before seen their reflections. Mirrors had not yet reached them; and they could not see their features in water because they inhabited a waterless plain. The Kazaks were just graduating from the nomad stage of civilization, but many of them still followed their flocks, and the Soviet government sent peripatetic hospitals after them, and wherever the Kazaks pitched their cylindrical felt yurts the hospitals halted to administer medical aid. What does democracy, what do votes, mean to such people? Nothing.

Liberty meant nothing to the Kazaks because they always enjoyed it and nobody had yet taken it away from them. The Moscow professor who needed freedom had much less than a Kazak. But the professor, taught by centuries of Russian oppression, made no demands. Russia's tradition of terror, Russia's vast sparsely settled areas, and Russia's low level of culture facilitated the work of the Bolshevik dictatorship. There was no active pressure from below for democracy. The Constitution was a gift from Olympus.

My article in *The Nation*, June 17, 1936, was the first printed anywhere in the world to reveal the contents of the new "Stalinist" Constitution. I had sent it from Moscow by mail and begged *The Nation* to use it without delay. The credit, however, is scarcely mine. Karl Radek simply told me about it. He said very little. But it enabled me to talk knowingly to Bukharin about the Constitution, and Bukharin, seeing I was informed, divulged more data on the document. So did Mikhalsky, like Bukharin and Radek a member of the Constitutional Drafting Commission. Then I went back to Radek and he, thinking he had given me all the facts I had, must have felt there was no use keeping the secret and spilled some more.

In the discussion that followed, I said to Radek, "The question of the Constitution is a question of the GPU."

Radek is a man who never stops talking and who knows all the answers. If I looked him up after a trip to America, he would ask me my impressions.

I might reply, "It seems to me that Roosevelt is facing a difficult choice." Whereupon Radek would explain in a half hour torrent just what Roosevelt's policy was and where America stood.

But when I said, "The question of the Constitution is a question of the GPU," he was dumbstruck. He walked up and down the room for full two minutes, and then exploded, "You are right."

The Soviet Constitution of 1936 is a significant state paper despite the fact that it has been honored in the breach. The practical results of its loud promulgation have been disappointingly negative. But the reasons for its failure supply the key to the prerequisites of success.

The Constitution, now the supreme law of the Soviet Union, does two things: it describes a system of government and it enunciates a bill of rights. The bill of rights is inspiring. But there is nothing in the system of government to safeguard the rights. The popular enjoyment of the rights therefore depends on the good will of the persons or person who control the government, and they have chosen to ignore the rights. One of the latest violations of the bill of rights is the introduction of payment for tuition in high schools and colleges. This contravenes Article 121 of the Constitution which says, "Citizens of the Soviet Union have a right to education. This right is implemented by universal, compulsory elementary education and by free education, including university education." The government did not ask the people or parliament whether it could introduce paid education. The Constitution was not amended to allow paid education. The government simply decreed paid tuition by ukase and that is all there was to it except for the pain in the hearts of many silent people.

How could anybody protest? The bill of rights in the Constitution grants and "guarantees by law" "freedom of speech, freedom of the press, freedom of assembly and meetings, and freedom of street marches and demonstrations." In life, these liberties are non-existent. If a citizen were to try to publish an article or letter or make a speech attacking the Soviet government for violating the Constitution by instituting paid tuition he would soon find himself in jail.

When the state or its subsidiaries own all the radio broadcasting stations, printing presses, printing paper, and meeting halls and when one party directs the state, civil rights are illusory. They can be suspended with impunity. The Constitution grants "the right to labor," "the right to leisure," "the right to old-age care," equality to women, and equality of race and nationality. Some of these rights do actually exist, and they are important. But not one of them is inalienable. They are all at the mercy of the dictator and could be scrapped without a squeak from the people. Indeed, such is the terror and the perversion of education, that men rise up to applaud whenever privileges are abridged or annulled.

The essence of democracy is the effective right to criticize, oppose, and oust the government in office and substitute another government based on another party or parties. The Soviet regime permits only a single political party. The trouble with democracy in the West is that the political parties on which it rests are frequently so corrupt, unrepresentative, and supine. But even where the ruling class, in the political garb of one party or the other, has an almost permanent tenure in office, the existence of an organized opposition, of free trade unions and of a free press, exercises a salutary sobering influence on government. Labor in the United States, for instance, has no major nation-wide party of its own, yet the competition between the Democratic and Republican parties, both of them capitalistic, impels them to consider the wishes and often yield to the pressure of labor whose votes might swing an election. As long as there are free elections a minority can fight for its rights. Indeed, where the rivalry between majority party and minority party is keen, a second minority, political or religious or professional, may dictate policy.

In the Soviet Union, there is no protection for a political minority. Therefore, there is no guarantee of democracy. There can be no democracy without a guarantee of democracy.

In the Soviet Union, political opponents and political minorities are purged by shooting, exile, or imprisonment. Purges are a permanent feature of dictatorship. They are the dictatorship's substitute for real elections.

The virility and viability of a democracy are determined by the relationship between executive, legislative, and judicial divisions of the state.

In most democracies—those that remain—parliament, fearing encroachment on its powers, is jealous of a strong executive. Actually, democracy has been destroyed where the executive was weak. In Germany and Italy, Fascism triumphed when hopelessly divided, obstreperous parliaments hampered and thwarted pusillanimous executives. A forceful chief executive can serve as a bulwark against dictatorship.

In Russia, however, the salutary give-and-take and friendly rivalry and balance between executive and legislative departments have never entered into popular experience. Czarist Russia never knew parliamentarism. The Duma was unimportant in national life. The Czarist administration was weak. The Kerensky government lacked backbone. Russia yearned for powerful leadership that would keep the country on an even keel. The Bolsheviks preached dictatorship and the nation accepted dictatorship as the inescapable alternative to chaos.

The voice of the people was to be expressed through the soviets. But soviets are executive contrivances. The village soviet is the village's government, and the city soviet is city hall. Independent legislatures reflecting the will of the people were never a feature of Bolshevik ideas or intentions. The Bolsheviks regard checks and balances as time-wasters.

The Constitution of 1936 did not change this in the slightest. Parliament does not control the executive departments. It merely elects them. But the dictator, elected by no one, runs the elections. He is chief executive because he holds in his hand all the sources of real power—secret police, army, party, treasury, propaganda. The courts, where they function at all, are subservient to the executive.

The Constitution of 1936 did nothing to curb the dictator. How could it? He wrote it.

Nevertheless, the Constitution was not all empty words and hollow promises. It gave the peasants equal voting rights with the workingmen; theretofore the vote of a factory hand had been worth five votes of a farm hand. It also restored the franchise to priests, former kulaks, and former officials of the Czarist regime.

At a meeting in the Kremlin of collectivized peasants, a farm boy making a speech revealed that his father had been a kulak. Without rising from his seat, Stalin exclaimed, "It doesn't matter whose son you are but who *you* are and how you work." This reversed the cruel Soviet practice of visiting the sins of the fathers on their children. The audience broke into cheers.

The internal enemy, defeated, could be treated with a touch of charity. That is why the Constitution looked like a new departure. Where there is less fear there can be more freedom. The chief change registered by the Constitution was the absorption of the peasantry—seventy percent of the population—into the Socialist system. Collectivization enabled Moscow to control the country's farms. It could never have controlled 130,000,000 individual peasants.

Collectivization, costly and bloody, promised to give Russia bread and rid it of famine. It promised to mitigate the fierce struggle between city and countryside. It promised domestic pacification. Hence the Constitution.

The Constitution was an attempt to stimulate peasant loyalty to the Soviet regime and to win over recalcitrant elements in the towns. The emphasis of Soviet propaganda now ceased to be upon Communist party supremacy and upon class rule. On May 4, 1935, Stalin drank a toast at a Kremlin reception of Red Army commanders to "non-party Bolsheviks." A non-member of the Communist party could be a Bolshevik. The Communist party thereby officially lost the political pre-eminence which it had already lost in fact. The Young Communist League had been told to keep out of politics. The Old Bolsheviks Society was suppressed. Non-Communists were being appointed to important industrial jobs. The regime charged leading Communists with sabotage and treachery. The Communist party was being purged continuously. That undermined its prestige.

The Communist party was now merged with the government. Lenin and Bukharin had always insisted on a strict demarcation between the functions of the party and those of the government so that the party could check, direct, and watch the government. But now party and government became one in personnel. Nobody could criticize the government from the outside, from party headquarters. *Izvestia*, the daily organ of the government, began to look like a carbon copy of *Pravda*, the daily organ of the party. Most of the important men in the party held pivotal government posts. Almost all, in fact, except—Stalin. He was not a government official. He was a party official. That enabled him to condemn the government's mistakes while refusing responsibility for them. He was the check and balance on the government; he alone. By merging the party with the state apparatus, Stalin enhanced his own power and destroyed the Communist party as a unique revolutionary instrument.

Thus the very same process which democratically equalized peasants with workers and non-Communists with Communists also lifted Stalin higher towards his goal of personal dictatorship.

The Constitution crowned a development which increased the political weight of the peasantry and of non-Communists. It was therefore a move to the Right, to conservatism. In literature, art, international affairs, and home politics the trend was likewise towards conservatism.

Stalin was attempting to dismantle the class state established in 1917 and create a nation. He wished to eliminate centrifugal, disruptive influences and substitute unity. He was impressed by the power which whipped-up nationalism gave Hitler and he wanted to acquire a similar power. He did not know how to do it. He tried history as a means to his end. He tried unifying patriotism. He tried to revive old traditions. He has even endeavored to brighten the memories of Czarist Russia and to regain the territories of Czarist Russia.

Stalin is the great centralizer. The central core of the Soviet Union is the old Russia of the ethnical unit called Great Russia. There are an estimated sixty-eight million Great Russians. But to the south are twenty-five million Ukrainians; to the west four million White Russians; on the Volga are the Tatars, Chuvashi, Mordvinians, and a host of other minor nationalities; in the warm Caucasus live eight million Georgians, Armenians, and Turks; Siberia has scores of nationalities.

To these non-Russians and to millions of Russian workingmen and peasants, the Russian nation had never meant anything. Nationalism and patriotism before the Revolution did not exist for them. The Czarist government was the symbol of oppression. There had been, up to 1917, a Russian nation in name, but not in fact.

Leninism is the doctrine of internationalism. The Soviet regime had always refrained from teaching patriotism or any type of nationalism. "Workers of the world, unite" was Moscow's primary slogan. If Soviet citizens boasted of Soviet achievements they attributed them to the superiority of Socialist methods and ideas, never to the fact that those methods and ideas were being applied in Russia. On the contrary, they always deplored the fact that backward Russia was the first country to introduce Socialism. In Germany, England, or America, they asserted, it would have brought better fruit.

Yet, beginning in 1935, first hesitantly, and then in roaring crescendo, the Soviet propaganda orchestra played patriotic themes. The word *"rodina"*—fatherland—emerged into official usage; not "socialist fatherland" as before, but simply fatherland. Poets sang "to our beautiful country." Editorials in 1935 urged "love of country." On May 1, 1935, an article by Vasilkovsky said, "There is no more grateful task and no more important political task than to encourage and fan the sacred flame of love of fatherland." Such terms were once anathema to Bolsheviks. D. Zaslavsky, an official journalist, believed that these words "once hated by millions, have lost their old meaning. . . . They sound different now." I doubt it. They still sounded reactionary to Soviet ears.

The new emphasis on "Soviet patriotism" was quickly followed by something far worse: Russian nationalism. This conformed to Stalin's strategy of doing a job in two or more installments. The first stage was called "Soviet patriotism." The second stage was Russian nationalism.

The campaign commenced with a bang in 1937. An editorial in the *Pravda* of January 15, 1937, was entitled, "The Great Russian People." It of course quoted Marx to prove the point of the greatness of the Russian people, and it attacked Hitler. "We love our homeland," it said. "We love our great, strong and picturesque Russian language. It is becoming an international language." But what about the scores of millions of Soviet citizens who were not Russians?

Sergei Eisenstein, with no great enthusiasm, was then working on his *Alexander Nevsky* film about a great battle on the ice of Lake Peipus (Chudskoe) in the thirteenth century between Russians under Nevsky and Teuton knights in armor. Unfortunately, Karl Marx had referred to this Baltic combat in one of his many writings, and this quotation was used repeatedly by the Soviet press in an effort to instill nationalistic and anti-German feelings. That was the purpose of the Eisenstein picture.

Glinka, whom *Pravda* proudly called "the creator of Russian national opera," had written *A Life for the Czar* which the students in pre-revolutionary days always booed from the gallery. The Czarist regime regarded it as a patriotic opera. The Big Theatre in Moscow prepared now to perform it under a new title, *Ivan Susanin*—the name of the hero. *Pravda* linked this performance, like everything else, with Stalin. It was part of his "orders to create a Soviet classic opera." So the creation of a Soviet classic opera consisted in changing the name of a chauvinistic Czarist opera.

March 11, 1937, was the two hundredth anniversary of the birth of a Russian architect named Bazhenov. The Bolshevik press declared that "Bazhenov's talents fill us, Soviet architects, with a feeling of national pride." Stalin was obviously attempting to induce Soviet art and science to drink at the ancient, rather muddy fountain of Russia's past. On March 14, 1937, an extensive *Pravda* article dealt with the great mathematician Lobachevsky, long dead, "whose discoveries are closely linked with the national nature of Russian science." A few days later—this intensity is characteristic of Communist propaganda—*Pravda* devoted another many-column article to Kovalevsky, a Russian paleontologist who died in 1883.

Two days later, *Pravda* launched a violent attack on Professor Pokrovsky, Soviet Russia's leading historian of Czarist Russia, and an old honored Bolshevik.

When Pokrovsky's *Brief History of Russia* first appeared—it was published by the International Publishers of New York in 1933—Lenin wrote him a letter which read, "Comrade Pokrovsky, I congratulate you very heartily on your success. I like your new book *Brief History of Russia* immensely. It reads with tremendous interest. It should, in my opinion, be translated into the European languages." But that was Lenin, and Lenin was dead. Now the Stalin press branded Pokrovsky as an "anti-Marxist." His school had engaged in "wrecking." What were his sins? He spoke of Czarist Russia as a country of "Oblomovs," sluggish and undynamic. He said that the blood of the Great Russians ("Great" ethnographically in contrast to the "Little Russians" or Ukrainians) was eighty percent Finnish. Pokrovsky, moreover, was not harsh to the invading Tatars. (In Czarist times there was a tradition of anti-Tatarism which the Soviet regime had formerly rejected.) Greatest crime of all: Pokrovsky described Czar Peter the Great as a reactionary. Karl Marx, according to *Pravda*, considered Russia's conquest of the Baltic provinces as a progressive move, whereas Pokrovsky looked upon it as simple robbery. The political purpose of this campaign now begins to emerge. The reinterpretation of patriotism in 1936 and the rewriting of Russian history in 1937, leads straight to the exploits of the Red Army after the Nazi-Soviet pact of August 23, 1939.

The one hundred and twenty-fifth anniversary of the Battle of

Borodino was celebrated for the first time in Soviet Russia on September 2, 1937. Soviet students, the press reported, placed flowers at the monuments of the Russian regiments that stopped Napoleon's army. This was "a glorious page of the past of our country." General Kutuzov, commander of the Russian army that resisted Napoleon, was lauded highly and in order to make this Czarist Prince—his title was omitted from the propaganda—palatable to a Soviet generation that had grown up to despise him, the press said that Czar Alexander I was envious of and opposed to him. "The Russian nation," said *Pravda*, "saved the independence of the fatherland in 1812. The great conqueror collided with a great nation and was beaten." This anti-Bolshevik version of history was intended to instill confidence in Soviet peoples for the struggle with Hitler. Actually, it sounded like Hitlerism and very little like the language of Bolshevism. It was the language in which the Czarist Russian encyclopedia referred to Napoleon and Prince Kutuzov.

Now commenced a Big Bertha barrage for the more extensive employment of the Russian language. Under the Leninist policy towards national minorities, the numerous ethnic units of the Soviet federation used their own tongues and learned Russian if they wished. This began to change. "Fascists and Trotzkyists" were accused of endeavoring to cleanse the Ukrainian language of "Russianisms." The bourgeois nationalists of the ethnic republics were interfering with the study of the Russian language. But the Russian language had "wonderful richness." It was "a treasury of world culture and had become the property of all the working people of the Soviet peoples." The policy theretofore had been to win the sympathy of Czarist Russia's subject peoples by making them feel they enjoyed cultural autonomy and did not have to speak Russian or accept Russian culture. Stalin was reverting to the hated Czarist policy of Russification which bred revolt in the hearts of non-Russians.

Apparently, Stalin imagined that if Soviet citizens were proud of Kutuzov, Peter the Great and the rout of the Teuton knights on Eisenstein's artificial ice they would be more loyal to the Bolshevik regime. Instead of meat he was giving them stale circuses.

This whole tendency revealed the narrow limitations of Stalin's mentality and statesmanship. He was searching for new psychological weapons to cement a national solidarity which he must have felt did not exist.

Brittle Marxists may react against concentration on Stalin's person as a clue to Soviet events. There is nothing in Marxism which denies the role of the individual in history. He is sometimes the vehicle for social forces. Sometimes he bends them to his purposes. Sometimes he misdirects them. Maybe Hitler is Germany's destiny. But maybe his judgment has been wrong; maybe he has made a mistake. When so much power is centered in one person, when his wishes, bad dreams, bad moods, and bad health influence state decisions it would be blind dogmatism to deny him a major part in his country's history. Without personal history, historic analysis becomes fatalism. Abstract social and economic circumstances are static without the impact of persons aiming to change them. A class or a party can alter history. Why not one man who monopolizes the power of the party and the class?

Suppose Lenin had never lived. Suppose Lenin were still alive. Suppose Stalin and Trotzky had never quarreled. Soviet history would, of course, be different. Has not the Bolshevik regime fixed its attitude towards persons in accordance with their birth and training? Do not Stalin's origin, biography and personal characteristics influence his acts? They do.

One evening, Stalin and Prime Minister Vyascheslav Molotov went to the opera, sat in a hidden box, and saw *Lady Macbeth of Mzensk* by Shostakovitch, a young man who had been hailed both at home and abroad as Soviet Russia's greatest composer. The opera, which burlesqued the vulgarity and emptiness of pre-Revolutionary Russian life, had been running throughout the Soviet Union since the spring of 1934, and had received enthusiastic reviews in the Bolshevik press. Soviet agencies helped to finance performances of it in foreign countries. Whenever prominent foreign musicians or theater people came to Moscow they were shown *Lady Macbeth*. But now Stalin saw it and didn't like it.

Stalin is about as much of a musician as I am. But since the opera did not find favor in his proletarian highness's ears it was taken off immediately. Two days after he attended the performance, the mighty *Pravda*, January 28, 1936, printed a smashing attack on Shostakovitch and his art. It was not music at all, just "a leftist muddle." Shostakovitch did not understand what the Soviet audience wanted. (They had packed every performance. He did not understand what Stalin wanted.) He was "formalistic," whatever that implies.

At this signal, all Soviet artists—musicians, authors, scenario writers, playwrights, poets—began beating their breasts in public and announcing that they too had sinned, they too were "formalist," "leftist." The Second Moscow Theatre, run by eager experimenters, closed down.

Stalin and Molotov again went to the opera. This time they viewed Djerzhinsky's *Quiet Flows the Don*. They liked its Russian folk tunes. Djerzhinsky was made a Soviet idol.

Stalin's wife, Nadezhda Alleluyeva, died after a very brief illness on November 9, 1932. She was thirty; he fifty-three. He was apparently very attached to her. She had studied in a textile institute, was modest, and always avoided the limelight. Her father had been a Russian revolutionary workingman. Wives in Russia play no role as wives. If they are not personally entitled to prominence or popularity, they are unknown; they do not enjoy any reflected glory from their husbands. The death of Stalin's wife was his personal tragedy and had nothing to do with the public life of the country. That was the Soviet code. Russians were therefore surprised and shocked when Alleluyeva received a large public funeral in which trade unions and government officials marched behind the bier. The Prime Minister of Turkey sent a telegram of condolence to Stalin. So did Matsuoka, chief of the Japanese delegation to Geneva and later Foreign Minister. So did many diplomats stationed in Moscow. Their expressions were printed in the Soviet press. Such publicity was startling. It had never happened before.

Alleluyeva was not cremated. Cremation—except in the case of Lenin—is a normal and accepted Bolshevik practice. Alleluyeva's family could not have objected on religious grounds because it was a revolutionary family. Stalin must have objected. I do not know the reason why and I have no psychological explanation. But probably there is one to be found deeply embedded in a Georgian atavism. Stalin's conduct and policies cannot be divorced entirely from his racial and cultural origins.

Stalin caused a pale pink marble bust to be erected on his wife's grave. It is not a likeness but rather a portrait of idealized womanhood.

When Alleluyeva died a Communist friend of mine who knew Stalin said to me, "This will affect Stalin and therefore all of us very much." Perhaps it has. I don't know.

The new conservative current deposited strange fish on Soviet shores. The Cossacks, symbol of tyranny and agents of Czarist Russian cruelty, were restored in their right to wear their ancient uniform and to appear in public as an organized unit.

Another step towards the rehabilitation of Czarist culture was the introduction of titles in the Red Army. Officers in the Bolshevik armed forces had formerly carried titles designating their functions: battalion commander, regimental commander, and so forth. Why? Because the old titles had a reactionary, hateful ring. Now the old names were revived. Red Army officers are now called Lieutenant, Captain, Major, and Colonel. To the Russian mind, the word "Colonel" summons up memories of Czarism. It is synonymous with Czarist rule. In the Soviet lexicon, it had been a word of opprobrium. It was in a class with "Prince" and "Baron." Stalin gave it Soviet franchise.

Then came a change which affected every Soviet woman, man, and child. It too marked the rightward course. It concerned sex relations. ZAGS in Russia means the official marriage, divorce, births, and deaths bureau. Each Moscow district has one. Most of them are old retail stores cleaned and repainted and broken up into cubicles separated by wooden partitions. Whenever I had nothing to do I would drop into a Zags and sit at the elbow of the registrar or woman lawyer who was there for free consultation. The employees were all women. They looked neat, worked efficiently, and took great pride in the attractive appearance of their bureaus. In several Zags bureaus they knew me from frequent visits throughout the years and I felt quite at home.

A woman holding a boy of six by the hand came in to register the birth of a child. She seemed very happy. I listened while she gave all the necessary information. She was sitting on a chair at the registrar's desk and I was sitting at the desk too.

"Why did you have the baby?" I asked the mother.

"I wanted it," she answered quite naturally.

"Do you know how not to have babies?" I inquired.

"Yes."

I asked her why she had waited so long between children. She said, "My husband received a raise last year and we got a second room."

Such a conversation was not unusual. Russians are quite uninhibited and they don't mind intimate questions. I once took an Open

Road tourist group to the Moscow Institute for the Care of Mother and Child which had interesting exhibits. While we were interviewing the director there was one Russian visitor, a young girl, viewing a collection of fetuses in jars.

"Are you a medical student?" I asked.

"No," she replied.

"What makes you so interested in the exhibits?"

"I am going to my village this summer when I get vacation from the university, and the peasants frequently ask about pregnancy, contraceptives, and such things, and I came here to look around."

"How old are you?" I asked.

"Nineteen," she replied.

"Have you had sexual intercourse?"

"No," she replied as simply as if I had asked her whether she had a job.

"Why not?" I inquired.

"Because I don't love anybody."

Then the director, Dr. Berkovitch, a brilliant woman, took up the question. I translated the interview to the Americans present. One of them said, "You ought to try those questions on an American college girl."

Because the Soviet peoples are so unspoiled and richly endowed, and because I have learned to love them I mourn all the more their prolonged and deep suffering.

Throughout the Revolution, sex relations in the Soviet Union have been abnormal on account of difficult living conditions. The Bolsheviks never tried to break up the family, and most of the Soviet leaders live orthodox family lives. But shortage of housing facilities and of commodities, as well as the storm of Revolution have shaken many family ties and prevented others from being made. The burgher who cannot marry without a four-room apartment and an eight-piece dining room set is silly. Four walls and a bed, or at least a mattress, however, are rather important prerequisites of the married life. But alas, in many Soviet cities, they are unobtainable. The rich have as many children as they can stand. But the poor have as many as they can afford. After that, in Russia, the women had abortions.

Russians marry early, and Russian men are often devoted fathers. But when wages are low and sleeping space is cramped, they live together without marrying or they marry and limit their offspring.

The number of abortions in the Soviet Union was excessive. The sensible or the Marxist way would have been to increase the sale of contraceptives or/and improve living standards. Birth-control information can be had for the asking in the Soviet Union. But contraceptives are scarce and often defective and were never sufficiently popularized.

With the normal Bolshevik penchant for going to extremes, the Soviet government swung from complete freedom of abortions to their complete abolition by the law of June 27, 1936. The Soviet alternative to no-abortions, however, was not birth control; it was a more-babies campaign, and the proscription of abortions was accompanied by prizes for bigger families just as in Fascist Italy.

The promulgation of the new anti-abortion law followed a month's public debate. The government published the draft of the law on May 26, and invited free nation-wide discussion. This was a very democratic procedure and encouraged the belief that the Constitution really meant something.

The Soviet government got more than it bargained for. The draft legislation was universally condemned. The Bolshevik press printed the denunciations. It published the resolutions adopted by factories and workers' clubs criticizing the law. "I have one child nearly three years old," wrote a woman in the *Moscow Daily News*, "and would be glad to have another. But we are already four people, including our maid, in one small room, and in my opinion it would be a crime to bring another child into the over-crowded room." Yet under the new law that woman would have to have a second and third and fourth child. For she is not entitled to an abortion, and in tightly packed rooms, without toilet facilities, even the best contraceptives may not work. "In a room of twenty square meters live my mother, my husband, and our two children, and I. I want another child but can I afford it in these circumstances?" wrote another Soviet mother.

Before 1936, the Soviet excess of births over deaths was officially stated to be over three million persons annually. Why should the Bolsheviks have wanted a still larger population? In my articles against the abortion law I made comparisons with the Nazi statutes in this field. I talked to Commissar of Health Kaminsky and vehemently attacked the law. He replied, "The Boss says we must have more children."

In the years that have elapsed since 1936, the shortage of rubber goods, babies' equipment, and apartment houses has been aggravated in Soviet Russia. But the number of babies has multiplied. More miserable mothers, more miserable fathers, more miserable children, more miserable doctors. Why? No valid reason, in fact no logical reason was ever given. In private, physicians and social workers were in despair.

For me, almost the worst aspect of the new anti-abortion statute was the way it reflected the Kremlin's contempt for the voice of the people. The people had been handed the draft law and told to criticize it freely. They did. The volume of negative criticism far exceeded the favorable criticism. But a month later the draft was republished, with two or three very minor changes, as the final law. Then what was the point of the discussion? The people felt defeated. Was this the manner in which the new democracy would function? I wrote that the law was "a mockery of the democratic discussion" and expressed the hope that Russia's first real Parliament would repeal the act and thus "redeem Soviet democracy." That was a naive hope. My treatment of this whole situation displayed the virtues and weakness of all my writing on Russia; it combined accurate reporting with oversanguine expectations.

And yet the Constitution was the result of an organic growth. In the summer of 1936, I traveled many thousands of miles through the Soviet Union together with an Open Road group of Americans. All were intelligent. Several—Helen Hall, who is Lillian Wald's successor at the Henry Street Settlement, Paul Kellogg, editor of *Survey Graphic*, Dr. John Lovejoy Elliott, president of the Ethical Culture Society of America, and Helen M. Harris, director of the Union Settlement and later of the National Youth Administration in New York City—had special training in social work and social investigations and approached Russia with critical, unbiased minds. They were favorably impressed by the enthusiasm of the Soviet people and by the prodigious official effort to improve conditions. I knew most of the places we visited from numerous previous visits; economic conditions were obviously better.

The peasants were in a quieter mood. They were reconciled to collectivization. They commenced to enjoy a few of its benefits. They still complained of the shortage of consumers' goods, but they hoped. The class struggle had abated. The terror had moderated. Soviet citizens talked more freely in private and did not hesitate to express their views in the presence of strangers.

The monthly magazine *Bolshevik* said, "Now that . . . our society consists solely of the free toilers of city and village—workers, peasants, and intellectuals—the former limitations on Soviet democracy are no longer necessary." That was true.

I think, therefore, that originally Stalin really intended the Soviet Constitution as a charter of greater freedom. I never believed that Russia would immediately become completely free and democratic. I did not anticipate the legalization of opposition parties. But I expected the training for democracy to begin. This would not have required Stalin to abdicate all his power. He could have remained in his supreme position and benevolently watched and nurtured the new democratic plant.

Instead, the development since the ratification of the Constitution has been altogether in the opposite direction, in the direction of more purges, greater repression, and worse economic conditions.

Two chief factors seem to have contributed to the change: Stalin's fear of personal rivals—hence the purges—and Stalin's fear of a foreign attack on the country—hence the new "nationalism." Apart from this, excessive individual power must simply have gone to his head. "Absolute power corrupts absolutely," Lord Acton wrote. On no other basis can one adequately explain his setting himself up as supreme musical critic. Moreover, the joy and seriousness with which the masses greeted the Constitution must have quickly convinced Stalin that more democracy would be achieved at the expense of his authority.

I have turned back to 1933—before the big trials and purges—and read the Soviet papers of a month chosen at random. No normal person with good taste would allow himself to be praised so fulsomely and loathsomely as Stalin did. It smacks of the pathological. The deletion of Trotzky's name from Soviet history was the opposite side of this medal. The Soviet Union did not need this. It was ready for democracy.

Yet just at the moment when the Constitution, product of more than a year's drafting, came into being, the personal dictatorship showed its ugliest face. Just as the country thrilled to the Constitution, Stalin staged the first Moscow trial of Bolshevik leaders in August, 1936. This was the beginning of the bloodiest purge in history.

Except for the big purge of June, 1934, there has been little violent reshuffling of Nazi leadership. Hitler took over the old bureaucracy, the old army, and the old industrial system. He changed them and added to them but, unlike the Bolsheviks, he did not scrap them and they functioned without the inefficiency of backward Russia. The more important explanation of the difference, however, is Stalin's sick mental attitude. Hitler is unique and every Nazi acknowledges his supremacy and indispensability. Stalin, on the other hand, would like to create the impression of his indispensability but realizes that he has not and cannot. The abnormal rancor and fear of rivals which this failure provokes in him have produced the abnormal phenomenon of the permanent purge. Every month sees a new batch of front-rank Bolsheviks consigned to the political dust heap.

I lived in Soviet Russia for fourteen years, with interruptions. I learned to know many people. I made many friends. I think if I returned now I would find few if any in office or in their homes. Most of them have been shot or exiled. I continue to read the Soviet newspapers from time to time. I hardly know any of the names, except for a handful of top leaders. The others have disappeared in the purge.

I was in Kiev when the August, 1936, trial of Zinoviev and Kamenev was announced. I debated with myself for a while whether to go back to Moscow for the proceedings or go to see the war in Spain. But I preferred a fight to a foregone conclusion. I felt instinctively that a very dark period of Soviet history was about to open. Spain was sad enough when I got there. But it was also noble. I was happy that a situation had arisen which took me away from Russia and took my mind off the disturbing events in Russia.

21. *Holy War*

THE war in Spain lasted from July, 1936, to March, 1939. It was a holy war because it was a war for peace. It was a holy war because it was a war for freedom. Spain had been free. It became Fascist. All those who helped Franco win contributed to the advent of the second World War. All those who helped Franco win helped to suppress democracy. Hitler and Mussolini regarded the Spanish War as a war to make Europe, and other continents, safe for war and autocracy.

Japan attacked Manchuria in 1931. But that was far away. Italy invaded Abyssinia in 1935. But Abyssinia was savage. Now, however, Hitler and Mussolini had dared to invade a European country, a country neighboring on France, a country from which the British and French empires could be threatened. Here, indeed, was a totalitarian challenge to the democracies. They took it lying down.

I was in Soviet Russia when General Francisco Franco broke his oath to the Spanish Republic. I decided immediately to go to Spain. But I could not go immediately because I was under contract to lead my Open Road tourist group through the Soviet Union. I left Russia with the tourists, stopped overnight in Warsaw, took a ten-day rest at a beautifully quiet health resort in Czechoslovakia where Markoosha had brought Vitya for a cure, and then flew to Paris.

In Paris I visited André Malraux, French novelist. Veteran of the Chinese nationalist struggle against Japan, he had thrown himself completely into the Spanish conflict. His apartment on the Rue de Bac was filled with ancient and pale graven images which he had brought from his explorations in Indo-China, with delicate old Chinese papyrus prints, and with paper editions of the world's best literature. Clara, his wife, told me he was busy in the next room. I waited.

"Will he be much longer? What is he doing in there?" I asked impatiently.

"He's buying tanks."

Malraux also bought airplanes with Loyalist money in Czechoslovakia, Belgium, and France. In France, to his eternal credit, Pierre Cot, French air minister, understood the meaning of patriotism and helped Malraux. Malraux applied the inventiveness of a great novelist to buying arms and gun running. He later served as a machine gunner on a Loyalist bomber. Though he was always soberly realistic, the proximity of death excited him. He has a machine-gun mind. It shoots out short sentences full of thought and penetration. He respects the intelligence of those who understand him. Born in 1895, he looked thirty at forty. His figure is trim and he moves with a quick glide. His long, distinguished-looking head is as full of nervous movement as of ideas; muscles in his neck involuntarily throw his head upward at frequent intervals. He has sallow skin, Basedow's-disease eyes, and a long skein of straight hair which falls down over his forehead as he talks. He never stops smoking, lighting one cigarette with the burning butt of its predecessor. He is not a Bohemian. Poet and philosopher, he is essentially a fighter and man of action, and he believes in discipline. He led, but he also served under others with a meekness and self-abnegation unusual in geniuses or in leftist writers. He despised wasted words, wasted effort, wasted time, and most writers. Self-sure but open to advice, he is an anarchist ready to wear harness for a cause, and anti-Fascism is the cause. In defeat he was as buoyant as when working for victory. Never a Communist, he worked closely with the Communists in France and Spain, but when the Soviet-Nazi pact was signed on August 23, 1939, he said to me in Paris, "We are back at zero." The Left movement was mortally wounded, he believed, but he wanted to start all over again. Too old for the air force, he enlisted in the French tank corps, and he hoped, after several months at the front, to go to America and explain the stakes which artists and radicals had in an Allied victory. In the great French military debacle, however, he was wounded, taken prisoner by the Nazis, and escaped.

With recommendations from Malraux and the Spanish Embassy in Paris I flew over the Pyrenees into Spain in mid-September, 1936. I stopped in Barcelona and Valencia, and finally reached Madrid. The first glance made it clear that Franco had succeeded in launching the social revolution which he and Azaña had hoped to prevent. For blue denim was on top, and the workingmen's quarters had moved into the center of the cities. Workingmen were not on tour in the fashionable avenues as they are Sunday afternoons on Unter den Linden in Berlin, where they gaze about as though visiting a foreign country. They had taken possession. They filled the cafés and lounged on street corners. Thousands of enlisted men wore a uniform which carried the factory into the army. It consisted of a one-piece blue overall, or "*mono*," with a long zipper down the front and zippers to close the pockets. (The men loved the zippers.) Middle-class and upper-class citizens thought it necessary to recognize the new trend by discarding neckties and hats and preferring their old suits.

Some of the men I had met on previous trips were now in the government. Caballero was Prime Minister, del Vayo Foreign Minister and Negrin Finance Minister. But the government was very little in evidence. The atmosphere was dominated by the political parties which tended to act as autonomous states. Each party had its own military insignia and its own strongly fortified headquarters. When the owners of hotels, industrial plants, and stores fled to join Franco or were killed or arrested because they supported Franco, the parties took over the abandoned property. Because the CNT, or anarcho-syndicalist trade union, was quickest on the trigger at the spot, it now managed the Gran Via Hotel. But the semi-Trotzkyist POUM had seized the Capitol Hotel, while the Communist party rushed in and appropriated the Catholic *El Debate's* printing presses. Even sectors of the front were divided among the parties. The Loyalists as a national government had yet to assert themselves.

After two months of war, what was the military situation in September, 1936? It revealed the Loyalists' strength and weaknesses. It explains why Franco could not win until spring, 1939.

The workingmen of Madrid, Barcelona and Bilbao, largest cities of the land, had seized the cities in July, 1936, when Franco rebelled. Armed with staves and stones, they attacked the barracks and routed the soldiers who offered only as much resistance as their officers could squeeze out of them. Other big towns—Valencia, Alicante, Malaga, Albacete, Cartagena, in fact, all important towns except Seville and Saragossa, were also in Loyalist hands. The urban population of the country consisting chiefly of factory workers, professional people, and middle class, did not, in its bulk, join Franco's camp.

The Loyalists held almost all the important units of the navy. When Franco rebelled, the officers tried to take the navy over to him. The sailors threw the officers into the sea or killed them or forced them to flee. The result was that the Loyalists had the ships but lacked experienced personnel for their use. Not until the Russians arrived months later did the fleet begin to function at all, and even then its performance was not important, and it never became a very proficient arm.

The Loyalist land forces consisted of a small number of loyal soldiers, a small number of loyal officers, and many thousands of volunteer militiamen whose zeal did not compensate for their Spanish abhorrence of discipline and their complete ignorance of warfare. The workingmen who had prevented Franco from establishing his sway over the cities were entering the militia and looking for the first time at a rifle. Some of them who had rifles actually fired a few rounds on ranges before rushing off to the front to face Franco's trained and ferocious Moors. Others waited in the rear for arms.

These militiamen, then, were organized not into one regular army but into several party armies. The Communists had their militia regiments, the Anarchists their columns, the Socialists and Republicans their own units. These obeyed the orders first of their party chiefs, and if the central government wanted the service of the units it had to negotiate with the parties. This phenomenon was the result of unusual circumstances. The bulk of the army went over to Franco. Before the vacillating government knew what had happened, the political organizations called for volunteers and began to train them. Yet this was so much in the spirit of Spain, that Largo Caballero, who became Prime Minister in September, 1936, long resisted the idea of a regular army, and it was only with difficulty that his Soviet military advisers persuaded him to abandon the popular but inefficient form of party armies. Even then the party military regiments persisted for a long time, and the International Brigade itself was in a sense a remnant of the early system.

The Loyalist army, such as it was, boasted a small air force. Many pilots stayed with the government. But their machines were old coffins. Here André Malraux performed an invaluable, historic service. His Foreign Legion of the Air, which he recruited abroad, and which flew the planes he purchased abroad, disputed the Fascists' mastery of the air and reinforced Loyalist resistance at a time when it might otherwise have collapsed in August, 1936.

The Loyalist air force, however, was no match for Franco's air force which consisted entirely of new German and Italian machines flown by skilled, highly trained men. Franco received planes from Germany and Italy at the very beginning of his revolt, and with their aid he ferried troops across the straits from Morocco to Spain. These troops quickly proceeded north towards Seville, and took Badajoz, Caceres, and other parts of Andalusia. Here they operated in areas filled with disgruntled, impecunious land-hungry peasants who were pro-Loyalist. Until the Moors arrived these republicans sided with Madrid against the disloyal generals.

The rebels themselves conceded this. *The Communist Atrocities*, a Franco book published in London "by the authority of the Committee of Investigation appointed by the government at Burgos" states, for instance, that in Almendralejo, province of Badajoz, "the arrests [of "anti-reds"] took place from July 18 to August 6, the eve of the entrance of the troops into city"—which means that the Loyalist civilian government continued in control until Franco brought in his Moors from Africa. Antequera, in the province of Malaga, "experienced the reign of red terror which lasted from July 18 until August 12." Likewise Azuaga, in the province of Badajoz, which "from the first day of the military rising, July 18, till December 24 . . . was in the hands of the Communist element." And Burguillos del Cerro, in the province of Badajoz, "was in the hands of the reds from July 15 till September 14, on which date the Nationalist army obtained possession of it."

Further, "the reign of Communists in Espejo, in the province of Cordoba, dates from July 22 . . . till September 25, the day on which our victorious troops occupied the town." "During a period of two months the inhabitants of Ronda, in the province of Malaga, were under the control of Communists." El Saucejo, a town of 6,588 inhabitants in the province of Seville, "was taken by the Nationalist forces on September 4." Until then the Loyalists ruled this place which is in the heart of Franco land. These instances could be multiplied endlessly. On the basis of Franco's own evidence it is clear that the Spaniards did not want Franco. There was not a single case where the civilian population rose up and took over power in the name of the insurgents. Franco's revolt was an army coup.

(It should be noted that "Nationalist" as used in this rebel publication always means the army of Moors, Nazi pilots, and paid mercenaries, while "Communist" is a synonym for the Popular Front, which consisted of many parties, including some strongly anti-Communist.)

As far as the civilian population was concerned, Franco had lost the war in July, 1936. But he immediately received Moroccan and foreign military aid and, together with the Spanish reactionaries who had always obstructed Spain's social progress, he commenced the conquest of his own country.

Having occupied Badajoz, Caceres, and other territory inhabited by pro-Loyalists, the Franco legions dashed northward and formed a junction with the northern provinces of Navarre and Aragon which were the traditional strongholds of agrarian reaction and royalism. Franco thus separated the Asturias mining area and the Basque region—both passionately Loyalist—from the rest of republican Spain. This divided the Loyalist strength, made co-ordinated defense impossible and ended with the occupation of the Basque region by the Fascists in the summer of 1937. In the first months of the war, accordingly, the Loyalists lost a considerable portion of their effective peasant support and at the end of the first year of the war a valuable portion of their proletarian support.

By September, 1936, Franco had taken Talavera and was moving on Toledo. Inside Toledo, a body of rebels had seized the Alcazar fortress, and the Loyalists were besieging the fortress.

With a note which Malraux gave me in Paris I got a room in the Florida Hotel, headquarters of Malraux's foreign air squadron. In the afternoon, I went with Clara Malraux and Martha Huysmans, daughter of the Socialist mayor of Antwerp, to the airfield at Barajas, outside Madrid. Beyond the city limits, the air was soft and fragrant, the sun shone bright, peasants nodded on their covered carts or threshed grain by pulling large cylinders of white stone over it. The scene was competely pastoral until we reached the camouflaged hangars of the airdrome.

We ate an excellent meal in the airfield restaurant and then adjourned to its cocktail lounge for liqueurs. Pilots lay on deck chairs on the terrace, slept or played cards or listened to radio jazz. Suddenly an airplane circled over the field. As it descended, men ran out to meet it and so did we. It was a beautiful tapering steel-color Fiat fighter. A handsome tall pilot pulled off his helmet and jumped out. First a stream of French oaths poured out of him. He was a rich Frenchman named Darré who flew for the Loyalists until 1939—unharmed. Nervously lighting a cigarette, he puffed and swore some more. "Five Italians attacked me, and not one of my machine guns would work. Every one jammed." I lifted myself up into the cockpit. It was a one-seater. The pilot was his own gunner. Near his elbow were four little black buttons. As he pushed one down, the machine gun whose nozzle stuck out from the plane wing would start firing. "Five Italians," Darré repeated, "and I couldn't get a single shot at them." A Spanish mechanic started looking over the plane. A big bomber came overhead. Darré had accompanied it. The pilot came out first, then three gunners with parachutes like big turtles on their backs. They called for help. They had two wounded inside. An ambulance raced towards the plane. Two men were quickly laid on operating tables in the airfield clinic and undressed. One gunner, a Frenchman, had a wound in the temple, a wound in the right shoulder, three in the right breast, and one in the left breast. All were only skin-deep and had glanced off and embedded themselves in the side of the airplane. The doctor dressed the wounds, put his right arm in a sling, and gave the airman a mixture of strong coffee and cognac. Later I saw him in the restaurant naked to the waist and wrapped in a white blanket, the center of a circle of friends to whom he was hero for an hour.

The pilot of the bomber was Abel Guidex, a French university graduate. He had been bombing Franco's front lines. He ordered the plane filled with bombs and petrol. He was going up again. Meanwhile he would have lunch. Clara Malraux, Martha Huysmans and I sat at the table with him. Both women were in love with him. He had a young, round, brown face and a boyish smile. He smiled almost incessantly. He ate heartily. Then we had coffee with him at the bar. He looked out to the field. The plane was being warmed up. The airfield commander asked two Spaniards whether they would go up in place of the wounded gunners. They said they had early evening appointments in Madrid. An Englishman and a Venezuelan volunteered. We saw them take off. Guidex waved a jolly farewell. I talked to him that evening in the Florida Hotel. He was an anti-Fascist, not a Communist; old friend of Malraux's. He flew every day on dangerous assignments. And came back smiling, until the day he was burned to cinders inside his plane. The Germans in northern Spain got him. They would never have got him if he had been armed. He had agreed to fly the commercial plane from Bordeaux to Loyalist-held Santander. Since he started on French territory, he could not carry machine guns. He nevertheless made the trip regularly for weeks. Each day, German spies at Bordeaux notified their friends in Spain that Guidex had just taken off. They waited for him in the air and attacked. He escaped. Friends warned him to quit. But he said the defenders of Santander needed the medical supplies and food he brought them every afternoon. Finally his machine was riddled by incendiary bullets and set on fire.

Martha Huysmans stayed in Spain until the very last day of the war, always going to the hottest sectors of the front and writing about her experiences in a Belgian paper. She was completely reckless after Guidex died. She was trying to die in Spain. It was not her fault that nothing hit her. Later she reported the Finnish war, and condemned the Soviet invasion. As a child she had fled from Antwerp when the Germans approached in 1914. In 1940, she fled again and took refuge, with her father, in London.

The first evening in Madrid I went to the Oro del Rhin. Every evening at eight Luis Araquistain, Caballero's friend, went there for a glass of beer. He sat there in peace-time. War did not break the habit. He was now Ambassador-designate to Paris. He discussed the internal political situation. The new Caballero government had slightly improved conditions, but the Anarchists, he said, seemed to be looking for trouble. The Socialists and Communists wished to avoid an open clash that would help Franco advance even more rapidly. Araquistain said the Anarchists of the FAI and CNT rejected discipline, committed murders, and defied the government.

"With a hundred airplanes," he declared, "we could win the war." But England, France, Germany, Italy, Russia, and lesser countries had organized the Non-Intervention Committee and agreed not to intervene in Spain. Up to date, this had meant that England and France and Russia had not intervened, while Germany and Italy had.

The next morning I drove out to the ancient Moorish city of Toledo, forty-seven miles from Madrid by excellent highway. When the revolt broke out in July, the Loyalists retained the city. A thousand rebels and their women folk, however, made a dash for the fortress which dominates the city. They were Civil Guards, army officers, landlords' sons and Fascists. They took with them five hundred hostages, women and children of loyal Republican Toledo families. The Alcazar had walls three yards thick and was built in a case of solid granite rock which extended some distance up its walls. There were three floors of subterranean cellars in the rock. Here the bulk of the defenders and the non-combatants remained while those on duty held positions in the debris of its battlements.

For six weeks, four to six thousand Loyalist troops had battered the eighteenth-century Alcazar unavailingly. First, Madrid had hoped to starve them into surrender. But now Franco was approaching Toledo.

The Alcazar was smoking. Three of its towers were gone; the fourth was intact, its steeple against the sky. With the exception of one wall, the whole superstructure had been reduced to one high heap of uneven blocks of brick and mortar, splinters of rock, and piles of broken plaster. At intervals of two minutes, shells burst in the debris with terrific impact. Thousands of rifles cracked incessantly, and little puffs of white dust jumped up where the bullets hit.

Miners from Asturias dug a tunnel under the citadel, filled it with six tons of dynamite, and ignited it. Debris flew thirty feet into the air. The streets of Toledo were sprinkled with glass and roof tile. The explosion was to have been preliminary to an assault on the Alcazar. But the three hundred men chosen for the task waited until the dust had settled, and by that time the defenders of the Alcazar had returned to their defense posts and met the attackers with withering machine-gun fire which drove them back. Barcelo, who commanded the attacking party was wounded in the leg. He passed the command to Luis Quintanilla, celebrated Spanish artist. But before Quintanilla could rally his men a sergeant ordered a retreat. I talked to the men later. They said the sergeant was a Fascist. Nobody could find him.

Toledo became a disease. Every morning I decided to stay in Madrid and see friends. But if Henry Buckley of the *London Observer* or Jan Yindrich of the United Press or some other correspondent phoned and said he was going out to the Alcazar and asked if I wanted to come along, I invariably said, "Yes."

On the second day, I toured Toledo with Yindrich, an Englishman who spoke excellent Spanish. We went from house to house making a semi-circular tour around the Alcazar. Every house was a fortress. Soldiers stood at its barricaded windows firing into the Alcazar with machine guns and rifles. When they weren't firing they lay down to sleep on the beds and sofas of the former residents. On the floor of one parlor I picked up a glossy sepia photograph of a newlywed couple. The bridegroom looks the typical workingman, short, wiry, with short-cropped black hair. He is wearing sandals. The bride is obviously frightened. Her big eyes are opened wide and her mouth is nervous. She is dressed in her best: bedroom slippers, a skirt and white waist. On the back of the portrait she wrote a message to her mother in a semi-literate hand. I stuck the photograph into my pocket. I have kept it on my table while writing about the Spanish War. These two people are my Spain. I often wonder what happened to them. Perhaps they are dead. A million Spaniards died in the Spanish War. One in every twenty-five inhabitants.

Yindrich and I passed the famous Cathedral, now closed and carefully guarded, the El Greco house still filled with priceless paintings but protected from ground to roof by walls of sandbags, and numerous private homes where we could see women in black sitting in blue patios knitting, sewing, and gossiping. Children played in the streets—the girls were nurses, the boys soldiers. But the boys had trouble because no one wanted to be a Fascist.

A plaza separated the Alcazar from a row of houses. The houses had been hit repeatedly by shots from the Alcazar. In front of one house stood an armored car spitting fire toward the fortress. We dashed across the street, caught one breath behind the armored car, and entered a house. Its short vestibule was covered to a height of several feet with broken blue tiles. Soldiers sat on the smooth surfaces and rested their chins on their rifles. (Yesterday one of them had inadvertently shot himself through the mouth that way.) Through a breach in the vestibule wall we climbed into the corner store. On a high wooden stool was perched an old man with gray porcupine hair. On the counter lay rolls or ribbons, cards of buttons, a measuring rod, chips of tile—all covered with fine dust. His money drawer was pulled back. The wooden money cups were empty. But he was there ready for business. The iron shutters were down. Occasionally a shot from the Alcazar hit the shutters or a ricocheting bullet rang against them. In the evening customers might come. What else had the old man to do?

We climbed upstairs. We saw the private lives of evacuated families. Books and students' copybooks, letters, and clothing on the floors; sideboards pushed against windows to protect soldiers inside; rice and sugar in containers that sat peacefully on kitchen shelves; and everywhere—photographs. Two soldiers followed us around. They were merely curious. Now and then one of them leaned against the window and fired towards the Alcazar.

"Do you see anything?"

"No," he replied, "but I received this Mexican rifle yesterday and I want to try it out." His buddy felt called upon to do likewise. "Shooting warms me up," he explained. The day was chilly and wet.

On the third day of my stay in Madrid, I called on Marcel Rosenberg, the Soviet Ambassador. He reproached me for not having come sooner. I told him I had been at Toledo most of the time, and besides I wanted to look around so as to have some basis for an intelligent conversation. Thereafter, I saw him practically every day until he left Madrid. We would talk either in his room which was also his office, or he would take me in his car to a park or a workingmen's quarter where we would walk. He was a very weak and sick man and he had to take a certain amount of mild exercise daily. When we drove, a guard of the Spanish intelligence service sat with the chauffeur and our car was followed by another fast car. It was filled with six young bodyguards. They jumped out of their car the moment Rosenberg's car stopped. They followed him wherever he went and he would sometimes turn around and shoo them away. If he stepped into a pissoir on the Cuatro Caminos, they surrounded its tin walls and waited.

Once we got out in a park where militiamen were training. They recognized him right away, saluted with the clenched fist and shouted, "*Viva Rusia.*"

"*Viva España,*" he yelled back. The men were amused.

"That's the Fascist cry," I told him. "You should say, '*Viva la Republica.*'"

"*Viva la Republica,*" he yelled.

We stopped at street corners to listen to people discuss the war and watched demonstrations and stood in front of stores.

"More goods in this shop after months of war than in the best Moscow store," I commented.

"Now, now," he smiled, "no counter-revolution."

In the Embassy, Rosenberg introduced me to two Embassy secretaries, Orlov and Belayev. I sat with them in a room and discussed Russia. Something made me talk about the GPU, and from the way they listened I knew that my guess was right; they were GPU men. Orlov, I later learned, was the chief of the GPU agents in Loyalist territory. He spoke English well, dressed dapperly, was good-looking and very intelligent. He also went by the name of Liova.

The Embassy military attaché was General Goriev. He spoke English with perfection, was tall and handsome. In his manner and appearance this pure Slav seemed more like a Britisher. He smoked a pipe, behaved nonchalantly, and smiled in the tensest situations. He talked freely to me about the disastrous position at the front.

"With a thousand fellows of the Red Army I would take the Alcazar in twenty-four hours," he said. Another foreign military attaché gave me the same estimate of the Loyalist forces at Toledo.

I repeated this to a high Loyalist official. He said, "One thousand good soldiers? We haven't got them. Besides, half might be killed in the attempt." Thousands were killed later because the attempt was not made.

At supper one evening in the Florida Hotel, a young Spanish woman told me that the chief physician of the Loyalist forces in Toledo had been executed. He had sent messages by secret radio to the rebels in the Alcazar and to Franco's headquarters. She had just brought his code to Madrid. Cases of sabotage and treachery in government ranks were numerous.

A little Chevrolet car was parked outside the hotel. Inside, a civilian read a newspaper. He leaned his shoulder against a hatless peroxide-blonde young woman; she was wearing a silk dress. On the radiator was a huge red flag and on the doors, in large letters, were painted the words EAGLETS OF DEATH.

The streets were filled with uniformed men and shrieking, hooting, speeding autos. There was no traffic control and each driver set his own speed limit. The big pavement cafés, drowned in sun, were filled with soldiers and workingmen sipping coffee and talking war and revolution. Numerous vendors did business on the cement pavements. One sold combs, razor blades, Sam Browne belts, soap, and toy rifles. His neighbor did a rushing business in maps of Spain. Women sold Madrid's numerous daily papers.

In the afternoon I went out to Toledo; I had given up resisting it. I spent much time in the Hospital of Santa Cruz right under the walls of the Alcazar. It is not a hospital but a museum filled with paintings, old armor, giant stone sarcophagi with ancient Hebrew characters still legible, Arab art. Tall Assault Guards in blue were lying about the big patio.

Outside the heavy gate of Santa Cruz a gray-haired artillery sergeant had placed a three-inch cannon. He promised to make headway against the Alcazar by piercing its walls with a ceaseless flow of shells. The granite walls were only 280 yards away. Young militiamen brought him the shells, and the air throbbed with the frequent explosions and the following crashes against the granite. A crowd of soldiers watched. Suddenly they opened a pathway. Largo Caballero, Prime Minister of Spain, had arrived. He stood and observed the action of the gun. Apparently the government was beginning to feel all the seriousness of the Alcazar situation. Caballero looked weary; he was sixty-nine.

He walked back to his car. Assault Guards and other soldiers followed him. He did not acknowledge their presence with a smile or a raised fist. They had expected him to say a few words. He merely sat down in the back of the automobile and sped away. Everybody was disappointed. The atmosphere was bad enough without that.

That evening I wrote in my diary, "If this continues Franco will soon win, which means Fascism in Europe will win, which means France, Russia, and England will lose. Spain is really the rehearsal for the next big international conflict. The victor in this preliminary battle will have gained an advantage in the vaster struggle to follow."

The next morning I revisited the airfield of Malraux's squadron. A giant German Junkers bomber rested on the ground. It had flown from Germany with other machines but lost its way and landed at Madrid with a crew of four. It had three motors. I climbed into it, moved some levers, touched the bomb racks.

"Why don't you use it?" I asked the commandant of the airdrome.

"We obey orders," he replied.

I talked to Foreign Minister Julio Alvarez del Vayo about the Junkers. He looked sad. "The French Embassy," he said to help me understand. It was still difficult to understand. Out of consideration for France, the Spanish Republic did not use a German machine. The machine had flown over France from Germany. It was concrete proof that Germany was violating "Non-Intervention." Yet the French Foreign Office had seen fit to warn Madrid not to complicate French relations with Germany by including the Junkers in its own air force.

I also asked del Vayo about Spanish Morocco. Franco held that colony and the Loyalists had no access to it. But they could proclaim its independence. That would make trouble for Franco among the Moors. However, the French government objected to that, too. They feared repercussions among the Moors in French Morocco. Besides it would be in violation of the Algeciras Convention of 1906.

Del Vayo and at least several other members of the Cabinet were staunch anti-imperialists and would have brushed aside this brittle legality but President Azaña insisted on it. Moreover, the Loyalists hesitated to offend France. They still hoped a change of French policy would enable them to get French help.

Several weeks later, the Nazis bombed the Madrid airfield and smashed their own Junkers.

I went for an interview with Finance Minister Juan Negrin. His duty now included the removal from circulation of all five-peseta silver duros, counterfeit and genuine. I indulged, as I often have with statesmen, in unsolicited criticism and advice-giving. I pointed out the disorganization in Madrid and at the front. No political leadership. No real military leadership at Toledo. No political propaganda among the troops at Toledo. A flabby Madrid press still using diplomatic language to describe a life-and-death struggle. The lies of the official communiqués; no communiqué admitted a defeat. "Soon, by adding up all the Loyalist victories announced in the war bulletins," I suggested, "Franco will be at the gates of Madrid." Negrin pleaded extenuating circumstances, but in 1939 when the war was over he recalled that conversation in 1936, and said to me, "I knew you were right. But I was a member of the government. I couldn't admit it to you." I felt at the time that he agreed with me. He was too intelligent not to know the truth.

I asked him how much money he had. Negrin said he would tell me because I was a friend but if I published it or otherwise let it be known, the Republic would suffer. He went to his desk, unlocked a little drawer, and took out a card covered with figures which he had written in ink. He said, "This is what we have, but when we mobilize all our resources, we will have more." They were taking over the assets of banks owned by Franco sympathizers and counting the jewels and stocks and bonds left behind by fleeing rebels. Not including these, Negrin said, "We have 2,446,000,000 pesetas in gold, and 25,000,000 pesetas in foreign currency."

"And silver?" I asked.

"And 656,000,000 pesetas in silver," he replied. The Spanish government's total assets in September, 1936, thus amounted to approximately 600,000,000 gold dollars or almost one billion paper dollars.

"Everything has been moved from Madrid," he volunteered.

"Does that mean that you will not fight for Madrid?"

"No," he replied, "but we can take no chances." The gold was moved to the naval base at Cartagena. Later it was shipped to Soviet Russia. It was used to pay the Bolsheviks for arms. It was also used to pay for Loyalist purchases in all countries. Soviet banks in London and Paris were the channels through which the Spanish Republic met many of its bills abroad. When the war came to a close in 1939, the Loyalists owed the Soviet government $120,000,000, which was never paid. Of this debt, $20,000,000, approximately, represented Loyalist imports of food and raw materials from Russia, and $100,000,000 imports of arms.

Negrin said, "We must be confident. We will win." That was Negrin's will power acting upon the national trait of optimism. If nine things go wrong and the tenth is right, the Spaniard usually concentrates on the tenth, wears a smile in his heart, and ignores the nine. If there is a speck of blue in the sky, he says the weather is fine. Negrin had will power and optimism. He also had faith in victory. Without faith there is no fight. The doubter is not a fighter.

That day the militiamen at Toledo entered the Alcazar walls and occupied a whole terrace. I went to see it the next day. It was a terrace on which the stables were located.

By this time, many of the soldiers recognized me as a foreign correspondent and asked to be photographed. Every day the Madrid newspapers printed photographs of individuals at the front. As soon as the soldiers had seized the terrace they removed the crosses from sixty fresh graves of rebels killed by the bombardment. This was senseless. It indicated the extent of the resentment which these born Catholics felt against the Catholic church. They regarded the church as Franco's ally.

I picked up some thin mimeographed sheets: the daily newspaper printed by the rebels inside the Alcazar. It contained radiograms from Franco, from Italian and German stations, orders of the day for their own officers, and a social column. Two children had been born during the siege, and three marriages had taken place. The rebels had parleyed with their besiegers through megaphones and the Loyalists had allowed a priest to go inside and baptize the babies.

Having got this far, General Asensio planned a further attack on the Alcazar. It was four in the afternoon. Shells whistled overhead. I heard them burst in the Alcazar. At the gate of Santa Cruz, a sixty-ton tank was preparing to go into action. It carried a light cannon and three machine guns. It stood within the building but near enough to the exit for the rebels to see it. It had been daubed

with camouflage and painted with names and slogans: "Viva Dimitrov," "El Partido Comunista," "CNT," "Viva la Republica." The
Popular Front on old ironsides.

I asked the driver when he was going into action. "At five," he
replied, although he should not have replied; he did not know me.
The handsome blue-uniformed Assault Guards were lining up, and
their officers had put in one of their rare appearances. I approached
a soldier and opened his haversack to see whether he was taking
any food along. No food. They had lunched at one. It was now
five. If they stormed new positions they might have to stay and hold
them. I mentioned this to one of the officers. He said they would be
relieved. But maybe the fight would be too hot to permit relief.

At five o'clock the artillery barrage had ceased by previous agreement so that the tank and the men could move into the Alcazar. Still
the tank did not move. I decided to participate in this attack. I
wanted to see how it felt. I asked nobody's permission. It was that
kind of war.

I walked out of Santa Cruz and hid between two ruined walls
not far from the Alcazar wall. Some young Communist troops,
"Pasionarias," had also taken temporary shelter here. They were
in fine mood, joked, laughed, and boxed with one another. After a
while, they moved up into the Alcazar enclosure. I waited for the
tank. Finally at 5:40 P.M., the tank lumbered out of Santa Cruz.
In the meantime, of course, the Alcazarites, driven from their posts
by the artillery barrage, could have returned to them.

The tank was now about one hundred yards away from me.
These one hundred yards were under the fire of Alcazar guns. I
was in tennis shoes. I jumped out of my cover, bounded quickly,
half-bent, over the debris, and overtook the tank. This dash was
for me the best part of the day, and I understood then how soldiers
go over the top with zest and animal passion. There is something
exhilarating in the combination of danger and muscular exertion.

There was a ledge sticking out from the back of the tank. I sat
down on it. So did an Assault Guard. The first thing he did was
to whip out his revolver and fire into the air. I felt the same way
only I had no revolver. The tank climbed and moaned and then
stopped. I heard the mechanics inside using a wrench and swearing. Then it creaked and moved again. We were going up and around
the terraces which led to the gardens around the Alcazar building.
The tank had to negotiate some hairpin bends and at such times

the back of the tank was exposed to fire from the Alcazar. The Assault Guard and I would then dismount and walk by the side of the tank. Occasionally it would slip and threaten to go down to the terrace below. We pushed ourselves away and leapt for safety.

The tank had now reached the terrace where the Pasionarias were stationed. They crouched behind a wall five-feet high which rose from one terrace to another. I joined them. The tank continued upward. Above, I could see Assault Guards holding on to the upright iron railings of a fence with one hand and hurling long aluminum-colored grenades with another.

A soldier came running down the road. Blood streamed behind his ear. Soon another came, his trouser leg reddening as he ran. On the terrace above us something hit the ground with a dull thud. A geyser of white smoke sprang up. Four men were wounded. They lifted themselves up and began hobbling downhill. Others, unhurt, wished to accompany them. Officers drew their revolvers, moved quickly from group to group and threatened to shoot anyone who ran away.

A wounded man on his way down stopped in front of me. Blood flowed from under his cap and made thin zigzag trickles down his face. His eyes looked wild. "*Arriba, arriba,*" he yelled hoarsely. "Up, up."

Two men skipped downward holding the arms of a third who had apparently become hysterical. Meanwhile, the hand-grenade bombardment above continued.

The officers succeeded in stopping the panic. They did it by threats and also by their own calm. The officer nearest me stepped away from the terrace wall into the middle of the road, lit a cigarette, puffed, and smiled. I walked over to him to ask what was happening. No soldier or untrained individual has any idea of the character of military action in which he is engaged. Before I could say a word to him something fell and pounded the road. Black smoke enveloped the men with whom I had been standing and when it cleared away five were stretched on the ground. I jumped down to the terrace below.

A second later, I thought to myself, "This won't do," and I climbed back to my terrace. A wounded man lay at my feet. Two soldiers and I lifted him up and started carrying him towards Santa Cruz. I had my arm around his waist. My right hand felt something warm, wet, and sticky. We were slipping in the sandy gravel of the road which the tank had plowed up. The wounded soldier asked us to open his belt. His gray *mono* showed a patch of blood over the heart. He was also bleeding at the knee. He groaned, opened his mouth, and said nothing. The three of us looked at one another and accelerated our pace. A soldier sat in our path calling for help. He was one of the wounded who had tried to get down by himself. Now he could go no further. One of the two men helping me left and went over to him. A stretcher-bearer was rushing up towards us with a stretcher. We deposited our wounded friend on it and ran with it into Santa Cruz. It was dark. We ran through the open patio into a big inside room, the first-aid station. Noise. Darkness. Confusion. One electric light burned dimly. We set down the stretcher and looked for a doctor. Everyone was shouting, "Med-ico, medico," while the three young medicos moved from one wounded man to the other. I grabbed the arm of one and brought him over to our man. We lifted the man on the operating table. His blood-drenched shirt was cut open. He had a superficial wound just over the heart which the doctor painted with iodine. Then the doctor opened the soldier's trouser leg. Part of his knee cap had been shot away. He painted that with iodine. The burn apparently woke the patient and he asked feebly for water. There was none at hand.

We removed our man from the operating table. Orderlies were carrying men to ambulances.

Somebody tugged at my sleeve. I turned and saw a wounded sol-der. Blood was flowing from his mouth. He sat on a chair and swayed and even in the bad light I could see how pale he was. I held both sides of his head. In a moment, the doctor returned to him with gauze and cotton and dressed a gash in the man's fore-head just where the hair begins.

I could hear the tank grinding in the patio. The patio and rooms of Santa Cruz were now filled with men. All the soldiers in the as-saulting party had come back. They stood in groups exclaiming, waving their hands, explaining why everything had gone wrong. Some sat in corners, portraits of desolation.

Nineteen men had been wounded in the attack. All but three were lightly wounded. The enemy, with uncanny accuracy, had fired four shells from a mortar. They had routed a battalion. The hand grenades, the artillery barrage, and the action of the tank were wasted.

As our car entered Madrid that evening, buses filled with soldiers passed us en route to the front. Torrijos, fifty-four miles from Madrid, had been taken by Franco that day. He could now march on Toledo. Would the wounded be evacuated in time? (When the Moors took Toledo they killed several hundred wounded Loyalists by throwing grenades into hospital beds.)

Before coming to Spain I had read in the Soviet press, and, too, in the press of Europe and America, about the heroism of Loyalist soldiers at the front. They had shown great bravery, it was reported, in the Guadarrama Mountains, at Talavera, and elsewhere. I looked for this heroism at Toledo and other fronts, but I never found it. I asked several correspondents whether they had seen any heroism. They hadn't. I asked Spaniards. They said they hadn't at the front, but that the Madrid workers had been brave in attacking the Montaña barracks in the first days of the insurrection. I asked Mikhail Koltzov, the correspondent of *Pravda*. His impression was the same as mine. I asked Malraux. He said, "Yes, a great deal. In the air." He recounted several instances of Loyalist pilots fighting against odds or volunteering for hazardous assignments.

A large body of soldiers has courage only if it is disciplined, well-organized, and operating under trustworthy officers. An aviator can be daring because once in the air he is king and depends on no one but himself. Then his nerves, his mental reactions, his physical state, his philosophy of life add up to courage or cowardice. A soldier in the ranks may be a personal hero, yet if there is chaos all around him, if his equipment is bad, if his officers have not won the confidence of the men, he will run with the rest of them. There are very few men who can stand when their comrades run.

Toledo fell to Franco on September 27, and the rebels came out of the Alcazar into the blinding light. Some of the women had gone mad.

The capture of Toledo was inevitable. The government had neither the arms nor the trained men with which to hold it. Now Madrid would soon be menaced. I drove out to see the environs. It was natural to expect that Franco would come up from the south, take Getafe, where there was an airfield, and then attack the capital. About a mile east of Getafe and ten miles from Madrid a rounded hill rose up from the plateau. I climbed up to look about. This was Cerro de los Angeles, reputed to be the geographical center of Spain.

On it had stood a huge monument to the Heart of Jesus. Rude hands tore it down after the war began. I could see to Madrid and far to the east, west, and south. The next day I persuaded Marcel Rosenberg to go out to the same spot with me. I said I thought it ought to be fortified for the defense of Madrid. He took a military specialist along.

I talked to Rosenberg every day about the danger to Madrid, and the danger to the whole cause if Madrid went the way of Toledo. He said, "Write me a memo. I'll send it to Moscow." I drafted it and gave it to him on September 30. He telegraphed it. I also talked with Koltzov, of *Pravda* who had influence in the Kremlin. He was on friendly terms with Stalin and War Commissar Voroshilov. His editor, Mekhlis, also carried much weight. I told him the Loyalists were through unless quick help came from abroad. He knew that himself. General Asensio, now in the Madrid Staff, had told me that Franco had twelve thousand soldiers on the Toledo front. French pilots who had flown over the area estimated the number at ten thousand. With these he could not take Madrid, if the government had airplanes and a few more arms. Madrid could be decisive and Madrid could be held. Koltzov asked me to write a letter which he would wire to *Pravda*. I gave it to him on October 4. He never sent it. I never discussed it with him, but I guessed the reason. On October 7, Ivan Maisky, the Soviet Ambassador to England, informed the International Non-Intervention Committee in London that the Non-Intervention agreement had been rendered virtually void by foreign aid to Franco. The Soviets could not agree "to turn the agreement into a screen shielding the military aid given to the rebels." If these violations were not "immediately stopped," Moscow would consider itself free from the agreement's obligations, Maisky said.

The Soviet government's decision to dispatch arms and other military assistance was accordingly taken in the first week of October, 1936. Rosenberg had been urging it all along.

Meanwhile, conditions at the front and in Madrid went from bad to worse. The spirit was bad. The soldiers played at war and lay around discussing politics but not digging trenches. In the city, the antagonism between the Communists and the Anarchists was growing. The Communists blamed the FAI—Federation of Iberian Anarchists—for the loss of Toledo, and called them "Fai-scists."

I wanted to meet an Anarchist leader. Old hands advised me to see Horacio Prieto—no relation of Air Minister Indalecio Prieto. I went to CNT headquarters with Horsfall Carter, an English anti-Fascist who knew Spain well. We asked to see a spokesman. One appeared, took us to a café, and answered questions. I said I would appreciate an interview with a national leader. He took us to the national office of the CNT. He introduced us to a man. I asked his name, but he said, "That is not important." We discussed the situation for forty-five minutes. I again asked his name. I promised not to publish it.

"Ah," he declaimed, "I am one of the nameless fighters of the revolution."

"Still," I insisted, "it can do no harm to tell us your name."

"Horacio Prieto," he said. He was romantic but sincere, and all the CNT fellows in and around both offices looked like working-men. They wore black-red bandanna handkerchiefs around their necks and carried black-red flags in their rifle muzzles. At Toledo, their political leaders held big revolvers at the ready even when they walked through streets far from the Alcazar. They did not trust the Communists nor did they trust their own men. Horacio Prieto admitted that Fascists might have entered their ranks for protection or for mischief. The Communists charged that the Anarchists were mercurial and independable. In civilian times, Communists charged, employers bribed Anarchist leaders to provoke strikes prematurely so that the strikes could be defeated. The Anarchists, on the other hand, said the Communists were reactionary. The Communists declared that at the front the Anarchists were flamboyant, theatrical, and cowardly. All these accusations, as far as I could learn, were partly true and partly untrue. But the important thing was that they revealed a serious split in the Loyalist camp. I frequently talked with Rosenberg about these unfortunate relations between Communists and Anarchists. The Anarchists were too important and numerous to be brushed aside or suppressed. Besides, I told Rosenberg, my impression was that they are a truly working-class party and that somehow or other—I knew it would be hard—a way could be found of collaborating with them. Rosenberg agreed. One day he said to me, "Why don't you go to Barcelona and see Emma Goldman about this?" The veteran American Anarchist had come to Spain on her first of two visits. I told Rosenberg I was ready to do anything that would help. He made inquiries, however, and ascertained that Emma Goldman had been taken ill and left Spain. I doubt whether I could have achieved much, for the trouble ran very deep.

Heads of states are often insufficiently informed. Those around them may keep the worst news from them until it is too late. I thought I might be of service to Spain by writing a letter to Prime Minister Caballero describing the critical situation as I saw it. I discussed the idea with del Vayo who welcomed it. On October 11, I had the rough draft ready in English and showed it to del Vayo. He removed his glasses, put his nose into the pages, and said, "This is excellent. But take out the reference to his age. It will pain him." People had been saying that Caballero was too old to run a war. I accompanied del Vayo to the War Ministry and then he ordered his driver to take me to the Palace Hotel. I met Rosenberg mounting the stairs with General Goriev, his military attaché. He was in good mood.

"You look like a cross between a CNT and the Apocalypse," he said to me. "Sometimes," he added, "you also remind me of a poem of Alexander Blok." I didn't ask him why, or what poem. I asked him what he thought of an inspiration that had come to me to write a letter to Caballero giving him some of my impressions. He said, "Fine idea."

In the morning, two Spanish friends worked on my letter to Caballero and rendered it into literary Castilian so that the Prime Minister would not have to go to the trouble of making a translation. The amended and completed English original reads as follows:

Madrid. Hotel Capitol.
October 12, 1936.

DEAR SENOR CABALLERO,

I have had the pleasure of talking with you several times and therefore I hope you remember me. You probably know my devotion to the Soviet Union and to the interests of anti-Fascist Spain. Because I am your friend I assume the liberty of writing to you frankly and freely. I am profoundly disturbed by the present state of affairs here. Many measures which could easily be taken, which must be taken, are not being taken. I have been to the front often and I have inspected the environs of Madrid. Objectively, the situation is far from hopeless. There is no reason why, with your vast resources of men and enthusiasm, you should not hold the enemy at least at the present line. But what I missed most in my three weeks here is the energy and determination which should characterize a revolution. I have studied the Russian Revolution in great detail. When Petrograd was threatened in 1919 every citizen was organized. Every man knew where he would fight, what was expected of him. Nor did they wait for the

Whites to come to them. Feverish political work accompanied tireless building of defenses, mobilizing of new men, training of old soldiers, and preparation of officers' cadres. Nothing was left undone. The city worked like a powerful motor. Again, when General Denikin moved towards Moscow in 1919, shock Communist regiments were sent to the front. The Bolshevik leaders left their offices and stayed with the troops. Nobody rested; everybody's first thought was of success in the field.

I tell you honestly I miss this spirit here. Of course, I know your difficulties and handicaps. You lack many necessary supplies. But you must do more than you have done. History will judge as criminals the men who will allow the enemy to take Madrid, or to postpone the victory of the revolution by allowing him to come too near Madrid without a titanic effort to stop him. I must say: if men whom I know to be sincere and faithful revolutionaries were not in this government I would be inclined to believe that traitors and saboteurs are in charge of defending this city and of holding the front intact. That is the impression an objective observer must get.

I want to ask you, for instance, this question: there are tens of thousands of building workers in Madrid. You have several cement and brick factories here. Why are you not building concrete trenches and dugouts? Why do you not stop all civilian construction work in Madrid and send the workingmen out to erect an iron "Hindenburg line" about thirty kilometers from Madrid which the enemy could not pass? In addition, the heights around the city should be fortified. All this could be accomplished in a relatively short period. It would improve the morale of the soldiers if they saw that you were doing things for them, and it would give them places in which to hide from air attacks.

These things are not difficult to do and they need to be done. Barbed-wire entanglements charged with electricity, the mining of bridges and roads, the creation of underground artillery nests—all these and many other measures can be undertaken. If Madrid is surrendered like Toledo, world socialism will condemn you and your colleagues. After that neither your best friends and followers nor the Spanish people will have any confidence in you. The leadership after that will pass to other hands, perhaps less able and less responsible.

This is not the time to be diplomatic—the moment is too grave. Many people in Madrid have already lost confidence in you. They criticize your policies and activities. One hears too all sorts of suspicions about Asensio. "Is he loyal?", it is asked. These sentiments reflect a very unhealthy situation. Madrid is not being talked to enough. The people have no contact with their government. I think your slogan should be: Let Madrid defend Madrid. Let Madrid organize itself into a committee of three hundred or four hundred and take the matter into its own hands. It will not discuss; it will act. Then initiative will be stimulated and enthusiasm aroused. Then you will get results.

I want to ask another question. The enemy has not many men. His front is thin. His lines of communication are long. In such circumstances, partizan fighting behind the lines could do great damage. In the Russian civil war there was as much fighting in the rear as on the fronts. Small partizan bands, consisting of several hundred men or less, armed with rifles, hand grenades, a few machine guns, etc. would operate behind the lines, blow up ammunition dumps and bridges, destroy small hostile detachments, stir up villages to revolt, interfere with railway and road traffic, and generally sow chaos and confusion. These tactics are especially effective at night. At one time, several large mounted partizan units sent out by Denikin under Generals Skuro and Mamontov, threatened to ruin the entire Bolshevik front in the Ukraine. Guerrilla fighting is natural in civil war, and it would be a powerful weapon in your hands. I know some attempts have been made here. But this should be launched on a vast scale, and right now when the enemy is near.

You understand why I write this way. I want you to win. I would help you to win. I think it is possible to win. But I think also that the methods of the past may result in the defeat of the revolution,

Salud, dear Senor Caballero,

LOUIS FISCHER.

My secretary delivered this letter to Captain Aguirre at 1.15 P.M. He took it in to Caballero immediately, came out after ten minutes with a long face, and said there would be no reply. I had expected none. I had expected Caballero to be angry, perhaps even deeply resentful. But I had to tell him what I knew many people were thinking.

At 4.15, I was sitting in the warm sunlight of my room reading the Oxford History of Napoleon's Peninsular War in Spain in 1808-09. The telephone rang. Aguirre calling. "The Prime Minister," he said, "wants to see you at seven o'clock. Del Vayo will interpret."

Del Vayo was waiting, and in a few minutes we were admitted. Caballero, dressed in a dark blue suit, was bent over and rummaging in a drawer. He straightened out, shook hands with us, and sat down at the head of a long polished table. Del Vayo took a chair at Caballero's right and I sat down next to del Vayo. Caballero had my letter in his jacket pocket. He brought it out and started reading aloud. When he reached "Petrograd was threatened," he said, "The advantage of the Bolsheviks was that they had only one party. We have many." He mumbled down the page and read distinctly, "You lack many supplies."

"You ask why we have not built trenches," he said with a pained expression on his fine face. "Do you know that two months ago, more than two months ago, we sent to Barcelona for shovels and haven't received them yet? You suggest barbed wire for entrenchments. Have we got barbed wire? We have ordered it in France. Inquire of your French friends when we can expect to receive it." He moved his head in a gesture which meant, "Don't think this job is so easy."

"But that's unbelievable," I said. "Spades and wire are not munitions. If you can't get those how can you hope to buy rifles and other weapons?"

"Rifles," he echoed. "Rifles? We received eighteen thousand from Mexico, the only country that has helped us. And now we have whole squads fishing them out of the Tagus and hunting for them in the fields where the men fleeing from Toledo threw them. For guerrilla warfare one needs arms and trained men. We have neither."

"Now as to the building operations in Madrid," he continued. "You try to deal with our trade unions. Their representatives were here this afternoon. They came to make demands on me."

"But," I remonstrated, "you should be making demands on them. Besides you are the leader of the Spanish trade-union movement. Surely they will listen to you if you ask them to construct fortifications instead of subways. If you have tools and materials for villas you have tools and materials for dugouts and trenches."

"That is more complicated than you suppose," he instructed me. "If the Socialist trade unions obey the government the anarcho-syndicalist trade unions, the CNT, will conduct propaganda against the socialists and try to attract their members. This is Spain. Our trade unions are more powerful than the political parties and it is difficult to control them."

"Maybe you are right," he went on, scanning my letter. "Perhaps 'people in Madrid have already lost confidence' in me. Let them choose somebody else in my place."

Del Vayo kicked me under the table and after translating Caballero's words, he added in English, "He is very sad. Cheer him up."

"I do not think the whole country has lost confidence in you," I remarked. "On the contrary, there is a feeling you are the only man for the job. But the people are not conscious of your leadership.

Nobody tells them what is happening. They have a feeling that the newspapers and official communiqués lie to them. You have not made a speech to the nation since you have been in office."

"No," he agreed, "I haven't. I am too busy. My room is always full of people who want to see me. There are other orators and better ones. Let del Vayo make speeches."

I reminded him that a nation at war needs to be in touch with its leader. He could speak on the radio from his office. It would not have to take more than fifteen minutes.

He shook his head.

He again dropped his eyes to the letter. "I have faith in Asensio," he declared. "I have been with him at the front. When bombs fall he stands still."

I suggested that this might be due to the fact that Asensio was a soldier and knew how few casualties result from bombs. "Besides," I added, "I do not say that Asensio is disloyal. I do not know enough to make such a statement. I only wrote that people are talking about him and that creates an unhealthy situation which must be cleared up, and it can only be cleared up if the leader of the nation explains matters and takes the country into his confidence."

He shook his head again. "There is already too much talking going on. You want a committee of three hundred for Madrid. They would never stop discussing. I am going to put the defense of Madrid into the hands of General Miaja."

I said that Miaja might handle the military side of the defense, but what about the political side? "If you have trouble with the trade unions, you, an experienced trade-union leader, they will twist Miaja around their little finger."

Caballero replied that Miaja would have expert political assistance. Throughout the interview the Prime Minister looked downcast. Now he sat up very straight, folded my letter, and put it back into his pocket. He looked at me and measured his words, "I can imagine that we look pretty bad to an outsider. We are slow to start. We need help. We have no experience in military affairs and many of our ministers have no experience in government. We have made mistakes and we will make more mistakes. I am glad you have spoken frankly with me. I am glad you are here. Stay with us and see whether we improve. If you have more criticism write me again, or come see me. I know you are a friend." He rose and shook my hand.

I was deeply moved. He was a noble person.

When I walked back into the anteroom, Captain Aguirre talked to me for a moment and asked whether I was comfortable and needed anything. I said I was all right but sometimes I had trouble getting a car to go to the front. The next day, Aguirre sent me a car with a chauffeur and an armed guard, and thereafter, until I left Spain, I always had an automobile at my disposal. It soon became known, too, that I had written the letter to the Prime Minister and that he had discussed it with me. (There are few secrets in Spain.) I think it gave me a unique position in Spain thereafter. I had, so to speak, been adopted by the Loyalists and they trusted me.

When I now reread my letter to Largo Caballero—after a lapse of more than four years, and what years!—I stop at the words, "victory of the revolution," and "defeat of the revolution." Six months later I could not have written that, for the Spanish conflict had commenced to place its chief emphasis on the war. Social change receded into the background; it became a by-product rather than a primary goal. Chaos, disorganization, and party individualism receded into the background. At the same time, Soviet military assistance commenced to arrive.

It was obvious from what Largo Caballero said to me, and also from the way he said it, that on October 12, 1936, the Spanish Republic was lost. If the Russians had not brought in their first airplanes, tanks, and military advisers that month the war in Spain would have ended in 1936 with a Fascist triumph, and then perhaps Czechoslovakia would have fallen earlier and the second World War would have started earlier.

There are those who would affirm that social radicalism was forced to retreat by the Russians and by the Spanish Communists whose prestige and power in Spain rose because Russia came to the Republic's rescue. I think this is a misconception. What happened was this: After months of vacillation and impotence, the central Loyalist government was beginning to take control of the situation. Soviet military intervention helped Caballero in the task of dominating the parties and trade unions. Moreover, radical social innovations antagonized part of the Loyalist population. The merchant class was largely anti-Franco, but it would not have remained so if the Loyalists had stopped all private trade. The peasantry also had good reason to be anti-Franco, for the landlords were pro-Franco. But

the peasants could not have been expected to support the Republican government if it had seized their small farms and formed socialist collectives. The peasants in Badajoz and Caceres might have welcomed collectives; they owned little land and slaved on the big estates. But the Loyalist-held rural districts of Catalonia, Valencia, and
the rest of the Levant, and even Castile included numerous small
farms, and while there was room for collectives here too, wholesale
socialism in the villages would have destroyed or weakened the
peasantry's inborn love of the Republic. In 1917, Lenin won the
peasantry by dispossessing the landlords and inviting the peasants to
take over, divide, and use the estates. Collectivization was not introduced until 1929, when the Soviet government had tremendous
strength, and even then there were enough difficulties. But in Spain,
the Anarchists and the POUM wanted to collectivize in the fall of
1936 when the war was being lost. The resultant turmoil would
certainly have ruined all Loyalist chances of further resistance. A
poor, unprepared, badly led Spanish Republic could not simultaneously fight a war and stage a revolution. Social change was inherent
in the war. Power was passing to different classes. Workers and
peasants shared the government with the small bourgeoisie and intellectuals. But the power had to be used with wise restraint, for it
would have been preposterous to introduce an anti-capitalist economy in September, 1936, and be defeated on the battlefield and put
in prison or executed by Franco in November, 1936. A full-fledged
revolution would have alienated the capitalist supporters of the Republic and thus spelled the doom of the Republic.

This issue remained very much alive throughout the Spanish struggle, and outside Spain it continues to be the subject of theoretical
debates which are only occasionally interspersed with facts.

From several directions, Franco's few men pressed ever closer to
Madrid. The city commenced to feel his proximity. There was a
tenseness in the air and a sensation of grim expectancy. Correspondents said, "Soon we will be able to go to the front by trolley." Air
raids started.

Among the correspondents was a tall, blond Englishman named
Hugh Slater, a Communist who wrote for Imprekorr, a Communist
news agency. He had a car of his own and wrote a great deal. One
day he disappeared without bidding farewell to anybody. We wondered what had happened. Then William Forrest of the *London*

Daily Express got a letter from Hugh posted in Barcelona. He said he wanted to return to Madrid but had no money and asked Forrest to send him funds. But very shortly thereafter he arrived in London where he frankly admitted that he was scared by the threatened closing of the iron ring around Madrid.

Harry Pollitt, the secretary of the British Communist party, talked to Hugh Slater and told him that if he wished to remain in the party he would have to return to Spain and prove that he was not a coward. Hugh came back and joined the International Brigade. He took a post of commander of an anti-tank unit. At Brunete and in other battles he fought gallantly, and he was officially cited for bravery.

When the European war started in 1939, Slater resigned from the Communist party and became assistant to Tom Wintringham, the commander of the great British school for Home Guards on an estate outside London. Hugh and Wintringham there taught hundreds of Englishmen the experience they had gained in Spain's International Brigade.

By October 16, correspondents visiting the front were not permitted to go beyond a point on the Navalcarnero road, twenty-five miles from Madrid. That day I went out by car with my secretary, a little Jew from the Argentine named Angel Rosenblatt. Pickets stopped us and we got out. A flock of soldiers on the road and on the banks overlooking it created the impression of disorderly retreat. But I heard the calm voice of an officer saying, "Disperse. Disperse. Lie down and don't move." That meant bombers. The men walked quietly out into the plowed fields and sat or lay down. I sat down. Two big bombers, black, their propellers shining in the sun, were circling over Valmajado, two miles away. Their altitude, I guessed, was two thousand feet. They were not afraid to come down low because they knew the government had no anti-aircraft guns. A bomb dropped from a plane. One heard a terrific crash and then a mountain of smoke rose from the earth. Having dropped one missile the airplane flew away, described a circle, came back, and then let fall another bomb. Several times we were within this circle. Would he drop the bomb just where I lay? I made myself as small as possible, put my knees under me and hunched my back. Then I pulled my coat collar over my head. That was pretty stupid. Yet when one is so helpless under a terrible monster one does things that one laughs at later. My Burberry raincoat would scarcely have saved my head from a hundred-pound projectile. But I had nothing better. I smelled the dry goldenrod. My nose was in it. Then I peeked out. He had passed. I lifted my eyes while scarcely raising my body. At that moment the earth shook. A bomb had hit the ground across the road, about a hundred yards from where I lay. I wondered whether any of the men had been killed. Here I was, whole and well, full of senses and ideas. I could move my muscles and I could see. The next moment my hands and intestines and lungs might be flying through the air and I would be finished. It would not be painful, I imagined. It would take only a second. I would probably not be aware of it. And was that all? I recalled a person I knew. Where was the plane? I could see it, a small black bird in the blue, graceful and fine to look at. The second plane dropped a bomb on Valmajado and sped away from us. I sat up and inspected the scene round about me. Men were stretched out about ten or fifteen feet from one another, cool and collected. I stood up and wanted to walk to what I thought was a better position. The soldiers yelled at me.

"He will see you. Lie down." I did so, and rolled a little in the direction of that position. A man sat behind a bush reading the morning *El Socialista*.

Two fellows were conversing. "We must have planes. We cannot fight without planes. Will Russia send them—that's the question now." The other said, "If the rebels win there will be an inquisition worse than anything Spain has ever experienced."

The plane was coming again. A government artillery battery had been firing that morning. He was searching for it. We were between him and the battery. He was directly over me. I was sure of it, but I also thought I might be wrong. For I was in my ostrich pose again and I could merely hear the purr of his motor. My ear followed his progress. He had passed. The noise gave me the distance. I sat up again. Both planes were now directly over the village of Valmajado. Both dropped bombs on it simultaneously. Then they moved away from one another, and while one soon became a speck in the sky the other came towards us and descended. Would he use his machine gun? In recent days the rebel airplanes had regularly fired off their machine guns after they had finished bombing. On Tuesday, a man threw himself face downward with his hands stretched out in front of him when a rebel plane came overhead. Fatal mistake. The aviator's machine gun drew a line of bullets across the soldier's wrists. Would that pilot up there do something similar?

I pulled myself inward. The roar of his motor was quite distinct. He dropped another bomb somewhere in the vicinity. The earth under me shook. Then his speed increased, the sound died away. The two machines had done their work and disappeared. The entire ordeal had lasted exactly twenty minutes. The soldiers stood up, about three hundred of them, and brushed their clothes. An officer called them. They gathered around him in perfect discipline.

The road back to Navalcarnero was filled with peasants who had left Valmajado before the bombing that morning. They preferred to become refugees than live under Franco. As the rebels approached, the peasants did not go to meet them. They fled in the opposite direction. They did not know where they were going. I saw them asleep evenings by the roadside. They had neither food nor money. They did not know what the morrow would bring. But they knew one thing: they did not want to be with Franco. Throughout these months, whole villages packed their poor belongings and moved towards Madrid. Their evacuation was a vote of non-confidence in Franco. Democracy is not merely the ballot box. There are many ways of voting. Dropping a slip of paper into an urn is the easiest and not always the most convincing way. Lenin once said that in 1917, "The Czarist army voted for peace with its legs. It ran away from the trenches." The Spaniards were voting for the Republic by running away from Franco.

The defense of Madrid was also a plebiscite. Loyalist resistance until 1939 against cruel odds was a plebiscite. Every day in Spain was election day. Franco advanced and took territory, but the people voted "No."

Votes minus arms, however, cannot fight Fascism. An unarmed democracy is an invitation to Fascism.

One evening Koltzov invited me to the special Russian dining room in the Palace Hotel. There were many recent arrivals. Their civilian clothes were new and seemed to make them uncomfortable. Soviet military assistance had come.

Still Franco moved towards Madrid. Air raids multiplied. Most of them occurred during the day. We had been put out of the Florida Hotel. I moved to the Capitol which was a sort of gridiron building that stuck out conspicuously into the Gran Via avenue. I was on the sixth floor and had a long balcony from which I could see a large section of Madrid. Whenever planes came overhead, men and women appeared on the roofs to watch. Once I watched an air raid while taking a shower.

Food got worse. The water was turned off several times a day and we had none at all from ten in the evening to eight in the morning.

The city was nervous. In the evenings, the blackout made everything gruesome. Several times, militiamen fired from the street into house windows where a light shone. Zeal and folly. The authorities suspected that Fascists were taking advantage of the darkness to commit murder and throw the blame on the Loyalists.

On October 24, I drove out towards Aranjuez. There had been fighting at Seseña and Pinto. I was with Geoffrey Cox, a correspondent of the *London Express*. Ten miles out from Madrid we saw two tanks coming towards us. At closer range we saw that one tank was towing the other. Approaching nearer, the tanks stopped and the drivers got out to tinker with their machines.

I looked at the drivers, walked up to one, and addressed him in Russian. He had an unmistakably Slav face. He answered in Russian with an Ukrainian accent. I said, "Ukrainian?"

He said, "Yes, yes. From Kiev." From Kiev! And fighting near Madrid! He told me they had been in a battle near Parla and one machine had gone out of order. This was the first time Soviet arms had gone into action in Loyalist Spain—October 24, 1936. We stood and chatted. The Soviet tank drivers liked the scenery and the Spanish people. Spanish peasants congregated looking very happy. "*Ruso, Ruso,*" they said and smiled. Presently, a car drew up with two German anti-Nazi photographers who were in the correspondents' group at Madrid. They took some photographs. The Soviet officer in charge of both tanks said he could not allow that and asked me to tell them that they would have to come along with him.

"You can't do that here," I explained to the Russian.

He was a bit bewildered by this strange announcement, and then he said, "In that case I must have their cameras." I translated, but the photographers produced official credentials from the Foreign Office which stated specifically that their cameras could not be taken away from them.

Nonplused, the Russian told me he would insist on having the exposed films. This the photographers regarded as a reasonable request. The tank driver said, "We cannot have such photographs printed abroad."

The next morning I was in the corridor of the Soviet Embassy. Orlov called me into his room. He showed me the developed films. He was the head of the GPU in Spain. He raged and said the photographers would have to leave the country. I assured him they were good anti-Fascists and certainly meant no harm. He explained that such pictures could do the Soviet Union and Spain a lot of harm if they got into the hands of the Non-Intervention Committee.

The photographers were not expelled.

After meeting the two tanks we proceeded towards Pinto. On our left was Cerro de los Angeles. Soldiers lay in trenches around the hill and a spiral of breastworks was slowly being dug up toward its summit. At the foot of the hill, in a small white house, I found Lister, commander of the Spanish troops in the area. He had been fighting a rearguard action to cover Madrid, and he was tired. He had been drinking. Lister spoke all languages except Spanish badly. He had shipped as a sailor to most of the countries of the world. He had worked as a laborer on the Dnieper dam construction in Soviet Russia. I spoke Russian with him. On this occasion, Lister's Soviet military adviser, "Fritz," a thin little man in a new blue suit, opened the staff map and explained the situation to me. The Loyalists were trying to delay Franco's approach to the gates of Madrid.

Geoffrey Cox and I walked to the top of the hill. Three black Junkers bombers appeared and headed, as we thought, straight for us. Geoffrey picked up his legs and ran along the crest and I ran away after him, and then we both stopped and burst into a laugh. If they had dropped bombs our running fifty yards wouldn't have helped. The Junkers flew on to Madrid and we saw their bombs fall on the city.

In Madrid at the time were: Vernon Bartlett, celebrated British radio commentator, later Independent Member of Parliament; Ludwig Renn, German Communist novelist; Gustav Regler, German Catholic turned Communist; Claude Cockburn, Communist editor of the Communist *The Week*, a mimeographed dope-sheet, and foreign editor of the *London Daily Worker*, who sometimes wrote under the name of Frank Pitcairn; and André Viollis, an elderly Frenchwoman who had written books on travel and had suddenly gone political and pro-Loyalist; Gerda Grepp, a Norwegian girl writing for an Oslo Socialist daily; and a dwindling group of bourgeois foreign correspondents. The bourgeois correspondents ate at the same restaurant almost every afternoon and evening; we were all losing weight.

The morning of November 5, Madrid was pallid with fright. Her friends seemed to be deserting her and she had to remain behind. Automobiles packed with occupants and laden high with mattresses and suitcases dashed toward the exits of the city. Peasants guided their donkey-drawn and ox-drawn carts through the streets. For them Madrid was a refuge.

No food in the hotel. Most foreigners and many Spaniards had left. Pedestrians hurried and did not look around them. Normal life was dying. Those leaving did not wish to see anybody. The sense of danger was not, I think, directly communicated by the situation. It made itself felt through the hasty departures of others. Those who could not leave had the look of persons in a trap and of saying to you, as you passed, "Tell me, please, what shall I do?" I felt the same way.

I walked over to the Palace Hotel. If anybody knew the military situation the Russians would. The whole staff of the Soviet Embassy had left. The rooms were in disarray. Only Orlov had remained behind; the GPU would be the last to leave the post of duty. The members of the Spanish government, Orlov told me, had left the night before. I asked him what I ought to do.

"Leave as soon as possible!" he advised. "There is no front. Madrid is the front."

I retraced my steps towards the Gran Via. I walked slowly. Was this the end? Would Madrid fall? If it did, could resistance continue elsewhere? Another defeat for the Left? Another victory for Fascism and evil? Did we always have to lose? How could Franco take Madrid if the militiamen fought for every avenue and apartment house? He did not have enough men. The city was quiet. If there were Fascists inside they had not yet stirred.

Suppose Franco takes Madrid, I thought. Would I be in danger? Probably not. I could be arrested and imprisoned. Whom would that benefit? Cold and hungry in a Madrid prison watched by rebels! The worst thing, it seemed to me, would be the looting and shooting before Franco restored order. That had happened at Toledo. I did not feel like taking chances with Moors, foreign legionnaires, and rebels on a rampage.

I looked into the large plate-glass window of the Gran Via Hotel. There sat Malraux smoking.

"What is the situation?" I asked.

"The enemy is in Carabanchel Alto," he announced in his usual communiqué style. That was about thirty-five minutes' walk from where we were standing.

"How do you know?"

"We bombed them there this morning," he replied. That was rather convincing, and equally distressing.

I asked him what I ought to do.

"Get out quickly," he said. "Get a car. If you can't get one I'll fly you out to the province tomorrow morning. But first you'll have to go bombing with us."

I had not yet decided definitely to leave but I had decided to leave by car if I did.

In the morning the city was still sadder and emptier. There was no coffee and no bread in the hotel. More oxcarts in the streets. I told Rosenblatt that I had decided to leave and invited him to come with me.

"I will stay here," he said.

That made it more difficult for me. I wondered whether I ought to change my mind and stay. "Don't be sentimental," I rebuked myself. "Suppose everybody behaved like you and departed?" I argued with myself. "But I am no soldier. What good would I do by remaining?"

By noon, we were preparing to leave. With me went Gerda Grepp, Ludwig Renn, Claude Cockburn, and a Spanish friend. We spent the night in Cuenca and the next day reached Albacete where I decided to stay.

22. I Enlist

TWO days after the beginning of the siege of Madrid, I enlisted in the International Brigade. I am as proud of that as I am of anything I have done in my life. A nation was bleeding. Machine guns were being mounted on the ivory tower. It was not enough to write.

For fifteen years I had written and spoken about what other people did. This limitation always irked me. But I never felt tempted to work in the Soviet Union or in any Communist movement. Now men were dying; I wanted to do something. Friends said my articles were a contribution to the cause. But I wished to contribute work as well as words.

I was the first American to enroll in the International Brigade. I went to André Marty, the French Communist deputy and chief commissar of the Brigade, and revealed my intention to him. He asked me what I could do. I said I could organize. He said, "We need a quartermaster." So I became quartermaster of the International Brigade. I never took any pay. I never swore allegiance to anything or anybody. I don't believe anyone in the brigade did. In the beginning, I continued to live in the Grand Hotel. But then Marty or Vidal, the chief of staff, would phone at seven in the morning and say, "Where are you? The staff is meeting." Seven A.M.! I was still in bed. So I moved to a room in the house on the edge of Albacete which was the Brigade's GHQ.

Several weeks later, an American named Dadiuk appeared at Albacete. He was an electrician, I believe, or a mechanic, and since I was in charge of the maintenance of barracks I asked him whether he would join my office force.

"I came here to fight," he said.

One of our problems was the refusal of most men to do office work. They preferred to train for the front. I finally persuaded a young German named Bauer, son of a rich farmer in Argentina, who had paid his own way from Buenos Aires to Madrid, to act as my assistant. But once Marty insulted him, and he quit and went back to his battalion. Shortly thereafter he left for the Madrid line.

My job was manifold. I had to feed the brigade in Albacete. We sometimes had as many as three thousand at the base. I had to clothe the new arrivals from head to foot, keep the barracks clean, and distribute arms. Each one of these tasks was a nightmare because of the disorganization, the shortage of supplies, and the crowding. To add to my troubles, the battalions at the front would send emissaries to me announcing that they had lost cooking utensils, clothing, and bedding in a battle. But I had nothing to give them. Once a battalion commander threatened to send an armed guard from the front to arrest me for failing to deliver the equipment he demanded. What could I do? I begged everywhere.

My best friend was Martinez Barrio. I had met him in April, 1936, in the Cortez. He was wearing formal diplomatic dress and looked the stiff statesman. He was Vice President of the Spanish Republic and President of Parliament. But now he was also civil governor of Albacete, and to him I turned in my distress. He sat beside a kerosene stove in a cold room, with a woolen blanket over his legs, a thick scarf around his neck, counting up figures and receiving countless officers and civilians.

"I must have four hundred pairs of socks tomorrow," I would say to the Vice President. "Four hundred Frenchmen and Poles are arriving in the morning."

Sometimes we would trade. In my storerooms I had five thousand pairs of army shoes sent by friends of Spain abroad.

On one occasion, a whole train-full of supplies came through from France to Albacete. It was sent by the French Communist party. It was my business to unload it and store it. I had no idea in advance what it contained. Squads of men gladly volunteered for the work. We found thousands of uniforms, several thousand gas masks—we were the only unit in Spain which had gas masks—(gas was never used in the war because both sides had gas and neither side had sufficient gas masks)—tinned food, woolen sweaters, blankets, woolen helmets, underwear, and field kitchens.

As we opened one bale, out came a baby's rompers. I thought: "Those fellows have gone crazy." Then a silk blouse. Then the barrel of a machine gun. They had smuggled through several dozen revolvers too. Marty took them and guarded them zealously. He gave me one; I gave it back. I had the rank of major or "commandante" but the men always addressed officers as "comrade." I wore a uniform consisting of corduroy jacket buttoned up to the neck, corduroy pantaloons that fell to the ankles and that had big patch pockets on the thighs, and heavy army boots. Marty complained because I wore nothing on my head.

When I enlisted I informed nobody abroad. I also stopped sending weekly dispatches to *The Nation*. *The Nation* wired me to Madrid but I was in Albacete. It suspected an accident. It asked the United Press in New York to investigate through its correspondents in Spain. It got in touch with the Spanish Ambassador in Washington who wired Valencia inquiring about my whereabouts. It sent out publicity which was printed in the papers: "Writer Lost in Spain." My sister in Philadelphia, frantic, wired Markoosha in Moscow who wired Rosenberg, the Soviet Ambassador in Valencia. My sister also got in touch with Oumansky, the Soviet Ambassador in Washington, who she knew was an old acquaintance of mine. He wired Moscow. Moscow wired Rosenberg.

Later people said to me, "What happened? How did you get lost?" "I wasn't lost," I replied. "I knew all the time where I was." Most friends winked as though to say, "I understand. You were off with a girl." I was in Albacete handing out shirts and blankets.

My chief headache was arms. The Twelfth Brigade, commanded by General "Lukach" (I had known him in Moscow as Mate Zalka, a Hungarian Communist author who had been living in Russia many years and had served in the Red Army cavalry), was leaving for the front. We had no rifles. Orders had arrived for the brigade to move to Madrid. And we obeyed the orders although it seemed stupid to let the men proceed unarmed. They were actually drawn up in the large uncovered courtyard of the Gaurdia Nationale barracks and the farewell speeches were being made—Ludwig Renn was in that outfit (he had enlisted the same day I did)—when trucks drew up with wooden crates filled with heavily-oiled rifles. The men "fell out" and each got a rifle and started rattling the bolt and looking down the muzzle and wiping off the grease. There was great jubilation.

I usually went to bed at about nine thirty. One night at one A.M. there was a loud impatient knock at my door, and I heard Marty's wife call out, "Everybody up, fully dressed."

I rushed downstairs. News had come from Valencia that the Italians had landed in the night on the coast, and the International Brigade had been instructed to "stand by." We were to go and intercept the Italians.

"With what?" was my first thought.

None of our men in Albacete had rifles. Marty ordered me to distribute what arms I had. I had several hundred old rifles in an old church where I had placed a heavy guard. Each rifle was catalogued. Some were marked "Oviedo, 1896." I remembered that because it was the year of my birth. But it wouldn't have been half so bad if they had all been of 1896 vintage. Some were younger, some were French, some American, some German. And besides I did not have bullets that fitted all of them. I handed out about 150 rifles.

The Internationals were quartered in several buildings, one the office of the Bank of Spain. I rushed around in my car to see whether the men were up and ready. They had to receive cold rations for the night march. My assistants handed out cheese, cans of tuna fish, bread, lemons, and wine. Without wine the French would neither fight, nor train, nor work. Some men who had arrived only recently were still short of articles of clothing which had to be distributed. Everybody worked with quiet efficiency. The men sat on the stone floors and in the courtyards with their packs on their backs, sleepy but excited. "Will we get rifles?" they asked me as I passed through.

I returned to the staff. Marty had thrown a heavy armed guard around the house. There was a complete blackout in the town. As I approached the house, a guard stuck his bayonet at my chest. They told me they had orders to shoot anybody who failed to answer their challenge immediately. I went inside and reminded Marty that the enemy was still hundreds of miles away on the coast, and that meantime we might have a silly accident here. He was the hysterical type; besides he thought he was being efficient and military.

Soon the Russians arrived. The International Brigade functioned under the friendly wing of three Soviet officers, who, however, made only occasional visits to Albacete. One was called Colonel Valois and though he spoke an excellent French that was not his name. I heard somebody call him Simonov. The other was called Petrovitch, and I have forgotten the name of the third.

Marty treated them and all Russians as though they were gods. He tried to keep everybody away from them. I behaved towards them as I did toward others who were here fighting for Spain, and since I spoke Russian they frequently consulted me about conditions and sentiment in the brigade. Marty resented it.

When they arrived that night I said to them, "Were you attacked by the guard outside?"

They laughed and said, "Who is responsible for that?"

Marty heard the question and rushed outside to send the guard away leaving only the usual sentry. The voices of the Russians introduced an atmosphere of calm. The Russians reported that the news about the Italians was still vague but we had to be in readiness. We were the most reliable unit this side of Madrid. I told them we had no rifles much less machine guns. They said they were seeing to that. After an hour, the order went out to let the men go to bed. The "state of alarm" continued.

The morning brought two items of good news. The landing of the Italians was a false alarm. And we had arms. They were waiting to be unloaded in the patio of the Guardia Nationale barracks. I dashed over. Tremendous joy among the men. There were several thousand rifles. But more. There were several hundred machine guns: Colts from America with a few parts missing, French guns, all new, a few Soviet Maxims—the first Soviet arms the brigade had had—and several dozen light machine guns carried on the shoulder. These last were Bergmanns—new, and made in Nazi Germany. The Nazis had sold them to the Poles, and the French Communist party, with Comintern money, had bought them from the Polish army. Warsaw needed money.

That day was a holiday in the brigade. Wherever I went, in the barracks, in the mess houses—most of the men ate in the Albacete bull ring—and in the streets, I was asked, "When do we go to the front?" Now that they had arms what were they waiting for? They went soon enough, and many of them never returned or returned as cripples.

The Loyalist government took arms wherever it could get them. Many of the purchases were made abroad by individual Spanish agents. Any Spaniard who said he had a friend in Antwerp or Athens or Amsterdam or Stockholm, who once knew a man who had worked for an arms merchant was given a commission and money to try to buy whatever was available. Some of these Spaniards were fraudulent adventurers who made off with a lot of funds, and some were well-intentioned failures. Only a few succeeded. Foreign friends of the Loyalists also did their best in all countries, with scant success. A few hundred machine guns or two artillery batteries were a big haul, but they amounted to very little at the front.

Among the successful left-wing Sir Basil Zaharoffs, apart from Malraux, was a French Communist deputy named Dutilleul. He had established contacts with Poland, Belgium, and other countries. He used money from the French Communist party and the Comintern. But this source was running dry, and when he came to Albacete in November, 1936, he asked me to introduce him to members of the Spanish government. I promised to go with him to Valencia. We made an appointment to leave Albacete early one afternoon. He was late. I waited for him in the staff building.

"Haven't you left yet?" Marty asked.

I told him I was waiting for Dutilleul.

"Where is Dutilleul?" he inquired angrily.

I told him he was making speeches to the men.

"What?" he yelled. "Who gave him permission? I am the one who makes speeches here."

He called an orderly. "Find Dutilleul and bring him to me immediately."

Marty was absurd. A French Communist deputy was addressing soldiers of the International Brigade. How could Marty object to that? Marty wanted to be the only boulder on the beach.

In Valencia I introduced Dutilleul to Foreign Minister del Vayo, and then the three of us went over to the office of Prime Minister Caballero. Dutilleul was asking for $30,000,000 with which to buy arms abroad. He told Caballero what he thought he could get with the money.

Caballero hastily called together the Inner War Cabinet and several attachés. Everybody arrived in short order. Those present were Caballero, del Vayo, Indalecio Prieto, Minister of Air and Navy, General José Asensio, assistant Minister of War, a representative of the air force, Julio Just, Minister of Public Works, Dutilleul and I. Caballero told me I could stay.

I had met Indalecio Prieto once before in Madrid. He had a tremendous, bald, egg-shaped head set on a blubbery diabetic body of gigantic dimensions. He was a right-wing socialist and Caballero was a left-wing socialist and they were regarded as bitter rivals for national leadership. With exemplary restraint and discipline, Prieto had nevertheless consented to serve under Caballero. At this meeting he did very little talking and when he did speak he showed a marked deference to Caballero. What Prieto said was the most intelligent contribution to the entire deliberation. He agreed that they ought to buy arms in endless quantities. "But our biggest need is to manufacture munitions at home," he declared. "Would it not be possible to purchase the mechanical equipment for a factory to manufacture rifles?"

Various technical matters were discussed and finally it was decided to instruct Negrin to make out a check for $30,000,000.

Dutilleul gave me itemized lists of the cargoes of freighters already chartered which would soon arrive in Loyalist ports. The staff of the International Brigade was eager to get as much as possible of this equipment for its own men. We were growing fast. By chance, for those were active days and I suppressed my instincts as a collector of documents, I kept several orders of the day. On November 19, for instance, 600 men were in Barcelona and would reach Albacete the next afternoon. Next day we learned that the detachment of 600 actually contained 1,080. Most of them were old soldiers or trained sportsmen and with a little drill they would soon be ready to go to the front. Madrid was holding, but nobody knew when a stiff Franco attack was coming. We needed arms. The S.S. Ramon was due from Danzig with artillery, machine guns, and hand grenades, and Marty asked me to go to Valencia and ask Caballero for most of its contents. Caballero promised about three-fifths of the precious goods. The ship was to dock in Valencia. But she was already several hours late. She had to pass through Gibraltar. Fascist airmen and submarines were patrolling the straits. Every minute of waiting became a terrific strain. I went to the Soviet Embassy at the Hotel Metropole. Kolya, I knew, was attached to the Loyalist fleet. I found him in his room. I told him the Ramon was late. Couldn't they send a plane from Cartagena to look for her and if she was located dispatch a destroyer to convoy her? Kolya got on the telephone to the main Loyalist naval base at Cartagena. They promised to send out a reconnaissance machine. I went away and sat in a café. In fifteen minutes, I was back again in Kolya's room. He phoned again. No news.

Kolya was a man of about thirty-three, blond, straight, and tall, pure Slav. He had learned Spanish. He was calm and simple. He was a bit perturbed too but did not show it. Kolya is Nicholas Kuznetzov, now Soviet admiral and the Soviet Union's Commissar of Navy.

A long hour elapsed while we talked about the Loyalist fleet. Finally, Cartagena called and reported that the Ramon had been sighted hugging the African coast. A fast destroyer had been detailed to meet her and a cruiser would be in readiness in case of attack.

The *Ramon* got in safely. I returned to Albacete. But the Spanish chief of staff at Albacete told me that he had received an order from General Asensio which countermanded Caballero's promise to me about the distribution of the cargo. The chief of staff showed me Asensio's telegram. The munitions would come to Albacete but the International Brigade was to get only a small portion of them. I argued with the chief of staff. I ran to Martinez Barrio. We had the best soldiers and they insisted on going to the fighting line without delay. In the end, we reached a compromise between Caballero's promise and Asensio's instructions.

I went to Madrid almost once a week. My first visit after the siege commenced was on November 15. In ten days, Madrid had changed its aspect. Frivolity gone! Barricades instead! Streets had been torn up and the granite blocks used to build walls across streets and in front of big buildings. Avenues were dug up to obstruct tanks. Most Madrileños refused to leave the city. The government actually arrested several noted artists and professors and took them to the coast where they were released. It did not want them to be hurt or killed. The art treasures of the Prado and other museums were moved out. This was no simple task. Some of the big Velasquez and Goyas could not be rolled without cracking the varnish and color. If they were transported in their frames in ordinary trucks they might be bombed or machine-gunned from the air. The Loyalist government therefore used specially armored trucks for this purpose.

Madrid was stripping for a long fight. On November 6, Franco could have entered the city without encountering any effective resistance. Instead he waited. Some said he wanted to take Madrid on November 7, just to "celebrate the Bolshevik revolution." Previously he had announced he would occupy it on October 12, Columbus Day. Spaniards relish these little pleasantries. But when Franco struck on November 8, it was too late. Spanish troops had occupied a strong position at Carabanchel thus obstructing rebel progress from the Toledo area, and an International Brigade unit had quickly manned the northern defenses of the city. When these Internationals marched through Madrid the civilians greeted them with "*Viva Rusia.*" Spaniards long regarded them as Soviet troops. Most of them were French. They numbered 1,900. The second International contingent—Lukach's Twelfth—reached the front on November 14. Its strength was then 1,550. They—a handful—saved the military situation. The first group suffered 900 casualties in its first four weeks under fire.

Lukach lost 750 men in the first three weeks. These fighters had left peaceful jobs and peaceful countries to die or lose their eyes and arms in the struggle against Fascism. But nobody used big words in the Brigade. It was a big, dirty, costly job. Flags were furled. The flags waved in the heart.

Throughout the centuries, men have left their homes to fight on foreign soil for liberty. Byron, Lafayette, Pulaski, von Steuben, Kosciusko, the Lafayette Esquadrille, the International Brigade—all had the same incentive and the same tradition. A police officer was pursuing Lafayette with a warrant for his arrest and arrived at a French port just as the Marquis sailed for America. That happened to many men who enlisted in the International Brigade. Often they had to climb the Pyrenees in the night in order to come down in Spain the next day. Those who could not make the long trek through the snow at high altitudes were carried by their comrades.

Especially in the first part of the war, the International Brigade performed an indispensable service in stemming the Franco tide until the Spanish regiments were better trained. Being a good soldier is often a matter of getting accustomed to the noise of shells and bombs. The human animal becomes accustomed to almost anything. The soldier must also feel what he is fighting for. At the front in Spain, men about to go into action would say to their officers, "Is this going to be important?" If tomorrow the official communiqué was going to say, "The Loyalists straightened their line on the X sector," or "Occasional skirmishes in the evening," he did not want to die for that. He wanted to die for victory, for a grand push.

The politics of a soldier likewise make a lot of difference. If he has any doubts about the government's policy, he fights with less bravery. That is why the Anarchists usually fought badly. They did not want to die for Caballero or Negrin or Martinez Barrio or the regimes personified by these men.

Several days after I enlisted, Marty placed heavy guards around all the International Brigade's premises: he had learned that Buenaventura Durutti, at the head of 10,000 Anarchists from Barcelona was stopping in Albacete en route to Madrid to check Franco. It turned out that there were not 10,000 but 3,000 and that they had no intentions against our brigade. They behaved like a lot of temperamental gentlemen but apart from that did nobody any harm. Marty, the Communist, was hypersuspicious of them.

Many Communists hated Marty. This was especially true of American Communist leaders whom he treated with calculated rudeness. The Americans in the Brigade resented the fact that he confiscated their United States passports and in hundreds of cases never returned them. The fate of those passports was a subject of much speculation. I believe Mr. Bullitt, not without reason, suspected that they had been presented to the GPU.

On November 15, I was in Madrid. I went to the War Office to see General Goriev who had taken command of the military situation. I asked an attendant where I could find General Goriev. He beckoned me to follow him and walked through long corridors calling out to everyone he met, "Have you seen the Russian general, have you seen the Russian general?" Goriev's presence there was a secret, but Spaniards hate secrets.

As I sat in Goriev's office, his Spanish interpreter and aide, Professor Robles of Johns Hopkins University, came in to tell him that Colonel Fuqua, the American military attaché, was outside and wanted to get the latest information. With the directness of an old army man, Fuqua had applied to the source. Goriev instructed Robles to talk to him.

Late that evening, I was in staff headquarters with Goriev. He was waiting for the latest news. Durutti had gone into action. A tall Circassian officer of Russia's Red Army served as his aide. The Anarchists were in front of Mt. Garabitas in the Casa de Campo which controlled the approaches to Madrid proper. They were fresh troops and Goriev had assigned an important sector to them.

After midnight, the Circassian arrived and reported that the Anarchists had fled in panic before a small force of Moors. This would allow Franco to enter the University City.

Durutti wanted his men to fight. That made him unpopular. I saw him frequently in the Gran Via Hotel in the evening. He had a large bodyguard with their fingers always on the triggers of their submachine guns.

Several days after the Anarchist debacle near Mt. Garabitas, Durutti was killed at the front. He was shot from the rear, and it was generally assumed that his own men assassinated him because he favored active Anarchist participation in the war and co-operation with Caballero. But many Anarchists were interested first of all in establishing an ideal libertarian republic in Spain and did not see eye to eye with the Socialists or the Communists or the bourgeois Republicans, and were none too enthusiastic about dying for the Caballero government. It was not "important."

My work as quartermaster in the brigade occupied all my attention, but lest I lose sight of the broader aspects of the Spanish situation, I took off one day a week, or two nights and a day, to visit Madrid or Valencia, the new capital.

One evening, at the dinner table in the Grand Hotel of Albacete, Ignacio Cisneros heard me say that I was going to Madrid the next morning. "Why not go by plane," he suggested. "There will be a plane at seven."

By car the trip took four hours. I would have to send my car to Madrid anyway so as to be able to get back. The plane trip would last an hour and a half, Cisneros told me. I added an hour for delays. Little time gained. But I grasped the opportunity. It sounded exciting.

The plane was an old crate that made only ninety miles an hour. It started ninety minutes late. It was a military machine used for reconnaissance and it had a huge hole in the rear of the roof through which a machine gun stuck out.

During the last half hour of the flight the pilot's assistant told each one of the eight passengers to watch a sector of the horizon for enemy aircraft and we hugged the earth, literally skimming the farm houses. Peasants gave us the clenched-fist salute. As we approached the airfield I saw a large semi-circle of pursuit planes parked on the outer rim with their noses pointed outward. I recognized them as the well-known stub-nosed Soviet Chatos. Every hangar had been hit by bombs and resembled a charred barn. This was the Russian airdrome at Alcala de Henares.

When we got out I addressed a man in Russian and asked when there would be a car for Madrid. There could have been no mistake about his nationality. He replied, "Right away." In a moment, a man in a brown leather coat beckoned to me and walked towards the center of the field. A huge Mauser revolver hung down the side of his leg. I said to myself, "GPU."

"Who are you?" he quizzed.

I took out my United States passport, showed him my Soviet visas, and explained that I was an American journalist. He wanted to know how I got into a military machine, what I intended to do in Madrid, and how I expected to get back. I told him.

His eyes photographed me for his memory, and then he told me it was all right. That evening I sat with Koltzov of *Pravda* and Carmen of *Izvestia* in their room in the Palace Hotel in Madrid when the same man walked in with mail for them from Russia.

Carmen lay on his bed reading letters and Moscow papers. Suddenly he exclaimed, "Fischer, here's something about you." He had started reading, in a fat Soviet monthly, an installment of Ilf and Petrov's account of their trip to America.

Somebody opened a window and we heard quick machine-gun fire which sounded like cavalry galloping over cobblestones. "Sounds nearer," Koltzov remarked gravely. It sounded to me like just around the corner.

"Close it," Carmen begged. "I want to read."

He read aloud from Ilf and Petrov. These two Soviet writers explained how they prepared for their trip to the United States. They looked up Walter Duranty in Moscow. "When you tell an American you are going to America," they wrote—I am quoting from memory —"he does not tell you what America is like, or what is of interest there. He sits down at his typewriter and gives you a letter to So-and-So and then another letter to XYZ, 'Yes and you must visit my friend ABC,' and he bangs out another letter of introduction. Louis Fischer did the same thing, and so did Sergei Eisenstein, the Soviet film director, and others. By the time we had to leave Moscow our single suitcase was so filled with these precious letters that we had trouble squeezing in our four shirts and four pairs of socks. In New York we revealed to Soviet Consul Arens our possession of these valuable letters and asked him what to do. He said, 'Give them to me. I will take care of that.' So Arens took the letters and invited the persons to whom they were addressed to a big cocktail party at the Soviet consulate. The appointed afternoon we, all nervous, stood at the head of the stairs with Arens. The writers, journalists, and artists of America started arriving. Arens introduced us. Each one shook hands with us and said, 'How do you do, Mr. Ilf. Glad to know you, Mr. Petrov,' and walked into the big reception room. They drank, smoked, talked, and laughed. We remained at the head of the stairs, for by the time the last one had arrived, the first one started going home, and then others went home, and each one, passing us on the way out, said, 'Pleased to have seen you, Mr. Ilf. It was a great pleasure, Mr. Petrov.' Soon everybody was gone. Our letters were gone too and we had not talked to a single person."

I interrupted Carmen's reading to tell him about an episode of the

Ilf-Petrov visit which had been reported to me in a personal letter from New York. My friend Alex Gumberg had taken Ilf and Petrov out to his country home in Connecticut. Petrov, who spoke some English, sat on a couch at one end of the large dining hall talking to American guests, while on a couch at the opposite end sat Ilf who knew no English. Next to Ilf was a pretty girl. Alex was there to translate.

The girl said, "Mr. Ilf, does the Soviet government really give you freedom to write as you please?" Alex, knowing the fruitlessness of such a discussion, translated to Ilf, "She says she loves you."

"But, Alex," said Ilf, "are American women usually so forward? What can I tell her?"

"He cannot discuss literature," Alex interpreted, "with such a beautiful girl. He'd much rather make love to you."

"Now, Alex, stop kidding," the girl said.

"She declares she wants to sleep with you," Alex said in Russian to Ilf.

Ilf blushed.

By now the girl understood that Alex was up to some mischief and turned to Ilf and said, "Don't listen to him; he's pulling your leg," and she tugged at Ilf's trousers.

"You see," Alex said in Russian to Ilf, "she wants you to take your pants off."

Somebody had again opened the window and the laughter mixed with noise of guns near-by. Koltzov wanted to know what was happening and called me to go with him to the War Ministry. We learned that the Moors had advanced in the University City but were now being held.

Next morning I went to General Goriev's apartment in the Ministry of War. He had just returned from a night's auto trip and was bathing. He came out brushing his hair. Then he put a net over his hair to keep it flat, and ordered a light breakfast. After breakfast, he lit his pipe, leaned back, and talked. He might have been an Englishman on a country estate. He had organized the defense of Madrid. More than any one man he was the savior of Madrid. (He was shot in the big Moscow purge.)

"Madrid will not be taken," he assured me. "It can never be taken. It can only be surrendered. And there is no mood of surrender."

He showed me the situation on the map.

A Russian entered who called himself Loti, Charles Loti. He spoke a perfect French but he was a Russian Jew named Rosenfeld. I withdrew while he consulted Goriev, and then he invited me to go to the Madrid front with him. En route, we stopped at several houses converted into military staff headquarters. The city had been divided into wards and each ward had its military command. Loti collected data from the commanders, listened to their complaints about the shortage of arms, and explained the general military position. Later he measured the depth of the trenches and found them too shallow.

"What is your job here?" I asked him.

"I am the second assistant of our commercial representative in Spain," he laughed. That was his official rank.

We drove through the Arguelles quarter towards the Casa de Campo front just outside the city limits. It was Sunday, December 6. Down one street people were running fast. The street emptied. Airplane motors roared overhead. Crash! A five-story building in front of us fell into itself like a pile of wooden blocks. We turned a corner. Another deafening bang. The air filled with brick and mortar dust which settled in one's throat. We were in the midst of a serious air raid. The driver stopped the car and we rushed into the vestibule of an apartment house. A bomb whistled near-by. It made my spine cold. I tried to force open a door which might lead to the cellar, but a column of air struck behind the door and made me recoil. A bomb had just fallen into the next house but one. Another bomb fell and from the thud it was clear that it had struck the street pavement outside. We crouched in the vestibule and heard parts of the paving hit the walls of the house in which we had taken refuge. A granite block came hurtling over the four-story roof and fell in the small courtyard to which the vestibule led. Half the block was blackened by the explosion. A woman in the vestibule said, "Barbarians."

A woman peeped out of a door which opened on the courtyard and motioned us to come into her apartment. We dashed diagonally across the court. She had two dark rooms. She was calm, at least as far as one could notice, but her younger sister was hysterical and screamed as each bomb struck.

The raid finally ceased and we returned to our car. A veil of dust still hung over the street. A military motorcyclist came up and commandeered our car for the wounded. I walked about. Automobiles were speeding away with the wounded who were propped up in the seats, or laid on the bottom of the car. I saw some who had lost limbs or parts of their faces and were bleeding profusely. When our car returned, the interior was covered with blood.

Women, old men, and little children started creeping out from the bombed homes. Everybody was white. Hair and faces powdered with white dust from ceilings that had collapsed on them. A girl of thirteen had saved a canary in its cage. In her other arm she carried a bottle of milk. A woman held a nursing baby. The baby howled and the mother howled. The mother had lost control. The mother's dress was whitened except for the black border where she held the child. A wrinkled old woman wrapped in a blanket cried. Her face muscles trembled.

"Where shall I go?" she asked me.

I put my arm into hers and we joined the stream of humanity that was moving toward the street-car line. We passed women in black standing at the entrances of houses. They wrung their hands and swayed from their waists in a rhythm of despair. Later the same thing happened to Warsaw, Rotterdam, London, Coventry, Berlin, Hamburg, and Haifa.

That day I cabled *The Nation* an article describing the bombing. "From outside comes no help," I exclaimed. "Where is the world which answered the call of Belgium? Where is the humanitarian heart of the millions who go to church and pray to God, or of the millions who call themselves idealists yet go about their business signing letters, having manicures, seeing cinemas, while a city of culture and beauty is ground into dust?"

Where?

Where? Waiting at home until bombs of the same manufacture and dropped by the same Luftwaffe would come to them.

My work in the International Brigade slowly acquired system. It was difficult to achieve complete order because of the necessary irregularity of the demands made on the quartermaster's office. Late in the evening, news would come that 500 men were arriving in the morning and had to be fully equipped. Or a hospital would send word that it had a hundred wounded members of the Brigade who had lost all their clothing. I had to supply our cantonments in villages within a circle of some thirty miles from Albacete—Madrigueras, Chinchilla de Monte Aragon where we had artillery training under a Czech captain named Miksche, a completely non-political friend of freedom, La Roda, Mahora, and other places. My principle of organization was that the more work I delegated to others the better the work would progress. I had no pride about doing it all myself and getting credit. One of my assistants in charge of the stores in the former Bank of Spain building was a Pole of about forty-five named Wolf. He labored hard and well. One morning he disappeared. My suspicions induced me to ask Marty, and Marty replied fiercely that he knew nothing. But I later learned the facts. In the middle of the night, three Polish comrades entered Wolf's room and instructed him to dress and come with them. First he refused but they told him he had to obey, and he understood. They had revolvers on their hips. He was arrested for "Trotzkyism." Marty had given the order. Four others were arrested that night.

My relations with Marty deteriorated steadily. I once said to him, "Listen, you are not a dictator nor am I a child." But he thought he was a Stalin. He knew I had had a friendly visit at the front with General Kleber. Marty and Kleber were at daggers drawn.

I sometimes dined at the Grand Hotel with Soviet army officers. That did not suit Marty. One morning the Order of the Day contained a reprimand for me. I had "neglected duty" the previous evening. The Frenchmen at the bull-ring mess complained that the meat in the evening stew was hard and I could not be found to receive their complaint.

A few days later, Marty returned from a trip to Valencia. He was cordial and warm when he met me, and called me into his office, and said, "I talked to some of your friends in Valencia. They feel it is such a pity for you to waste your time with kitchen problems and clothing distribution when you could be doing far more important things."

I saw the point.

In forty-eight hours I had handed over the job to my successor. But I continued to be interested in the International Brigade and did everything I could to augment its strength and make its members comfortable.

23. *The First Battle of the Second World War*

SADLY, I bade farewell to the International Brigade and to my shirts, spoons, and blankets and returned to my trade, journalism.

I decided to go to Geneva. Foreign Minister Alvarez del Vayo had already left Valencia for Switzerland to place the Loyalist case before the League of Nations and plead for the scrapping of Non-Intervention which had quickly acquired quotation marks.

I had spent three months in Spain. Nothing else had existed for me. A nation fought for its life and millions of its citizens for their lives. England and France looked on passively while Germany and Italy attacked a democracy. The League had put Spain on the Council's agenda. History would be made. There would be tremendous doings, intense curiosity. Everybody would be interested in Spain.

I rushed from my hotel in Geneva to the League Council meeting. Correspondents stood in small groups and diplomats stood in small groups. Occasionally, diplomats *and* correspondents stood in the same small groups. I approached one group where I saw an acquaintance. They were talking about "Wallis." Who was that? I asked. Somebody said, "Mrs. Simpson." I moved to another group. "When is the broadcast?" "Will he abdicate?" Nobody mentioned Spain. Nobody cared about Madrid. Everybody was in Buckingham Palace.

Late that afternoon, December 12, 1936, at the home of Ludwik Rajchman, chief of the League of Nations health department, I heard King Edward the Eighth's abdication address: "The woman I love." It was unique and impressive. But he was pro-Franco, and was he a Fascist? Rumor had it that he sympathized with Hitler and that through Mrs. Simpson Ribbentrop influenced British policy. Such things were going on in France. Why not in England?

Geneva did not hear the bombs bursting in the air of Spain. I felt lonely and cold. Switzerland seemed so quiet and clean and abnormal. Spain had become normal for me. Some friends in Geneva lived with Spain as I did. Their society comforted me. But they were the intellectual élite, the League patriots, the internationalists, the anti-appeasers.

I attended the session in the marble conference hall of the League. At a long, crescent table sat the delegates to the League. But between them sat the black women of Madrid. Behind Delbos I saw Malraux's nervous face and cigarette. When Viscount Cranborne spoke for England he read from a paper. After del Vayo spoke, Delbos answered from a paper prepared before he had heard del Vayo's address. A secretary in the cool of the Quai d'Orsay was answering a million voices that rang in del Vayo's appeal. I wanted to do more for Spain, to devote all my time and energy to Spain.

Before going to America on a lecture tour, where I hoped I could make appeals for funds for Spanish relief and urge men to volunteer for the International Brigade, I went to see my family in Moscow. Moscow was not Geneva. Moscow lived in Spain. Everybody talked Spain. My boys asked me to come to their schools and give little speeches on Spain. At least eight Soviet friends asked me how they could go and fight in Spain. The director of a museum came to see me and inquired whether I had any posters or documents relating to the Spanish War. The apartment was filled with people all the time, and no one let me ask questions about Russia. "Spain is more important," they said. "If we win in Spain we will be happy here." The newspapers were filled with endless articles and reports on the Spanish situation. An American friend, Bob Merriman, my tennis partner of former years, phoned to find out how he could get to Spain. He had been an instructor in economics at the University of California, a smiling, shy, tall person, always eager to assure me, when he defeated me on the courts, that I really played better than he did. (He later became the commander of the American volunteers in the International Brigade and was killed in action.) Spain was stirring Russia as no Soviet issue in recent years had stirred it. I never believed that the Kremlin could succeed in converting Soviet citizens to old-style narrow nationalism. Russians understood Spain, a poor country whose progress was obstructed by a backward class. The Spanish civil war was like the Soviet civil war, reactionaries fighting the people and foreign powers aiding the reactionaries while nobody helped the people.

Communist friends in Spain had urged me to see Dimitrov in Moscow and give him my impressions of the Spanish situation. I had first met Dimitrov in Russia in 1935. John Gunther, collecting material for *Inside Europe*, wanted to interview him and we went together to the sanatorium where Dimitrov was recuperating from his experiences in Nazi prisons. Dimitrov was now head of the Third International. Gunther told him that he had covered the Leipzig trial and Dimitrov said, "I remember your face. I watched you from the prisoners' box. The sympathy on the faces of the foreign correspondents was encouraging." That trial made history. Dimitrov had long been held in jail by the Nazis on the charge of setting fire to the Reichstag in the early days of the Fascist regime. His captors had put him in chains. He was asthmatic and suffered torture from confinement. At the trial, however, his robust figure, leonine head with black hair, and free, frank face spoke defiance. Dimitrov's testimony drove his prosecutors into a rage. He attacked the Nazi regime and analyzed its anti-proletarian, war-making character. He interpolated remarks that upset the case they were building up. He charged that the whole trial was a farcical frame-up. Hermann Goering himself took the witness stand. Dimitrov, the prisoner, the man at the mercy of the Nazis, was calm. But Goering lost his temper and threatened Dimitrov. Turning the tables, Dimitrov accused Goering of burning the Reichstag and using the miserable, doped van der Lubbe as a foil. Goering's intemperance left the world with the distinct impression that Dimitrov's thrust had struck home. Reports of the trial filled the world press for weeks.

The Hitler government did not dare sentence Dimitrov to death. British officials urged Berlin to release this prominent Bulgarian Communist. The Nazis freed him and allowed him to fly to Moscow.

I went out to Dimitrov's log-cabin country home on the outskirts of Moscow. He was in a suit of bad Soviet blue serge with a jacket that buttoned up to the neck. There was something heroic and historic about him, a man made of one piece. I had the same feeling when I met Winston Churchill. But since Dimitrov is simpler than Churchill, the impression of unity is greater. Dimitrov is the old-type Balkan peasant-revolutionist equipped with a modern weapon—organized Communism. He is, above all, a fighter, and Moscow ruined his personality by making the Third International a rubber stamp.

We talked for several hours. He asked about numerous Spaniards and foreigners in Spain, particularly about Marty and Kleber. Obviously, reports of the Marty-Kleber feud were on his desk. (Very soon, Kleber was recalled from Spain, and then, as often happens,

Marty was recalled too. Later Marty returned. But Kleber did not. There was a rumor that he had been shot in Moscow.)

Dimitrov said the anti-militarism of foreign Communists had kept them out of armies, navies, national guards, and officers' training corps. They therefore had too few people to draw on for the International Brigade. The countries with conscription were an exception, he added. That is why, apart from geography, the French constituted the bulk of the Brigade. He hoped America would send many thousands of volunteers. He hoped there would be more non-Communists than Communists, and he stressed the political wisdom of the enlistment of American socialists, liberals, and Jewish nationalists. "We can then build the American Popular Front on the Spanish battlefield," he said.

In practice that proved difficult. American Communists and foreign Communists in America were none too anxious to have socialists, who might be Trotskyists, in the International Brigade. And the socialists had very few men for enlistment anyway because their organizations were so weak.

I went to see Maxim Litvinov, Commissar for Foreign Affairs. He wore the same kind of blue serge suit as Dimitrov. Apparently, a Soviet factory had turned out a first order. Litvinov looked depressed. He is the buoyant, energetic, positive type of person. Now he seemed pessimistic. The purge was beginning to creep towards his commissariat.

Litvinov put an endless chain of questions to me about the morale of the Loyalist soldiers and civilians, the material damage from bombings, the behavior of individual Russians in Spain, the quality of Spanish leaders. Finally, he asked me whether I had seen Uritzky in Moscow. I said, "Who is he?" Litvinov replied, "He's an interesting person," and offered to fix an appointment for me with him.

The next day Boris Mironov of the Foreign Office press department phoned and told me he would take me to see Uritzky. We drove to the Soviet War Commissariat. From his office and his personality I concluded that Uritzky did not merely hold general's rank —the four diamond-shaped tabs on his collar showed that—but was one of the top chiefs of the Commissariat. I learned later that all Soviet military affairs in Spain, including the shipping of materials and men, were directly in his charge.

Uritzky too asked questions. He began with the International Brigade. After about a quarter of an hour had elapsed, he asked me whether I would mind if a stenographer took notes, and he summoned a stenographer and begged me to repeat everything I had said. Then the questioning continued. Uritzky intimated that he wanted the stenographic record for his superiors. The interview lasted three hours, broken only by glasses of tea and cake.

I did most of the giving in this meeting. But I learned from his questions. And he also answered some of mine. When he asked, for instance, whether the International Brigade could furnish tank drivers and mechanics and whether the Spaniards would make good tank drivers I deduced that the Soviet government intended sending more material and few men. I said that the Spaniards were naturally good mechanics and that many of the foreigners could drive automobiles and trucks. "But," I added, "everything depends on how much equipment you send." To which he replied that transportation presented the chief problem. The Italians, he declared, had their spies at Constantinople and watched every ship that came out of the Black Sea. Moscow had a big bureau which did nothing else but devise means of disguising war munitions and the vessels that carried them. They sometimes rebuilt freighters, giving them a false deck, and placed arms between the two decks. Tanks were immersed in the oil of tankers, and so on. But airplanes could scarcely be hidden. I wondered whether big bombers might not fly from the nearest Soviet point to the nearest Loyalist airfield. He said it was physically impossible. Nor could they land in Czechoslovakia. The Czechs would not allow it for fear of antagonizing Germany. No Soviet airplanes flew from Russia to Spain at any time during the Spanish War. Uritzky explained that if a Soviet machine made one forced landing anywhere in Europe the whole world would squeal and "Litvinov wouldn't like that." This made it clear to me that Soviet aid to the Loyalists would remain within the limited legal-illegal bounds of Non-Intervention. There would be subterfuge and lying and therefore delays and scarcity of supplies. Moscow apparently would not go "all out on Spain." On December 14, 1936, the Soviet S.S. *Komsomol*, carrying munitions to Spain, had been set on fire and sunk in the Mediterranean by the Italian navy. Moscow was deterred. Russian aid to Spain depended on Anglo-French co-operation in the Mediterranean or transit overland through France.

I told Uritzky the Loyalists needed submarines and other craft to protect the coast against the Italian and German navies and to convoy ships. He said, "We have already sent four submarines and we have ten more for shipment. But the Spanish leaders must understand that we can only give them supplies if they ask for them. Even in the case of Outer Mongolia we do not take the initiative and suggest that it buy arms. It orders them on its own. You might explain in Valencia that they must be more aggressive with us."

Uritzky inquired about Cisneros, the commander of the Loyalist air force who necessarily co-operated closely with the Russian air fleet in Spain. We talked about him for a while, and then he said that Luli Cisneros lived in his family with another Spanish girl, Charito. "Since I became their guardian," he said, "I have been the most unpopular man in the Soviet Union."

"Why?" I asked in astonishment.

Uritzky told me that all his colleagues complained; he had taken unfair advantage of his position to get Spanish children. Why couldn't they get Spanish children? And why should he have two?

Uritzky explained to them that one girl of eleven who didn't speak Russian would be unhappy alone and so Luli and Charito stayed together with him. But that satisfied nobody. "I'll take three," a member of the Red Army general staff assured him. He said he would never have peace until he could distribute a big contingent of Spanish children among his friends.

I told Uritzky that I had to visit Luli because I was going back to Valencia where I would see her parents, Constancia de la Mora and her husband, Ignacio Hidalgo de Cisneros. I was leaving Moscow to go abroad on January 1, and since most Russians celebrate New Year's Eve very late, we agreed to meet at noon on the first with all members of our families at the Red Army rest home outside Moscow where the Uritzkys were spending the holiday week.

A car fetched us and took us out through beautiful snow-carpeted woods to the rest house. Luli and Charito were out in the woods. I saw them coming home across the snow, little Spanish girls in fur caps and squirrel coats that reached down to their heels. Charito was smaller than Luli but older. Her father had been killed in a dog fight with a Franco pilot but she did not know it. They seemed happy and fatter than most Spanish children I had seen in recent months. Charito refused to sing or dance though she reportedly did both well, and I did not blame her. Uritzky's wife prepared tea for her family and mine (in Russia any time is tea time), while he beat me easily at billiards, and then we all sat around a huge table laden with pastries and sandwiches. Before long we were the center of attraction for uniformed and non-uniformed men and women at other tables, who were obviously very fond of the little girls. When the crowd was big enough Luli and Charito discreetly slipped away to their rooms. Such affairs rarely interest children.

That morning's Moscow newspapers had carried a list of seventeen Red Army men who were created "Heroes of the Soviet Union," the Soviet govenment's highest distinction, for "exemplary fulfillment of special and difficult government tasks with a view to strengthening the military might of the Soviet Union and the display of heroism in their performance." No. 4 on the list was Sergei Tarkhov.

I mentioned the honor list and said to Uritzky, "I knew Tarkhov. He died in Madrid." Uritzky drew in his lips and nodded. I inquired whether he knew the circumstances of Tarkhov's end, and he urged me to recount them.

It was in November, 1936. I arrived one day in Madrid from Albacete and went to the Palace Hotel to look for Russian friends who had lived there. I peered into several rooms of the second floor and found them all occupied by wounded soldiers. A nurse in white stuck her head out of a door and asked whether she could help me. I said I was looking for some Russian comrades.

"Russian comrades," she burst forth. "There is one here. Please come in."

A man was lying in bed and mumbling—just coming out of ether. "Russian aviator," the nurse said. "Three shots in the stomach." She wanted me to return because she expected to have trouble making herself understood to him.

I came back in the afternoon. I greeted him in Russian, and his first question was, "What is the situation at the front?" I assured him without regard to realities that it was all right.

"Very bad time for me to have been knocked out, eh?"

"You'll be back soon," I promised. He smiled feebly. I could see he had a powerful build, broad neck, round head, big chest. "Tell him," the nurse begged, "he must wear his pajama coat." He complained that he had never been able to get accustomed to pajamas. The nurse sat on his bed and fondled his hair. "Very strong man," she said.

That evening I asked a Russian officer about the wounded pilot. He told me the story. The pilot was in an attack plane over the outskirts of Madrid when his motor went dead and he bailed out. He declared that when he jumped he was unwounded. But as he floated downward, helpless in his parachute, he was hit in the stomach by shots from the ground. When he reached the ground he was captured, beaten, and forced to walk a long distance. His captors delivered him to a big building. This was the Loyalist War Ministry but he did not know it. His captors were Loyalists and they had fired at him while he dangled in the air. When he came down they addressed him in Spanish and since he failed to open his mouth they assumed he was German.

Inside the Ministry, officers interrogated him. Dazed, and in excruciating pain, he remembered the instructions he had received in Moscow, "Don't talk." Russians came in and swore at him. But there were two kinds of Russians; Soviet Russians and Whites, and Franco was reputed to have White Russians. Tarkhov kept his mouth tightly shut except for occasional moans. At this moment, the chief of the Soviet air squadrons in Spain entered the room, and seeing the wounded man, shouted, "Tarkhov, thou!"

He was immediately taken to the Palace hospital and operated on. The same evening the Loyalist government published a sharply worded decree cautioning soldiers and home guards against shooting or attacking parachutists.

I visited Tarkhov again the next day. "You must impress on him," the nurse expostulated, "that he is not permitted to get up in the night." He had risen to go to the lavatory. Only a Russian giant could have mustered the strength. I told him not to do it again, and he said, "If I lie here motionless too long my muscles will get weak and then I won't be able to return to my squadron so soon."

The way the nurse talked about him it was clear that she had fallen in love with him. "I have promised to go with him to Russia," she told me, and she obviously meant it and hoped he would take her. She showed me his clinical chart. The fever curve was mounting. He asked me what it said and I assured him that he would soon be well.

The next day he died.

"Let's play billiards," Uritzky exclaimed. There were tears in his eyes.

He beat me again. I had to go and prepare for my departure. As we shook hands near the door he put his left hand on my shoulder and kissed me on the lips. The kiss was for Spain. (Uritzky disappeared in the big purge.)

During my Moscow stay, everybody, including Markoosha, displayed a reluctance to discuss Soviet conditions. Markoosha finally relented. The new Constitution still filled many hearts with hope, she said. One hundred and fifty-four thousand proposals for amendment and improvement of its text had been submitted by individual citizens. At the Congress where Stalin, on November 25, 1936, presented the Constitution for adoption, the delegates were better dressed than ever before. Each article of the Constitution was read separately and received wild applause—except Article 124 which was received in silence. It grants freedom of religious worship. All speeches at the Congress were filled with attacks on Fascism. N. N. Liubchenko, chief of the Ukrainian delegation said, "Just as a pig can never look at the sky so Hitler will never see our cabbage patch." Litvinov condemned the anti-Comintern triangle pact.

Nevertheless, Markoosha said, the air was full of foreboding. The Zinoviev-Kamenev trial had come and gone, and now a second big trial of leading Bolsheviks was being bruited. It would involve Piatakov, leader of Soviet industry, Karl Radek, publicist, Gregory Sokolnikov, former Finance Commissar and Ambassador to London, L. P. Serebyakov, an old co-worker of Lenin's, and others.

Zinoviev had been cordially disliked even by many Communists. Kamenev was highly respected. They had constituted, with Stalin, the triumvirate which took over control when Lenin died. They had had their doubts about the wisdom of making a revolution in 1917, and Lenin flayed them mercilessly. But after that Lenin worked with them, and so did Stalin.

When they joined forces with Trotzky in 1926, Stalin sent Kamenev as ambassador to Rome, and Zinoviev was removed from Leningrad. First step. In January, 1928, they were exiled to Siberia. Second step. In June, 1928, after proper recantations, they were brought back to Moscow. Kamenev worked in a publishing house and Zinoviev held a minor job in the co-operative movement. Both wrote nauseatingly pro-Stalin articles in the press. When Kirov was assassinated in 1934, they were sentenced to a ten-year exile. Third step. On August 14, 1936, they sat on the stage in the Moscow Hall of Nobles on trial for their lives. On August 24, they were sentenced to death. Fourth and last step.

They and others were accused of plotting to assassinate Stalin, Voroshilov, Ordjonekidze, Kaganovitch, Postishev, Kossior, Zhdanov, and others. They plotted with several German Communists, it was charged.

Fritz David, a German Communist on trial, confessed that on instructions from Trotzky, he had come to Moscow to shoot Stalin. Moses Luria, another German Communist, confessed that with the help of the Nazi Gestapo he had planned to kill Voroshilov. Yevdokimov, another defendant, former President of the Leningrad Soviet, described how the defendants had vied with one another for "the honor" of assassinating Stalin. Zinoviev admitted to being a Fascist. "Trotzkyism plus terrorism is Fascism," he affirmed.

Prosecutor Vishinsky demanded the death sentence for all of them. "The mad dogs must be shot," he shouted. But this was mild compared to the self-denunciations of the defendants themselves. They dramatically proclaimed their guilt, and if one of their number seemed to insist on his own execution with too little passion his comrade-defendants fell upon him wrathfully. The death sentences were announced in their presence at three in the morning. Kamenev rose and appealed to his three sons "to die, if necessary, under the banner of Stalin."

(I shall deal with the phenomenon of confessions in another chapter.)

The trial touched off mass arrests of German, Polish, and other foreign Communists in Moscow. Government officials in the offices where the defendants had been employed were arrested in hundreds.

It was the first time in Soviet history that front-rank Bolsheviks had been executed. Moscow had a gruesome feeling that anything might happen now. No man's past services, whether to the Revolution or to Stalin, protected him. It was open season. A paralyzing nervousness began to spread.

I left Moscow with a sense of relief. I was sorry for the people who were being arrested. And I was even more sorry for those of my friends who saw safety in publicly defending the trials and the arrests.

Before going to America to lecture I wanted to have a pleasanter picture in my mind. Bombs over Valencia were far less disturbing than the echo of shots in the GPU cellars on Lubianka Square.

It was only a short trip from Paris. The express left the Quai d'Orsay station in the evening. Early in the morning it arrived at

Toulouse. The Air France plane, skimming the snow-covered peaks of the Pyrenees, reached Valencia in time for lunch.

I stayed a week. I interviewed Caballero, Prieto, del Vayo, Negrin, and many others. When I told Caballero that Uritzky had told me in Moscow the Spanish government must ask for more munitions, he registered surprise. "We've asked for everything. But it is very difficult to talk to Rosenberg. He listens and says nothing." It did not occur to Caballero that that was the limited function of a wise Soviet Ambassador. Rosenberg's reticence, however, often irritated expansive Spaniards.

Prieto was pleased to hear that Uritzky had promised more submarines. "We also need speedboats," he said. Prieto too complained that the Russians were slow in sending material.

I told Rosenberg their reactions.

General Grishin, the ranking Soviet military officer in Spain, took me to his office and asked my impressions of Moscow. Then I asked him about the military situation in Spain. He was satisfied with the progress. While we talked, the door leading to the next room was open and I could hear an assistant taking down a telephonic report of a battle north of Madrid in the Las Rozas section. I heard him repeat the information. He was told how many Loyalist soldiers were engaged, what arms they had, how the Soviet airplanes collaborated, how the soldiers fought, how the rebels fought, and what booty was taken. It was a Loyalist victory that day.

Valencia felt more confident. The Republican army began to function like an army. The International Brigade continued to grow.

Crossing the Atlantic, I received a radio message from New York inviting me to address a dinner the night of my arrival in honor of Soviet Ambassador Troyanovsky. I accepted. Upon disembarkation, a representative of the arrangements committee told me that I was not to speak on Russia because the Ambassador would do that, and I was not to speak on Spain because that would embarrass the Ambassador. I promised to speak on the stormy trans-Atlantic crossing.

So with sea air in my lungs and in fresh evening clothes, I rose at the banquet and said, "In the eyes of many of us who have been devoted to Russia, Spain was the test. Russia is meeting the test successfully."

Most of the diners were friends of the Soviet Union and radicals. I knew from their applause and from what they said to me later that they were relieved. The Communist and Soviet press had denied there was Russian help to Spain. The Fascists affirmed it. These people did not know what to believe. They knew I had just come from Spain and had seen the evidence of Russian aid. They were happy. For a Soviet Russia that failed to help struggling Republican Spain would have forfeited the right to the friendship of liberals, intellectuals, and Communists.

If the egotistical patriotism which I saw emerging from Bolshevik headquarters in 1935 and 1936 as the new national dogma had barred the way to Soviet participation in the Spanish struggle in 1936, I would have despaired of Russia, and I think I would have turned away from Russia then. I would have known that Moscow had forsaken the internationalism which was its grace, that Moscow's soul had been corroded. To protect a victim of Fascist attack was Soviet Russia's intimate concern. It was the concern of every anti-Fascist. It was the proof of anti-Fascism. The statesmen of the democracies did not furnish the proof.

For me personally, Spain was salvation. I was glad to leave Russia and immerse myself in a new, vibrant situation where Russia showed its finest face. The Bolsheviks who worked and fought for Spain were glorious human beings. They could not have fought for their native land with more self-sacrifice and heroism. They identified themselves with Spain. It was their adopted country.

Before long, André Malraux arrived in New York to make propaganda for the Loyalist cause, and *The Nation* arranged a dinner for him. He delivered a beautifully poetic speech. I had preceded him with a factual address outlining the history and background of the Spanish conflict.

When the meeting was adjourned, Malcolm Cowley of *The New Republic* asked me whether he could have the text of my speech to print in the magazine. I said I would try to write it up and let him know. But *The Nation* protested, reasonably enough. I continued to work on it until I decided to expand it into a pamphlet. I had offers from two publishers for a book on Spain, but what I could write at the moment was too tentative to dignify with permanence. If America printed and read more pamphlets it would be afflicted with fewer of those books which are really nothing more than padded magazine articles or watered pamphlets. Besides, a ten-cent pamphlet gets a bigger circulation and I was interested in reaching the largest possible audience with the facts on Spain. The pamphlet was published in the United States in May, 1937, by *The Nation,* and in London, and in Paris in both French and German. I dictated most of it on the roof of the Mayflower Hotel in New York while sick with arthritis, and the income from it paid all the expense of a ten-weeks' illness, chiefly because my good doctor charged me little more than his carfare and laboratory costs.

In this pamphlet, I declared that "the first battle of the second World War is now being fought in Spain." For the British edition, I went further, "The fate of Spain is thus intimately related to the fate of Czechoslovakia and Austria. The victory of the legal Spanish government would make warlike ventures in the rest of Europe more unlikely and lend resistance to the geographic status quo. This the Fascist aggressors must at all cost prevent."

My joints were still swollen when Fernando de los Rios, the Loyalist Ambassador in Washington, told me the government had called him to Valencia for a conference of its diplomatic representatives. I felt so jealous of his going back to Spain that I painfully picked myself up and sailed with him. It was difficult for de los Rios even to eat celery without discussing Spain in the seventeenth century, and between Sandy Hook and Cherbourg the learned professor gave me a course in the history of the 1600's. He looked with a kind of academic disdain on the more recent centuries, the disdain of an expert on Egypt of the Pharoahs toward the modern Rome of the Caesars.

A few weeks after leaving New York I was bumping in a baby Fiat from Valencia to the Madrid front, and that finally cured me. Señor de los Rios, incidentally, did not content himself, as he easily might have, with debating politics in Valencia. He visited almost all the fronts, sharing the hardships and dangers of the troops.

24. *The Sins of Democracy*

I HAVE lived in all the major dictatorships: Soviet Russia, Nazi Germany, and Fascist Italy. I am convinced that dictatorships are costly to individuals, bad for countries and dangerous to world peace. I believe that democracy is better than dictatorship. Democracy is better, but I am not sure it is good.

Between 1936 and 1939 I watched democracy in Spain lose a war. I watched democracy in Europe and America make a war. Democracy is heavily laden with sins of commission and omission. It takes two to make a war and two to lose a war. The aggressors alone could not have made the World War of 1939. They had help from the democracies. Franco alone would not have won the Spanish War. He received help from Hitler, Mussolini, Chamberlain, and Daladier.

Arrived in Valencia from New York in June, 1937, I asked Negrin for an appointment, and he invited me to have dinner and spend the night at Naquera, a small town near the capital where he could sleep undisturbed by nocturnal air raids. Negrin had an Hispano-Slav disregard of time, and it was ten before we got away to Naquera. Carabineros in light green uniforms jumped smartly to attention as his big car rolled into the grounds. The house had a tremendous porch overgrown with tropical vines. Salamanders darted across the wall under the bright electric lights. Trees grew in huge tile pots that stood on the tile floor of the porch.

During dinner, served by Carabineros, Negrin fitfully looked at his watch. Something disturbed him. At midnight he said to me, "Two men are being executed now. It had to be. We are at war." He reverted to the men twice in the subsequent course of our conversation.

I told him I was glad he had become Prime Minister. My only regret, I declared, was that del Vayo had not been included as Foreign Minister. "José Giral may be a good pharmacist, but you must admit," I said, "he makes a rather colorless and ignorant Foreign Minister."

He did not admit it except by not denying it.

415

I asked him how he was chosen to head the government and how he picked his ministers. The explanation lasted half an hour.

The Communists, many Socialists, and many Republicans felt that Caballero was too dilatory and weak as War Minister. Negrin was suggested as War Minister. But Caballero refused to relinquish the post. He contended that a Prime Minister who was not War Minister in time of war would become a figurehead. The Communists thereupon withdrew their support from Caballero.

The Communists also refused to back Prieto for Premier. He was too anti-Communist. President Azaña, accordingly, summoned Don Juan Negrin.

"That slightly overwhelmed me," Negrin said. "I had never dreamed of being a Prime Minister. But I accepted and started interviewing the heads of the various political parties and of the two big trade-union organizations"—UGT, the Socialist trade union, and CNT, the anarcho-syndicalist trade union.

Under Caballero's influence, the UGT abstained from participation in the Negrin government. The Socialist party designated three ministers: Negrin as Premier and Finance Minister, Prieto as War Minister, and Zugazagoitia as Minister of Interior. "Zuga," as friends called him, was a young Prieto man from Prieto's Basque country, and like Prieto, a newspaper editor. The Communists designated Jesus Hernandez, Minister of Education, and Vincente Uribe, Minister of Agriculture. The bourgeois Republicans designated Giral, Foreign Minister, and Giner de los Rios, Minister of Public Works and Communications. The Catholic Basque Nationalists named Manuel Irujo, who became Minister of Justice. The Catalan bourgeois named Jaime Ayguade, whom Negrin appointed Minister of Labor. Negrin did not want a big Cabinet and limited it to nine posts.

"I could not include del Vayo," Negrin explained, "because he could only have come in as representative of the UGT, and the UGT rebuffed my offer of collaboration." That was the formal reason. The reason was that Azaña and Prieto were opposed to del Vayo. They suspected that he was too sympathetic to the Communists. Moreover, Azaña wanted to be his own Foreign Minister, and to achieve this he had to have somebody who knew nothing about foreign affairs.

The Negrin government was thus constructed by the same method of give-and-take and party and personal bargaining that France knew so well. It was the democratic method. It had many disadvantages.

But it had this advantage: one party could not dominate all the others and in the end eliminate all the others. Throughout the war, the Communists or Socialists or Republicans could have overthrown any Cabinet by withdrawing their support from it. This was a safeguard against dictatorship.

Negrin told me he did not want the Anarchists in his government. They might come in later when they learned to collaborate. Prieto was of the same mind. Prieto explained his stand to me. He said, "We are a coalition government. Each minister brings the government the support of his party. But an Anarchist minister does not do this; his party is an unorganized flock; part goes in one direction, part in another. The Anarchist leaders have no influence over their own people. When the May rising occurred in Barcelona Garcia Oliver and Federica Montseny, then Anarchist ministers in the Caballero government, went to Barcelona to quell the disturbances. But they soon came back to Valencia and the first thing they did they asked for food. Their Barcelona comrades not only did not listen to them; they refused to feed them."

Negrin was the symbol of Spanish resistance to foreign invasion and Fascism. Statements that the Negrin government would be a tool of Great Britain and France, though widely circulated, deserve no notice now because it was not.

Negrin's cabinet, as constituted in May, 1937, disguised two major conflicts. One was the conflict between Negrin and Azaña. President Azaña was an appeaser. He wanted to use British and French good offices to arrange an armistice. Giral served this purpose. Del Vayo would not have. Prieto stood halfway between Azaña and Negrin. His health and his whole mentality made him a pessimist. He lacked faith in the cause. Yet being a born fighter he fought on.

There was a second major conflict intertwined with the first: anti-Communists versus Communists. In a war so shot through with politics, control of the army meant everything. The Communists were trying to get control of the Loyalist army. Prieto, Minister of National Defense, obstructed their efforts. He enjoyed the backing of Azaña and of the four bourgeois members of the Cabinet, four out of nine. Prieto's vote made five. "Zuga's" might make six. Prieto could thus dominate the Cabinet and clash with Negrin who, although Prieto's superior, had great respect for Prieto's personality, ability, and sterling qualities. It took Negrin almost a year to break the Azaña-Prieto stranglehold on his power. Negrin also had enemies outside the Cabinet: Caballero, Luis Araquistain who resigned as Ambassador to Paris when Caballero fell, and the Anarchists.

Negrin, burdened with the back-breaking task of directing a country at war, of fighting a powerful domestic-foreign enemy, and of organizing a good army, faced the additional hardship of balancing the hostile forces in his own democratic government. When the war was over, sitting in his room in the Hotel Plaza in New York, I asked Negrin whether, if he had the whole thing to do over again, he would suppress the political parties.

Negrin said emphatically, "No. We could not, in fighting, destroy the things we were fighting for."

I had a lot of trouble getting an interview with Azaña. He was President now, and as such never saw journalists. Negrin said he could not ask Azaña to see me. But one night, Negrin stopped at Azaña's country place on the way out to Naquera, and when Azaña's secretary came out to greet Negrin I reminded him that I had written a letter to Azaña requesting an interview. In a few days, a message came giving me an appointment.

Azaña was late arriving at his executive mansion on account—so his secretary said—of the long night air raid. I waited with Rosenblatt in the antechamber. Presently, uniformed heralds blew loud notes on their horns, and guards and stiff attachés in diplomatic garb stood to attention.

When the first visitor was ushered into the President's office I asked the secretary who he was. A judge from the province of Jaen. He came out in three minutes. The next visitor was a general. Rosenblatt, Azaña's secretary, and I played guesses as to how long the general would stay. Before we were through guessing the general passed us on the way out of the building. He had been in for five minutes. The third caller was José Domenchina, a Spanish poet. He remained closeted with Azaña for twenty minutes. How long would my audience last? If it was too short I would not get what I wanted; if too long I would miss my lunch at the hotel.

When he saw me, Azaña exclaimed, "Ola, Fischer" (pronouncing it, as Spaniards did—Featcher), and slapped me on the back. This is Spanish for a friendly handshake. He complimented me on my Spanish. I said I was glad to see him in Valencia.

We sat down near a window on soft gilded chairs. "Tell me what you think of the situation," he began. I said that is what I wanted him to do. We kept this up a while and finally I said I would tell him what I thought if he would tell me what he thought. He agreed, but he stipulated that nothing he said was for immediate publication. I could only write that I had been received by him.

Azaña had a great mind yet somehow one did not respect him as a person. He was not brave like Negrin or noble like Caballero or unique like Prieto. Brain alone carried him very high. But without heart and fortitude he never reached the pinnacle and never captured the imagination or the loyalty of the nation.

I told Azaña that it embarrassed me to tell him what was happening in Spain, but if he insisted I would try. To me, the most interesting process was the emergence of a Spanish nation. Andalusians were mixing with Asturians, Madrileños with Catalans, and all had a dawning sense of their country in danger. Second, I thought the bourgeoisie was losing its political ascendancy and most of its political power. Third, I thought the Communists were becoming increasingly bourgeois. Fourth, Loyalist foreign policy impressed me as being too timid. Fifth, he ought to mix with the people more, visit hospitals and convalescent homes, and talk to the soldiers. (I thought, but I did not say, that it might stiffen his morale.)

"Now you tell me," I said.

He unbuttoned his jacket and I saw the initials of his name on his silk shirt. I once saw initials on the dirty undershirt of a peasant boy in a Spanish village. There are few Spanish men who do not have initials embroidered on their shirts. Is it Spanish individualism or what?

"Undoubtedly," Azaña declared, "a Spanish nation is being born. Franco is completing Napoleon's job. The task commenced in one war, and interrupted because Spain resisted the French Revolution, is being completed in this war. The Spaniard is beginning to say, 'I am a Spaniard,' and not, 'I am a Valenciano' or, 'I am a Castilian.' "

"Spain and Russia," Azaña went on, "defeated Napoleon and in that way defeated their own futures. Both countries failed to become nations. Today in Spain we are struggling against foreign domination. That feeds nationalist sentiment. I," he declared, "am the super-expression of the new Spanish nation."

"You say the bourgeoisie is losing its power and the Communists are becoming bourgeoisie. An intriguing paradox," he continued. "But in Spain, one must learn to translate well-known terms. The Germans and the Italians made the mistake of thinking that if the army went over to Franco they would win the war in two weeks. When they thought 'army,' they saw organized, disciplined regiments sitting in barracks awaiting orders. Well, they have the army. But it has not meant victory. In the same way, 'Communist' means something different in Spain. The Communists are supposed to be atheists. In Spain, the Communist party was the first to demand the reopening of the churches and the loudest to decry the unnecessary assaults on the church in the beginning of the war.

"The Spanish Communists," President Azaña asserted further, "have advocated protection of private property on the land. Spain needs more than that. Some of our larger industries must be nationalized."

"That," I suggested, "sounds like the program of the Communists. Why don't you join the Communist party?"

"Oh, no," he replied, "that would be misunderstood abroad." I told him I had not meant it seriously.

He assumed a grave demeanor and explained that he differed most with the Communists and other Spanish friends on the question of continuing the war. He had sent Julian Besteiro, moderate Socialist leader, to represent Spain at the coronation of King George VI in London, in May, 1937. "On my instructions," Azaña said, "Besteiro had a conference with Mr. Anthony Eden and outlined my peace plan to the British minister. A truce between the government and the rebels was to be declared. All foreign troops and volunteers serving on both sides would then be withdrawn from the country. During the truce no battle lines would be shifted. England, France, Germany, Italy, and the Soviet Union would thereupon devise a scheme, which the Republic promised in advance to accept, whereby the will of the entire Spanish nation on its political future would be ascertained."

"But," Azaña exclaimed indignantly, "my representative did not even receive a reply from the British government. Do they think I am an Armand Fallières?"

I did not know who Armand Fallières was. I learned later that he was President of France in 1913 and that his name served as a synonym for a rubber stamp.

I expressed doubt whether Franco would ever accept such a proposal or whether Hitler and Mussolini would allow him to do so. The Fascists knew a plebiscite would go against them, and they had not invested their men and arms in Spain to be voted out of it. "Nor would I trust them," I continued, "to repatriate their so-called volunteers if they promised it, or to keep their lines intact during the truce."

We talked of many more things until my grumbling stomach informed me that it was past lunch time in the hotel. I had already spent an hour and a quarter with Azaña. I took my leave, and since it was so late I went across the street to Negrin's Presidencia. Negrin always ate late. I found him at the table.

Negrin asked me whether I had seen Azaña and then inquired what Azaña had said. I gave him a general summary of the conversation. Negrin was especially incensed by Azaña's steps in relation to England. A Spanish President had no independence of action in foreign affairs or any other province. The Spanish President was not an executive but a sort of Republican King of England who was a symbol of the state without any administrative function.

I asked Negrin his opinion on my characterization of the Communists. He replied, "Left and Right have become very confused concepts. You remember when we met in the spring of 1936 I commented on my being called a right-wing Socialist. The difference between me and the left-wing was that they marched the youth organization through the streets in beautiful blue shirts and red ties, while I said, 'Stop marching and get arms.'"

"Now too," Negrin continued, "names are misleading. In many respects, the Communists go too far to the Right. I dislike the forced village collectivization of the Anarchists. It has turned some peasants against us. But I also dislike the Communist agitation against collectivization. In general, I believe in doing things quietly by economic measures and without revolutionary disturbances. Russia has lost much by the violence, suddenness, and one hundred percent character of its reforms. We will slowly absorb all the banks. When the war broke out, workingmen's committees, often Anarchist, took over the factories. Production fell. They paid themselves in wages everything they took in from sales. Now they have no money. They are coming to me for running expenses and for raw materials. We will take advantage of their plight to gain control of the factories. Catalan industry is in chaos and as a result we have to depend far too much on imports which, as you know, are expensive even when we can get them."

Negrin then brought up the question of the purges and trials in the Soviet Union. We discussed this subject for over an hour. His refrain was, "This will do us a lot of harm." I had one refrain too, "The purges and trials are the overhead of dictatorship. It is necessary, above all, to prevent the rise of a dictatorship in Republican Spain." Negrin agreed. We reverted to this matter many times during the course of 1937 and 1938.

Not one of the world dictators is a highly educated man or a person of varied experience and broad culture. They are narrow individuals. But Negrin speaks a dozen languages and has traveled the world. In Paris, after the Loyalist defeat, he started studying Greek, Chinese, and Arabic. His room is always heaped high with the latest books. He has his share of skepticism, cynicism, and philosophy. He has the modesty of one who knows his limitations. A dictator never looks into a mirror. Negrin does, and laughs.

However, Negrin felt he was the right man in the right place as Prime Minister of Spain. He believes today that he still has a role to play in the future of his country. That makes for confidence and energy. Negrin wants to do things. He is a man of action. On occasions, he procrastinates. In his relations with Azaña and Prieto he displayed caution and the ability to wait and prepare. On the other hand, he takes delight in quick decisions without consulting others. He consults them later. He cuts red tape. He is an executive. He inspires great personal loyalty to himself. He knows how to delegate authority. This is a rare quality in modern statesmen. He does not always know how to choose his delegates. Spain is rich in fine human beings and poor in administrators and civil leaders. That is its backwardness.

Negrin shuns the limelight. He hates to be photographed. He hates to make speeches. He does not strut or boast. He has a sense of his own inadequacy and his being a small speck in a big world. He does not intrigue. The complicated interplay of conflicting party-political forces is a strange new field to him and he abhors it. During the war he frequently ignored it. Once there was a cabinet crisis. He disappeared for four days and went to a mountain home. Meanwhile Barcelona boiled. Everybody whispered the names of new ministers. Negrin kept his ears shut. When he returned he solved the crisis in a morning.

One evening in July, 1937, Negrin invited me to dinner in his office in the Finance Ministry. Other guests were War Minister Prieto, Education Minister Jesus Hernandez, Arthur Stashevsky,

Soviet trade representative in Spain, and a colonel of the Carabineros. Excellent food was served, and excellent wines followed by liqueurs. Prieto was in fine fettle and kept the company amused with quick quips and anecdotes, some of which Negrin had time to explain to me. As the evening grew old, Prieto sang Basque songs and others joined. We were still at the table when Hernandez, sitting next to Prieto, leaned over to him and said, "You know, Prieto, in 1917 I plotted to assassinate you."

Prieto, his tremendous spherical bald head gleaming, looked the giant beside young little Hernandez with his curly black hair, eye glasses, and pinched face. Prieto guffawed, put his big arm around the leather coat Hernandez wore, and exclaimed, "*Bueno, camarada, bueno.*"

I was going up to Madrid by car and told Negrin that I would be there three days. He said, "You may be there longer. I am going soon too, but don't tell anybody." This made it pretty plain, and if I had any doubts the heavy traffic on the road from Valencia to Madrid would have dispelled it; the Loyalists were planning an offensive in the central sector.

We detoured because the rebels were shelling part of the Valencia-Madrid road. En route, a truck driver stopped us. He was having engine trouble. It was a pitch-dark night. Men on top of the truckload were speaking English. Members of the International Brigade.

"Where are you from?" "New York." "Chicago." "Los Angeles."

I heard a voice that had no American accent. "Is that you, Ralph?", I asked. It was Ralph Bates, talented British novelist, commissar and lecturer on politics in the Brigade. We made the rest of the trip together in the car.

Madrid was black. Pickets stopped us, examined our papers, turned their flashlights on us, and asked for the password. "Madrid is the heart . . ." the picket said. ". . . of the defense of a free Spain," our driver answered. "Pass," said the picket.

The next morning I strolled through the streets and walked down to the Casa de Campo front. Madrid was transformed. Its face and arms were covered with old scratches and scars and fresh wounds. But it walked erect, eyes unafraid and white. It had become thin and gaunt, but its muscles were hard as steel and its trigger finger unerring. Its heart never skipped a beat. "*No Pasaran,*" proclaimed in the frivolous days of October, 1936, had become a fact. Madrid could not be taken, was never taken.

(Winston Churchill, Prime Minister of Great Britain, was driving through the streets of London in August, 1940, with H. R. Knickerbocker, American correspondent, as his passenger. They passed several pillboxes. Churchill turned to Knickerbocker and said, "London will be defended at every street corner if necessary. London will be a second Madrid." Madrid was a symbol and an inspiration to London—after it had been the victim of London.)

In Madrid, friends told me later that week that Negrin was in the city. I phoned him and went to see him; we had a very bad breakfast together. Food was much worse in Madrid than in Valencia. I reminded him that he had asked me to keep his stay in Madrid secret, but many people knew about it. He said, "To make folks feel that everything was normal I went to a café in the evening." Negrin is a Madrileño by adoption and he could not resist a café.

The offensive had started in the Brunete district west of Madrid. The Loyalists hoped to gain ground and raise morale, but the real ambition was to get behind the besiegers of Madrid and lift the siege. Spain being the least discreet of countries, the correspondents were not only prohibited from going to the front but even prevented from telegraphing more than the uncommunicative communiqués. We chafed. I asked Negrin whether he could give me a pass to the front and he swore to me that the cabinet had ruled that no one could go to the front without a personal pass from Prieto. He promised, however, to talk to him, and the next day Negrin handed me the permission signed by Prieto which I still have as a souvenir.

Negrin's office lent me a big open Rolls-Royce and, dressed in a white shirt for some silly reason—so that I could be seen better from the air, I suppose—I started out. The driver took a very circuitous route, by way of Colmenar Viejo and through hills with startling rock formations in which each boulder suggested the shape of some animal or object. The sun beat down mercilessly. Within many miles of the area of combat the olive groves were filled with more military equipment than I had ever seen in Spain—tanks, cannon, trucks filled with oil drums, and boxes of ammunition covered with branches and twigs. Even the guards had leaves sticking in their headgear and shoulder straps. Hostile aircraft was overhead most of the time.

Villanueva de la Cañada was being shelled as we drove in. Every single house had been hit. There were no inhabitants left in it. Here a roof had been knocked in, here a wall battered down. The men told me that they were shelling the enemy and the enemy was shelling them. At first I could not distinguish which was which, but in a few minutes I knew when the Loyalists were firing and when I had to duck behind a wall.

If we followed the road till we got to a pond and then along the left side of a cemetery we would reach Brunete where an attack was now proceeding, the soldiers informed us. My chauffeur suddenly developed an interest in his car, and he did not know whether he would have enough gas. This was an old story; drivers always slowed up as they approached the front but never carried complaint to the point of refusal. On the edge of Brunete I got out and walked. Soldiers behind a hill said everything was quiet; only a little activity in the air which apparently did not bother them for they were on the lee of the hill. I asked about Americans and they thought I might find some in the town. All the streets were empty. I looked into two houses and they were empty. The third was a farmer's hut. As I walked in I called out in Spanish, "Are there any Americans here?" and then I heard, "Yeh, whatchya lookin' for?"

A young man in tin helmet and khaki uniform was sitting on a pile of large tins—jam captured from Franco, writing a letter. I introduced myself and he asked: "Of *The Nation?*" He introduced himself. He had worked on the main crane at the Republic Steel works in Chicago. How was the Little Steel strike going, he wanted to know. I disclosed what I had read and then he continued the story. He inquired about the new Negrin government. Would it be energetic? The Spaniards behaved like "namby-pambies." So far, he said, the offensive had been "so-so." Whenever hard fighting had to be done they threw in the International Brigade.

We went out into the yard to listen to the shelling. We heard sharp machine gunning. About a half mile to the west of us, an airplane dove to earth. "They're strafing our men in the trenches out there," the crane driver explained. A moment later a second airplane dove and then a third. I stood up on a box to get a better view. He pulled me down and into the house. "Hey," he exclaimed, "in two seconds it could be over us."

The heat was breathtaking and flies and bees buzzed around the jam cans. I suggested that he finish the letter and let me take it with me. I would be in Paris in three days. His eyes said, "Lucky guy."

"But I haven't got an envelope," he replied.

I suggested that he write the address on the letter and I would put it into the envelope in Paris. Before I mailed it I did an improper thing and read the letter. It was about eight lines long and it read something like this:

DEAR SWEETHEART,

Your last letter worries me. You are getting thin. You don't eat enough. You must not get thin. Please promise me that. I don't want you to be sick. How much do you weigh now? Please write often. I'm OKay.

Love and kisses. . . .

As I drove back into Madrid at about six in the evening, Negrin in a car packed tight with assistants, and followed by another automobile, passed on the way to the front. His staff did not allow him to go to the front during the height of day when he would have to be dodging airplanes. The next morning I had breakfast with him in the Presidencia. He said he was satisfied with the progress of the battle. The troops were becoming seasoned and learning to use the new material. We also discussed the political situation. He told me he wanted to move the capital from Valencia to Barcelona. But Azaña and Prieto were opposed.

My first reaction was, "In Catalonia you will have no political support. The Socialist party there is too weak."

He replied, "Yes, but I will find the support. We will enlarge the *Vanguardia* [official organ of the government] into an attractive big-circulation newspaper. Moreover, people will judge us by our acts. But the important consideration is that unless Catalonia participates more actively in the war we cannot win it."

Wags in Madrid said that the only state which really practiced Non-Intervention was Catalonia. This was not strictly true, but it was true enough to be a terrific handicap. Catalonia did not pull its weight. Catalonia was the largest Loyalist industrial center. But it had not mobilized its resources for war. It had not, actually, gone to war.

Two factors made this possible, Catalan separatism and Anarchist policy. Spain was becoming a nation but Catalonia, with a strong nationalist tradition of its own, lagged behind the other provinces. Catalans even had the effrontery and indelicacy to paste up a poster in Madrid showing a map of the fighting in Barcelona in July, 1936, and saying in the appended text that now it was Madrid's turn to display the same heroism. But Barcelona's epic lasted three days and then the same old light-heartedness returned. Madrid had been suffering for twelve months with very little help from Catalonia. Indeed, the Catalans obstructed the war effort.

Catalonia was the traditional Spanish hearth of anarchism. The Anarchists were romantic revolutionists and therefore never got anywhere. Revolution without discipline is chaos. (With too much discipline it is death.) The Anarchists objected on principle to discipline. Their worship of egalitarianism was so dogmatic that Durutti, even when he was commanding thousands of men at the front, had to waste his time standing in line, plate in hand, for his stew.

Many Anarchists, opposed to government of any kind, objected to participation in the Loyalist government which they regarded as reactionary. Towards the end of 1936, Caballero took the Anarchists into his cabinet. He suspected them. When I saw him in Valencia in December, 1936, he pointed to several hand grenades on his mantelpiece and said, "You see those. The Anarchists are manufacturing them for themselves, perhaps for fighting against some of our own people, but they do not send them to the front. They hold up munitions that come in from France or by sea. They have seized tanks which we need at Madrid." Nevertheless, Caballero on occasions tried to play off the Anarchists against the Communists. That is politics. Even war does not stop it.

The Catalan Anarchists controlled transport from the French border to the rest of Spain. General Grishin, the Soviet Chief of Staff in Spain, told me that when the Anarchists agreed to collaborate and bring matériel through, they were quick, reliable, and faithful to their promises. But it was difficult to get them to promise.

In January, 1937, I had a long talk with Garcia Oliver, Anarchist Minister of Justice in Caballero's cabinet. Madame del Vayo interpreted for me. We discussed every conceivable political topic, and then, out of politeness, I asked him about the work of his ministry. He said, "I have organized an artillery school." An artillery school in the Ministry of Justice! It was, of course, a school for Anarchists. There were other army artillery schools. Garcia Oliver got them guns for training purposes.

I once met Garcia Oliver in Paris. He went there to buy arms for his party. He had the money from the proceeds of Catalan exports which, by law, should have gone into the federal treasury. To stop such traffic, Negrin, as Finance Minister, created a corps of Carabineros who patrolled ports and frontiers.

The Anarchists were romantic in their ideas but hardboiled and tough in practice, and it was difficult to handle them. The root of the trouble was their approach to politics. They wanted an immediate social revolution in Spain and meanwhile they neglected the war against Franco. They kept their arms and their men for the revolution while Franco won victories which would wipe out all social gains.

This attitude bore bloody fruit in the May, 1937, uprising in Barcelona. Anarchist dissidents, working with the POUM, tried to capture the city. It was definitely a move against the central Loyalist government and intended as such. A POUM regiment withdrew from the front, against staff orders, and moved on the city. Several hundred men were killed in the streets and more wounded. The insurrection was soon suppressed. Had it succeeded it would have divided Loyalist Spain to Franco's advantage.

The POUM men were semi-Trotzkyists. They differed with Trotzky on many matters, and he did not altogether approve of them. But they were near to Trotzkyism, and the Communists identified them with Trotzky.

After the revolt several of their leaders were arrested. Their trial took place in October, 1938. They were accused of being paid agents of Franco and of plotting to kill Prieto and two Communist generals in the Loyalist army. This had a Moscow Trial ring. The Spanish Communist Party printed a book of documents purporting to prove that the POUM were Fascists in the employ of Franco. A prominent Soviet citizen, whose name I do not mention because he may still be alive in Russia, told me in Spain at the time that the) documents were forged by the Spanish Communists. The accused were given a fair trial with adequate defense. They denied everything except that they had, together with the Anarchists, fomented the May, 1937, revolt. Two were acquitted, one sentenced to eleven years' imprisonment, four to fifteen years in prison. They were all soon released.

It was in order to put Catalonia to work, to stamp out the anarchy of the Anarchists and the POUM, and to be nearer France, Loyalist Spain's only land frontier, that Negrin wanted to move the federal capital to Barcelona. This was done in November, 1937. It was a stroke of genius: it made continued Loyalist life possible.

Bitterly opposed to the tactics of the Anarchists and the POUM, Negrin nevertheless deeply regretted lawless acts against POUM leaders. Andrés Nin, little POUM leader whom I had known in

Moscow when he was Trotzky's intimate co-worker, was arrested and interned in the prison at Alcala de Henares. Later he was taken from the prison, and he has not been heard of since. The POUM said Communists kidnapped him and shot him. The Communists said he had been stolen from prison by his followers and escaped to Paris. I do not know which version is correct. I am inclined to believe he was killed in Spain, but I cannot prove it. The GPU is known to have assassinated people abroad, and a Trotzkyist, or Trotzky himself, would be welcome targets for their revolvers. Whatever happened, the Loyalist government had nothing to do with it. Too many armed men were walking about Loyalist Spain for one government, torn internally and bent under cruel tasks, to hold all of them in check.

Mark Rein, son of the Russian Menshevik leader Abramovitch, also disappeared mysteriously in Spain. Negrin gave every facility to those who conducted the unsuccessful search for Rein, and apologized and tried to make amends for the tragedy. Abramovitch himself came to Spain twice and the Loyalist authorities assisted him in his vain quest.

Another unsolved Spanish war mystery is the case of José Robles, Professor of Spanish Literature at Johns Hopkins University. When the civil war broke out he was spending the summer in Spain with his family, and he immediately offered his services to the Loyalists. He had never belonged to any party and never participated in political life. In October, 1936, and later, he worked as English interpreter for General Goriev, the Soviet officer in command at Madrid. Goriev trusted him. Robles had a fine open face and pleasant personality, and looked the disinterested idealist.

In the spring of 1937, a story was circulated in Valencia that he had been shot as a spy. He was not shot by the government, and I do not know whether he was shot, but he vanished at about that time without leaving a trace. People affirmed that he had been smuggled out of Spain against his will and taken by boat to Russia. Whispers said he had talked too much and revealed military secrets in Madrid cafés. If that could have been proved it might have warranted turning him over to the Spanish government for trial, but not taking him for a ride. American friends of Robles, notably John Dos Passos, have interested themselves in the case but have not been able to establish the facts. A careful investigation was impossible.

The anti-Communists attribute Robles' disappearance to the Communists.

This accusation notwithstanding, Robles' young daughter joined the Spanish Communist youth organization and came to America in 1938 as a member of its delegation to the Youth Congress. Robles' son, aged 18, also worked with the Communists. He was employed for a time by Constancia de la Mora in the press department of the Foreign Office, but finding this too tame he volunteered for guerrilla fighting behind Franco's lines and operated with a band of brave partizans who slipped into the rebel-held city of Saragossa to set fires, bomb electric power stations, and otherwise harass the enemy. In 1938, the rebels caught him and sentenced him to death. Mrs. Robles and her daughter are now in Mexico. They do not know whether the boy has been executed, and they naturally cannot altogether abandon the slim hope of seeing Professor Robles again.

Whenever the question of Nin or Rein or Robles came up for discussion Negrin was mortified. When his administration was inaugurated he quickly clamped down on illegal acts. Superfluous pickets on roads were suppressed, and guard duty taken over by his trusted Carabineros. In 1936, arbitrary shootings were frequent. But in the early months of 1937, they became the exception. Nin, Rein, and Robles were isolated and regretted instances of an evil war-time phenomenon that had been wiped out by the middle of 1937.

I returned to Paris early on the morning of July 14, the national holiday of the Third Republic. Lines of armored cars, big tanks, and small tanks filled the streets. I went to the Champs Elysées to view the annual parade. Squadrons of airplanes flew overhead. Frenchmen applauded. Then the army marched; "the best army in Europe," officials called it. French regulars, Cadets, Zouaves in colorful costumes, Senegalese black troops in khaki and red fez, Moroccan cavalry, artillery, machine guns, light machine guns, rifles. Twenty percent of the military establishment that paraded that morning would have enabled the Loyalists to win the war in three months.

But the French said they did not want to interfere "in other people's wars." I spoke to deputies and journalists. "This is your war," I argue. "Fight it in Spain. Otherwise it will come to France."

"No," they replied, "we will keep our arms for ourselves."

The Fall of France. The Tragedy of France. Many books have

been written on the subject. It did not begin when Hitler's Panzer divisions crashed into French territory. It began at Versailles. It began in the Ruhr. It began on March 7, 1936, when Hitler remilitarized the Rhineland. It continued in 1937 and 1938, when France and England starved the Spanish Republic.

In 1940, I heard a broadcast to America from Paris by Léon Blum, French leader. "Des Avions pour La France," he begged. But in 1936 and 1937, when Blum was Premier of France, friends of France and of Spain begged, "Des Avions pour l'Espagne." Blum said No. Daladier, his successor, said No. That was the tragedy of France.

It was right that America sell airplanes to an embattled France. It was good for American defense. But why did not France sell arms to Spain? Spain is nearer to France than France to America. Free France did not die because it was weak. It became weak because it was blind. It did not see that it had commenced to die when Hitler became Chancellor, when Mussolini violated Abyssinia, and when Franco brought the Moors across the Straits and Nazi bombers across France. I think I know why.

25. Black Moscow

I HAD not seen my family for seven months, and so I went to Moscow in August, 1937.

Red had ceased to be the correct adjective for Moscow. It was black.

Whenever I was not in a log cabin in the pine woods outside Moscow I sat on the balcony in shorts taking the sun. On a balcony near by sat another man, an important Soviet official. He had a large apartment. He had had his own official car. He was waiting on the balcony to be arrested. His little bundle of clothing and toilet articles was packed in readiness for the GPU's nocturnal visit. Waiting was killing him. He waited three more weeks while the GPU watched and while his wife wasted away. Then the GPU came.

He was one of thousands. We lived in an eight-story apartment house with eight entrances and about one hundred and sixty apartments. The GPU had laid its hand on more than half of them. And our house was no exception.

Despite the cheering sun, heavy gloom pervaded Moscow. Friends and acquaintances did not want to meet one another. How could anyone know who was under surveillance? You might be incriminated by associating with a person who was scheduled to be arrested in a fortnight and in the meantime was being shadowed. People withdrew into themselves and the family circle. But could you be sure about members of the family? The press reported denunciations of arrested husbands by their wives, and denunciations by children of their arrested parents. Then perhaps it would be better not to share all one's troubles, worries, and impressions with the wife or with one's grown-up son.

The newspapers were dull where they had always been exciting. They gave less attention to foreign news, and an endless amount of space to the names of tractor drivers, cow hands, beet harvesters, and locomotive drivers who had won decorations for distinguished services. The phenomenon of giving public praise to common men was highly laudable. But when several times a week one or two pages of an eight-page newspaper were devoted to these lists, citizens yawned and threw the paper away after a few minutes.

Reading had been a great Soviet pleasure. But some writers had been arrested, and the others felt that it was safer not to write. "Better not" became the rule of conduct. Bureaucratic fear of responsibility paralyzed initiative. When an official was asked his opinion of a project he most frequently refrained from a positive recommendation lest its failure be pinned on him. He would say, "I have no objection." That was the old formula of Czarist officials.

Into this deadening atmosphere of dread, the GPU threw a spy scare. The Soviet newspapers published an unending chain of articles by GPU "experts" on spies. Foreign governments, they explained, had innumerable spies in Russia. Many Russians had emigrated from Russia before the Revolution. The secret services of foreign countries had them in their grip. They wrote to their relatives in Soviet Russia and their relatives wrote back, and how did you know when you wrote back you had not revealed important information to the enemy? Russians stopped all communication with foreign countries and with foreigners inside. Foreign scientific journals were kept from Soviet universities. Soviet scientists were discouraged from attending international scientific congresses.

American Communists who had lived in Soviet Russia for a long time were clearing out, first because the Bolsheviks did not want them to stay, and also because they themselves had had enough. By this time most Polish, Hungarian, and German Communists had been arrested. A German Communist friend of mine discussed this, informally, with a GPU official who was a friend of hers. He said, "If German Communists are ready to build socialism in Germany they can do it in Siberia too." The revolutionary attitude towards foreign Communists had given way to this ugly cynicism. Yet the Soviet Constitution gave "the right of asylum to foreign citizens persecuted for furthering the interest of workers." But then it also guaranteed the "inviolability of homes and the secrecy of correspondence," as well as the "inviolability of persons." The GPU spat on all these rights. If it wished to seize anyone it did. If it wished to enter a home it did so. Never in Soviet history had insecurity been greater than in the summer of 1937.

The year 1937 had begun with a sensational trial of leading Bolsheviks—Piatakov, until his arrest assistant chief of the Soviet industrial system and for many years an outstanding Bolshevik, Radek, noted publicist, Sololnikov, member of the inner Bolshevik group which staged the Revolution in 1917, former Finance Commissar, former Ambassador to London, once Stalin's candidate for Soviet representative to the League of Nations, Serebyakov, another Bolshevik veteran and front-rank industrialist, together with thirteen others. They were accused of "wrecking," of espionage on behalf of foreign powers and Trotzky, and of plotting to kill Soviet leaders.

Radek had been foreign editor of the government newspaper, *Izvestia*. He ran a bureau in the party's Central Committee which supplied Stalin with information on the international situation. When Radek was arrested his associates in these undertakings were purged. For they might have known about his "counter-revolutionary" activities. *Izvestia* became still duller.

Sokolnikov's wife was the former wife of Serebyakov. She was a prominent author who wrote under the name of Galina Serebyakova. She had published a book on Karl Marx's youth which the Soviet press praised highly. When Sokolnikov was arrested she disappeared and her book was condemned. Friends and official collaborators of Sokolnikov, of Serebyakov, of Piatakov, and of every other defendant likewise disappeared. Piatakov had appointed thousands of factory managers, engineers, inspectors. Now he confessed treason: he had conspired with Germany and Japan to wreck the Soviet regime, tear the Ukraine and the Far Eastern provinces from Russia, and sabotage Soviet industry. Many workingmen believed this confession. Then they had to say to themselves that he probably appointed the engineers and managers to assist in his treachery. Then these engineers and managers had to be purged else faith in the confessions and trials would be undermined. Moreover, if the engineer had been a "wrecker" his friends and subordinates became suspect too. He could not sabotage alone. He needed helpers. He had had confidants. Who were they? Livshitz, a defendant in the Piatakov-Radek trial, admitted to having staged about thirty-five hundred railway accidents. He needed thousands of underlings to accomplish this feat. They had to be found and punished.

Every trial, every purge, every arrest started a long chain of more purges and more arrests.

Russia had lived badly since 1916. It had made innumerable sacrifices in living conditions and health. Its spirit and nerves had been subjected to heavy strain. The Five Year Plan and agrarian collectivization, 1929 to 1932, redoubled the tension. The tension was not relaxed at the end of that hard period. It continued. By 1935, I had an almost physical sensation that the Soviet Union was simply very tired. It wanted to sit still. It wanted to eat better, live better, and be left alone. It did not wish to be bombarded each day with radical changes, new appeals, new demands. There was a great yearning for silence and peace. That is why the economic improvement of 1935 and 1936 and the Constitution of 1936 brought so much joy. The regime had turned a corner, people said. And that is why the purges, trials and intensified terror of 1937 and 1938 broke so many hearts. "Will it never end?" Soviet citizens asked.

1916 to 1937—twenty-one years of hardships, turmoil, and spiritual travail. Oh, for some quiet and solace! Women I knew, fine intellectual women with government jobs, would meet after hours and just drink themselves into a stupor. Citizens who had always followed politics at home and abroad with keen interest escaped into apathy. Suicides multiplied. Youth took refuge in cynicism. Everybody played for Safety First. Lying, hypocrisy, humiliating obeisances, violence towards one's deepest convictions, and disloyalty to friends were a small price to pay for keeping out of prison. To divert suspicion from yourself you accused the other fellow. You yelled loudest at meetings when resolutions were voted calling on the government to execute Piatakov, Radek, and their accomplices. When Stalin's name was mentioned you applauded, and you did not dare to stop even though it might go on for ten minutes.

It seemed that the country had lost the capacity to be shocked. If Lenin's closest collaborators could be shot, if Radek who had led the newspaper cheering for Stalin could get ten years for plotting to kill Stalin, then anything could happen. Yet nobody was prepared for the sharpest shock of all. On June 12, 1937, Assistant Commissar of War and Chief of Staff and Marshal of the Red Army, M. Tukhachevsky, hero at twenty-seven of the great advance on Warsaw in 1920, was executed for treason. With him were executed seven other of the highest generals in the army. General Gamarnik, also of the supreme command, committed suicide, the papers said, when the police came to fetch him. The nine generals had participated, the official announcement read, in a "military-fascist organization" connected with a foreign power, understood to be Germany. They wanted a pact with the Nazis. The published statement said they confessed to all this, although their trial was a secret court martial. They were tried by a special high court of eight military leaders.

At least three of these eight are known to have been executed for treason since then.

The execution of Tukhachevsky and the generals amounted to the decapitation of the Red Army. Tukhachevsky was first demoted on May 11, 1937, and sent to the Volga district as a regional commander. Stalin was preparing the army for the removal of its leaders. Within a fortnight Tukhachevsky was brought back to Moscow for secret trial. The decree of May 11 announcing his demotion contained a second important order; political commissars were reintroduced into the army. During the Soviet civil war in 1917-1921, the Bolsheviks, compelled to create an army quickly, enlisted the aid of Czarist officers. They could lead troops but politically they were untrustworthy, and so the Bolsheviks attached a political commissar to each Czarist officer. The commissar watched the officer and also conducted Soviet propaganda among the soldiers. When peace came in 1921 the commissars themselves took military courses. Also, young men who had matured since the Revolution and were reliable politically entered the military academies. Professional knowledge and political loyalty were then combined in one and the same person, and commissars were accordingly abolished. Now, when Tukhachevsky was about to be purged, Stalin reintroduced the system of commissars. *Pravda* stated that the commissars "are the eyes and ears of the Communist party in the army." This meant that Stalin suspected the officers of loyalty to Tukhachevsky and put in his own henchmen to spy on them. It is not surprising, therefore, that many of these suspected officers were arrested at the time of the execution of the generals. The estimated number of officers arrested is thirty thousand. It was a holocaust, and it affected the quality of the army for a long time to come. Officers are not manufactured overnight.

Tukhachevsky had been abroad the year before his death and made a good impression on the British and French General Staffs. When he and his comrades were shot the efficiency and striking power of the Red Army were marked down by foreign experts. The trials and the purges also shook the foreign friends of the Soviet regime and many turned away from it.

Literally a massacre of Soviet talent occurred in 1937. The mere arrest of a man was scarcely noticed. Most of the people purged simply disappeared. They may have been shot. They may still be in prison or exile. Thousands of victims are still unaccounted for, and their families probably still hope. Take the case of my friend Marcel Rosenberg, Soviet Ambassador to Spain. He was recalled in February, 1937. Rumor had it that he was executed. But I met him in the Metropole Café during my August, 1937, visit to Moscow. He told me he had been appointed to represent the Foreign Office in Tiflis. But he never occupied that post, and he has been "lost" since 1937. Is he dead? Who knows? His family does not know. This uncertainty is one of the most harrowing features of the Soviet purges.

Only a small proportion of arrests and executions were ever recorded in the Soviet press. I have myself checked several Soviet provincial dailies for May to December, 1937, inclusive. They list 1,313 executions in the districts they serve. The Moscow papers, much more circumspect, list only thirty-four during the same period although the figure must have run into thousands.

On January 19, 1937, Bukharin, editor of *Izvestia*, beloved of Lenin and the entire Soviet youth, leading Bolshevik theoretician, was dismissed. The *Great Soviet Encyclopedia* said of him that he was "one of the leading participants in the 1917 Revolution, a distinguished theoretician of Communism." His arrest in January, 1937, was the first step to his trial for "Fascist treason" in April, 1938, and his death sentence.

On March 5, 1937, G. Smirnov was appointed chairman of the State Planning Commission. That is the only indirect notice the world has had of the purge of Mezhlauk. Valeri Mezhlauk, young teacher of Greek and Latin before the Revolution, soon rose to high rank when the Soviets came to power. He came to America to negotiate important contracts with Henry Ford and Owen D. Young. He was recognized as one of the outstanding industrialists of Russia. At the time of his purge he was Assistant Prime Minister of the Soviet Union and Chairman of the State Planning Commission, the general staff of the entire economic system. He has disappeared. Nobody knows what happened. It is as if a Knudsen or Owen D. Young had vanished one night and was never heard of again though years passed. Mezhlauk's brother, also a prominent industrialist, has also disappeared.

On March 15, Gregory Kaminsky, Commissar of Health, was removed from office. Since he was not at the same time appointed to another job—the normal Soviet procedure—he was assumed to have been purged. He is another of the missing. On March 19, 1937, Postishev, second Bolshevik of the Ukraine, was demoted. Later he was purged. On March 28, Krestinsky, Litvinov's assistant in the Foreign Office, was appointed assistant Commissar of Justice. This was another method of initiating a purge. In June he was arrested. In 1938, he was tried and sentenced to death.

You had to know how to read the press. Anyone branded "an enemy of the people" had been arrested although the press did not say so. If a new book was subjected to bitter political attack the author had probably been purged. Experience taught that most of these "probabilities" received subsequent confirmation. In April, 1937, Kalmanovitch, Commissar of State Farms, was purged. At the same time, the President of the State Bank, the Soviet bank of issue, was arrested.

In May, Kirshon, a prominent Soviet playwright, was tried and has not since been heard from. Two locomotive drivers were shot for deliberately causing train wrecks; forty-four were shot and many more arrested in Siberia for espionage in the pay of Japan; twenty-two shot for a train wreck in Georgia. All the high officials of the trade-union movement except Shvernik were arrested.

The budget for June, 1937: Cherviakov, the President of the White Russian government, "committed suicide." By a "coincidence," the whole government of White Russia, was simultaneously arrested. The Commissar of Social Welfare of the Crimea, and Unschlicht, the acting secretary of the Federal Central Executive Committee, likewise disappeared that month. The president of the Far Eastern Coal Trust, the head of the Suchan coal mines, the head of the Far Eastern timber trust, and unnamed others were publicly accused of "wrecking" which was tantamount to a death sentence. Also: the apartment of Lapinsky (Mikhalsky), prominent Soviet journalist, well-known in Washington and New York, was searched; he had been arrested and is still missing. A new assistant commissar of the defense industries was appointed. Ergo, his predecessor is no more. Ruzdutak, of the Bolshevik big ten, arrested; later executed. Assistant Foreign Commissar Leo Karakhan, arrested; later executed. Thirty party officials in Rostov arrested. Trials of "Trotzkyist wreckers" in Tashkent, Tomsk, Archangel, and other cities. Thirty-six employees of the Siberian railway shot. I omit many more.

July: Doletzky, for many years the director of TASS, the Soviet telegraphic agency, and his assistants accused by a provincial paper of being "Trotzkyist bandits and Fascist agents." The translation of that is "executed." It is said Doletzky shot himself when the GPU knocked at his door in the night. Assistant Commissar of Finance Maryasin, arrested for "sabotage." Budu Mdivani, old Georgian Bolshevik and ancient enemy of Stalin, executed with seven associates. Feinberg, Ilinsky, Lukyatov, popular Youth League leaders, charged with being "enemies of the people." That meant they were shot. Later their successors were arrested. Twenty-two more employees of the Trans-Siberian railway officially announced as executed. Likewise executed: sixty-four officials in the Far East charged with aid to Japan. Finnish Soviet writers denounced for nationalism; their fate is hardly to be doubted. Several dozen "mass trials"—ten to thirty defendants each—are being held in various parts of the country. Each results in a large proportion of death sentences.

August, 1937—the month I spent in Moscow: Kraval, assistant chairman of the State Planning Commission, Troitzky, chief of the Financial Plan, and ten other heads of departments who worked with Valeri Mezhlauk, excoriated as "enemies of the people." A black shroud covers their fate. Seventy-two shot in Irkutsk, Siberia, for train wrecks. Six shot in Minsk, White Russia, for feeding poisoned food to soldiers. Thirty-four more executed in Irkutsk. Eight shot in Leningrad for "counter-revolutionary acts." *Pravda* attacks Dibetz, the director of automobile and tractor industry of the entire country. Since then no more has been heard of him. Two women shot in Leningrad for feeding poisoned food to children in schools. Hundreds of other arrests reported in the papers and thousands not so reported.

But these gruesome facts are mere child's play compared with the bloody pogrom which blackened the face of Russia in the fall of 1937 and throughout 1938, and which continues to this day under a thick veil of secrecy lifted only occasionally by the Kremlin or penetrated by stray bits of information which reach outsiders.

For years I had been on warm terms with many Russians. One of them would phone and say, "What are you doing this evening?" and if I said I was reading or working, he might say, "Why don't you come over?" or I would suggest he come to me, or we might compromise on a café. These Russians often told me their innermost political views because a man has to talk when his heart is full and they preferred to talk to one who, unlike Soviet citizens, was under no obligation to reveal secrets. (The moment a Russian is arrested his intimates and acquaintances are expected to go to the

GPU and report everything incriminating they know about him.)
Several of these dear friends of mine had now been executed.

A man has spent many long evenings in your study drinking tea
or stretched out on your couch telling stories or boxing with your
kids in their room. He has talked to you of his ambitions and hopes,
of his family problems. He has opened his soul. Now you see him,
you see him day and night, walking down a corridor in the GPU
prison with a uniformed guard behind him. They walk to the cellar,
the guard with a finger on his revolver trigger. Your friend has
walked this road before to be cross-examined by his investigator. And
he has returned to his cell. It has happened every day for months.
This time the guard, on orders from above, draws the revolver and
shoots your friend through the back of the neck—and that is all. That
happened to many of my friends, and I still see their faces.

It was better not to call on Soviet friends and acquaintances. The
visit of a foreigner might get them into trouble. Always, literally
always in the past, our apartment was filled with Russians when I
arrived from abroad. They came just to welcome me back, but also
to get the latest news and impressions of the international scene. This
time nobody came. I read Lenin, walked the streets, and played
tennis.

Litvinov received me and so did Dimitrov. We talked only about
Spain and the international situation, not a word about purges or
trials or declining rates of Soviet production. Litvinov complained
that the Loyalists never won battles. They advanced and then retired. I explained the difficulties: a new army, insufficient equipment, new officers. Franco, on the other hand, had more arms than
he could use. Litvinov asked many questions. He said we would meet
soon again in Geneva at the regular League session. I said, "Negrin
will be there and he can tell you more than I can."

Before leaving Spain I had talked with Negrin about Communist
party politics. I had told him I would soon be going to Moscow to
see my family. He said, "Tell the people there to call off the Spanish Communists and this fusion propaganda. Our Socialists are against
it. We want collaboration with the Communists but we wish to
retain our identity as a separate party."

I told this to Litvinov but merely that he might know about it. I
told it to Dimitrov because he was in part responsible for the situation and might countermand the Communist instructions for the
fusion campaign. "But why does Negrin object?" Dimitrov asked.

I replied that when the Socialists and Communists of Catalonia fused, the result was one Communist party which joined the Third International, and that when the Socialist and Communist youth organizations of Spain amalgamated the whole became a purely Communist group.

"That was," Dimitrov said. "But it can change. There is no reason why Negrin should not be the leader of a united Socialist-Communist party." I objected that he would then be regarded a Communist puppet. "No," Dimitrov assured, "the party born of the merger could join the Second International." This seemed startling and I made sure that I had correctly understood Dimitrov. He meant just that. "All Spanish Marxists adhere to the Second International."

It appeared to me that if, as a result of such action, the Comintern had no Spanish section, and if, with parallel success of the fusion campaign in France, it had no French section, then little would be left of the Comintern. Dimitrov's strategy spelled the death of the Comintern or, euphemistically, its "union" with the Second socialist, reformist International. After the Spanish and French Communist parties entered the Second International, the small Communist parties—British, Belgian, and others—would try to do likewise, and then Moscow would be rid of the Third International. Many circumstances indicated that the Kremlin regarded the Comintern as more of a nuisance and less of an asset than ever. Dimitrov was definitely under an official cloud. He engaged in fewer activities. Often he did not go to the Comintern office but remained at home to see visitors.

The merging of Socialist and Communist parties would have been the Popular Front with a vengeance. Moscow still believed in the Popular Front. Moscow saw the Popular Front as the best guarantee of collective security and an anti-Fascist policy in democratic countries.

The Comintern interfered with friendlier relations with England, France, and the United States. Other circumstances hampered these relations more. But the Comintern did interfere, and Stalin had in recent years shown no great enthusiasm for Dimitrov or for the Comintern. One cause of this attitude was Dimitrov's refusal, after arriving in Moscow from his triumphant trial at Leipzig, to participate in the nauseating Stalin worship. Dimitrov in the end had to bow his big noble head, for the alternative would have been complete silence and inactivity for him. But I do not think he was very happy in Moscow conditions. When I saw him again in Moscow in May, 1938, he seemed even more depressed and more removed from the center of power.

Dimitrov's idea of liquidating the Third International by transferring its most important foreign parties to the Second International may have been his personal view. He was a true proletarian revolutionist and he must have realized that a Comintern harnessed to the Soviet government had less influence on the working class of the world and was less free than it would have if its constituents joined the Socialist International. He must have seen that the Comintern was losing its own personality and increasingly becoming an automatic mouthpiece of Stalin's dictatorship and an instrument of the GPU.

But Dimitrov's idea also reflected Stalinist policy. Foreign Communists in Russia were under a cloud. Hundreds, probably thousands, of them had been arrested. A cartoon in the Moscow evening paper apropos of the annual masquerade carnival held in the Park of Culture and Rest depicted a Nazi spy looking at a series of masks and wondering which one he should wear. The masks were marked "foreign specialist," "tourist," "writer," and "victim of Fascism." That made it all very simple; these categories were suspect and Soviet citizens would do well to avoid them. But victims of Fascism whom the Soviet Union admitted were all Communists and many were prominent figures in the Comintern. Since no cartoon or printed word appears in Moscow which does not conform to official policy this little sketch indicated a new hostile attitude towards foreign Communists. As such it merely supplemented a much more concrete indication: the wholesale imprisonment or banishment of the bulk of Polish, Hungarian, and German Communists in the Soviet Union and of the Viennese Schutzbuendler or Socialist Defense Corps members who fled from Austria after February, 1934. Other Communists were leaving as fast as they could.

I was glad there was a Spain to work in and work for. It would have been mental torture to live in Moscow's atmosphere. The alternative would have been to go away and attack the Soviet regime in my writings and lectures. I was not yet ready to do that. In Moscow, I met Joseph Barnes, resident correspondent of the *New York Herald Tribune*. He thought the purge had come to an end. I differed with him; but it was only my opinion against his. In 1930, the engineers and intellectuals had been subjected to a violent purge. Thousands were arrested. Factories were paralyzed as a result. Then Stalin made a speech and it stopped. Perhaps this too would stop. I had invested fourteen years of hope in Soviet Russia. The present black phase was about a year old. I would wait. Besides there was Spain. Every nation was kicking Spain, and only Russia helped. It did not help enough but it helped, and the Loyalists were grateful. If I had come out as a public enemy of Russia many non-Communist doors would be closed to me in Spain. It would have been embarrassing for numerous Spaniards to be on friendly terms with a person who attacked Russia. I was losing Russia. I did not want at the same time to lose Spain.

26. Nyon Light

HITLER understands only one language, the language of force. That is true of all dictators. They are cynical about words. They know too well the crimes against words which they themselves have committed.

In the dictatorships it is guns instead of butter. In the democracies it was, for too long, words instead of guns. Speeches, conferences, notes, treaties. The dictators replied with tanks and bombers.

Only once the democracies saw the light: at Nyon, in September, 1937. They acted. They stopped talking and acted—and the dictatorships became very small.

The matter started in this way. "Unknown" submarines had been torpedoing ships in the Mediterranean which carried food, raw materials, and arms to the Loyalists. Foreign correspondents in Rome said jestingly that Mussolini proposed to erect a monument to the "unknown" submarine next to the monument to the unknown soldier. Mussolini was called the "unknown" statesman. When the Loyalists took Blackshirt prisoners they called them prisoners of "unknown" origin. Everybody in the world knew that the "unknown" submarines were Italian. But the British and French, and of course the Italians, the Germans, and the Non-Intervention Committee, observed the amenities and called them "unknown." The Soviet press called them Italian.

The Mediterranean had become unsafe. Between July 27 and September 3—thirty-nine days—eighteen ships were attacked. Some were British and French. London and Paris did not like the idea of Italy converting their "artery" into Mare Nostrum. There was still plenty of resentment against Italy in the British Foreign Office on account of Abyssinia. In Geneva, before the Nyon conference, Anthony Eden made a broadcast punctuated with anti-Italian barbs. When he finished he turned to the *London Times* correspondent who was in the studio and said with obvious glee, "I hope Musso heard that." To curb Eden, London sent Sir Robert Vansittart to Nyon. Eden was Foreign Minister; Vansittart was permanent chief of the Foreign

Office—Eden's first assistant. Vansittart, urbane, learned, skilled diplomat, as handsome in his burly way as Eden in his, excelled in his passion against Germany and would have courted Italy in order to break the Axis and reconstitute the Stresa front: England, France, and Italy against Germany. But at Nyon, Eden won the day.

Edgar Ansel Mowrer, of the *Chicago Daily News*, used to drive me out in the rain from Geneva to the near-by town of Nyon (pronounced Neon) where the international conference took place in the assembly hall of the little local schoolhouse. The stage on which the principal stands to conduct exercises and where Swiss children present amateur plays was not used, but the hall itself—seating capacity four hundred—was divided into two unequal parts, the larger for the two tables at which the foreign ministers and their secretaries sat, and the smaller for the crowded newspapermen of all nations. Many journalists could not get accommodations and stayed away.

Here in the schoolhouse the governments adopted measures to stop the exploits of the "unknown" submarines. Italy, Germany, and Japan were not represented. Litvinov was glad. He had maneuvered to keep them out. Moscow had sent Rome two sizzling notes prior to Nyon in which the Soviet government declared it had positive proof that the Soviet steamers sunk in the Mediterranean had been sunk by Italian craft. A Soviet ambassador told me that the Soviet government did not have any proof. But the Italians did not challenge Moscow to produce the evidence; Litvinov had gambled on that. He did not want Italy at Nyon. He never believed in the need of "universality." When League officials or other diplomats argued that the League could not be effective because the aggressor powers had withdrawn, he scoffed. He always regretted the absence of the United States from Geneva, but he contended that if the Fascist nuisances remained away the others could accomplish more—if they wished. Nyon proved it. At Nyon, the assembled delegates simply decided to patrol the Mediterranean and sink any marauding submarines on sight. The patrol was carried out by the British and French navies. The torpedoings stopped. They simply stopped. Mussolini understood the smoke of British cruisers better than the perfumed notes of the British Foreign Office. Mussolini saw that the British meant business and that the French, at last, were playing ball with the British.

(These were the same British and French navies which, according to the lame excuses of the appeasers, would have been in such terrific peril if oil sanctions had put Mussolini in bad temper in 1936. One cannot say too often that appeasement was not a matter of a weak arm but of a weak brain and a weak will.)

Nyon pointed the way to a method of checking Fascist aggression. It was a stinging answer to those who maintained that to halt the totalitarian dictatorships it was necessary to go to war. Nyon was not war. Yet Mussolini pulled in his horns.

Yvon Delbos, French Foreign Minister, said at Geneva that month, "To prevent war [the nations wanting peace] must check its impetus by displaying the force which their union constitutes. The sum of our energies, if they converge resolutely towards the same end, is greater than any other force." This was common sense. It was collective security. It was a permanent Nyon. It could have prevented Munich. It could have saved Spain. It could have staved off the European war.

But Nyon proved to be only a flashlight, not a fixed beacon. The Anglo-French allies were apparently frightened by their own success. They were ready to put a stop to Italian piracy in the Mediterranean. But they were not ready to put a stop to Italo-German intervention in Spain. The presence of both Eden and Vansittart at Nyon reflected the divisions in London. Nyon decided on patrolling the Mediterranean. But then England invited Italy to join the patrol. Mussolini was invited to hunt down his own submarines. This was a stupid gesture of friendship to Rome, and it watered down the moral lesson of Nyon. London and Paris were incapable of a sustained firmness because they had no firm convictions about Fascist aggression and about Spain.

What had happened to make Nyon possible? The Loyalists' military position had improved. At Brunete the Republican troops registered some gains. It had become obvious that Spain would not be a walk-over for the Fascists. Barzini, the *Popolo d'Italia's* Burgos correspondent had wired his paper, "We must not imagine an easy, rapid victory. [Loyalist] resistance can become very solid and very tenacious."

Even the British and French governments had to consider realities sometimes. When Franco's early victory seemed assured, London and Paris were ready to help Franco win. The sooner the War in Spain was over the better. But now that the conclusion seemed in doubt the so-called statesmen wavered.

The British admirals, moreover, disliked the idea of Italy behaving like the mistress of the Mediterranean and sinking British ships. The French were alarmed by the dimensions of Italo-German "non-intervention" in Spain. Edouard Daladier, addressing the executive committee of his Radical Socialist party on September 10, 1937 said, "Despite our real and sincere desire to remain faithful to the Non-Intervention policy . . . we cannot permit it to end in the destruction of the freedom of our communications with our African empire or create a menace on our Pyrenean frontier. In the life of a people resolved to maintain its greatness, there comes a time when it must say 'No.' "

Bravo, Monsieur Daladier! At Nyon, his country said No, and it worked. But then he got frightened and said Yes, and again Yes.

France was perturbed by the entrenchment of Italy and Germany in Spain. The Italians, eager to convince an unbelieving world that they were good soldiers, boasted a bit too blatantly of their part in the conquest of Bilbao and the Basque district. "Woe to the weak," Daladier cried in the same speech. (Then why did he not arm? He was Minister of War.)

Nyon was a moment of sanity, a burst of realism. The national and imperial interests of France and England were threatened in Spain. In the summer of 1937, Franco had conquered the Basque coast of Spain and driven the Loyalists from Bilbao and Santander. Now the Republic could get arms from Russia only via the Mediterranean. If Mussolini cut that route, the Loyalists would be finished. That explains Nyon. France and England wished to see Russia continue her aid to Spain.

But they were not prepared to give direct aid themselves. They did not mind a prolongation of the war at the expense of Germany and Italy, and of Russia. But they would not send arms themselves. And before long they had also changed their minds about the sinking of ships. Soon the old arguments were repeated; the Loyalists were "Reds" and had burned churches. What about the cutting of France's life-line to Africa? What about the menace on the Pyrenean frontier? Class hatreds and economic prejudices apparently weighed more in the balance. If the Loyalists won under the guidance of the Popular Front, the Popular Front would be stronger in France too. Compared with that threat to their power at home what did the Right reactionaries care about the national and imperial interests of France? They defended their class interests at the expense of France.

But some Frenchmen did care. The Frenchmen in the International Brigade cared. Many of them were Communists. Yet in effect they were better Frenchmen than the French appeasers and French supporters of Franco. Edouard Herriot, speaker of the Chamber of Deputies, cared. Pierre Cot cared.

The foreign policy of a country, especially of a democracy—though not only of a democracy—can never be understood unless it is seen as the product in part of a struggle between contending domestic forces. Sometimes one wins, sometimes the other. Sometimes, both shape policy. While President Roosevelt made anti-appeasement speeches, certain gentlemen in the United States State Department were busily appeasing. While Chamberlain appeased, Churchill fought appeasement, and in the end Churchill was called upon to direct the war which Chamberlain's appeasement made inevitable. Occasionally, one and the same man may be torn between two tendencies. Léon Blum, Socialist Premier of France, was undoubtedly pro-Loyalist at heart. But by sponsoring Non-Intervention he helped kill Loyalist Spain. He did it because of pressure from England and because he was cowardly. His Popular Front government came into office in 1936 with a vast majority. But he was afraid that aid to the Spanish Republic would split the country. It split the country anyway. It ruined the country. That was Hitler's goal. The Spanish struggle divided England and France into two hostile camps. That made it easier to conquer France and attack England. The civil war in Spain was matched by civil wars in the democracies, not civil wars fought with machine guns and bombs, but nevertheless internecine strife which disrupted internal unity and obstructed the formulation of a strong national policy. It became more important to the French conservatives to defeat the friends of Loyalist Spain in France than to defend France. *Gringoire, Candide*, and other pro-Fascist French weeklies and dailies attacked Blum and Cot much more violently than they attacked Hitler and Mussolini. They energetically abetted the Fascist victory over Spain although that victory was a prologue to the Fascist victory over France.

Pierre Cot was Minister of Air from June, 1936, to January, 1938. Cot tells me that he was instrumental in sending one hundred French airplanes to the Loyalists. Seventy of these went in 1936, thirty in 1937. Of the seventy, fifty were sold by private French companies with the consent of the French government. Thirty-five of these were new pursuit planes and fifteen were good bombers and reconnaissance machines. The other twenty were old and were sold unofficially to André Malraux.

A striking detail: The French Senate was informed about the sale of the thirty-five fighters. They were sold to the Loyalists officially. But the Senate was told that this was in execution of a pre-war contract with the Spanish government—and no such contract existed. The fifteen bombers had been manufactured for Lithuania. Cot told Lithuania that it would have to wait, and gave the Spanish Republic priority.

In 1937, it became even more difficult for pro-Loyalists in France to help Spain. The thirty French planes delivered by France to Spain in that year were "contraband." Then this source dried up. Altogether, France sold the Spanish republic one hundred airplanes. Léon Blum approved. But if the entire French cabinet had been consulted a much smaller number would have gone.

When the Spanish War broke out, Blum sent a delegation to London to co-ordinate French and British policies on Spain. The delegation consisted of Yvon Delbos who was weak, Corbin, the French Ambassador in London, who was a reactionary, and Admiral Darlan, who remained to serve the Vichy government of Marshal Pétain. Pierre Cot says that Darlan was impressed by the sensational accounts he heard from British naval men of the manner in which the Loyalist sailors had killed their officers. That makes policy too. So this French delegation worked out the details of Non-Intervention. Later, Blum would have liked to rid himself of this incubus. But the British government and numerous Frenchmen of the Right and Left, even Socialists, did not let him.

The League of Nations session held at the same time as the Nyon conference was, as usual, a battleground on which the Loyalists fought for their rights as a sovereign state to buy arms for self-defense. This is an elementary rule of international law, but the democracies broke it when they sanctioned Non-Intervention, and the United States infringed it when it refused to sell arms to a legally established government resisting foreign aggression.

The *London Times* Geneva correspondent reported to his paper that the Loyalist government was represented at the League deliberations by a strong delegation, including Prime Minister Juan Negrin and Alvarez del Vayo. He did not even mention José Giral, Spanish Foreign Minister who also attended. Del Vayo was a sort of ambassador-at-large. People like him. He is warm. Everybody who knows him, from his cook and elevator boy to foregin diplomats, learns to be fond of him. He is honest, frank, humble, and modest. On the platform and at Geneva sessions he speaks with passion and force. He is a good journalist and writes quickly. His addresses of Geneva were among the memorable ones of those hectic years in which the League died because it refused to do what it was created for—work for peace and not just to please England or France. Del Vayo wrote most of the speeches himself. But he also enjoyed the able assistance of Pablo Azacarate, Loyalist Ambassador in London, who had been employed by the League for fourteen years and was once its Deputy General-Secretary. Azcarate, tall, thin, bald, knew all the tricks and techniques of the Geneva racket and contributed the legal touches to Vayo's speeches. Azcarate was responsible for some of Spain's cleverest maneuvers at Geneva. I often saw the speeches before they were delivered and occasionally offered suggestions which were included in the final draft.

At the September, 1937, League session, it was Spain's turn to preside at the Council sessions, and Prime Minister Negrin came specially to Geneva for this purpose. He had delivered only two or three speeches in his life, but he performed very well in this his first foreign forensic experience.

I usually phoned Negrin at breakfast time and he would often ask me to come down to his suite immediately. Several times I found him in the bathroom shaving and wearing only his pajama pants. To remove the lather after the shave, he would duck first one side of his head, then the other side into a sink full of water. Next he got into a hot bath and scrubbed himself and talked with gusto while I sat on a bathstool or stood against the wall. Occasionally, a secretary would come in with a telegram, bend over the bathtub and hold it while Negrin read it. Negrin was very natural and simple about all this. In Barcelona too I had a session with him in a bathroom together with Otero, a gynecologist who during the war became chief of the armaments section of the War Ministry. Otero felt all right during the shaving process but when the Prime Minister got ready for the bath he was rather shocked.

One evening I invited Negrin and Martha Dodd to dinner at the Bavaria. The Bavaria is the restaurant to which statesmen and journalists attending League sessions came to exchange views, news and glances. Even Litvinov went. Its walls are covered with the originals of caricatures and sketches of famous Geneva visitors made by Derso and Kellen and other artists. At a table near us sat a man who didn't seem to belong in this atmosphere. He eyed Negrin without interruption. One could not help being aware of it. "That's the special bodyguard the Swiss government has assigned to me," Negrin said. "I never say anything to him but he turns up wherever I go." Del Vayo used to take his guard along in his car. The guard was a German Swiss and so is Madame del Vayo; they got acquainted and his life was simplified when he was included in the family group. Del Vayo often pleaded with him that it was not necessary to come along, but the detective replied that he had strict instructions from the government never to relax his vigilance. Besides, he was beginning to enjoy himself.

One evening Negrin gave a dinner to about twenty friends. I sat next to an unofficial adviser of the Chinese government. I think I did not say two words until the dessert was served. I was having a brain wave. The Loyalists were short of arms. The transportation of Soviet arms to Spain encountered innumerable obstacles. China was getting arms from Russia. China was able to buy arms anywhere because no Non-Intervention operated against her. The Chinese had little money. The Loyalists had plenty of money. Couldn't the Chinese buy arms for the Loyalists? Russia could send to China the arms it would normally send Spain; no transport difficulties there; and then China could purchase the same amount of arms in the United States or elsewhere and ship them via the Mediterranean or France to the Loyalists.

I outlined this scheme to my neighbor at dinner. He saw possible mutual advantages. After dinner I went to Negrin's room and talked to him about it. He greeted it enthusiastically. I asked him what he would be ready to pay the Chinese for their assistance in obtaining arms for Spain. He said, "Well, it would be worth up to fifteen percent to us." Negrin suggested that I sound Litvinov on the idea.

The next day I saw Litvinov. Dr. Kung, the Chinese Finance Minister, had just left Litvinov. The unofficial Chinese adviser had already talked to Kung, and Litvinov had already heard of my scheme. Litvinov said, however, that munitions matters were not his province. He intimated that I might consult a Soviet military man in Paris. Litvinov was always like that, but it did not mean that he was unsympathetic or that he would not take it up in Moscow.

In Paris, several days later, Dr. Lee visited me. Lee was a Peking professor with a sparse gray beard of very long hairs and a round

dumpling face. He was leaving for Moscow where he had appointments with Stalin and War Commissar Voroshilov with whom he
hoped to arrange for more munitions deliveries.

I put the whole plan on the basis of the solidarity and sympathy
that ought to exist between two nations which were fighting totalitarian aggression. He was a liberal and agreed. But he intimated that
China needed money.

Then I had an interview with Dr. Wellington Koo, the Chinese
Ambassador in Paris. With him, I discussed collaboration between
Spain and China in general terms only. With General Semenov, the
Soviet military attaché in Paris, the conversation got down to brass
tacks, but he simply listened, and promised to report to Moscow.

Meanwhile, Negrin authorized Pablo Azcarate, his envoy in London, to handle the negotiations. I went to London where Azcarate
and I met the unofficial Chinese adviser.

One of the problems involved was transit through France. Suppose
China bought airplanes in America. Normally, a freighter would take
them via the Pacific to China. Would France allow them to land on
its territory, ostensibly for transshipment to Asia but actually for
Spain?

President Roosevelt once vaguely hinted to Fernando de los Rios,
Loyalist Ambassador in Washington—but in no connection with this
Spain-China-Russia scheme—that if France supplied arms to the Loy-
alists it might replenish its stocks with purchases in the United States.
All sorts of variations of the scheme were therefore possible.

As usual, a lot of breath and time was wasted on talk. The Chinese
referred everything by cable to China. It appeared that a certain
amount of rivalry existed between Dr. Kung, Finance Minister, and
T. V. Soong, President of the Bank of China, who was in Hong
Kong. The Chinese in Europe were closer to Soong than to Kung.
Dr. Kung hoped to buy arms in Germany. The whole triangular or
quadrangular scheme therefore remained in abeyance until December.

All this volunteer dabbling in diplomacy gave me an illusion of
activity, but I was fully aware of the fact that many well-meant
efforts to obtain war munitions for Republican Spain had never graduated from the conversation phase. So while this affair excited me
I still kept my feet on the earth, studied the European situation and
Spanish developments, and sent frequent articles to *The Nation* and
the usual carbon copies to my little private syndicate.

In October, 1937, I took a trip to Spain.

27. Confidence and Hunger

WE are going to save the world," said Negrin, addressing the Cortes in Valencia on October 1, 1937. "We shall wake from the lethargy in which we have lived for two centuries. I have faith in Spain. I have faith in victory." There had been bombs that night over the city. When I flew in from Paris just as the Cortes session was opening, the pilot made a detour over the sea to avoid enemy craft.

Negrin felt confident, and Parliament echoed his optimism. But this reliance was not based on a realistic study of the situation, which might have encouraged some and sobered others with a sense of mounting hardships. What spoke in Negrin was Spain's destiny. It was like a child in the womb that had to be born. Spain was beginning to stir. It was rousing itself from centuries of sleep. Fascist bombs had awakened it. Negrin knew that an elemental force urged Spain on to life. Therefore he had trust in victory. Without victory the child would die before birth.

Already, Spain suffered hunger. The Loyalists held the large cities which consumed much food, but Franco held the great meat-producing and wheat-producing regions. The Loyalists therefore had to import food. But they imported less than they needed because they had to have enough money for munitions. Good men were compelled to make this cruel decision. The Loyalists never got anything for nothing. They paid Soviet Russia for arms, and they usually overpaid for arms bought elsewhere. Sometimes they paid twice or three times for the same arms. Thus: a Loyalist agency bought and paid cash for several batteries of artillery in Belgium. Since this was illegal, the Belgian government seized the goods. The seller, suspected of having bribed a high official to make the seizure, now informed the Loyalist agency that he could get the guns released if he paid their full value plus a bribe to several officials equal to half the value of the batteries. The agency had no choice but to pay cost and a half in addition to the original payment.

Franco arranged an exhibition of the arms he had captured from

453

the Republicans. It looked like a museum; it included Krupp cannon of 1880, the oldest howitzers ever manufactured, and machine guns held together with wire. The Republic ransacked the arsenals of Europe and paid fancy prices for the worst possible junk. Franco, on the other hand, had more arms than his men could use. He got them for nothing from Hitler and Mussolini; they would cash in later—they hoped. It was, unfortunately, not simply talk to say that the Loyalists had to oppose the flesh of their men to the steel of the Fascists. And now the flesh was hungry, too.

On this visit to Valencia I lived in the Presidencia, Negrin's head-quarters, and took most meals with him. Otto Katz, a German author who devoted his abilities to Loyalist propaganda abroad, and several of Negrin's secretaries and military advisers also ate at the Premier's table. Negrin likes company and likes to share his opinions with others. In private, we frequently talked about Soviet Russia. Several high Soviet officials in Spain had been recalled and were reportedly purged when they got home. Negrin would say, "We trusted these men implicitly. Now they are condemned as traitors. How are we to know whether the men who have succeeded them here can be trusted?" I told him this was the very doubt which crept into the minds of millions of Soviet citizens.

I saw a lot of War Minister Prieto on that trip. He was an interesting and unusual personality. I understood his Spanish but did not know enough of the language to express myself well, so Gisela Bauer, a Viennese woman married to a Spaniard, acted as interpreter. Gisela was Prieto's private secretary and opened his secret mail and telegrams. She spoke English, French, German, and Spanish fluently. I had made inquiries in Paris for Prieto about the possibility of enlisting Latin American officers in the Loyalist forces. Several Mexican officers had served brilliantly in the Republican army. Prieto wanted more from Mexico and other Spanish-speaking countries. I had also spoken to a member of the French Cabinet about recruiting French reserve officers for Spain. Negrin had asked me to do that, and he suggested that the experience might stand the French army in good stead. The Loyalists several times put this proposition to the French military: "Germany and Italy are trying out new weapons in Spain. Thousands of Nazi pilots are coming to Spain for graduate courses in actual combat. Why can't you send some of your people here? That would help you and us." The French refused. France had a new airplane equipped with a cannon. Pierre Cot proposed that it be put through its trials in the Loyalist air force. The French government said No.

Whenever a novel airplane type or an anti-aircraft gun was captured by the Loyalists, the Russians packed it off to Russia for analysis. The Loyalists offered the British and French the same facilities. They never accepted.

I talked to Prieto about all these matters and about domestic politics. I put one question, "Why is it that the Spanish Socialists and Communists, who would seem to be so close to one another, are such bitter enemies?" He took an hour to answer. He delivered an oration. It was a wonderful performance and a privilege to see his huge bulk, sunk deep into a soft chair, bounce up and down and sway from side to side as he explained his views. He said he had once favored merging the Socialist and Communist parties. But now he violently opposed that. He did not trust the Communists. He gave instances. He told me how they tried to get control of the army through the officers and commissars. He resisted their efforts.

I said I had observed at the front that commissars improved the morale of the troops. He replied, "But why must the vast majority of them be Communists?"

I said, "Lister, Campensino and Modesto are doing the job of generals. But you refuse to give them the rank of generals. They are kept down on the colonel level." He explained that that was due to old Spanish army regulations. It was not an answer, but it revealed his bias.

I had overstayed the ninety minutes granted me, and yet I had not had enough and hoped he would find time tomorrow to take me out to his country home in Vetera where he would not be interrupted by telephone calls and secretaries. He told me to come tomorrow at five.

Next day however, Prieto said he was afraid to leave his office; he expected news from the front and wanted to be near the telegraph. But he would promise me an hour without interruptions. There was one interruption: the young secretary who had been instructed to keep visitors away himself burst like a cyclone into the room and waved a telegram. "My wife's given birth. It's a girl," he exclaimed. Prieto hoisted himself out of the depression in the sofa, embraced the secretary, and congratulated him.

Among other things, we talked about del Vayo. Del Vayo undertook occasional missions abroad, wrote articles, and spoke on the radio, but his energy, enthusiasm, and excellent knowledge of world politics were not being used to the full. He was Commissar General of War and all the commissars were under him. But Prieto interfered so much with the work of the commissars that del Vayo could do very little except go to the front and address the troops in the trenches. I suggested to Prieto that it would solve a problem for him and del Vayo if the latter became Foreign Minister or, at least, Ambassador in Paris—the Loyalists' most pivotal diplomatic post. Negrin and I had discussed this matter several times.

Prieto is a great actor, and he imitated the way del Vayo speaks. I told him that if he could see del Vayo at a League of Nations Council session he would change his mind about him. Prieto finally declared that he had no objection to del Vayo as Foreign Minister or Ambassador, but it was not his affair.

As a matter of fact, Negrin wanted del Vayo in the Foreign Office, but could not appoint him over Azaña's veto. Prieto had originally shared Azaña's opposition. Negrin, however, could not insist on del Vayo's appointment because he had not yet won his battle with President Azaña. Negrin's prestige was rising. He was quickly forging ahead as the popular leader, but the process was not yet complete. He still had to consider Azaña's wishes.

My hour with Prieto passed all too quickly. Brazenly I said he had been very kind to me but still I thought that we could have a real talk only in the relaxed atmosphere of the country. He told me to come the next afternoon at five.

I was walking in a street in Valencia the next morning when I met Constancia de la Mora. Surprised at finding her away from her desk at such an hour, and reading distress in her face, I asked what had happened.

"I've been discharged," she exclaimed.

"What for?" I asked.

"Prieto did it," she said bitterly.

This episode is to me the most interesting in Constancia de la Mora's official career although I find no mention of it in her autobiographical book, *In Place of Splendor*. At the beginning of the war, Constancia took care of refugee children. Then she was put in charge of a hospital near Alicante for wounded Soviet pilots. But so many of them were killed outright that she had little to do. One day in January, 1937, she requested me to speak to del Vayo and recommend her for work in the Foreign Office press department.

I did. Del Vayo is a gorgeous human being, but he often procrastinates, and I talked to him several times, and also to his wife Luisy, urging Constancia's appointment. Finally, he appointed her, and she was a brilliant success. She knew languages and the psychology of foreigners, and the correspondents liked her.

Now she had been fired.

This is what happened: Within the Loyalist Cabinet, Prieto and his friends had been engaged in a struggle with the Communists to curtail the prerogative of the army's political commissars. Prieto had just succeeded in pushing through a decree to this effect. The press published the decree over his signature and on behalf of the entire cabinet. But when the foreign newspapermen wanted to wire the news abroad, Constancia did not allow it. In other words, she was censoring her own government. She was putting her devotion to the Communist party above her duty as a state official. Prieto lifted the telephone, talked with José Giral, and Giral dismissed her.

A few hours after Constancia told me of her dismissal I was at lunch in the Presidencia. Negrin came in late and sat down next to me. After he had settled down to his meager first course, I said to him in German—Otto Katz and others heard it, "Prieto did a very foolish thing today."

"What's that?" he asked.

"He has had Constancia de la Mora discharged."

"I would have put her in prison," Negrin flashed.

I told Negrin I believed she had behaved unpardonably. "But she is irreplaceable in the press department. All the foreign visitors and journalists are pleased with her and there is nobody who would do nearly as well in her job. I do not defend her action. But I think she ought to be taken back."

We argued all through lunch until Negrin said, "Well, it's up to Prieto anyway. Talk to him."

That evening at five, I called on Prieto by appointment, and hoped that we would go out to his country villa. We did. We got into his big black limousine with Gisela (Prieto told her to take a warm coat). An open car filled with detectives followed.

Prieto said, "I don't know what more you expect to get out of me. You have squeezed me dry like a lemon." He was in good humor. After a half-hour ride, we arrived in the little town of Vetera.

We entered through a small swing gate. A level walk of bright red tiles led to the broad, low tile-walled house. On either side of the walk stretched large gardens filled with rose beds and very green evergreen dwarf bushes. The housekeeper came to meet us and Prieto immediately ordered her to collect a bouquet of roses for Señora Bauer.

I said, "Somebody must be cursing you."

Prieto said, "Who?"

"The owner of this fine house."

"Here he is," Prieto said. He beckoned me to follow him into the house. In the front lobby he switched on a light. The light hung in a corner niche and under it was a small wax figure of a man in a toga with a wire halo around his head. "That's the owner. He had it made," Prieto exclaimed.

"I hope you will never do such a thing."

"Oh, there wouldn't be enough wax for me," he laughed.

I remarked that many European statesmen had gone much further along the road of self-glorification. He said, "No, I have never wanted to be first." While he and I moved a heavy marble-topped table and three chairs into position on the porch, he mentioned several instances in his political career where he had stepped down and refused to take the lead.

He asked me whether I drank. He said he never drank either, but added, "Let's have some cognac." Gisela drained her glass straight down while Prieto and I sipped slowly. He sat looking into the distant hills. Twilight was setting in and the hills were purple and brown. "Four hundred years from now, nobody will know I ever lived," Prieto mused aloud, "and in Afghanistan nobody today knows that I am alive. It is so peaceful here. I'm glad you made me come."

Nobody talked. The housekeeper brought the roses, and Prieto said they were too pale. Couldn't some brighter ones be found?

Silence again. Presently he turned his face from the hills, looked at me, and said, "What do you think of me?"

I puckered my lips and thought for a moment or two, but when I was about to open my mouth he interrupted. "No," he said, "I didn't want you to think. I wanted it to spill forth," and then he talked incessantly himself. He told several Spanish anecdotes. When he gave me a chance, I said, "You probably believed I was looking for good things to say and couldn't find them and that's why I hesitated. On the contrary. I always refrain from paying compliments to statesmen lest they imagine I am currying favor with them. I said that to Negrin only yesterday. I wanted to speak of your faults."

"Go ahead."

"As I see it," I began, "you have two major shortcomings: your limited acquaintance with the outside world and your limited ambition."

He asked Gisela to explain what I meant by limited ambition. She asked me. I reminded him of his own statement that he didn't want to be first. He didn't fight enough. "You are a pessimist and a philosopher. That makes you a fine person but it doesn't exactly help win a war. You are an Arab."

When Gisela translated "Arab" he winced. No Spaniard is pleased to be classified so close to a Moor. "You take the Communists," I proposed. "A considerable number of them wear blinkers. They see less but fight better. You see Afghans and wonder about 2300 A.D. Could that be one explanation of your differences with the Communists?"

"Don't be so polite," he cautioned. "It's not like you."

"The Communists are the best fighters in Spain."

"Also the best intriguers," he added. Then he went into a reverie, and when he came out of it he said, "You think I am a pessimist. My people are hungry. Whoever wins this war, Spain will be laid low by famine when it is over. Day by day, I watch everybody around me growing thinner. . . . I am the only exception," he chuckled, clasping his fat flanks.

"The Fascists want our raw materials," he asserted. "Well, perhaps there is a maldistribution of the wealth of the world. Perhaps an adjustment could be found which would cost fewer human lives."

This idea of Fascist "Have-nots" is a profound fallacy. It is not for raw materials or colonization that the totalitarians want new territories. Italy did not go to Abyssinia for wealth. Prieto did not insist on his point of view. He was not in a controversial mood.

It grew cold. We finished our cognac and Prieto said he had to go back to Valencia to work. In the car, I said, "I want to talk to you about an unpleasant subject."

"Namely?"

"Constancia."

He looked up in astonishment. I assured him I agreed that she had violated every canon, but it would be difficult to find a substitute for her and Loyalist propaganda abroad would suffer.

"I swear to you," he declared with customary emphasis, "that I did not act out of personal motives. Only this morning I sat at the sick-bed of Ignacio, her husband. I admire his work and respect him. I have nothing against Constancia either. But she is a Maura and like her famous grandfather Don Antonio Maura, Prime Minister of Spain, she is brusque. And sometimes hysterical. She does things this way." He threw his arm swiftly from one side of the car to the other and shouted, "Bah, bah, bah."

"Anyway," Prieto agreed after more conversation on the matter, "it's up to Negrin. Let him do as he pleases." This was exactly what I hoped he would say. That evening I repeated this to Negrin. Negrin said he wanted to establish a press department in the Presidencia and might take Constancia into that, but in any case her services would not be lost. "I will take the matter up with Giral tomorrow," Negrin declared.

I asked Negrin whether it would help if the correspondents signed a petition asking for the reinstatement of Madame de la Mora. He thought it wouldn't hurt. Early that afternoon, a blond young United Press correspondent, whose name I have forgotten, had been collecting correspondents' signatures on such a petition. My experience was chiefly Russian, and in Moscow an official who had sinned would be endangered by the support of foreign journalists. So I advised the U.P. man to hold up the petition. Now I went back to him, signed it, urged him to get all the men to sign and also to telephone Madrid and get the signatures of Herbert Matthews, Ernest Hemingway, and the other correspondents there. In a few days, Constancia was back at her job in the Foreign Office press section.

(When I returned to Spain in December, 1937, one of my first visits was to Constancia. She received me with calculated rudeness. I said, "What's the matter?" Her chin quivered and she said, "You had me discharged." The injustice of the accusation sickened me. I asked her what made her think so. She said I had refused to sign the petition. I told her about my conversations with Negrin. She could ask Otto Katz and others about one of them or Negrin about all of them. She could ask her close friend, Gisela Bauer, about my argument with Prieto about her.

"Besides," I begged, "ask the U.P. correspondent whether I didn't sign the petition in the end." I explained why I hadn't in the first place.

She said she took my word for it, but our relations thenceforth were always frigid and troubled. Constancia's animosity had a deeper root than her ignorance of my efforts to have her restored to office.

The Spanish Communists resented my good relations with Negrin, Prieto, Azaña, and other Loyalist leaders, and tried to interfere with them. Constancia told American visitors that my friendship with Negrin had been spoiled, and when in May, 1939, I arrived in New York on the *Normandie* with Negrin, thus giving the lie to such canards, she refused to speak to me. She has not spoken to me since. I had never done her any harm. In fact, despite her hostility towards me, I persuaded del Vayo to take her to Geneva as press aide in May, 1938, because I thought she would be effective there.)

In addition to Negrin, Prieto, and del Vayo, I saw many Spanish and non-Spanish friends. I noticed that since my last visit in July, 1937, the compromisers among the Loyalists had abandoned their hope for a negotiated peace. They had realized that Hitler, Mussolini, and Franco were not businessmen seeking money or peace, but power men after power and strategic positions. The skeptics of the type of Prieto, Azaña, and Giral had shifted; they thought the Loyalists could win the war by waiting and remaining on the defensive.

I found documentary proof of this attitude in a report which Foreign Minister Giral had submitted to the Loyalist government about his trip to Czechoslovakia to represent Spain at the funeral of Thomas Masaryk in September, 1937. Negrin gave me a copy which I have before me. Giral had a cordial interview with President Beneš. Beneš had always been pro-Loyalist. The probable sequence of events in Europe did not elude his keen eye, and he knew that the fate of his own country hung on Spain. He helped the Loyalists to get arms, but his Prime Minister Hodza and other reactionaries interfered when they could. Full of sympathy, Beneš inquired after Loyalist prospects. Giral said that the military situation had reached an equilibrium. The Republicans expected Franco to encounter mounting troubles with his civilian population and in that way succumb.

In Prague, Giral also talked with Léon Blum. Blum asked about the political situation in the Loyalist zone. Giral said that Republican policy "far from being in the hands of the Communists, was directed by men like Prieto and Negrin who were actuated by the highest nationalist sentiments and by an independence of character which did not admit of foreign pressure." He thought offensives too expensive; the Loyalists could win the war if they strived only for local military gains, meanwhile doing what they could to undermine morale in Franco territory.

Giral asked Blum whether it was true that several members of the French cabinet desired the exclusion of the Communist members of the Loyalist government. Blum declared that the retirement of the Communists would make no difference in the general attitude towards Spain.

(Several months later, Clement R. Attlee, the British labor leader, returning from his visit to Spain, dropped in to see Blum in Paris, and Blum put to Attlee the question which Giral had put to him in Prague. Attlee replied just as Blum had, "It doesn't make much difference who constitutes the Loyalist cabinet; to the reactionaries it will always be a 'Red' government.")

The Loyalists were now convinced that the war would last at least another year and perhaps two. I asked Negrin whether the money would last. He said it depended on the rate of expenditure, but he trusted that they could make ends meet for nearly two years. With this in view, they were stimulating the export of fruit, mercury, potash, and other products.

Imports, on the other hand, were being curtailed, and the result showed in the sad thin faces of Spaniards. Yet there was enthusiasm and faith everywhere, and the nearer one got to the front the better grew the spirit. I looked at these people and I said to myself, "They are, after all, fighting and suffering for things that are mine, that are important to me. They are resisting Fascism and upholding freedom. They pay heavily for it. If only the world could be made to realize this. If only the democracies could see Spain in this light. Spain was paying to fight the battle of the democratic world. Couldn't the democracies share some of the cost. Did the Spaniards have to stand the bombs, feel the steel, and also go hungry? At least the world could send food."

I felt this more poignantly when I left Spain and saw the full-stocked stores and the fat bellies and sated looks of the French and then of the British. Charity alone should have sent trainloads of food into Spain, and political considerations should have made the trains longer, heavier, more numerous. Yet to the end, Spanish stomachs grumbled with emptiness while bombs crashed and shells burst. Mothers in black refused to give up their places in food queues when the air-raid alarm sounded. In Madrid, I saw five women killed in a milk queue, and blood from their bodies ran down into the gutter to mingle with streams of milk from their pitchers. We are all callous hypocrites, and we enjoy life though we are aware of the homeless and hungry below our windows. But those who saw the misery and glory of the Spanish Republic could not be silent or idle. Many of the foreign correspondents who visited the Franco zone became Loyalists, but practically all of the numerous journalists and other visitors who went into Loyalist Spain became active friends of the cause. Even the foreign diplomats and military attachés scarcely disguised their admiration. Only a soulless idiot could have failed to understand and sympathize.

In Paris, Madame Genevieve Tabouis, diplomatic correspondent of the liberal *L'Œuvre*, was a consistent protagonist of the Spanish Republic. She knew everybody of importance in France and was an old friend of ex-Premier Herriot. She could phone foreign ministers, cabinet members, and diplomats and ask them for information and opinions which the next day appeared in her column. Frequently she invited such people to her apartment. One evening in November, 1937, she gave a dinner attended by Herriot, the Spanish Ambassador Ossorio y Gallardo, the Soviet Ambassador Suritz, ex-Premier Nitti of Italy, M. Paul-Boncour, former Prime Minister and Foreign Minister of France, and several other ambassadors and journalists. I sat next to Nitti. Ossorio held the floor often throughout the evening. He was a conservative Catholic and fiery advocate with a loud voice and no inhibiting discretion. Much to the obvious embarrassment of his colleague Suritz, Ossorio disclosed that two Soviet ships were waiting in Channel ports to unload airplanes for Spain but could not get the permission to do so. Herriot was surprised. Ossorio told how a single customs official in a Pyrenees town or an employee of the Finance Ministry might hold up valuable munitions shipments. "And now the French frontier is open," Ossorio remarked sarcastically. "You can imagine what happens when it is closed." Herriot promised to make inquiries. He was Speaker of Parliament and exercised considerable influence. But he was fat and lazy and shrank from political responsibility.

A few days later I flew over to London. In international affairs, France had become the trailer behind England's auto. That did not mean that Paris had no independence. It meant that it had less independence.

The British co-operative movement was collecting money for food for Spain. Labor was starting to campaign for Spain. A Popular Front committee, consisting of Communists, Laborites, Liberals like Wilfrid Roberts, M.P., and Conservatives like Katherine, Duchess of Atholl, was especially active. I went to see them to talk of Spain's sufferings and needs.

Clement R. Attlee, the leader of the Labor Party, had written an introduction to my "Why Spain Fights On" pamphlet. I called on him in the big office given to him by the government in the House of Commons. While I talked he sucked his pipe and said, "Quite" and "Right." I had a card to him from Negrin, and in Negrin's name invited him to lead a Labor delegation to Spain. He was noncommittal, but later he accepted, and in December he took the trip with Philip Noel-Baker, M.P., and Ellen Wilkinson, M.P.

Ellen Wilkinson, diminutive redhead, was the heart and fire of the pro-Loyalist work in England throughout the Spanish War. (In 1940, she was the only woman member of the British war government.) As a member of the executive committee of the British Labor party, she exercised influence among the leaders, and her oratory, fervor, and hard work made her very popular among workingmen. She is indefatigable. She addressed meetings, wrote articles, organized committees, called committee meetings, traveled up and down the country, and shot brilliant questions at complacent ministers in the House of Commons.

Question Time often is the most interesting period in the British Parliament. The House meets at 2.45 P.M. every weekday, except Friday and sometimes Thursday when it assembles at 11 A.M. It usually adjourns at 11 P.M. After the bewigged speaker has slow-marched into the chamber followed by a somber individual carrying his train, another carrying a sword, and a third the gold (or is it gilded?) mace of authority, and taken his padded seat on an elevated and canopied throne, the first thing on the agenda is Questions. Most of the M.P.'s are there, tightly packed together on tiers of long benches covered with black leather. The government supporters are on the Speaker's right. Facing them is the Opposition: Labor, Liberals, and the sole Communist. A broad aisle down the center separates the two "hostile camps." Ministers, and Attlee, often put their feet on the secretaries' table that forms the barrier between the ministers' Front Bench and the Opposition Front Bench.

The few visitors occupy galleries running around the walls of the small chamber. Those with very good hearing can catch much of what is said below. Questions have been submitted in advance. Ministers must answer all questions unless it is "not in the public interest" to do so. The questions of the government supporters serve to bring out the achievements of the government. But others may nettle their ministers. The Opposition questions are calculated to embarrass the government and elicit information that might be useful to attack the government's policy. Ministers' replies arouse noisy approval from their friends, and laughter or cries of "Shame" or angry replies from the Opposition. Questions are frequently put down to get publicity for some outrage at home or abroad. In this way, many of the most flagrant British sins of commission and omission are brought to the public's attention.

England is the land of clubs. Every gentleman feels that he must belong to a club. It is his café, restaurant, meeting place, and reading place. The House of Commons, they say, is England's best club. Deep in its recesses are spacious smoking rooms where no women are admitted and where tea and alcohol are served. It has a restaurant in which, by English standards, fair food is served. None of these places admits a visitor who is not accompanied by an M.P. and in none can you make even a pretense at paying the bill. The M.P. pays.

To the dark central lobby of the House of Commons—from which a corridor leads to the less important, neglected House of Lords—come people from all parts of the country, the empire, and the world. They fill out a green card and give it to a giant Bobby. He is the page. Soon the M.P. comes out to lead you to the tea room or terrace over the Thames for a drink or into the gallery to listen. Privileged visitors are taken to the inner lobby where the M.P.'s congregate.

In the House any afternoon I would meet a dozen interesting and influential people who had the same sympathies as I had. One afternoon, the Duchess of Atholl invited me to tea in the House. Her husband, the Duke, is one of the biggest landholders in Scotland, and she is no radical. But she had gone to Madrid and thenceforth she worked as hard for Loyalist Spain as anybody in the realm. In her oldfashioned black silk dress that fell to her shoetops she would sit on the platform, at Spain meetings, with Communists, left-wing socialists, workingmen, and demobilized International Brigaders and appeal for help for the Republicans. She would interrogate everybody who had been to Spain and hang on their words and note many of them in a book filled with her illegible scrawl.

The Duchess was pro-Loyalist on humanitarian grounds and because she is a good British imperialist. At one time she had led the crusade in the House of Commons against Soviet Russia, but now she said to me, "When they call me an agent of the Comintern because I am a friend of the Spanish Republic I think of how wrong I may have been when I accused people of being Comintern agents."

We sat drinking tea and eating buttered toast. "That's General Speers," she said, indicating a stately gentleman. Speers is a Conservative M.P., prominent friend of France and especially of Czechoslovakia. He and I exchanged a few sentences and then he invited me to have a drink with him the next afternoon. After questions, the M.P.'s troop out in scores to keep such appointments in various corners of the House labyrinth. When I saw him I emphasized the relationship between Spain and Czechoslovakia. He was skeptical. (We met again after Munich, and he said, "I'm afraid you were right.")

Sir Archibald Sinclair, poised Liberal statesman, Minister of Air during the second World War, took me to dinner in the House dining room and asked about Loyalist problems. He offered to have me meet Lloyd George. I was delighted. Lloyd George's secretary telephoned in the morning and gave me an appointment for November 26, at 4 P.M. in the House. Lloyd George had his own private office there. He inquired about domestic manufacture of munitions in Spain. "I was Minister of Munitions, you know," he said. He complained that he was beginning to forget names, but he thought that some of the experts who helped him in 1916, 1917, and 1918 might give their services now to the Republicans. "Go and see Sir Walter Layton," he urged. Layton had been his right-hand man in the Ministry of Munitions. (He was a key member of the British Purchasing agency in the United States in the second World War.) Layton edited the *London Economist* and the daily *News Chronicle*. Lloyd George's secretary made the appointment for me, and Layton asked me to dinner at his club on Pall Mall.

My date book shows that during that fortnight in London I saw: Philip Noel-Baker; Attlee—twice; John Middleton, secretary of the Labor party, who was remarkably well-read in American magazines; Robert Boothby, Conservative M.P.; D. N. Pritt; Sir Stafford Cripps and George Russell Strauss, left-wing Labor M.P.'s; Victor Gordon-Lennox, diplomatic correspondent of the conservative *Daily Telegraph;* Captain Liddell Hart, military correspondent of the *London Times*, and, unlike his paper, pro-Loyalist; J. B. S. Haldane, the Communist scientist; Paul Robeson; Vernon Bartlett, liberal columnist and broadcaster; Ivan Maisky, Soviet Ambassador; Pablo

Azcarate, Spanish Ambassador; Lord Kinouel, Labor peer; Eleanor Rathbone, Independent M.P.; Stephen Spender, radical poet; Herbert Morrison, Labor leader; Irene Ward and Macnamara, Conservative M.P.'s; Harold J. Laski, in his London school; A. V. Alexander, M.P. (First Lord of the Admiralty in the Labor government and again in the second World War); Tabouis who had come to London on a visit; Kingsley Martin, editor of the *New Statesman and Nation;* Harry Pollitt, secretary of the British Communist party, a fine workingman type; H. Noel Brailsford, Labor publicist; W. Dobbie, an ex-workingman, jolly and round, passionately devoted to his class and to Spain, now a Labor M.P.; and the Duchess and Ellen Wilkinson several times.

Brailsford combines fine intellect and a deep romantic strain. He is a Byron. He enlisted in the Greek army during the 1921 war with Turkey. He wished to enlist in the International Brigade and was dissuaded only with difficulty by his friends who told him he was no longer young. He had been very pro-Soviet and written pro-Soviet articles and books. The Moscow purges caused him suffering. He turned against Russia. My own views were such that I could not differ with him too radically. Yet I pleaded for "a truce on Russia because of Spain." We had to concentrate on positive work for Spain instead of on negative work against Russia. Once we went together by taxi to a Spain conference in the Friends' House near Euston where he was to speak. We paid the driver two shillings. The driver saw the crowd outside. "Will there be a collection for Spain?" the driver asked, and when Brailsford said yes, he handed us back the coin and told us it was his contribution.

Ivan Maisky, the Soviet envoy in London, was one of the first Soviet officials I had met in 1922 when he worked in the press department of the Commissariat of Foreign Affairs. A former Menshevik, like several other Soviet envoys abroad, ability, hard work, and discretion lifted him high in Bolshevik rank. A Soviet Ambassador in England during the appeasement years and the Spanish War needed a great deal of patience and restraint and a gullet that could swallow jibes, rebuffs, and insults. Maisky had these qualities. Maisky's services to Loyalist Spain are not forgotten even by those who now abhor Russia's foreign policy; Maisky as a member of the Non-Intervention Committee at times devoted as much time to Spanish affairs as to Soviet politics, and he was in a way a second Loyalist Ambassador in London. Diligently and with infinite care, he cultivated numerous important individuals in British political life. His attractive wife added to his popularity in high society.

Every ambassador anywhere is a lobbyist and propagandist. Usually he works at teas and dinners. But in London an ambassador has another arena, the House of Commons. Compared to London, Paris was always politically dead. Members of Parliament had their eyes and ears wide open and liked to listen. If Edgar A. Mowrer had a scheme to help China or boiled over with indignation about some French stupidity he flew to London to see Winston Churchill or Hugh Dalton, the Laborite, or some other British politician. Reuter's man Swire came back from Barcelona and looked for air-raid shelters in London and found none and made himself a one-citizen committee to interview Eden and others on this deficiency. In Paris such business was always backstairs intrigue or worse.

In the first fortnight of December, I was back in Barcelona. The Loyalists, fighting like lions on ice-covered crags, had captured Teruel, a city at the point of a dangerous salient threatening Valencia. The Republicans had also stepped up their home production of munitions and were beginning to turn out airplanes modeled on the Soviet Chato. Army discipline was tighter. "The war will probably go on until 1939," I wired *The Nation*. This, I said, irked Hitler and Mussolini. "Germany and Italy are eager to see the end. If they swallow Spain, Germany will be free to launch the next adventure. Czechoslovakia, Austria . . ."; the cost of intervention in Spain "weighs heavily on Italy." Arms were coming down from France into Catalonia—Soviet arms and Czech arms. "The new French stand . . . raises the price of intervention to Germany and Italy. Poor Spain is sapping the vitality of world Fascism. Should China resist as long as Spain has, the international outlook would grow much brighter. . . . If the non-Fascist, status quo, pacifist nations got together, the unholy triple alliance of territory-grabbing pirates could be stopped. Spain's heroic fight has made this a concrete possibility."

I was in New York for Christmas. I still get excitement out of these quick jumps from one world into another, from bombs in Barcelona to crowds in Times Square.

28. What Would Happen If . . . ?

I THINK the most widespread American disease is the desire to know what will happen. The most frequent question at lectures in the United States is, "What would happen if . . .?" "Will a defeated Germany go Bolshevik?" "Will England adopt socialism if it wins the war?" "What will Russia do?"

Now a lecturer has a question, "What would happen if you knew what would happen? Suppose I or I and a thousand others told you what would happen if. Would it make any difference?"

This is one of the gravest problems of modern democracies. What is the duty of those who think they know what will happen if? Pertinax, Emile Buré, and Genevieve Tabouis told France that further appeasement would kill her. Pierre Cot, Georges Mandel, and a few other French politicians issued similar warnings from ministerial offices. Nobody paid any heed. In England Winston Churchill beat the tom-toms, Sir Archibald Sinclair sounded the alarm, Labor party spokesmen painted the future in sinister colors. But Neville Chamberlain, Sir Horace Wilson, Sir John Simon, Sir Samuel Hoare gaily went on appeasing forever until they appeased themselves and innocent millions into the worst war in history.

If nobody had foreseen what would happen if, the tragedy would not be so horrible. But hundreds delineated the exact contours of the tragedy that would lead to the second World War. And it didn't help.

General Douglas MacArthur, former U. S. Chief of Staff, has said, "The history of failure in war can almost be summed up in two words: Too Late." Those two little words also sum up the history of our late peace. If those who now understand would have understood two years earlier, three years earlier, many calamities might have been avoided; the great calamity might have been avoided. I do not believe the War was inevitable.

President Roosevelt, practically alone among the democratic statesmen in office, foresaw the gathering storm. He spoke of it in a message to Congress in January, 1936. He pointed directly to it in his famous Chicago speech on October 5, 1937. "The present reign of terror and lawlessness began several years ago," he said, ". . . and has now reached a stage where the very foundations of civilization are seriously threatened." He obviously referred to Abyssinia, Spain, and China. "Civilians, including women and children, are being ruthlessly murdered with bombs from the air. In times of so-called peace ships are being attacked and sunk by submarines without cause or notice. Nations are fomenting and taking sides in civil warfare in nations that have never done them any harm." That could only mean Spain. "Nations claiming freedom for themselves deny it to others"—a smack at Hitler yearning to impose a worse Versailles on others.

The President called on peace-loving nations to "make a concerted effort." The peace, freedom, and security of ninety percent of the population of the world was "being jeopardized by the remaining ten percent who are threatening a breakdown of all international law and order." He therefore advocated a "quarantine" of the aggressor nations. This policy, if adopted, could have preserved the peace of the world. But Europe did not hear. Even America refused to listen.

Roosevelt was bitterly opposed to appeasement from the very beginning. But his two most important ambassadors in Europe were not. Joseph P. Kennedy admired and abetted Chamberlain's appeasement policy. William C. Bullitt praised Daladier's foreign policy. He did so talking to me and to others. And of course gentlemen occupying important jobs in the State Department did not see eye to eye with the President. One might think that did not matter. They were his public servants. No. The man who executes policy day by day in notes and negotiations can thwart the will of his chief. "A government" is an abstraction. It consists of officials representing various trends, often conflicting trends, and some of them get an opportunity to implement their personal views in opposition to the avowed policy of the head of the state.

Appeasement in relation to Spain took the form of Non-Intervention which enabled Germany and Italy to intervene on behalf of Franco, and Russia to intervene on behalf of the Loyalists. But since Russia encountered difficulties of transport and transit, this gave the advantage to Fascism. America's counterpart to Non-Intervention was the embargo on arms shipments to Spain. We refused to sell arms to either side. That looked like neutrality. But since Franco had all the arms he needed and the Republic did not, it was actually unfair to the legal Spanish anti-Fascist government. The United States embargo helped Franco win. It helped Hitler and Mussolini to win in Spain. It therefore accelerated the war crisis of September, 1939.

Those who knew Europe predicted this in so many words. We foretold exactly what would happen if Spain fell. But the appeasers were busy in Washington and in U. S. embassies abroad.

President Roosevelt has said it. "We have learned the lesson of recent years. We know now that if we seek to appease them by withholding aid from those who stand in their way we only hasten the day of their attack on us."—Dayton, October 12, 1940. Spain taught America that lesson.

"You cannot appease the unappeasable," Mr. Bullitt said at Chicago on October 21, 1940. Too true . . . and too late. To appease a totalitarian dictator was "useless," Bullitt said. He should have known that simple truth much earlier.

"Timidity, weakness, and short-sightedness . . . governed the policy of the confused reactionary governments in France and England before the war," President Roosevelt said in New York on October 29, 1940. That fact was discovered too late in France. It was discovered just in time in Great Britain.

Appeasement helped to make the second World War. In Spain, the United States had an opportunity to turn England and France away from appeasement. The question of the American embargo on Spain transcended Spain. If the President had lifted the embargo he would have indicated to London and Paris that he wanted Loyalist Spain to win. He would have indicated his open and strong disapproval of appeasement. He would have become the ally, the powerful ally, of Winston Churchill who was fighting Neville Chamberlain and of the true French democrats who were fighting Daladier and Bonnet.

This is not hindsight. On January 13, 1939, in Washington, Major George Fielding Eliot spoke at a private dinner of the Foreign Policy Association. Journalists, State Department officials, some senators, including Floor Leader Senator Barkley and a few others—about thirty in all—were present, and William T. Stone presided. I got into an agitated public argument with Jerome N. Frank, chairman of the SEC, on American foreign affairs, and I declared, "By lifting the embargo on Spain we can oust Chamberlain." To prevent this,

Chamberlain's crew in Washington worked hard, and effectively, against the lifting of the embargo. Catholics in America were the other great force that prevented the lifting of the embargo.

Secretary of State Hull declared on October 26, 1940, "By 1938 there was no longer any doubt that the existence of the arms embargo provision was definitely having the effect of making widespread war more likely." The embargo was applied only to Spain. I talked with Mr. Hull in the State Department on January 24, 1939, and even then he was in favor of lifting the embargo.

The Gallup Poll sounded American opinion on the Spanish struggle three times: in February, 1937, February, 1938, and December, 1938. The first time 40% expressed views, the second time 50%, the third time 66%. The first time, 65% of those who had views were pro-Loyalist, the second time 75%, the third time 76%. The majority of Americans favored the lifting of the embargo. Logic and common sense favored it. President Roosevelt and Secretary Hull favored it. But it was not lifted.

Jay Allen, Hamilton Fish Armstrong, Dorothy Thompson, Professor Walter B. Cannon of Harvard, Archibald MacLeish, Henry L. Stimson, Josephine Schain, Raymond Leslie Buell, Guy Emery Shipler, A. A. Heller, Bishop Francis J. McConnell, Paul J. Kern, Secretary Ickes, Dorothy Kenyon, Herman F. Reissig, Congressman Jerry O'Connell, Ernest Sutherland Bates, Paul Kellogg, Helen Hall, Freda Kirchwey, John Dewey, Francis J. Gorman, Frank P. Walsh, Catholic attorney, Miles Sherover, hundreds of newspaper men and editors, and many thousands of other Americans tried to induce the United States government to cease hampering the Spanish Republic's efforts to defend itself against brutal aggressors. I did what little I could towards the same end. I spoke on the platform, wrote articles, talked to senators and representatives in Washington, and on February 24, 1938, made a plea to Mrs. Roosevelt in the White House.

I have always admired and applauded President Roosevelt's numerous speeches and messages on foreign policy. I like his personality. I believe, however, that history will record the failure to lift the embargo as a blunder. A democratic leader must give ear to dissenting minorities and to approving majorities. When very much is at stake—and peace for Europe was the stake in Spain—he is warranted in ignoring dissenters in the hope that acts will convert them where words have not. The dictators, unfortunately, do not wait for the democracies to be educated. They take advantage of our lack of knowledge.

I have seen one bomb turn a Barcelona woman's coolness for the Republic into flaming hatred of Franco. Fifty pounds of TNT taught her more than a ton of educational propaganda.

The day after my talk with Mrs. Roosevelt I kept an appointment with Mrs. Carrie Chapman Catt, militant pacifist, a remarkable and venerable fighter. She too thought the embargo ought to be repealed. An increasing number of Americans felt that our neutrality rendered unneutral aid to the aggressors. In private, numerous Catholics also saw the wisdom of repealing the so-called neutrality legislation. They knew that some British Catholics and the bulk of French Catholics were pro-Loyalist. The Basque Catholics were fighting on the Loyalist side. Hitler was persectuing Catholics in Germany; he could not be working for them in Spain. Franco saving Catholic Spain with Nazi pagans and infidel Moors was a spectacle that revolted many Catholics. But the discipline of the Roman church is strict and few American Catholics expressed pro-Loyalist sentiments in public.

One reaction to the Catholic attitude on Spain disturbed me profoundly. I discovered that wide sections of America are potentially very anti-Catholic. This applies not only to the South or to Masons. Religious intolerance is an ugly animal, and once aroused it can divide a country as nothing else can. I met Americans of all shades of political opinion who were irked by the activity of Catholic churchmen in such political issues as those of the Supreme Court, the World Court, child labor, and American foreign policy towards Spain. Catholics, needless to say, can do anything they please within the law. But the charges I heard made reference to sermons in churches, speeches by Catholic leaders, propaganda in the Catholic press, and pressure by Catholic groups. Cardinal O'Connell said flatly, in an interview published March 19, 1938, several days after Franco's airplanes killed hundreds of civilians in Barcelona, that the report "is a lie." This injudicious statement still makes me angry. The bombing is an historic and confirmed truth. Such bombings happened too many times, and not only in Barcelona. Hundreds of towns were bombed. "General Franco," the Cardinal continued, "would not dare do a thing like that. . . . Franco is fighting for Christian civilization in Spain." What horrifying nonsense! Franco was fighting *against* Christianity, *against* civilization, *against* Spain, and *against* peace.

(I never believed that the Catholic church would benefit from a Franco victory. It has not. Camille M. Cianfarra telegraphed from Rome to his paper, the *New York Times,* on January 26, 1940: "A distressing picture of the political aftermath of Generalissimo Francisco Franco's victory in Spain has reached the Vatican. According to information given to the Papal Secretariat by 'a very reliable Spanish source,' there are at present 500,000 political prisoners in Spain. . . . Priests still held in Carmona jails number sixty. . . . Two thousand women, it is said, are in the Bilbao jails, waiting to learn their fate. In December, twenty-five persons were executed.

"The Vatican's relations with Spain," the dispatch, obviously based on Papal information, continued, "leave much to be desired, according to some Vatican quarters, where it was noted with regret that in General Franco's recent speeches and in those of other authoritative representatives of his government, no mention was made of the religious reconstruction that should be undertaken in war-torn Spain." Obviously. Franco's hands are too red with the blood of innocent Spaniards. His right hand is befouled by the touch of Hitler.)

Catholic opposition notwithstanding, the pro-Loyalist movement assumed vast proportions in the United States. Americans inspired by love of the underdog, love of freedom, passionate hatred of Fascism, and a concern for world peace gave to the Spanish Republic their money, time, sympathy, and blood. In many ways, and for many people, pro-Loyalism represented the highest peak of idealism in America between the first World War and the second. Loyalist Spain was an unusually attractive cause. A poor people, long ground under the heel of tyrants, was fighting oath-breaking generals. The generals were aided by Hitler, Mussolini, and the Moors. The Republic fought against cruel odds. It suffered discriminations. It bounced back after the worst reverses. Its leaders were men of culture and ideals. Its soldiers were brave, barefooted, ill-equipped, and hungry. Its women suffered stoically and bent their haggard bodies over their young to stay the shrapnel of Fascist bombs. America saw them in the newsreels rushing to shelter across the streets of Madrid, dragging children by the hand. Barbarism had descended on a civilized country. Spain pleaded for aid and the western governments refused. The finest hearts ached for the Spanish people, and the finest minds worried about it. Powerless to do much they sought with all the greater passion to do more. The list of Americans who helped the

Loyalists is a roll of honor. The passing of time, and the softness of some other nations in resisting Fascist attack, make the Spanish struggle stand out in ever more glowing colors.

I am happy I did my bit. I am sorry it was so small. I would have given all that I had for a democratic victory in Spain. In the dark days when the Spanish government's strategy was being crippled by the Alcazar siege—September, 1936—a group of correspondents was returning from Toledo in a car. We asked one another what we would give to have the Loyalists take the Alcazar. Would you give a finger? Would you let your right arm be cut off? (Would you today allow your right arm to be hacked off if that would relieve London of air raids for a week?) Such questions are easy to answer because you know they are rhetorical. I hate to sound romantic and grandiloquent. Yet I think I would have been ready to die to defeat Hitler, Mussolini, and Franco in Spain.

I returned from America to Paris in the middle of March, 1938. That week Barcelona suffered the worst three days in its life. For seventy-two hours Italian and German giant bombers hammered the big city with heavy bombs. Hundreds of thousands cowered in the subways for days and nights. Others fled to the hills and slept there. Work in offices and factories languished. French newspapers carried gruesome details of the slaughter and long lists of casualties. On the third day of the bombing the telephone operator in my Paris hotel rang and said Barcelona was calling me and would I accept the call. Of course I would. Who could be calling me? What had happened? Panic. Fire destroying the whole city? The government fleeing? Some dear friends mangled by bombs? I walked up and down the room, then tried without success to read. The telephone. The voice from Barcelona: "Hello, this is Ivor Montagu."

"Ivor, what has happened?" I shouted.

"Listen, Louis," he softly replied, "do you think we could find a market in the United States for a long educational film I have been turning here. If yes, the Spaniards will help me finance the enterprise."

My first impulse was to tell him to go to hell. My next was to be endlessly grateful. Ivor's inquiry had told what I wanted to know about the situation in Barcelona.

A week later I was in Barcelona myself. The moment I crossed from the French town of Le Perthus to the Spanish frontier town of La Jonquera I got quiet inside. The spirit of the people obviously was unbroken—and the customs official put on white cotton gloves before he examined the things in my suitcase. He had not had them the last time.

A town en route to Barcelona had been badly bombed just before we rode into it, and the highway was littered with glass bits, rock, and telegraph wires. Women in black dug their fingers into their cheeks. Clanging ambulances rushed towards the big hospital in Barcelona. Barcelona itself was quiet and wounded. I first went to the scenes of the recent bombings. In the Calle de las Corts Catalanas several tremendous apartment houses had been completely wrecked and in places pulverized. A Spanish woman who had gone down there immediately after a bombing told me that she had waded to her shoetops in blood. Scores were killed in this street alone. The broad street was still roped off. I went through by ignoring the policemen's summons and started taking photographs. But a plainclothes man quickly overtook me and arrested me. I took him in my car to Constancia de la Mora's office and she had him release me. At the Corts Catalanas one saw the sight that always follows bombings of homes: women digging in the debris searching for clothes. A woman would find a sleeve and then dig more carefully until she brought out a dress or her husband's shirt. Children dug for their toys and for pillows. I asked a little girl what she was doing. "I'm looking for my doll," she said.

The bombing had been exceptionally destructive and foreign military journals declared the Germans had been experimenting with new explosives. Hitler used Spain as a testing ground for weapons and men. The Nazi pilots who bombed Poland, Holland, and London got their first experience in Spain. Guernica was a rehearsal for Coventry; Hitler wanted to see how thoroughly a small town could be wiped out from the air.

Negrin looked depressed. It was the first time I had seen him so. "We simply haven't enough airplanes," he said. "If France doesn't help quickly we are lost." The Loyalists had practically no good bombers and only one-third as many fighters as the Fascist rebels. After the Teruel victory, Hitler and Mussolini had poured vast quantities of stuff into Spain. They had retaken Teruel. They then started pushing on the Aragon front with the intention of reaching the east coast and cutting off Catalonia from Valencia and Madrid. In this Aragon offensive, the American contingent of the International Brigade took a terrific beating and lost many men in killed and imprisoned.

Wavering Loyalists wavered some more. The Barcelona bombings shook civilian morale. At a cabinet meeting several ministers called for an immediate armistice. (Foreign newspapers thereupon reported that Barcelona was suing for peace.)

In the midst of this crisis, Negrin climbed into his camouflaged Douglas and flew non-stop to Paris. He outlined the situation to Léon Blum, who was again Premier of France. Blum cried. Negrin had little time. But the French pondered. While waiting, Negrin wandered into Brentano's bookstore on the Avenue de L'Opéra where Colonel Charles Sweeny, an American army officer who fought in the French army in the first World War, then in the American army in France and had gone down to Spain to ask for a command in the Loyalist forces—he organized the Eagle Air Squadron of Americans in England in 1940—saw Negrin buying the latest political books in English.

Blum promised Negrin help. Three shiploads of Soviet bombers and pursuit planes had been held up in Channel ports for several weeks. These would be released. Soviet cannon would be allowed to pass. Whispers filled Paris. The French staff, it was said, had decided to send three divisions into Spain to drive the Italians out of the Aragon. The French military were always sensitive to what happened on their Catalan frontier. Rumor had it that the French navy wished to occupy the island of Minorca in the Balearics so as to offset Italy's control of near-by Majorca Island.

While the generals and admirals debated, Foreign Minister Paul-Boncour told British Ambassador Sir Eric Phipps about their debates. Sir Eric held up his hands in holy dismay. Suppose France got involved with Italy and Germany by precipitous action on behalf of the Loyalists, Phipps protested. Conveniently, news of impending German mobilization plans were circulated in Paris. The franc rocked. French military moves might kill it, the reactionaries argued. Jouhaux, leader of the French trade unions—five million members—informed Blum that the workingmen would produce more arms if they were told that some of those added arms would go to fight France's enemies in Spain. The Paris Metal Workers' Union announced that its members would do an hour's overtime each day without pay if the extra munitions were sold to Barcelona.

But the Paris daily *Journal*, financed by Mussolini—no secret—declared it would revolt if France marched to the aid of Republican Spain. "France," I wired, "is divided and pacifist, and young men basking in the glorious spring sunshine with their girls think how terrible it would be to have to go to the trenches. This makes government policy." This made France fall in 1940.

The French Right did not want the Loyalists to win; that might strengthen the Left in France. The Left in France was afraid to antagonize the Right. France, thus disunited, "invited His Majesty's Government to state its views," and H.M.G. said No. Blum therefore moved timidly and ineffectively. We gave transit to some Soviet material. He did not want Franco to rule Spain. But he did nothing to save Spain decisively. Nor did Edouard Daladier whom Blum had included in his cabinet as Minister of War.

So Negrin came back to Barcelona bringing a few welcome gifts for the army, and an armful of books. Everything depended on the resistance of the hungry people and on the spirit of the army and the government.

In one of my talks with Dr. Negrin during the last week of March, 1938, I told him that friends of Spain in Paris wanted me to inquire what he thought of the idea of buying a Paris daily for a year. He said they must make no arrangements for more than a month. So it was as bad as that?

I went down to the Ebro at Tortosa and interviewed soldiers. I busied myself seeing people in Barcelona. I saw the del Vayos. They invited me to meals often; del Vayo was on a strict diet and ate little more than bananas and so there was food for me. Vayo felt confident. That reflected his irrepressible temperament, but he also had his ear close to the people's heart.

In those critical days, the *Frente Rojo*, Communist morning paper in Barcelona, asked del Vayo for a statement approving the death sentence passed at the Moscow trial on Bukharin, Rykov, Yagoda, and others. He asked my opinion and I said, "Don't do it." He was not inclined to do it anyway, and didn't.

The Loyalists needed a tonic. War Minister Prieto had been telling his staff officers that the war could not be won and would soon be lost! On the battlefield at Teruel he had said to his assistants that they would soon lose Teruel again. That proved true. But when officers are sending men to their death in obedience to the War Minister's orders the War Minister himself cannot tell them that these efforts are vain. I also heard a report that news of Prieto's dark views on the future of the struggle had been passed on to the pro-Loyalist French Ambassador Eric Labonne, and this when France's attitude was so vital. President Azaña, naturally, was even more defeatist than Prieto.

The next time I saw Negrin I therefore said to him I thought the country needed a change of government. If the head men were defeatist the army's morale would deteriorate. I had seen a lot of mismanagement at the front. The town of Fraga, pivotal center, had been left in the hands of four hundred raw recruits and a major who bolted at the first shot. A shift of ministers would have a tonic effect. "If Azaña objects," I ventured, "you can throw a guard around his house and cut off his telephone. The situation requires something drastic. You cannot stop at formalities when so much is at stake. This is no time to be tired."

"I am not tired," he snapped back. Then he asked, "Have you been speaking to Zuga?"

Zugazagoitia had preceded me in Negrin's office. "No, why?"

"Zuga is talking to Prieto," Negrin replied. "Stay here a few days longer." That was clear enough. The next week, Prieto left the government and Negrin took over the War Ministry. Negrin is very loyal to his friends and the dismissal of Prieto caused him pain. The unpleasant task of breaking the news to Prieto was performed by Zugazagoitia and Marcelino Pascua, the Loyalist Ambassador in Paris.

(Zuga, a young man of about forty, was seized by the Gestapo in the occupied French zone in 1940 and handed over to Franco. He was executed without trial in Madrid.)

I was in Paris in the first week of April when Prieto left the cabinet and del Vayo became Foreign Minister in place of Giral. I advised my friends to buy the Paris daily for a year in the interests of the Loyalist cause. The paper was pro-Loyalist and anti-appeasement. It needed money to keep alive and to broaden its influence.

On April 6, 1938, I addressed a meeting in the House of Commons at the invitation of the Duchess of Atholl. Major Hills, an old Conservative M.P., was in the chair. He and I sat behind a long high wooden counter, and in front of us on wooden school chairs—the kind with one large arm—sat twenty-five M.P.'s, all supporters of the Chamberlain government, among them Harold Nicolson, who was very pro-Loyalist, Wing Commander James, who was very pro-Franco, and Marcus Samuel, who was very anti-Soviet.

I made an introductory statement of about half an hour. I said I had just been to Spain and felt certain that the Loyalists would continue to fight even though Franco thought he had won. The government still had reserves of men and enthusiasm as well as material whereas Franco could not grasp victory because of limited man-power which reflected lack of sympathy for his cause in the large part of Spain he had conquered.

Great inequality existed in the air, however, and that was the Loyalists' chief difficulty. They had ninety planes, most of them fighters, and most of them old, and all of them had done more flying than was good for them. Franco's air force, if one could call it Franco's—it really belonged to Mussolini and Hitler and was simply using Spanish territory to operate from—numbered at least five hundred machines and perhaps as many as eight hundred. In addition, some of the Italian bombers flew from Sardinia, bombed Loyalist centers, and returned to their airfields without ever touching Franco's soil.

The Spanish government, I added, suffered likewise from a shortage of artillery, in fact from a shortage of everything but money, determination, and public support. I dilated on both these subjects: the military situation which favored Franco, the domestic political situation which demonstrated Franco's weakness. Hitler and Mussolini had set him up and they held him up. Spain did not need a Franco regime. Spain's great need was the solution of the land problem and Franco could not solve that.

I saw the question "Why?" on several faces in front of me.

"Why?" I said. "Because Franco would have to deprive his own supporters of their wealth and social position. He would thereby undermine his sole political backing. No government deliberately destroys its own social base. That is why Franco will keep Spain eternally dissatisfied."

I then turned to the international phase of the Spanish problem. "Hitler and Mussolini are not in Spain to fight Bolshevism. They say that to delude you. They are in Spain to fight you and France." The *Paris Temps* of April 5, 1938, had printed an excerpt from the Italian *Gazetta del Popolo* which affirmed that for Italy Anglo-French sovereignty in Spain was no less menacing than Communism.

At this point, I was asked if it was not true that Italy was in Spain to get commercial advantages. I replied that for this purpose traveling salesmen would be better than flying bombs. If Mussolini devoted to penetration into Spanish business only a part of the millions he was spending on the smashing of Spanish economy he could have most of it. But he was pursuing military-imperialist aims; he coveted the Western Mediterranean. The Franco people were talking of restoring Gibraltar to Spain. For Mussolini, Spain was a continuation of the Ethiopian campaign and both were facets of an ambitious Roman conception.

A member suggested that England could oust Italy from Spain by peaceful means. "If Mussolini were ready to quit Spain at England's behest," I replied, "why should he have gone there in the first place? He knew in advance you wouldn't like it. I think one of the dangers of England's world position is her confidence in it." I spied several wry faces.

I had said that Franco started the rebellion and was responsible for it. "But," one M.P. challenged, "is it not true that the Loyalists provoked the Nationalists by the assassination of Calvo Sotelo, the Monarchist leader?"

This was a well-oiled legend. Sotelo was shot in Madrid on July 14. The revolt started in Morocco on the 17th. But Franco, the Germans, and the Italians had had more preparation than seventy-two hours. Italian planes received orders on July 15, to fly to Morocco to aid Franco. Besides, we had the testimony of Captain C. W. H. Bebb, in a signed article in the *London News Chronicle* of November 7, 1936. I had the clipping in my pocket.

Bebb was a pilot of the Olley Air Service in England. "On the afternoon of July 9," he wrote, "a Spaniard walked into our office at Croydon airdrome and asked to see Captain Olley. Ten minutes later I was called into the office and asked if I would undertake a secret flight to the Canary Islands. . . . We started at dawn on July 11. . . . On the 14th, we left Casablanca for Las Palmas, via Cap Juby, and arrived at Las Palmas at 2 P.M. on the 14th. While I was waiting at Las Palmas, José Calvo Sotelo, leader of the Right, was murdered in Madrid. I gathered the impression later on that the murder of this man caused General Franco and his staff to start the revolution several days before they had originally intended." Then Captain Bebb describes how he flew General Franco from Las Palmas to Casablanca and Tetuan. He had been hired for that purpose on the 9th. The murder of Calvo Sotelo was an incident, not a cause. It may have advanced the date of Franco's rising. Nothing else.

"Tell us about religion in Loyalist Spain," some one called out.

"I have never understood," I began, "how an institution like the Vatican which is anti-revolutionary and stands, presumably, for law and order, can support a clique of rebellious generals who have broken their oath to the government in a peaceful country. . . . The Vatican is situated in Italy. The Pope is always an Italian. Most of the cardinals are Italians. The Roman church supported Italian expansion in Abyssinia and behaves the same way now in Spain. Mistakenly the Vatican regards the world struggle as one between Fascism and Communism. Its choice is obvious. The Catholic leaders of the pro-Franco movement in the United States are at the same time appeasers and foes of liberalism.

"In Spain, the Catholic church is definitely aligned with Franco. It was always aligned with the Francos. It always supported the reactionary monarchy against the people. It was an established church which lived on subsidies from the state. It was an owner of factories, power stations, and much land, one of the biggest landlords of Spain. Hence it identified itself with the landlords' cause. Hence the people identified it with their enemies.

"The Catholic hierarchy of Spain has done much harm to Catholicism in Spain. The Loyalists are not anti-religious. In Soviet Russia the regime is frankly atheistic. One will look in vain, however, for anti-God sentiments in the declarations of the Loyalist government or of its leaders. But the church has taken the side of the generals, the Nazi pagans, the infidel Moors and Mussolini. This will react to the disadvantage of the church. The people will distrust the church. A Franco victory will hurt the church in Spain. It will die in the hearts of common men. Only a liberal triumph could enable Catholicism in Spain to attempt to redeem itself.

"When the civil war broke out, the people did not burn banks or commercial houses. They burned churches. I regret this. But this has happened before in Spain and in Mexico and elsewhere. Where popular wrath overflowed it attacked the church which was closer to the higher-ups than to the underdog.

"The church in Spain behaved like a political party," I said, "and it has to pay the penalties. It is in the front line of battle fighting under the Fascist banner. It cannot complain if it is struck by bullets."

"Why does Moscow help the Loyalists?" Marcus Samuel asked.

I explained that a general ideological affinity of course existed, although the Spanish Republic was in no sense Communistic. Moscow's chief concern, however, was to weaken the aggressor states so that they might not catapult Europe into a major war. I dealt with this at length and closed by suggesting that the best way to insure world peace would be to strengthen the resistance of the Chinese and Spanish governments.

When Chairman Major Hills adjourned the meeting a group of M.P.'s gathered around. A rapid exchange ensued. Hitler had seized Austria the previous month; the M.P.'s were somewhat worried.

When the members started to disperse, a tall, handsome M.P. whose demeanor during the meeting made me think he was pro-Loyalist, introduced himself as Colonel Ropner, Conservative, and invited me to have dinner with him in the House the next evening. He said he would have four M.P.'s with him. The following morning he phoned and told me there would be twenty M.P.'s, including Sir Thomas Inskip, Minister for the Co-ordination of Defense, and several junior ministers. "Did I mind?" No. And would I mind if a friend of his asked me to his office? I soon received a telephone call from Colonel Clark, chief of the intelligence service of the War Office.

I went over to see Clark in Whitehall. For almost an hour he and a gentleman who had once been in Spain as military attaché plied me with questions. They were most eager to learn about the qualities of the officers and non-commissioned officers of the Loyalist army.

I submitted willingly to their queries. When they seemed to have had enough I said, "Now I would like to ask you one." Colonel Clark nodded. "Why," I inquired, "do you allow enemies of the British empire to advance towards its defenses?"

"We in the War Office, you know," Colonel Clark asserted, "do not make policy. But I would like to ask you this. In your opinion, would it be better if Franco won quickly or if Spain remained an open wound through which the poisons of Europe could escape?"

The question was calculated to reveal a lot to me. The alternatives he outlined obviously represented the views of two schools of thought in British military circles, and from the tone of his voice I gathered that he belonged to the school which hoped that Italy and Germany might be weakened by the expenditure of effort and material in Spain.

That evening I met Colonel Ropner by appointment shortly before eight. He led me out to the House terrace overlooking the Thames river. He first begged my forgiveness, but there would be thirty-one M.P.'s and some were bringing their wives. "Did I mind?" On the contrary I felt complimented. Colonel Ropner then told me that he had visited Russia recently. He thought well of the Red Army, what he saw of it, yet he wondered whether bad transport facilities would not handicap it in a war. He had also been to Germany recently and received friendly treatment there. He said, "I'm pro-Fascist, but I'm all with you on Spain." Colonel Ropner's imperialism was stouter than his class prejudices.

Inside, we took sherries and then occupied places at the long table. Sir Thomas Inskip was at Colonel Ropner's right and my left. On my right sat Sir Arnold Wilson, the leader of the Franco forces in Britain. Among the others present were: the Duchess of Atholl, Vyvyan Adams, R. H. Cross, Vice Chamberlain of the Royal Household, the Marquess of Hartington, Parliamentary Under-secretary for the Dominions, Lieutenant Colonel Muirhead, Under-secretary of State for Air, G. H. Shakespeare, Parliamentary and Financial secretary of the Admiralty, Rear-Admiral Sir Murray F. Sueter, Captain Euan Wallace, Parliamentary secretary of the Board of Trade, Captain G. Waterhouse, Comptroller of the Royal Household, and H. G. Strauss.

During the first part of the dinner, an M.P. across the narrow table kept Inskip busily engaged in conversation, and so Sir Arnold and I concentrated on one another. He talked about everything but Spain. He assumed, without a word, that we had better agree to disagree. He said he had written books on Persia and had quoted my *Oil Imperialism* in one. He knew my *Soviets in World Affairs* too. Wilson had spent much time in the East as British Imperial official and also as an official of the Anglo-Persian Oil Company. Though fifty-three, and a Member of Parliament since 1933, he was firmly built, dark, and energetic-looking. He had visited Hitler and been received several times by Benito Mussolini. His book, *Walks and Talks Abroad*, published in 1936, urged appeasement of the Fascist powers.

(In September, 1939, the second World War broke out. It destroyed every pro-appeasement argument, for appeasement was based on the assumption that war would be postponed for a long time. If appeasement merely postponed war for a short time, then England should have armed faster and sought more allies. The British and French did not do this because they really believed that appeasement meant "peace for our time." The outbreak of war demonstrated the complete bankruptcy of appeasement. Being an honest man, Sir Arnold recognized this, and early in the war, he, veteran of the 1914-1918 conflict, and far beyond the enlistment or conscription age, volunteered in the Royal Air Force and deliberately took the most dangerous post it could offer—rear gunner on a bombing plane. He did this, he told friends, to atone for his sins of appeasement. Hitler and Mussolini had disappointed him. In the most crucial period of his country's history, Wilson, unlike Churchill, had been wrong. His country would pay for his mistake. He himself wanted to pay too. He did. On June 4, 1940, Lieutenant Colonel Sir Arnold Wilson, brave man because he faced not only the enemy but also his own mistake, was posted as missing. He has not been heard of since.)

As the roast beef and red wine were being served, Inskip turned to me and asked about my experiences in air raids in Spain. The efficacy of various types of shelters interested him a good deal, but most of his questions were directed to the matter of civilian morale. I described some scenes in Madrid, Barcelona, and Valencia where temperamental, undernourished Spaniards displayed a combination of British-like stolidity, Moorish fatalism, and American race-track passion.

I asked Inskip whether government circles were very much interested in Spain. He replied that there was great interest and great difference of opinion. "Many people believe," he affirmed, "that the government are pro-Fascist on Spain. The truth is that five or six members of the cabinet are pro-Franco, five or six neutral, and twelve pro-Republican." He followed this with a long exposition, between bites and swallows, of British policy towards foreign civil wars. The policy had always been, he asserted, to help the government against the insurrectionists. He gave instances. "If we were to send arms to anybody," he made it plain, "it would be to the Spanish government." But the state of British armaments, he added, and the antagonisms in Europe were such that "we prefer to sell arms to neither side." I replied that none expected England to sell arms to the Loyalists, but they could cease deterring the French from doing so and cease using their influence in Washington to hinder the lifting of the arms embargo.

Inskip said the French had been sending large quantities of arms to Spain. Apologizing for differing with him, I said I thought this was not so. He answered that he had recently seen the figures. I told him that I knew arms were going through France, but France was not selling the arms. The arms were from Russia, Czechoslovakia, and Poland. "Maybe you're right," he conceded. "Maybe the figures I saw referred to supplies passing through France." It interested me that he should have had a detailed report on arms traffic in France.

Colonel Ropner introduced me as an American and "a man of the Left just as we are people of the Right." Jolly cries of "No, no" and laughter protested they were not of the "Right."

I spoke for half an hour, watching the faces around me. At one point I stated that France had done very little for the Loyalists. In recent weeks, however, the Spanish government, I said, had succeeded in buying a few guns in France. An M.P. opposite me, who had been doing a great deal of writhing while I spoke, called out, "Non-intervention." "It's just a little drop of the non-intervention which the Germans and Italians have been practicing." (If I had had more courage I would have added "with your help.") "The life of France would be threatened by a Franco victory, and the law of international affairs now is that a nation breaks treaties to safeguard its national interests." For this I was rewarded with several "Hear, hear" exclamations, one of them from Inskip who rocked on his chair. When I sat down, the audience applauded lustily, some pounding their palms on the table. They were being polite Britishers. Ropner asked for questions.

The gentleman who had intimated that only the Nazis and Fascists ought to "non-intervene" in Spain, posed the first one with a little speech. He spoke as follows, "You are an American journalist. Do you know your colleague Mr. Knoblauch? [I nodded.] Do you know his recent book on Spain? [I nodded again.] In it he says that sixty thousand citizens of Madrid were murdered by the Loyalists during the first weeks of the civil war. Do you accept that figure?"

I replied that I would rather deal with the whole problem of atrocities than answer yes or no.

"You invite us to sympathize with the Loyalists," the M.P. interjected with irritation. "I want to know what sort of people the Loyalists are. I therefore ask you about the sixty thousand murders and you refuse a reply."

Inskip exclaimed, "Oh, oh," and several guests cried, "Let the gentleman answer as he sees fit."

I arose and said, "There have been many atrocities on both sides." A chorus of "Hear, hear" interrupted me. "I cannot give you a reply about the alleged sixty thousand. No layman knows what sixty thousand of anything is. If I told you that sixty thousand people in London were doing this or that, or sixty thousand automobiles were circulating on Piccadilly you would not know whether I was telling the truth, unless a government statistician or official toll-taker assembled the data. Especially during the chaos that followed the advent of the civil war, nobody was in a position to have any reliable figures in Madrid. Only the Loyalist authorities could have had statistics on killings and they would not publish them. They did not even have them. The sixty thousand, therefore, is merely the private guess of partisans and I am not disposed to accept its historical accuracy." More "hear, hears" told me that I had made my point. Inskip contributed a loud grumble of assent.

"Civil war breaks out in a country when the government is weak. The civil war further weakens the government. Moreover, civil war is, by definition, a clash between two bitterly opposed sections of the population. The fighting of the civil war exacerbates that bitterness. In America, too, we had plenty of cruelty during the civil war. The Spanish conflict is no friendly picnic. Hosts of marked Loyalists were caught by the civil war in Franco territory, and vice versa.

"You have heard of the Fifth Column. As General Mola, Franco's able strategist, advanced on Madrid in October, 1936, he could not suppress his temperament, and with true Spanish expansiveness, announced that his forces were converging upon the city in four marching columns. But a 'Fifth Column' inside Madrid, he added, would greet them as they approached and take the city from within. The Loyalists knew this without Mola. During the early months of the civil war, after the army and the police had deserted the government, individual Loyalists took the law into their own hands and dealt roughly with these fifth columnists.

"When I first arrived in Madrid in September, 1936, an atmosphere of uncertainty and fear pervaded the city. Nightly, murders took place. The city was blacked-out and violent elements made hay in the dark. But gradually, the government took hold of the situation. All the atrocities committed in Loyalist territory antedate May, 1937. Since that date there have been no atrocities in Republican Spain." For this I was again rewarded—"Hear, hear"—from a surprisingly large number of those present.

I had not yet exhausted the subject of atrocities. "The atrocities in Loyalist Spain," I contended, "were the concomitant of transitory weakness. But Franco's atrocities are not an accident. They are a policy. Franco rules against the wish of the majority." Several heads moved in dissent. I addressed them, "It would be instructive if you superimposed a map of divided Spain today on the electoral map of February 16, 1936. You would find that a large part of the zone now held by Franco voted for the Popular Front, that is, for the government against which the generals rebelled. I urge you to consult that map. Why is it that Franco has not won the war after almost two years of effort? He had the army from the very beginning. Hitler and Mussolini have given him much more help than the Loyalists have received from Russia. The answer is that Franco has too few soldiers, and he has too few soldiers because the population is not with him. That is why I believe there is no peace in Franco. If he wins his regime will rest on bayonets and force just as it does today. He keeps his people subjugated by constant terror. But you would be surprised at the freedom the Loyalist government grants its citizens. Some would say, indeed, that there is too much democracy.

"One final word on atrocities," I begged. "Atrocities may be disputed pro and con. But there can be no argument about the continued bombings of civilians in Barcelona or of the repeated shellings of civilians in Madrid. Those are among history's worst atrocities. The Loyalists cannot defend themselves because they lack the weapons."

I sat down.

The M.P.'s began to compete with one another for the chance to put questions. "Isn't it true," I was asked, "that former Prime Minister Lerroux of Spain has denounced the 1936 elections as corrupt?"

I replied, "Mr. Lerroux is certainly an authority on election corruption because he has staged so many corrupt elections himself. But on February 16, 1936, Portela Valladares was Prime Minister, and he opposed the Popular Front, so that if there was any fraud it was at the expense of the parties now in the Loyalist coalition."

I made two *faux pas* during this period of questions. At American lectures I stand up when a questioner stands up. I did the same at the dinner in the House of Commons. But in the British Parliament no two persons may be standing at the same time, and when one rises the other sits down. Once when an M.P. stood up I stood up, and he immediately sat down. Colonel Ropner told me to sit down till the questioner resumed his seat. My second mistake was to refer to those present as "gentlemen." They are all "honorable gentlemen" and some were "right honorable gentlemen." I realized it when I returned to my hotel room. And I also thought of all the clever remarks I should have made.

An M.P. said, "You have alluded to intervention on both sides. Why have the Bolsheviks helped the Republicans?"

I tried to be brief. "The Russians started helping the Loyalists late in October, 1936, when the Non-Intervention Agreement had been reduced to a complete farce by large-scale Italian and German aid for Franco. Nobody can adduce proof of Soviet intervention in Spain before October. Nor is it logical to suggest that a revolt initiated by Franco was Moscow-made. Russia's role in Spain is part of a larger conception of the world situation. There is, of course, a general ideological affinity. But the Bolsheviks are also sending arms to Chiang Kai-shek who has executed more Communists than any other non-Communist and who is far from Left. The Bolsheviks do not want a Soviet Spain. Their participation in the Spanish conflict is calculated to prevent yet another Fascist victory and another encouragement to aggressors which might result in a major war. If France is surrounded on three sides by hostile powers—Germany, Italy, and Spain—it would be easier for Germany to attack Russia. A Fascist Spain would partially immobilize the British fleet. . . . The only method of safeguarding peace is to bolster the resistance of the victims of aggression. That will weaken the striking power of the aggressors. It will teach them that further predatory adventures will be costly. China's stand hampers Japan's ability to strike elsewhere, and if the Loyalists could hold out for another year we would have less to fear from Germany and Italy."

I am quoting from a long entry in my diary about this dinner. "This is no time to talk peace or yearn for peace," it goes on. "The only way to guarantee peace is to stop the countries that have made wars and are likely to make more wars." I got a great deal of assent on that. "The Loyalists are taking arms where they can get them. If you and the French sold arms to them the political situation in Spain would be affected thereby."

"The danger of Communism exists everywhere," an M.P. announced. "You surely cannot expect us to be sympathetic to an attempt to implant it in another country."

"The Spanish Communists," I replied, "are more conservative than some French socialists and than many British Laborites. They are a petty bourgeois party in some respects. They are defending private property against those who wish to confiscate or collectivize it. The Spanish Communist leader Hernandez has tried to construct a theory against agrarian collectivization. But that is really not the point. The British government and the British capitalists must decide whether Communism threatens them more than Fascism. It is Hitler's clever game to make you believe it does. The Soviet Union and Bolshevism have not been and are not a threat to the British Empire or to British capitalism. The contrary is the case. Czarist Russia was more of a menace to India than is Red Russia. I do not see where or how the regime in Russia has harmed or weakened the British social system. The Soviet government could be your ally. Even if Spain went Soviet—which is almost precluded—it would be better for England than a Franco-Fascist Spain under Hitler's and Mussolini's thumbs."

Next question explained much British indifference toward the Spanish struggle which translated itself into a pro-Franco policy. "You gave it as your considered opinion that Italy and Germany will not retire from Spain after the war. But is it not likely that the nations which have intervened in the struggle will arouse the resentment of the Spaniards who will ultimately expel them, whereas we, whose hands are clean and have remained aloof, will reap the benefit of our neutrality? Despite attempts to subjugate it, Spain has remained independent for centuries. The Spaniards resist yokes. Moreover, Franco would need money for reconstruction and he would have to come to London for it."

I replied that the mass of Spaniards were almost as anti-French and anti-British as they were anti-Fascist; they held England and France responsible for the slaughter of poorly armed Republicans. Besides, Mussolini and Hitler were in Spain to get something. Why should they leave because the British and French wished it? As to money, "I have not yet seen Mussolini in the City. You thought he would come after the Abyssinian war. Faith in its financial power is one of the causes of England's bad diplomacy." Eyebrows lifted.

After several further questions, Chairman Colonel Ropner adjourned the proceedings by saying, "Before the dinner, someone told me that Mr. Fischer was both intelligent and brave. I am sure you will agree with me that he is."

My neighbor on the right, Sir Arnold Wilson, Franco supporter No. 1, rose and moved a vote of thanks to me.

Though I had told others that the Loyalists would hold out, in my heart I was worried and I therefore went down again to Barcelona. I got a room in the sixth floor of the Majestic Hotel. The elevator did not work because of electricity shortage. In the evening, the lights went out—sometimes for a few minutes, sometimes for hours. The trolleys began to look like Moscow street cars, tightly packed inside, with men and women hanging on in front, in the back, on the sides and on the roof. The food situation was no better and no worse, but distribution was better, and the government had started importing more food.

Everybody asked about the possibility of getting airplanes and other arms from America, Russia, France. "The answer," I wrote, "will determine the fate of Spain for a generation. It will also determine the next phase of European history."

The rebels, with the help of Italian aviation and highly motorized infantry, had broken through to the sea. The Loyalists therefore could not go by land from Barcelona to the Valencia and Madrid regions. But it was characteristic of Republican resilience and vigor that they said, "It is better so. Each half of Loyalist Spain will work harder and fight harder because it must depend on its own resources." I found Negrin more optimistic than a month earlier. Negrin, del Vayo, and other political leaders, and many military leaders flew regularly over rebel lines from one section to the other. Once a cabinet meeting was held in Madrid. That electrified the besieged city. To carry mail from Catalonia to Valencia, the Republic fitted out a special submarine and printed an appropriate postage stamp. Despite the Fascist blockade, a regular passenger and freight service was established between Barcelona and Valencia.

Throughout my stay in Barcelona, I visited the Foreign Office every day, and every day I saw Ivor Montagu sitting in del Vayo's antechamber still waiting for permission from the War Department to take moving pictures at the front. Frequently I found Ivor reading Pushkin's poems in English translation. Once he said to me, "You know, it seems to me that the Loyalist government ought to enunciate its war aims, a sort of Fourteen Points program like Woodrow Wilson's."

"Wonderful idea," I said, "why has it never occurred to anybody?"

I passed the idea on to del Vayo. "*Stupendo*," he exclaimed. He talked to Negrin. Negrin said, "Fine, write them." Vayo drafted ten points and showed them to Negrin. Negrin said, "We must have thirteen to show that we are not superstitious," and he added three himself. The Thirteen Points were published on May 1, 1938, and became the cardinal principles of the Republic. Negrin frequently referred to them in speeches. They were communicated officially to foreign governments, and pro-Loyalist propaganda abroad often took them as its text. The war and peace aims were: Absolute independence for Spain. Expulsion of foreign military forces. "Pure democracy" on the basis of universal suffrage. No reprisals after the war on individuals who took part in it. Respect for regional liberties of Spanish provinces, a guarantee of civil rights. "Liberty of conscience and the free exercise of religious belief and practice." Encouragement of "the development of small properties" by private capitalists but no big trusts that can control the government. An agrarian reform to "abolish the former aristocratic and semi-feudal system of land ownership." Guaranteed rights of workingmen. "The cultural, physical and moral improvement of the race." An unpolitical army. Renunciation of war. Co-operation with the League of Nations. Finally, a "complete amnesty" for enemies on the Franco side.

Loyalist Spain was civilized.

29. Farewell to Moscow

TIME to see Moscow again. It was destined to be my last trip to the Soviet Union.

I flew to Prague on Saturday, May 21. That day I called on an old friend, Soviet Ambassador Alexandrovsky who had been at his post for several years. He told me that the Czechs had mobilized their entire army during the night of Friday to Saturday. "Between ourselves," he said, "they have summoned to the colors not only the classes mentioned in the official communiqué, but all their reserves." The government expected a German invasion, and this was its answer. Czechoslovakia would fight. Alexandrovsky stated that he had been consulted, that he had consulted Moscow, and that Russia had advised Czechoslovakia to order a general mobilization. Russia promised assistance.

I visited Czech press officials. They were calm and determined. They had done their duty to meet the menace. Now it was up to Hitler.

Sunday afternoon, I passed down Wencel Street, the main thoroughfare of Prague, and saw Camille Hoffmann sitting on the terrace of a café. I sat down to have a coffee with him. Hoffmann was the Czech press attaché in Berlin, a Socialist and a Jew. He had come to the capital to see his superiors.

His first question was about Barcelona. "It must be tense in Spain," he suggested. That struck me as funny. I said, "People in America are probably listening to broadcasts about the explosive atmosphere here—soldiers at their posts, the Czech Maginot line manned, anti-aircraft batteries stripped for action. But we sip coffee on the sunny terrace and look at those rejoicing couples on the pavement."

We watched the well-dressed Sunday crowds stroll up one side of the pavement and down the other. Peasants in folk costume were selling flowers. They looked happy. As Europe went, they were prosperous, and they certainly ate and dressed well. I suppose that annoyed Hitler.

It was a weekend of crisis and quiet. Those strollers knew that

493

Nazi bombers might darken the sky at any moment. They were calm. Their slogan that day was "Pleasure as usual." Self-defense was axiomatic. Who could have thought that this Czechoslovakia would surrender its prosperity and liberty without a blow! Left to themselves, they would have behaved in September as they did in May. But in September, they submitted to the stupid mercies of Chamberlain, Daladier, and Lord Runciman.

Hitler suffered a rebuff. He thought Prague would be another Vienna. But the Czechs had decided to stand their ground. Hitler therefore recoiled. Another Nyon. The President Beneš of treaties talked this time through soldiers and generals. Hitler, subsequently, denied his evil intentions in May. Of course. Admission of defeat would have clouded his aura of invincibility. But the Czechs had exact reports of Reichswehr concentrations on their frontiers. They would not have mobilized for nothing.

This Prague episode was encouraging.

I went on to Warsaw where I saw American Embassy people and some Poles and then made that long boring journey across the flat face of Poland and Russia to Moscow. In that stretch I knew every railway station, every waiter in the railway station restaurants, and a great many of the porters. I was an old customer.

Markoosha and the boys met me on my arrival in Moscow, and straightway Markoosha started pouring dark news into my ear. "How is So-and-So?" I asked. Disappeared. "And X?" He had been shot. His wife? In exile.

No Russian friends came to see me. They were afraid to see a foreigner. And they had broken off relations with Markoosha because she was the wife of a foreigner and corresponded with "abroad." A Soviet woman was in Markoosha's study once when the phone bell rang. I was calling from Paris. The woman picked up her bag and rushed out. To be in a room where a conversation with a foreign country was proceeding! The idea frightened her.

On the fourth day of my stay I received my first Soviet visitor, Mikhail Koltzov. He had to know about Spain. He wanted to kiss me but I hate this European custom and he embraced me instead. He was still "all right." That is why he dared to come. (He was purged the same year. His articles and books are no longer published and most of his friends think he has been shot. Next to Radek he was probably the most influential Soviet journalist. Koltzov, incidentally, is the "Karkov" of Ernest Hemingway's *For Whom the*

Bell Tolls. Koltzov was very emotional about Spain. But when talking to strangers he wrapped himself in a smoke-screen which consisted of equal parts of brittle *Pravda*—editorial prose and literary spoofing. That made him seem pompous and cynical.)

Markoosha told me how Russians now gauged the intensity of the purge. When the Kirov was assassinated in 1934, many hundreds of well-to-do Muscovites took special trips to Leningrad to buy furniture, paintings, carpets, hangings, and other properties, which people sent into exile after the murder had to sell quickly at low prices. The purge in Leningrad almost solved that city's housing problem. Now the pawnshops and commission shops in Moscow were full of pre-Revolutionary interior decorations, fur coats, and similar effects which the Moscow victims of the purge were getting rid of in a hurry. Apartments vacated by executed, imprisoned, or banished persons were usually given to GPU officials. If the head of a family disappeared his family was rarely permitted to retain its home.

Litvinov seemed to be empty inside when I interviewed him in the Foreign Commissariat. It was not surprising. The ground had been taken from under his feet. His appointees and assistants were being removed and imprisoned. Yurenev, Ambassador to Japan, Davtyan, Ambassador to Poland, and Karsky, Minister to Lithuania were arrested in November, 1937. A little while later, Asmus, Minister to Finland, disappeared. Brodovsky, Minister to Latvia, was recalled in the same period and reported shot. He was an old friend of mine. Barmine, Soviet Chargé d'Affaires in Greece, received orders to return home in December, 1937. He refused and lost his citizenship. Boris Skvirsky, loyal servant of the Soviet government in Washington, later appointed Minister to Afghanistan, left that post by request late in 1937. Bogomolov, Ambassador to China, was dismissed. Minister to Denmark Tikhmenev was dismissed in December, 1937, Minister to Hungary Bekzadian was dismissed the same month. Minister to Norway Yakubovitch was dismissed simultaneously and charged with Fascist conspiracy. In January, 1938, Ostrovsky was withdrawn from the Soviet Legation in Rumania. Every one of these men has vanished. On April 5, 1938, Feodor Raskolnikov, Soviet Minister to Bulgaria, ousted from his position, refused to obey orders and forfeited his Soviet citizenship. Raskolnikov was a young and fiery revolutionist. An officer in the Czarist fleet, he brought one of the Czar's cruisers over to the Bolsheviks in November, 1917.

The British captured him. Then they exchanged him for eight British officers. He took command of the Soviet flotilla in the Caspian and fought with great daring in Persian waters. Later he became a prominent Soviet author. This flaming Bolshevik fighter broke with his country. He died in mysterious circumstances in a hospital in Nice a few months later.

Leo Karakhan, Ambassador to Turkey, was shot in December, 1937. N. Krestinsky, Litvinov's assistant commissar, had been sentenced to be shot. Litvinov's private secretary, Gershelman, had been arrested. Several of his secretaries and translators had been arrested in his own office. Most of the heads of departments in the Foreign Commissariat had been arrested.

With the exceptions of Maisky in London, Suritz in Paris, and Boris Stein in Rome—Stein was removed later—all Litvinov's appointees as heads of Soviet foreign missions had been replaced, and replaced not by foreign office men but usually by GPU agents. The Soviet diplomatic service is now dominated by the secret police. A few appointments have also gone to the army. Litvinov had successfully fought the influence of the GPU in his commissariat for many years and he even resented the presence of GPU agents in minor positions in Soviet foreign missions. In this latter respect he failed, but he nevertheless kept Soviet diplomacy firmly in hand. Now it had been taken from him.

Small wonder Litvinov seemed empty inside. Always when a high Soviet official was purged, most of the personnel of his department was purged after him. Guilty or not, they were punished because he was, for no man in prominent position is merely an individual. He creates his own system and has a loyal following. To destroy the individual the Kremlin felt it had to destroy his system. In the case of Yagoda, chief of the GPU, this meant the dismissal or arrest and execution of many, many tens of thousands. In the case of Litvinov it meant hundreds. But in Litvinov's instance, the process was reversed. Litvinov's system was smashed while he remained. He remained because both at home and abroad he had been identified with a popular Soviet foreign policy. At every lecture I delivered in the United States during 1939 and 1940, I was asked what had happened to Litvinov. Because of his popularity he was retained in office until Stalin was ready to sign with Hitler and scuttle Litvinov's foreign policy. By that time Litvinov had become merely one person. He had been shorn of influence and power. It was there-

·ore unnecessary to shoot him and he was permitted to engage "in iterary activity."

I asked Litvinov whether he was not pleased with the firm stand :aken by Czechoslovakia. He said yes, but he distrusted England ind France. "Hitler is not through yet," he declared. "The British ind French want an agreement with Germany."

"And your own country," he added bitterly. "Your President delivers eloquent orations against the aggressors but America continues to ship munitions, oil and scrap iron to Japan."

He also felt sour about Spain. "Always defeats, always retreats," he said. We always spoke English.

I said, "The reason for all the defeats and retreats is Franco's air superiority. If you gave the Loyalists five hundred airplanes they could win the war."

"Five hundred airplanes. Five hundred airplanes would do us more good in China."

I argued on that point. Finally he said, "I will talk with my higher-ups. I have no airplanes. You know what I am. I merely hand on diplomatic documents."

Impassioned enemies of the Soviet government have charged that it withheld airplanes and other munitions from the Loyalists in order to bring about changes in Spanish domestic politics which would enhance the strength of the Spanish Communists. There is no proof of this, and I believe the accusation is incorrect.

Many circumstances affected Soviet munitions sales to Spain. The war in China commenced in July, 1937. A quick Japanese victory would have been detrimental to Soviet Russia's defense interests. Moscow sent hundreds of planes and pilots to serve Chiang Kai-shek. That left fewer machines for export to Spain. Soviet industrial capacity is limited.

The Czechoslovak crisis started in May, 1938, and continued through Munich to October, 1938. During that period, a European war might have involved Russia. Stalin therefore reduced his munitions deliveries to Spain. He also had to send planes to Czechoslovakia.

A serious obstacle to Russia's arms trade with Spain was the problem of transit. Spain's supplies depended on passage through France, Loyalist Spain's only land neighbor. And too often the French closed that one frontier. The Soviet government repeatedly quarreled with France over this question during 1937 and 1938. Ships heavily laden with Russian munitions stood in French channel ports, usually Dunkirk, for weeks because Georges Bonnet refused to let them be unloaded. Sometimes, the French customs authorities, acting on instructions from Paris, would allow the boats to be unloaded and the goods to move south, but then the French customs authorities on the Spanish border, also on instructions from Paris, refused to permit them to go into Spain. During the great Fascist offensive in December, 1938, which ended in the fall of Catalonia, millions of dollars' worth of Soviet arms were lying around in southern France waiting for clearance papers for Spain. With these arms Catalonia might have been saved. And France might have been saved.

At no time during the Spanish War were there more than seven hundred Soviet Russians in Spain. Normally there were less. But they were key-men. I met many of them in staff headquarters, at the front, and in the Palace and Gaylord Hotels in Madrid, the Metropole in Valencia, and the Majestic in Barcelona. They never talked revolution or used big words. They did their work. They were men of iron. Eighteen hours a day on duty, weeks at the front, bombing twice a day—they did not stop as long as there was something to do. Then they bathed and relaxed; they did not talk revolution. They had done revolution. . . . Some were purged when they returned to Russia.

The purge in 1938 ranged free and far, and Litvinov's Foreign Office was not the only sufferer. The "Stalin" Constitution of 1936 had been drafted by a Commission of twenty-seven, Stalin and twenty-six others. Of the twenty-six, fifteen had been purged by 1938. They were all leaders of the Bolshevik regime.

Liubchenko, the Prime Minister of the Ukraine, "committed suicide" on September 2, 1937. I put it in quotation marks because he was mentioned in one of the Moscow trials as an active traitor which probably meant that he was shot. The same month ten important officials of the Leningrad electric power plant were reported executed. Also seven Bolsheviks in the city of Ordjonekidze for belonging to a "rightist wrecking society" under the leadership of Hermann Mgaloblishvili. That meant that Mgaloblishvili, President of Georgia, whom I had interviewed every year for years when I visited Tiflis, was no more. Twenty "wreckers" executed in the Far East. Four executed and six imprisoned in Ossetia for damaging a grain elevator. Four executed in Leningrad for poisoning sailors of the Baltic fleet with bad meat. Nineteen railway workers shot at

Vladivostok as "Trotzkyist terrorists." About a hundred more exe-cutions were recorded in September, 1937. This month was typical.

In the period between August, 1937, and May, 1938, the Presi-dent and Vice-President of the Adjaristan Republic were executed. Bubnov, Commissar of Education disappeared—the eighth of seven-teen members of the Russian cabinet to go. Rukhimovitch, Com-missar of Defense Industries, was removed and not reappointed—i.e., purged. The head of the GPU at Sukhum was executed with many of his assistants. Grad, who succeeded Cherviakov as Presi-dent of White Russia, removed. Yakovlev, Commissar of Agricul-ture, arrested. Arens, former Consul in New York, purged. Leo Karakhan, former assistant Commissar of Foreign Affairs, executed. Yenukidze, a big blond Georgian, secretary of the Soviet govern-ment, executed. General Alksnis executed. Zuckerman, chief of the Central Asian department of the Foreign Office, executed. Shebol-dayev, chief of the Communist party of the North Caucasus, exe-cuted. Lubimov, Commissar of Light Industry, and his aides dis-missed. Ostrovsky, keeper of the Moscow Zoo, and the animal feeders dismissed "for cruelty." Professor Vavilov, member of the Academy of Science, agriculturist with an international reputation, accused of "wrecking." Krylenko, famed prosecutor in former Mos-cow trials, removed and since unheard of. Admiral Orlov executed. Admiral Sivikov executed. General Yegorov, Marshal of the Red Army, executed. Commissar of Agriculture Eiche discharged. Gen-eral Lushkov of the Far Eastern Red Army flees to Japan; and his subordinates in Russia reported executed. Petrovsky, President of the Ukraine, purged. Natalie Satz, charming and gifted director of the Moscow Children's Theatre, exiled. Dynamic Betty Glan, direc-tor of the Moscow Park of Culture, purged. These are only the prominent ones. The executions and arrests of smaller people add up to thousands.

And between March 2 and 13, 1938, the greatest of all Moscow trials had taken place. Nicholas Bukharin, former member of the supreme Bolshevik leadership, editor of *Pravda* and *Izvestia*, dearly beloved by Lenin, leading Bolshevik philosopher; Alexis Rykov, Prime Minister of the Soviet Union; Yagoda, head of the GPU for many years; Krestinsky, Ambassador to Berlin and assistant Foreign Commissar; Christian G. Rakovsky, Ambassador to London and Paris; Rosengoltz, Commissar of Foreign Trade; Chernov, Com-missar of Agriculture; Grinko, Commissar of Finance; and thirteen others—all were found guilty of all the crimes in the Soviet calen dar. Eighteen were sentenced to be shot. Rakovsky, one of the three exceptions, got a twenty-year prison sentence, Bessonov, former Counselor in the Berlin Embassy, fifteen years, and Professor Plet nev, Russia's best-known heart specialist, a man over seventy, twen ty-five years. (The maximum prison sentence had been raised from ten to twenty-five years.)

Markoosha did not want to live in Soviet Russia any longer. She had previously connected her life and future with it. She was a Soviet citizen. Marriage with me in November, 1922, did not make her an American citizen. We expected that our two boys, George and Victor, would make Russia their permanent home, and Markoosha did not want them to be foreigners in it. She therefore thought it unnecessary to register them at the United States con sulate.

But in May, 1938, I told her definitely that no matter what hap pened in Spain, and even if the struggle there were to end soon in defeat, I had no intention of coming back to the Soviet Union. I would not return to Moscow and write about the sort of develop ments that now darkened the horizon. I could not write about them favorably because I disapproved of them and if I stayed and wrote about them unfavorably, my life would lose many of its joys. I refused to report a perpetual funeral.

Markoosha accordingly decided that she wanted to leave for good. She too had changed her mind about Russia. In fact, she, with her deep intuition and keen sensitivity, had turned against Stalin's policy before I had. For her, the Revolution meant first of all the human side, and it was being trampled in the gutter. Women, culture, lit erature, people's feelings, personal dignity were offended every day, and these, as she used to tell me when I was carried away by the success of the Five Year Plans, were more important to her than increased steel and coal production or even the construction of new cities.

At Markoosha's request I accordingly wrote a letter to Yezhov, head of the GPU or Commissariat of Home Affairs, as it had been rechristened, telling him that my work would henceforth keep me abroad and that I therefore wanted my family to emigrate. Markoosha needed a Soviet foreign passport. The boys, as my children, were American citizens, but the Soviet government might dispute this and try to keep them in Russia. I deposited my letter in Yezhov's personal mail box outside the GPU headquarters. I never received a reply or an acknowledgment. I was resolved, however, to pursue the matter much further. I expected many difficulties.

Markoosha and I naturally spent much time discussing the sensational trials and concessions. I have thought about them in all the years since. They were a political tragedy but for me they were also a personal tragedy. Of the twenty-one defendants in the Bukharin-Rykov trial, I knew six fairly well. My friends Radek and Sokolnikov had figured in a former trial. Many good acquaintances of mine had been mentioned in the trials and executed as a result.

What was the inner meaning of these horrible trials? Why did they confess?

30. *The Moscow Trials and Confessions*

I NEVER approved of the big Stalin purge. I did not write a word about the Moscow trials of leading Bolsheviks. I did not condone the trials, nor did I undertake to explain them. Neither did I condemn them. I suspended judgment because I was not sure in my own mind what they were.

I read the records of the trials when they occurred. I read the opinions of those who regarded them as frame-ups and the statements of those who accepted them as truth. Now I have reread the stenographic records of the Moscow court proceedings. I have again studied the literature on both sides. I have a perspective now on the effects of the trials and the purges which I could not have had at the time.

Nobody has satisfactorily explained the confessions. If the confessions are true that is explanation enough. But why did they confess if it was all a tissue of lies? None of the Trotzkyist propaganda or any other material on the subject provides a conclusive, logical solution of the confession puzzle. One of America's greatest jurists and legal minds has said to me that the Moscow trials were "the greatest judicial mystery of all time."

Karl Kindermann, Theodore Volscht, both German, and Max von Ditmar, an Esthonian of German origin, were arrested in November, 1924, entering Soviet Russia. They claimed to be Wandervoegel, young German hitch-hikers seeing the world. But the GPU arrested them and charged them with plotting to assassinate Trotzky and Stalin. Their trial took place in Moscow in June, 1925. It received tremendous publicity. The press in Germany fumed, and branded the charges as shamefully flimsy. Von Ditmar turned state's witness. Germans said he was a GPU agent. All three defendants were sentenced to death.

Later they were exchanged for a Soviet citizen named Skobelevsky. Skobelevsky was a high GPU official who had gone to Germany in 1923 to participate in the revolution. The Germans put him in prison. Stalin, with a primitive sense of loyalty to one who got into trouble for him, wanted Skobelevsky freed. The three German students, therefore, were arrested and condemned so that Russia could exchange them for Skobelevsky. I was told all this by a Soviet official who followed the whole matter at close range from the inside as part of his job.

On June 6, 1928, I was sitting in the gigantic resplendent Hall of the Columns in Moscow, watching the Shakhti trial. Several score Soviet engineers, charged with sabotage and espionage, were on trial for their lives. I did not know how much to believe. I believed part; I wondered about the remainder. One of the defendants was an old Jew, past seventy, named Rabinovitch. He fought for his life. Or, rather, he fought for his name. He refused to die as a spy of the Polish intelligence service. Rabinovitch, defiant and Talmudistic, engaged in a running duel with Procurator Krylenko, diminutive, sneering, bald-headed Slav in hunting costume. Rabinovitch challenged Krylenko at every step. Defendants at Soviet trials are permitted to do that, and to make speeches and call witnesses and cross-examine them. The score was certainly in Rabinovitch's favor, and some Soviet journalists took a secret delight in the great Krylenko's discomfiture.

One afternoon, a GPU soldier, with bayoneted rifle by his side, marched in a witness named Mukhin. To this day I have remembered his name and his sallow pasty face. He had been in prison for months on a charge unrelated to the Shakhti trial. Sworn in, he testified that he, Mukhin, had handed money to Rabinovitch as a bribe and for distribution to other saboteurs.

Rabinovitch rose, walked to within two feet of Mukhin, looked him in the eye, and said, "Tell me, please, about whom are you speaking, me or somebody else?"

"I am talking about you."

"Why do you lie, eh?" exclaimed Rabinovitch. "Who told you to lie? You know you gave me no money."

Mukhin, speaking in a monotone like an automaton, stuck to his story. The GPU soldier marched him out. Krylenko looked crestfallen. It had not worked. It was obvious to everybody that Mukhin had repeated what was rehearsed in the GPU cellar. I said this to a Soviet Foreign Office chief who was present. He kept quiet. That is the way a Bolshevik assents on a ticklish subject.

A trial of Soviet citizens took place in March, 1931, in the same Moscow Hall of Columns. They were charged with Menshevism, or anti-Bolshevism. They confessed. They disclosed, indeed, that Rafael Abramovitch, exiled Russian Menshevik leader, had come into the Soviet Union illegally and stayed with them from the middle of July to the middle of August, 1928. They described in detail how they met him and where, what he said to them, and what they said to him.

Abramovitch, living in permanent exile outside of Russia, gave a detailed interview to the foreign press in which he stated that he could not have been in Russia during that period. He was on vacation in the little German town of Plau, Mecklenburg. The police record, the registry of the boarding house, and the affidavits of friends who had seen him there every day confirmed this. He had participated in the International Socialist Congress at Brussels, spoke almost every day at the public sessions, and was often photographed and seen with the delegates. The minutes of the Congress, the affidavits of delegates, and his passport confirmed that. Abramovitch added that neither had he gone into the Soviet Union at any other time.

In 1929, when I visited Christian G. Rakovsky in exile at Saratov, he could have recanted his Trotskyism and returned to Moscow to work as a rehabilitated Bolshevik. But he suffered Siberian exile for five more years. At his trial in April, 1938, he confessed that he had been a British spy since 1924. If he was a spy why did he not, in 1929, seize the chance to resume work in Moscow?

I approached the Moscow trials with considerable skepticism. But it is one thing to have doubts and another to be certain that all the trials were frame-ups based on false evidence and forced admissions of guilt.

First of all, why the trials?

Since there is no abstract justice under Bolshevism—no absolute sins and, unfortunately, no absolute virtues—it is necessary to ask what the Soviet regime tried to achieve by the trials. Many Bolsheviks have been executed without trials, and the defendants in the trials could have been executed without trials. Why the trials?

The chief defendant in all the three Moscow trials of leading Bolsheviks was Leon Trotzky. Men sat in the dock and made statements and received sentences. Yet Trotzky was the person the court wished to condemn. The edifice of guilt which the state prosecutor André Vishinsky sought to construct was an enormous leaning skyscraper. Its numerous floors and underground cellars were often connected with one another, but sometimes not. Threads from them all ended in the hand of Trotzky. It was a case of remote control.

The scheme, as it emerged from the confessions, was this: The Trotzkyists in the Soviet Union would hasten a foreign attack on Russia. The attackers—Germany and Japan—would help Trotzky and his friends to rule defeated Russia. Trotzky would give the Ukraine to Germany and the Far Eastern provinces and Amur district to Japan. The Germans would also get economic concessions in Russia.

Radek, testifying under the eyes of sixteen co-defendants, the judges of the Supreme Court, the prosecuting attorney Vishinsky, and his assistants, scores of Soviet and foreign journalists, a group of foreign diplomats, and hundreds of Soviet spectators, declared that he had frequently been in touch with Trotzky and received several letters from Trotzky by secret emissaries. "In 1935," said Radek, "the question was raised of going back to capitalism." Vishinsky: "To what limits?"

Radek: "What Trotzy proposed was without limits. To such limits as the enemy might require." The enemy was Germany and Japan. Trotzky, according to Radek, advised a complete sell-out to Russia's foes and to world Fascism.

How was this to be achieved? Trotzky wanted the Soviet leaders assassinated, the accused in the three trials deposed. Kill Stalin, Voroshilov, Molotov, Kirov, Kaganovitch, Zhdanov, and the others. Commit acts of sabotage. Wreck trains and factories. Blow up bridges. Poison soldiers. Give military information to Berlin and Tokio. Crush Bolshevism. Subjugate Russia. Then Trotzky and his accomplices, as puppets of Hitler and the Mikado, would govern this capitalistic, truncated, weakened Russia.

This was not just a paper scheme. Trotzky himself, it was alleged, had discussed the whole matter with Rudolf Hess, Hitler's first assistant. (Molotov saw Hess in Berlin in November, 1940.) They had worked out a plan. Trotzky also had contacts with the Japanese government. In April, 1934, Gregory Sokolnikov—so he reported at the trial—received the Japanese Ambassador in the Commissariat of Foreign Affairs. Sokolnikov was then Vice-Commissar of Foreign Affairs. At the end of the interview the interpreters went out, and the Ambassador asked Sokolnikov whether he knew that Trotzky had made certain proposals to his government. Sokolnikov replied, "Yes." The Ambassador, you see, was trying to find out whether

Trotzky was acting on his personal behalf or whether he had strong backing in Soviet Russia.

Think of the members of this anti-Bolshevik, pro-Nazi, pro-Japanese conspiracy! Rykov, Prime Minister of the whole country. Yagoda, head of the mighty GPU. Tukhachevsky and his eight leading generals. The Number Two man in Soviet industry. The President and Prime Minister of White Russia. The Prime Minister of the Ukraine. The Prime Minister of Uzbekistan. The Prime Minister of Tadjikistan. The Federal Commissar of Finance. The Federal Commissar of Agriculture. The Secretary of the Soviet government. The commander of the military guard of the Kremlin. Two assistant commissars of foreign affairs. Several Soviet ambassadors. Hundreds of factory managers. Each one of these had numerous subordinates. Yagoda could put the entire secret police of the nation at the disposal of the plotters. Tukhachevsky was the key-man in the Red Army.

Why did they fail?

Fritz David, a German Communist, defendant in the 1936 Zinoviev-Kamenev trial, admitted in the public hearings that Trotzky had chosen him for the "historic mission" of killing Stalin. David actually got to a Third International congress in Moscow attended by Stalin. He had a Browning revolver in his pocket. But he was too far away to get a good aim, he said.

All right. But Yagoda's men guarded every entrance and exit of the Kremlin and of Stalin's apartment. They were posted at frequent intervals along the road which leads from Moscow to Stalin's country home. They guarded the country home. Yagoda himself, Tukhachevsky himself, Piatakov, and many other accused had carried arms and were regularly in Stalin's intimate company. Why didn't they kill him? There is no answer. At the trials the question was not even asked. Why hire a poor German Communist for a job of assassination when you have the whole Kremlin guard and army chiefs and the secret police?

From Turkey, France, and Norway, Trotzky allegedly gave orders, and in Moscow, Leningrad, Siberia, and Turkestan they were executed by the highest officials of the Soviet government, by men who had signed his deportation order, who had condemned him in speeches and articles, who maligned and swore against him each day. The prosecution thus unwittingly paid a tribute to Trotzky's personality. But—Trotzky has branded as a lie every accusation leveled against him at the trials! He called all the trials gigantic frame-ups.

There was in Berlin a swarthy young man named Bukhartsev, correspondent of *Izvestia*, as fervent a Bolshevik as I have ever met. In addition to his work as correspondent, he spied on the Nazis and got young American ladies to help him. But at the trial, Bukhartsev testified that he had been a partner in this big pro-Nazi, anti-Bolshevik, Trotzkyist plot to restore capitalism in Russia. In December, 1935, Yuri Piatakov, Soviet Vice-Commissar of Heavy Industry, went to Berlin on official business, to buy equipment. Bukhartsev met him and took him to the Tiergarten, Berlin's central park, where they saw one of the Trotzky's undercover men. This man said that Trotzky wished to see Piatakov. He would make all the arrangements. So he got Piatakov a false German passport, chartered a private plane, and Piatakov flew non-stop to Oslo where he talked with Trotzky for two hours. Then he came back to Moscow and reported to Radek and Sokolnikov the details of the conversation. He gave the details to the court. Radek and Sokolnikov confirmed what Piatakov said. He had said it to them at the time.

But Trotzky denied that he ever met Piatakov in Oslo or anywhere else in 1935 or any other year of his exile. The director of the Oslo airport told newspapermen that no airplane from Berlin, in fact, no foreign airplane, landed on his field in December, 1935. The Norwegian family with whom Trotzky was living swore out affidavits to the effect that Trotzky never received a visit from any Russian and never went away from them to meet anybody.

Vladimir Romm, a Soviet correspondent in Geneva and Washington, testified in court that he met Trotzky in Paris by secret appointment. He named the place, the Bois de Boulogne. Date: end of July, 1933. Romm went with Trotzky's son, Leo Sedov, to the park and there they met Trotzky. Trotzky gave Romm instructions for Radek. He also gave Romm a letter for Radek. The letter was pasted in the cover of Novikov Priboi's novel *Tsusima*. Romm brought the letter to Radek in Moscow. Radek in the witness stand confirmed this testimony by Romm and described the contents of the letter.

But Trotzky swore that he never met Romm, never in his life, never even heard of him, and never wrote any letters to Radek from exile. Romm went all the way from Washington to Moscow on a GPU summons to testify at this trial and to incriminate himself. Since the day he appeared in court he has not been heard of again. He expected trouble before he left America and told his American friends so. They advised him not to go. He went because he could not disobey the GPU. It can compel obedience. It has murdered men abroad. I know that because I know of one case in all its gruesome, bloody particulars.

The GPU killed Ludwig. That was the only name by which I knew him. So when the French press announced in September, 1937, that a Czech named Hans Eberhardt has been killed under mysterious circumstances near Lausanne, I thought nothing more of it. Several months later, I learned that Eberhardt's real name was Ignace Reiss, and that he was the Ludwig whom I had known since 1931. I met him in Berlin through German Communists. He was introduced simply as "Ludwig." That was not unusual in such circles, and one asked no questions. Ludwig was a round, jovial Polish Jew with a most keen intelligence. I enjoyed discussing politics with him. He invited me to a café once, and took me to an expensive one. He also dressed well. His conversation, his interests, his manner made me think he worked for the GPU.

When Hitler arrived, Ludwig left Germany. Several times he visited us in Moscow. He was an interesting person and an idealist. In 1935, I met him in Paris. He had made Paris his headquarters. He never told me what he did and I never inquired, but in France he spoke less guardedly and I deduced that he was engaged in military espionage for the Soviet government with special emphasis on Hitler's war preparations. For months he would disappear, and then he telephoned me and we met in the café of the Hotel Lutetia where I lived or in a café on the Champs Elysées. I also met his wife, a brave intelligent woman. She knew the danger he courted every day. He traveled across Europe on false passports, stole across borders, used false names, and lived illegally in Paris. There was always the possibility that a foreign agent of the German Gestapo would shoot him or that the police of some country would arrest him.

During our Paris meetings in 1936, Ludwig spoke very critically of the Soviet regime. Until then he had been completely loyal and devoted. When I returned from America in June, 1937, he called me up and we had a sitting of several hours. The Zinoviev-Kamenev trial in August, 1936, had deeply upset him. On its heels came the Piatakov-Radek-Sokolnikov trial in January, 1937. Stalin was destroying the old revolutionists and, with them, the Revolution, Ludwig stormed. Stalin was using the trials to wipe out all potential rivals and everybody who had ever disagreed with him or agreed with Trotzky. Even Hitler did not commit such atrocities, he said. He regarded the Moscow trials as frameups and the confessions as fakes.

I warned him to be cautious. If he talked that way he could easily be reported. I suspected how perilous it was for an agent of the secret police to turn against his masters. Since he knew many secrets they would try to destroy him. I would have been even more perturbed about this fine person if I had known then, what I learned subsequently, that he was the chief of the Soviet military intelligence work abroad. When such a man goes anti-Stalin he signs his death warrant.

I pleaded with Ludwig to hold his tongue. I also said to him that there was still Spain and that Russia was aiding Spain. "Not sufficiently," he said.

"Still," I urged, "wait till I come back from Spain. Don't do anything rash until we have another talk." His mood made me think he might kick over the traces.

I never had any way of reaching him. I did not have his address or telephone number. But he always managed to know when I arrived in Paris. This time, on my return from Brunete and Madrid, he got in touch with me immediately. "Don't tell me about Spain. They have shot Tukhachevsky, Yakir, Kork, and the others. And Gamarnik committed suicide. Silly. I knew Gamarnik. He would never have committed suicide." All restraint was now gone. He was out-and-out anti-Stalin. He wondered whether Voroshilov would be next.

He talked about his comrades in Moscow. He had worked closely in the GPU with several Polish friends and he realized that whatever he did would react against them. He obviously contemplated some desperate deed, but I had no idea what it might be.

The rest I know from the officially announced findings of the Swiss police and from Victor Serge's book on Ignace Reiss. Ludwig had worked sixteen years for the GPU. On July 17, 1937, he wrote a letter to the Soviet government full of vituperation against Stalin and denouncing the purges. He was joining Trotzky, he said. He was returning the decoration he had received for distinguished work on behalf of the Revolution. The courage he had displayed in serving the GPU he now displayed in breaking with it. He wrote the letter and delivered it at the Soviet Embassy in Paris.

That evening he sat in his hotel room. The telephone rang. He answered. No one spoke. Five minutes later it rang again. He answered. Not a sound. This happened four times. The GPU employees in Paris who had opened Ludwig's letter had had a council of war that evening to decide on their course of action. One of them, a friend of Ludwig, left the meeting, walked down a boulevard, stopped in a pay station, called Ludwig and when Ludwig said "Hello" he hung up. He walked two blocks and telephoned again. Ludwig answered "Hello"; the friend slowly put down the receiver. Then he called again in another pay station, and again. He wanted to make Ludwig uneasy. But he did not dare to speak to him. How did he know whether Ludwig's phone had been tapped by the GPU? If his voice were heard he would be doomed, for he had just come from the meeting which determined the fate of Ludwig. Or perhaps the meeting was a trap. Perhaps the GPU was testing him. Perhaps Ludwig was a party to the trap. If he spoke to Ludwig over the telephone the GPU would know that he revealed its secret. Ludwig understood the meaning of these telephone signals. The next morning he took a train for Switzerland. He assumed he would be safer there.

In Lausanne, an old woman friend, Gertrude Schildbach, likewise a GPU agent, visited him. He had talked to her about the pain which the Moscow trials had caused him and she expressed sympathy and understanding. He wanted to talk to her now. He took her out to dinner. After dinner they walked down a country road. An automobile stopped and the men in it, and Gertrude Schildbach, pushed Ludwig into the car. There they opened up on him with submachine guns. He struggled, and under his fingernails the Swiss police found pieces of Miss Schildbach's hair. Then the murderers threw Ludwig's body into the road and abandoned the car.

I lived in Lutetia until after the second World War commenced. And every time I passed the café downstairs I thought of Ludwig's body with bullet holes in it lying in a Swiss road.

So Vladimir Romm knew he had to go to Moscow when the GPU in Washington told him to go. If he refused he would suffer the consequences. At the trial Romm described in detail his encounter with Trotzky in the Paris Bois. But Trotzky denied it. Trotzky denied any contact with Rudolf Hess, the Nazi leader. He denied any contact with Japan. Trotzky declared he was opposed to personal terror and assassination. Nor did he wish the defeat of the Soviet

Union in war. (He did not want to see Russia defeated in Finland.) And of course he was a Communist, anti-Fascist, and anti-capitalist, and indignantly disclaimed any wish to restore capitalism in the Soviet Union.

It was for the Soviet prosecutor to prove his charges. He submitted no proofs, no documents, no evidence—except the confessions of defendants and witnesses. All the trials were based on the statements which the accused made in the preliminary hearings in prison. The procedure in court consisted in getting each defendant to repeat publicly what he had already said in the secret investigation chambers, and in getting other defendants to corroborate these statements. Not one of the witnesses was a free man. Even witnesses like Romm and Bukhartsev had committed crimes against the Soviet state by being in touch with Trotzky.

Everything depends, therefore, on how one looks at the confessions. In ordinary jurisprudence, a confession in itself is not sufficient to convict. Nevertheless a confession is not necessarily untrue.

The men in the dock—not a single woman—had written numerous bright pages in the annals of Bolshevism. Forty years or less, they sacrificed and labored for the cause, many by the side of Lenin, many in the company of Stalin. But now they did not merely blacken their records with admission of treachery and counter-revolution. They assassinated their own characters. They spat on their whole lives and dragged their names through the vilest filth.

Take Rakovsky. An old revolutionist and recognized as such by the world and in Russia, he admitted at the trial that he betrayed the labor movement before 1917. Also, he was a landlord. "Well, of course, I was an exploiter," he exclaimed in the witness stand. He further testified that in 1924, while Soviet Ambassador in England, he signed up as a British spy. Scotland Yard recruited him in a restaurant. Two men just walked up to him and said he had to work for the British intelligence service and he agreed. That is how he described it in court. Then he went into exile as a Trotzkyist, first in Saratov, later in Barnaul. In 1934, he recanted. "This telegram [of recantation]," he said at the trial, "was insincere. I was lying. . . . It was my deliberate intention to hide from the Party and the government my association with the [British] intelligence service ever since 1924, and Trotzky's association with the [British] intelligence service since 1926." After this insincere recantation, the Soviet government sent him on a mission to Tokio. There the Japanese intelligence service recruited him. "I returned from Tokio," he seemed to boast, "with the credentials of a Japanese spy in my pocket."

But that was Rakovsky's complete career. Before the Revolution he was anti-labor and an exploiting capitalist; after the Revolution a spy who conspired against his government and the Revolution. Why did he damn himself forever in this wise?

Bukharin is testifying at the March, 1938, trial. In the dock he was no less witty and scintillating than at his desk or at a mass meeting. Bukharin denied complicity in the assassination of Kirov. He denied plotting to kill Lenin or Stalin. He denied being a foreign spy as the indictment alleged. But he admitted his participation in a revolt of rich peasants in the Kuban region. He did wish to overthrow the Soviet regime and turn it over to Germany and Japan. For all this "I am responsible," he exclaimed, "as one of the leaders and not merely as a cog." Heaven forbid that anyone give him too little discredit! "I do not want to minimize my guilt," he declared in court. "I want to aggravate it."

Prosecutor Vishinsky had a difficult time with Bukharin. He insisted that Bukharin discuss what he had done, not what he had not done.

BUKHARIN: "Yes, but every negation contains an affirmation, Citizen Procurator. Spinoza once said that in the sphere of determination . . ."

VISHINSKY: "Speak concretely. How were you preparing the seizure of power?"

Again, when Rykov confessed a certain crime, Vishinsky asked Bukharin for corroboration.

BUKHARIN: "If Rykov said it, I have no ground for not believing him."

VISHINSKY: "Can you answer me without philosophy?"

BUKHARIN: "This is not philosophy."

VISHINSKY: "Without philosophical twists and turns."

BUKHARIN: "I have testified that I had explanations on this question."

VISHINSKY: "Answer me No."

BUKHARIN: "I cannot say No, and I cannot deny that it did take place."

VISHINSKY: "So the answer is neither Yes nor No."

BUKHARIN: "Nothing of the kind. Because facts exist regardless of whether they are in anybody's mind. This is a problem of the reality of the outer world. I am no solipsist."

On another occasion Bukharin had admitted that he contemplated arresting Lenin for twenty-four hours in 1918; however, "as regards assassination, I know nothing whatever."

VISHINSKY: "But the atmosphere was . . ."

BUKHARIN, *interrupting:* "The atmosphere was the atmosphere."

Still another encounter between angry hunter and playful quarry:

VISHINSKY: "I am not asking you about conversations in general but about this conversation."

BUKHARIN: "In Hegel's *Logic* the word 'this' is considered to be the most difficult word. . . ."

VISHINSKY: "I ask the court to explain to the Accused Bukharin that he is here not in the capacity of a philosopher, but a criminal. . . ."

BUKHARIN: "A philosopher may be a criminal. . . ."

VISHINSKY: "Yes, that is to say, those who imagine themselves to be philosophers turn out to be spies. Philosophy is out of place here. I am asking you about that conversation of which Khodjayev just spoke. Do you confirm it or do you deny it?"

BUKHARIN: "I do not understand the word 'that' . . ."

At one time, both gentlemen began to lose their tempers. Said Bukharin to Vishinsky, "I beg your pardon. It is I who am speaking and not you." The Chief Justice called Bukharin to order. But a moment later, Bukharin again reprimanded Vishinsky. "There is nothing for you to gesticulate about," he yelled to the federal prosecutor. Vishinsky got his revenge when he said a moment later, "You are obviously a spy of an intelligence service. So stop pettifogging."

BUKHARIN: "I never considered myself a spy, nor do I now."

VISHINSKY: "It would be more correct if you did."

BUKHARIN: "That is your opinion, but my opinion is different."

VISHINSKY: "We shall see what the opinion of the court is."

The accused were, for the most part, men of big caliber and great intellect and they did not show the least sign of physical torture or of having been drugged or doped. They were keen and quick. They tripped up one another, made brilliant speeches, and displayed good memories. And always they insisted they were traitors and criminals.

Rykov said he worked for the Polish Intelligence Service while Prime Minister of the Soviet Union. Krestinsky said he had been a German spy since 1921, and that he was in Germany's pay while serving as Soviet Ambassador in Berlin. In return for this he received a quarter of a million marks per annum from General von Seeckt, the commander-in-chief of the Reichswehr. "I used to take it to Moscow myself and hand it to Trotzky." (He said this in the preliminary hearings but omitted it at the trial and Vishinsky himself failed to bring out this quaint bit of testimony regarding the German army's financing of Trotzky.) Foreign Trade Commissar Rosengoltz said he had supplied information on the Soviet air force to General von Seeckt in 1922 on instructions from Trotzky. Other defendants heaped equally damaging admissions upon their heads.

In all this symphony of self-denunciation and self-condemnation only one fully discordant note was struck. Krestinsky, former envoy to Germany, former Assistant Commissar for Foreign Affairs, had, at his first interrogation in prison—June 5 to 9, 1937—within a week after his arrest, confessed to every crime of which the preliminary investigator accused him. The public trial started on the morning of March 2, 1938. All the defendants pleaded guilty. Except Krestinsky. He pleaded not guilty.

Prosecutor Vishinsky called Accused Bessonov as the first witness. Bessonov had been Krestinsky's Counselor in Berlin. Under Vishinsky's cross-examination, he declared that he and Krestinsky had engaged in Trotzkyist activity in Germany. Krestinsky, summoned to the side of Bessonov to testify, denied Bessonov's statements. Vishinsky reminded him that in the preliminary secret hearings he had admitted his crimes.

"My testimony of June 5 or 9," Krestinsky affirmed, "is false from beginning to end." He had given false testimony in prison in the first week of his GPU detention. He stuck to it all the time he was in prison. Why? Here is a clue to the secret of the trials.

VISHINSKY: "And then you stuck to it."

KRESTINSKY: "And then I stuck to it because from personal experience I had arrived at the conviction that before the trial . . . I would not succeed in refuting my testimony." Now, in court, he declared he was not a Trotzkyite and not a conspirator or criminal.

Vishinsky called Rosengoltz to the stand.

VISHINSKY: "Do you take it that Krestinsky was a Trotzkyite?"

ROSENGOLTZ: "He is a Trotzkyite."

VISHINSKY: "Accused Krestinsky, I ask you to listen, because you will be saying that you did not hear." (Krestinsky had previously complained that he could not hear Bessonov's testimony.)

KRESTINSKY: "I don't feel well."

VISHINSKY: "If the Accused declares that he doesn't feel well, I have no right to question him."

KRESTINSKY: "I have only to take a pill and I shall be able to continue."

VISHINSKY: "Do you request not to be questioned for the present?"

KRESTINSKY: "For a few minutes."

A few minutes later Krestinsky was back at the stand denying charges and making lengthy intricate explanations in refutation of accusations leveled against him by his comrades in the dock. Vishinsky reverted to the question of why Krestinsky had given false testimony in prison. Why did he mislead the prosecutor?

KRESTINSKY: "I simply considered that if I were to say what I am saying today—that it [his early confession in prison] was not in accordance with the facts—my declaration would not reach the leaders of the Party and the Government."

In other words, he had made his untrue confession in prison because anything else would have been more difficult, and now, before the eyes of the foreign and Soviet press he was saying it was all a lie. He was not guilty.

The court adjourned for two hours. Evening session, March 2, 1938. More charges are made against Krestinsky and still he disclaims all. "Today I am telling the truth," he insists.

VISHINSKY: "Since twelve o'clock?"

KRESTINSKY: "Yes, in this court."

Court is dismissed. Krestinsky spends the night in his cell. The next morning, hearings are resumed. Krestinsky is not called on that morning. In the evening session, Accused Rakovsky reports on conspiratorial connections he had had with Krestinsky in the interests of Trotzkyism. Krestinsky thereupon confirms Rakovsky's declarations. He adds, "I fully confirm the testimony I gave in the preliminary investigation." But all day yesterday he had denied that testimony. What had happened? Vishinsky also wanted to know. He asked Krestinsky the meaning of this sudden shift since yesterday.

"Yesterday," Krestinsky replied, "under the influence of a momentary keen feeling of false shame evoked by the atmosphere of the dock and the painful impression created by the public reading of the indictment, which was aggravated by my poor health, I could not bring myself to tell the truth. . . . In the face of world public opinion, I had not the strength to admit the truth that I had been conducting a Trotzkyite struggle all along. . . . I admit my complete responsibility for the treason and treachery I have committed."

After that, for the subsequent eight days of the trial, Krestinsky behaved like all the other defendants and accepted a mountainous burden of guilt.

When did Krestinsky tell the truth, when he retracted his confession on the first day of the trial or when he confirmed it during all the remaining days of the trial? What had happened to Krestinsky between the morning he pleaded not guilty in court and the next evening when he accepted his guilt as he had during the preliminary investigations?

How did the authorities extract the confessions from the accused? The man who knew was Yagoda, the head of the GPU for many years. He himself had staged numerous public trials including the trial of the Zinoviev-Kamenev group. Now he himself was on trial. And he confessed.

Imagine how much Yagoda might have disclosed! But he sat through the trial bored and listless and was rarely called on to speak. He did not open his mouth until late on the fifth day of trial even though others had mentioned him and it is normal procedure in Soviet courts to ask an accused person to corroborate or reject accusations made against him in the witness stand. Brought to his feet on the fifth day by Vishinsky he helped Vishinsky by disputing Bukharin's and Rykov's assertion of innocence in the Kirov murder.

"Both Rykov and Bukharin are telling lies," Yagoda stated. "Rykov and Yenukidze were present of the meeting of the center where the question of the assassination of S. M. Kirov was discussed."

VISHINSKY: "Did the Accused Rykov and Bukharin in particular have any relation to the assassination?"

YAGODA: "A direct relation."

VISHINSKY: "Did you?"

YAGODA: "I did."

Then Yagoda sat down and was not heard from again until the seventh day of the public trial. On that day, Drs. Levin and Kazakov, two Soviet physicians, were testifying about their alleged efforts to kill Maxim Gorky, revered Russian author, Menzhinsky, chief of the GPU, Kuibishev, a member of the Politbureau, and Max Peshkov, Gorky's son. Levin, a venerable man past seventy who had treated Lenin and who was an honored figure in Moscow, as well as Kazakov testified that they had acted on Yagoda's instructions.

Yagoda said it was true he conspired to kill Gorky and Kuibishev but not Peshkov or Menzhinsky. Vishinsky read from Yagoda's preliminary evidence in prison: "But he (Levin) said he had no access to Menzhinsky, that the physician in attendance was Kazakov without whom nothing could be done. I instructed Levin to enlist Kazakov for this purpose."

VISHINSKY: "Did you depose this, Accused Yagoda?"

YAGODA: "I said that I did, but it is not true."

VISHINSKY: "Why did you make this deposition if it is not true?"

YAGODA: "I don't know why."

VISHINSKY: "Be seated."

Dr. Kazakov in court described in great detail a conference he had with Yagoda in Yagoda's office and he repeated the instructions Yagoda had then given him. In prison, Yagoda had corroborated Kazakov's information. "I summoned Kazakov and confirmed my orders. . . . He did his work. Menzhinsky died," Yagoda had said. But now at the trial Yagoda declared that he had never set eyes on Kazakov before he saw him here in the dock. Vishinsky read out Yagoda's statement in prison.

VISHINSKY: "Did you depose this?"

YAGODA: "I did."

VISHINSKY: "Hence you met Kazakov?"

YAGODA: "No."

VISHINSKY: "Why did you make a false deposition?"

YAGODA: "Permit me not to answer this question."

VISHINSKY: "So you deny that you organized the murder of Menzhinsky?"

YAGODA: "I do."

VISHINSKY: "Did you admit it in the deposition?"

YAGODA: "Yes."

The same questions came up again. Vishinsky said to Yagoda, "At the preliminary investigation you . . ."

YAGODA: "I lied."

VISHINSKY: "And now?"

YAGODA: "I am telling the truth."

VISHINSKY: "Why did you lie at the preliminary investigation?"

YAGODA: "I have already said: permit me not to reply to this question."

Mystery. The man who knew most said least. He could have talked as much as he pleased. He could have explained why he lied. Vishinsky asked him to explain. Yagoda could not have feared incriminating himself. He had admitted enough to justify a death sentence. Then why did he not talk freely?

A little episode now occurred in court which lifts the veil behind the secret of the Moscow trials and confessions. Doctor Levin was still in the stand explaining how, on Yagoda's orders, he killed Gorky, Gorky's son, Menzhinsky, and Kuibishev. Any men accused in a Soviet trial may put questions at any time to another accused or to a witness. Yagoda rose. "May I put a question to Levin?" "When Levin finishes his testimony," the presiding Chief Justice replied. Normally, Yagoda could have put his question immediately. Yagoda therefore insists: "This concerns Maxim Gorky's death." "When the Accused Levin finishes, then by all means," the Chief Justice assured him.

Levin continued with his testimony. When he finished, however, the President did not give Yagoda an opportunity to ask his question. Instead, he adjourned the session for thirty minutes. When the court reconvened after this interval, Yagoda was permitted to put his query to Levin. Yagoda said, "I ask Levin to answer in what year the Kremlin Medical Commission attached him, Levin, to me as my doctor, and to whom else he was attached."

Levin did not remember. That was the end of Yagoda's questioning. He did *not* put that question to Levin about the death of Maxim Gorky. He substituted another irrelevant, unimportant question.

What happened in that thirty-minute recess? Obviously, Yagoda promised the authorities not to put the question. This confirms my belief that the key to the Moscow trials and confessions is that an understanding existed between the accused and the prosecution. There was an agreement between them on how to run the trial. All the defendants had turned state's witnesses. They did this for a consideration. They were promised their lives. The court would condemn them to death. That was necessary for the sake of public opinion. But they would not be shot. And I therefore do not think that all the many leading Bolsheviks who figured as confessed culprits in the Moscow trials were immediately executed. Some may still be alive.

During the Bukharin-Rykov-Yagoda trial in March, 1938, Boris Kamkov and Vladimir Karelin appeared as witnesses against Bukharin. Kamkov and Karelin were the two former leaders of the Left Social Revolutionary party. This party had participated in the first Soviet government in 1917 which was a coalition government. Then, in July, 1918, the Left Social Revolutionaries killed Count Mirbach, the German Ambassador in Moscow, and revolted against the Soviets as a protest against the Brest-Litovsk peace with the Kaiser. Kamkov and Karelin were arrested and sentenced in 1922. For the next sixteen years, nobody ever heard of them or from them. Then suddenly they appeared from out of the depths, pallid, ghost-like apparitions brought specially to the Hall of Columns from Siberia, to testify that in 1918 Bukharin wished to kill Lenin and Stalin.

It is not difficult to see how men bearing false names could be hidden away for many years in a strictly supervised, hermetically sealed country like the Soviet Union. Few people have ever escaped from the Soviet Union, and most of the accused were old men whose families were in Russia.

What induced the accused Bolsheviks to enter into a bargain with the authorities?

They were offered the alternative: Confession or Death. Trotzky, who knew many of the accused intimately, and who understood Soviet methods better than anyone outside Russia, said to the American Preliminary Commission of Inquiry—Professor John Dewey, Carleton Beals, Otto Ruehle, Benjamin Stolberg, and Suzanne La Follette—which interrogated him in Mexico in April, 1937, "When anybody has to choose between death at one hundred percent and death at ninety-nine percent when he is in the hands of the GPU, he will choose the ninety-nine percent against the one hundred percent." The defendants in the Moscow trials chose the ninety-nine percent of living death because if they had not confessed they would have been shot immediately.

There was, for instance, Leo Karakhan, former Vice Commissar of

Foreign Affairs. At the Bukharin trial, several defendants stated that Karakhan was a German spy and that he conducted all the treasonable negotiations with the Nazis. Then he should have been in the dock with the others. But he was not. He had been shot together with Yenukidze, who, it was alleged by the prosecution and by the defendants, had been the key-man in the entire conspiracy. They were executed in prison on December 19, 1937. That was just when the defendants in the Bukharin-Rykov trial were being cross-examined in the GPU prison for the March, 1938, trial. If Karakhan and Yenukidze had confessed they would have been in the dock. They refused to confess. They were executed. This cannot have been without its effect on the preliminary prison cross-examinations.

Bessonov, one of the defendants in the March, 1938, trial, stated in court that he refused to confess from February 28, 1937, to December 30, 1937, when he was confronted with Krestinsky's confession. But this is incorrect. For Krestinsky confessed in June, 1937, and had finished testifying by October. I am sure it was the execution of Karakhan and Yenukidze on December 19 which induced Bessonov's breakdown on December 30. The publication of the story of the execution in *Pravda* was an unusual expedient. It served to intimidate those who still refused to confess. I can imagine what it meant to Bessonov when a copy of *Pravda* with the news of the Karakhan-Yenukidze execution was introduced into his cell. He must have read it and said to himself, "This is my last chance. If I do not confess now they will shoot me as they have Karakhan and Yenukidze. They are promising me my life if I confess. Maybe they will keep the promise. I have a one percent chance to live if I confess according to dictation."

Or take the case of my dear friend Boris Mironov, whom many foreign correspondents knew as assistant chief of the Press Department under Oumansky. He was witty and highly educated and very much in love with his wife Celia. We used to visit one another often. Then he was arrested. At the trial, Krestinsky asserted that he had kept in touch with Trotzky through foreign correspondents and that Mironov had arranged all this. What correspondent? Vishinsky asked.

KRESTINSKY: "I cannot tell definitely. He left for America."

Some people thought it was I. But I never had anything to do with it. Moreover, they assumed that there were such activities, and that Mironov engaged in conspiracy. If he had, it would have been natural for him to be brought in as a witness when Krestinsky referred to him. Romm and Bukhartsev who allegedly served similar liaison functions had testified. Why didn't Mironov testify? Because he refused to confess to lies. Mironov is dead.

Innumerable Bolsheviks were shot without trials. Only those who confessed were tried. Nobody who did not confess was ever tried. In the three big Moscow trials, fifty-five persons were accused. Of these, only twenty-five had been important leaders and officials. They constituted a small fraction of the men who had made and led the Revolution. They constituted a small fraction of those who were arrested and who were asked to confess. The confessors were far fewer than the non-confessors. It is quite possible that even persons who confessed were not brought to public trial because the GPU suspected that they might use the trial to deny their guilt. The GPU studies the psychology of its victims. It put on public trial only those whom it could fully trust. It almost made a mistake in the case of Krestinsky.

How did the confessors know that the Soviet government would keep its part of the compact and let them live? They could not be sure. But there was that one percent chance and they grabbed it. Yagoda must have known, and others too, that in Soviet Russia many state's witnesses had been spared. When I was in Moscow in December, 1936, a highly placed Bolshevik intimated to me that the German Communists who had confessed in the Zinoviev-Kamenev trial had been rewarded with clemency. Radek and Sokolnikov, in the second trial, were condemned to ten years' imprisonment which must have encouraged the defendants in the third. In the third, Rakovsky, Bessonov, and Pletnev were officially given prison sentences.

The Soviet government needed the Moscow trials and confessions, or thought it did, and the accused met the government's need. They behaved in most respects just as the Kremlin would have wanted them to. In a Soviet court the defendant can at one time or another say anything he pleases. But in these trials, the defendants were interrupted on several occasions by Vishinsky when they approached ticklish subjects—Bukharin's dispute with Stalin, for instance—and they never reverted to them. That was part of the bargain.

From Stalin's viewpoint, the ideal result of the trials would have been high praise of Stalin, condemnation of Trotzky, and acceptance by the accused of the accidents, economic difficulties, shortages, and political disturbances which had occurred in the country during the past seven or eight years. This *was* the result.

The dictator is infallible; the dictatorship can make no mistakes. That is the official Stalin credo. But there had been hundreds of train wrecks. "We deliberately staged them," the defendants said. From the beginning of Bolshevik time winter goods had been offered to customers in the summer, and summer goods in the winter. "That is," said Vishinsky at the trial, "the public was offered felt boots in the summer and summer shoes in the winter." "Yes," replied Accused Zelensky, head of the co-operative stores. This, he confessed, was part of the conspiracy. He thus absolved the Soviet government of a shortcoming for which many citizens cursed it. The Commissariat of Finance had adopted certain measures with regard to savings banks in which millions of individual depositors were interested. Commissar of Finance Grinko, accused, declared that he did it deliberately because "it caused irritation among the broad masses of the population." Now the broad masses would understand and no longer blame Stalin for their irritation. Stalin must be without blame. They would blame Grinko, the puppet of Trotzky; whatever went wrong in Russia was Trotzky's doing. The peasants in collective farms had complained that they were underpaid. Grinko testified that Rykov ordered this to sow discontent. There had been a bread shortage. Didn't you do that, Vishinsky probed. Of course, Grinko asserted, I did it with Zelensky. Tractors which served the farm collectives broke down frequently and the peasants always had trouble providing for tractor services. Ex-Commissar of Agriculture Chernov revealed that he did this purposely and put men of his own illegal, rightist, Trotzkyist organizations in charge of the tractors with a view to spoiling the government's relations with the peasants. "As regards stock breeding," he added, "the aim was to kill pedigree breeding stock and to strive for high cattle mortality." That should satisfy the peasants who had complained that beasts in collectives died too fast. There had been a shortage of paper. Ivanov testified that he arranged that on Bukharin's orders. Peasant revolts in Siberia and the Kuban? Bukharin did that too. "The kulaks," said Ivanov, "were in an angry mood." Bukharin exploited this mood. The government had distributed impure seed in the villages. "I did it," affirmed Accused Zubarev. In White Russia, the number of livestock had been disastrously reduced. It was done at the wish of the Polish Secret Service, several defendants deposed. Thirty thousand horses died of anemia in 1936 in White Russia. "My work," Accused Sha-rangovich admitted. This admission was then headlined in White Russia's newspapers and radio broadcasts. In a mining district, some children were digging in the dirt and struck some dynamite which killed a large number of them. Shestov took this crime on his shoulders. The accused damaged the cotton crop of Turkestan and the silk production of Uzbekistan, delayed the construction of a giant water-power station in Ferghana, put nails and glass in butter, gave short weight and measure in retail stores, and committed hundreds of similar acts.

All right. The accused have been removed forever from Soviet administration. But the Soviet press in 1939 and 1940 continued to announce arrests for train wrecks, venality in co-operative stores, poisonings. The *New York Times* of December 14, 1940, reported from Moscow that the Soviet newspaper *Soviet Agriculture* charged the "capitalist world" with "trying to send to our country not only spies and terrorists; the enemy is trying to wreck with anything possible . . . seeds infected with pink worms, lemons with larva of the Mediterranean fruit fly, and infected potatoes" . . . and diseased cotton had been shipped into the country. The guilty nations this time were America, England, and the Netherlands. Apparently, Soviet farming had again suffered some setbacks for which a scapegoat and explanation had to be found. These setbacks—and excuses—seem to be a permanent feature of Soviet life. In 1936, 1937, and 1938 the Soviet dictatorship hoped to pass the blame to those who confessed. Stalin must be blameless.

In court, Accused Bukharin said they planned to open the front to the Germans in case of war, and then "it would be expedient to try those guilty of the defeat at the front. This would enable us to win over the masses by playing on patriotic slogans."

Bukharin, in other words, allegedly also intended to stage Moscow trials if he and his friends overthrew Stalin. The trials would help them rally the population to their cause. Big Soviet trials have nothing to do with justice. They are forms of super-propaganda. They are not, primarily a product of bad economic conditions. They serve to rewrite history. The Bolsheviks have been very energetic in rewriting history. They serve to alter the political record, to white-wash Stalin, to blacken his enemies, to frighten potential enemies. The trials undertook to demonstrate that the Soviet administration is perfect; the only trouble is that some Trotzkyists are still at liberty.

For these purposes Stalin needed the trials and the confessions. If the accused had been dangerous they could have been removed without public ceremonies. But they were assets to Stalin. The only problem was to induce them to perform in the required fashion. He paid them for their efforts. He asked them for confessions and promised them their lives as a reward. They hoped he would keep the promise.

The accused, accordingly, were very accommodating throughout the trials. They frequently insisted, for instance, that the moment any Soviet citizen makes the first short step against the Soviet regime he is bound to end up as a great criminal and traitor. This was a warning to everybody against committing the original sin.

Above all, the accused, many of them old friends of Trotzky, outbid one another in maligning Trotzky. This was certainly very pleasing to Stalin. Thus Piatakov: "I only deeply regret that he, the main criminal, the unregenerate and hardened offender, Trotzky, is not sitting beside us in the dock." Sokolnikov: "I express the conviction, or at any rate the hope that not one person will now be found in the Soviet Union who would attempt to take up the Trotzky banner. I think that Trotzkyism in other countries too has been exposed by this trial, and that Trotzky himself has been exposed as an ally of capitalism, as the vilest agent of Fascism." Rakovsky, for thirty-four years a devoted friend of Trotzky: "I share the State Prosecutor's regret that the enemy of the people, Trotzky, is not here in the dock with us. The picture of our trial loses in completeness and depth because of the fact that the ataman of our gang is not present here." Rosengoltz: "Trotzky . . . is the vilest agent of Fascism. . . Rakovsky was right when he said that here in the dock it is Trotzky in the first place who is missing. Trotzkyism is not a political current but an unscrupulous dirty gang of murderers, spies, provocateurs, and poisoners. . . . Long live the Bolshevik party with the best traditions of enthusiasm, heroism, self-sacrifice which can only be found in the world under Stalin's leadership." Bukharin: "In reality the whole country stands behind Stalin. He is the hope of the world. He is a creator. . . . Everybody perceives the wise leadership of the country that is ensured by Stalin." That is how Stalin felt about it. Bulanov, Yagoda's assistant in the GPU, throws a bouquet to Yezhov, Yagoda's successor: "The Russian worker, the Russian peasants are fortunate that Nicholai Ivanovitch Yezhov caught us in time and put us in the dock." Radek: "We all know of the tremendous work which the railways had accomplished under the direction of Kaganovitch," Kaganovitch was No. 2, or perhaps No. 3, Bolshevik.

These stuffy tributes to Yezhov and Stalin and these denunciations of Trotzky were in the spirit of *Pravda* editorials and official propaganda generally. The defendants were doing what was expected of them. If the confessions are true these statements are hypocritical. Sincere men could not thus fawn on Stalin after they had been ready to kill him. They would not condemn Trotzky after they had been ready to commit murder and treason simply because he asked it.

The Soviet government obviously realized that the confessions heavily taxed the credulity even of Soviet citizens who did not hear the counter-arguments. The state prosecutor, and especially the accused, used every opportunity to try to make the confessions appear more plausible. Bukharin, Radek, and many of the accused obligingly devoted long impassioned speeches to an attempt to dispel the doubts about the truth of their confessions. "Please believe us," they cried in appeals directed to the outside world and to their own country. But how could one believe them? While allegedly serving as dupes of Fascism, while allegedly plotting to overthrow the Soviets and assassinate Stalin they had written and spoken in public in fulsome praise of Stalin and behaved as enemies of Fascism and staunch Bolsheviks. Perhaps they were no less hypocritical now.

The defendants, and others, have given two unsatisfactory explanations of the confessions. It has been said that they confessed because they were confronted by others who had confessed; the weight of the evidence broke them down. Not at all. At the Zinoviev-Kamenev trial, the defendants publicly accused Radek, Sokolnikov, Piatakov, and Serebyakov who figured in a subsequent trial. But when these men were arrested they did not plead guilty. On the contrary, they denied their guilt, denied it for many months.

In prison, during the preliminary investigations, Radek was confronted with Sokolnikov who had already confessed. Yet Radek refused to confess for three months. He did not confess until a month before his public trial opened when the authorities probably told him that this was his last chance: he could confess or be shot. It is hard to say, "Shoot me." Krestinsky confessed in his cell in June, 1937. Bessonov was brought to him. He accused Bessonov. Yet Bessonov remained adamant until December 30, 1937, after the official announcement of Karakhan's execution. Bukharin resisted too. Others had confessed before him and dragged his name in. "For three months," nevertheless, he said at the trial, "I refused to say anything. Then I began to testify." Muralov, a commander in the Red Army, the former chief of the Moscow garrison, refused to talk for eight months of imprisonment and then made an abject confession. Rakovsky did not confess until his ninth month of imprisonment. So it was not that evidence was piling up against them. It had piled up long before they confessed. Nor could it have been physical torture. That would get a man down in a week or so, or two months at most. It was the cynical feeling that further resistance in defense of one's honor and name was foolish when all the others had submitted and accepted the better end of the Confession or Death offer. It is quite likely that a man like Bukharin was also motivated by other than selfish considerations. He may have said to himself, "My chief concern is to keep alive. Who knows what changes will take place in the future?" Perhaps it was with a view to the political role he might still be called on to play that he did not wish to admit being a spy. Overthrow the Soviet regime? Yes, that could be interpreted as a revolutionary measure against Stalin. But a spy wears a black badge forever.

The second unsatisfactory explanation of the confessions is this: the defendants were good revolutionists. They were imprisoned and told that they would be shot for their crimes but they could perform one last service to the Revolution—admit guilt and error, glorify Stalin, and excoriate Trotzky. I think this is downright rot. All the leading defendants were highly intelligent men and every one of them knew that the trials were doing the Revolution and Bolshevism great harm at home and abroad. If they had all refused to confess and if there had consequently been no trials it would have been much better for the Revolution. The trials offer this choice: either many of the leading survivors of 1917—except Stalin, of course—were base traitors and Fascists, or the Soviet government manufactured the evidence and extorted the confessions. Neither choice is complimentary to the Revolution. No! If the defendants had behaved as good revolutionists they would have refused to confess.

The confessions emphasize the degradation of spirit caused by the Stalin regime. Some of these Bolsheviks and other revolutionists had, when arrested by the Czarist police, declined to open their mouths, declined even to give their names. Men spent their lives in Czarist dungeons because they refused to budge one millimeter from their ideals. Was it simply that the GPU's technique of torture was finer than the Okhrana's? Lengthy cross-examinations in prison, cruel prison regimes, no reading matter or visitors, threats of reprisals against families certainly had something to do with the final decision to confess. But these forms of pressure existed in Czarist times too, yet true revolutionists refused to confess. Moreover, if they had confessed under torture they could have said so to the world at the public trials. The only way of making sure that a defendant would not tip over the whole delicate applecart by revealing everything at the public court hearings was to promise him his life if he didn't and promise him torture after the trial if he did. I do not think Krestinsky would have confessed in order to save his wife who was herself a revolutionist. He knew that she would not have wished to be saved by an act that would damn him forever in revolutionary history.

It was easy to defy the Czarist Okhrana. It was the hated enemy. But when your own Soviet secret police asked you to confess falsely in order to save Stalin's face it broke your heart first and then broke your will.

The spine of many of the accused Bolsheviks had been crushed even before they were arrested. A mild illustration: Michael Borodin, a man of powerful build and striking presence, had been sent by Moscow to China. He quickly became the real master of nationalist China. He twisted provincial war lords around his little finger; the big men of China deferred to his political sagacity. In 1927, he returned to Moscow and became the scapegoat for the failure of Stalin's policy in China. He was put in charge of a Soviet paper-manufacturing trust and, of course, he made a mess of it because he lacked business experience. Then he got another but smaller economic job which he likewise mishandled. This was all part of a deliberate scheme of humiliation. Finally he landed in the editor's chair of the *Moscow Daily News*. Two little Communists were introduced into the office to hamper every step he made and to check and irritate him. Before he could print an editorial he had to consult the Central Committee of the party. He was barred from any initiative. Just as a man may rise and grow when given a big task so he may shrink when he is a dismal misfit in a small one. I was present once in Borodin's office in the *Moscow Daily News* when an American radical, a lad of twenty-three who worked on the paper, came in. Borodin scolded him for falling down on a story. The American argued. Borodin became angry. The American yelled, "You can't talk to me that way." Borodin yelled back. They both waxed hot. Borodin finally threw his hands above his head and shouted, "Get out of here. You're fired." The great statesman who had ruled millions at war and molded big Chinese minds to his will could not manage a cub reporter.

Magnify this many times. Rykov took Lenin's job as Prime Minister and held it from 1924 to 1930. He was under constant attack as an oppositionist, until he was removed December 19, 1930. He was unemployed for several months and then was appointed Commissar of Posts and Telegraphs, notoriously a Soviet job of no political importance. The attacks in the press and at meetings continued. His best friends shunned him. On a vacation in the Caucasus, he slipped into a public celebration on the anniversary of the Revolution. People moved away from him. Nobody talked to him. The orators flayed him. In August, 1936, his name was mentioned in the Zinoviev-Kamenev trial as one of the leading conspirators. On September 27, 1936, he was dismissed from the Post Office. He sat home, did nothing, and waited. He waited for five months. He was not arrested until February 27, 1937, and arrest must have come as a relief from morose suspense. He stayed in prison for a year before his trial opened. After all this he naturally had very gloomy and cynical ideas about what had happened to the Revolution, and rather than feel inspired to help the Revolution by self-flagellation and self-immolation his mood was rather: "Oh, what's the use. If Stalin wants me to confess and say thus-and-so, I'll do it. Why should I die for this?"

When Rykov left the Commissariat of Posts and Telegraphs, Yagoda took his place. The Commissariat of Posts was a sort of halfway house to prison. Soon, accordingly, Yagoda was ousted from it and charged with embezzling funds. Later he was arrested and charged with murder and treason. He and Rykov were defendants in the same trial in March, 1938, and sentenced to death. The trial was staged by Yezhov, who succeeded Yagoda as head of the GPU. But on July 25, 1938, Yezhov was dismissed from the GPU and appointed to head the Commissariat of Water Transport, which is another non-political sideshow like the Commissariat of Posts and Telegraphs. Later Yezhov disappeared.

Stalin's technique of slow-motion destruction demoralized his victims long before they entered their prison cells. No ordinary third-degree would have produced the confessions. It was a third-degree that lasted for years, a third-degree to which the entire country was and is today submitted. The Moscow trials and confessions were merely the sensational, highly-silhouetted shape of an everyday Soviet phenomenon, and it is only against the background of this phenomenon that the confessions can be understood. Millions of Soviet citizens live lies every day to save their lives and their jobs. They make false confessions day in and day out. They write lies, speak lies. They lie to one another and know it. They lie to themselves and get accustomed to it. They lose their illusions and succumb to the sole cynical goal of self-preservation until a better day. The assassination of character and the annihilation of personality is the dictatorship's chief weapon which it never forgets. The further a Soviet citizen is from the center of the regime the less he feels its blows. The peasants are least exposed to it. The workers more. The officials much more. And for the highest officials like Rykov, Yagoda, and Krestinsky the destruction of personality and character took the intensified, telescoped form of trial and confession. The wonder of it is that so few confessed.

The Bolshevik dictatorship has become a personal dictatorship. It was not that in the beginning. In a personal dictatorship, all persons are effaced to save one person's face.

But the effect of the Moscow trials was to undermine confidence in the Soviet regime. For years Yagoda was "the flaming sword of the revolution." He put Zinoviev, Kamenev, and others on trial. Now he himself was in the dock as a traitor. Could he have staged the trials to harm the Revolution? Yagoda was succeeded by Yezhov, and Yezhov became "the flaming sword of the revolution." Then Yezhov disappeared in disgrace from the GPU. Whom could one trust?

During the many years he had tortured Russia as head of the GPU, Yagoda executed, exiled, and arrested millions of men, women, and children. The dead could not be resurrected. But were the cases of prisoners and exiles reviewed after it was allegedly discovered and proved that Yagoda had long been a traitor in league with Fascists? Hadn't he falsely accused and punished innocent people? A few dozen individuals were granted clemency after Yagoda's eclipse. But the vast bulk went on serving their sentences. How did the wives feel whose husbands had been sent away by Yagoda? How did the families feel whose members had been shot by him? They got no redress and no comfort.

Thousands of Soviet authors, journalists, party speakers, and provincial leaders had been purged as "enemies of the people." Then how could the ordinary Soviet citizen know that the man whose article he was reading in the morning's paper or whose speech he was listening to over the radio would not be annihilated tomorrow as an "enemy of the people." Should he believe what he was reading or hearing?

The purges and trials produced a serious crisis of faith in the Soviet Union which continues to this day. Since everybody is a potential spy and traitor then it is best to distrust everybody. This has been ruinous to economic activity and morale. Keep as far as possible from responsibility; do as little as won't hurt you. Be a hypocrite if need be. *Sauve qui peut*. These became the guiding rules of Russian life.

The Soviet masses and intellectuals took refuge in indifference and passivity. The Communist party became more and more of a rubber stamp. Citizens did not care what happened as long as they were left out of it personally. Stalin's pact with the Nazis in 1939? "Well, the hell with it. I'm all mixed up. It's not my business. I'm taking care of myself."

The trial of the "Trotzkyist criminals" who allegedly made a pact with the Nazis led ultimately to Stalin's pact with the Nazis.

Why, instead of holding my tongue, did I not come out in 1937 or 1938 as a critic of the Soviet regime? It is not so easy to throw away the vision to which one has been attached for fifteen years. Moreover, in 1938, the Soviet government's foreign policy was still effectively anti-appeasement and anti-Fascist, much more so than England's or France's or America's. It helped China with arms to fight Japanese aggression. It helped Spain with arms to fight the Nazis and Mussolini. It encouraged Czechoslovakia to stand firm against Hitler. I did not know how long it would last. But while it lasted, I hesitated to throw stones in public. Even now I think I was right. In private, if asked, I made it clear that I had cooled toward Soviet domestic policy. My friends can confirm that and so, if they will, can some of my ex-friends.

Divorce may be a sudden rupture or a gradual estrangement. My divorce from Russia was gradual. It has caused me many a heartache nevertheless. When I did begin criticizing Russia, I was chided by certain people, including a great lady who writes a syndicated column, for not delaying longer.

Some persons have whispered that I refrained from open criticism of Soviet Russia because my wife and two boys were still in Moscow, and I feared reprisals against them. There would have been nothing reprehensible in such restraint on my part. But the whisper was untrue.

31. *Mr. Lloyd George*

IN America, as in many other free countries, the War in Spain attracted the support of many of the finest men. During the years of the Spanish struggle, I met in Paris numerous literary men and artists who were about to go down into Spain. I met most of them again in Spain and most of them when they came back up to Paris. The list of these people is a roll of honor: Lillian Hellman, Richard Watts, Jr., Ernest Hemingway, Bennett Cerf, Vincent Sheean, Diana Sheean, Meyer Levin, Ernst Toller, Erskine Caldwell, Sylvia Townsend Warner, Martha Gellhorn, Dorothy Parker, Alan Campbell, Elliot Paul, Barbara Wertheim, Stephen Spender, Waldo Frank, Erika Mann, Klaus Mann, Richard Mowrer, and Jo Davidson. There were more.

Jo Davidson is pure American and yet nearly pure French. With his beard, he is the image of Karl Marx. He had made busts of Gandhi, Mussolini, Franklin D. Roosevelt, Rockefeller, Foch, Pershing, Litvinov, Chicherin, Walt Whitman, Shaw, Wells, Sinclair Lewis, Radek, Clemenceau, Lloyd George—the list is endless. He can do a head in three hours if necessary. He went to the front in Spain and did Lister, Campesino, and Modesto in almost no time. The Loyalist soldiers who watched the work called him "Sculptomoton." He also made busts of President Azaña, del Vayo, Pasionaria, and Constancia de la Mora. Negrin would not sit for him. (I once accompanied Negrin to a rest home of the International Brigade. I suggested he take along a photographer. He said, "I'd rather lose the war." But some of the men had cameras and whenever they asked him he stood still and let them take snapshots.) In New York, after the war, Negrin did sit for him. Davidson presented the Spanish busts to the American committee which was collecting money for the Loyalists. He also collected money for Spain at private gatherings in the United States.

One morning in July, 1938, I received a letter in Paris from Ellen Wilkinson, Labor M.P., asking me to come to London to see Mr. David Lloyd George. Some one had told him of the meeting and dinner I had addressed in the House of Commons in April. He was inviting me to lunch at his farm in Churt.

I flew over to London, and Ellen Wilkinson drove me down in her tiny car. My concern was twofold: to keep my feet from going through the frail floor into the motor and to keep the windshield dry, for the rain descended in sheets. I had met Lloyd George in November, 1937, but as we approached Churt the prospect of spending several hours with him excited me more than the anticipation of any encounter I had ever had with a statesman. He was not in office, had no great power, but a page of world history would always belong to him, and he looked the part.

At Churt, Lloyd George has a very big farm which is tilled under his expert direction. On the piano in the reception room stood framed, autographed portraits of the famous men of the epoch. We waited a minute and then he came in with springy step. He was dressed like a young man in bright fashionable clothes. He is short but stately. His face is ruddy and sheathed in smiles. He wears pince nez from which dangles a wide black ribbon. His long silver white hair falls straight and lustrous to his collar. An electric current went through the air as he entered the room.

He took out a big cigar, bit off the end, spat and offered me one. I said I didn't smoke. There then followed the colloquy I have had ten thousand times in life, but Lloyd George gave it his own ending.

"Have some sherry," he said, pouring Ellen a glass. I told him I didn't usually drink.

"No vices," he said.

"No visible ones," I said.

"Well, I have them all, visible and invisible," he exclaimed with a rich laugh, "and that's why I feel so good at seventy-five."

He immediately asked about Spain. First about the army. He put questions on the soldiers, on the officers, on rifles, cannon, machine guns, airplanes, everything in detail. "What kind of anti-tank guns have they?" he inquired. I replied as well as I could.

"When I was Minister of Munitions in 1915," he recounted, "I could get no money from the government for the anti-tank gun. However, an Indian maharajah gave me a million pounds to develop and manufacture it, and when it proved a success the Treasury allocated funds for further production."

Captain Liddell Hart says this is the story of the quick-firing trench mortar. But I am sure we never mentioned trench mortars.

Liddell Hart's facts are probably correct, however. Lloyd George's memory must have taken him into the error.

Lloyd George asked about the Loyalist officers and I told him that they presented a great problem, for most of the officers of the old regular army had gone over to Franco and it was difficult to create an officers' corps quickly.

He said, "General staffs are usually reactionary. They are built on the caste system. In the World War, our generals endeavored to keep down all high officers except those of their own class. The only exception was Sir William Robertson, who was the son of a butler and who rose from cavalry sergeant-major to Chief of Staff. In the battle of Passchendaele only General Monash could have extricated the British army. But Monash was a Jew and the staff held him at arm's length."

After each one of my answers he talked about his own experiences in leading Britain during the first World War. "But you must not let me reminisce in this manner. It is the way of an old man." I encouraged it.

"In Spain," he declared, "a class war is raging and the upper classes are fighting the people. I have been in the same fight here all my life. The landed aristocracy, conservative churchmen, and the vested industrial and financial interests have always fought me. And I them," he chuckled.

We went in for lunch where we were joined by Miss Stevenson, Lloyd George's secretary. First he discussed farming, and he told us how much of the food we ate he raised himself. Then he recalled his meetings with Woodrow Wilson. I think he did not like Wilson. Later he mentioned a visit to Churt by Mahatma Gandhi. "All the maids came in to shake his hands," Lloyd George said. "As Gandhi sat on the couch with his legs under him, a black cat which we had never seen before came in through that window and sat in his lap. When he went it disappeared. Some weeks later Miss Slade, Gandhi's secretary, visited us and the same black cat returned and then disappeared."

He took an interest in Soviet Ambassador Maisky who, at the time, was on vacation in Russia; he hoped Maisky would not be arrested there. He had high praise for Pablo Azcarate, the Loyalist Ambassador in London.

Lloyd George said he would wish to visit Loyalist Spain. He was going by car to the French Riviera soon and might connect the two trips. I explained that he could enter Spain on a morning, go to Barcelona by auto in three hours, and leave Spain again the same evening. His visit would mean a lot to the Spaniards. It would buoy them up. "But," he exclaimed, "I would go to the front. I would stay more than a day"; and he reminisced on his front experiences in the World War.

Miss Stevenson told me that was the trouble. If he went he would stay too long and place himself in danger. His daughter, Megan, and son, Gwilym, she said, therefore objected to his going. I turned to Lloyd George and said, "Miss Stevenson and I have just decided that Negrin will arrest you after twenty-four hours in Spain and deport you." He laughed uproariously. He inquired about Negrin. "The Continent, at last," he declared, "has produced a fighting democratic statesman. How old is he?"

"Forty-five," I replied.

He made a calculation by visibly turning his eyes up and backward into his memory, and said, "I was Prime Minister at fifty-four. It is a good age."

"Negrin is the only big man who has emerged from the Spanish War," I commented a moment later.

"Sometimes," he said with a smile, "it is better when there is only one. I had much trouble with the others."

On the way back from the dining room to the parlor we passed a large enlargement of a snapshot taken at the French front in 1916, showing Lloyd George, General Haig, the French General Joffre, and French Minister Albert Thomas. Lloyd George paused to let us look at it. I said, "They seem to be trying to sell you something." On the picture, Lloyd George wore a skeptical amused look.

He apparently did not understand the connotation of "sell." "No," he replied, "they were trying to convince me that in a few days they would throw in the French cavalry, smash the German lines, and drive the Germans out of France. Haig agreed with them and looked for victory in 1916. I did not." He pointed to Haig's highly polished boots. "Haig was brilliant," Lloyd George remarked, "down here."

It had stopped raining and we went out to see the view. One could see far in the direction of London. He drew in a deep breath and sighed and said, "It is beautiful here. I hate going down to London and I do so only when there is a debate on Spain in the House." He was spending much time reading last proofs of his latest book of World War memoirs. He figured out the number of words he had to read. He was pleased that an earlier volume had sold so well. He turned to Ellen Wilkinson and instructed her to call on him without hesitation whenever he could do something for the Spanish Republicans. "Nothing is more important for Great Britain," he stated firmly.

In the house again he showed us several score of gold and silver cases elaborately shaped and adorned which had been presented to him by British cities in recognition of his war efforts. Some took the form of celebrated municipal buildings and churches. He said, "Not one of them is for my work in peacetime." He mentioned his contributions to social reform. "I have been honored only for killing my fellow-men. Here," he pointed, "is the war case from the city of Birmingham. It was given to me in the same hall where in my early years they shouted me down and threatened me with violence for voicing humanitarian impulses."

In another room, he stopped in front of a painting of a North African town. "That was painted by Winston," he said. Lloyd George and Churchill had gone on a vacation together. The painting was very good and sensitive. Lloyd George talked about Churchill. He displayed a deep affection for him. "Winston also plays the violin," Lloyd George said. "Few men in England write or speak as well as he does." Turning to Ellen, he asked, "Why do we keep him down?" She suggested that British people do not ordinarily trust brilliance.

Conversation drifted to Harry Pollitt, the leader of the British Communist party. "The Communists," Lloyd George volunteered, "are the Liberals of the twentieth century in that they have inherited our former capacity for indignation."

He asked us to sign his visitors' book, first showing us some of the interesting names. He bent over and watched as I wrote my name, and said, "Wait. Write—*Louis Fischer, Barcelona.*" The idea of having a signature from Barcelona delighted him. He was young despite his age.

He stood on the porch as Ellen went through the long process of warming up the car. Then he waved good-by. He looked a colorful, excitingly magnetic, and beautiful personality. It was a stimulating experience to have met him.

Churchill is the political descendant of David Lloyd George. Both are dynamic and talented British imperialists yet they are moved by a passion for freedom. They are isolated fruit on an old tree. The late Chamberlain, the late Lord Lothian, Halifax, Sir Nevile Henderson, Sir John Simon, Hoare, and others of the same crop seem to be made of very inferior stuff when set beside Churchill and Lloyd George. But another tree is growing in England which is not upper class and which may yield a new, hardy fruit.

Lenin wrote, "Mr. Lloyd George is not only a very wise man but one who has learned much from the Marxists. It would not hurt us to learn something from him."

I remained in London until July 12 when I addressed a meeting in the House of Commons attended by seventy-two members of Parliament from all parties. The next morning I took the train to Paris.

That same month, a Congress for Peace and Freedom met in Paris. It illustrated the widespread support which the pro-Loyalist movement had found throughout the world; it also illustrated the disunity of the Left. Robert, Lord Cecil, presided at most of the sessions. He reminded the French of the recent visit of the British royal sovereigns to France and thanked them for the warm welcome which France had accorded the monarchs. The French delegates knew that Daladier had wanted the royal visit to strengthen his hand and that, as part of the *quid pro quo*, London had demanded the closing of the French frontier with Loyalist Spain. The French complied.

After Cecil, Jawaharlal Nehru, Indian Nationalist leader, rose to speak. "I come not to speak in the names of kings and princes," he began, "but on behalf of several hundred million downtrodden Indians." The Hindu revolutionist was answering the British lord.

England sent the Duchess of Atholl, Philip Noel-Baker, Wilfrid Roberts, George Russell Strauss, Ellen Wilkinson, and other M.P.'s. Only one important representative came from the United States, Bishop Oldham of the Protestant Episcopal church. Spain's delegation included: Pasionaria, Martinez Barrio, the President of Parliament, and Madame Luisy del Vayo.

The presidium had decided against an address by Pasionaria. She was the best orator there, a chip of Spain, symbol of the womanhood of suffering Spain, but a Communist leader. The delegates demanded Pasionaria. No, said the chairman, Pierre Cot. Interruptions, ovations, obstructions. Loud cries for Pasionaria. Cot adjourned the meeting. Little Ellen Wilkinson was hoisted on the platform to re-open the meeting unofficially and give Pasionaria the floor. Two attendants took her under the arms and carried her behind the stage. Then Nehru walked on. Nobody would dare touch him. He was oriental dignity itself, olive-skin face, dream eyes, thin gray hair. But he was angry. Cecil wished to demonstrate that the Communists did not dominate the peace movement. Nehru wished to assert the right of free speech for Communists fighting Fascism. An attendant disconnected the loudspeaker and another extinguished the lights.

At the next session, Martinez Barrio announced that the Spanish delegation would not insist on making a special statement of its views, and instead, Madame del Vayo, white and shaking—it was her first public performance—read a long resolution drafted by the Loyalist representatives. Pasionaria had stepped down and the Communists had agreed upon conciliation. But under the oil the sea seethed.

Nehru is not a Communist but in my many years in Russia and Europe I have rarely seen a truer revolutionist. Privilege plagues his big country, the privilege of caste, raj, prince, and rich man. He struggles against it. He went to Spain and promised the Loyalists help. India sent help. I suggested to him once that a letter from Gandhi to the Spanish government would be good propaganda. Gandhi sent the letter to Negrin.

I think certain southern races take a more tolerant view of corruption and venality than northern puritans be they Christian, Jewish, or Bolshevik. In like manner, it has always seemed to me that Hindus are more honest than westerners, more self-critical and honest with themselves, more selfless. Nehru writes a pamphlet and says he has not been radical enough, he has made mistakes, he must retire from politics for a while, think things over, get straight with himself. He does it. It would be funny if a Bonnet or Flandin or Sir Samuel Hoare behaved that way.

Georges Bonnet, Foreign Minister of France, gave a lunch to several of the people attending the peace congress as delegates or journalists. About fifteen persons were present, among them Lord Cecil, Pierre Cot, Walter Lippmann, Theodore Dreiser, Edgar Ansel Mowrer of the *Chicago Daily News*, Alexander Werth, Paris correspondent of the *Manchester Guardian*, Pierre de Lanux, French lecturer in the United States, and Bishop G. Ashton Oldham. After

food and wine had been consumed in heavy volume, Bonnet said
he would answer questions "off the record."

Theodore Dreiser got in his question first. "Mr. Minister," he
began in a big booming midwestern drawl, "I have a question. Would
you say that France is a democracy?" Bonnet would much rather
have been asked about a secret treaty or whether he got bribes.

"Eh, ah, *sûrement*," Bonnet muttered, "of course, eh, ha, ha."

"Mr. Minister," Dreiser kept on, and the answer obviously did
not matter to him, "would you say that America is a democracy
and could you prove it in a court of law?"

General laughter made a reply unnecessary. Dreiser now subsided
into a heavy silence, while Werth and Edgar, champion appease-
ment-haters, got after Bonnet. Mowrer made this point: France was
not helping the democracies in Spain and Czechoslovakia. There was
strong sentiment in America for both countries. The fall of those
two countries would reinforce American isolationism, and then,
perhaps, when France needed help the United States would adopt
the same attitude as Mr. Bonnet now does towards European victims of Fascist attacks and threats.

Bonnet replied that he was for peace. (But everyone is for peace.
Every scoundrel is. Hitler is.) The United States talked, he said
politely, but did nothing. He cited the recent Brussels conference
on the Far East as an example. Washington wanted the powers to
assume a firm attitude towards Japan. "But we say to your State
Department," Monsieur Bonnet said, " 'Will you help us if we get
in trouble with Japan? Will you help us if Japan seizes the island
of Hainan?' Your State Department says, 'No, pardon me.' " Then
he spun beautiful phrases about his eternal admiration and friendship
for the "great American people." Sadly enough, the minister won
that little bout. America did not yet practice the policy of collective
security by aiding countries which resisted Fascist aggression. I
remarked, "You could win America for collective security by practicing it yourself."

"We try, we try," Bonnet said. "It is *très difficile, n'est-ce pas?*
Ha, ha."

32. Ebro: River of Blood

FOR the Spanish heart, or for the pro-Spanish heart, there was not much balm in London or Paris. But on the Ebro River which marks off Catalonia from the rest of Spain, the Loyalist army had struck hard at Franco. If the Republicans held firm for a while longer perhaps the world would open its eyes and see the danger that lurked for Europe in a Fascist victory over Iberia. On this hope, all Loyalist resistance was predicated; alone, the Republic could never win. Would the blood of Spain wash away the blindness of the West?

At two o'clock, early on the morning of July 25—while Bonnet slept and the Paris Peace Congress rested from its talk—Spanish government units started crossing the Ebro in the face of an entrenched enemy. For two months everything had been meticulously prepared. During the night, two pontoon bridges were silently slung above one hundred and fifty yards of rushing river. The first soldiers ran over them at full gallop. They met opposition. Soldiers waiting on the Loyalist side listened to the firing but were unable to cross because of the heavy traffic on the narrow bridges. They listened and could not stand it. A large number of men, especially Americans in the International Brigade, waded in. They propelled themselves forward along the pontoons and in places swam with their thickly-oiled rifles above their necks.

The Loyalist bank was low, the rebel shore steep and protected by sand bags and barbed wire. But normally the Spanish War was a trade-union war. The armies took two hours off for lunch, quit at five P.M. and slept tightly all night. If you attacked during off-hours, you won the initial advantage of surprise.

The Loyalists attacked with so much passion that the rebels quickly abandoned their positions and surrendered or fled. The official Franco bulletin charged that the military feat was not as great as it sounded because disloyal peasants—disloyal to Franco—helped to dislodge the Fascist forces. Stupid of Franco to admit this.

It was a considerable victory and aroused great enthusiasm among the Republicans. In six days the offensive reached its maximum expansion with the occupation of 250 square miles of territory. In those six days, the Loyalists lost only 66 dead and 4,965 wounded, most of them light cases. The Loyalists, on the other hand, took 5,000 prisoners and inflicted 6,000 casualties on the enemy.

Then the Fascist aviation arrived in force. When I saw Prime Minister Negrin in Barcelona in the first week of August, he told me the government had fewer than 400 airplanes, most of them much-used. Franco had 500 Italian airplanes and 300 German, Negrin estimated. Franco concentrated this gigantic armada on the narrow Ebro front. After the initial surprise, he wheeled his artillery into position. He vowed to retake the lost Ebro ground.

On August 7, I went to the Ebro front in a conspicuously new Ford auto belonging to Joe North of *New Masses*. With us were a French writer and a British journalist. We reached the river at midnight and waited our turn to cross. Tanks and trucks had dug deep ruts in the road. Bombs from Fascist airplanes made deep craters in it. The ruts and craters multiplied as we approached the river bank. Men in shorts repaired the road during the night. Feverish work also proceeded at the water edge where the bridge ended. The Loyalists had built three bridges across the Ebro, two on pontoons, one on trestles. They also had put up a sham bridge which looked like a bridge from above but wasn't. The Fascist bombers wasted their ammunition trying to hit it. They dropped tons of bombs on the river in an effort to destroy the bridges. The river bank and the river beaches were pocked with deep bomb holes which sometimes filled with water. The engineers labored up to the waist in the river fastening new tow-ropes and replacing broken pontoons. The work proceeded in complete darkness lest a light attract hostile bombers.

Finally, our Ford rattled on to the bridge. The chauffeur told us to watch through the windows on either side. There were not more than three inches between the tires and the edges of the bridge. The bridge consisted of isolated, loosely fastened planks like the metal strips of a xylophone, and as the car rolled forward it struck a note on each plank, the same note again and again and again until, steering clear of craters, and with a helping push from a few strong arms, it climbed up on the opposite bank.

We took the road to Corbera, a town at the front. The night was black and quiet. Occasionally, we veered around a truck covered with huge tarpaulin—probably a gun going up to the line. After a few miles, the road became more populated with vehicles and men. New battalions were moving to the front. The men walked without much order. Officers shouted "Keep together." The sand on the hard road crunched under their feet. Each time our driver flashed on a dim light to avoid hitting someone, the soldiers yelled, "*Apagar la luz.*" They did not want to be discovered by bombers that might be hovering above for just such prey. Nearer the front, we encountered tired men coming out of the line. The road became thick with soldiers and trucks. We heard foreign languages too. We stopped the car, called a soldier, gave him a cigarette, and said, "American?" No, he was a Greek, had enlisted in Athens, but the Americans were right behind. They were coming out of the line too tonight, being relieved by a Spanish brigade.

Soon we heard New Yorkese and Chicagoese in the Spanish blackout. We picked up Milt Wolf, the captain of the Americans. His men had been in battle since the first day of the offensive. Thirteen days of constant combat without undressing, without bathing, sleeping on rocks and hard ground under an unending rain of shells! Milt asked us to look him up later that morning. He said the Americans would be held in reserve somewhere in an olive grove further down the road.

We drove on. Spanish units were moving into the line; others were coming out. As we proceeded, the thud of cannon shells became more pronounced. Each thud answered itself—thud, thud. Pause. Then a deeper thud-thud; Franco's guns were replying. And always the crunch of boots on the hard road. Trucks and speeding cars threw up clouds of dust. I felt the grit far down in my throat. Suddenly I heard a baby crying. A baby in the war? We were at a crossroads where the highway forked to Corbera and Flix. I got out of the car. A tall, thin Spanish woman stood against a post holding a child of about two. Near by, a boy of four or five sat on a milestone.

She had left Barcelona in 1937 and gone to the Corbera region where her family lived in a village. She would eat better there. Her husband was in the Loyalist army. She had been caught by the fighting and she wanted to get a lift to Barcelona. Couldn't I help? We were going the other way. I went back to the car to fetch a jar of hard candy which I had brought in from Paris to tide over hungry hours between meals. She wanted no candy. She wanted to get into a truck and go home to Barcelona. Because the little boy saw his mother refuse the candy he would take none. He relented when I put one into my mouth. I talked to the soldier who regulated traffic in the darkness at the crossroads. He said he was looking out for the family and would try to find place for them in a lorry.

It was now about two-thirty in the morning and we were all pretty tired. The driver decided to find the Anglo-American cook-house. It was located on a side lane. A sentry recognized our driver and Joe North, and brought out some blankets. Joe North, the Frenchman, and the Englishman lay down on the ground to sleep. The driver slept at his wheel—that was instructions. I slept in the back seat of the car.

I awoke several hours later when day broke. A Franco recon-naissance plane circled high overhead. A bird sang in a near-by tree. A tall Spanish cook killed a lamb and drained the blood into a big pan. I washed my teeth with some coffee and my face with oily water.

Men started to appear. They had slept in personal air-raid shelters hollowed out in the brown earthen bank overlooking the road. They put on their shoes and were dressed. The cookhouse had been bombed the week before and three men killed.

Our Frenchman wished to find Modesto, the officer in command of the whole Loyalist army on the Ebro. But Joe North preferred to talk to the Americans and get material for a cable to the New York *Daily Worker*. They had argued far into the night about this, and now they resumed the argument. I hoped we would do both. I suggested we locate Modesto first.

We found him at breakfast in staff headquarters in a yellow house which stood alone on a hill. He ordered out more ham and sherry—all captured from Franco's retreating hosts. We had a tremendous meal and more than an hour of talk. Modesto loved to talk and curse. He was a handsome, jovial little fellow in his thirties, a woodworker who had been a corporal in Spain's pre-war Foreign Legion of toughs. Now he belonged to the Communist party; he knew a few words of Russian. At the table sat Maximov and two Soviet aides. Maximov was a general in the Russian Red Army and had succeeded Grigorovitch as highest Soviet military adviser in Loyalist Spain. We discussed politics over the meal and when it was over he told me about the war situation. I asked whether the Republican victory on the Ebro could be regarded as significant by purely military stand-ards. "Decidedly," he said. To cross such a river and to hold a newly seized bridgehead on the other side against overwhelming odds in the air was a real achievement. Loyalist supplies all came from across the Ebro and that complicated the conduct of the operation. The real heroes were the engineers who maintained the bridges intact. Several times, he told me, the bridges had been destroyed. The engineers had a pact: the moment a bridge was hit, whether it was day or night, whether the raid had ended or not, they immediately started rebuilding it, for if the Republican army in the newly conquered zone were cut off for even a day its very existence might be jeopardized. Maximov said the Loyalists were short of cannon and anti-aircraft guns. But the soldiers had learned to lie still under bombs. They were becoming excellent fighters. Bombs rarely killed, he explained. Their worst effect is on the nerves.

I asked him whether the Loyalists could hold the new territory on the Ebro. He replied, "No military man would answer such a question. It all depends on how much Franco is ready to pay to get it back and how much we are ready to pay to keep it."

He added that Franco's artillery fire was sometimes as heavy as in major World War battles. Apparently, Franco feared the effect which an unretrieved defeat might have on his civilian and army morale and on the attitude of the Western Powers. If his chances of victory became dimmed, the appeasers in London and Paris would lose influence and the Left would gain influence. To encourage the appeasers Hitler and Mussolini threw more arms to Franco.

It was August, 1938, a month before Munich, a month before the vivisection of Czechoslovakia. A setback for Fascism on the Ebro would inspire resistance to Fascism elsewhere. Fascism always made capital out of its invincibility. No use trying to stop us; we are the future, Hitler and Mussolini asserted. Better to come to an understanding with us, they told Chamberlain and Daladier. We always win. It is fate. It is our strength. Give us what we ask or else . . .

The crunch of bombs, the thud of shells, and the blood that ran into the Ebro made policy on the Thames and the Seine, on the Spree and the Moldau, perhaps even on the Potomac.

Loyalist victories reinforced the political position of Englishmen and Frenchmen who wanted the Loyalists to gain victories. Often as I listened to Questions and debates in the House of Commons it seemed to me as though some Conservatives took a mischievous delight in the sinking of British ships in Spanish waters.

For the Liberals and Laborites protested such sinkings and tried to prod the unwilling Chamberlain into demanding compensation or taking steps for safety on the seas. Anything that discomfited the Opposition or demonstrated its impotence gave pleasure to many supporters of Neville Chamberlain. They were on Franco's side because their political opponents in England were on Negrin's side. They were pro-Franco for other reasons too. But Franco gains and Loyalist defeats were sticks with which to beat the anti-Fascists of Britain.

The issue of Spain divided England. It divided France. The fear of a Left triumph in Spain made many Englishmen and Frenchmen more pro-Hitler and more pro-Mussolini. Spain split the democracies. Democratic disunity was one of the goals of Italo-German intervention in Spain. Weren't Hitler and Mussolini fighting Communism and Russia in Spain? Wasn't that a worthy aim? Shouldn't anti-Communists everywhere help? Shouldn't anti-Communists support Hitler and Mussolini in other things too? The appeasers fell for this bunk. Then Hitler thumbed his nose at them by signing a pact with Communism and Russia.

The Ebro was the Marne of peace.

We went from Modesto's headquarters to seek the Americans. Modesto had told us it was a quiet day in the air. But we had to get out several times and lie on the ground while rebel planes hovered overhead. We found the Americans in an olive grove. Many were still asleep. They slept in their clothes, and the sun was now high, and when they got up there was nothing to eat or drink, not even water, and one could see them massaging the insides of their mouths with their tongues. I distributed American cigarettes. I always brought in a few cartons from France.

These men had been in the front line for a fortnight. One would expect them to talk first of all about women and what they would do if they could get to Barcelona. "Tell us about Czechoslovakia," was their greeting to me. They asked Joe North about strikes in America. They were tired, and everyone of them yearned to return to America. But they knew they would be back in the front in a few days. This was only a brief respite. While we sat on the ground and talked, airplanes came over. The men lay down on their backs and watched. Others started digging in. They told us about men who had been killed and wounded. They talked about Jim Lardner.

I had met Jim Lardner in Paris. He was the twenty-three-year-old son of Ring Lardner. He worked for the *Herald Tribune*. He went to Barcelona to report on the war. It gripped him as it did everybody. I watched him sitting in the lobby of the Hotel Majestic. For days he sat and didn't talk. Then friends and journalistic colleagues started talking to him. For he had decided to join the International Brigade. Most persons tried to dissuade him. Even soldiers of the Brigade told him to write about them instead of shooting with them. He listened. Then he went around the corner and enlisted. He was wounded in battle, lay in the hospital, recuperated, and returned to the front. There he was killed. He was the essence of America. He looked, thought, and wrote American. The presence of Americans in the Loyalist army stirred the American in him; they were fighting for bleeding, wounded Spain. They were also fighting for the United States. America was paying back Europe for the Lafayettes, the von Steubens, the Kosciuskos. He paid an American debt. Spain owes him a debt. America owes him a debt.

I sat under an olive tree and listened to Alvah Bessie. I had known him in New York where he worked on the *Brooklyn Daily Eagle*. He had been in the Ebro offensive from the beginning, and kept a diary. He read us some pages. They later served as material for his book on the Spanish War, *Men in Battle*.

The sun waxed hot. Men stripped and searched for lice in the seams of their clothes. A Spanish barber made his appearance and started cutting hair. Johnny Gates, chief commissar, promised water soon, and even food. Some fellows were writing letters home. Others daydreamed and did nothing: life-long friends from Boston or Los Angeles had been killed at their sides. "He might have been here if that damned Fascist had aimed different," one said to me when I crouched and asked what he was thinking about. "Or I might be dead," he added with a philosophical and satisfied wave of the head.

Human beings grow accustomed to death if they see enough of it. The peasant dreads death less than the cultured urbanite because he encounters it oftener in the animal world. The more primitive the man the less his fear of death. The Moors were the best soldiers in Spain because they were so sure of the hereafter, I suppose. Russian tank drivers used to tell me how astonished they were at the bravery of the Moors. The treads of their tanks, they said, were sometimes filled with ground bits of human flesh; the Moors had stood still and fought till the iron caterpillar monsters rode over them.

The Moors fought well because of a something in their blood, tradition and faith. The Americans and the other Internationals fought well because of a belief in peace, decency, and the human rights of common people. As I looked at the Americans lying there among olive trees as old, gnarled, and twisted as those I had seen in Gethsemane, I thought of my own role in the Brigade. I had obtained considerable sums of money for the transportation of volunteers to Spain. At one public meeting in the Hippodrome in New York I had urged men to enlist. Some of those were probably dead now. I had helped to send demobilized and wounded Americans back to the United States at the expense of the Spanish Republic and to get them spending money on board ship and a $25 bonus per man to tide over the difficult period immediately after landing in America. It was a responsibility to bring men out of their homes into a battlefield, and on the Ebro that day my feelings of pride were mixed with sorrow.

Joe North, the boss of the Ford auto, now insisted on returning to Barcelona, and the Frenchman, Englishman, and I concurred. The morning was gone. We pointed the car to the river. Occasionally, the chauffeur reminded us to crane our necks out of the windows to watch for airplanes. Usually, one was guided by the trucks. If a truck ahead of you stopped with a jerk and its occupants dashed out into the fields you knew they had sighted a plane. But the road was empty and we had to keep a lookout ourselves. As we approached a spot where a side road intersected our main highway I noticed that a soldier and a boy who had been sitting on a culvert quickly jumped up and ran. I shouted to the driver and he turned off his motor. The moment he did so we heard a much bigger and louder motor zooming above us. We threw open the doors and bolted, hoping to get to the open field, for a road is dangerous because it is so clearly visible from the air and offers no protection. But we could not get as far as the field. The plane had opened up its machine guns and was strafing us. I had been under bombs many times, but this was the first time I had been strafed and it was pretty awful. We all lay in the stinking ditch by the side of the road. I thought to myself, "I don't want to be crippled or blinded. It's better to die." The plane was laying down a field of fire around us. We were his lone target. I hunched my back, put my head as close as possible to the stench, covered my eyes with one hand and the top of my head with the other. How long did it last? Probably not more than two minutes. But they can be very long. He closed his guns. We looked up. A bomb separated itself from the fuselage of the plane and fell with a whining whistle. It hit somewhere near. But that was all. No explosion. Another bomb dropped from the plane. "He must be down to about one thousand feet," Joe said. The bomb whistled, struck earth. Silence. A third bomb and a fourth bomb. He resumed altitude and made off. Two of us ran into the field. But he was through with us. He had dropped four duds. We decided he must have been an Italian. We found all four bombs. One had fallen on the side road about twenty yards from where we lay. The other three had fallen in the field near the road. If one had exploded it would have killed or maimed us all. One bomb had imbedded itself in the ground and was standing with its point upward. A bomb is so constructed that it should strike point-first. All the bombs were defective. They were hundred pounders and their shells were rusty.

After an experience like that you have a desire to get as far from the scene as possible. But when we reached a small town on the Ebro, a sentry told us the bridge had just been wrecked by bombs and we would have to retrace our steps and go by way of Flix. The sentry was covered with white powdery dust from the buildings that had been hit in the bombing. He was the only living soul to be seen. The entire town had been deserted.

The detour via Flix meant about two hours' more travel, and our chauffeur did not have enough gasoline for the extra mileage. To obtain gasoline we needed a slip from the military authorities and so we drove back to Modesto's staff house and reached it just in time for a powerful lunch such as one never got in Barcelona. The Russians had gone to the river to see the effects of the bridge bombing, but Modesto was there, in fine shape and mood.

Near the gasoline depot there was a temporary prison, and the official in charge of the depot invited us to interview two recently captured Germans. They were surly and refused to talk. When we got back to the car at the gasoline station, the air throbbed with planes. We tried to count. We lost count because they were so high—three miles, we estimated for some—and because they were racing fast in all directions across the sky. Apparently, a tremendous squadron of Fascist bombers, protected by fighters, was attempting to bomb the bridges, and a considerable number of Loyalist fighters was trying to stop them. There must have been at least fifty all told. Twos or threes from each side separated from the main bodies, found corners in the air for themselves and circled and circled looking for a chance to attack. Sometimes two would head towards one another, pass one another, corkscrew to earth and then straighten out with their machine guns blazing at one another. You never knew which was rebel and which Republican. Meanwhile the bombers "laid their eggs." Where? Had they demolished another bridge?

The air felt as though it consisted of huge solid chunks which pounded each other and sent solid air-waves against one's ears. The planes moved so fast that the sky seemed full of them. I had been caught behind a tree when the whole thing started. A woman in a little wooden shack called to me. Several soldiers had taken refuge there too, but the woman was anxious about an ancient mother who kept going upstairs and coming downstairs and looking out and retiring into the shack. I decided to go back to the tree. Near by lay two old rubber automobile tires. I sat down and leaned them against me. That was all the protection I could find. On this occasion I timed the raid. It lasted twenty-three minutes. Then the planes disappeared.

We drove fast to Flix hoping the bridge was intact. Flix had been bombed often. We stopped in one house overlooking the high bank of the river. A mother and two children lived in it. The mother said she had stayed because the food was more plentiful than in the big cities. Here the soldiers fed her. And the air-raid shelter, dug by the Fascists into the solid rock of a hill, was the best I ever saw in Spain. Rats ran around in the streets; the raids had broken up their life.

The bridge was intact. All traffic had been diverted to it and we had to wait. Two little specks appeared in the air. Were they coming to bomb the bridge? No, Loyalist patrol fighters. Flix was the best bridge; built on supports in the river bed. Our car dashed across. The beach and the shores were continuous bomb craters. Having got over, we again had to jump out of the Ford when bombers appeared, but it was now beginning to grow dark and the raiding ceased. The bombing crews were going home for dinner. We passed a huge cave with a wide mouth that had been converted into a hospital. White nurses moved about inside. It afforded perfect protection against raids. Only shrapnel from a chance bomb that fell right at the entrance could do any damage. We did not stop because it was late. We detoured at Falset which had just been raided. The chauffeur was tired and sleepy. I swayed in the front seat and slept and woke and slept. The chauffeur asked me to talk to him lest he fall asleep at the wheel. We arrived at the Majestic Hotel after two in the morning.

That day I lunched with Dr. Negrin at his villa on the outskirts of Barcelona. I told him about our experience with the four dud bombs. He said, "Don't write about that now. The Fascists might be able to trace the bombs." Workingmen in factories in Italy, he said, are deliberately spoiling bombs. "We have opened dud bombs made for Franco in Portugal in which the workingmen inserted notes saying, 'Friend, this bomb won't hurt you.'"

Every day, about an hour before dinner, the hotel lobby began to fill, and everybody sat waiting eagerly for the restaurant to start serving dinner. As you took your place at the table, the headwaiter, in evening dress, approached and bowed, greeted you amiably and handed you the menu card. It was made of heavy glazed paper with embossing in gold, and on it the names of the dishes were typed. One specimen I kept offers: Potage Garbour, Medaillon Grillé, artichauts Farçies Provençale, and noissetes. There was no choice, but the waiter handed you the card anyway and you always said, "I'll take all of it." Foreigners supplemented this shrunken fare with imported delicacies. This applied especially to Herbert L. Matthews, tall, thin, silent, efficient, hard-working, much-eating correspondent of the *New York Times*, the best journalist in Spain. We usually sat four or five or even eight at a table and pooled our commissaries. Then we had coffee in the lobby. The lights were weak and sometimes they went out completely. It was difficult to read. After 10 P.M. the electric current ceased altogether. The regular correspondents then drove off to the press department to get the war bulletin and phone the day's news to Paris.

The Loyalist army was holding the rebels on the Valencia front. Sagunto, important steel center, had been saved from Fascist capture. The army also clutched to its Ebro gains. The Republic gave an impression of calm and strength. The soldiers, the women, the officials voiced two slogans: our aims are just, and the world is unjust to us.

Catalonia was tired. Mercifully, Barcelona experienced only six air raids during the fortnight I spent there. Citizens had grown accustomed to them. When the sirens blew people walked to the shelters or continued on their business. Once I was caught in a tropical downpour of rain. The Spaniards ran faster than when bombs fell.

I bought an imported French dress for Markoosha who was in Moscow and sent it to her through Anna Louise Strong. (I usually bought Markoosha's clothes, even evening dresses and shoes, in Paris or London or New York and brought them to her when she could not leave Russia.) Normal life fought for itself. Despite the sharp shortage of soap, women were fragrantly clean and richly made-up. Jewelry and paintings could still be had in the stores. On the streets, couples smiled and laughed. The cafés were jammed although they served no coffee, no food, and only a few cheap, watery alcoholic drinks. Photographers did a rushing trade. Two foreign lovers who lived in the Majestic bought bunches of flowers for one another on the much-bombed Rambla de Flores. Cinemas operated until dark. Symphonic orchestras gave concerts. The newspapers printed articles on economic conditions in foreign countries and odes by old poets and warrior poets, odes to a sunset, odes to a fair maiden. Beautifully printed books appeared in Barcelona. Along the road back to the frontier, government employees pruned the fat sycamore trees. The customs official had washed his white gloves.

I remained in Paris three days. Paris was quiet in August and I wanted some relaxation. So I flew down to Cannes on the French Mediterranean Riviera. Every day I played tennis with an instructor for two hours in the broiling sun, ate lunch on the way home, took a shower, and then fell asleep. When I awoke at about three I went to the beach, rented a *pedalo*, which is a sort of skiff or canoe equipped with foot paddles, and went out several miles to sea. After about an hour of this strenuous exercise, I swam, came home for a shower, slept for thirty minutes, went out to dinner, roller-skated all evening, came home for my third shower, and slept soundly through the night. Several times friends at San Ary, a near-by resort on the Riviera, phoned and asked me to visit them. Ellen Wilkinson, Otto Katz, and Friedrich Wolf were there and they could not understand why I wouldn't come over. For me a vacation is a vacation from people. I wanted to be alone, and throughout the stay I never talked to anybody except waiters, my tennis teacher, and the hotel personnel.

My tennis instructor told me this one: Borotra, the French tennis ace, played as Swedish King Gustav's doubles partner. "More to the left, Your Majesty, more to the left," Borotra instructed. "Yes, I know, I know," King Gustav commented. "That's what my Socialist ministers always say to me."

One afternoon I was awakened by a phone call. My room had no phone and I went out into the corridor. It was a call from London. But I told the London operator it wasn't for me; the person wanted had a three-pronged name which I didn't hear very distinctly, but the first part was Leon and not Louis. A few minutes later I was again summoned to the phone. The operator said it was for me. Was I Fischer? The call was for Leon Trotzky Fischer, and at the London end was Vincent Sheean who just wanted to have some fun.

I spent thirteen happy days at Cannes. But I read newspapers, and I began to feel that something was brewing in Europe. I think a correspondent develops a special sense for political climate. His bones feel coming crises and storms—just as a rheumatic person may have a premonition of rain. I sensed approaching bad weather, and reluctantly returned to Paris. In a few days, the prelude to Munich commenced. Storm over Prague. Tempest over Czechoslovakia. Cyclone in Germany. Hitler over Europe. Chamberlain making speeches.

33. *The Fall of France*

BY an infamous agreement dated Munich, September 29, 1938, Chamberlain and Daladier gave the Sudetenland to Hitler and thus killed a free nation, Czechoslovakia. On the thirtieth, Mr. Chamberlain, pink and self-satisfied, flew back to England. When he alighted at the Croydon airdrome he was wreathed in smiles which reflected real happiness. He waved a scrap of paper signed by Hitler and himself and exclaimed, "I believe it is peace for our time." "Our time" lasted exactly eleven months.

The appeasers would like to make it appear that at Munich the Anglo-French yielded to superior force. They say: Hitler threatened war if he did not get the Sudetenland; France and England could not fight because they were unprepared. This is a dishonest argument because it is only partially true and is largely untrue.

The British and French governments actively assisted in bringing about Munich. They did so long before the Czechoslovak crisis arose.

The excuse of inferiority was also employed at the time of Abyssinia. Could England have gone to war on account of Abyssinia, the appeasers asked. The answer is Yes. That would have been the best time for it. Germany was not yet rearmed. In January, 1935, Goering said Germany had no air force. War in 1935 might have saved Europe from a deadlier war in 1939. England and France were ten times stronger than Italy in 1935. England alone was stronger. Mussolini would probably have desisted if the British had shown any intention of resisting him. It was not that the British and French could not stop Italy. They did not wish to. Indeed, Pierre Laval told Mussolini to take Abyssinia in January, 1935, ten months before the invasion of Abyssinia commenced, and the British, who knew all along about preparations for the conquest, made no effort to interfere.

The same thing happened in regard to Czechoslovakia. In November, 1937, Lord Halifax, who was the King's "Master of Foxhounds," went to Berlin to see a hunting exhibition. He also visited

553

Hitler at Berchtesgaden and indicated clearly to him that England had no interests in the Danube area. That made it open season for Hitler in Austria and Czechoslovakia. Hitler commenced to prepare. Yet he hesitated. He was merely beginning his career as international bandit and he proceeded cautiously. He wanted to be quite sure there would be no opposition. So he told the British and French what he proposed to do. He announced, on February 20, 1938, that he regarded himself the guardian of the ten million Germans of Austria and Czechoslovakia.

How did Chamberlain react? Did he warn Hitler to keep hands off? No. He said in the House of Commons two days later, "If I am right, and I am confident I am, in saying that the League as constituted today is unable to provide collective security for anybody, then I say we must not try to delude ourselves, and still more, we must not try to delude weak nations into thinking that they will be protected against aggression and acting accordingly when we know that nothing of the kind can be expected."

This was Chamberlain's reply to Hitler. Go ahead, Mr. Hitler, he was saying, take those ten million Germans in Austria and Czechoslovakia. We will not do a thing about it. Mr. Chamberlain made this statement in reply to Anthony Eden who, the day before, had resigned as Foreign Minister on account of sharp differences of opinion with Chamberlain about Spain, Italy, and the League of Nations. Eden would have tried to prevent the rape of Austria and Czechoslovakia.

Three weeks later, Hitler, not wishing to disappoint Chamberlain, annexed his "beloved" Austria.

To any politically literate person this signified that Czechoslovakia was in peril. Hitler had taken seven of the ten million Germans. The other three million lived in the Sudetenland. Czechoslovakia's frontier with Austria had been unfortified. Now, therefore, it was more exposed to German attack.

Accordingly, the Soviet government on March 18, five days after the annexation of Austria, proposed a conference of the major powers to consider the new situation. The British and French governments rejected the proposal; Chamberlain announced in the House of Commons that Marshal Goering had assured the Czechs no harm would be done to them. And Goering, Sir Nevile Henderson, British Ambassador in Germany, assured London, was an honorable man. Not at all like that maniac Hitler. "I had a real personal liking for him," wrote Henderson of Goering. So everything was all right.

England and France neither protested against the annexation of Austria nor admonished Hitler for wiping out an independent state and member of the League of Nations, nor warned him against repeating the stunt. This was encouragement enough for Hitler. But not enough for Chamberlain. He was lavish in his gifts to Mussolini and Hitler.

Lady Nancy Astor gave a party at her house in May, 1938, so that Prime Minister Chamberlain might get acquainted with the American correspondents in London and they with him. They asked him questions. One journalist "spilled" the story. It was Joseph Driscoll of the *New York Herald Tribune*, and when Chamberlain was asked in the House of Commons about Driscoll's dispatch he did not deny it. According to Driscoll, the correspondents asked Chamberlain whether he thought France and Russia would fight for the Czechs. Chamberlain replied that they would not fight for the Czechs because they had no geographical contact with Czechoslovakia. "Besides," Chamberlain added, "the Russians have shot their best generals." But Russia could send planes. Ah, Chamberlain replied, the Czechs lack sufficient airfields. "Nothing seems clearer," Joseph Driscoll summarized, "than that the British do not expect to fight for Czechoslovakia and do not anticipate that Russia or France will either. That being so, the Czechs must accede to the German demands, if reasonable." With the excellent German espionage service in London every word Chamberlain uttered at Lady Astor's was very likely known to Hitler the same day.

In the third week of May, the German army displayed considerable activity. These movements, Berlin explained, were "routine." "But," comments Hamilton Fish Armstrong in his succinct, brilliant and useful little book, *When There Is No Peace*, "Beneš had learnt something from watching the fate of Austria after 'routine' movements of German troops. . . ." President Beneš therefore ordered the full mobilization of the Czechoslovak army. The Russians advised him to do this.

The "routine" movements remained routine. Hitler for once drew in his horns.

Pierre Cot, the former French Minister of Air, tells me that between this May episode and the Munich crisis in September, the

Soviet government delivered 300 military planes to Czechoslovakia. Mr. Cot had this information from high Czech authorities.

The British and the French, on the other hand, continued to undermine the Czechs' confidence and bolster up Hitler's. Officially, the French said they would support Czechoslovakia. Actually, Daladier, and especially Georges Bonnet, who became Foreign Minister of France just about this time—April 10—the wrong time—urged Prague to yield. Hitler was making use of a gigantic Trojan Horse he had in Czechoslovakia, the Nazi party of the Sudeten Germans led by Konrad Henlein. The Sudeten Germans had had their grievances in the past as every national minority may have. But their complaints had been neither loud nor insistent until the annexation of Austria when, under the lashing of Hitler's whip, the Sudeten Fascists commenced making impossible demands. Beneš was conciliatory. But whenever he accepted a demand, Konrad Henlein asked for more. In August, the British government delegated Lord Runciman to Prague as intermediary between the Czech government and the Sudeten. He never once sought to moderate the pressure of Hitler or Henlein on Prague. He conceived his task as squeezing more concessions from Czechoslovakia.

Frederick T. Birchall wired the *New York Times* on August 11, "In the inner circles of the democratic governments, despite French pledges and British sympathy, the preservation of Czechoslovakia as an independent state has already been virtually given up." High British and French officials told this, "off the record," to numerous visitors, and German ears were wide open in London and Paris.

Meanwhile, Hitler accelerated the building of the fortifications of the Western Wall facing France. From all over Germany, young men conscripted into labor battalions were rushed down to do this job. Hitler later said they numbered 462,000. Hitler examined the new forts on August 28, and appeared demonstratively at Kehl, opposite the Maginot Line. Throughout Germany, the army engaged in extensive maneuvers.

Was Hitler staging a gigantic bluff or did he intend to fight?

I believed throughout that Hitler knew England and France would not go to war on behalf of Czechoslovakia. A fortnight after Munich I wrote defending the thesis that Germany had never expected to wage war with the Western Powers over Czechoslovakia. In December, 1938, I wrote again on the subject, quoting these words from Winston Churchill in the *London Daily Telegraph* of December 1, 1938: "It is now known that during the late crisis Herr Hitler concentrated three-quarters of his armies against Czechoslovakia, and left on the French frontier, to guard his uncompleted defenses, a force far inferior to the French army. . . . Either Herr Hitler must be a desperate gambler or he must have been pretty sure that he would be let alone to work his will on the Czech republic." Hitler was more than pretty sure. He was sure.

Hitler discounted every Anglo-French gesture of support to Beneš because he knew what went on behind the scenes. I was at the Blackpool British Trade Union Congress in the first days of September. The trade unions wanted the government to stand fast for Spain and Czechoslovakia. Resolutions to that effect were adopted and submitted to 10 Downing Street. But Attlee, Citrine, and others at the Congress realized that Chamberlain would yield. For on September 7, an editorial in the *London Times* urged the Czechs to give up the Sudetenland to Hitler. It was later denied that this editorial represented the view of the British government. Every serious person in England, Germany, France, and Czechoslovakia believed that it did. Munich proved that it did. The denial confirmed the belief.

However, powerful groups and persons in the western countries opposed the Chamberlain policy of war-making appeasement. Chamberlain walked the straight and narrow path to Munich. But even Halifax and Daladier had their doubts. Bonnet never. Hitler's speeches, tours, maneuvers, blusterings were designed to break down the opposition to Chamberlain and Bonnet and to break the heart of the Czechs.

In France, as in England, the spokesmen of labor insisted on help to Czechoslovakia. After Munich, Jouhaux, the leader of the French trade unions—the C.G.T.—revealed in a published speech that he had visited Premier Daladier during the tense days before the surrender. Jouhaux reminded Daladier that France had an alliance with the Czechs and that it had been concluded for just such cases as this. "Yes," replied Daladier, "we are bound by treaties, but treaties can be interpreted."

"France," Jouhaux objected, "does not interpret her signature." The Left was more patriotic than the Right.

"Listen," Daladier said finally, "I will read you a report by General Gamelin." Gamelin was then French chief of staff. The Premier opened a drawer in his desk and drew out a thick document. He read the first page to Jouhaux. It outlined the difficulties created for France by the loss of the Saar, the remilitarization of the Rhineland, and the annexation of Austria by Germany.

"But read on," Jouhaux demanded. "What does Gamelin recommend?"

"Despite these difficulties," Daladier read, "it is necessary to intervene."

That was the view of the French army staff. Reserves had been called up and the Maginot Line was fully manned. It was the view of Georges Mandel, Minister of Colonies, Paul Reynaud, Minister of Finance, César Campinchi, Minister of the Navy, Champetier de Ribes, Minister of Pensions, and others in the government, outside the government, in the press, in the public.

France was divided on the question of Czechoslovakia. So was England. So, indeed, was Czechoslovakia itself. And so was Germany. I think this is the essential clue to the Munich crisis. Even individuals, sometimes key individuals in politics, were divided within themselves counseling resistance in the evening and surrender the next morning, or vice versa.

Hitler's purpose, Chamberlain's purpose, Bonnet's purpose during the pre-Munich crisis was to bring the waverers off the fence into the surrender camp and to frighten the resisters into passivity or flight. Towards this end it became necessary to convince British and French citizens that Czechoslovakia was not so important, that Germany was extremely powerful, that England and France were very weak, and that Russia, which advocated the defense of the Czechs, did not mean it. Hitler likewise faced opposition at home. Propaganda Minister Goebbels said so in a speech on October 11, after the event. Hitler subsequently spoke in public of the generals who advised against action. *Das Schwarze Korps,* organ of the S.S. guards, on September 22, 1938, condemned as "short-sighted, unpolitical ostriches" those who asked, "Why now? Why the hurry? Did we not wait in the case of Austria until the fruit was ripe, and cannot the Sudeten Germans carry on a few years longer until Czechoslovakia falls apart of itself?" There must have been many "ostriches" for this magazine to take cognizance of them. "Don't be fools," the paper replied. "Much more is involved than the Sudetenland." A fatal blow was being struck at France. To win over his own public and army staff, Hitler had to intimate, without saying it, that there would be no war. The public and the army feared war for good reason, but Hitler was a much better psychologist than they; he had a woman's intuition about old men's weaknesses and he knew that by a last moment "twist," as Germans called it, the Nazis would win without shedding German blood. Munich was the last moment "twist" which saved Hitler from the exposure of his bluff. Flabby German democracy which had presented its own head to Hitler on a charger taught him to expect similar favors from flabby foreign democracies.

The game in France and England, therefore, was to make citizens quail before the imminence of air raids. The authorities ordered inadequate shelters dug in the mud of city parks. Paris extinguished its lights. But Berlin did not. Germany took no precautions. Hitler was "pretty sure" he would have no need of them.

Bullitt, the United States Ambassador in Paris, had revealed his concept of the European situation to many persons: it was easier for France to agree with Germany than with Soviet Russia. This was also the guiding thought of Bonnet and of all appeasers. To convert it into policy, reports of German might and Soviet collapse would help. Herein Colonel Charles A. Lindbergh played his little role.

Lindbergh had paid visits to Russia and Germany. In each country, he saw airplanes, airfields, and aviation factories. When he returned from these investigations, Americans in Paris and Americans in London introduced Lindbergh into the highest official circles. For instance, Ambassador Kennedy saw to it that he got to Neville Chamberlain. What Lindbergh said to the upper levels immediately filtered down to the lower strata. Lindbergh said the Soviet air force was poor and that Germany had ten thousand first-line planes and could turn out twenty thousand planes a year.

Obviously, the Russians did not tell Lindbergh that their aviation was bad. Obviously, the Germans did tell him that they had ten thousand planes. That is the only way he could have found out. In any country it is difficult to ascertain the strength of an air force. In a dictatorship it is particularly difficult except through persons authorized by the dictatorship to talk. No stranger can count ten thousand planes in different parts of Germany. Somebody has to tell him. Somebody told Lindbergh. He believed it and repeated it. But it was not true. It was, however, gleefully accepted by the appeasers in London and Paris because it bolstered their positions against the non-appeasers, against the fifty percent-appeasers and against the twenty-five percent-appeasers.

As the pre-Munich crisis advanced, the anti-appeasers lost ground. Before going to Geneva for a League of Nations session I went to see Georges Mandel in Paris. He was the arch-enemy of the appeasers. He is a swarthy man, crafty, energetic, and was much-feared and much-hated because he knew so much. He collected information, mostly unsavory, about French politicians. Rumor has it that he kept these files abroad.

I interviewed him in the Ministry of Colonies. Richard Mowrer, born in France, accompanied me. I asked Mandel what he thought would happen to Spain in the event of a European war. He replied quite frankly that Germans and Italians in Spain would inconvenience a France that had to bring African troops across the Mediterranean to the motherland. All anti-appeasers felt that by saving Czechoslovakia they would also save the Spanish Republic. That constituted an additional reason for the appeasers not to save Czechoslovakia. I gathered the impression that Mandel, usually buoyant and confident, was depressed. The tide was going against his kind.

On Sunday, September 11, French Foreign Minister Bonnet dropped down on Geneva for a few hours. He met Maxim Litvinov, Señor Alvarez del Vayo, the Loyalist Foreign Minister, Nicolas Petrescu-Comnen, the Rumanian Foreign Minister and Delegate to Geneva, and several journalists. Litvinov told Bonnet that Russia was ready to help Czechoslovakia with armed force. The Rumanian Foreign Minister told Bonnet that Rumania would give transit rights to the Soviet troops and weapons. The next day Bonnet told a meeting of the French Cabinet that Russia would not help and that Rumania opposed Soviet transit. Later when it became known that Bonnet had lied three Cabinet members threatened to resign—but did not. Hamilton Fish Armstrong states that a faction of the French Cabinet and the French General Staff was believed to favor "strong support of Czechoslovakia." He also declares that the Soviet and Rumanian Foreign Ministers are "believed to have reached an understanding with regard to the passage of Russian troops through Rumania in case of a general war." The *London Times* correspondent in Geneva telegraphed his paper that "in case of aggression against Czechoslovakia neither Soviet Russia nor Rumania would remain neutral." Nevertheless, Bonnet gave the Cabinet the exactly opposite impression because the prospect of Soviet aid might cause the entire appeasement structure to totter.

I had snatches of conversations with Litvinov in the League corridors during the sessions, but on September 16, he received me for a real talk. I inquired particularly after his opinion of what might happen to Spain if a European war broke out. He said he hoped the French would have enough sense to send immediate help to the Loyalists and that England would do likewise. We discussed this for a while, but then he brushed it all aside with one of his usual gruff explosions, "All this is not realistic," he said. "There will be no war now. They have sold out Czechoslovakia." He had a way of smiling which showed his bitter contempt. "I know the Chamberlains," his smile signified.

Nevertheless, I pursued the matter further and asked what Russia would do if war came over Czechoslovakia. He declared that the Poles would not grant transit to the Red Army because they feared social complications. They could not allow armed workers and peasants, Litvinov explained, to pass through Polish areas in which Polish and Ukrainian workers and peasants were oppressed. "It would take us a month," he estimated, "to force our way through Poland in order to help the Czechs. The Rumanians, not so hostile to the Czechs, will probably let us pass. But the Rumanian railroads are poor and our heavy tanks would have difficulty on their poor bridges and highways. But we could help in the air," he added.

"However," he smiled again, "this is also unrealistic. Don't you say in America, 'They have sold it down the river'? Well, they have already sold Czechoslovakia down the river." That was on September 16, 1938, fourteen days before the Munich sell-out was signed. Diplomats and journalists in Geneva changed their minds many times during those crazy pre-Munich days. One afternoon, depending on what Hitler had said in his last speech, some would see war as certain. That same evening, having seen the latest news, they might predict peace. Even Soviet ambassadors attending the League sessions reflected the gyrations of diplomacy and events. But Litvinov never shifted from his conviction that there would be a sell-out.

The sell-out was complete, abject and useless.

The sell-out operated on Hitler's well-known technique of "raising the ante." In the beginning of the crisis, Hitler's Henlein presented various plans for Sudeten autonomy within Czechoslovakia. On September 12, Hitler, addressing the annual Nazi congress at Nuremberg in the presence of several pro-Nazi British lords who told him England would not fight for the Czechs, went a step further. "I demand," he shouted, "that the oppression of three and a half million Germans in Czechoslovakia shall cease and be replaced by the free right of self-determinatoin. . . . It is up to the Czechoslovak government to discuss matters with the authorized representatives of the Sudeten Germans. . . ." The method proposed was still that of negotiations.

So Hitler raised the flag of self-determination. When Schuschnigg had proclaimed a plebiscite whereby Austria might self-determine if she wished to join the Reich, Hitler seized Austria to prevent the balloting. What was he doing in Spain if he believed in self-determination? Did he believe in self-determination when he annexed Czechs and Slovaks, the Poles, the Norwegians, Danes, Dutch, Belgians, and French? Yet people in France and England took Hitler at his word when he urged self-determination for the Sudeten. Hitler is the greatest liar in Christendom. When he needed the excuse he inveighed against Versailles in order to win the soft hearts of liberals and others who were ashamed of the peace treaty. When he needed it he proclaimed himself an anti-Communist so as to win the capitalist reactionaries in the democracies. When he needed it he appealed to the West as a "have-not." When he had more than Germany or any country had ever had he still wanted more. Still later he lied about the "new order in Europe," and again about "the revolution." Hitler has tanks, planes, guns, and words. He uses them all in the same way—to shoot down individuals who do not defend themselves.

So now Hitler asked self-determination for the Sudeten. Accordingly, Neville Chamberlain, aged sixty-nine, got into an airplane for the first time in his life and flew to see Hitler at Berchtesgaden. The leader of the mighty British empire bowed to Hitler who drew his conclusions. That day, for the first time, Hitler's Henlein announced, "We want to go home to the Reich."

Chamberlain took this message back to London. He would deliberate with his colleagues. Meanwhile, messages went from Berlin to the Sudetenland where the local Nazis forthwith intensified their riots and atrocities. Hitler also stirred up Poland and Hungary to make demands on Czechoslovakia. Frightened, London and Paris decided to capitulate. At 2.15 A.M. on the morning of September 21, the British and French Ministers in Prague routed Beneš out of bed and delivered an ultimatum to him: If Czechoslovakia did not surrender the Sudetenland it would be "solely responsible for the war which will ensue" and in any case neither England nor France would fight. Beneš had to yield to this diplomatic atrocity.

Chamberlain, back at Godesburg, Germany, on September 22, was asked by Hitler if the British and French governments had in effect agreed to the transfer of the Sudeten territory to Germany.

"Yes," Chamberlain replied.

"*Es tut mir furchtbar leid*," Hitler said sharply, "*aber das geht nicht mehr.*" "I am very sorry, but that is no longer any good." Hitler, having made sure that he was getting all he had asked, asked for more. He wanted more than the Sudetenland for himself and he wanted Poland and Hungary to receive strips of Czechoslovakia. He, obviously, was breaking up Czechoslovakia. He had become a great idealist. Self-determination for Germans? That wasn't enough. There must also be self-determination for Poles and Hungarians otherwise the rump of Czechoslovakia might be too strong. Chamberlain was taken aback by the deceit of Hitler. Powerful forces in England and France demanded the rejection of the Godesberg terms. Soviet Russia offered to collaborate against Germany. The Czechs remanned their fortifications on the German frontier. But Hitler pulled a few more drastic tricks. He threatened war, world war. (Yet he never ordered a general mobilization. He did not wish to worry his own subjects.) Again Chamberlain and Daladier acquiesced. And by the Munich *dictat*, which in substance and procedure was more cruel than Versailles, he got everything he asked at Godesberg.

If I were asked whether the Britain and French should have fought to prevent the break-up of Czechoslovakia, I would reply: first, they should never have allowed it to come to Munich. That catastrophe was the product of earlier appeasement. The Rhineland, Spain, China, Ethiopia, the supine acceptance of Austria's fate, the rebuffs to Russia, the British courtship of the Nazis—these gave Hitler the insolence and strength to stage Munich. Second, knowing what the totalitarian Japanese-German-Italian triangle had already done and planned to do, the democracies should have been better armed at the time of Munich. Third, the anti-German combination possible at the time of Munich was very probably much stronger than the combination which declared war on Germany eleven months later.

The day before France declared war on Germany in September, 1939, Daladier said to the Chamber of Deputies, "France and England cannot accept the destruction of a friendly nation which would presage new enterprises of violence directed against them. Is this, in effect, only a German-Polish conflict? No, gentlemen, this is only a new phase in the onward march of the Hitler dictatorship toward the domination of Europe and the world." Quite right. And every word of this statement applies equally to the Czechoslovak crisis.

U. S. Ambassador Joseph P. Kennedy affirmed in a speech in support of President Roosevelt's election for a third term that, "if Mr. Chamberlain had had five thousand first-line planes at home when he conferred at Munich we would have truly seen 'peace in our time.'" This declaration carries an implied criticism of appeasement by the No. 1 American appeaser. But apart from that, why did not Mr. Chamberlain have five thousand planes at the time of Munich? He could have had them. British factories were capable of turning them out. The world had for years been full of wars and rumors of wars. Ambassador Kennedy's son, John F. Kennedy, has outlined the partial reply in a book entitled, *Why England Slept*. England slept because Chamberlain was Prime Minister and Chamberlain was an appeaser. Churchill and others had continually urged the establishment of a Ministry of Supply with special powers to stimulate the production of munitions and airplanes. But, said Mr. Chamberlain on May 25, 1938—just after the first Czech crisis, "I doubt very much whether we would be justified in asking for such powers, or whether, if we did ask for them Parliament" (—whose majority he controlled—) "would give them to us in time of peace. The analogy of wartime is really misleading. We are not at war." Here is Chamberlain's fundamental error. They were at war. Germany had been at war for years. Europe was at war. Chamberlain refused to see it. He thought he could prevent hostilities with words.

France was even more neglectful of its armaments. France, to be sure, lacked the powerful industry of Britain and Germany. But it could make good planes and it could have bought good planes. Who is to blame that it did not?

Some answer: The Popular Front, Léon Blum. This is one of those accusations so easy to make and so difficult to prove. God forbid that the accusers look into a table of statistics! Facts might upset them. The Popular Front took office under Blum on June 6, 1936, and remained in office throughout 1937. Léon Blum himself was Premier from June, 1936, to June, 1937, when he was succeeded by Chautemps. He returned for a short interval in 1938. During

1938, the attack on the Popular Front succeeded in robbing it of cohesion and strength, and Blum's labor reforms were gradually whittled down. But the League of Nations annual almanacs show that French production rose during the Popular Front regime. Thus, the general index of industrial production was 75.2 in 1934, 72.5 in 1935, 78 in 1936, 81.7 in 1937, but 76.1 in 1938. Pig iron was 62 in 1934, 58 in 1935, 63 in 1936, 79 in 1937, but 61 in 1938. Steel was 65 in 1934, 66 in 1935, 71 in 1936, 84 in 1937, but 66 in 1938. Output rose during 1937, which was the real Blum year, and fell thereafter.

No. The trouble was not with the Popular Front or with the forty-hour week. It lay elsewhere.

Pierre Cot, French Minister of Air in 1936 and 1937, writes me, "In 1936 and 1937, France did not buy a single airplane in the United States. I simply bought patents for motors, etc. Requests to buy airplanes in the United States were vetoed by M. Georges Bonnet, Minister of Finance."

The appeasers also sabotaged production at home. Pierre Cot has given me the copy of an official letter which he, as Minister of Air, wrote on December 6, 1937, to Premier Camille Chautemps. In it he reveals his sad experiences during his eighteen months as Air Minister. He complained that the budget of French aviation constituted only twenty-two percent of the national defense outlays compared to thirty-four percent in England and much higher proportions in Germany.

In June, 1936, the French government adopted a plan for the manufacture of two hundred and fifty military planes per year during the next five years. In August, in view of the rapid strides of German aviation, this schedule was doubled. The Cabinet agreed to make the Air Ministry a supplementary allocation of seven billion one hundred million francs. The first yearly installment was to be one billion two hundred million francs. Cot received only five hundred million francs.

To finance the expansion of aviation plants, it had been decided by the government to give credits to industry. Instead of releasing them in June, 1937, as agreed, they were made available in October, 1937. But worse. These credits were cut in half by the Ministry of Finance. "In the coming year," Cot wrote to Chautemps, "we may accordingly expect a fall in production." Further: "The credits which I have received will not permit me to turn out five hundred military planes in 1938."

In 1936-37, Cot wrote in his letter, the budget for preliminary work in the aviation industry—making of models and industrial mobilization—was reduced 1,298,000,000 francs "or thirty percent of the total." In the same period, other credits were reduced 1,852,-000,000 francs. And this while Goering worked at top speed.

Depressed by Germany's supreme air effort, Cot constantly pressed the government to intensify airplane production and to grant a three-billion credit for air raid defenses. But the General Staff of the army refused. On February 15, 1937, the Supreme Military Commission decided "that there is no intention to modify or extend the plan for expanding the army of the air."

Why?

Daladier, Minister of War and later Premier, frequently told Pierre Cot that "the Spanish War proved that the role of aviation remained very secondary." And Bonnet said there was no money in the exchequer.

The chief evil in France was neither financial nor military. It was political and psychological. In 1914, the general staffs of all armies were wedded to the idea of the attack, "always the attack." That was the Napoleonic tradition. The Kaiser began the war by smashing into Belgium, the Russians by advancing towards East Prussia, and the French and British, at the first opportunity, by taking the offensive throughout 1915 and 1916 in France and Flanders. Then the defensive stage of the first World War intervened. The war descended into the trench. France won. Victory in 1918 through defensive strategy made the French nation and general staff trench-minded. Hence the Maginot Line, which was an enlarged and improved trench.

Germany, on the other hand, lost in 1918 because it could not continue the offensive. In another war, success would have to depend on sustained and rapid attack. That is why the Blitzkrieg dominated German army psychology. While France sought to develop the most resistant steel and concrete for fortifications, Germany concentrated on giant tanks and giant bombers, weapons, par excellence, of offense.

Even after the outbreak of the second World War, as Pertinax testifies, the "Maginot Credo" persisted. He says, "Since the Maginot fortifications"—according to this credo—"couldn't be captured, the French government felt at liberty to take its time."

Cot shouted, More planes. Colonel Charles de Gaulle cried, Produce tanks. The appeasers, the defeatists, the defensivists replied, We have the Maginot Line. Besides we will come to an agreement with Germany and then all will be well. Why should we, in the meantime, waste our precious francs on weapons that will never be used?

Then, at least, their opponents insisted, extend the Maginot Line along the Belgian frontier to the sea. No, no, came the answer. Whenever this question came up in French Cabinet deliberations, majority opinion felt that such a prolongation of the Maginot Line would seem to serve notice on Belgium that France had no intention of marching to her defense in case of a German attack. That would throw Belgium into the arms of Germany. So France built a few pill-boxes and gun emplacements opposite the Belgian frontier but left herself exposed to a repetition of the traditional German Schlieffen Plan which was her undoing in May, 1940.

France and England paved the way to Munich by neglecting their rearmament, by surrendering invaluable strategic positions in Asia, Africa, and Europe to the aggressors, and by feeding Hitler's contempt for the democracies. If Hitler himself had drafted a scheme of Anglo-French behavior it could not have been more pro-Nazi.

Nevertheless, the Western Powers should have stood by Czechoslovakia.

The reason the British and French gave for not doing so was the superiority of Germany in the air. Figures for airplanes have a universal tendency to multiply themselves in the imagination. The Nazis consciously encouraged this bad arithmetic. The Nazis are the best propagandists in the world because lying with them is a principle. They lied to Colonel Lindbergh, to General Victor Vuillemin, chief of the French air force who visited Germany at Goering's invitation, and to others. They lied about the ten thousand first-line planes they were supposed to have. They exaggerated their strength to frighten their victims.

In the official organ of the Italian air force, *L'Ala d'Italia,* published in Fascist Rome, Signor Mario Muratori printed an article on the size of the German air force. He put the front-line strength at 3,000 and said it would be 6,000 in 1940-41. The German *Essener*

National Zeitung, organ of Marshal Goering, the creator of Nazi aviation, republished this article on October 25, 1938—*after Munich!*

When Premier Chautemps returned from London late in 1937, he told Pierre Cot that England was producing 300 planes a month. Cot's letter to Chautemps dated December 6, 1937, states that according to the French secret service, "Deuxième Bureau," the British Royal Air Force in the British Isles consisted of 1,550 first-line planes, and 1,450 second-line older machines. France, Cot continued, had at that moment 1,350 first-line planes of which 450 were light fighters, 170 medium bombers, and 730 heavy bombers and 1,750 other planes.

In 1938, the French Intelligence Service, according to a letter which I have from Pierre Cot, reported that the Nazi Luftwaffe numbered 3,600 front-line planes. Only 2,500 of these, however, were armed and manned. For the others, Goering had no pilots.

Thus, even if one takes the highest figure for Germany—3,600 first-line machines—and compare it with the combined Franco-British air fleet—2,900—the discrepancy is not overwhelming.

But there was also Czechoslovakia. Hitler disclosed in an address on April 28, 1939, after he had seized all of Czechoslovakia, that in that country Germany had come into possession of 1,582 Czech planes, 501 anti-aircraft guns, 2,175 light and heavy cannon, 785 mine throwers, 469 tanks, 43,875 machine guns, 114,000 automatic pistols, 1,090,000 rifles, one billion rounds of rifle ammunition, three million artillery shells and vast quantities of searchlights, bridge-building equipment, motor vehicles, automobiles.

How heartbreaking it was to the Czechoslovaks to lay down all these arms and to abandon, without fighting, their carefully constructed line of fortifications just because the British and French forced them to do so before Munich!

Since German airplane production exceeded the Anglo-French aviation output, the gap between the Nazi Luftwaffe and the combined air fleets of France and England was far greater in September, 1939, when the Allies went to war than in September, 1938, when they did not. Besides, Hitler had the 1,582 Czech airplanes. At Munich-time, they would have been, for all purposes, Anglo-French planes. Pertinax said in the *New York Herald Tribune* of November 24, 1940, "As is well-known, the relative military power of the Western democracies never did increase in the twelve months that elapsed between the Munich settlement of September 29, 1938, and the outbreak of the hostilities. It shrank instead." He, like Cot, thinks it would have been better to go to war in 1938.

But it is not merely a matter of counting planes, guns, and soldiers. Munich demoralized France and made it even more defeatist. That applied to some extent to England too. The small countries of Europe had less confidence in the stamina and courage of the big Western Powers. Spirit can often be weighed against planes.

And then this further consideration. If the democracies had forcibly obstructed the vivisection of Czechoslovakia it is fairly safe to assume that Poland, which went to war with alacrity against Germany in September, 1939, would have joined the anti-Nazi coalition. Not that Polish leaders were all anti-Nazi. Quite the contrary. But Warsaw had always regarded Germany as the great foe and had always indicated that it would side with France and England if they resisted Germany. When they appeased Germany, frail Poland, foolishly but pardonably obedient to Hitler, swallowed his bait and cut itself a slice of Czechoslovakia thus helping to seal its own doom. If Poland had not fought on the Allied side in 1938, it could easily have been kept neutral by Russia. Moscow had warned it in September not to move against Czechoslovakia. It is more than likely, too, that Rumania and even Yugoslavia would have joined the Allies.

In 1938, Loyalist Spain would have contributed its meager best to the Allied cause. If Hitler and Mussolini had continued to support Franco that would have drained their resources for the struggle with the major powers. If the Loyalists had won, the Allied position in the Mediterranean would have been immeasurably improved. In September, 1939, however, Loyalist Spain was gone.

Last, but of course not least, Russia.

At the outbreak of the second World War, Soviet Russia was not with the Allies. If anything, it was against the Allies. How would Russia have behaved in September, 1938? It is always difficult to make a precise statement about something that did not happen. There is evidence from excellent sources, however, to support the belief that Czechoslovakia would have had Soviet aid.

The *Chicago Daily News* of April 18, 1938, printed an interview by Erika Mann, daughter of Thomas Mann, with Edouard Beneš, the former President of Czechoslovakia. Dr. Beneš was then teaching at the University of Chicago, and the *News* submitted Miss

Mann's text to him for approval. He gave it. Dr. Beneš said, "Russia was faithful to the very last moment; I knew that."

"Dr. Beneš," the interview proceeds, "said he was assured by Russia that it would have sent military assistance even though France and England failed to do so."

But many Czech reactionaries, not Beneš, were afraid of this very contingency. Says Miss Mann, "I was told in Prague a few days before Munich, by persons belonging to the government, that they feared Czechoslovakia, if she offered resistance with Russia's aid alone, would have become a second Spain."

For further reference—Communists later argued that Russia should not assist conservative Britain and France—be it noted that Moscow would have been prepared to give help to Czechoslovakia although some of the most powerful Prague leaders were so reactionary that they preferred their country to die without a struggle rather than accept Soviet help.

It is known now that several mighty squadrons of Soviet planes were actually standing on Czechoslovak airfields at the time of Munich. Litvinov urged in his speech at the League of Nations on September 21, 1938, and again and again in diplomatic encounters, that England, France, and Russia enter into immediate military staff negotiations with a view to joint action.

The British Foreign Office itself announced Russia's readiness to co-operate. On September 26, three days before Munich, a Foreign Office communiqué asserted that "if, in spite of all efforts made by the British Prime Minister, a German attack is made upon Czechoslovakia, the immediate result must be that France will be bound to come to her assistance and that Great Britain and Russia will certainly stand by France." The French Foreign Office inspired the French press either to deny the authenticity of this communiqué or play it down. But it was true. Bonnet and Daladier knew it was true. Lord Halifax would not have made that announcement without Moscow's consent. The British and French would appease to the very end, and did, but if nothing worked and Hitler actually attacked, Russia would fight. Hamilton Fish Armstrong, a keen and careful expert, takes for granted that this official British Foreign Office communiqué amounted to a "categorical pledge" by England and Russia to back up France and Czechoslovakia. He thinks that "so solid a coalition" would either "have called Hitler's bluff" or quickly defeated Germany.

For Stalin, the situation at Munich in no way resembled the situation in September, 1939. Germany was relatively weaker at Munich. Moreover, Russia's steadfastness was required in 1938 to instill some courage into the Western Powers, and she therefore felt inclined to act first, even before they did, whereas in 1939, the Allies had guaranteed Poland, appeasement was receding, and the Allies officially assured Stalin that they would go to war first. That being the case, Stalin decided not to go in at all. If he wanted a war which would enfeeble Germany he had to participate in 1938 but did not have to participate in 1939.

The European anti-German and anti-Axis combination was stronger at Munich-time than it would ever be again.

That, among other reasons, is why Munich was such an unmitigated calamity. It did no good and did a lot of harm. It changed the entire course of world history. It marks the end of an era. One might call the years before Munich A.M. and after Munich P.M.

If, after Munich, Chamberlain and Daladier had at least said, "We have been defeated and now we must get busy and do something about it," some of the lost ground might have been retrieved. But Chamberlain thought it was "peace for our time." Then why hurry rearmament? Under pressure from Churchill and like-minded Englishmen, the defense program was somewhat accelerated, but compared with the pervading imminent menace it was ludicrously slow. Anthony Eden and others said so publicly.

Daladier apparently knew he had betrayed France at Munich. When he flew back from that fateful conference he looked down as his plane circled over the Paris airfield at Le Bourget and, seeing the immense crowd awaiting him, he said to Etienne de Croy, a French Foreign Office official, *"Ils sont venu me conspuer."* "They have come here to hiss and abuse me." He expected a hostile reception. He had sold out France and he realized it.

But Daladier misunderstood; the mob was not there to lynch him. It came to hail him as a hero returning from peace. His progress through Paris in an open auto with the grinning Bonnet by his side resembled a triumphal procession. Vain, weak man, it turned his head. Popular acclaim is a dangerous potion. Daladier now concentrated on retaining the adulation of the mass.

One raucous discord marred this vast chorus of praise; the Communists reviled Daladier for his Munich role. They wanted him to resist Hitler. That embittered him. At the first opportunity he replied with an unusual and vitriolic attack. It was at the annual Radical Socialist Congress in Marseilles, October 28, 1938. The significance of his words transcended domestic policy; they gave a preview of French policy towards Germany and Russia.

He said, "One party tells me that it always advocated intransigence even at the cost of war and that it disapproved of the negotiations. That was the Communist party. . . . The violence and intransigence of this party have paralyzed my work. Did it not weaken the position of France when Communist papers and orators rudely attacked Mr. Neville Chamberlain who toiled with such admirable faith for peace?"

Posters immediately appeared throughout France demanding the suppression of the Communist party.

At Munich, Daladier went on, he could not help feeling "that there were strong reasons why France and Germany should get together." This statement, coupled with his attack on the Communists, meant that the French government would persist in appeasement, would continue to court Germany and would not court Russia. Indeed, Nazi Foreign Minister Joachim von Ribbentrop drove through deserted Paris streets on December 6, 1938, and with Bonnet signed a Franco-German pact of friendship. Munich had not taught the French that Germany was the enemy. Therefore, they rebuffed the Russians. Daladier often told Pierre Cot, who in Cabinet meetings repeatedly suggested the wisdom of better relations with Moscow, that "negotiations with the Russians would create difficulties with Germany and England." "This argument," Cot writes me, "was always taken up by M. Chautemps." And, of course, it was the one thought in Bonnet's head.

More appeasement after Munich. How Hitler must have laughed! What a spectacle for the gods! Germany getting ready for war on France. France appeasing Germany. France signing treaties of "friendship" with Germany. France refusing to try for the active friendship of Russia.

Was it merely stupidity and blindness? Or madness? Or corruption? Pertinax openly accuses Bonnet of "sinisterly" engaging in "*de facto* underhand complicity with Nazi imperialism." I do not know at all whether there is any truth in charges that a prominent appeaser took direct bribes from French bankers and others. Pertinax, the most honest and the most capable French newspaper commentator, refers, in *Liberty*, November 2, 1940, to a former French minister "who to the knowledge of the competent services, had direct exchanges with the enemy." These circumstances and the machinations of such Nazi agents as Otto Abetz, later Nazi Ambassador to the Vichy of the Pétain of Verdun, undoubtedly oiled the ways of appeasement.

The roots of the problem nevertheless ran much deeper. And again it is Pertinax, in the same *Liberty* article, who touches the spot. "For huge sections of the conservative classes," he writes, "Hitler's warlike preparations receded far into the background compared with the social danger, and newspapers were paid by German and Italian agents to foster that outlook." These French conservatives feared Blum and the Communists more than they feared Hitler especially since to defeat Hitler they would have to work hand in glove with Blum and the Communists. Without the Communist party, or against the Communist party—one of the most powerful in the country—France's war-making capacity was circumscribed. That is why Daladier would never have launched a verbal assault on the Communists if he had thought a war imminent. The French conservatives hated the French Communists too much to fight shoulder to shoulder with them for France. A real alliance with the Soviet Union would have given bourgeois France the support of the French Communists in a war. That was another good reason for preferring even an expensive compromise with Hitler. Only after all hope of appeasing Hitler was exploded by his seizure of Czechoslovakia in March, 1939, did England and France become serious about Soviet collaboration. Then it was too late.

Neville Chamberlain was a sincere pacifist on general religious and humanitarian grounds but chiefly because he feared the effects of a war on the British social system. Somewhere in *Gone With the Wind*, Rhett Butler says that no matter who won the war the South they loved would perish. It did. Chamberlain feared the death of his England in a war. He appeased to prolong its life. He appeased until even he saw that Hitler did not wish Chamberlain's England or any England to live. In France, the military collapse of 1940 revealed the true visage of numerous Frenchmen who had always preferred a second-class Fascist France dominated by Hitler to a France free and democratic.

The appeasers were bad Englishmen and bad Frenchmen. Hitler, in the month of Munich, took a chance on their victory over true

Englishmen and Frenchmen who were anti-Hitler for reasons of social principle and others who were anti-Hitler for imperialistic and nationalistic reasons. This combination forced Chamberlain and Daladier to declare war on Hitler in September, 1939. Hitler was not sure that the bad democrats would give him his Munich. Goebbels revealed in a speech on October 11, 1938, that "the Fuehrer and his advisers pursued a risky policy. But nobody can win a lottery if he doesn't buy a ticket. It was a test of nerves for the nation and its leaders." There is the story of Munich. Hitler gambled on the nervous collapse of the British and French governments. His nerves held longer.

H. R. Bruce Lockhart, author of *British Agent*, tells this story: A Yugoslav diplomat once politely warned Hermann Goering that Nazi tactics might some day arouse the democracies into fighting.

"Bah," Goering scoffed. "You have only to bang your fist on the table. Then the democratic countries make a few speeches in Parliament and nothing happens."

Goering and Hitler and Goebbels tried that procedure once too often and thrust the entire world into war.

Czechoslovakia and France were allies. France and England were allies. Whatever weakened Czechoslovakia weakened France and England. If Hitler's goal was an attack on France he would first attack Czechoslovakia and thus deprive France of an invaluable partner.

Alone France was no match for Germany. With Czechoslovakia and England it had a chance. That is why Hitler disliked the Czech-French alliance. That is why he broke up Czechoslovakia. Yet France and England did nothing to save Czechoslovakia. Indeed, they did everything to kill it.

When the second World War came, Daladier, Bonnet, and the rest, looked for fifth columnists in France. Diplomatic dwarfs pointed to unhappy refugees as dangerous enemies within the walls. But Daladier and Bonnet themselves were the fifth column. They did more than neglect to blow up a bridge over the Meuse or at Sedan. They handed the enemy a whole line of fortifications, the Czech "Maginot Line" which was France's line too. They presented Hitler with all of Czechoslovakia's arms and arms factories. It was treason on a huge scale.

34. *Just Before Christmas: 1938*

RAYMOND GRAM SWING, radio commentator, well-known correspondent, composer, and authority on Mother Goose poetry—he of the calm voice and worried countenance—dropped in on Geneva during the Munich crisis. He was en route to Prague. We sat on the hotel's broad green sunny lawn, which lies in a bowl below the Alps, and groused about the stupidity of world leaders. Geneva was a rialto and caravanserai. Every evening at the Bavaria Café, diplomats and journalists discussed and fretted. Above the din and through the smoke, Robert Dell of the *Manchester Guardian*, aged 73, excelled all competitors in the vehemence and acidity of his remarks against Chamberlain, Halifax, Bonnet, Daladier. Dell had grown up in the tradition of the French revolutionary syndicalists and until only a few weeks before his death in New York his temper was strong and unhampered.

The League of Nations itself did not even take up the question of Czechoslovakia, a "member state." The League was polite society and never handled dirty linen. Every time Chamberlain retreated in the face of Hitler's bluster, the delegates and officials breathed with relief; it meant so much less for them to do.

Alvarez del Vayo, Pablo Azcarate, and other Loyalist leaders attending the League session were disconsolate in the realization that the battle of Spain was being lost at Berchtesgaden and Godesberg. They were true internationalists. They fought Fascism because it had assailed their country. They would have fought it elsewhere too. That is why an anti-Fascist like myself was as welcome in their midst as a Spaniard. Del Vayo's speeches were patriotic and at the same time universal.

At League meetings delegates tried hard to kill time with dignity. They waited till others elsewhere made the big decisions on Czechoslovakia and Spain. It was a humiliating spectacle. The delegates felt like dry leaves in the diplomatic storm. No will of their own, no color, no life. Then suddenly a dynamo was turned on. A voice spoke with power, pride, and fight. The voice of Spain. The voice

575

of Negrin. He had come from conducting the war. He was dressed in cutaway and striped trousers, a cultured, urbane scholar and gentleman. Yet even the blasé Assembly of the League, with de Valera presiding, recognized Negrin as Spanish Militiaman No. 1, and the Latin American delegates especially thrilled to his words.

He made a plea for Spain. But he also offered a plan for justice. The Loyalist government was sending home the members of the International Brigade and all foreigners in its service. It invited the League to dispatch a commission to count them as they left Spain and to confirm the fact that none remained. The Loyalists would do this no matter what Franco did. But they hoped their action would induce the powers to insist on a similar withdrawal of the Germans and Italians in Spain.

Needless to say, Franco did not respond, nor did the powers. But the International Brigade was disbanded. When its men bade farewell to Spain they left behind them, to lie forever in Spanish soil, some of the finest sons of our tormented modern age. They had known what it was all about. They had known that they would get nothing out of it. "The manner of their death was the crowning glory of their lives." Those who came back can be proud that they were able to see when the rest were blind and that they acted under no compulsion except that of inner conviction and devotion to a good cause. The Brigade's life stands as an untarnished epic.

The official report of the League of Nations Commission sent to Spain stated that on January 12, 1939, when it finished its labors, it had counted 12,673 foreigners in the service of the Loyalists! This number included male and female nurses and doctors, foreign personnel in units other than the International Brigade, and more than 3,000 wounded Internationals. The effective soldiers in the International Brigade when Negrin spoke at Geneva thus numbered approximately 7,000.

About 40,000 foreigners entered Spain during the war to join the International Brigade. Of those no less than 3,000 were from the United States. I estimate, roughly, that almost half the Americans were killed in action or died from wounds received in action. The percentage of casualties for the entire Brigade was high because in the beginning of the war they bore the brunt of the fighting while the Loyalists trained Spaniards for the army.

Sir Arnold Wilson, M.P., wrote in the *London Observer* of October 23, 1938, that Franco had captured 50,000 foreign prisoners of whom 25,000 were French. Since he had been my neighbor at dinner a few months back I sent him a letter saying these figures were impossible and asking for his source. He mailed me a Franco throw-out published in England which stated that "over 47,000 are foreigners and of those more than half are French." Sir Arnold added three thousand for good measure. Franco could not have taken more foreigners than ever entered the Loyalist army. As a matter of fact, Franco has now released all his foreign prisoners—with the possible exception of a dozen. Their total was several hundred, certainly under one thousand.

I had had some awkward experiences at the front and in bombings in Spain and escaped without a scratch. But in Geneva, during the Munich month, I was playing tennis one afternoon when a ball hit my right eye and injured the cornea. The oculist told me not to read, not to move, not to bathe, not to get excited, and to stay in bed. And this was a week before Munich. The Vayos lent me their radio. A girl friend came in to read the French papers to me and another to read the English press, and friendly colleagues telephoned regularly to give me the news. I missed the smoke, gossip, and noise of the Bavaria.

On September 27, Geneva was blacked-out. Chamberlain, speaking over the radio that evening, had sounded as if he were weeping. "How horrible, fantastic, incredible it is that we should be digging trenches and trying on gas masks here because of a quarrel in a far-away country between people of whom we know nothing!" What a statement from a British statesman! England's great leaders of the eighteenth and nineteenth centuries must have revolved in their graves. (Did Chamberlain know more about Poland a year later?) He was resolved not to fight. He begged Hitler not to fight.

Throughout the month of October, 1938, all Europe suffered from a "hangover." It was the morning after the Munich before. Europe smelled like a noisome swamp. People like Edgar Mowrer and myself who had grown attached to Europe from years of life with it got together and simply mourned. We said it was no use staying abroad any longer. Europe was entering a hideous, dark age.

When my eye healed, I went down to Spain. By a gigantic expenditure of materials and men, Franco had driven the Loyalists back over the Ebro. Bombs fell daily and nightly on Barcelona. Yet for some reason Spain seemed healthier than the rest of the world. Republican Spain stood and took it. The others groveled before the Fascist tyrants. Spain was a light in the universal gloom. But the light was soon to go out. It is hard to take it for two and a half years. President Azaña, weakest of Loyalist chiefs, nevertheless reflected the spirit of Spain in a phrase, "The important thing is to be right." But how many outside Spain cared about that?

The end of November, 1938. "Do your Christmas shopping early," Americans were being told. "Gifts for HIM," the stores advertised. Barcelona was getting gifts from HIM, from Benito Mussolini.— Sunday: Good Barcelona Catholics had gone to church. In the previous week the city had been bombed forty times. They prayed for some peace and good will. Then the sirens sounded and the bombers came, and they cursed HIM.

Wednesday morning: During the night two raids had taken place, they told me. I slept through one. But an anti-aircraft gun on a roof near-by had pumped so insistently in the second attack that I awoke and put on a robe and went downstairs into the lobby. I slept late in the morning, came down for substitute coffee and dry rolls and then walked out, coatless, into the bright warm sun of the boulevard. Nobody looked up. If the planes came, they came. Faces were haggard but relaxed. Girls laughed and soldiers on leave flirted. Suddently, the siren. Unless you are hit, the siren is much the worse part of an air raid. I stood at the entrance of the hotel. The invading bombers were behind us and we could not see them. We could only hear the anti-aircraft guns booming overhead. But the people across the street could see the squadron, and I watched the raid through their reactions. They hung from balconies and out of windows craning their necks and making excited exclamations. Presently they began to point. They waved their fists in evident pleasure. A group of us rushed across the broad Paseo de Gracia. "See it," they said to us, "see, there are five and one is lagging behind. It has been hit." The Spaniards pranced and forgot about their safety. The eyes of one young fellow were almost popping. The evening communiqué said, "One bomber visibly lost height and speed and may have descended at sea."

Barcelona had had many months of air murder. But it still thrilled to the discomfiture of the enemy. Many people never went into an underground shelter. Except to inspect them, I was never in one during the entire war period. The Spaniards were so frivolous and so eager to see the bullfight of the air that the government issued instructions to ministers and important officials threatening reprisals if they did not betake themselves to a shelter the moment an alarm sounded. The War Office had a shelter equipped with telephone, electric light from an independent motor, desk, chairs, and other conveniences, and the minister could descend into it by special elevator from his private office.

The five bombers disappeared out to sea, and ambulances, clanging fiercely, dashed by to the scenes where the bombs had fallen. The wartime grapevine was perfect, and in a few minutes we knew at the hotel that a 400-pound bomb had hit the Via Durutti. Several correspondents drove to it. Not more than five minutes had elapsed from the time the bomb crashed. A police cordon surrounded the area. Women were sweeping up the splintered glass into neat piles. A fire-engine ladder rested against a third-floor window, and firemen were carrying down wounded and dead. The rungs were slippery with blood. One room in another building had been exposed to view when its front wall fell in bits to the pavement; a dressmaker's fitting figure was whole and upright; a picture remained hanging; a child had been killed.

We drove to the morgue. Two Englishmen with us squeamishly refused to go in unless the Swedish woman in our group stayed out. She withdrew. Stretchers red with blood lined the courtyard. We brushed past the stockinged feet of a dead woman. Two children about five years old lay on an inclined plane covered with tin. The little boy had on a polka-dotted blouse. An attendant in white apron moved one finger to the right and left indicating that these were not victims of today's bombing. "They've been there for three days," he said. Nobody had claimed them. He beckoned us into a deeper chamber. It was dimly lighted. The dead lay side by side on a stone floor. Assuming that we were in search of relatives he lit his cigarette lighter, stopped and threw a few rays on the face of the victim. Where the body was headless or the face smashed back into the skull beyond recognition he tried to bring the light on a conspicuous article of clothing. Each body had a number. The last number was thirty-nine. Thirty-nine dead in a single morning raid. One girl, as far as I could see, was intact. Her face now had a greenish pallor. She was a Catalan beauty and twenty minutes ago soldiers home from leave and men out on a stroll had probably called her "guapa" and flirted with her. Another girl's stockingless legs had been broken below the knees and above the ankles. A man in a cheap brown suit with his thighs shattered. An attendant entered carrying in front of him a shallow wicker basket; its contents had been a human being this morning. Number forty.

These victims of Rome had left their homes to go to work, to shop, to go to school, or to pay a friendly visit. Their families would not miss them until the evening. We went back into the street. The same sort of people were going about their business, carrying food bundles, gossiping on corners, smiling, flirting. Before long they might be stretched out on the marble slabs of the morgue. And we too. Civilization.

I spent the morning with the two Englishmen. One was the brother of a member of the Chamberlain government, and the other a Conservative party Parliamentary candidate named Michael Weaver. In May, they had spent three weeks in Franco territory. "This morning," they announced when we left the morgue, "has made us pro-Loyalists." Weaver went back to England and made propaganda for the Republic. The alternative would have been to support and love the regimes that had sent those innocent men and women into the morgue. Many Britons did that.

This raid, the government announced, had lasted three minutes. Forty dead in three minutes. A second raid at 12.45 P.M. A third at 7.20 P.M. That day alone—325 dead and several hundred wounded. Throughout the night there were so many sirens that I did not know, lying in bed, whether they were coming or going. Breakfast the next morning. The planes attacked twice again. Eleven raids in twenty-four hours. This was unusual. It was November 23, and Neville Chamberlain was due in Paris that day to discuss Spain with Daladier. Mussolini wished to make himself felt in those Paris discussions. "I will dictate the outcome of the Spanish struggle," Mussolini was saying. But he did not say it in a diplomatic note; he said it with bombs, and 325 persons were stretched on marble slabs.

That evening I dined at the Ritz with the League of Nations Commission which was evacuating the International Brigaders. A bellboy brought in two objects and showed them to the members of the commission: one, a part of an Italian bomb, two, the time-delay fuse of an anti-aircraft gun stamped with Russian letters. Both influenced Spanish domestic politics.

On every visit to Spain, I went to see Luis Araquistain and his wife Trudi. Both were violently anti-Negrin and pro-appeasement, but somehow we got along well.

Araquistain, Negrin, and del Vayo had been gay young men together and had frequented the Madrid night clubs and cabarets. Araquistain, I think, could never rid his mind of this memory, and he never thought highly of Negrin. How could a Lothario conduct a war? It was like saying, "That fellow can't be a good surgeon. I remember him when he wet his diapers." Negrin had been a frivolous youth and was all the more serious now.

Araquistain and del Vayo, brothers-in-law, had worked closely with Caballero when he was the undisputed leader of the Spanish workers. Araquistain always considered himself del Vayo's superior. He swung a mighty pen. Del Vayo was the better orator, despite his teeth. Araquistain had been Ambassador to Berlin; del Vayo, Ambassador to Mexico. But when Caballero became Prime Minister in September, 1936, he appointed del Vayo Foreign Minister and Araquistain Ambassador to Paris. Trudi was with her sister, Luisy del Vayo, in Biarritz when this news reached them and Trudi was shocked; del Vayo would be Araquistain's boss. Araquistain nevertheless took the job and did it well. When Caballero fell, Araquistain quit in protest, and thereafter, throughout the civil war, he was unemployed. Able men were few. He sulked and did not serve the cause. I never understood that and said so each time I saw him and Trudi.

Our meetings always followed the same pattern: they would say I had had Araquistain appointed to Paris. "Yes, you and Marcel Rosenberg," Trudi would emphasize with a beautiful smile. I invariably protested; I was not even in Spain when the appointments were made! I gave them my opinion of the real reason; Prieto and Araquistain could not bear the sight of one another. Prieto was too important to keep out of Caballero's Cabinet. Therefore Araquistain had to stay out. They did not refute this interpretation. It was common knowledge.

Trudi and Luisy no longer spoke to one another. Once they met at a dressmaker's in Barcelona. They kissed one another and cried but did not talk. Both of them would have been ready to die for the Loyalist cause, and they still loved each other. But party politics had torn them apart. I was very welcome in both households because I could tell Trudi about Luisy and Luisy about Trudi. Each wanted to know everything about the other. The children visited their aunts.

Then Araquistain used to say to me that I had helped to overthrow Caballero! I was sick with arthritis in the Hotel Mayflower in New York when it happened. I could scarcely have done it had I been well in Valencia. Because of my access to key-men in Spain and Moscow, people attributed to me powers and designs which I did not have. My contacts enriched my life. I cultivated those contacts zealously and refrained from spoiling them by indiscretions or boasts. My experiences with men of stature helped me grow and I look back on them with great pleasure and gratitude. I think I enjoyed the confidence of Communists, non-Communists, and anti-Communists because I resisted party clichés and narrow loyalties. There is nothing heavier than a party card and I never carried one.

Araquistain was violently anti-Communist. But his denunciations of the "Reds" sounded like love hymns when Trudi launched into an anti-Communist tirade. They argued that Moscow was prolonging the war in Spain. They wanted it to end. How? Would you surrender? Would you beg Mussolini and Hitler for a truce? They did not know how; it was not in their hands. But once they had had a plan. To wit: When Araquistain was ambassador in Paris, he employed an intermediary named Shapiro to approach Hjalmar Schacht, the Nazi financier, with a view to buying Hitler out of Spain. The Loyalists would pay Germany and Italy several hundred million dollars to get out. Léon Blum also knew of the scheme and, according to Araquistain, approved it. I always thought it was childish and told them so. Regimes bent on world conquest cannot be bribed with cash. They were not even bribed with Abyssinia, Spain, Austria, Czechoslovakia, Albania, Memel, and Manchuria. They want more, more, more.

The Araquistains' son Finki worked as a physician in the big Barcelona hospital. He invited me to visit it. I entered a room occupied by a single patient. He had thick, shining black hair—Spanish hair—then two eyes without expression, a nose and an upper lip. Below the upper lip was a gaping red hole. The entire mouth and lower jaw had been shot away by an explosive bullet in the Ebro battle. When you see something like that you know what war means and you do not make up your mind lightly about wanting your country to go to war. This man could neither talk, smile, smoke nor eat. He would undergo plastic surgery. Trudi Araquistain's London friends had contributed very expensive and modern surgical equipment to this institution. In another room, a doctor was dressing a wound: shrapnel had torn away the soldier's nose. Everywhere I saw hideous human faces without cheeks, without chins, without eyes.

The hospital cared for 2,000 patients. A corporal wounded at Teruel, in December, 1937, still lay there helpless in December, 1938. His left leg had been amputated up to the hip and the stump was gangrenous. The doctor said it had to be exposed to the air. Many other amputations were due to feet freezing in the battle of Teruel; Loyalist soldiers in rope-soled canvas shoes had fought in the mountain ice and snow for days without relief. In the corridor a man with broad shoulders and big frame was learning to walk again. He had lost both legs. I thought of myself in such a situation; how would I feel? The specialist told me that legless and armless men developed neuroses. The legless men sometimes refused to leave their beds. The armless men looked darkly into a future where they would have to be fed, clothed, and taken to the lavatory.

I was in New York for Christmas and peace and good will.

35. *The Death of a Nation*

I SPOKE on Russia at Ford Hall, Boston, on January 1, 1939, and began the year auspiciously by surprising both Trotzkyists and Stalinites. "FISCHER SHOCKS FAITHFUL BY SWING FROM STALIN LINE," the Trotzkyist *Socialist Review* said in a crudely sensational headline. The story announced that I had "developed a new orientation." It recorded that when a member of the audience asked me why the Soviet government did not admit refugees from Hitler-ruled countries, I replied, "I have not heard a satisfactory explanation why the Soviet government does not admit them." I was asked about the Moscow trials. I replied, "I do not approve of everything that is going on in the Soviet Union." I was asked about the settlement of Jews in Biro-bijan, the Far East Siberian territory. I expressed pessimism about its prospects.

"During the question period," continued the *Socialist Review*, "Dwyer, of the *Daily Worker*, took the floor and bitterly attacked Fischer."

Much against her own wish and mine, Markoosha was still in Russia. I had written to Yezhov, chief of the GPU, in May, 1938, asking him to allow my family to leave the Soviet Union. No answer. I had spoken to Litvinov about it in Geneva in September, 1938. He said he could do nothing and advised me to write to Stalin. I wrote to Stalin, by registered letter from Paris, in November, 1938. He got the letter. No reply. All Soviet channels were thus exhausted. I kept receiving letters and then cables from Markoosha in Moscow which showed her mounting desperation. I had to do something and quickly. Markoosha's nerves had been under a severe strain. She had applied for a passport and received a refusal. I was worried.

I knew that if I asked the State Department to intercede it would act through the United States Embassy in Moscow or get in touch with Soviet Ambassador Oumansky in Washington. Such démarches could be easily rejected by the Soviets, and then Markoosha would be in worse plight because a foreign government had intervened on her behalf. The approach to the Soviets had to be made in such a manner that it could not be repulsed.

On January 3, 1939, I wrote a letter to Mrs. Eleanor Roosevelt begging her to receive me "on a purely private matter which is urgent and very important to me." I got a wire soon saying that Mrs. Roosevelt would see me at the White House at four-thirty P.M. on January 6.

Mrs. Roosevelt had been showing several visitors through the rooms of the lower floor of the house and when they left I could hear her say to the Chief Usher, "Has Mr. Fischer arrived yet?" We sat down on a sofa and I quickly explained my family's predicament to her. What impressed me most was the way in which she immediately grasped all the implications of the situation. "The older boy is sixteen. That means he will soon be of military age," she remarked, for instance. She had studied in Germany and lived abroad, but the Soviet regime was a very distant phenomenon to her and yet she understood. I felt grateful and warm towards her for her instant and profound human comprehension. Mrs. Roosevelt said she would do what she could.

On January 18, I received an urgent telephone message to call Oumansky at the Soviet Consulate in New York. He wanted to see me. I went over. We talked for an hour about everything on the map but not about Markoosha and the boys. When I brought up the question he said, "Why haven't you mentioned it to me before?"

"Listen," I replied, "if your boss can't do anything why should I suppose you could!"

"All right," he said, "let's drop the subject. But tell me, why don't you write something about the Soviet Union?" It was the same subject.

I told him Spain monopolized my attention and I didn't feel like writing about Russia. He argued, coaxed, and complimented. He suggested that many Americans were wondering why I didn't write about the Soviet Union. They waited for a word from me about recent developments. I replied that I wouldn't write.

"Moscow will be very interested to learn that Louis Fischer refuses to write about the Soviet Union," Oumansky hinted.

"You can report anything you like," I declared. I wrote nothing.

The morning of January 21 brought a radiant telegram from Markoosha to the effect that she had been promised passports for three. I immediately sent the news to Mrs. Roosevelt. She wrote back suggesting I inform her when the whole family was reunited in the United States. (I did so in May, and Markoosha, George, Victor, and I were invited for a private dinner in the White House with Mrs. Roosevelt and the President. Eleanor Roosevelt would be the first lady of the land even if she were not First Lady.)

By cable I made an appointment to meet my family in London, and sailed for England on the *Queen Mary* on February 10. Lord Lothian and U. S. Ambassador Joseph P. Kennedy were on board. They spent much time together. I had one good talk with Lothian. We discussed many phases of the international situation. He was still an appeaser. I said, "After traveling through the country for lectures and talking to people in New York, I have the definite impression that most Americans are anti-Chamberlain and anti-appeasement." He said he too had traversed the country in recent months. But he had found that the only persons opposed to Chamberlain were the "Jews and radicals." After the war commenced, when he was Ambassador in Washington, Lothian expressed the same view to Maurice Hindus. To him, Lothian said that the only people who disliked Chamberlain were "radicals, Jews, and lecturers." There must be millions of lecturers in America.

Lothian and I also wrangled about Spain. Lothian said, "In April, 1936, Bullitt came to us from Moscow and told us that the Bolsheviks were preparing a revolution in Spain."

I did not inquire about the identity of "us." It might have meant the so-called "Cliveden set" of which Lothian was a member—the Astors, the *Observer* and *Times* people, and a number of outstanding British aristocrats. Or it might have meant British official circles. Bullitt, having broken with Russia and switched to an anti-Soviet position, informed important responsible persons in England, according to Lothian, that Moscow was preparing trouble in Spain. When the trouble came the British appeasers naturally concluded that it was this which Bullitt had foreseen. Bullitt thus made ample contribution to the Fascist victory in Spain.

"There are two answers to Bullitt's statement," I argued with Lothian. "One is that the war in Spain was started by Franco and not by the Communists or the Republicans. In the second place, if the Russians had been preparing a rebellion, how would they have prepared? They would have shipped arms to Spain. But the fact is that the Loyalists started the war with no arms at all."

Lothian did not say a word in reply. He asked me to come see him in London, which I did.

Two days after my arrival in England, I went to Harwich to meet the family, en route from Denmark. They had seen Helsingfors, Stockholm, and Copenhagen. The boys liked Helsingfors especially. They bought some good clothes there. Capitalism didn't seem as bad as it was painted in Moscow. Markoosha was sad for the friends she had left behind. Her own experiences had been more harrowing than I suspected. The GPU did not like the idea of her leaving; it resented the necessity of opening a little breach in the Chinese wall that surrounded the country.

On their third day in England, George and Victor, age sixteen and fifteen, went to a Sunday afternoon open-air meeting in Trafalgar Square. Under the statue of Nelson, workingmen and others gathered to advance the cause of the anti-Fascist Popular Front. This movement was led by Sir Stafford Cripps. When the boys got back to our hotel room, they reported to me about the meeting. In a whisper they said, "Papa, the people yelled, 'Chamberlain Must Go.'" They translated that into their own backgrounds; it was the equivalent of a demonstration on the Moscow Red Square shouting, "Stalin Must Go." No wonder they were surprised.

The next Sunday, Trafaglar Square saw another labor meeting, this time for Loyalist Spain. Attlee and Herbert Morrison addressed the thousands who assembled. The meeting adopted a resolution of protest against Chamberlain's Non-Intervention policy. The Labor leaders, followed by bands and sympathizers, then walked down Whitehall to deliver the resolution at Chamberlain's residence in 10 Downing Street. At this point, I went back to the hotel, but my kids got to the very door of the Prime Minister's home. Democracy was fun.

To tell the next story about the boys, I must first state that I have a reputation with them for mischief-making and pranks. We had guests one evening for dinner. At the end of the meal, the waiter brought finger bowls with water and a slice of lemon in them. I put my hand in the bowl. George laughed and said, "Just like papa." This was his first encounter with the bourgeois institution of washing hands in lemonade!

Markoosha and the boys had booked passage on the *Queen Mary*, sailing for New York on April 15. But Victor wanted the excitement of making the trip alone even though he knew only a few words of English. We let them have most of their wishes. So he went alone. I saw him off on the *Queen Mary* at Southampton, put his tip money for the ship personnel in separate envelopes, and bade him a calm farewell. Friends met him at the pier in New York. Markoosha caught up with him in New York a fortnight later, and I caught up with them another fortnight later.

On March 17, Markoosha and I were sitting in our London hotel when Ellen Wilkinson telephoned and said, "Chamberlain's making an important speech. D'you want to hear it?"

"Yes, how?" I replied.

"Just listen," she said. She put her telephone to her radio and I sat for at least half an hour listening to an address in Birmingham by Prime Minister Neville Chamberlain. It *was* important; it was his first step away from appeasement. On March 15, Hitler had invaded and annexed what remained of Czechoslovakia after Munich. This violated Hitler's own pledges. It shattered his oft-repeated assurances. "We are not interested in suppressing other nations," Hitler said in Berlin on September 26, 1938—four days before Munich. Why did he say it? To make Munich easier. To fool Chamberlain. "The Sudetenland is the last territorial claim which I have to make in Europe," he declared in the same speech for the same reason. "I have assured Mr. Chamberlain," Hitler continued, "and I emphasize it now, when this problem is solved, Germany has no more territorial problems in Europe. We don't want any Czechs."

So! And now he had taken all of Czechoslovakia. How did Chamberlain react? The day of the violent occupation of Czechoslovakia, Chamberlain rose in the House of Commons and made a statement. In the Birmingham speech forty-eight hours later—the one which I heard over Ellen Wilkinson's telephone—he himself described that first statement as "cool and objective." He called it "a very restrained and cautious exposition." At Birmingham he apologized for it. "I hope to correct that mistake tonight," he said.

The forty-eight hours had altered Chamberlain's reaction. His Birmingham speech was firm, and critical of Hitler. But the change in Chamberlain had been induced by events near home; active revolt brewed in the Conservative party. "His speech at Birmingham on Friday," wrote the *New Statesman*, "was a political necessity." Englishmen and upper-class Englishwomen picketed the House of Commons wearing cardboard placards front and back. The placards carried one word, "Churchill." The press demanded Churchill. The Labor party demanded action. The people cried, "Stop Hitler." Chamberlain could not see very far. But his hearing was excellent. A politician thinks first about his own political backing. Chamberlain heard the warning. In Birmingham he bent to the violent anti-appeasement tempest that raged over Britain. The country felt convinced that "that man" Hitler would have to be destroyed some day and it was better not to wait. So Chamberlain now asked "what reliance can be placed upon other assurances" by Hitler? "Is this the end of an old adventure, or is it the beginning of the new?" he wondered. He wasn't sure yet. "Is this, in fact, a step in the direction of an attempt to dominate the world by force?" He should have asked a Nazi high-school boy or a newspaper vendor on the Strand. Churchill had been answering those questions for years.

Chamberlain, however, had learned. He had learned that "we are not disinterested in what goes on in southeastern Europe," in the Balkans. He reminded Hitler that England would fight. He went so far as to suggest that "appeasement" was "not . . . a very happy term."

In a democracy, neither death nor birth is instantaneous. An old policy dies slowly. The pregnant period of a new one is prolonged. The policy of any government, sometimes even of a dictatorship, is like a moving ticker tape. The new policy comes in when the old is still visible. For a time both are valid. (Unlike the usual telegraph ticker tape, the ribbon of policy may travel in two directions.)

When Chamberlain spoke on March 17 at Birmingham, the ticker started typing out a new policy. The old policy had not yet been torn off. Some officials and some sections of the public still fought for appeasement. The type in which the new was printed seemed pale. But I have a wider circle of acquaintances in England than in any other country, and I felt certain that appeasement was on the decline. "This year," I wired to *The Nation* from London on March 4, before Chamberlain spoke in Birmingham, "marks the end of the era of map-carving by blackmail." After 1939 it would be too late for more Munichs. I therefore expected new demands from Germany and Italy in 1939, and since England and France would be stiffer, I expected trouble. Where? "Germany," I cabled, "is looking westward. The Ukraine has dropped out of the headlines."

Most observers predicted that after Munich Hitler would turn East. *Drang nach Osten.* I always thought this an illusion. On January 30, 1939, speaking in the Reichstag, Hitler demanded colonies. In *Mein Kampf* he had derided the idea of colonies. They had never done Germany any good, he stated correctly. He wanted the Ukraine instead. But now he turned westward. It was from England that he could get colonies. On January 30, likewise, Hitler promised that "a war against Italy, from whatever motive, will find Germany at her side." This meant that Hitler would support Mussolini in an offensive war too. Hitler, departing from his custom, refrained from anti-Soviet abuse in that speech.

It was when France and England awoke to the fact that Hitler was aiming at them, and not at Russia, that the ticker tape of appeasement started moving out. Simultaneously, Moscow said, "Hitler is looking West. We can breathe more freely. We don't need England and France as badly as before." Ivan Maisky, the astute Soviet Ambassador in London, told me in March, 1939, that the Soviet Union was in an "isolationist" mood. It leaned to neither side. I could see that between the lines of the Moscow newspapers which I read in London. Chamberlain and Daladier had believed Hitler's "anti-Comintern" and "anti-Communist" bluff. Suddenly, poor dear Neville Chamberlain discovered that he was the "Comintern," that Hitler meant him. No British Prime Minister had ever gone to a reception in the Soviet Embassy in London. On March 1, Chamberlain did, and allowed himself to be endlessly photographed in Maisky's parlors.

Things were happening.

Hitler was turning his "attention"—that meant his army—to Poland. Rumors of an impending invasion of Poland circulated widely. Prime Minister Chamberlain announced in the House of Commons on March 31, 1939, that if Poland resisted "His Majesty's Government would feel themselves bound at once to lend the Polish government all support in their power." For England to give such a guarantee was a striking departure both from precedent and from appeasement. The policy of appeasement was not yet dead. It was merely dying. Attempts would be made to save it. But the guarantee to Poland showed how far Chamberlain and his Tory party had traveled since Munich, indeed since March 15. Communists, Laborites, Liberals, and, on the Right, imperialists of the Churchill-Amery-Eden-Duff Cooper type continued to press the appeasers to abandon the vestiges of appeasement and make no more concessions to Hitler, Mussolini, and Japan.

I went to Paris, and on April 20, I saw Ambassador Bullitt in the

U. S. Embassy on the Place de la Concorde. He was, as usual, very affable.

Premier Daladier had warned the French Chamber of Deputies on February 24, "The next few months or even weeks would bring some redoubtable reefs to be faced, and peace would have to be defended with vigilance." The French were worried. The French government had great confidence in Bullitt and listened to his views. He felt very close to the French government. He exercised much more influence than any ambassador in Paris. Bullitt, being the sensitive artist, reacts to atmosphere and is influenced while he influences.

Bullitt devoted most of his conversation with me to an analysis and praise of Daladier. We didn't understand Daladier and underestimated him. He had been firm at Munich. At least in the morning. The deliberations at Munich, Bullitt told me, began with a speech by Hitler which was in the nature of an ultimatum. Daladier didn't like it and left the room. He said he had not come to Munich to hear ultimatums. Goering went out to calm Daladier and bring him back. Daladier resisted. (In other words, Daladier grasped the terrible significance of Hitler's demand.)

So far Bullitt. But in the evening, Daladier relented and surrendered. A tale gained currency that Daladier was drunk in the evening. Some people believed the story because they knew that Daladier occasionally did get drunk in the latter part of the day. But Chamberlain was not drunk at Munich; he probably was incapable of getting drunk. Yet he surrendered too, and he played the main appeasement role.

Bullitt indicated in his conversation with me that France would be firm. "Louis," he said to me, "why don't you go to London and tell your British Labor friends to stop opposing peacetime conscription?" In a conference with Sir Eric Phipps, the British Ambassador in Paris, Daladier had officially requested Britain to introduce conscription. France expected war. Bullitt knew it.

Three days before my talk with Bullitt, President Roosevelt had issued a peace appeal to Hitler and Mussolini. "Did you see the President's definition of Munich?" I said to Bullitt.

"No, where?" he replied.

I pulled from my pocket a clipping from the *London Times* of April 17 on which I had marked these words in the peace appeal: ". . . international problems can be solved at the council table. It is therefore not necessary to the plea for peaceful discussion for one side to plead that unless they receive assurances beforehand that the verdict will be theirs they will not lay aside their arms." This had been one feature of Munich; Chamberlain had undertaken in advance to give Hitler what he asked.

"In conference rooms, as in courts," Mr. Roosevelt continued, "it is necessary that both sides enter upon discussion in good faith, assuming that substantial justice will accrue to both, and it is customary and necessary that they leave their arms outside the room where they confer." Hitler had taken his planes, machine guns, and bombs into the room where he conferred with Chamberlain and Daladier at Munich.

Bullitt read the marked passage and said, "Yes."

Munichism was on the way out as the official French policy, and as the official British policy. Bullitt's attitude too had changed. With customary felicity of phrase, he formulated his new attitude in a speech on May 28, 1939, at the American Legion monument in Neuilly Cemetery, "To Americans the acceptance of war is a less horrible alternative than the acceptance of enslavement." And Czechoslovakia? "We therefore understand and sympathize with nations which, whatever the odds, prefer to fight for their freedom rather than to submit to the heel of the conqueror." Bravo! And Czechoslovakia? And Spain?

Spain was finished. Just about the week it died, Hitler seized the rump of Czechoslovakia.

Dr. Juan Negrin, Julio Alvarez del Vayo, President Azaña, and many other Loyalist leaders now resided in France as refugees—they and almost half a million more Spaniards who had fled from Catalonia shortly after Barcelona fell on January 26, 1939. Franco's Catalan forces attacked late in December with an unprecedented weight of arms. In his book, *Freedom's Battle*, Alvarez del Vayo recounts a visit to the Catalan front which he made with Prime Minister Negrin at the height of the offensive. They held a conference with General Rojo, Chief of Staff, and General Sarabia, commander. Negrin asked how many rifles the Loyalist army in Catalonia possessed.

"Thirty-seven thousand," Sarabia replied.

Thirty-seven thousand rifles for over a hundred thousand men. At Igualada, del Vayo records, two battalions of highly trained machine-gunners stood idle "for want of a single machine gun or rifle." The rebels, he reports, had from ten to twenty times as many planes as the Republic and thirty times as many tanks. The disproportion in all other branches was no less heartbreaking. No wonder Franco reached Barcelona and then the French frontier.

Madrid and the central Loyalist zone still held. For more than two years Madrid had been a crown on the head of the Spanish Republic and a thorn in the flesh of Franco. Suppose Madrid and the territory around it could have stood off Franco until September 3, when France and England went to war. Would France and England have saved it? Maybe. Maybe not.

The alternative was to surrender at once to Franco. That meant delivering to him many thousands of Republican heads. Franco had personally told James I. Miller, director of the United Press, in an interview printed in the *New York World-Telegram* of November 7, 1938, "We have more than two million persons card-indexed with proofs of their crimes and the names of witnesses." Commented Mr. Miller: Franco "revealed that the Republicans would not escape scot free after the war."

Negrin and Vayo could not hand over two million people to the Fascist executioner. But Madrid and its hinterland were exhausted. Thirty months of shells, bombs, encircling peril, and hunger! It was too much to ask human beings to go on when they could see no chance of victory.

It was a cruel dilemma. Negrin and del Vayo hoped, by holding out a little while longer, to extract a promise of mercy and clemency from Franco and to win time for the flight of those with a price on their heads. But their slogan was "Resist, resist, resist," and that had been the slogan from the beginning of the war. The people wanted peace. The Communists nevertheless favored resistance until the end of their strength. Negrin and del Vayo agreed to carry on in the hope that, with the intervention of the British and French which they had requested, Loyalists trapped in the central zone would be able to escape abroad.

The Communists occupied a commanding position in the central zone. Army Chief General Miaja was under Communist influence and carried a Communist party card though he probably knew as much about Communism as Francisco Franco. Communist propaganda had inflated him into a myth. Jesus Hernandez served as Communist party leader in Madrid and he wielded real power.

But the domination of the Communists weakened their popularity. This, to me, was the proof of the irrepressible democracy of the Spaniards. As soon as one group acquired a political monopoly in a certain region it lost influence with the people and was booted out. This happened to the Anarchists in the Aragon in 1937, and now to the Communists in the Madrid area.

From France, after the Catalan debacle, Negrin and del Vayo flew to Alicante where Negrin phoned Colonel Casado, the military commander at Madrid. Casado said, "I have revolted."

"Against whom?" Negrin asked.

"Against you," Casado replied.

Negrin phoned Valencia, Murcia, Albacete, and Estremadura. They replied in much the same manner. Miaja stood with Casado.

Negrin and del Vayo wanted no blood shed and they flew back to France. But the Communists in Madrid fought against the forces under Casado. Individual Socialists and bourgeois Republicans also opposed Casado with arms. For many days, men who had stood shoulder to shoulder resisting Franco fired upon one another. The few remaining Loyalist planes dropped bombs on Loyalists. The streets of Madrid, which no rebel had trod, ran with Republican blood. Victorious, Casado and the Socialist leader Besteiro surrendered Madrid to Franco. Franco immediately took reprisals. The first victim was Besteiro who died in a Fascist prison. Casado fled to London.

It was a miserable close for a saga of national heroism. The Spanish people rose to great heights in the great struggle. It showed that centuries of poverty had not killed its pride, honor, and self-respect. Now Franco would undertake to eradicate these through Fascism.

In Paris, after the heartrending final episode of the Casado-Besteiro revolt, I had tea in a Champs Elysées café with Trudi Araquistain, Madame del Vayo's sister. She approved of Casado. She was passionately anti-Communist. "Oh, I'm sorry Pasionaria escaped," Trudi said about the Spanish woman Communist leader. "I'm sorry she wasn't shot in Madrid."

This is a measure of the bitterness engendered among Spanish anti-Fascists by the fight against Fascism. The Loyalists in exile now entered upon the sad role of émigrés. The law of all emigrations is: Man Eats Man, Friend Assails Friend. Parties split into fractions, the fractions into factions, the factions into groups, the groups into grouplets. In the *Daily Worker*, André Marty called del Vayo a "wretch" while Pasionaria attacked Negrin from Moscow for his pro-British sentiments. More conservative Loyalists criticized Negrin for collaborating with Communists at a time when they did too.

Everybody blamed everybody else for the defeat. Everybody made wild accusations. Everyone thinks the Spain of the future is his. Meanwhile many must fret about their permit to stay in the country of asylum and worry about the next meal.

A nation died when Franco won. But nations have been reborn.

36. *A Yachtful of Diamonds and Pearls*

TOWARDS the end of 1938, the Spanish Republican government rented a handsome villa in Deauville, one of the most fashionable seashore resorts in France. In the villa lived several well-dressed men and several beautiful Spanish ladies. They led the life of rich South Americans spending the season at the playground of Europe's high society.

As Franco's army pushed closer to Barcelona in December, 1938, Negrin, Loyalist Prime Minister, started worrying about the government's treasures. When the civil war started in 1936, many wealthy Spanish aristocrats, landlords, and industrial magnates fled Republican territory precipitously and could not smuggle out their jewels. The Republic gathered up these fabulously valuable gems. It ransacked private mansions and palaces in the mountains. Its agents tapped walls to find secret safes. In the deserted house of a countess of ancient lineage in Madrid they confiscated a cache including a necklace of black pearls, a diamond tiara, and other like knickknacks worth several million dollars. Similar finery left in bank vaults by Fascists who had been executed or imprisoned were added to the government hoard. Some of the jewels were family heirlooms that had been brought from the Golconda in India when sixteenth-century Spanish explorers sailed around the Cape of Good Hope in search of the wealth of the East.

Each piece of jewelry was carefully catalogued and described. A special guard responsible to Negrin was put in charge. Negrin told them they would pay with their lives for any theft or loss.

The entire treasure was kept in Figueras, near the French border. It had been transferred to that city shortly after the beginning of the siege of Madrid. There was a hoary fortress at Figueras with several subterranean levels which no aerial bomb could demolish.

No one person ever had access to the treasure. Nothing could be taken from it without the written permission of the entire Board of Custody which consisted of officials of the Finance Ministry. When the League of Nations Commission which counted the foreign volunteers in Loyalist Spain had finished its labors, Negrin and Foreign Minister del Vayo wished to show their appreciation of the impartial efforts of the Commission by giving its Chairman, the Finnish General Jalander, and its Secretary, Lieutenant Colonel Basch of France, two small presents in the form of inexpensive trinkets. They had to make a special request of the Board of Custody which voted to grant it.

As the front crept nearer to Figueras, Negrin gave orders to have the entire treasure transported to the chic villa in Deauville. But this was merely a temporary expedient. For if the Loyalist regime collapsed the jewels would not be safe from the French authorities or from Franco spies. Spanish Fascists had been reported loitering in the vicinity of the villa. There were spies everywhere. Negrin accordingly gave instructions for the purchase of an ocean-going yacht.

Catalonia fell. France was hostile to the Loyalists. Negrin immediately ordered his officials to remove the jewels from France to the Western Hemisphere.

One night in the second week of February, 1939, the well-dressed inhabitants of the Deauville villa put on working clothes and carried huge cases filled with diamonds, sapphires, emeralds, pearls, and gold and platinum jewelry down to the sea and loaded them on the yacht *Vita*. The estimated value of the jewels was $50,000,000. The cargo also contained strong boxes packed tight with stocks and bonds.

The treasure on the *Vita* was in charge of Señor Puente, a young officer in the Carabineros who had just been promoted to the rank of colonel. He belonged to the Spanish Socialist party, and Negrin trusted him. Negrin told Colonel Puente to place the jewels in the safe-keeping of President Cardenas of Mexico. They would remain in Mexico until a favorable turn in the wheel of history made it possible for the anti-Fascist Republicans to return to Spain and set up a government. Then the treasure would constitute the Republic's financial foundation stone.

The *Vita* under Colonel Puente left Deauville at full speed. Its swift engines carried it quickly away from the shores of Europe toward America. Then it slackened its pace and cruised leisurely. It stopped in a West Indies port to refuel and take on fresh water and food. Meanwhile, Dr. José Puche, Chief of the Health Service of the Republic army, was racing from Europe to Mexico to act as Negrin's contact man with President Cárdenas.

But Colonel Puente was an old admirer of Indalecio Prieto, veteran

Socialist leader and former Loyalist Minister of War. Prieto had been ousted from the government by Negrin and sent as Spain's special plenipotentiary to the inauguration of Pedro Aguirre Cerda, the new Chilean Popular Front president. That decorative mission completed, Prieto, filled with resentment against Negrin for having superseded him and eliminated him from active participation in Spanish politics, took up residence in Mexico City.

From the high seas, Colonel Puente sent a radio to Prieto in Mexico. When the yacht *Vita* anchored at a Mexican port, its jewels were turned over to Prieto. Negrin's special emissary, Dr. Puche, arrived too late.

When the Spanish War ended, Negrin himself went to Mexico and saw President Cárdenas, He also tried to see Prieto. However, Prieto refused to meet Negrin. An acrimonious exchange of letters took place between Prieto and Negrin. One of Negrin's letters was thirty-eight pages long. Nothing helped. Technically, the *Vita's* treasure is in the custody of the Mexican state. Actually, Prieto has access to it and can from time to time attempt to market its gems and valuable papers. Negrin has lost it. Prieto could use the money to assist Spanish refugees.

The beautiful *Vita*, flying the flag of Panama, rides at anchor in the harbor of Acapulco, Mexico.

37. Settling Down in America

MY friends have always predicted that some day I would "settle down"—and I suppose gather moss. I arrived in New York on May 1, aboard the *S.S. Normandie*, which also carried Negrin and a party of Loyalists who were en route to Mexico to see about the *Vita* treasure. I love the heat of summer. I played tennis, swam, canoed, and thought of settling down. Meanwhile, I scampered about America delivering lectures.

What would I have to do to settle down? Live in one place and take a job? My record was still pretty good. My last steady job was in 1921. In 1928, Frederick R. Kuh, in charge of the United Press bureau in Berlin, summoned me from Moscow to substitute for him, at an enormous salary, while he went on vacation to Chicago. I stayed in his office for three days and found it intolerable. So I took the night train to Heidelberg, my favorite spot in Germany, rowed on the Neckar, walked on Philosophenhoehe, and expanded in the sun for two weeks. That supplied me with the necessary *Sitzfleisch* to occupy Kuh's chair for the next two months.

I like to impose discipline on myself. I hate others to impose it on me. I can work hard if nobody drives me. I would never take steady work just to earn money. I don't need money that badly. I spend freely when I have the means, but I can also reduce my standards to my means. I have no possessions and few clothes. My most expensive vice is taxis. I spend no money on tobacco or drink—and very little on women. Come to think of it, that is not quite true—since 1929 I have been contributing to the support of my wife. But that should end soon. She is writing a book.

In June, the second month of my settling-down, I delivered an address at the annual conference of Settlement Workers which met in Jamestown, New York, under the presidency of Helen Hall. A few days later I repeated it at the annual conference of Social Workers which met in Buffalo under the presidency of her husband, Paul Kellogg. It was a general survey of the international scene. But I also revealed changes that were taking place inside me. I discussed Fascism and Sovietism. Russia had demonstrated that "an economy from which private capitalism has been eliminated can build up a country and produce on a large scale. . . . On the other hand, Soviet production for the daily use of the population is woefully inadequate. The flow of consumers' goods is irregular and insufficient and has shown no tendency to satisfy the nation's requirements. Above all, the Soviet government's significant economic and social progress and the successful defense of its territories in a hostile environment have been achieved at great expense to the liberties of men and to intellectual and artistic freedom. The restrictions, far from being relaxed in accordance with the promise of the 1936 Constitution, and as domestic stability and invulnerability against foreign attack grew, have actually been tightened."

Then my true confession: "These aspects of the world situation . . . have radically altered our sense of values. . . . Those who once said, 'Yes, we have the freedom of the press but . . . ,' those who daily argued about the weaknesses of parliamentary regimes have been educated by bitter events. The operations of dictatorships have taught anti-capitalists and leftists to treasure freedom above all else. Without civil rights there is no economic security even when unemployment has disappeared, and peace and national security are tenuous where the will of the people is ignored. The dictatorships have made us love democracy more."

Further in my address to the conferences in June, I declared, "It looks as if we are today approaching another major international crisis reminiscent of September, 1938. . . . Russia holds the key to the war-or-peace situation. I do not know whether the Anglo-Soviet pact will be concluded. But if the negotiations fail, world peace will be in grave danger. The Fascists will take advantage of the disunity. . . . The Russians are torn between the wisdom of isolation and the necessity of co-operation. The British are torn between their passionate dislike of the Bolsheviks and the imperative need of another mighty ally. . . . If Russia stays out the responsibilities of the United States will be greater." I felt that the question of war or peace hung by the outcome of Russia's talks with the powers. The role of Russia was paramount.

Dashiell Hammett, Mary van Kleeck, Vincent Sheean, Corliss Lamont, Donald Ogden Stewart and several others addressed an open letter in July, 1939, to "all active friends of democracy and peace" asking them to sign, for publication, a statement setting forth the differences between the Soviet Union and Fascist states. I looked down the list of the ten who initiated the open letter and found that at least half of them knew nothing or little about Soviet conditions. Then I read the ten pages of text elaborating the contrast between Bolshevist Russia and Fascist countries, and I writhed. I discussed it with Markoosha in a New York apartment we had rented for the summer. Her reaction was the same as mine. I would not sign. I started to write my reply. I kept the rough draft, "After careful consideration, I have decided not to sign your letter because it contains a number of statements whose categorical nature results in a departure from the complicated truth." July 17, 1939. I didn't like the formulation very much and let it lie and in the end sent nothing. Four hundred Americans, mostly liberals, did sign. Max Lerner subsequently said to me that I should have protested publicly at the time. He was probably right. But I still hesitated; Russia had not yet aligned itself with Hitler.

I could have accepted the Open Letter's declaration that the Soviet Union "has eliminated racial and national prejudice within its borders." But the proposition that trade unions in the Soviet Union are free is ridiculous and untrue. They are passive, unprotesting instruments of the government and the Communist party. Point Nine sang a hymn to Soviet democracy and the Constitution. How could I subscribe to that after the purges and trials and the terror? "The Soviet Union has emancipated woman and the family." Yes, but part of that was on paper. The compulsion to raise large families—since abortions had been prohibited and sufficient contraceptives were not available—fettered women anew, and difficult material conditions which necessitated long standing in queues, hard housework in badly built and badly equipped apartments and a constant struggle with shortages vitiated many of the benefits of progressive legislation. A frigidaire, an electric washing machine, green vegetables, a doctor for the children when you want him, easy shopping, a pleasant bathroom, and a home and political atmosphere without excessive tension also make women free. Economic conditions in Russia were not improving. On the contrary.

Above all, my mind protested against the implications of the Open Letter. The Soviet regime was founded to produce a better human being. Now it was assassinating the human being—sometimes with bullets, sometimes with lies and false confessions.

(The Open Letter with its four hundred signatures was published in the press the day before the news of the Soviet-Nazi pact shocked the world!)

And now all my thoughts about settling down were interrupted. The radio and the newspapers recorded the rising temperature of a patient I had known for a long time: Europe. On August 9, I sailed for Europe on the *Queen Mary*. I did not know that the second World War was three weeks off. But I felt that something was coming which I must not miss.

38. *Europe Slips into War*

MONDAY, August 14, 1939, the day of my arrival in Paris, I had dinner with the H. R. Knickerbockers. Walter Duranty was there. We discussed Bullitt. I said he had, until lately, been an appeaser. He was the only important foreign diplomat present at Le Bourget when Daladier landed there from Munich. He had defended Munich in conversation with me. Knickerbocker said he didn't believe Bullitt had been at Le Bourget. I said, "Call and find out." Knick phoned and asked for Bullitt's secretary. "He is out," the answer came. "Is there any message?"

"Please tell him Knickerbocker telephoned."

"Hello, Knick, this is Bill."

Knickerbocker told Bullitt our conversation and asked about Le Bourget. Bullitt confirmed it.

A few days later, I called on Soviet Ambassador Suritz. I had known Suritz for many years. When he was in the Berlin Embassy in 1934, I had lunch with him one day and talked about the possibility of a close alliance between Germany, Italy, and Japan. It is one of my regrets that I failed to write an article along these lines at that time. I sketched for Suritz what the three self-styled "Havenots" might gain by co-operating in Europe, in the Mediterranean, and against India. Suritz disagreed. After lunch he called in Bessonov, his Counselor, who also disagreed, and a debate went on for another hour. When the Fascist triangle actually emerged in 1936, I rose in Suritz's estimation, and in Paris, during the Spanish struggle, we used to have long intimate conversations about international events.

Now I went to him to ask about the situation. Did he think Hitler would attack Poland? He did not know. "But in any case," he said with emphasis, "the line should be clear. If France and England want to stop Hitler from going into Poland they should sign an agreement with the Soviet government. If he goes into Poland, they should of course reach an understanding with the Soviet government."

That was August 19.

I had gone to bed when Knickerbocker telephoned at midnight on the twenty-first to tell me that Ribbentrop was flying to Moscow. I immediately saw a picture of the Nazi who had fashioned the anti-Comintern pact being welcomed in the Kremlin where the Comintern was wont to meet. Ten minutes later the telephone rang again. A friend was calling from New York to ask whether Ribbentrop's flight to Russia meant war in Europe. I walked my room for an hour after that. It seemed a day of doom.

Suritz had been perfectly sincere. Soviet embassies are rarely informed about goings-on in Moscow. The negotiations between the Soviets and the democracies had proceeded in parallel with the negotiations between the Soviets and Hitler. Stalin did not tell his left fingers what his right hand was doing.

Colonel Charles Sweeny, professional soldier, lover of France, anti-appeaser and staunch pro-Loyalist by healthy instinct, took me on August 23 to the Anglo-American Press Club luncheon. The permanent British and American correspondents in Paris met regularly at lunch for comradeship and exchange of views. On this occasion, I remember among those present P. J. Philip, Englishman, correspondent of the *New York Times*, Jo Davidson, Edmond Taylor, of the *Chicago Tribune* and author, subsequently, of that sensitive, intelligent book, *The Strategy of Terror*, and John Elliott of the *New York Herald Tribune*. Arthur Sweetser was the guest speaker. He was a high American official of the League of Nations and had just returned from America. He spoke on conditions at home. Then the chairman asked me to say a few words on the Nazi-Soviet pact. I was surprised; I had not expected to be called upon. I was in no mood to say anything. The text of the pact had not yet appeared in the Paris press. The purpose and general contents of the document, however, were known.

Ed Taylor records the following in his book, "Louis Fischer also spoke at the Press Club, said German-Soviet pact was a terrible blow, terrible encouragement to aggression. Even said it was 'criminal' to make such an alliance at such a time. Seemed very despondent." I recall my concluding sentence, "I see only unrelieved blackness." I expected the worst. Two days later I wrote an article analyzing and assailing the pact.

The Soviet-Nazi pact of August 23, 1939, was not merely an arrangement for future deeds. Every diplomatic agreement is of the future, present, and past. Stalin's agreement with Hitler was a product of the Moscow trials and purges and of the deep social phenomena which brought them about. The pact was the beginning of something but also the end of something. Russia ceased struggling with itself.

The young rebel because they have much time. The old say, "We will not see the results anyway." Youth, with a whole life to spend, chucks it into the fight. The aged, who have least to lose, count costs. The Bolshevik Revolution was a revolt against Russia. Its primary purpose was to overcome Russia by destroying the ugly material, psychological, and cultural heritage of Czarism. But revolution is the line of most resistance. Revolutions may grow old and tired. Then they sign an armistice with the enemy. Bolshevism's enemy was Russia.

Stalin is a mixture of revolution and Russia. He is Karl Marx superimposed on Peter the Great. They are in conflict within him as they are in conflict within the country. There were times when Marx's pull was stronger. Now Peter is on top.

Stalin had led a vigorous crusade against the physical vestiges of Russia's past; he introduced the five-year plans and agrarian reorganization. But he succumbed to the spirit of old Russia. He surrendered to Russian nationalism. He has adopted, and perfected, some of Czarism's worst methods of repression. If the revolution had destroyed more of Russia, Stalin could have destroyed less of the revolution.

The Nazi-Soviet pact was prepared by the years of revolutionary ebb in Russia between 1936 and 1939. The pact was a symptom of the advanced state of corruption resulting from Stalin's personal dictatorship. But that only partially explains it. It took three to make that agreement: Stalin, Hitler, and Chamberlain-Daladier.

The case of Hitler is very simple. He contemplated an assault on Poland which might result in a major war. He knew, and every German knew, that Germany lost the first World War because it fought Russia in the East and England and France in the West. In another two-front war, Germany was sure to lose again. Hitler wanted a war on one front. The pact with Stalin gave it to him.

The French *Yellow Book*, published by the French Foreign Office after the outbreak of war, contains a striking report sent by Robert Coulondre, the French Ambassador, from Berlin to Paris on June 1, 1939. His reporting was reliable and most of his prognostications proved correct. He passed on, as "positively truthful information," this: "It is believed in the upper circle here that if there is an armed conflict with Poland on account of Danzig the result will be a general war. Hitler asked General Keitel, chief of the staff, and General von Brauchitsch, commander-in-chief of the Reichswehr, if, under present conditions, Germany could win a general war. Both said it depended on whether Russia stayed out or came into the war. In case she stayed out Keitel's answer was 'Yes,' while Brauchitsch (whose opinion is worth more) answered 'Probably.' Both generals stated that if Germany had to fight against Russia too it would have little chance of victory."

Hitler accordingly bent every effort towards keeping Russia out of the war. It is possible that but for the pact with Stalin, Hitler would not have gone to war in 1939. Hitler probably hoped that a pact with Stalin would frighten the Western Powers out of going to war when he invaded Poland. Stalin may have had similar expectations. The Nazi-Bolshevik pact was a maneuver designed to restore appeasement to full power in England and France. Its primary purpose was to bring about a Polish Munich. When that failed to eventuate, it brought about the second World War in which, however, Germany had no eastern front.

Although the Soviets and Germany were the only two governments to sign the pact of August 23, 1939, others helped to make it. Chamberlain and Daladier, personal symbols of the reactionary appeasers of their democratic countries, made a twofold contribution: first, they contributed to it by appeasing, and then, they contributed to it by ceasing to appease. The attitude of Great Britain and France in crises affecting Ethiopia, China, Spain, and Czechoslovakia disgusted everybody in the Soviet Union—and particularly Maxim Litvinov. The cold rebuffs administered to Moscow by London and Paris irritated the Soviet government. Stalin had preached collective security as the only hopeful alternative to Hitler's bi-lateral treaties which led to aggression. But Chamberlain and Daladier rejected all of Stalin's and Litvinov's offers. The Kremlin, chagrined, nevertheless hoped stubbornly for an understanding with the Western Powers against the Fascist Powers. Stalin pursued the policy of courting England and France long after Munich. Russia feared the Fascist Powers. Russia feared an attack by Germany with the connivance or encouragement of England and France. The friends of Russia in England and France, the friends of peace, and the friends of the British

and French empires directed their efforts towards the abandonment
of appeasement; they urged aid to the victims of Fascist attack.

Then, gradually, the British and French started abandoning appeasement. The friends of Russia, the enemies of Fascism, and the
orthodox British and French imperialists were winning the day
against Chamberlain and Daladier. Chamberlain and Daladier themselves began to realize that Hitler could never be appeased. Appeasement was going out the window. England and France were generat-
ing a mood of resistance to further totalitarian violence. In March,
1939, England gave a guarantee to Poland. This made good news in
Moscow. If England and France would fight over Poland then Russia
had nothing to fear from Germany. Germany, after eating up Poland,
would have to turn around against France. In that case, Germany
needed Russia's friendship to insure against a two-front war. Hence
the pact.

The end of appeasement, which was the beginning of the second
World War, meant that Germany would be busy fighting the Allies
and would not be in a position to concentrate on Russia. For the
first time in years, therefore, Stalin had a choice in foreign affairs.
Formerly, he could not have been pro-German because Hitler did
not want him. Hitler wanted the anti-Communist slogan which lulled
Chamberlain and Daladier into appeasement. Stalin, accordingly,
could only have been pro-Ally. But now he could be pro-Ally or
pro-German.

This was a wonderful opportunity to remain truly neutral. Europe
would be engaged in war and Russia could stay out. I criticize Stalin's
new foreign policy because he threw away this opportunity. Instead
of remaining at peace, he went to war in Poland and Finland. Instead
of remaining neutral, he rebuffed one belligerent group and made a
compact with the other. Instead of keeping aloof he smiled on Hitler
and engaged in aggression.

Soviet Russia helped Hitler by giving him access to its meager surpluses of oil, fodder, cotton, iron, and other materials. It helped Hitler, as the *Pravda* editorial boasted on August 23, 1940, the anniversary of the signature of the pact, by "guaranteeing Germany undisturbed security in the East." It helped Germany by inducing Communists in England, France, the United States, and smaller countries
to sabotage the war effort against Hitler. It helped Germany by acting as a transit country for German imports.

Since the signing of the Soviet-Nazi pact, Soviet newspapers and spokesmen have refrained from condemning Hitler and Mussolini. Anti-Fascist agitation has been curbed in the Soviet Union. The country had been taught to abhor every manifestation of Fascism. This propaganda then ceased, and in its place came virulent diatribes against France, England, and the United States.

Nazi aggression was not merely passively condoned. The Bolsheviks justified it. The *New York Sunday Worker* of May 12, 1940, printed a two-page article by George Dimitrov, secretary-general of the Comintern, on the war situation. It is one long attack on the Western Powers. It contains only two references to Germany: the first, a factual mention of the conclusion of the Nazi-Bolshevik pact; the second, "The French and British war incendiaries are exerting unparalleled pressure on the small neutral states and have openly trampled the neutrality of the Scandinavian countries underfoot. Germany has retaliated by occupying Denmark and a large part of Norway." Dimitrov exculpating Hitler and Goering! What a spectacle!

The same issue of the same paper carried an article wired from Moscow the previous day by André Marty, French Communist leader. "Already," he complains, "the Lofoten Isles and Iceland are 'under the protection' of Chamberlain." The Lofoten Isles are dots in the harbor of Narvik. This is the greatest of all crimes. The Lofoten Isles! But Marty does not even mention the Nazi occupation of Holland, Belgium, Norway, and Denmark. That was all right. That was done by Hitler. Later the Communists similarly contended that the Greeks had provoked Mussolini into attacking them. Sweet Mussolini. He never attacks unless provoked. Ask the Loyalists. Ask the Abyssinians. Ask the Albanians. Ask the Italians.

For me, the essential and shocking incongruity of the Nazi-Soviet pact was the intimacy it inaugurated between a state founded as a workers' regime and a state that had smashed workers' political parties and trade unions and imprisoned, tortured, and murdered many thousands of Communists and Socialists; between a state that gave equality to nationalities and a state based on the principle of the supremacy of one Aryan race; between a state that spoke in the name of a new culture and a state that behaved like a mechanized barbarian. The pact, moreover, denies the most fundamental idea of world peace—that only a union of non-aggressors can guarantee individual nations against aggression. This is what Litvinov had always preached. This is what Stalin had preached.

I felt immediately that Moscow's treaty with Fascist Germany was bad for Russia as a country and bad for the labor movement abroad. "We are back to zero," André Malraux said to me in Paris.

"It is the war," the cashier in my hotel sighed when she read the news of the pact. She had lived in Russia before 1914 and spoke a few words of Russian still and had some sympathy with the Left. Thousands of Frenchmen called to the colors within two days after Ribbentrop and Molotov affixed their signatures to the document naturally blamed it for their personal misfortune. Communists were confused and waited for a cue from Moscow. When the Soviet Ambassador in London heard of Ribbentrop's flight to Moscow he said it couldn't be true. When it was confirmed, the Communists said the treaty would contain an escape clause making the whole treaty invalid in case Germany went to war. But it contained no escape clause. The Communists defended the pact nevertheless, and found virtues in it and in the reprehensible acts that flowed from it. If a single Communist had advocated such a Nazi-Soviet arrangement before it was concluded I might have respected the Communist defense of it later on. But all Communists condemned anybody who suggested the remote likelihood of an agreement between Moscow and Berlin. In June, 1939, at the University of Virginia Institute of Politics, Earl Browder said publicly that there was as much chance of such a pact as there was of his becoming President of the United States Chamber of Commerce. Yet he defended it when it came. When I had met Browder at Charlottesville he criticized the passage in my speeches in which I had suggested the possibility that Moscow would not sign with the Allies.

The first duty of every chief of state is to safeguard his state. But they can make mistakes. Chamberlain and Daladier blundered through appeasement into war. History, I believe, will show that Hitler committed an error when he seized the rest of Czechoslovakia. I think Stalin made a fatal blunder by aligning himself with Hitler. Suppose he had not signed with Hitler, nor, at least for a time, signed with the Western Powers? Suppose he had remained truly neutral and within his own frontiers instead of occupying small nations whose independence he himself, as late as March 10, 1938, had pledged the Soviet government to defend? What would have happened?

If Stalin was in a position to force Hitler to retire from his position in the Baltic states and the eastern half of Poland he would certainly have been able to get less from Hitler, to wit: no German penetration into these territories. This would have given Russia buffers against Germany instead of a common frontier. It might be argued that if Russia had not actually taken over these countries Hitler could do so in the future. But if England and France had not declared war on Germany on September 3, 1939, what would have prevented Hitler from vetoing the Russian occupation of the Baltic states and Eastern Poland? Germany is stronger than Russia. The pact itself was no protection. The pact is a piece of paper. The value of such a piece of paper depends on circumstances. The circumstance that invested the pact with validity was the war in the West on which Hitler had to concentrate. If there had been no pact at all the same thing would have been true; Hitler engaged in the West could not have molested Russia. It was not the pact, accordingly, which gave Russia safety. It merely gave Russia the opportunity of stealing foreign territory and of suppressing small nations. Neutrality without a pact would have been just as safe for the Soviet Union and much more honorable. At a later stage in the war—if the war had come without the pact—the Bolsheviks could have assumed a less neutral and more pro-Allied stand. For Germany and Japan are potential national menaces to Russia. Hitler has announced his designs on Soviet territory. The Japanese are aggressive neighbors; the United States, England, and France are not.

The photographs of Stalin smiling on Ribbentrop in the Kremlin were an indictment. Stalin did not have to be present at the signing of the pact. He had never before attended the signing of a treaty. He did it with a purpose: to show how loyal he intended to remain to Hitler. My friends in Moscow—those that remained—had been taught to abominate the swastika. Now they saw it intertwined with the red flag.

When the Soviet-Nazi pact was signed I expected war. Nevertheless, or perhaps therefore, I went by car with the del Vayos the next day to La Baule on the Brittany coast to enjoy the last week of summer and the last week of peace. Pablo Azcarate, the former Loyalist envoy in London, was spending the summer at La Baule with his family. To salve my journalist's conscience I told myself that it would be a good idea to see the province on the eve of war.

On the beach at La Baule, I bet Azcarate five hundred francs that major European powers would be at war within six weeks. (Within a week he sent me the money by messenger. Suspecting that I would hesitate to accept it, he wrote, "I have lost. I have, therefore, to pay. It is one of the oldest and best established laws in the world.")

Along the highway to Brittany old women were pasting official mobilization posters on telegraph poles and walls. Only a few classes were being summoned. On our way back from La Baule, on August 31, new posters summoned more and more classes. The men of France were going off to war—again. The women bade them farewell again, and did not know whether they would return. At the little monuments to the dead of 1914-18—there is one in every town and village of France—women in black were laying little bunches of fresh flowers. The memory of those dead became more poignant as young men went up to stand where their fathers had fallen. France, which had been bled white in 1914-18, would give its blood again.

The next morning at five, the Nazis marched into Poland. The employees of my hotel were pale. I felt the nervousness of Paris as one may feel the nervousness of a person to whom one is talking. I walked the streets most of the day. Luggage stores were doing a rushing business. Many taxis had been requisitioned and others hired to take Parisians out to the country. The trains were packed with soldiers. I went to the Gare d'Est. From this station soldiers departed for the Maginot Line. Men in civilian clothes with heavy hobnailed military shoes and little suitcases at their feet sat with their girls or wives and children at little marble-covered tables in cafés in the streets leading to the station. No one smiled. They knew what it had meant in the last war. The station and the area around it were like one sprawling funeral. It was much more depressing than an air raid in Spain.

September 3, at 11.00 A.M., Great Britain declared war on Germany. France held back. Georges Bonnet, the arch-appeaser, and Mussolini were trying to leave England isolated so that the full weight of the Nazi attack would fall immediately on England. This would accord with the Hitler principle of "knock them out one by one." I spent the afternoon of September 3—it was on Sunday that war came—at the La Phaisanderie estate of Lucien Vogel, Condé Nast representative in Paris. We were sitting in the open at 5 P.M. A lone plane flew overhead. The radio announced France at war. Bonnet had lost.

Going back to town, we saw women along the streets of little towns gazing morosely into nowhere. Some bit their fingernails. Some cried. At one point traffic was held up. Our car halted alongside a line of farm horses that had been requisitioned for army use. Heavy, well-groomed, powerful horses. A farmer put his arms around the neck of his horse, put his cheek against its head, and talked into its ear. The horse shook its head up and down. They were saying good-by.

I dined that evening with the Knickerbockers and later found a taxi in the blackout to take me back to the hotel. Before going to bed I laid out my clothes so that I could dress easily in the dark in case of a raid and I put my flashlight within reach. I had done this so often in Spain. Now war had come to Paris. In 1937, I had suggested to French friends a poster for distribution in France. It showed Madrid being bombed, and the title was, "After Madrid, Paris?" "Propaganda," some people said contemptuously. In the night I heard the siren, but it did not sound serious, and I stayed in bed.

Downstairs, in the morning, everybody was exchanging impressions. What they had said in the shelter. How the anti-aircraft fired. Someone had seen a plane shot down. "I swear I did." One told where bombs had fallen. The official bulletin said the planes had been intercepted before they reached Paris.

Paris had the jitters visibly. Autos crammed with human beings and baggage were rushing out of town. No taxis. Many small traffic accidents: cars scraping one another, bumping into one another; bad driving because of bad nerves.

France went to war without rejoicing, without enthusiasm, without any sentiment except a desire for animal safety.

So Europe was again at war. The war did not have to be. The governments of Europe, and governments outside of Europe, are responsible for it. Hitler alone could not have made the war. Nor could there have been a Hitler in Germany but for events and policies in other countries. Two wars in twenty-six years are a blot on civilization. They condemn the statesmen and the social forces which control our world and which led mankind into this massacre. Until August 23, 1939, it might have been said that capitalism bore the guilt. Now Bolshevism shares the guilt. Russia, in fact, made war on Poland and Finland. Fascism, Communism, and Capitalism are responsible for the second World War. That is why we are "back to zero."

How, then, can wars be prevented? I strongly favor those who fight Hitler. But human beings are too precious, and the machines their minds can now create are too destructive, for the world to go to war once or twice in a generation. It is necessary now to oust the maniacal tyrant. But simultaneously a new social order and a new international organization must be evolved which will make Kaisers as well as Hitlers, Czars as well as Stalins, Chamberlains as well as Poincarés forever impossible.

39. *Europe at War*

I STAYED in Paris from September 3, 1939, the day France and England declared war, to September 21, and was bored throughout. No excitement. No important changes. Just bad news from Poland to disturb the day, and a few air-raid alarms to disturb some nights.

Immediately after the outbreak of war I stopped playing tennis, because it would have been inconceivable to play tennis in Spain during the war. You would have offended the people. But here in Paris Edmond Taylor, Walter Kerr, William Henry Chamberlin and Hubert R. Knickerbocker played straight on, and finally I decided that it was foolish not to play and joined them. Some Frenchmen played too.

The spirit in Paris was simply rotten. A young French newspaper editor who spoke English revealed his innermost hope to me; he wanted to be attached to the British Staff with headquarters at the grand Hotel Crillon in Paris. Too many men had been mobilized and the government had no accommodations or work for them. Fist-fights occurred in the workingmen's districts between Communists and anti-Communists. The government seemed without leadership and without initiative.

Petty, reactionary army officers were now in charge of censorship in the Hotel Continental. They took luscious revenge on their political opponents of the Left, unnecessary revenge. Léon Blum's daily article in the Socialist *Populaire* once appeared as a two-column white blank with his name under it. Blum was pro-war and, of course, anti-Nazi. But the censor was anti-Blum. Blum wanted the Chamber of Deputies to meet as the House of Commons did in London. The censor blocked that. The polemic continued. It created bad blood. The bourgeois *L'Œuvre* seconded Blum's appeal. "The entire republic," this daily wrote, "would be happy to see the people's elected representatives associated in the work of national defense." M. Martinaud-Deplat, chief censor, tried to stop this agitation. Frenchmen had to plead for what, in Britain, was the automatic rule of political life. The French government had no faith in the people; the people had no faith in the French leaders. The same leaders had betrayed France in Spain and Czechoslovakia. Was there any guarantee that they would not betray France again?

With added war powers to inflate him, Daladier was making himself a putty dictator. He could pout and be silent like a dictator. But he was weak. He postponed reaching a decision. When he finally made a decision he ate out his heart lest it be the wrong one. Strong minds took advantage of Daladier's weakness. They imposed on him and misled him. "Liberté, Egalité, Fraternité," was the French revolutionary motto. Now wits changed that and said, "Egalité, Fraternité, Daladier." He was a bad substitute.

Anti-Fascist propaganda was unwelcome to the French authorities. France, they said, was fighting Germany, not Fascism. German anti-Fascist refugees, more anti-Hitler than most Frenchmen, were clapped into jail and concentration camps although they would have eagerly joined the struggle against Hitler.

Organizational chaos pervaded the national scene. No leader stirred the country to great effort or to higher emotions. The whole tone of France was flat. Officers on leave after short sojourns in the Maginot Line said that Germany's West Wall could never be pierced; it bristled with electrically operated guns. A heavy pall of defeatism hung over Paris.

There was no sense in remaining in Paris and I went to London, crossing the Channel through a cordon of British destroyers. My first evening there, John Gunther and Knickerbocker gave a dinner to Stephen Litauer, the leading Polish correspondent in London. Poland had been knocked out by German and Soviet collusion, and the dinner was a little tribute to his country and to him. Major Cazallet, Conservative M.P., was there, also Vernon Bartlett, Independent M.P. and journalist, Victor Gordon-Lennox, diplomatic correspondent of the *Daily Telegraph*, Ex-Premier Van Zeeland of Belgium, Webb Miller of the United Press, who later met death in a blackout accident, Frederick Kuh of the United Press, Fred Bate of an American radio company, and Charles Peake, chief of the press department of the Foreign Office. We talked until midnight. Criticism was divided pretty evenly between the British government, for stupidity, and France, for inactivity. Van Zeeland said Belgium would fight if invaded and he did not mind being quoted.

The frankness with which the British spoke astounded me. Political life flowed on. The war had not congealed thought; it had not, therefore, paralyzed action or banished the possibility of change. England was freer in war than under the tight-fisted, one-man appeasement regime of Neville Chamberlain. From M.P. to bus driver and hotel waiter, men fearlessly expressed views opposed to those of the government. You could be pro-war, anti-war, for immediate peace with Hitler; you could justify Hitler, praise Stalin, condemn Halifax, swear at Churchill, say what you pleased. Totalitarian neck muscles were completely undeveloped. (They were beginning to develop in Paris.) No one looked around to see whether anybody was listening or watching. Aneurin Bevan, wasp-tongued, tempestuous, brilliant husband of Jenny Lee and left-wing Labor M.P., banged his fist on the marble table of the Café Royal and yelled, "This bloody war will be over by Christmas. I'll bet you a quid the Chamberlains will sell us out again."

The war, I felt, brought England a sense of exhilaration. Retreat had ended. Bloodless surrender in the face of the threats of marauding Fascist despots had ceased. The British people had enjoyed the peace which Chamberlain gave them but they were ashamed of the way he got it. They put no faith in its permanence. It ran against the grain of the average Englishman to betray the Spaniards, Czechs, and Chinese and to scrap the League of Nations, while exposing the Empire to growing perils.

With the outbreak of the war the British people seemed to come into its own. It gained in self-respect because it gained in responsibility. Nowadays nations do not go to war. War comes to them. There are no restricted battlefields off in the farmlands where few people live. Every street is a battlefield. Every backyard is a trench. The people fight. People fight better if they rule. British political genius understood this; France did not understand it. Britain girded its loins for action. It was fighting first for survival. But the British people were also fighting for what Hitler took away from Germans and would take away from them: trade unions, political parties, and the freedom to do and say what they pleased:

The British Communist party, always an enemy of appeasement and an advocate of resistance to Fascist aggression, naturally supported the war from the start. A manifesto issued by the Communist Central Committee on September 2, 1939 said, "Now that the war has come, we have no hesitation in stating the policy of the Communist party. We are in support of all necessary measures to secure the victory of democracy over Fascism." (They still called it democracy and Fascism.)

Harry Pollitt, secretary of the British Communist party, published a pamphlet with the imprint of his organization, entitled, "How to Win the War." Pollitt is a former workingman and was very popular and respected even among non-Communists. Written after September 3, and widely distributed by Communists, the pamphlet declared that, "The Communist party supports the war, believing it to be a just war which should be supported by the whole working class and all friends of democracy in Britain."

But some Trotzkyists and ultra-radicals might oppose the war as an imperialist war. Harry Pollitt answered them. "To stand aside from this conflict," he wrote, "to contribute only revolutionary-sounding phrases while the Fascist beasts ride roughshod over Europe, would be a betrayal of everything our forbears have fought to achieve in the course of long years of struggle against capitalism." But today Pollitt's party, and other Communist parties, are using those "revolutionary-sounding phrases" and are standing aside.

When did the betrayal commence? On September 17, 1939, when orders came from Moscow for a new line. What had changed? The war was the same on September 17 as on September 3. Chamberlain was no more reactionary, the British empire no more imperialistic. The Nazi-Soviet pact had been signed before September 3. Everything was the same. But the instructions from Moscow were different.

"The British workers," wrote Harry Pollitt in his pamphlet, "are in this war to defeat Hitler, for a German victory would mean that Fascism would be imposed on the defeated countries." But after September 17, the British Communists apparently did not mind that; they began to sabotage Britain's war effort and to use "revolutionary-sounding phrases." They wanted the war to end with a negotiated peace which, inevitably, would be a Hitler victory. Pollitt, however, had asserted that the Communist party "will do everything it can to bring the war to a speedy conclusion, but only by the defeat and destruction of Hitler." It is not Pollitt alone who said these things. Communist parties throughout the world follow the same general line decreed by Moscow; Pollitt revealed what Moscow thought at the time, except that Moscow was a bit late in this case in countermanding earlier instructions. On September 17, by virtue of a foreign radiogram, the war became an imperialist war, no longer a just war, no longer a war for democracy, no longer a people's war.

When the Communist government of Russia engaged in aggression, Communists elsewhere took a more charitable view of Hitler aggression. The Communists discontinued their boycott of German goods. They did not, however, discontinue their boycott of Japanese goods. Why not? Was Germany less of an aggressor than Japan? No. But the Soviet government had not yet settled its differences with Japan.

The blackout in London was really black, much blacker than in Paris, and you either tried to develop a sense of touch in your sole as you pushed towards a curb or you turned on your pocket flashlight at regular intervals. Few people entertained, and events on the world stage rather made the theater a lesser attraction. I usually dined and spent the evening in the Café Royal which was frequented by journalists, artists, Bohemians, and people who came to look at them. I would grope down the Strand and across Piccadilly Circus and then, late at night, often with Frank Hanighen, grope back again. At one corner, a soprano voice called out, "Hello, darling," and its owner lit up her face with a flashlight. The next second a deep bass tone cried, *"Daily Worker."* On the Strand and in other main thoroughfares, Communists sold the *Daily Worker* day and night, and I often saw them push it into the faces of soldiers in uniform. The British government was too secure in its faith in the common sense of its citizens to fear their conversion to the Communist policy of peace with Hitler. Peace with Hitler, the people said, means Hitler in England, terror, torture, anti-Semitism, lower standards of living, private life according to official instructions. "Is that what the Communists now want?" London asked. Chamberlain did not dread a Communist-inspired defeatist, pacifist movement among the masses because he knew too well that he had declared war on Hitler under the pressure from those very masses. Let the Communists drown in their own drivel, was the British tactic.

I spent the weekend of September 23, 24, and 25 in the straw-thatched country cottage of Kingsley Martin, editor of the *New Statesman and Nation*. Kingsley gloried in the leaning walls, wormwood beams and creaking floors of the hut which dated back centuries. Before dinner every evening he went to the pub near by to play games and talk with the farmers who came in for their bitter or ale. The city had invaded the country. First the children arrived, évacués from London. Then the parents visited the children. The two kingdoms—city and country—were for the first time getting acquainted with one another. The beginning of knowledge was irritation. The kids got in the way of the animals or pulled their tails and let them loose into the fields. Mamma's arrival robbed Mr. Smith of his traditional Sunday afternoon nap. A schoolmaster dropped in on Kingsley. The war had provoked a feud between urban and village teachers. The London schoolteachers thought they were far superior to the village pedagogues. But these, in turn, saw at every turn the ignorance and helplessness of the metropolitan educators. Gradually, however, things were getting ironed out. Walls of brick and mortar were tumbling in England as a result of the war. Social walls too were beginning to topple.

One afternoon Kingsley Martin, Dorothy Woodman, and I drove the short distance to the country home of Harold J. Laski and stayed for dinner. The professor of political science and master of English had a new assignment; he had taken in two young Cockney boys from Whitechapel and his ambition was to teach them not to drop their H's.

With Kingsley and Laski the war as a topic of conversation soon yielded to Soviet policy and the new Communist line. In 1937, Laski had asked me to explain the Moscow trials and purges and now he quoted one phrase back at me. I had attributed them, in part, to Stalin's "pathological psychology"; Trotzky was a major phobia in his mental make-up.

"Is it weakness due to the purges," Laski wondered, "that produced the pact with Hitler?" It was that and Moscow's desire to appeal to the Russian nationalism of the peasant masses by regaining old Russian lands; it was the temptation to grab what could be grabbed; it was the hope that territorial acquisitions would make citizens forget the economic stagnation arising out of the purges; it was the great lure of appeasement, of staying out of war a little while longer. Englishmen ought to understand that best. It had been their policy for years.

Laski liked Harry Pollitt. So did many Laborites. A week earlier Harry Pollitt had been dismissed as secretary and chief of the Communist party. But he had merely been expressing the party's Moscow viewpoint until it changed. In the October, 1938, *Labour Monthly*, official organ of the British Communists, he had written,

"It is said that democracy, so long as it rests on the basis of capitalist economy, is not worth defending. It is worth while dealing with this is in some detail. . . . Democracy is not abstract. . . . It means that the people have definite rights, the right to organize, the right to strike, the right to vote, the right to free speech. Those that tell us there is nothing to choose between Fascism and bourgeois democracy should take the trouble to find out what the workers suffer in Fascist countries. . . . Our party can take its stand in the forefront of the fight for democracy against Fascism." This was good Communist sense. In contra-distinction, the present Communist line is hypocrisy. And nonsense.

The policy of "revolutionary-sounding phrases" followed inevitably on the Nazi-Soviet pact. The Communists outside Russia could not remain pro-democratic and anti-Fascist after August 23, 1939. For if the foreign Communist parties had supported England, France, and the United States against Germany and Italy, they would have been faced with the unanswerable question, "And why isn't Soviet Russia also against Germany and Italy?" Weakness? But Communists would not admit the weakness of the Soviet regime. Reaction in Soviet Russia? Communists would not admit that. The non-Soviet Communists had to take the same line as the Soviet government or expose the faults of the Soviet government. To justify their anti-British position, however, the Communists did not say, "We are not pro-British because Russia is not pro-British." Instead they said, "We are not pro-British because England is imperialistic and reactionary."

John Strachey and his wife Celia came over Saturday afternoon and we argued for hours. John, cricket champion and Marxist interpreter, accepted the new Communist stand. He said if Russia was a Socialist country then everything it did was in the interest of socialism. We threw Marx and Lenin quotations at one another and engaged in verbal dog-fights. John was not to be dissuaded. Months later, however, he saw things very differently and enlisted in the British home defense and later in the RAF.

Those who continue, in violation of fact and logic, to justify Stalin, involve themselves in contradictions. In September, 1938, Russia was ready to fight on the side of England and France for Czechoslovakia. Did that mean that England and France were less reactionary and imperialistic in 1938 than in 1939? Obviously not. In 1938, Soviet Defense Commissar Voroshilov complained that Poland would not permit the Red Army to enter its territory and save it from aggression. Later Moscow called Poland a semi-Fascist state. So the Bolsheviks wished to protect a semi-Fascist state against attack. Then why not help England and France? The Soviet government was delivering large quantities of arms to Chiang Kai-shek. But Chiang Kai-shek had executed more Communists than any non-Communist in the world. Yet Communists say, without blushing, that they cannot side with England because it is bourgeois and reactionary?

The same insincerity characterized Communist defense of the Soviet attack on Finland later in 1939. The Communists and the other defenders of Russian policy alleged that it was necessary for Stalin to seize certain portions of Finland because they menaced Leningrad, the second largest Soviet city. In June, 1930, Stalin said, "we do not want a single foot of foreign territory but we will not surrender a single inch of our territory to anyone." This immediately became a popular slogan. It was carried on banners and posters. It became the subject of articles, speeches, and pamphlets. It was repeated millions of times throughout the years, until 1939. Stalin did not say we want no foreign territory except the Mannerheim Line. He did not say we want no foreign territory except a section of Finland from which Leningrad can be attacked. He said, "We want not a single foot of foreign territory."

I lived in the Soviet Union for fourteen years. I never once heard the argument that Leningrad was menaced by Finland. I never heard that the British and French built the Mannerheim Line. Soviet sources suspected, on the contrary, that the Germans had a hand in constructing it. Moscow charged that England and France had helped Finland to arm. But we know from Soviet official sources that England and France also helped Russia to arm. Normally, arms merchants sell to all who pay.

The workingmen of England were staunchly behind the war. They grumbled against hardships and defended their rights. They hoped the war would end with more democracy and real people's rule. They were fighting Hitler and Chamberlain, the Fascists abroad and the Tories at home. The alternative was to surrender to Hitler and lose everything.

On the Right wing of the Labor party there were still some appeasers, and the fact that Russia had adopted an appeaser role made these conservative Laborites more pro-Soviet. But I must have spoken at length to at least twenty Labor M.P.'s and they all declared that their constituents were strongly pro-war. To obtain data on this point I went to John Middleton, secretary of the Labor party whom I had known before. He sat at his desk and read thousands of letters from individual workingmen and from Labor party leaders, speakers, and organizers in the provinces. He said the sentiment was overwhelmingly for the energetic prosecution of the war, but also for non-participation in a government with Chamberlain. Labor remembered the decorative role which its representatives played in the Cabinet during the first World War.

Herbert Morrison held the same view. Ellen Wilkinson arranged a small lunch in the House of Commons so that I could have a long talk with Morrison. I asked her to invite Leland Stowe of the *Chicago Daily News* and *New York Post*, which she did. I sat at Morrison's left, on the side of his one seeing eye. "Herb," or " 'Erb," as Londoners know him, is a former workingman. He looks and reacts like a workingman. He is chairman of the London County Council which involves the tremendous administrative job of running the whole economy of the second largest city of the world. If one man is responsible for London's being able to "take it," he is Herbert Morrison who equipped the city with the fire-fighting apparatus, the transportation facilities, sanitation, and other requirements for standing up under Hitler's murderous bombardments.

Morrison said to me, "I think Labor should not enter the government. We ought to keep our hands clean for the time, which will come in this war, when vast social changes must be made." He became a leading figure in the Churchill government a few months later. The social changes had started not in a sudden cataclysmic form but with gradual insistence. Moreover, Labor's collaboration was necessary to get Chamberlain out of No. 10 Downing Street and Churchill into it. Morrison early understood that the war was more than an international war. It was concurrently a civil war. Class was competing with class for political power while at the same time the classes collaborated against a foreign enemy who wished to destroy them all. In 1917, Lenin urged converting the imperialist war into a civil war in each country. The second World War was both simultaneously. To conduct only one meant to lose the other. To conduct the war only as an imperialist war—as Daladier tried to do—robbed the government of popular support. To conduct it only as a civil war would open the door to Hitler. Lenin's civil war in Russia actually did open the door to the Kaiser who imposed the

Brest-Litovsk treaty and took the Ukraine and the Crimea from the Bolsheviks while the Turks seized part of the Caucasus. If Germany had won that war, it would very probably have crushed the Bolshevik revolution. It is a strange paradox that the United States by helping the Allies win in 1918, saved the Bolshevik regime.

After the lunch I walked with Herbert Morrison down the corridor to the central lobby of the House and asked him whether he would not try to get me an appointment with Winston Churchill. He immediately walked into the Members' writing room, and wrote me a letter of introduction which I could mail to Churchill. Then he entered the chamber. I stood talking to Ellen Wilkinson. Before long Morrison came out and said to me, "I just talked to Winston. He wants you to communicate with his secretary."

I wrote to Brendan Bracken, M.P., Churchill's young secretary. I used to meet Bracken at John Strachey's house in Westminster when John was a Labor M.P.

Bracken wrote that Churchill would see me at the Admiralty at 5 P.M. on October 12. The morning of that day I was instructed to present myself at 3.30 instead. Later the hour was altered to 6.30. I arrived at 6.15, and Churchill received me immediately.

I had no sooner entered the big room than Churchill said, "Have a drink?" And he walked over to a small table on which stood a bottle of whiskey, several glasses and a soda siphon. I said I rarely drank. He said, "Will you?" I said, "Yes." He had just poured in the whiskey when Bracken opened the door and told him that Margesson was on the phone. David Margesson was the chief Conservative whip in the House of Commons, in other words, the boss of the Conservative party. Churchill left the room to take the call and I remained alone. I squirted some soda into the glass—it was the first time I ever made a whiskey-and-soda—and perched myself on the ledge of a bookcase that stood against the back wall of the room and looked around at the large papier-mâché globe brown with age, the big chairs covered with bright red leather, the large wall maps, and the huge desk.

When Churchill came back after a few minutes, he said, "Have you had your drink?"

"I have it," I replied. "Shall I pour you one?"

"No," he said. "I've had mine this afternoon."

We sat opposite one another at a small round table. He smoked a very fat cigar and dropped ashes on his vest and occasionally brushed them off with the back of his hand. Across his vest was a gold chain of big links. His eyes look watery and tired. His face is huge and flabby and the lips have a fleshy droop. Yet the total impression is power. The upper half of his face is intellect, the lower half British bulldog. He speaks with a slight impediment, and his s's have a suspicion of s-h. He let me stay for thirty minutes. I talked much in the first five minutes and the rest of the time he replied to my brief questions. I enjoyed his English. He rolls out an ordinary sentence with the rounded finish and force of a carefully polished work of art. Churchill's English has the simple power of the language of the Bible. His nouns are pictures and his verbs work.

I think his strength lies in the fact that he doubts and does not doubt. He is coldly critical of his own country's weaknesses and mistakes. Enthusiasm does not blunt analysis; hopes do not distort facts. He thinks while he fights. He dares to have thoughts and doubts about conditions because he has no doubts about his course of action. He knows what he wants to do. There is no way back. There is only the struggle. The civilized brain in the upper story does not hamper the animal determination in the lower story.

Neville Chamberlain could not be a good war leader because he had prepared his mind for peace. But ever since the advent of Hitler in 1933, Winston Churchill had prepared his mind, and had wished to prepare his country, for war. When war came Churchill was brought into the government. Soon Churchill headed the government and spoke for England. He is England. The Englishman is narrowly insular, yet made broadly international by the empire and trade. He is rooted deep in the old rock of the isle but he reacts to changes in the world's weather. For every Conservative Briton who looks backward there are at least three who see national survival in terms of progress and adaptation. In social legislation and civil liberties, Great Britain was always far in advance of any other great power. Churchill, I could see, is a fervid devotee of freedom. It is not merely a war motto or a war aim, but a component part of his life fiber. Of course, there is India. That is a serious blemish. But whose mentality has no blind spots? Like Lloyd George, Churchill is capable of indignation, passion, hard work, and bluntness. He convinces others not so much with words as by the contagiously axiomatic nature of his own convictions. "There will always be an England" is very Churchillian—and very British.

Two weeks before I saw Churchill he said in a speech, "Russia is a riddle wrapped in mystery inside an enigma. But," he added, "there is a key." I discussed the key with him. We discussed other subjects too.

Unfortunately, my interview with Churchill was "off the record." I asked him whether I could quote one striking sentence and he said, "Better not." At the end of twenty minutes, Bracken stuck in his red head and announced, "You have another appointment, sir," but we had not yet circumnavigated the globe and Churchill could not drop me in a distant country. He took me home to the United States.

During this wartime stay in London I also had an interview with Sir Robert Vansittart, the chief diplomatic officer of the British Foreign Office. I liked him very much. He is informal and possesses a prodigious knowledge of diplomacy, history, and geography. For that reason probably, and also because he was one hundred percent anti-German during the worst Chamberlain era of appeasement, he was unceremoniously shelved and allowed to sit in his office doing very little of importance while Chamberlain used Sir Horace Wilson, an official labor disputes arbitrator, as his diplomatic adviser. Sir Horace accompanied Chamberlain to Germany, went as Chamberlain's special emissary to Hitler in the last week of September, 1938, and was more active in foreign affairs than Vansittart or even Halifax. Meanwhile Vansittart used the time that lay heavily on his hands writing plays, movie scenarios, and poems. He looks as a poet never should, burly and tough.

British permanent officials cannot talk for publication even when they are very angry, and that was the understanding on which Vansittart agreed to see me. He talked of many things with wisdom and penetration, and asked me to come back again.

That same week, Kennedy received me in the United States Embassy. He feared that "world economy would soon take a nose dive." The essential component element in the appeasers' "peace for our time" was money for our time. Kennedy's concern on this score exceeded even Chamberlain's. He had more sympathy for the policy of Chamberlain and did more for it than for that of Roosevelt. He saw the world through the bars of the dollar mark. He got on best with Chamberlain and worst with Churchill.

I had tea one afternoon with Sir Stafford Cripps in the House of Commons and then he invited me to lunch with Lady Cripps at the

English Speaking Union. Cripps is gaunt, gentle, smiling, idealistic, and able. One of Britain's best lawyers, he used to give half his earnings—said to be $100,000 a year—to various Left causes. When the war started he dropped all his professional work and devoted himself to politics. People trust his integrity. Like Lord Halifax, he is an Anglo-Catholic. The two of them are friends. He had been seeing Halifax often and was preparing to go on a world trip which would take him to India for conversations with Gandhi, Nehru, and the Viceroy, to China for talks with Chiang Kai-shek, and to Moscow for an audience with Molotov. On the return trip he came through New York where he breakfasted with me in my hotel room. He eats only raw vegetables and raw fruit, and drinks coffee copiously. In London, I exposed Soviet foreign policy in the realistic light in which I thought I saw it. Sir Stafford, however, was sanguine. His subsequent appointment as British Ambassador to Moscow demonstrated that Churchill did not hesitate to go as far to the Left as possible in picking a man *persona grata* to the Bolsheviks. If Cripps got nowhere, it would prove that the difficulty was not personal.

Tea in the House of Commons with Lady Rhondda, owner of coal mines and of the weekly journal *Time and Tide*. But neither I nor she could pay for it. We had to wait till a friendly M.P. arrived to pay the check. . . . I went to the Ivy Restaurant with a fellow journalist. At the end of the meal I said, "Check, please," to the waiter. After ten minutes I hadn't yet received it. Finally, he brought me a blank check. All sorts of whispered negotiations had gone on to ascertain whether I was a steady customer whose check was good. I had wanted the bill. . . . Lunch with Sir Archibald Sinclair, later Minister of Air, and Wilfrid Roberts, both Liberal M.P.'s. . . . Dinner with Sefton Delmer of the *Daily Express* and his wife. He showed movies he had taken while flying with Hitler in an airplane. He told us Hitler does not like to be seen eating. . . . Interview with Rushdi Aras, the Turkish Ambassador. Interview with Raschinsky, the Polish Ambassador. Dinner with Helen Kirkpatrick of the *Chicago Daily News* and Victor Gordon-Lennox. Tea with Hamish Hamilton, publisher, who had volunteered for the R.A.F., and Miss Jean Forbes-Robertson, sister of Diana Sheean. Dinner with Labor M.P. Dobbie, a former railway worker who beamed because I had nicknamed him "Doctor" in Spain. Talks with Hugh Dalton, Admiral Keyes, Eleanor Rathbone, Robert Boothby, and Edith Summerskill, M.P.'s of various political hues. Dinner, finally, with Frederick Kuh of the United Press and his wife, Renata. London was full of excitement, information, impressions, political life, political events. After three weeks of it, I went back to Paris.

My London experiences, especially the talk with Churchill, made me more than ever certain that something was wrong with France. I aired my apprehension to André Malraux. He said, "You must tell this to André Maurois." Maurois, the noted French author, was at the Hotel Continental in the press department but also close to the General Staff and the government. He had just been appointed liaison officer with the British army. Malraux arranged a date for me. I gave Maurois my impressions of England and spoke of the contrast I saw between the live democracy of England and the dull "dictatorship" of Daladier. He said, "You must speak with Herriot."

"There is no use," I replied, "complaining to someone who agrees with you."

He said, "Then you must see Paul Reynaud." He also offered to arrange an interview for me with Alexis Leger, the permanent chief of the French Foreign Office, Vansittart's opposite number. I saw Reynaud in his big cabinet in the Finance Ministry on October 24. I remained with him an hour. Reynaud is a thin, dapperly dressed little man with quick movements, most unlike Churchill in appearance. It is often impossible to determine a person's nationality by his looks. (Accent is a better guide.) You spot a man as a Swede and he turns out to be Czech. Madame Tabouis could be an English-woman, until you hear her speak. Stalin might be a Greek. But Churchill could not be French, and Reynaud could scarcely be British.

Reynaud speaks an excellent and fluent English. The interview with him was also "off the record," but either he thought he had to use stiff official verbiage with me or he thought I was stupid enough to take it at its face value. When I suggested that part of what he said was contradicted by facts we both knew, he stepped down into charming, communicative informality. He even said I could quote several of his specific statements.

I asked him how long France could go on paying cash for purchases in America.

He said, "At the present rate, for two years."

I said, "It's a pity you didn't spend some of this money a few years ago buying airplanes in the United States."

"Ah," he commented, "that is another matter. I was not in the government then."

Most of the interview was spent in comparing the internal regimes of England and France. I said that one of Europe's chief ills since 1919 had been the divergence of policy between London and Paris. Now they were allies fighing side by side. But the attitude towards the war and towards civil liberties was so different in the two countries that I could foresee potential clashes between them on the conduct of the war and certainly in the formulation of the peace.

I gave as an illustration the circumstance that Parliament in England functioned with real effectiveness whereas in France it was almost an offense to demand the convocation of the Chamber. He told me the Chamber would meet on November 30. I argued that it depended on whether it would meet merely as a rubber stamp for the semi-dictatorship or as the mouthpiece and essential weapon of democracy.

Reynaud said cryptically, "Parliamentarism is shaped by the relationship between the head of the government and the leader of the opposition. In England Mr. Chamberlain and Mr. Attlee get along well together."

This was a large part of the story: Daladier could not stomach Blum. Reynaud and Blum were on friendly terms. The implication of Reynaud's statement was that if he became premier democracy would be revived. Paris knew that Reynaud's ambition tended in this direction. Powerful elements in the General Staff preferred Reynaud's sprightly dynamism to Daladier's sluggish sullenness. It was said that Gamelin and Reynaud would not have driven the French Communist party underground where it could work efficiently and pose as a persecuted martyr.

Reynaud thought America would be in grave danger if Germany won the war. "In 1914," he recalled, "we never dreamed of the arms that we were using in 1918. This war will see the birth of new weapons and the perfection of old ones which will bring the United States within easier range of European armed forces."

I went to talk to Reynaud, and later to Alexis Leger, because I hope to make them aware of what I regarded as a disturbing discrepancy between the public tempers of England and France. When I got back to America I wrote a long article called, "England and France—A Contrast." It was submitted to several monthly magazines but they turned it down. Events in Europe were moving fast, and editors believed that my sad tale of French flabbiness might soon be out of date.

It was not difficult to forgive France for the heavy heart with which her people entered the war. I wrote in that article, "When France goes to war her whole manhood is engaged. I take my hotel as a typical example. It normally employs 310 people. By September 7, four days after the declaration of war, 208 of these had been summoned into the army. Of the 102 who remained in the hotel, 25 were women, 15 minors, and the others men over age. But one of the managers who is fifty-five showed me his reservist's card. In certain circumstances he too would have to go.

"A single waiter was left for the floor service of the entire big hotel. He ran, puffing, from room to room doing his bit to please the remaining guests who stuck it out in perturbed times. He was thirty-seven. Five of his brothers were mobilized. He said, 'My health is bad. Lungs. But my turn may also come soon.' On my return from three weeks in London he was gone. His turn had come."

Several hours before leaving for Italy I had an interview with Alexis Leger. Leger had held his position as real inner master of the international affairs of his country for many years. That position is one to conjure up a picture of parchment-skinned face, of a man buried in treaty texts and technical formulas, of a crafty, scheming statesman engaged in world-wide intrigue, of a cold bureaucrat and office automaton. Under the pseudonym of St. Jean Perse, however, Leger wrote a long poem entitled *Anabase* which was translated into English by T. S. Eliot and has influenced the work of British poets, of Archibald MacLeish in America and many others. He has also published poems under the name of St. Leger Leger. He speaks an exquisite French with a somewhat un-French accent. He was born in Martinique in 1887, and the scenes of his life and work—the East and the West Indies—are more suggestive of romance and exotic dances than of cobweb-covered archives and the mazes of diplomacy.

Now he is an exile, robbed of his French citizenship by the authorities in Vichy. If he had had his way there would have been little appeasement and perhaps therefore no Vichy. But while France was crawling before Germany in the pre-1939 days, French Foreign Ministers used him as an executive secretary rather than as a diplomat with initiative. Downing Street did the same with Vansittart.

I sat with Leger for an hour and a half. I scarcely opened my mouth. André Maurois had given me a good introduction, and Leger, besides, knew my *Soviets in World Affairs*. After we had exchanged initial greetings I simply told him that I was going to Rome that evening and would appreciate his views on the Italian situation. He gave me an analysis that was worthy of a wider audience. I could see the perfect mechanism of his mind sort out the facts, place them before me, establish the proper relationship between them, and then sew them all together. He did this with the Polish situation too, and the Russian. He had gone to Moscow with Laval, whom he passionately detests, in May, 1935, and participated in the negotiations with Stalin. I believe he has also negotiated with Mussolini and Hitler; he is one of the few diplomats, accordingly, who has met all three dictators. President Roosevelt once entertained the piquant idea of bringing them all to Washington, D. C., together with the Prime Ministers of England and France. That was before the war. Among journalists and writers who have met all three dictators, I can think only of Roy W. Howard and Anne O'Hare McCormick of the *New York Times*.

From France-at-war I traveled to "neutral" Italy. Twenty-seven hours from Paris to Rome. During the night it snowed heavily in the Alps but in the morning the express pulled through the long Simplon Pass into the cuddling warmth of Lombardy. The waters of Lago Maggiore were a deep blue set off by the green trees and bright flowers. I was tempted to get off and stay and play at Stresa.

I was in the diner when the train entered Italy from Switzerland. I had ordered coffee. If the waiter had moved just a bit faster I could have had it on my table in Switzerland and drunk it in Italy. But now he came to me and said it was against the law to serve coffee in Italy. I looked at him angrily and then suggestively. He poured me one cup, and later another. But elsewhere in the kingdom of Il Duce, the injunction is strictly observed. In Naples I was offered "autarchic coffee," the first mouthful of which I spat into my napkin.

The train stopped at Milan for three hours. I rushed to the famous, beautiful cathedral. A squadron of Savoia-Marchetti bombers flew over the city. The same type had dropped bombs on Valencia, Barcelona, Figueras, and Tarragona during my visits there. Now the Italian people were paying for those bombs, and for the costs of Guadalajara, Danakil, and Ogaden. Italy had ordained two meatless days a week. Public dancing had been prohibited. Life was too serious for dancing. A federal regulation required all clothing and textiles to contain an admixture of hemp and other crude domestic fibers. Coal imports had been pared and homes were cold. The government rationed petrol. As a result, thirteen out of every fourteen automobiles were withdrawn from circulation. But what did all that matter when Mussolini was founding another Roman Empire?

In Rome, I interviewed William Phillips, the United States Ambassador, whom I had met in Berlin; François-Poncet, the French Ambassador whom I had also first met in Berlin; Sir Noel Charles, the British Chargé d'Affaires, whom I had known in Moscow; several foreign military attachés, and a few Italians. An official in one embassy allowed me to read all the confidential reports he had been sending to superiors in his home country for the last nine months. They were a mixture of interesting gossip and invaluable serious data. I also saw the American correspondents, particularly Herbert L. Matthews who had covered the Spanish War for the *New York Times*. Not all foreign journalists working in the capital of a dictatorship are brave; Matthews possessed moral courage, just as at the front in Spain he had displayed great physical courage.

As often as I could tear myself away from viewing the sites of ancient Rome and trying to solve the puzzle of modern Rome, I sat in shirtsleeves on my sun roof reading the manuscript of Matthews' book on the Spanish War. It is a noble book by a noble person about a noble people. I could raise my eyes and without moving see the Palazzo Venezia and the Vatican. Their occupants intervened against Spain and against Europe. From my hotel roof I gazed long at Mussolini's and Pacelli's brown walls, and my mind went back to the tragic streets of barricaded Madrid, to the bloody morgue of Barcelona, to the battlefields of Castile, Aragon, and the Ebro, and to the decency and the cemeteries of Republican Spain. I saw Spanish faces, the faces of women and children livid with fear, waiting for death's missiles as Mussolini's bombers hover above them. I saw the Loyalist leaders striving against discouraging odds to serve their country. They were now outcasts in a world that courted "neutral" Mussolini. What a world! Mussolini would soon stab it in the back.

The British and French were granting credits to Mussolini. They had opened a breach in their Mediterranean blockade for his benefit. They should have crushed him immediately the war broke out. They should have known him as Hitler's bloody blood-brother. But Lord Halifax, the British Foreign Secretary, wrote an introduction to a war book by Lord Lloyd, called *The British Case*, which praised Mussolini and his work. And Anatole de Monzie, a member of the French government, "promised" the Cabinet in Paris that Italy would remain neutral. General Gamelin, chief of the French General Staff, urged the government to allow him to march into Italy in September, 1939, while Germany was busy seizing Poland. He said that France should either subdue Italy, or demand firm guarantee from Mussolini in the shape, perhaps, of control of the Italian fleet, so that Italy would not go to war later when it suited her purposes.

Gamelin reportedly declared, "I can smash Italy with ten divisions. If Italy remains neutral we will have to watch her with fifteen divisions. If she comes in on our side we will have to help her with twenty divisions." But de Monzie advocated the continued courtship of Mussolini. Enough appeasement remained in Paris to enable de Monzie to win his point against Gamelin. Fools in the British Foreign Office, the Quai D'Orsay, and the U. S. State Department had always believed they could break the Axis. The only way to break the Axis was to break Mussolini. It would not have been difficult. Italy is poor. The Fascist regime is weak. I was impressed by the unanimity on this subject. One outstanding diplomat in Rome told me that the regime was "shaky." Another, speaking English, called it "wobbly." A third said, "Do you think the regime is in danger?" He was not asking me. His question was his way of telling me. Mussolini, however, was receiving help from the Allies as well as from Hitler.

"Mussolini," one correspondent laughed, "will gallantly rush to the aid of the victor." When he knew which side was winning he would join it. On June 10, 1940, he thought he knew, for France had collapsed and was flat on her back. He had to lift her up a bit so as to insert the stiletto in the back. But what a blunder! He jumped too soon. He miscalculated. He had wanted to be in on the kill. He knew his Hitler. The Nazis would not allow even a friendly "neutral" to share in the spoils of victory. Unfortunately for Mussolini, the kill was not yet.

One of the reports sent by my diplomatic friend to his government stated that in August, 1939, Marshal Badoglio, supreme commander of the Italian armed forces, informed Mussolini that the army would not put its heart into war on the side of Germany. The people did not want any more war on anybody's side, and Hitler is the most hated man in Italy. The daily organ of the Vatican, the

Osservatore Romano boosted its circulation from 40,000 before the war to 130,000 when I was in Rome simply because it printed news favorable to England and France. Even high Fascist circles doubted the wisdom of aligning Italy with Germany. Count Ciano, Foreign Minister and Mussolini's son-in-law, was said to be anti-Hitler. In May, 1939, Ciano went to see Hitler. They took lunch together. Ciano told Hitler that a European war would be protracted and that Italy could not afford to join it. "*Du bist ein Esel*," Hitler said to Ciano. "You are a jackass."

Spoiled, handsome Ciano didn't like that. What Ciano disliked especially was that instead of being allowed to relax and luxuriate after lunch, Hitler walked him over hill and dale for two hours, lecturing and berating him all the while. Ciano had other ways of expending his energy, but Hitler didn't. So deflated did Ciano feel after this visit with Hitler that on his return to Rome he did not keep several appointments with top-rank diplomats made before his journey to Germany but went to the seashore and lay around on the beach—with four blondes, according to diplomatic report—until his ego was restored.

It was known, too, that the King and many in his entourage were anti-German. While I was in Rome, Mussolini appeared theatrically on the balcony of the Palazzo Venetia and delivered a speech of exactly fifty-eight words, "Fascism," he cried, "asks only one privilege for itself: to construct and to act in all circumstances with the people and for the people." Abraham Lincoln's most essential "by the people" was omitted.

What did Mussolini intend to say? "To construct" means not to go to war. "With the people" means not to offend their desire for peace. Mussolini bowed to what he knew was the will of the country. But the necessity of doing so irritated him. He hoped, some day, to be able to enter the conflict.

The terror, accordingly, was intensified. When I walked into the big office of M. François-Poncet, the French Ambassador, in the glorious villa built by Michelangelo, he first pulled his telephone plug out and then came to meet me. The telephone, even with the receiver on the hook, might register our conversation for the Italian secret police. But this form of espionage was mild compared with what Italian citizens had to fear. In literally all restaurants and cafés I saw a placard distributed by the Fascist party which read, "Here one does not make predictions or discuss high policy and high strategy." In other words: "Shut up." In the provinces, the notices were more blunt, "For habitual propagators of fantastic reports who consciously or unconsciously alarm the country, hard days are in store. The Squadrismo [Strong Arm Squad] of [here the name of the town was given] is very much alive and some individuals already have reason to know how very alive it is." Coffee and petrol were scarce in Italy but castor oil flowed freely. It sometimes killed people to whom it was forcibly administered by the Squadristi.

Mussolini himself spoke in Bologna on September 23 and promised to "clean up . . . the riffraff." At Genoa he stated that apathy would not be tolerated. His newspaper, the *Popolo d'Italia* inveighed against "bellyachers, rumor-mongers, toy strategists, and members of a certain lounge-lizard snobbery."

People were "bellyaching" about the declining standard of living, rising inconveniences, and shorter macaroni. They were protesting against the regime's pro-Germanism because they feared it would in the end lead them into war. Italians like to talk and express themselves. The heightened restraint irked them.

But in the absence of a government "of the people," the people could do nothing; the secret police and the dictator overruled popular wishes, the generals' wishes, and royalty's wishes.

Italy did not want the war. It did not want Hitler. But Mussolini wanted the war because he was Mussolini and because he was Hitler's puppet. So Italy went to war, and paid.

November 2, 1939. I was leaving Europe-at-war. I was standing on the top deck of the majestic *Rex* still loading in the bay of Naples. As I looked now in the direction of Vesuvius, now towards nine "unknown" submarines that rocked near by, someone tapped on my shoulder, and there stood Kostya Oumansky returning from Moscow to the Soviet Embassy in Washington.

"I hear," he began, "that you have been attacking my country."

"I have always said what I think about your country," I announced. "When I liked it I praised it. Now I condemn it."

"So Prince Radziwill is better than collective farms," he sneered. (Prince Radziwill is one of the rich land-owning nobles of Poland.)

"Listen," I said, "I have just come from Rome. The Fascists tell me that they are putting the Abyssinians into trousers and building schools and roads for them. The conqueror and imperialist always affirms that he is out to help the conquered."

"Hm, hm," muttered Oumansky. It was clear to him where I stood. "Will you be going to the Soviet Union soon," he inquired sweetly.

"Just now I am going home."

"Well," he smiled, "anytime you want to go you can depend on me to veto the trip."

"Thanks," I exclaimed. (Pause.) "Tell me, how's Moscow?" I demanded.

"Fine."

"Did you see Litvinov?" I inquired.

"No."

"Why? I thought he was your old patron and friend."

"Yes," Oumansky explained, "but you know Moscow. I was very busy and he is busy and he lives out of town."

"What's Litvinov doing?" I asked.

"He's doing literary work."

"What's Troyanovsky doing?" (Troyanovsky was Oumansky's predecessor in Washington.)

"He's doing literary work," Oumansky replied.

"What's Boris Stein doing?" (Stein was Soviet Ambassador in Rome and a mutual friend of ours.)

"He's doing literary work."

I roared hilariously.

"What are you doing?" Oumansky asked me after a long pause.

"I'm doing literary work," I said. "But I'm not an ex-commissar nor an ex-ambassador."

Oumansky spoke of the beautiful scenery. On that, at last, we could agree. Dust was blowing into our eyes.

"Well," Oumansky declared, "I suppose I won't be seeing much of you after we land in New York."

"Oumansky," I said, "you are always the diplomat. You mean that we can meet on the boat."

He nodded assent and went below. But I felt there was no use talking to him.

Americans have better and more information about the war than the nations of Europe. That is the achievement of the radio and the newspapers. Americans have more news about England than most Englishmen and certainly learn more about events in Germany than most Germans. Only Americans hear regular broadcasts from belligerent capitals. And only American correspondents have the courage and initiative to fly, like the lamented Ralph Barnes, in loaded bombers, or like him and others, sail in warships and submarines.

The radio gives headlines, features, and commentary. It could thus be a substitute, as far as foreign news goes, for the tabloid, for some columns, and for the editorials of weekly magazines. It has not yet, however, been able to take the place of the big morning newspaper. The *New York Times* and *New York Herald Tribune* are reporting the war more fully, with less bias and with richer information than any other newspapers in the world. Late radio news bulletins and even the scanty telegrams in the afternoon press sometimes moderate the "kick" I get from the morning papers. I have always seen international affairs as a vast drama. The newspapers raise the curtain and carry the story forward another day. They are the next installment of the thriller. The newspaper is a magic carpet which takes me to five countries on the first page, and to more and more countries as I turn the pages. I read a paper straight through and never read the continuation of page one on page six until I reach page six.

No country reads and listens as much as America. The Czechoslovak crisis, the suffering of Spain, and the horror of China involved America spiritually as they did few overseas nations. Whatever we are mentally, Americans are temperamentally members of the big fraternity of mankind. The radio and newspapers do not create this feeling. They cater to it.

Ten countries lost their independence in the first twelve months of the war: Poland, Denmark, Norway, Luxembourg, Holland, Belgium, France, Latvia, Lithuania, and Esthonia. Three others—Finland, Bulgaria, and Rumania lost large stretches of territory. As each of these nations was invaded by aggressors, always on excuses that sounded as good as propaganda ministers could make them, Americans lent sympathy and sent aid. In the second year of the war, more countries joined the lengthening list of areas subjected to the "new order" or the "revolution." America's desire to aid victims of assault is fine sentiment, good sportsmanship, and excellent policy. The greater the obstacles placed in the path of the aggressors the less likely they are to roam further afield. This is now the axiomatic rule of many columnists, commentators, lecturers, authors, ministers, politicians, and statesmen, who, if they had advocated it a few years earlier, might have helped avert the black catastrophe.

When France fell some Americans regarded the event as a criticism of democracy. But it was merely a condemnation of the manner in which French democracy functioned. The difference between France under Hitler's boot and France fighting off the Nazis amounted to five thousand planes and ten thousand tanks which France could have bought or made. Everything depends on who runs a democracy, on whether it is run by the people or by leaders who can be distinguished only with difficulty from the national enemy.

Politics often is shaped by mistakes, and these can be based on too little faith. One of the reasons why France signed the armistice with Germany was military defeat. The other was the belief that England too would soon be defeated. In the same expectation Italy entered the war on June 10, 1940. England's firmness has made all the difference to conquered France, to Italy, to Germany, to Russia, and to the United States and Japan.

England stood firm because it was protected by the English Channel and had more time to gear its superior industry to war needs. But it also had greater self-confidence. The fate of France, moreover, served as a frightening example to England. Great Britain could do something about it because the Conservatives had had the the sense to give the people, through Labor and Liberals, a larger share in the conduct of the war and of the nation's affairs. Britain's future depends on whether the ordinary citizen, the man-in-the-street, the woman-in-the-shelter, the soldier-in-the-barracks, thinks that it is his war and that he will make the peace.

A soldier's ideas on the eve of battle are simple and searching. If he decides that the cause and the leaders are not his own he will not fight with enthusiasm. He may even run away at the first chance or throw away his rifle. That is why good leadership and a clear vision of the future are as indispensable to military success as guns and planes. This is particularly true with women at the front line in millions. They want to know what it is all about and what will come of it. They remember, or were told of, the first World War. Two major wars in a generation! Will there be a third?

Conclusion

To Be . . .

PERHAPS the most interesting document that has come out of the blood and suffering of the second World War is the proclamation made by Prime Minister Winston Churchill on June 16, 1940. He said, "The two governments declare that France and Great Britain shall no longer be two, but one Franco-British Union. . . . Every citizen of France will enjoy immediately citizenship of Great Britain; every British subject will become a citizen of France." True, this offer was made in a highly desperate moment; it came too late to ward off France's premature capitulation to Hitler. But after the War, all of Europe will be in a no less desperate plight. Europe will be faced with the relentless alternative of union or chaos.

The War has shown that the nations of the European Continent, with all their paraphernalia of sovereignty, were dependent upon Hitler's will and deeds, while Great Britain, with all its empire and riches, is dependent on the United States. The farce of independence in isolation has thus been completely exposed. Millions of Americans, moreover, are convinced that the prosperity and security of the United States depend to some extent on conditions beyond its frontiers. The realization of interdependence is more widespread than ever. This is the soil in which the new war aim, or peace aim, of internationalism has sprouted. Leslie Hore-Belisha put it aptly on October 21, 1939, when he was British War Minister. "This is not a war about a map," he said. The purpose of this War is not a victory which will enable one side to write a better or worse Versailles. It is a war for the rebuilding of the life of Europe, and then of the entire world, on a new foundation. Even Neville Chamberlain, before his death, spoke of the necessity of "a new international order."

The failure of nationalism to protect nations from assault has been amply demonstrated by events since 1938. As the planes and tanks raced across boundaries, nations realized how silly those boundaries had been in peacetime. The "neutrality" of small countries and the "safety" of large ones proved a costly myth. In the heat of war Europe has quickly grown ripe for federation.

Because war is the lowest activity of the human race it often provokes the loftiest dreams. Attractive slogans and utopias are therefore suspect. If the idea of federal union were based on the hope that the insane asylum of Europe would change into a love nest I would despair of its prospects. If its realization depended on the upsurge of practical idealism from blood-soaked ruins it would enjoy scant chance of success. There is little love or idealism in politics. The United States of Europe has become a realistic goal because the national selfishness of the past has so obviously defeated itself.

A good way to kill myself would be to take care only of myself. I must, to keep alive and well, also take care of the traffic cop, of the man with a contagious disease in Buffalo, of the criminal with a submachine gun in Memphis, of the unemployed in Texas, and of the soldier in California. In any country this is the universally accepted rule of human society. But not between countries. The nations of the world concentrated on their own narrow interests. This egotistical nationalism caused the death of many nations. The only safety for nations is in internationalism.

People do learn from experience. Mistakes which cost millions of homes and lives have opened many European eyes. The second World War is unlike the first if only because it is the second. If a person contracted pneumonia, recovered, and six weeks later got pneumonia again, the second attack would be different because the person would be different. Europe after the second World War will be weaker than in 1919 but also wiser. Bitter experience is teaching nations that only in union is there survival and peace.

In this era of shortened distance and interlaced economies, Europe with its multitude of exclusively nationalistic and selfishly independent nations is as much an anachronism as the sovereign counties and duchies of the Middle Ages would have been in the succeeding era of industrialism. The crazy-quilt map of pre-1939 Europe was antiquated and destructive. The territory of the United States, cut up into forty-eight nations obeying no federal laws and boxed off by forty-eight tariff walls, would provide a parallel to the disunity of the old Europe.

Economic nationalism is now recognized as no less harmful than political nationalism. The extreme form of economic nationalism is Fascism. But Hitler did not want raw materials. He wanted war materials. For purposes of peace it is not necessary for each country to own the supplies it consumes. No equitable adjustment of the purely fortuitous distribution of the world's natural wealth can be achieved by the shifting of frontiers. Such an adjustment would require every nation to obtain possession of its proportionate share of the world's oil, timber, nickel, coffee, and all other forms of wealth. Germany, for instance, would occupy a strip of the Texas oil field, a section of Canada's nickel mines, an area of Brazil's coffee lands, and so forth. This is manifestly absurd. But it is the logical corollary of the "have and have-not" fable. The alternative to such madness is freely flowing international trade; nations buy what they do not own. Fascism has confronted mankind with this choice: either the strong nations seize the materials they lack or all nations engage in a normal exchange of products. In centuries past, empires have robbed aplenty, and Britain is no exception. But the cure is not for the Germans to rob from the British what the British have robbed from others. The cure is to stop all robbery, and to grant to all who need materials the free and equal right to purchase these materials. Under such conditions parts of national empires would soon become parts of an international federation. The thesis that the Germans or Italians arrived late, as nations, on the historic scene and are now therefore entitled to their turn at imperial banditry must mean interminable wars, for not only will the acts of brigandage be resisted; other nations will want their turn after Germany and Italy.

The economic and political disunity of Europe is at an end. We have reached a parting of the ways in world history. The world will never be the same whoever wins the second World War. Europe will either be united under the heel and whip of Hitler or will unite itself into a voluntary federation wherein each country, while retaining its identity, will surrender sufficient sovereignty to keep it from running amuck.

The League of Nations was merely a rostrum. It was not an organization. Diplomats, often tired and gray, came to Geneva at irregular intervals to breathe the mountain air, to make speeches, and to intrigue. League members did occasionally combine to collect statistics or study labor problems or consult on opium sales, but they never attacked the question of war prevention. The League was a failure not, as so many Europeans have said, because the United States refused to join, although that was a factor in its weakness; it failed because its member states did not implement the Covenant when they had the power to do so. The statutes of the League provided for sanctions against an aggressor. Those sanctions were applied once in 1935 when Italy invaded Abyssinia. But they were applied so half-heartedly by England and France that they failed of their purpose and discredited sanctions as a means of coercing an aggressor. From then the descent to war was steep.

The League was not a union or a unit. In fact, it emphasized the world's lack of unity. It was a playground full of seesaws, balance-of-power seesaws. The statesmen were playing the old, old game that had caused so much trouble.

When I first went to Europe as a journalist, in 1921, I expected to find all statesmen and many private persons pondering such questions as these:

"How did the world get itself in the recent terrible war?"

"How can we avoid another massacre of the same kind?"

I was disappointed. A few individuals and some small groups in western countries preached pacifism, international friendship, socialism, or Communism as a means of averting war. But the politicians were more concerned with remaining in office, retaining their territorial gains or wiping out their territorial losses, stealing foreign markets, and collecting debts from other countries while not paying their own.

Once more, the statesmen were slowly stoking the furnaces of war. Once more, the people let them do it.

Europe after 1918 was not very different from the Europe of before 1914. A few boundaries had been pushed around and a few crowned heads were gone. In the place of the Czar was Lenin. In the place of the Kaiser was a democratic Republic. But the rivalry and friction between nations continued unabated. Within each nation, economic maladjustment, racial animosities, and social injustices were heaping up the same old poisons. Such a situation had produced the war of 1914. There was no reason to suppose that it would not produce another war. It did.

Unless Europe and other continents are reorganized after the present war and unless nations establish more decent and more civilized conditions at home there is no reason to suppose that a third World War will not follow the second.

Appendix

Letters from Mrs. Eleanor Roosevelt

DOROTHY Rosenman (Mrs. Samuel I. Rosenman) arranged an interview for me with Mrs. Eleanor Roosevelt for February 24, 1938 in the White House. The substance of the conversation and the exchange of letters that followed could not, I knew, be published in *Men and Politics* when it first appeared in 1941 or in its fifth edition in 1946. The material should be of interest now.

When I was ushered into Mrs. Roosevelt's presence a younger Mrs. Roosevelt, holding in her lap a little girl of four who had "a tummy ache," was also present. They soon left and I had an hour alone with the First Lady. She sat in a big chair and served tea. A table laden with many varieties of sweet cookies and tiny sandwiches stood within arm's reach.

I began by saying I had spent some times in Spain recently. "Please don't tell me about Spain," Mrs. Roosevelt interrupted. "Martha Gellhorn has talked to me about it."

For a moment I was taken aback by this stern injunction. But in a flash I realized that Mrs. Roosevelt was being direct and honest while intimating where her sympathies lay. Her remark actually brought me more quickly than I had expected to the purpose of my visit: the effect on the Spanish Republic of the United States arms embargo. I had, I began, seen murderous raids in Madrid and Valencia. As soon as two Loyalist planes took to the air the Italian, (or were they German?) bombers fled. Barcelona was a city swollen by refugees to a population of two million. At times it had as few as eight anti-aircraft guns and never during the fighting since 1936 did it have more than forty. America's inability, under the Neutrality Act, to sell arms to the legitimate Spanish government meant that Nazi and Fascist airmen in the service of Franco could slaughter Loyalist citizens with impunity. The government of the Republic, which possessed some bombers, refused to use them against civilian targets.

Mrs. Roosevelt and I discussed aspects of this question during tea. She was friendly throughout. She wondered whether the lifting

642

of the embargo would enjoy enough public support in the United States. As I stood up to go she promised to tell the President what I had said.

(I went back to the Mayflower Hotel and typed out a diary entry on the conversation.)

Four days later I received this letter:

THE WHITE HOUSE
WASHINGTON

February 28, 1938

My dear Mr. Fischer:

I talked to the President and told him what you said. He agrees with you, but feels that it would be absolutely impossible to repeal the Neutrality Act, because the people of this country feel that it was designed to keep us out of war, and, on the whole, it is the best instrument to accomplish that end. He feels certain that we could not get the people to change this point of view without a period of education and perhaps from experiences which they have not as yet had.

I am sorry that this is the case.

Very sincerely yours,

Signed,
Eleanor Roosevelt

"History," I noted in my diary, "will record President Roosevelt's failure to lift the arms embargo as a blunder. . . . A democratic leader must give ear to dissenting minorities and to approving majorities. But when so much is at stake—and peace in Europe is at stake in Spain—he is warranted in ignoring dissenters in the hope that acts will convert them where words have not. The dictators, unfortunately, do not wait for democracies to be educated. . . ."

Replying to Mrs. Roosevelt from aboard the Queen Mary sailing for Europe, I thanked her for the letter which revealed "the President's favorable view and your own friendly sentiments." I suggested that the process of education had already commenced. I noted that we were supplying arms to Chiang Kai-shek and metal scrap to Japan. "In regard to Spain," I wrote, "the effect of the Act is unneutral and anti-Loyalist."

"I am on my way back to Spain," I concluded, "where amidst death and suffering one nevertheless enjoys the exhilaration of being in harmony with the sole people that has dared to say 'No' to the Fascist aggressors."

If the Spanish Republic had received adequate support from the Western democracies they might not have had to say "No" to the same aggressors after free Spain fell.

Another letter to me from Mrs. Eleanor Roosevelt dealt with the difficulties my wife and two sons had encountered in leaving the Soviet Union. Since President Roosevelt and Mrs. Roosevelt helped to get them out of that country, I typed out the story and sent it to Mrs. Roosevelt for approval. Her reply follows:

THE WHITE HOUSE
WASHINGTON

December 16, 1940

My dear Mr. Fischer:

I hate to spoil anything you have written, but I would rather you left out my letter and any reference to the President. I do not want more than a mention of the fact that you came to see me and I said I would do what I could. I do not want it said that I interfered.

Very sincerely yours,

Signed,
Eleanor Roosevelt

In accordance with Mrs. Roosevelt's request I amended my account as it appears on page 585 of this volume. Now I believe no harm can be done by restoring what I had deleted at the First Lady's justified request. She did indeed understand immediately the situation of my family in Moscow and said, "I'll talk to Sumner" (Under-Secretary of State Sumner Welles, a close friend of the Roosevelt family).

"Thanks," I said. "But if Mr. Welles speaks to the Soviet Embassy here or if he urges our embassy in Moscow to approach the Soviet authorities my wife may be refused and then she will be in a worse plight, for it means that a foreign government had interceded on her behalf. The request has to be made so as to preclude any rejection."

I did not have to explain any further. "I shall talk to Franklin at dinner and let you know tomorrow morning."

The next morning at ten the telephone bell rang in my room in the Mayflower Hotel and a voice said, "Hello, this is Eleanor Roosevelt." In Europe, or in many places in America, somebody would first have asked me who I was and then announced who would speak. "I spoke to Franklin yesterday," Mrs. Roosevelt announced. "He is ready to do what is necessary but he doesn't like Oumansky [Soviet Ambassador Constantine Oumansky]. He will see Oumansky if you think it necessary, but he would prefer not to, and I suggested that I might see Mrs. Oumansky."

I was quite moved and showed it by saying, "You are very sweet. Could you tell Mrs. Oumansky that you were making the request on behalf of the President?"

Mrs. Roosevelt, "Yes," and I said, "That will be fine." She promised to give me the news as soon as there was any.

On January 11, Mrs. Roosevelt wrote: "The lady I tried to see, Mrs. Oumansky, is away, but I will see her on her return and let you know immediately what transpires." Below her signature she added, "She is coming to tea tomorrow."

Mrs. Roosevelt felt that I was eager for news. This sensitive consideration on the part of a person who received a mountain of mail each day was one of the qualities that made her a great woman.

On January 18, I had an urgent telephone message to call Ambassador Oumansky at the Soviet Consulate in New York. He wanted to see me. I went over. We talked for an hour about everything on the map except Markoosha and my boys. Finally I said,

"How did Raya like Mrs. Roosevelt?"

"Fischer," Oumansky exclaimed feigning surprise, "so it's you." As though Raya Oumansky's tea talk in the White House could have been carried on in blank anonymity. "Why haven't you mentioned it to me before." He promised to do "everything I can for you." I was sure he would. The President's request had already undoubtedly gone to Stalin.

When I received Markoosha's telegram of January 21 (Moscow can move fast when necessary) I passed the news to Mrs. Roosevelt. My letter crossed one of hers in which she wrote, "I hope you will let me know how things work out as I shall be interested." Then, below her signature, she added by hand, "Just came back on the plane with Oumansky who told me he thought your 'little matter' was arranged. Have you heard anything definite?"

I wrote her that I happily had.

Subsequently members of my family and I met Mrs. Roosevelt on many private occasions.

Index